INVENTING AFTERLIVES

INVENTING AFTERLIVES

THE STORIES
WE TELL
OURSELVES
ABOUT LIFE
AFTER DEATH

REGINA M. JANES

Columbia University Press
New York

Columbia University Press
Publishers Since 1893
New York   Chichester, West Sussex
cup.columbia.edu

Copyright © 2018 Columbia University Press

"Gabriel" from *Gabriel: A Poem* by Edward Hirsch, copyright © 2014 by Edward Hirsch. Used by permission of Alfred A. Knopf, an imprint of the Knopf Doubleday Publishing Group, a division of Penguin Random House LLC. All rights reserved.

I Am a Cat, by Natsume Sōseki, copyright © 2002 by Aiko Ito and Graeme Wilson. Used by permission of Tuttle Publishing, a division of Periplus Editions (HK) Ltd. All rights reserved

Library of Congress Cataloging-in-Publication Data
Names: Janes, Regina M., author.
Title: Inventing afterlives : the stories we tell ourselves about life after death / Regina M. Janes.
Description: 1 [edition]. | New York : Columbia University Press, 2018. | Includes bibliographical references and index.
Identifiers: LCCN 2018000804 (print) | LCCN 2018009938 (e-book) | ISBN 9780231546294 (e-book) | ISBN 9780231185707 (cloth) | ISBN 9780231185714 (paperback)
Subjects: LCSH: Future life.
Classification: LCC BL535 (e-book) | LCC BL535 .J35 2018 (print) | DDC 202/.3—dc23
LC record available at https://lccn.loc.gov/2018000804

Cover design: Lisa Hamm
Cover image: Amy Weiss/Trevillion Images

IN MEMORIAM DALE E. WOOLLEY

AND FOR CHARLES, THE ONLY AFTERLIFE
DALE EVER TOOK AN INTEREST IN

CONTENTS

Preface ix

1. CONCERNING THE PRESENT STATE OF LIFE AFTER DEATH 1

2. IMPERMANENT ETERNITIES: EGYPT, SUMER, AND BABYLON, ANCIENT ISRAEL, GREECE, AND ROME 28

3. TOURING ASIAN AFTERLIVES: ETERNAL IMPERMANENCE 132

4. PURSUING HAPPINESS: HOW THE ENLIGHTENMENT INVENTED AN AFTERLIFE TO WISH FOR 197

5. *WANDÂFURU RAIFU* OR *AFTERLIFE* INVENTIONS AND VARIATIONS 256

Notes 291
Index 353

PREFACE

LEO *(July 23–Aug. 22)*

The FBI will have to ask you some tough questions next week, such as whether true love really exists and what happens after we die.

HOROSCOPE, *THE ONION*, OCTOBER 13-19, 2011, 9.

David Hume had an answer for the FBI. The single most famous event in that British philosopher's life was a visit James Boswell, Samuel Johnson's biographer-to-be, paid him in 1776. "Nothing endears so much a friend as sorrow for his death," Hume had observed,[1] yet it was not sorrow moving Boswell to Hume's side, but curiosity. As Hume lay dying, Boswell came to see how an atheist died. Serenely and cheerfully, was the answer, with no itchy desire after eternal life, no fear of roasting in flames, no apprehensions about annihilation, and no dread of the gaping gap of vanished consciousness. Boswell had bad dreams for a week.

To begin a book about afterlives with someone who did not believe in one may seem perverse, but it has a purpose. Everyone has some belief, or beliefs, about what happens after death, even if the belief is that nothing at all happens or that nothing can be known about what happens or that there is no point even thinking about it. Once death becomes a phenomenon that human beings can think and talk about, we inevitably ask, "So what comes next; what's after that?" The question applies both to the dead and to the survivors, and answers range from "nothing" to "eternities." Whatever the answer, it establishes our relationship to the cosmos we live in: what it means, what it is for, and how we are to live within it while we live.

Death, of course, has at once everything and nothing to do with the afterlife. Afterlives are narratives made by the living in order to define the relationship between the living and the dead, between the self and the prospect of its own death, between survivors and those who have disappeared from the social unit. Death is the limit that provokes those fictions. Out of death's blank wall, we want to make a gate, and then we demand to know what is on the other side of the gate. Hume vanished without fear. Boswell lived less happily, complaining of his melancholy the year before Hume died, "[A]ll the doubts which have ever disturbed thinking men, come upon me. I awake in the night, dreading annihilation or being thrown into some horrible state of being."[2] Some of us know exactly what and whom to expect—and may be praying that we've got it wrong and there will be a loophole through which we can wriggle out of our just deserts into paradise.[3] Many presume on paradise.

The word *afterlife* presupposes some posthumous existence, pleasant or unpleasant, but beliefs about what happens "after life" include the denial of any such existence. Whether an afterlife is affirmed or denied, the afterlife narrative overcomes death, dominates it, and reintegrates death and the dead into the continuing self-conceptions of the living. When blurb writers exclaim, "This book is not about death, it's really about how to live!" they are describing not a happy accident but a necessary fact.

As a word denoting what happens after death, rather than in later life, "after life" comes tardily to English. It is not used until 1598, in an introduction to Christopher Marlowe's posthumous works, where it refers to the memory of the author and the man.[4] Literary studies still use the word most frequently to refer to authors' reputations.[5] Not until 1611 does the term refer to the state of a soul after death, when it turns up in the wondering words of a pagan, surprised by Christian missionaries who tell "vs strange things, and giue vs faire promises of after life, when this life shall be ended."[6] Christians, firmly possessed of "eternal life," a phrase first attested in 1479,[7] had no need to meddle with any life that was merely "after." For seventeenth-century writers, "after life" designated the speculations of heathens and the denials of Epicureans and Sadducees.[8] The preferred generic term for their own afterlife expectations was "future state," a phrase that the *OED* gives to Alexander Pope's *Essay on Man* (1733), but that already appears in 1588 in Gervase Babington's exposition of the Lord's Prayer, sandwiched between one's future state in this life (1567) and the future state of England (1589), also very much in this life.[9] Christians start using the term *afterlife* to refer to their future and eternal state only in the mid-eighteenth century.[10] As the word changes, so does the concept, less "state" and more "life."

In religious studies, afterlives accompany the complex and nuanced understanding of a religious tradition over time and in time. Scholars maintain a careful professional agnosticism as to the reality of intrinsically unverifiable afterlives and the claims of contending traditions. What a tradition maintains as to immortality is accepted as given, while its chops and changes, responses to political and intellectual ferment, differences from itself from moment to moment, form the object of study. Creating new knowledge through meticulous detail, religious-studies scholars are rightly suspicious of grand historical narratives and ahistorical cognitive arguments. This study proceeds otherwise.

It proposes a fable of origins in cognitive studies because the irreligious, too, need to be accounted for. As unbelievers like Hume demonstrate, there is no "hard wiring" of afterlife belief (or God), but afterlife beliefs (like God) do originate in human sociality and cognition, that is, language. Other primates recognize death and dislike it, but they have nothing to say about it. Human afterlife talk weaves death into life's narrative, if only to write FINIS, as Walter Benjamin implies. Religious traditions occasionally recount the origins of their afterlife beliefs, while those outside those traditions (and outside of religious studies) commonly explain away those beliefs in functional terms ranging from condescending to paranoid: as compensatory or consoling or ethical or controlling or imitative or stolen.

Yet the earliest attested afterlife beliefs (and some still current) are not compensatory, consoling, ethical, or controlling. Nor can we know what they may imitate or from whom they may have been stolen. They neither satisfy human desires nor have anything to do with justice or morality. Some other explanation is necessary, for people wanting explanations. The human mind seems the place to look. But not just the mind: human minds are always (already) social. Proposed is an ahistorical account that accommodates both the cognitive quandary death poses and the social injury it creates.

This ahistorical deep structure (a modern mythos) supports, but does not determine, the variety afterlives display in changing socio-political and economic circumstances. That morality and the afterlife originate independently is not immediately obvious. The misery of some early afterlives we have never known, and we have forgotten the horrors of earlier iterations of our own. Only very lately—and still not universally—do justice and morality attach themselves to afterlife beliefs, and only in the enlightenment does human happiness come to dominate afterlife expectations. These claims require demonstration that only a narrative traversing many places and times can supply, if they are to persuade.

Applying the cognitive and collective insights of the first chapter to pre-Christian western afterlives, we see how western afterlife beliefs develop moralistic immortality and contend with empirical skepticism up to the advent of Christianity. The parallel but far more complex processes on the other half of the globe are briefly charted, with Hume's tribute to "the Metempsychosis." Once western moralistic immortality is in place, afterlife imaginings proliferate without fulfilling all human wishes. More famous for resisting priestcraft than for piety, the enlightened eighteenth century pursued happiness all the way into the next world. Putting into place the consolatory clichés about the afterlife that moderns take for granted and assume are eternal, Enlightenment invented the wish-fulfilling afterlife attacked in the next century by Marx, Engels, Freud, et al. Now we live with and without afterlives, and the final chapter celebrates the flourishing of afterlives no one believes in found in recent film and fiction.

Dispelled are a number of common misconceptions about the afterlife, including the assumptions that afterlife beliefs are universal and all cultures subscribe to some promise of life after death, that afterlives originate to console the dying and their mourners, that afterlives originate as a form of wish fulfillment, that afterlives are necessary for morality, that afterlives are a construct of power to control the minds and behavior of the living. Many of these misconceptions are a product of the afterlife that the Enlightenment put in place three hundred years ago, and there is something to be said for each of them, as a purpose such beliefs have served. Their grudging attitude obscures, however, the very interesting work an afterlife can do, the creation *ex nihilo* of great imaginative fabrics. They also underestimate the persistent note of skepticism that accompanies afterlife affirmations. More damagingly, they have sometimes inhibited modern atheists from developing their own afterlife narratives independent of, though derivative from, their culture's traditional religions. The calligraphy for FINIS can be as elaborate as one likes, as extensive as the mind can reach.

Chapter 1, "Concerning the Present State of Life After Death," takes up the current proliferation of afterlives, proposes an origin for afterlife theorization in primate behavior and theory of mind relative to dead bodies, sketches the prehistoric evidence for afterlife beliefs, assesses the role of afterlife beliefs relative to morality, and indicates the insufficiency—and necessity—of anti-afterlife arguments from John Toland to Karl Marx and Sigmund Freud. The questions here are why we construct afterlives at all and what they do for us. The argument is that afterlives originate in empathy with the socialized dead body and respond to a cognitive and social demand: what has happened to the life that animated this body? What now is the community's relationship to that body? Justice and morality have originally no connection with death. Death comes like the sun and the rain equally to the just and the unjust, the moral and the immoral. Death levels; it does not differentiate. The connection to justice and morality is self-consciously patched in at different times and places; thereafter it sticks like a burr. For this argument to be persuasive, it needs to be held against actual afterlife conceptions as they developed through time.

Chapter 2, "Impermanent Eternities," sketches the transformations in western afterlives from the Egyptians and Sumerians through Jews, Greeks, and Romans, ending when Christianity arrives. When such well-informed writers as S. Jay Olshanky and Bruce A. Carnes assure readers that concepts of life after death emerged to "soften [death's] harsh reality,"[11] only acquaintance with harsh early concepts can provide the necessary corrective. Early afterlives are dismal everywhere but Egypt. Even Egypt lacks initially any correlation between justice and death, although it will model exploiting the afterlife for social control. Elsewhere afterlife fates were more likely to correlate with how one died and how fecund one had been. Post-Homeric philosophers and poets belatedly meted out justice after life to Greeks and Romans, but ancient Israel zealously erased its traditional justice-free afterlife beliefs as it compiled the Torah and Prophets, leaving only traces of disapproval. Analogous to *varnashrama-dharma's* role in Hinduism, lineage and the law gave Israel all the meaning and morality it needed. Post-exilic Deuteronomic ideology linked God, life, and law with temporal reward, apostasy with temporal punishment and death. When those linkages broke down in the Hellenistic period and diaspora (reported in Esther, Daniel, and Maccabees), a new concept was borrowed: resurrection. Life became for the first time eternal and linear. Having infiltrated Judaism, eternal life and resurrection defined Christianity and Gabriel's message to Muhammad. After a brief tour of Asia, fast forward seventeen hundred years.

Chapter 3, "Touring Asian Afterlives: Eternal Impermanence," visits that part of the world where "afterlife" is a misnomer. "Afterlife" assumes an ending. Asia adopts rebirth, the endless, visible burgeoning of life from life, and then sets about putting an end to it as the highest philosophical attainment. A better life may be in prospect the next time around—or much worse. Morality is sometimes supposed to depend on rebirth: what other guard is there on behavior? Life continues, or the consequences of actions, though bodies do not. Consequences unfold into the future, well beyond the individual performing an action. Tracing the ancestors, rebirth, and such key concepts as dharma, karma, non-self, emptiness, and Pure Land, from the Vedas through Buddhism, Jainism, and Hinduism in their travels from India, the chapter jogs to China to pick up Confucianism, Daoism, and new varieties of Buddhism, hovers over Tibet, and on to Japan, ending with two encounters between Buddhism and the Christian west that validate Buddhist insight.

Chapter 4, "Pursuing Happiness: How the Enlightenment Invented an Afterlife to Wish For," exposes a neglected but crucial period in the development of modern afterlives. In the eighteenth century, British thinkers created the wish-fulfilling afterlife that we now take to be eternal and that Marx and Freud attacked with such energy in the nineteenth and early twentieth centuries. The traditional Christian afterlife damned to eternal sulfurous flames all non-Christians and many Christians (almost all, among Calvinists); for the devout, the faithful, the repentant, or the elect, it was theocentric. The beatific visions that close the biblical book of Revelation (c. 100 CE) and Dante's *Paradiso* (set in 1300) are paradigmatic. Dying, one encountered God, at best met Jesus and the souls of good men made perfect, and enjoyed eternal, unimaginable ecstasies. (Whether these meetings took place immediately upon death or only at the Last Judgment puzzled Protestants.) Those rigorous God-centered raptures yielded to an afterlife that accommodated friends, relations, children, and current intellectual movements, all the secular delights of love, life, and mind. As Keith Thomas observed, "only in the early modern period [was] stress . . . laid on the reunion of the nuclear family. As earthly values changed, so did conceptions of heavenly felicity."[12] Particularly significant for conceptualizing historical change is that improvements came from below, moving from popular discourse into mainstream theological acceptance. Theology bent to desire, led by women, sealed by men. A pivotal moment in the human demand for happiness after death as well as in life, the eighteenth century located the truth of the afterlife in the human mind, where the argument of this book begins, but in a different drawer. Their drawer was labeled "wishing makes it so, because of the organization of the human mind and the benevolence of God." Unnoticed, Adam Smith re-filed it where it is found today.

Chapter 5, "*Wandâfuru Raifu* or *Afterlife* Inventions and Variations," asks what use afterlives are if we do not believe in them. Freed from that odd couple theology and reality, afterlives in which no one believes function as usefully as, but less threateningly than, afterlives in which almost everyone believes. Representing the dazzling variety of modern reinterpretations of afterlives are Hirokazu Kore-eda and Spike Jonze, J. M. Coetzee and Milan Kundera, Steve Stern and George Saunders; meanwhile Samuel Beckett sneers. Unlike traditional afterlives, the modern ones pretend to no explanatory power, but they continue to dissipate death's terrors by articulating and reinforcing values that shape living in the present. Certain behaviors are rewarded, others punished, and the project elicits reflection and self-examination from reader or viewer, as to the quality and character of life as it is lived. Authors approaching death as their topic disclose their deepest concerns as artists and, perhaps, as human beings in their fantasies of last things, beyond the end. Some modern writers, Nadine Gordimer and Julian Barnes come to mind, carp at the afterlife, sour grapes in the sky, but do not leave it alone.

Some fascinating topics are no more than glimpsed. Only in America are the dead tormented by "unfinished business," like *Carousel*'s Billy Bigelow.[13] When Europeans come back from the dead, as in Pedro

Almodóvar's *Volver*, Guillaume Canet's *Ne dis personne*, or Stieg Larsson's *Girl with the Dragon Tattoo*, the person has not really died, though someone else is likely to have been murdered. An afterlife is a narrative of destination, the reciprocal of a myth of origins. Cultures want stories about where they came from; so they want stories about where their members go when they are no longer here. Giving up Genesis, we cling to a Big Bang. Why develop whole other worlds for the dead? is much the same question as why tell stories about characters as imaginary as the dead have become.

A study that traverses this much terrain temporally and geographically is evidently much indebted to the work of other scholars in many fields; their ghosts appear in the notes and bibliography. The literature on death and the afterlife is vast: it would require several lives perfectly to control it. Primary material begins in prehistory and continues to the present. Modern secondary material has a briefer history but has multiplied exponentially in the last fifty years. Philippe Ariès's complaint in the 1970s that death cannot be spoken or addressed transformed the world it entered and generated numerous studies of dying practices and beliefs. Studies now document death and afterlife beliefs from the Egyptians and Sumerians to the present.[14] This study does not pretend to analyze in detail the death rites or beliefs of a single culture or religious tradition but rather ranges widely across cultures and times and traditions, ending in mere literature and movies. Why? In our end is our beginning.

Once upon a time, renting all the Japanese films at the local video store to keep company with a son away in Japan, I came across one that made me ask: what course can I teach that will let me show this film? *After Life* is the mistranslated English title of Hirokazu Kore-eda's *Wandâfuru raifu*. Ten years earlier, a children's version of *Gilgamesh* had astonished me, much as the first translations had astonished the nineteenth century. Familiar with biblical and classical traditions, passionate for John Dryden's translations of Lucretius, and curious about the power of this Japanese film, I began looking into primatology and the origins of morality, Terror Management Theory, with its important discovery of mortality salience and odd insistence on death's terrors, and such current standard works as Alan Segal's *Life After Death* (2004), Colleen McDannell and Bernhard Lang's *Heaven: A History* (1988, 2001), and John Bowker's *Meanings of Death* (1991), among many others. I found myself troubled by certain absences.

The insights and scrupulous accuracy of these authors move with a teleological thrust toward the afterlife most Christians now enjoy. There seemed no place for the tradition of afterlife denial or the afterlife fantasies of afterlife deniers or the inventions that emerge outside religious traditions. John Bowker seemed almost discontented when he observed that "Virtually everything that *can* be imagined about death *has* been imagined."[15]

What a literary scholar finds, of course, is narrative. Once language possesses us, it expresses individuals' thoughts and concerns, but more importantly it makes a society cohere through shared stories and their meanings. Afterlives are stories we tell each other and ourselves about death, a word so powerful that it elicits as strong a physio-psychological response as a life-threatening situation or the thing itself. These stories may be Aristotelian in form, their meaning produced by the end, or they may be cyclic, unfolding endlessly, their meanings in process, provisional, momentary. Traditionally, afterlives have been presented as something to be believed, nor is this study exempt, though it leans the wrong way. Those who believe in their disbelief are also represented here. All that we know of any afterlife is the stories we tell now, and they are perhaps afterlife more than enough.

As to Kore-eda's film, it is worth traversing millennia of afterlives to reach it. Whether or not you read this book, do see the movie. But be warned—it is a Japanese movie, and so it is slow, very slow. Some viewers will regard it as taking an eternity to come to an end.

ACKNOWLEDGMENTS

Errors, gaffes, and inadmissible inferences remain all my own, but for suggestions, inspiration, encouragement, assistance, and correction that they themselves may have forgotten by now, I should like to thank Kathryn Davis, Bill Fox, Alexandra Golcher, Steve Goodwin, Joshua Katz, Eliza Kent, Leslie Mechem, Francine Lichtert, Robert Mahony, Claude Rawson, Rebecca Schiffenhaus, the Skidmore Help Desk, Joel Smith, Adrienne Stefani, John Taylor, Charles E.Z. Woolley, and Eric Zencey.

INVENTING AFTERLIVES

1

CONCERNING THE PRESENT STATE OF LIFE AFTER DEATH

When a lot of different remedies are suggested for a disease, that means it can't be cured ... I have plenty of remedies, any number of them, and that means I haven't really got one.

—ANTONIN CHEKHOV, THE CHERRY ORCHARD

When your heart stops beating, you'll keep tweeting.

—LIVESON WEBSITE (A "SOON TO LAUNCH SERVICE THAT PROMISES TO TWEET ON YOUR BEHALF EVEN AFTER YOU DIE"), QUOTED IN EVGENY MOROZOV, "THE PERILS OF PERFECTION," NEW YORK TIMES[1]

All life is good, even if it is fictitious.

—ANITA BROOKNER, INCIDENTS IN THE RUE LAUGIER

Let me make one thing perfectly clear: there is no life after death. Saying so, I realize, costs me many readers. They are already closing this book, forgoing what remains of this sentence, hopeful that their lives will continue, somehow, beyond the grave. One could be coy and noncommittal, but let me not cheat anyone into hoping that beyond the next page lies an answer or a promise. I am no Dinesh D'Souza or Deepak Chopra nor even Mary Roach conceding a little hopeful uncertainty at the end of *Spook*. I do not practice the professional agnosticism of religious studies. There is, of course, lots of life after death; it is just not one's own.

For something that does not exist, life after death has never been in better health than at present. Deservedly so, for in the afterlife human creativity manifests all its variety and much of its purpose, entertaining, instructing, and distracting us. What we imagine about the afterlife—and all afterlives are imaginary, especially those that do or do not exist—is fundamental to how we situate ourselves in our own lives and in the world in which that life takes place. We cannot think about any afterlife without defining a universe. Whether we trust in an afterlife or smash it by denying personal or impersonal immortality, we shape our place in a cosmos. These days, the afterlife is an extra room—a refinished attic play area or media space—added to the houses in which we live. So let us first check out the furnishings: current afterlife beliefs and their proliferating possibilities, erroneous but conventional assumptions about afterlife origins, and afterlives' more probable cognitive origins and social, collective purposes.

Afterlives originate in a question the dead raise and do not answer: where did the person I knew as this body go? Something has gone missing from the body, absconded, kidnapped, set off on a journey, or gone into hiding. The most likely explanation is a journey; more hopeful or fearful is hiding nearby; frequent is theft by malevolent witchcraft. Where do the dead journey? To their own kind, probably, so as not to be lonely; they acquire a territory, though they may also cling to their bones, to us. Is their land like the land of the living, the only world we know, or unlike it, since it is occupied by the dead? Are the dead like the living or, being dead, their opposite? The body decaying, speculation feeds speculation. As Pliny observed, "After men are buried, great diversitie there is in opinion, what is become of their souls & ghosts, wandering some this way and others that."[2] Originating with language, these questions are renewed every time someone dies. We are born into cultures that have already answered such questions for us.

Like all beliefs, beliefs about the afterlife originate in the human mind, working over certain features of human existence, in this case the complex tangle of the individual, society, and death. Nothing about the mind's workings determines what those beliefs will be, but the intrusiveness of death demands some cognitive response. Unlike beliefs about, say, New

York City or Paris, beliefs about the afterlife can neither be verified nor refuted. But like New York City or Paris, people who have never visited the afterlife may nevertheless have strong views: the world to come may be terrifying or idealized or even doubted. Why should I believe in a hive of glass towers, where the sunlight never reaches the ground? Or a bejeweled city of gold, constantly illuminated, with a river running through it? Like most of what we think we know, we take our beliefs on authority, regarding as our own what others make or know (*my* smartphone), rejecting one authority for another.

Most modern accounts of afterlife origins address either the individual or society, but fail to situate their own skepticism about the afterlife. At the level of the individual, afterlives are believed to console survivors, to soothe existential anxiety over dying, and to pander to psychological neediness by fulfilling unsatisfied desires. At the cultural level, morality is thought to require afterlives, and all cultures are thought to have them. Once afterlife beliefs develop, they do all these things, but they do not originate in these good deeds. They originate in recognizing death and thinking about past and future or, more precisely, in the human inability to think without thinking about the future. Once developed, afterlives proliferate in our consumer culture so vertiginously that a recent CBS/*Vanity Fair* poll asks not what respondents believe about immortality but what immortality they would prefer.[3]

"The psychic next door said that my sister is a new soul, but I am an old soul, so I'm really my own great-grandmother," reports a skeptical modern-day undergraduate, otherwise quite certain that life ends at death.[4] A recent Ipsos/Reuters poll finds that 51 percent of the world's citizens say they believe in some form of afterlife. Claiming ignorance are 26 percent. The remaining 23 percent are sure "you simply cease to exist." Among the believers, 23 percent believe in an afterlife "but not specifically in a heaven or hell"; 19 percent believe "you go to heaven or hell" (41 percent in the United States say they believe this); 7 percent believe "you are ultimately reincarnated," and a surprisingly low 2 percent believe in "heaven but not hell" (here the United States ranks highest, at 4 percent). In 2014, more Americans believed in heaven (80 percent) than in life after death (73 percent). Polls differ, but Americans are more religious and more certain of their afterlife prospects than citizens of any other developed country.[5]

As belief prospers, disbelief surfaces, and representations of afterlives diversify. From the pulpit, clergy still assure their congregants that the dead shall again see each other in God, and Southern billboards promise eternal life, John 6:47: "He that believeth on me hath everlasting life." From these familiar traditions, afterlives have broken free. Now they course through movies (*Defending Your Life, Wristcutters: A Love Story, What Dreams May Come, A Ghost Story, Coco*), TV series (*Six Feet Under, Buffy the Vampire Slayer, Dead Like Me, The Good Place*), young adult novels (*Sabriel*), popular and serious fiction (Mitch Albom, *The Five People You Meet in Heaven*; Julian Barnes, *History of the World in 10½ Chapters*; George Saunders, *Lincoln in the Bardo*; Nadine Gordimer's essay "Afterlife" and John Updike's short story collection *The Afterlife and Other Stories*), plays (Conor McPherson, *Seafarer*; Michael Frayn, *Afterlife*; Daniel Alexander Jones, *Duat*), graphic novels (Anders Brekhus Nilsen, *Big Questions, Or, Asomatognosia: Whose Hand Is It Anyway?*), nonfiction (Mary Roach, *Spook*), comic nonfiction (Thomas Cathcart and Daniel Klein, *Heidegger and a Hippo Walk Through Those Pearly Gates*), memoirs (Don Piper, *90 Minutes in Heaven*; Julian Barnes, *Nothing to Be Frightened Of*), scientific accounts of near-death experiences, or NDEs (Raymond Moody, *Life After Life*; Kenneth Ring, *Life at Death*; Lee Bailey and Jenny Yates, eds., *The Near-Death Experience*; Bruce Greyson and C. P. Flynn, eds., *The Near-Death Experience*), or incidental accounts of NDEs (Oliver Sacks, *Musicophilia*). Thanks to Dante, Philip Larkin, Seamus Heaney, Peg Boyers, Billy Collins, and others, poems still outnumber internet sites. Orpheus's descent has long been an operatic subgenre while musical comedies such as *Carousel* share stages with chamber operas, such as *Charlie Parker's Yardbird*.

To make the *New York Times* nonfiction best-seller list, a positive report from the afterlife helps. September 2011 saw at number one *Heaven Is for Real*: "A boy's encounter with Jesus and the angels"; at number eight *The Boy Who Came Back from Heaven*: "A boy who awoke from a coma two months after a car accident had an incredible story to share"; and at number nineteen bringing up the rear but on the list for 209 weeks, *90 Minutes in Heaven*: "A Baptist minister describes the otherworldly experience he had after a car accident."[6] By April 2013, *Heaven Is for Real* had sunk to number sixteen (on the list for ninety-six weeks), the boy and the minister had disappeared, but a neurologist was making a strong showing at number two, on the list for twenty-three weeks, with his return from death in *Proof of Heaven*.[7]

An afterlife ex machina wraps up the mysterious, long-running, obsession-creating TV series *Lost*.[8] In *Sum: Tales from the Afterlives*, David Eagleman invents forty fascinating new afterlives, forty thieves of time. Like Orpheus pursuing Eurydice into the underworld (Monteverdi, Gluck, Offenbach, Glass), *Sum* is soon to be an opera. Equally orphic, Eagleman has generated a new religious orientation, "possibilianism," with at least one convert and a website.[9] Economic theorists ponder the role of scarcity in heaven (Scott Gordon, "Economics of the Afterlife") or question the invention of hell (Brooks B. Hull and Frederick Bold, "Hell, Religion and Cultural Change"). Moral philosophers debate the desirability of immortality (Bernard Williams, "The Makropulos Case: Reflections on the Tedium of Immortality") or affirm that we need an afterlife for our species more than we need personal immortality (Samuel Scheffler, *Death and the Afterlife*). Vampires and zombies, ghosts and ancestors stalk through subgenres of immortality. It was once said that in the midst of life we are in death; we are now certainly in the midst of afterlives.

What are afterlives that we should be surrounded and invaded by them? As narratives that adjust an individual's and a society's relationship to death, afterlives are as inescapable as death itself, but—also like death—they need not take up very much attention. "O Death, thou comest when I had thee least in mind!" The medieval Everyman was healthily oblivious to death's certainty, and that obliviousness does him no harm in his play (*Everyman*, c. 1500): his Good Deed saves him handily. Jesus himself commented testily on men's preferring to plan great new barns as they lie down on the last night of their lives, indifferent to storehouses in heaven or anywhere other than here (Luke 12:16–21). Memento mori would be unnecessary if people were not inclined to forget death in the midst of life. Death always comes as a surprise, being in equal parts inevitable and astonishing. As these examples suggest, if we are inclined to forget about death, some spoilsport will leap forward to remind us or someone will die.

In the second decade of the twenty-first century, death intrudes in new ways as a public-policy issue. The demographic bulge of the postwar period, its members now entering old age, approaches death, puzzles over the unconscionable survival rate of their parents, and dooms younger cohorts to monotonous meditations on mortality. The numbers, political slant, and discursive freedom are new; the process is ancient. Durable traditions deliver afterlives to us, but their hegemony has collapsed while the questions they addressed persist. As a society, we are engaged in renegotiating our contract with death, individually, collectively, and globally. Remembering death may terrify or depress, but, as we will see below, it also invigorates. It jolts the system into attention and activity.

Afterlives are neither as eternal nor as universal as they seem. For the last two thousand years, today's major religions, Christianity, Islam, Judaism, Buddhism, Hinduism, have endorsed various forms of life's continuing after death. Christianity and Islam are specifically predicated on promises of eternal life and personal immortality. Hinduism and Buddhism are premised on the impersonal immortality of rebirth; some variants (Vaishnavism, Pure Land) accommodate continuing personal identity in a heaven. Two thousand years is as close to eternity as most of us can imagine. Thus we tend to assume that afterlives are universal and all cultures at all times have had them.[10] Folded into that assumption are desire and the democratic criterion of truth: the more people who believe something, the more likely it is to be true. So, if belief in an afterlife is as universal as, say, the belief that the sun rises every day in the east and sets in the west, then it must be as true.

Since the seventeenth century, however, explorers and anthropologists have turned up cultures in which nothing happens after death. Seventeenth-century Sami (Laplanders) infuriated European explorers by declining to know anything of an afterlife. They hold that "men and beasts go the same way, and will not be persuaded that there is any life after this."[11] Today's A'rna of Nigeria mock their Muslim neighbors' afterlife certainties and wonder how they can know what happens beyond death: "If one of our ancestors would come back and tell us, we could tell you; but if one has never seen an ancestor, how can he know that his ancestors are yet alive somewhere, much less what lies on the other side of death?"[12] One eighteenth-century response was that the general views of mankind should not be called into question by a handful of obscure savages.

More recently, Human Relations Area Files anthropological data from nonindustrial cultures, past and present, report only 2 percent of cultures fail to elaborate an afterlife. Another 18 percent propose a simple afterlife of sleep or joining the spirits that is the same for everyone (as in ancient Israel and Shinto); another 30 percent propose an afterlife that is uniformly pleasant or unpleasant for everyone. *Gilgamesh* and Homer fall into this category, on the unpleasant side, Australian aborigines on the pleasant. Another 29 percent propose pleasant and unpleasant alternatives, with sometimes a third possibility (Christian, Muslim, Platonic, and Virgilian afterlives), and the final 21 percent elaborate complex systems with multiple stages and souls.[13] Early and late Egyptian mortuary practices fall here, as well as Hindu and Buddhist systems. That 80 percent of human cultures elaborate afterlives of ever increasing complexity suggests that once people start thinking about afterlives, they find it difficult to stop. Most recently, the moral philosopher Samuel Scheffler has traded in the familiar personal immortality of an individual or transmigration's discontinuous but ongoing existence, for "afterlife" defined as the continuing life of the human species.[14]

Even within cultures that have afterlife beliefs, not everyone believes them. Disbelief was so common in ancient Rome as to have, like RIP, its own epitaphic abbreviation, NF NS NC: *Non fui, non sum, non curo,* or "I was not, I am not, I care not" (in other words, "I did not exist before I was born, I no longer exist, and I don't care one way or the other"). Modern accounts usually attribute belief to individuals' emotional needs, whether to console themselves for loss, to fend off terror of death (their own and others'), or to give meaning to an otherwise meaningless life. Or they chalk up belief to wider social purposes: to heal the social rupture caused by death, to reinforce morality and acquiescence in the social status quo. Jay Olshansky and Bruce Carnes tell us that afterlives are "idealized worlds, created to soften the reality of life in a world filled with pain and suffering."[15] For Sigmund Freud, belief counters infantile human helplessness before "pitiless . . . nature."[16] For Karl Marx, religion is "the halo" of life's "vale of woe"; life after death must then be the twelve stars in the virgin's crown.[17] If the afterlife makes people feel better, it has also been thought to make them act better.

"No afterlife, no morality" is a slogan defending the afterlife that twists to undermine it. In Dostoyevsky's uneasy world, everything is permitted in the absence of immortality (and God).[18] As in Dostoyevsky's subordination of God to immortality, *atheist* long meant someone who denied the afterlife, no matter the gods. Lucretius might dedicate *De Rerum Natura* to Venus as passionately as he pleased; he was still called atheist for denying providence and a future state. Modern classicists who smugly affirm that Lucretius was no atheist forget the wider early meanings of the term.[19] Atheists, it was clear, were immoralists who disbelieved in order to commit the nefarious acts believers virtuously denied themselves.

Dostoyevsky's view still has adherents as well as antecedents. "Who would not commit all the excesses to which he is prompted by his natural inclinations, if he may do them with security while he is alive, and be incapable of punishment after he is dead? . . . [N]o man will be contain'd within the bounds of duty, when he may safely transgress them."[20] So John Dryden in 1685 anticipated Dostoyevsky's terrifying desire. Freud echoed the expectation in *Future of an Illusion* (1929). Social constraints chafe; men long to shrug them off; only fear keeps them from gratifying every forbidden desire. Moralizing the afterlife supplements the neighbor's watchful eye with God's. He will punish or reward no matter what society does or fails to do or to see. We now know to put pictured eyes near a coffee machine to persuade more people to contribute to the payment pot.[21] Michel Foucault would cover those eyes (*Surveiller et punir: Naissance de la prison* [Paris: Gallimard, 1975]), but large-scale societies without effective police early added the watchful eyes of high gods to monitor behavior.

Arguments for a moralized afterlife come from both sides of the aisle—from religious who deplore atheism, and atheists who deplore religion. Christopher Marlowe scoffed that the first origin of religion was "to keep men in awe."[22] Rejecting the community's commonly held beliefs on a point as tender as death incurs suspicion about solidarity and reliability. Should disbelief itself be a prohibited category, affirming disbelief enacts alienation from the community, and the community reciprocates that hostility. Rarely among eighteenth-century thinkers even after Pierre Bayle, Catherine Trotter Cockburn argued that an atheist might be virtuous. Now a minor sociological cottage industry undertakes to prove that atheists are rather more moral than less so.[23] Yet skeptics confident of their own virtue are not always sure of that of others, especially if the others are poor.

Henry St. John, Viscount Bolingbroke, a mid-eighteenth-century deist, thought the common people should be left their afterlife for the sake of their behavior.[24] Henry Fielding, a borderline Christian-deist, saw social revolution as the consequence of persuading the poor that they had no compensatory afterlife to look forward to.[25] When urban agglomerations lacked effective police, and industrialization had not yet disciplined bodies, Christianity for the masses was, says Simon Dickie, "almost a mainstream Enlightenment position."[26] The moral argument turns the afterlife into a plot to keep the disadvantaged obedient and to control minds. Why should the afterlife differ from other ideologies? Yet afterlife denial fulfills all the ends attributed to belief, except policing morality.

Thus Freud, at the end of *The Future of an Illusion*, urges mankind to give up acres in heaven in favor of cultivating Candide's garden plot here. Let us liberate this world from oppression and declare "without regret," quoting Heinrich Heine, "We leave Heaven to the Angels and the Sparrows." Vigorously denying an afterlife, Freud appropriates all the illusory benefits he attributes to afterlife belief. Heaven renounced, the survivor is consoled and reconciled to that loss in the affirmation of his garden. Turning from imaginary heavens to the real earth, he fulfills his wishes through social action, enforces morality in the world's liberation (farewell, police), strengthens the social order by human solidarity, and affirms meaning that extends beyond the self through the human world, defining contours for the cosmos. Heaven is for angels and sparrows, earth for the rest and the real. Contemplating an afterlife, or denying one, we look after our psycho-socio-moral needs. Afterlife denial is as energizing, invigorating, and life-affirming as any afterlife belief. But if the same psycho-social-moral needs are met by both belief and denial, those needs cannot be the source of belief. An origin is called for that comprehends both believers and deniers, as well as the generous variety of developed afterlife beliefs.

Afterlives perform multiple functions in contemporary and earlier societies, but their primary, original role is cognitive—to explain what happens at and after death. That cognition is not isolated, but socialized. The afterlife narrative adjusts how to behave at death's approach for the dying and for the surviving community, and it defines the relationship existing between the living and the dead. In this sense, societies without afterlife beliefs still have them. They know that they do not know, and they deny, when asked, the possibility of knowing. Freud did not believe in an afterlife, but he had firm beliefs about the afterlife. There is no distressing uncertainty about the matter. Other people's certainties may even become, as for the A'rna and the Sami (and Epicureans and *New Yorker* cartoons), a source of mirth.[27] It is vital for individuals and cultures to know "what's next" because death reminders are powerful. It is easy to ignore death—we do so most of the time—but when we are reminded, we experience a little life-enhancing jolt. Freud recognized as much when he elaborated his theory of a death instinct. Thoughts of death, like thoughts of sex, stimulate. But unlike sex they bind the individual to the community and the self rather than to an immediate object of desire.

Across cultures, being reminded of death ("mortality salience") strengthens ideological biases, cognitive psychologists have shown.[28] Drop a word associated with death during a psychology experiment and participants adhere more fiercely to their own core values and those of their group. Lexical association performs, on its own, the community-strengthening socio-political ends attributed to afterlives. Death, when evoked, brings the tribe together; group solidarity is its own reward, isolation its own punishment. Adam Grant, an organizational psychologist at the Wharton School of the University of Pennsylvania, has explored "whether death awareness affects people at work."[29] Deadlines, anyone? It certainly affects almost everything else.

Death awareness makes religious fundamentalists more fundamentalist.[30] It inclines people to conform to the opinions of others in their group—but not to the opinions of those outside their group.[31] It makes men more hostile to women's studies and women more supportive.[32] It increases one's preference for allocating scarce resources to members of one's own group.[33] It makes one adhere more firmly to cultural norms, whatever they may be.[34] Thus afterlife denial offends deeply when belief is normative. It explains the preference given tragedy over comedy that puzzled Hume.[35] Death awareness also, paradoxically, explains why skeptics embrace ending life, their own or others', with dignity, while many religious Christians, clinging to comatose loved ones, fend off Jesus's welcome to eternal life.

Happy afterlife beliefs do not correlate with any hurry to get there. In a seeming paradox, pro-life militants do not imagine a loving Jesus welcoming to his presence aborted fetuses, terminal sufferers, and comatose patients, or restoring the vegetative to their conscious souls. If they did, their opposition to abortion, euthanasia, end-of-life consultations ("death panels"), and shutting down artificial life-support systems should be far less vehement. They would not resist heaven with such fervor and at such expense. If there ought to be "no atheists in foxholes," there should equally be "no Christians in intensive-care units." Yet studies of terminally ill patients confirm that the religious seek more aggressive, life-prolonging care than the less religious. Intent on staving off death through the very last week of life, they are also less likely to have living wills and end-of-life directives.[36] From Dinesh D'Souza to the Baptist preachers and their young children who keep returning from heaven, a firm grip on the next life carries over into the demand for the continuation of this one. While skeptics fit their own fantasied or assisted deaths into natural, cosmic cycles, ideologues of life cling religiously to life here or there, but especially now.

The conventionally religious have no monopoly on afterlife cravings. Some nontheists are as determined to live forever as those who believe in someone who has already arranged an eternity for them. Scientific analogies serve as well as any other. If the mind or soul is information and not matter, quantum theory forbids its destruction. In *The Physics of Immortality* (1994), Frank J. Tipler proposes that we will be resurrected as computer simulations, our quantum states reactivated, though our being has dispersed. Resurrection will occur when computers can "store all possible human simulations [as] an insignificant fraction of the entire capacity," shortly before "the final Omega Point singularity." Much depends on what the Omega Point wants: what age our emulated body is, where our emulated brain is placed, whether we come with ancestors and descendants, whether our emulation is real or a fantasy, and whether the Omega Point decides to let us continue running eternally. Tipler expects the Omega Point to love us. Hans Moravec, in *Mind Children*, thinks the resurrection will occur sooner, since simulations need not emulate the quantum state. John Leslie, in *Immortality Defended*, argues that "our life patterns are but an aspect of an 'existentially unified' cosmos that will persist after our death." Radio waves persist after the radio has been smashed; light from the Big Bang is still arriving. Although nothing new emanates from the smashed radio, traces continue, so brain product endures when we, the union of brain and body, do not.[37]

In sum, death awareness makes people come together with others of their kind, erasing their differences, enlarging their generosity, and enhancing alienation from those not of our kind. The evolutionary utility to groups of such attitudes seems patent: hunting and warfare and childbirth are risky businesses that require enhanced collaboration for success. The individual, fleeing in terror, bent on saving his own skin, is easily picked off by a coordinated group intent on attack or by the bear pursuing one of five scattering friends in New York in 2014.[38] Enhanced identification with others when one is under threat serves both the self and the group. It would indeed be astonishing if the brain did not react to life-threatening stress, but it is highly instructive that the changes that do occur link not to self-preservation (the individual) but to group solidarity (the other, but not Other).[39] Terror Management Theory initiated these inquiries and discovered the phenomenon, but it attributed the effects to existential anxiety at the prospect of one's own death, an individualist account. Fear of death varies among individuals. In a survey of the fears of modern undergraduates, fear of speaking in front of a group beat out fear of death.[40] Nor had it yet been discovered that in addition to enhancing group identification, death reminders generate happy thoughts. Death reminds us what we value about life, irresistibly.

One Terror Management theorist works hard to drum up anxiety in the otherwise calm reader in this engaging account of the losses death incurs. Fear of death is different from other aversive events, like not finding a mate

> because there is nothing one can do to reduce the probability of death to less than 100 percent certain. Humans know that this is one thing that will definitely happen and this one thing might well be the end of their existence, a disconnection from every thing and person they care about and love, a final thwarting of all of their desires and favorites: belonging, sex, pleasure, control, love, aesthetic enjoyment, learning, exploration, sports, travel, theater, music, significance, reading *Psychological Inquiry*, ad infinitum.[41]

Anyone not made a little existentially anxious by that account either has strong nerves or is snacking while reading. Death-awareness effects diminish if one is given something good to eat at the same time.[42] More surprisingly, death awareness also cheers us up: those happy thoughts come irresistibly to mind, unsought. Some unconscious mechanism provokes those reminded of death to produce ideas associated with happiness, filling a blank third letter after *jo* with *y* rather than with *b*.[43] The sting of imagined loss elicits its antithesis. So, in spite of his scary intentions, the Terror Management theorist ends his screed with "belonging, sex, pleasure . . .

ad infinitum," travel and theater, world without end. Instead of ending on the loss with which he threatened us, he fills our imaginations with all the things we love and want to possess forever. If we cannot possess them forever, those who live after us will. And if all human life is doomed, plants and animals will flourish anew, and the planets spin on.[44] There is a reason, or at least a psychological mechanism, that explains the assault of the mantra "Live every day as if it were your last." Thinking on the last day cheers this one. There is a minority among us whom thoughts of death paralyze, but even they draw near to what terrifies them. Mortality salience animates, but it does not produce any afterlife concepts.

Actual mortality raises its own cognitive questions: What has happened? Where did the person who animated this body go? Edward Hirsch catches that moment in *Gabriel*, his elegy on the death of his son, when he records the moment he sees his twenty-two-year-old son's body:

> I peered down into his face
> And for a moment I was taken aback
> Because it was not Gabriel
>
> It was just some poor kid
> Whose face looked like a room
> That had been vacated.[45]

We call what has happened *death*, a term that signally fails to answer the second, more pressing question, "Where is the person who used to be here?"

Afterlife concepts derive from the coincidence of how the mind works and what happens at others' deaths. That seemingly dead bodies occasionally recover is the clincher. Most simply put, when someone dies, something goes missing that has been the medium of interaction with that person. When something goes missing, we ask where it is, we look for it, and failing to find it, we wait for it to reappear.[46] Things, we know, do not disappear into thin air. They must be somewhere, and we often find them. The logic of human experience requires that whatever it is that vanishes when someone dies, soul, consciousness, breath, heartbeat, response, has gone to some other place. On this principle, we declare laws of conservation of matter and energy, and quantum physics claims that information never vanishes. If death puts out the candle's flame, the soul must be the smoke drifting up from the snuffed wick. Reincarnation or metempsychosis becomes entirely plausible, for soul or life force disappearing here must reappear over there—or perhaps over there. Even David Hume thought metempsychosis a logical possibility, "the only system of this kind, that philosophy can so much as hearken to."[47] When someone seemingly dead recovers, a rare and therefore remarkable occurrence, whatever went away has come back.

In Emmanuel Levinas's terms, in death the face of the other has ceased to respond. "Death is the *no-response*."[48] What remains is an untoward and uncanny presence, a socialized body without sociality. Vanished is that aspect of the other that responds to the self, that defines the self through its responses, and, distributed through many bodies, creates the self within society. The face that no longer responds is both a face and not a face; it is no longer the face we looked into to find ourselves. But we know ourselves only in the face of the other, the earliest mirrors of mankind, and if the face does not respond, we are not there. Death for Levinas is not possible, but "an ever open *possibility*."[49] Our own deaths, to the anxiety over which Terror Management Theory attributes so much, transfer to ourselves the non-knowledge of death given by the death of the other, a transference "not mechanical [*une mécanique*] but [that] rather belongs to the intrigue or the intrication [*sic*] of My-self [*Moi-même*] and comes to cut the thread of my own duration, or ties a knot in this thread, as though the time in which the 'I' [*moi*] endures dragged out its length."[50] It is a moment that can always and only be imagined, but the nonresponse of others is all too visible.

The primacy of Levinas's responsive face is also neurological. The brain allocates the fusiform gyrus area to recognizing faces, especially eyes, mouths, and their movements. At five months, infants' brains light up when a face flashes in front of them in the same two-phase recognition process as adults.[51] Babies are slower: they take 1.3 seconds to complete a reaction that adults finish in 0.3 seconds. Faces are the first abstraction an infant recognizes, and in the bonding of infant and mother, eye to eye and mouth to breast are equally important. The blind touch each other's faces. In prosopagnosia, the afflicted cannot recognize faces. Relying on other cues to identify persons they know, they helplessly offend people to whom they have been often introduced but can never recognize. When the face no longer responds, the open eyes no longer see, the mouth no longer closes. A change has occurred that must be accounted for.

For this accounting, cognitive psychology currently provides a stripped-down model of the mind's processes in causal agency, agent detection, and, for primates, theory of mind. Like cows and crows and chimps, we need these processes to act in the world, and without them our world would be both unworkable and unrecognizable. *Causal agency* means that events have causes; *agent detection* assumes an agent exists and refers to the search for whatever caused the event. Absent in cows and crows but common to people and chimps, *theory of mind* attributes mental states like our own to others and recognizes that the contents of others' minds may be different from our own. This fundamental aspect of human sociality and cognition develops around age four and suffers impairment in autism. Empathy, which Frans de Waal identifies as "the original, prelinguistic form of inter-individual linkage,"[52] the capacity to feel what another is feeling, underpins all social interaction. Making it happen, mirror neurons ensure that we mime internally the actions we observe others performing. In death, theory of mind does a double take.

Causal agency and agent detection are closely linked, and theory of mind imposes sociability and community on causation, humanizing it. When we bump into a table and bruise our shin, we look for a cause for our pain—the bumping—and an agent—the table. Animating the agent, we often blame the table for putting itself in the way: "Where did that wretched table come from?" Some people even impose eternal suffering on the table in question: "Where did that [God-] damned table come from?" Activating theory of mind, we attribute malevolence to the traveling table, and people have been known to kick the table in retaliation. More benignly, we realize some person moved the table because guests are coming.

In death, an agent has vanished. I wait for the reply, and it does not come. An entity to which I attributed consciousness like my own has absconded.[53] So, faced with the disappearance of the animating principle, our ancestors wondered where it had gone. Who had taken it? What was become of it? Where was it? What was it doing? It could not just be gone. Or perhaps it is just gone, poured out like water. In the answers to such questions, and in a society's need, as Robert Hertz argues, to prevent its own diminution by loss, afterlife narratives originate.[54] Michael Shermer calls people "natural-born immortalists," but that is not quite right.[55] We are natural-born questioners of mortality, and a substantial minority persist in doubting the immortality solution.

Our speechless primate cousins can neither pose nor answer such questions, but they recognize death and do not like it. In their silences, our feelings are visible without our words. Chimpanzees wait for life to reappear in dead conspecifics; they act aggressively to provoke signs of life; they touch the dead gently, hoot softly, leave them lingeringly.[56] They lick the wounds of the injured, but not of the dead. In their unsettled and uncertain responses, we see from another, prelinguistic angle the situation our afterlife narratives address. Elephants stroke the bones of other dead elephants and render themselves vulnerable to poachers by returning to the site where their dead were slaughtered.[57] Whales are said to grieve.[58] Among macaques, gorillas, chimpanzees, langurs, even baboons, mothers and male caretakers may carry dead infants for several days, and grieving primates exhibit the same physiological indicators as humans (temperature, blood pressure, heart rate).[59] Not surprisingly, the most frequently reported accounts of primates' responses to death are of mothers carrying dead infants, days extending to months if the corpse mummifies.[60] That such reports are more common than those for adult primates is not just interspecific empathy or human sentimentality in action. Mothers carrying dead infants for days are visible to observers, while most primate deaths in the wild are not.

In the wild, chimps retire into their nests or deep vegetation when they are injured, ill, or old.[61] Accident, predation, and murder ("intergroup violence") create rare exceptions and opportunities for observation. Chimpanzees killing a chimpanzee from another group (and not cannibalizing it) abandon the corpse, often within an hour.[62] Deaths by accident and interspecific predation are, by contrast, marked by waiting, vocalizing, and anxiety for a reaction from the dead conspecific, even to violent interventions.

At a riverbank, as two groups met, an adult male falling from a tree broke his neck on an upturned rock. No one touched him, but for ten minutes, they kept up an unusual, intense, shrill, unique distress call ("wraah"); then they gathered silently around the body, sitting and gazing at it for another ten minutes, as one continued the special "wraah" call.[63] After twenty minutes, life began to resume, with sporadic feeding, grooming, mating. Periodically individuals, especially younger ones, approached the corpse, sniffed it, stared at it. For four hours, the group stayed near the corpse, adolescents still paying close attention to it as time passed, older adults grooming, feeding, nearby. Then they left. A young adult male, a paralytic adult male, and an adolescent female were the last to leave, each departing after a final gaze at the corpse.[64]

For Freudians, especially interesting is the persistent copulation in the presence of the dead. The group consisted of fourteen males and two females, one adolescent, one adult with an infant; eleven males mated with the adult female sixteen times at intervals ranging from three to forty minutes over the four-hour period, some several times. Unfortunately, the author of the study does not indicate whether such rates of copulation are ordinary or represent exceptional, stress-induced sex.[65] They certainly suggest resurgent "happy thoughts," that mechanism of mental movement to positive affect.

By contrast, predation and a natural, anticipated death induced both mild and violent contact with the body. A leopard's killing an adolescent female provoked "intense mass excitement." "[S]ome displaying males even dragged [her] over short distances."[66] Others gently shook the hand and leg, looked in the face and groomed the body, removing fly cases. Six hours elapsed before they abandoned the body.[67] A natural death in captivity showed responses that were similar, the authors observe, to human reactions to an expected death. As an old chimp grew lethargic, her three companions, a daughter and a mother-son pair, groomed her frequently, orienting themselves towards the dying chimp's head. The two female chimps gradually ceased grooming and moved slightly away. After about ten minutes, the male charged the platform where the dead chimp lay, pounded her torso with both hands, and then ran away from the platform, an act he repeated twice during the night. The daughter sat beside the body all night, without grooming it. The mother of the mother-son pair groomed her son longer than usual. The three survivors' sleep was disturbed, and in the morning they removed straw from the body, "cleaning the corpse." Once the body was removed, for several days they avoided the old sleeping area.[68]

As Anne Zeller observes, primates experience grief at loss of individuals, but lack mourning as a communal response or recognized "group activity": "Since mourning is the culturally constructed social and public response to the loss of an individual, it rests in a social and symbolic context which is not available to primates."[69] Primates respond to the breakdown of social responses by waiting for those responses to reappear and crying out or by trying to provoke some response through violent, expressive actions. Different causes of death—predation, accident, natural in captivity—elicit different reactions: fury, wonder, anxious resignation. As with us, primate theory of mind demands a response that death frustrates. But our few surviving primate relations do not bury each other. They just move on.

Like them we howl—and move on—but we also touch, prepare, and dispose of the body that unites survivors by its presence. Funeral rituals form a community around the dead, separate the living from the dead, re-situate the dead relative to the living. Protecting the survivors from death and the dead, they fulfill the obligations of the living to the dead, which are obligations to the community created and threatened by death. Wakes, sitting shivah, and cemeteries close the gap created in the community, as dirt fills the grave. The greater the loss to the community, the greater the need to fill the grave with gifts, to secure life with magic. When the community feels no loss, when the dead does not signify to the collective, the mere individuals who care may scatter ashes where they will, or they may keep the body close by.

Funerary rituals rarely articulate but always presuppose a narrative about what next happens to the person gone missing. Jonathan Swift, the Dean of St. Patrick's, Dublin, imagined his friends disposing of him in lines as rapid as grief: "The Dean is dead; . . . he ran his race,/ We hope he's in a better place."[70] In the popular western view, soul and body separate abruptly at death; death is precisely that separation. The soul flies off with a devil or an angel; the body "remains." The modern medical West understands death as a process before a final shutting down. Medically defined, brain death enables organs to be harvested for reuse before death has progressed too far through the body.[71] Organ donors are not being harvested while they are still alive.

Some materialists send a nonexistent soul into nonexistence. So Hiraga Gennai in eighteenth-century Japan called on Buddhist imagery of flame, of material sparks: "Life comes into being the same way a spark does when stone and metal are rubbed together. Life continues as long as the firewood burns, but when the fire goes out, nothing is left but burned-up charcoal—yes, that's right, your body."[72] Michael Graziano and Daniel Dennett take consciousness to be the attention the brain pays to its own processes, which ceases when the brain ceases processing. [73] In the funerary practices most familiar today, departure is assumed, and the body is burned, buried, or, more rarely, exposed (among the Maasai, on the Parsis' Towers of Silence, both burned and exposed among Tibetan Buddhists). Cremation continues the process of burning up the charcoal. Burial puts it out of sight. Exposure integrates it with other living beings. In many earlier afterlives, multiple souls take different directions; some remain, others depart the body. Empathy with the body underlies the aversion to burning attested in the earliest recorded afterlives or, until recently, in Roman Catholicism, for the sake of the resurrected body. God is now trusted to be able to reassemble ashes as well as naturally decomposed dust.

Other cultures understand death as a process that continues over time, a gradual separating. Peter Ramsden contrasts the twentieth-century Canadian belief in abrupt separation with the seventeenth-century Huron view that there are stages in death, recognized by points at which bodies are reburied, their bones rewrapped and moved to different resting places.[74] Certain contemporary Indonesians, who visit and periodically rewrap corpses, are horrified by western practices of cremation or burial: "How could you? How do you love (*kaboro'*) and remember (*kilala*) your forebears if you cannot hold (*toe*) them and see (*tiro*) them as we do?"[75] The soul-person is still in some way present in the bones; through care of the bones a relationship continues. Unlike the skull that brings only death to mind in the western memento mori, these bones are not anonymous. Such empathic identification with what is left undergirds the veneration of relics, literally "what is left behind" (from *relinquere*). In the Chapel of Relics in St. Trophîme, Arles, a note carefully explains to hordes of wondering tourists—Protestant, Buddhist, atheist—that Catholics venerate relics in anticipation of the resurrection of the dead and as the presence of the saints among them. Such an explanation was once unnecessary.

Consciousness ceases in the dead, but it has not ceased in the living. The living continue to attribute to the dead—and to themselves as dead—some aspect of the consciousness they cannot imagine (being) without. The dead glide along our memories on well-established neurological pathways of recollection. Theory of mind leads us to attribute consciousness to the dead, motivating the decoration of corpses and their provisioning with grave goods, while the practice of agent detection leads to events' being attributed to the now invisible dead, as to the always invisible gods. The dead must have gone someplace else, but they are also still beside us. In fact, they are inside us. Our frustrated empathy with the dead also leads us to believe, not mistakenly, that where they have gone, we will follow. It is not surprising that traces of afterlife belief are both very common and extend very far back.

How far back do afterlife beliefs go? Barely five thousand years for written accounts: unambiguous testimonies to beliefs about an afterlife appear in Egypt and Sumer after 2500 BCE (mid-third millennium BCE) and develop rapidly, enriching and complicating details and imagery. Tomb inscriptions, books of the dead, amulets and magic spells, poems about visiting the world of the dead—many genres take up that terminal question. In Sumer and Babylon through at least the sixth century BCE, afterlife conditions depended on how the living cared for the dead and how the dead had died. In Egypt, within a few hundred years of their first appearance around 2350, magic spells ensuring the pharaoh's ascent to the sky had been appropriated by queens and nobles. As access to an agreeable afterlife democratized, the conditions of access were moralized and complicated.[76] In China, written evidence attesting to afterlife beliefs and ancestors' influence appears on oracle bones in the Shang dynasty (c. 1200–1045 BCE), with the first grave offerings appearing around 5800 BCE. Their successors, the Zhou, limited commoners to two generations of ancestors, royals to seven.[77]

Before writing, archeology provides evidence of death's social context. Skull rings, burials, and cremations disclose a community's consciousness of death. Yet it is not always clear whether a body was intentionally buried. Are the bones in a shaft in Spain from four hundred thousand years ago signs of burial or simply "bin-ends," left behind?[78]

The earliest burials that seem clearly intentional occurred ninety thousand to one hundred thousand years ago, performed by Neanderthals and early modern humans.[79] An early-modern human holds a boar's jaw in his hands, and a young Mousterian woman is buried with an infant at her feet. Neither those faint intimations of cause and effect or of desire, nor the ibex ring perhaps associated with a Neanderthal burial, nor the rose petals perhaps scattered by Neanderthals disclose any certain information.[80] About 74,000 years ago, a four- to six-month-old infant was buried with a seashell ornament in KwaZulu-Natal.[81] By thirty thousand years ago, bodies are elaborately decorated with ochre and ivory, beads and baubles, but the decoration does not speak for itself to clarify what it means, beyond the community's willingness to dedicate valuable resources to this body. (And where is everyone else?) The beautifully bedecked corpses of thirty thousand years ago may be arrayed for a festival of the gods or a meeting with other dead of which we will never know the particulars. The community may be asserting itself among the dead or placating greedy divinities or soothing the aggrieved dead or assuaging social panic at the loss of a key personage. Some eleven thousand years ago, at Gobekli Tepe in southwestern Turkey, hunter-gatherers carved vultures, spiders, and snakes on t-shaped stones that they then buried. Bits of human bone have been found in the dirt, and the site, once dismissed as a medieval cemetery, may have served both as temple and for the dead.[82] Grave goods, objects placed with the dead in a burial, are somewhat more suggestive, seconded by the proximity of burials to dwellings, either in them or nearby.

Like a decorated body, grave goods show symbolism in action, and they attribute to the corpse—or to the gods underground—desires that remain powerful in the living. In themselves, they do not prove a belief that the dead continue as conscious beings. Personal objects may be regarded as polluted by contact with the dead and so buried with them. Survivors wistfully project this life's lost desires on to the dead, as when a nineteenth-century French mother buried her daughter with a sou so that "she could have some fun in Paradise."[83] Still, when the dead are put in the grave accompanied by objects they found useful in life, or when traces of food or drink remain in the grave, some continuing life seems to be attributed to the dead. When a pipe for pouring libations extends from the surface into the grave, some necessary service is being performed. The dead need feeding; they become thirsty. Theory of mind, or empathy, considers what I would like or need were I in this situation. Burials in houses or very near them keep the dead close for some purpose, for power or influence attributed to them or for the comfort of their presence, staving off loss to individuals as to the community. The dead, too, may want to stay nearby. From Iwo Jima, the Japanese general wrote his family about what to do with his remains, "If I have a soul, it will stay near you and the children, so enshrining me in the house that you're living in will be fine. (And then there's always Yasukuni shrine.)"[84]

Studying the last fifty thousand years of funerary practices, V. Gordon Childe found simple grave goods in Paleolithic graves, joints of meat, unspecialized scrapers, lumps of ochre as toiletries. Practical, reusable items began appearing in abundance about seven thousand years ago: food, drink, pots, weapons, tweezers, rings and beads and necklaces, dice, lamps, buttons, amulets, and figurines. Absent from graves, though frequent in other domestic sites, were work tools. Either tools were too valuable to place in graves, or working in the next life was not part of the plan, neither imagined nor projected nor desired. Childe also found that after an initial elaboration and enrichment of grave goods, quality fell off. As societies grew rich, complex, and stable, they replaced real goods, like human sacrifices, with symbolic—and cheaper—models of human beings, animals, implements, jewels, and foodstuffs.[85] Greek grave goods of the first millennium shrink beside the glittering Mycenaean royal tombs of the thirteenth century BCE.[86] The seventh century BCE saw a woeful "falling off in number and value of goods offered to the dead," a modern classicist laments.[87] The great gold hordes of Afghan nomadic tribes eclipse contemporaneous burials by richer urban peoples in the first century CE.[88] Sixteen centuries later, reforming burghers rejected buying indulgences for the dead to hasten the soul's release from the pains of purgatory. Provisioning the dead shifts from human sacrifice to roast meats to water to prayer, and finally even prayer is denied utility.

Less happily, archeologists have found corpses that seem to be mutilated so they cannot come back. Their legs are broken; their bodies are bound; their heads are removed. Rather than trusted ancestors or fortunate infants buried in the walls of the house, these seem to be dangerous corpses, dismembered and disabled to prevent their making their way back to the precincts of life and taking their places among the living.[89] Such burial treatments seem to be signs of a different narrative about the dead. The dead are hostile and may impede others' route to the afterlife.[90] The dead are hungry, ravenous for the taste of the living, whom they would devour if they could. So Homer's shades surge towards blood, and the gods quail when Ishtar threatens to break open the underworld to let the dead up to eat the living. The dead, in sum, feel all the anger, rage, and resentment toward the living that the living feel toward death. They may be hostile, unforgiving, and vengeful. They may have it in for us, rejoicing in our failures, as malevolent as those living friends in whose misfortunes we take a secret pleasure. "As *Rochefoucault* his Maxims drew/From Nature, I believe 'em true:.... This Maxim more than all the rest/Is thought too base for human Breast;/'In all Distresses of our Friends/'We first consult our private Ends,/'While Nature kindly bent to ease us,/'Points out some Circumstance to please us.' "[91] The dead, after all, are dead, and we are not—how can they help hating us? Therefore, the living need to protect themselves.

All such speculations are merely speculative, in the absence of words or stories. Words, too, can be misleading. The common Christian tombstone inscription "requiescat in pace," or "rest in peace," proposes eternal sleep rather than eternal life. Addressing the body until its resurrection, the inscription skips the question of what the soul is doing in the meantime. Is it sleeping or dead with the body, awaiting the body in heaven, hell, purgatory, or enjoying some other intermediate state? Islam proposes the simplest burials and among the most beautifully elaborated afterlives. Yet while the Taj Mahal creates paradise on earth, the stones outlining the shape of a body over a simple Maghreb grave tell no afterlife tales. In Rabat, the richer dead have proper tombs, white or brightly tiled, blue, orange, green. The tombs take the shape of a body, a vertical stone at the head, the body a rectangular outline above ground. In the center of new graves, a little indentation holds water. In older graves, the center fills with growing vegetation, foliage flourishing, overflowing the sides, green life growing abundantly from death. Exquisitely consonant with Islam's faith in eternal life, the striking exuberance of this sign of life's conquest of death is perhaps misleading in its theology.

Cultures often have elaborate death rituals and beliefs that leave no physical evidence ten years later, much less ten thousand. In *Ten Canoes* (2006), the aboriginal Australians who collaborated on the film tell a story of cyclical origins. People are born from fish; they occupy water holes in the water and slip into the mother's vagina when the father dreams them. When people die, their souls go back into the water hole as little fishes and wait to be reborn. At death, until they collapse, the dying sing and dance. Then others take up the dance and death song that summons the fathers, all the spirits, who find the soul and take it, flying—sometimes it has to be brushed away from the body, with bunches of leaves dusting it off—back to the water hole, into the water. Birth and death participate in a cycle playing through water and fathers' dreams and mothers' dark, deep holes.[92] No morality is enforced, no priests empowered, the destination common to all and not undesirable. One could wish to be a little fish. Elaborate, intricate systems of afterlife beliefs may disappear without a trace.

Writing reveals what archeology intimates—the variety and variability over time, within and between cultures of afterlife narratives. Among the surprises of ancient afterlives is how grim they often were and how amoral. However watchful the earliest high gods were, they looked out only for the living and paid no mind to the dead, hived off to their own god(s) and left there. It was long before afterlives were integrated with other means of social control, and it was patchily done. The still common assumption that an afterlife is necessary to enforce morality is a back-formation from the afterlife's late adaptation to policing people's behavior. It seems necessary because it has been in place for a long time. Yet it was not always so.

That afterlives and morality merged only gradually, cobbled together at various places and times by persuasive thinkers, indicates their disparate evolutionary origins. Morality or our social rules proceed from the need to govern relations among the living, to adjudicate the interests of individuals and of the group through which alone individuals survive. Morality has little to do with the dead or dying, except to define correct treatment for the dead within the community. The living know that their actions affect the circumstances of the dead, who may be starved or denied burial rites. The power of the dead to control their own future state by premortem actions develops in Egypt by the third millennium (the twenty-first century) and elsewhere around the sixth century BCE, in a few places east and west.

Morality antedates afterlife narratives, developing independently long before afterlives begin to flicker on cognitive horizons. Evolutionary psychologists trace morality's origins in our primate cousins, related social species dependent on each other and the community for survival.[93] Frans de Waal's primate studies show the basic elements of human morality—and immorality—turning up in primate sociality. Others have marked the stages of spontaneous moral development in the behavior of young children and located moral decision centers neurologically in older parts of the brain.[94] Primate sociality signifies as precursor to our morality, long recognized as social.

Adam Smith argued for the inherent sociality of morality in 1759 (*Theory of Moral Sentiments*). Disputing Francis Hutcheson's concept of a "moral sense," Thomas Hobbes' and Bernard Mandeville's individualist selfishness, Rousseau's asocial autonomy, and David Hume's utility, Smith called our involuntary wincing at a blow aimed at another "sympathy." So the watching crowd twist and writhe along with the balancing tightrope walker, and delicate gentlefolk feel themselves itch where beggars are scratching their scabs.[95] That unconscious, irresistible slipping into another person's perspective (underlying "theory of mind") Smith made foundational to the formation of conscience and the self. Without society, there would be no occasion for morality. In society, however, we seek others' approval and avoid their disapproval, first to survive, then to prosper.

Monkeys were not on Smith's mind as he developed a concept of morality based on what we now call not "sympathy," but "empathy" (coined in 1895), but monkey morality suggests that human morality must antedate reward-and-punishment afterlife narratives, and why such narratives, once found, are so compelling. Primatologists, minding monkeys and other primates, have found robust moral systems governing intraspecific and even interspecific behavior. Chimpanzees make friends with—and have been known to assist—birds, cats, and people, as well as other chimpanzees. Primate morality has unwritten, unspoken rules that regulate behavior within the group—freeloaders are punished, the helpful are helped, hierarchy is recognized but also manipulated by cultivating allies and competing for dominance.[96] Chimpanzees share more readily with those who have recently groomed them. Adult chimpanzees punish adolescent chimpanzees who stay out late and delay every one's dinner: they beat them, and the next night the young chimps come dutifully in on time. Fairness, the expectation of equal distribution, animates the capuchin monkey who receives a cucumber slice, sees his neighbor given a grape, and then shakes the cage and hurls the cucumber slice that was once entirely satisfactory.[97] Those rules enable cooperation against other groups and individuals. Chimpanzees hunt monkeys, attack foreign chimpanzees, seize their females, and murder their infants; they also risk themselves to defend members of their own group. Females may rescue a trapped male and trap or chase other females. Many will risk drowning to save an infant. Sometimes they exhibit behavior that humans call immoral. Female gorillas may conceal themselves in the bush to dally with a nondominant male, out of sight and hearing of the male who claims exclusive access. Female chimps may visit other groups of chimpanzees for surreptitious matings.[98] They, too, know to avoid watchful, censorious eyes.

Chimpanzees lack the higher reaches of human self-denial and group identification, but then, so do many people. We admire our species-specific altruism because it is uncommon, or we begrudge it, denying its existence or impugning its motives or calculating its probabilities.[99] Primates share the groundwork of our morality, but they have no rules for coping with the dead, apart from watching to see if their companion comes back and moving away when it is clear that there will be no return. Morality is for the living.

That does not cease to be true among the higher primates. Almost 50 percent of human afterlives do not distinguish pleasant and unpleasant situations for their dead. No one is rewarded or punished; everyone is in the same situation. Such unfairness has a powerful empirical warrant. Everybody dies, the just and the unjust, those who help and those who hurt. Their bodies undergo the same process of dissolution. There are no distinctions in death, so why should there be distinctions after death? If such distinctions are to exist, they must be invented in defiance of death's evident leveling. There are two exceptions: people die in different ways, and bodies receive diverse treatments in death.

Primates respond differently to different kinds of deaths—natural and expected, accidental, and by predation, those they suffer and those they cause. Some afterlives catalogue such distinctions. For example, in ancient Sumer, among the earliest human afterlives on record, individuals experience different conditions depending on how death happened. So, too, the condition of the dead depends upon the care taken by the living. What matters to the dead is that others perform the proper rites. Chinese (and Indian) ancestors die if the rites are not performed.[100] Sumerians sip muddy water.

To make the leap from differences in afterlife conditions depending on how one died to differences depending on how one lived required considerable ingenuity. It seems to have occurred first in Egypt. Several millennia later, Plato promoted it, and Virgil codified it. Judaism linked the law and life. Afterlife was otiose so long as the linkage held. When it broke, and obedience to the law brought martyrdom and death rather than life,

Judaism too adopted a system of rewards in another life for the righteous. Once the leap was made, binding a logical explanation to a moral imperative, the combination was immensely seductive and has remained so. Threatening to remove a moralizing afterlife feels like a divorce or the death of a spouse—it wasn't always there, but you are now quite certain you cannot live without it. Removing it—or threatening to remove it—shakes the foundations of the life that one has come to know as one's own and that claims one as its own.

In their origins, afterlives do not take the shapes we expect: they neither comfort survivors nor fulfill the wishes of the dying. They rarely have any moral component, while the most moralizing of ancient peoples, the Jews, had no afterlife at all. (Properly speaking, the severest moralists erased the traces of earlier beliefs and practices on ideological grounds.) Instead, the earliest afterlives enhance the solidarity of the community in rites observed for the dead, engage empathy with the socialized dead body, and meet a cognitive demand as to the present whereabouts of what once lived in the now dead body, the absent person. Unsocialized bodies are abandoned or, when expelled from the community, desecrated. That the primary demand is cognitive accounts for a recurrent note of skepticism, sometimes soft, sometimes brassy, chiming ever more loudly the more elaborate the afterlife systems. Afterlife disbelief is as ancient as belief, if less visible. Some people and cultures prefer not to go beyond the empirical evidence. That persistent skepticism emerges even when afterlives turn hopeful. Belief in immortality has steeled many a virgin martyr, while skepticism has kept her brothers safe at home, to live and reproduce. To make this good, we need to attend to the oddities in some forgotten afterlives that look like our own, but somehow just do not quite get it right.

2

IMPERMANENT ETERNITIES: EGYPT, SUMER, AND BABYLON, ANCIENT ISRAEL, GREECE, AND ROME

I have always taken a particular Pleasure in examining the Opinions which Men of different Religions, different Ages, and different Countries, have entertained concerning the Immortality of the Soul, and the State of Happiness which they promise themselves in another World.
—JOSEPH ADDISON, *SPECTATOR*

[I]n origin the major continuing religious traditions, both East and West, had no belief that there would be a worthwhile existence after death. They could not deny that in some sense there is a trace of the dead, in memory and dreams, or in the resemblance of offspring to ancestors; but whatever state the dead may be in, it is a condition of extreme weakness. . . . [G]radually both traditions came to realize that there may be about us that which does endure through the process of time and therefore perhaps through the event of death.
"AFTERLIFE," *THE OXFORD DICTIONARY OF WORLD RELIGIONS*

O Gilgameš, where are you wandering?
You cannot find the life that you seek:
when the gods created mankind,
for mankind they established death,
life they kept for themselves.
You, Gilgameš, let your belly be full,

keep enjoying yourself, day and night!
Every day make merry,
dance and play day and night!
Let your clothes be clean!
Let your head be washed, may you be bathed in water!
Gaze on the little one who holds your hand!
Let a wife enjoy your repeated embrace!
Such is the destiny [*of mortal men*].

—SIDURI, ALEWIFE GODDESS, TO GILGAMESH[1]

Happy ever afterlives required inventing. When Joseph Addison trusted that men the world over promised themselves eternal happiness in another life, he had 1700 years of Christian doctrine supporting him, and he forgot about hell. To Addison and to us the morally inflected, compensatory afterlives we now enjoy seem eternal. Gilgamesh knew better. The gods kept life for themselves and gave mankind death. Digging up dead afterlives reveals how grim ancient afterlives were, how inextricable body and soul, and how remote moral considerations. It also reveals how changeable they were. Of the four principal coexisting and ultimately intersecting western afterlives that Christianity displaced—Egypt, Sumer/Babylon, Israel, Greece/Rome—each underwent significant transformations, tending to both public purposes and private anxieties, the private imbricated in the public. Discontented with their first responses to questions about death, our ancestors corrected the answers on the quiz.

Literary materials represent a late stage in the development of afterlife concepts, but it is possible to tease out earlier views already being modified in the earliest texts. No matter how permanent an afterlife seems to be—the great model is Egypt (or Christianity)—its surviving texts reveal continuing transformation, responsive to environmental influences, political changes, ideological shifts. In Egypt, Sumer, Babylon, Judea, Greece, and Rome, priests, philosophers, and poets quarreled bitterly about persistence through death and the conditions to be encountered in the grave. They revised their views of the next world in response to their ideas about this one, marking ideological and sociological rifts, as they adopted or scorned the inventions of their neighbors. Afterlives have been evolving since they were first imagined. Visibly in time, they democratize, they terrorize, they provide new hopes, and they provoke skepticism. They are even, as in ancient Judea, repressed on religious grounds.

Where the story we know best usually begins, this chapter ends: on the brink of Christianity and the triumph of the moralized afterlife in the monotheistic religions. Christianity originates in the middle of first-century Jewish debates about the dead and resurrection (discussed below). Its afterlife concepts have undergone multiple transformations, the last—or most recent—during the enlightenment (chapter 4, below). In turn, Christianity reshaped Judaism's take on the afterlife, while Islam's paradise reinforced the other religions of the book that preceded it. The Christian and Muslim traditions have prospered by proposing in their sacred texts doctrinally required beliefs about an afterlife, promising salvation and threatening damnation.[2] For a period, even Jews were persuaded. The Mishnah, in a self-fulfilling paradox as witty as Pascal's wager, excludes from "the World to come" those who say, "There is no resurrection of the dead" (Sanh.11).[3] In the twelfth century, Maimonides included resurrection among his Thirteen Principles of Faith fundamental to Jewish belief.[4] Since then, without textual support in the Torah and prophets, afterlife has reverted to the margins, as an option, but not a requirement, in Judaism. Those embracing the option usually consider it a requirement. Others rejoice in alternatives. As one rabbi responded when asked about Judaism's position on the afterlife, "Ask two Jews, and you'll get three answers."[5]

These familiar afterlives have long obscured their antecedents. From annihilation to reincarnation, from dreary sleep under the earth to agonizing punishments and blissful rewards, the ancients rang changes on the possibilities. They blurred the line between what they believed or feared really happened and what they clearly understood as afterlife fictions, mythic embellishments serving a philosophical or practical or satirical purpose. Sometimes, as in Plato, the afterlife is modified and improved on explicitly ideological grounds. Elsewhere, among Sumerians and Egyptians, the afterlife improves in ways that have evident ideological implications, although no author survives like Plato to explain why these changes are necessary. Israel flaunted its prohibition of once flourishing contact with the dead in its theo-ideological shift to monotheism.[6] Erased, the underworld gods left traces in prohibitions and poetic imagery, and YHWH's dead stayed imprisoned, unconscious, silenced, below the ground.

Egypt and Sumer, Greece and Rome, Judea with its claim of Egyptian experience and actual Mesopotamian connections: these represent only a few views west of the Tigris and Euphrates, spread through writing in major urban centers. Views in the suburbs and back alleys of empire were still more various and idiosyncratic, as attest the traces they have left in the ground as artifacts and in mysterious textual references (e.g., the Gospel Matthew's binding curses). Everywhere, from cities to wilderness, flourished magical practices, numerologies, demonologies, spells, incantations, offerings, curses, fortunetelling, prophecies, and oracles. Others have detailed such popular practices,[7] and much remains to be discovered about the beliefs and practices of the ancestors. Yet texts still provide the clearest evidence of change. The ancients recorded their afterlives in some remarkable literary works very much worth knowing as they imagined realms the living can never see—the land where the dead live. By the time those texts appear, the afterlife has been conquered and colonized, but it never stays still.

JUSTICE IN EGYPT, NILOTIC DISCIPLINE

Four thousand years of Egyptian difference; probable environmental and socio-political factors; the afterlife pharaoh escapes, followed by others; enhancing social controls; tomb-robbers and the emergence of skepticism; spread of Egyptian cults in Europe

Among the ancients, the Egyptians were the only people to invent an afterlife worth having—or dying for. Their moralized afterlife provided eternal life, justice, and happiness in another world, with punishments for those who deserved them. The care they lavished on their dead is familiar to every museum visitor and child passionate for pyramids. They have been called "obsessed with death," "obsessed with the afterlife," and more justly by Salina Ikram "obsessed with life and its continuation."[8] As a recent Field Museum wall text (2013) avers, the Egyptian project was to reproduce a life close to this one, but better, in the next world. Elaborated very early, their resilient and dynamic system lasted a long time. It will be another two thousand years before Christian imaginings surpass the duration of Egypt's.[9]

The Egyptians, then, would seem to cast serious doubt on claims that blissful afterlives require invention, that afterlives develop over time, originating in identification with the body, and that morality and justice are a late addition to afterlives and not always present. Happily, the generous labors of Egyptologists have uncovered such transformations, charted in Egyptian mortuary and literary texts, or inferable from them. The process is already complete in outline by the time the first documents appear. Although a *New Yorker* writer laments "that it wasn't until the Middle Kingdom (2010–1630 BC) that average Egyptians even dared to hope for the promise of an afterlife,"[10] an afterlife that seems a "promise" rather than a threat is Egypt's invention. How Egypt devised so early an expectation of eternal happiness continues to puzzle and fascinate Egyptologists.[11] Two factors seem critical.

Among the earliest large-scale complex societies, the ancient Egyptians succeeded better than their neighbors in controlling their environment, and that control they extended to the next world. Social discipline mastered and exploited the Nile in prehistoric times, enabling kings to unify and tax a settled, productive population and supporting the priestly magical sciences that made Egypt fabled in the ancient world. When Moses and Aaron defeated the Egyptian magicians, who saw in action the finger of God (Exod. 8:19), they accomplished a far greater feat than crossing the Red Sea dry shod. The Nile was erratic, sometimes with too much water, sometimes too little, and famine periodically threatened the enlarged population that the river made possible, yet a disciplined social organization freed Egypt from the arbitrary vagaries of rainfall and erratic flooding. In certain temples, priests maintained instruments and records that tracked the Nile's flooding patterns, the famous "Nilometers," invented in pharaonic times and further systematized under Islam.[12] Such routine predictability through the disciplining of nature, coupled with anxiety since nature can never be entirely disciplined, informs the Egyptian extension of control from life into death.[13] A divinized pharaoh, demanding to join the gods, benefited from a priestly and technological class empowered to ensure he succeeded, and continuously improving their methods. Ultimately their *Books of Going Forth by Day* (a.k.a. *of the Dead*) map the journey through the next world with a precision that will not be seen again until Virgil and Dante.

As crucial to the Egyptian difference was another environmental factor. Bodies buried in desert sand dry up and shrivel, but do not rot. A body preserved is a self visibly preserved: something remains. From the possibility of preserving the body proceeds its desirability. What cannot be imagined is difficult to desire. The earliest Egyptian burial dates from 55,000 BP (before the present).[14] Naturally mummified, desert-buried bodies with grave goods, food, drink, weapons, and ornaments appear around 4500–3300 BCE. Bodies buried in coffins, safely out of reach of the sand, putrefied, as loathsome as rotting bodies elsewhere. Eventually someone, doubtless collaboratively, devised artificial embalming and succeeded in re-creating eternity. According to John Taylor, around 2600 BCE extraction of the inner organs permitted successful artificial mummification, with techniques continuing to improve until they reached a peak about 1000 BCE.[15]

As Egyptians theorized the afterlife, the physical body was necessary to support its multiple souls, the *ka*, requiring nourishment and staying with the body, and the *ba*, winged for flying to the stars. The body preserved as mummy was a divine being, and so was the heart, center of morality, intellect, and conscience, "the god which is in man."[16] Empathy with the body is enabled by its preservation, and the souls are at once still with the preserved body and departed from it to other realms.

When the first afterlife texts appear (the Pyramid Texts, c. 2350 BCE), Egyptians had enjoyed 300 years of successfully mummifying bodies, and pharaohs had distinguished themselves from other dead by building the pyramids that were a wonder of the ancient world. The texts on the walls of Unis's small pyramid confirm V. Gordon Childe's finding that as societies become richer, their material investment in grave goods diminishes.[17] At first, with its cultural investment in burials, Egypt seems an exception, but the great pyramids are almost the earliest pyramids. Completed by 2525 BCE, some 175 years before the Pyramid Texts, Khufu's great pyramid at Giza remained, Toby Wilkinson observes, the tallest building in the world until 1889, when the Eiffel Tower surpassed it. Khufu's son Khafra completed the Giza complex with the Sphinx and a pyramid on a higher elevation than his father's.[18] From 2450 BCE, after the intergenerational competition of Khufu, his father, and his sons, Egyptian pyramids diminish in size. The great era of pyramid building was over. As the pyramids shrink, Pyramid Texts abruptly appear on the walls of the burial chamber, guiding pharaoh (Unis d. 2345 BCE) symbolically to Osiris and Ra.[19] Later periods will witness grave goods peaking, then turning mass produced and shoddy, as a new fashion arises.

Egypt's four thousand–year afterlife is usually regarded as confined to Egypt and immobile as its pyramids. Yet as Stephen Quirke, John Taylor, and others demonstrate, within Egypt it was a fluid, constantly developing tradition, intensely responsive to political changes. Even pyramids saw fashionable revivals. After Khufu, one king put pyramids in every town, and the Twelfth and Seventeenth dynasties saw revivals, almost a thousand years later, 1938–1755 and 1650–1550.[20] Funerary texts disappear sometimes for several centuries, especially in periods of foreign invasion and social unrest, and then become a way to reassert national identity when the invaders are repelled. So in the seventh, fifth, and first centuries BCE, new texts and very ancient ones were brought together, sometimes deliberately archaized.[21] Saving souls depended on a highly specialized treatment of the body by a cadre of experts, who mastered a literature of spells, meaningful decoration, and ritual procedures. The preserved body preserved the souls, and around the Mediterranean Egypt monopolized that technology of the body. Outside Egypt, from the fourth century BCE, perhaps winged by new Greek theories, its promise of eternal life spread, freed from the body.

Some chronological markers may be helpful, between the first Egyptian burials found, about fifty thousand years ago, and the seventh century CE, when Islam displaced Christianity as Egypt's official and dominant religion. The first burials with grave goods date from 4500–3300 BCE, suggesting some conceptual system. A thousand years later, pyramids rise for Old Kingdom pharaohs (2686–2181 BCE). After the completion of the Giza complex (2450), the Pyramid Texts suddenly accompany Unis, who had no son (2345 BCE). Through known dangers that hem the dead, only pharaoh goes to the stars. That changes in the sixth, and last so-called, of the Pyramid Texts. Neith, the half-sister and queen of Pepi II (c. 2260–2175 BCE), appropriates pharaoh's spells. With no accommodation for gender, she is sent off in precisely the terms used for pharaoh. The texts spread to priests, officials, nobles in their tombs: democratization has begun.[22] Old Kingdom burial becomes so valued that the official Sabni travels to sub-Saharan Africa to bring back his father Mekhu's body to preserve his father's life.²³ Without the body, life vanishes. In the tale of Sinuhe, the self-exiled traveler is lured back to Egypt: "Think of your corpse, come back!"²⁴ By 2000 BCE in the Middle Kingdom, spells multiply from 800 to 1200, and the Coffin Texts appear, written on coffins, rather than pyramid walls.²⁵ One no longer needs a pyramid of one's own. A coffin will do.

In the New Kingdom (1580–1090), the so-called Books of the Dead appear, rolled papyri placed beside the mummy in coffins, rather than written on the coffin, and the scene of judgment takes place before the gods.²⁶ This period, especially between 1550 and 1300 BCE, sees a new emphasis on morality and judgment, annihilation vying with increasingly hideous punishments, as Osiris's enemies are decapitated or plunged into the darkness of an eternal pit.²⁷ As the afterlife becomes ever more desirable and ever more accessible to persons of different social classes, the terrors and dangers of the journey sharpen. Nor did technological innovation cease. By 1000 BCE with mummification techniques perfected, bodies no longer had to be hollowed out, stomach, lungs, liver, and intestines placed in separate jars, each protected by a different god. Canopic jars become symbolic.

Conquered by Persia in the sixth century BCE (c. 525 BCE, expelled 402 BCE), Egypt gained the camel, the first Suez Canal, and Herodotus as reporter of its traditional burials.²⁸ Happily, the Persian presence justified Herodotus's fascinated excursus on Egypt in his *Persian Wars*, Book II. About 430 BCE, Herodotus reports the full commercialization of the afterlife, as descending Egyptian classes laid claim to eternity. Access was equally available to bodies treated at very different prices. Herodotus reports three classes of treatment, three price categories, and precisely detailed procedures for removing the brain with hooks, draining, stuffing, and submerging the body in natrum. The cheapest bodies are just "given to those who come to fetch [them] away." More expensively treated bodies are encased and propped in a tomb.²⁹

As Alexander invaded Egypt, Isis invaded Europe: a temple opened in Piraeus, near Athens, about 333 BCE. Osiris was the murdered god the dead aspired to; jackal-headed Anubis oversaw the judgment of the dead, but Isis was the sister-mother goddess who had gathered Osiris's scattered parts and revived him to father Horus with her. Isis cults spread through the Mediterranean and beyond, reaching Rome in the second century BCE.³⁰ Ending native Egyptian rule, Alexander the Great consulted the bull god Apis and the oracle of Amun to confirm his divinity as he named after himself a city of the Nile delta (331 BCE). His successors, the syncretistic, adaptive, library-building Ptolemies, integrated Greek science and Egyptian belief (323–30 BCE) and were displaced in turn by the Romans (31 BCE, Actium).

In the Roman period, from the first to the fourth century CE, the quality of mummification declined, as realistic portraits displaced the god's image on the coffins of Hellenized Egyptians intermarried with Greeks.[31] The Fayyum mummy portraits combine Greco-Roman portrait painting with Egyptian burial preparation: modern eclecticism. From Hawara in the first or second century CE, on a funeral shroud a bearded man in Roman dress looks out; he is surrounded by Egyptian deities, architecture, and imagery, including falcons with the double crowns of upper and lower Egypt. From the same time and place, a beautiful female portrait mummy's wrappings form diamond shapes with a brass boss at the center of each, and no Egyptian iconography at all, apart from the fact of a mummy.[32] Marking a shift from the body to its representation, the decorative canopic jars used from about 1000 BCE disappear. Funeral papyri shrink to passports and then disappear after the second century CE.[33] As late as the fourth century CE, elaborate mummies with coffins and portraits survive.[34] Then the Christians came to power. Surviving third-century Roman persecution, Christianity turned shrines to Isis into altar bases and temples of Amun into chapels, looted Alexandrian temples of Serapis, and murdered their priests, as well as Hypatia, the female Neoplatonic philosopher.[35] In the seventh century, Arab conquest oversaw mosques built in the angles of temples. In the nineteenth century, Lucie Duff Gordon marveled at the past's traces, a Muslim saint as patron of crocodiles, Osiris's festivals under a new name, birth and burial ceremonies that were not Muslim but ancient Egyptian.[36]

At the heart of the system, and equally the source of modernity's continued fascination with Egypt's ancient practices, is the preserved body.[37] The spells chant body parts, the souls are defined by their relationship to the body, the aspects of personhood to be preserved are parts of the body. Images, too, had power. In early tombs, dangerous animals are often pictured mutilated or incomplete, missing the parts that would threaten the tomb's inhabitant.[38] Modern filmmakers imitate ancient fears when they reanimate mummies disturbed within their tombs.

In the Pyramid Texts a horrific vision of life among the dead motivates pharaoh's escape to the stars. Stephen Quirke proposes that the Pyramid Texts are the afterlife of chants that hymned the gods, celebrated feast days, and protected the living from such dangers as insects and snakes. Turned liturgies to accompany the burial of dead kings, they finally appear on the walls of the king's tomb.[39] In their new place within a tomb, they reveal pervasive anxieties about death, the body, and judgment. They sketch an obsession with death's leveling powers and even pharaoh's potential vulnerability to the judgment of others. Egyptians, they suggest, well knew a dismal and terrifying afterlife.

The first pharaoh protected by texts, Unis flew effortlessly to the sky, his own misdeeds erased. What he escapes, however, what does not happen to him, reveals the conditions of the other dead. Osiris protects him from "the wrath of the dead."[40] "The Great Lake's wrath has missed him" (p. 47, #172). He will not eat excrement and urine; he will not suffer hunger and thirst (p. 30, #143, 144). The apes who sever heads will leave him in peace, for his head is tied on his neck, and his neck is on his torso (p. 44, #165). Heads separate from their decaying bodies at the top of the spine, the verses recognize. He will not travel in darkness; he will not see those who are upside down, i.e., those in the underworld (p. 47, #170). The dark place of the dead reverses the physical order of the world above. Significantly, a judicial process is adumbrated from which he is exempt. *Maat* [justice] is with him, and he will "not sit (to be judged) in the god's court"; there are no accusations against him (p. 47, #170; p. 46, #169; p. 50, #177); he will not be given to the fire (p. 47, #170). There is no case against him, there is no guilty verdict against him; he is not at the head of the gods of disturbance, but at the head of the Sun's followers (p. 56, #207; p. 50, #179). He has destroyed "the one against (his) ascending to the sky" (p. 56, #207). He is also lord of semen, who takes women from their husbands as it pleases him (p. 60, #222).

Somewhere, then, there is a place of judgment that reverses life's norms, except for judgment. People are upside down and travel in darkness, not light; they hunger and thirst and eat excrement and urine; accusations are made and the gods sit in judgment. Troublemakers, disturbers of the peace are abhorrent. None of this has anything to do with pharaoh, and he escapes it all, but it is clearly waiting for someone. Social control extends beyond the grave to create a chamber of horrors more disturbing than anything in Mesopotamian or early Greek imaginings. Pharaoh escapes a world darker and more grotesque than even the dreary Sumerian afterlife finding literary form at the same period (c. 2100 BCE). Perhaps because pharaoh escapes: Sumerian kings enter their afterlife along with the common dead.

Pepi I, in the third and longest of all the Pyramid Texts, required more encouragement than his predecessors. He had to be told repeatedly to "Live! Live—you have not really died!" He had to be promised that his body would not decompose, his decay would not ooze, his smell would not be bad. Early mummification was still imperfect. He had to be promised that he would not be made a king among the dead (the fate of Gilgamesh and Ur-Namma in Sumer), but would rise to the gods. He had to be assured that he would not be accused, arrested or taken before officials or found guilty, and his opponents would not be justified.[41] By exempting him from what others anticipated, the priests and scribes responsible for the texts, inadvertently or purposely, assimilated the pharaoh to the judicial system affecting others. As access to the afterlife reached down the social ladder, the judicial process changed its character. Instead of answering the voices of individual accusers, as in a village council, a king's court or durbar, or other open forum, the soul endures an objective judgment before the gods. The Coffin Texts balance the two forms of judgment; the later Books of the Dead emphasize the gods' judgment in a full scale judicial review.[42] Who is watching shifts from the community or court to the high gods.[43]

The Field of Reeds, mirror of Egypt, a destination alternative to the stars and gods, also appears for the first time in the Pyramid Text of Pepi I (pp. 105–07, #31). Unis passes by the Marsh of Offerings (p. 30, #143). Pharaoh might escape to the stars, but a destination in a world that looked more like Egypt came to be favored.

Negotiating the transition from pharaoh's wishful afterlife to everyman's, the great Egyptian poem variously titled "Dispute between a Man and his Ba," "A Sufferer and his Soul," dates from the Middle Kingdom sometime between 2050 and 1800 BCE, the period of the earlier Coffin Texts. The sufferer is confident, his Ba skeptical about the sufferer's access to justice. Like Job, the sufferer demands a hearing, but he knows those who hear him and what they will do. Unlike poor Job, he has great confidence in the outcome, and the gods do not undermine that confidence by silencing him out of a whirlwind, though his own soul tries:

> Let Thoth, the divine judge, hear my case,
> Let Khonsu, guardian of pharaohs, protect me.
> Let Ra, the divine boatman, judge me,
> Let Isis . . . defend me.[44]

The sufferer knows who will look out for him: he names the names. The soul mocks this claim as pretentious, struggling against a democratizing afterlife: "It is so foolish for an ordinary human like you/ To want the funeral of a pharaoh." The sufferer insists that his heir will bury him properly and the soul had best let him die: "If you continue to oppose my death,/ You will never find rest in the land of the dead./Trust me, my soul, my companion . . ."

The sufferer laments his own miserable personal situation, his literally stinking life, like "bird drop on a hot day . . . rotten fish in the full sun . . . the breath of a crocodile," his reputation abused, worse than "accusing a faithful woman of adultery, calling a legitimate child a bastard, plotting to overthrow the government." General social conditions are worst of all: the just perish, fools thrive, everyone chooses evil and rejects good, crimes outrage no one, and sins make everyone laugh. Contrasted with current social conditions is the beauty of death: health to the sick, freedom to the prisoner, home to the traveler, his native land to an exile. Scented like myrrh, death is a soldier returning home, clear skies after rain. It offers justice, wealth, and wisdom:

> Surely whoever goes to the land of the dead
>   Will live with the divine assembly,
>   Will judge the sins of the wicked.
> Surely whoever goes to the land of the dead
>   Will ride in the Barque of the Sun,
>   Will collect gifts offered at temples.
> Surely whoever goes to the land of the dead
>   Will be wise,
>   Will have a hearing before Ra the creator.

To this paean, the soul can only give way, urging the sufferer once again to stop thinking about dying, and promising the outcome the sufferer desires, but not yet:

> When it is time for you to die,
> When your body returns to the earth,
> Then I will travel with you,
> Then we shall live together forever.

Curiously, the soul, not the sufferer, wants to stay above ground, as if life insists on staying in the light, no matter the sufferings endured by the body or the knowledge that somewhere else is better.

Other Egyptian works also figure death as a relief: "Death long-desired arrives like water for the thirsty/ . . . like the first drop of milk on a baby's tongue."[45] Contemplating death, we know, keeps people alive and lively. So, too, the miserable and powerless soul entertaining suicide gains power over its situation. The intolerable need not be endured, and that thought enables endurance of the unendurable. Time enough, there will be "time for you to die,/When your body returns to the earth."

In the Coffin Texts, the outline sketched in the Pyramid Texts is filled in, codified, and developed. Proposing a subterranean mirror of Egypt or a celestial destination among the stars, the Coffin Texts promise reunion with loved ones in the Field of Reeds. "A man does what he wishes in the land of the dead," proclaims one coffin from about 2000 BCE.[46] The Coffin Texts provide maps of the route to the afterlife, supply passwords for critical junctures and instructions on how to walk upside down.[47] They tell the sun's path, the division of hours, the solar boat.[48] The judicial element expands: more demons threaten the soul, and a hippo-crocodile-lion monster gapes to swallow up the wicked.[49] Justice also opens a moral system, what one should do, and what one must not, most fully elaborated in the scrolls of the Books of Going Forth by Day.

From those books unrolls a lively picture of ancient personality types, stepping out from the walls of their tombs or rising up in their coffins. In the judgment before Osiris, Egypt integrated social and moral codes with the treatment of the dead. The deceased, male or female, stands before Osiris and forty-two judges who represent an aspect of cosmic balance or *maat*. She must name the judges and declare innocence as her heart is weighed against the feather of *maat*. If the heart is heavier than the feather, the deceased is consumed by Ammit, the waiting monster of annihilation. If the heart is light with conscious innocence, she proceeds into the afterlife. The deceased makes his "negative confession": he has "*not* lied, borne false witness, stolen, cheated, or robbed."[50] Nor, with a stunning thoroughness, quite beyond the Ten Commandments, has he "sulked, stolen the bread ration, instilled fear in another, sexually abused a young boy, been abusive of another, been too hasty, said too much, committed treason, bathed in water reserved for drinking, raised my voice, cursed the divine assembly, been boastful."[51] An ideally submissive, social personality emerges, entwined with anticipated, dreaded deviations—the loud boastful bully and the fearful subordinate, the assertive, rebellious individual and the conciliating honest man, the traitor-blasphemer and the loyal, pious citizen. The Egyptian facing judgment cannot claim he was never warned.[52] If only the dead read these rules, the living transcribed them, at length and often, and they seem to be drawn from the life.

As judgment developed more details, the journey more hazards, and the destination more similarity to Egypt, one concern that had not occurred to pharaoh emerged (post 1990 BCE): the horrid possibility of eternal labor in the Field of Reeds. Reflecting their hierarchical and bureaucratic social structure, Egyptians delegated. They avoided labor in the Field of Reeds through *shabtis* (a doll substitute or slave for the person) and magic formulae. Originally a stick substitute for the mummy itself, a place for ka and ba in case of damage, shabtis lose their mummiform shape when they go to work.[53] The first *shabti* spell appeared between 1990 and 1780 BCE (Dynasty XII, Spell 472 of the Coffin Texts), becoming chapter 6 of the Book of the Dead in Dynasty XVII (1650–1550 BCE). Chapter 5 bears the title "The Chapter of Not Allowing the Deceased to Do Work in the Underworld," followed by chapter 6, "The Chapter of Making *Ushabti* Figures Do Work for a Man in the Underworld."[54] In Ikram's summary, the spells show a clear knowledge of the organized and meticulous labor Egyptian fields required and an equally deep desire to evade that labor: "O *shabti*, if [the deceased] is commanded to do any work in the realm of the dead: to prepare the fields, to irrigate the land or to convey sand from east to west; 'Here I am' you shall say."[55] Life was not easy for *shabti*. One tomb contained 401 *shabtis*: one for every day of the year and 36 overseers, identified by their more elaborate costumes and whips.[56] *Shabtis* sometimes had their own coffins, where they rested the other 364 days. By 1000 BCE, *shabtis*, now called *ushabtis* ("ushabti" to answer, "here I am" being the answer anticipated), were mass produced, crude, and plentiful. They answered the call to work with the reliability of Abraham or Samuel or Mary replying to God, and they enabled an easeful afterlife. No one intended any longer to convey sand from east to west or to begin doing so for the first time in another world. Men carouse, eat, drink, plow, and reap, and the individual need have no fear. He expects justice and knows the names of his gods.

Yet however determined elite and lower status Egyptians were on their easeful eternity and their names' survival, other Egyptians often failed to accord them due respect, and skepticism flourished beside belief. Tombs and coffins were recycled; mummifying materials embezzled; grave goods palmed, by those in positions of authority and with access. Tomb-robbers plundered tombs, blithely preferring the goods of the present to others' eternal welfare. Those who robbed tombs were often those entrusted with building and guarding them, such as the Chief Doorkeeper of the Temple of Amun, Djehuty-hotep, brought before Pharoah.[57] The punishment for tomb robbers was severe: erasure of individual identity, now and eternally. "Five cuts" removed the facial features: nose, ears, lips. The living person was impaled, and the name was expunged, removing the person from the worlds of the living and the dead.[58] Only pharaoh could impose death or mutilation.[59] The first evidence of capital punishment in Egypt appears as a tomb inscription setting out punishment for tomb violations.[60] Bribery saved the tomb-robber stone-mason Amenpnufer to return to his practice and be caught again. When human police failed, curses invoked the gods for enforcement.[61] Natural anxiety over death transferred itself to anxiety over one's tomb and its security, as problems deriving from status and class differentials continued into eternity.

The intrepid continued to look out for their interests in this world, regardless of consequences in this life or the next. Something like skepticism, as well as greed and desire, may have animated the breakers of tombs. Certainly, class resentment at ontological difference moved some. Robbers took the gold and jewels from the body "of this god" and looted household stuffs and silver wrapping from the singers of Amun Re. Some enjoyed disrupting the afterlife of these gods, schadenfreude with profits. Amenpnufer set fire to the coffins of the mummy of this god and his queen and boasted the city's complicity.⁶² Setting fire to the mummy-body destroyed the souls; burning meant annihilation. Actively hostile, from others' harm they did themselves some good, making merry with what they gathered riskily from others' tombs.

Skepticism emerges within the tombs of the New Kingdom (1580–1090 BCE), ironic mummies engaging confident ones. The songs of the Harpers flourish in the New Kingdom, advising the dead to make merry, feast, and drink, because generation succeeds generation, men are forgotten, their walls crumble, their places know them no more, their property passes to others, and no one returns from the dead. Often called "heretical" for representing the fate of the dead as "dubious," the songs engage a dialectic of life and death in which life dominates but death is not deprecated.⁶³ Addressing the Osiris within the tomb, the dead person as god, the songs advise him, happy in death with wife, child, feasting, and pyramid, to enjoy life while he lives it. That curious double time recognizes that in many cases the tomb's future occupant selected the songs' advice to live now that would accompany him when he was dead. So, too, survivors visiting the tomb to feed the dead found themselves advised how to live in the shadow of death.

Miriam Lichtheim argued that the first Middle Kingdom harper's song of Antef, surviving in two New Kingdom copies and inspiring a genre, was a secular poem transferred to a funerary context.⁶⁴ Except for one phrase in some songs, "the land that loveth silence," the songs suggest no apprehension about the fate of the dead. Their skeptical empiricism concerns this life. However fundamental it may be to Christianity, returning from the dead was never an Egyptian expectation. Grave goods are recognized as symbolic. Still, the original is chilling:

> Make holiday, and weary not therein!
> Behold, it is not given to a man to take his property with him.
> Behold, there is not one who departs who comes back again!⁶⁵

Only in the Ptolemaic period does the harper theme explicitly reject the traditional Egyptian afterlife. In a unique funerary stele for the wife of a high priest of Ptah, dying at the age of 30 in 42 BCE, every expectation of consciousness, pleasure, and familial reunions characteristic of Egypt vanishes, replaced by a land where one lies unconscious in the dark, wrapped in eternal sleep. Dead, Taimouthes advises her surviving spouse in the familiar terms of the harper songs: "Cease not to drink, to eat, to get drunk, to enjoy sex, to make the day joyful, to follow your inclination day and night; do not allow grief to enter your heart." Suddenly, however, she seems to have returned from the dead to report a mistake: "The West land is a land of sleep and of darkness, a place whose inhabitants lie still. Sleeping in their form of mummies, they do not wake to see their brothers; they are conscious neither of their father nor their mother; their heart forgets their wives and children."[66] The afterlife in the West land and the mummified body mark the stele as traditionally Egyptian, and the forgetful heart has a terrible poignancy as the seat of consciousness closes down.

That the stele should be a priest's wife's is curious. It could scarcely be erected without priestly complicity, and it praises "Apis-Osiris-Khentamenti, King of Gods,/ Lord of eternity, ruler of everlastingness." Yet, like some other inscriptions, especially for those dying young, it finds darkness where others expected glad justice.[67] Wilkinson regards the stele as signaling a new fear of death, but Taimouthes, or her spouse, seems more sadly resigned than fearful.[68] Death's certainty enhances life's precarious pleasures and brings to mind what is most dear, getting drunk or fathers and mothers, wives and children, but in depreciating the West land, something has been lost. A priest so enlightened may reflect the waning moral and political significance of the priesthood in Ptolemaic Egypt, reduced to marginality in a political-intellectual world where power is located elsewhere. Or he may indicate a priestly family negotiating two worlds, integrating the heterogeneous views circulating in contemporaneous Epicurean Greek and Roman thought.[69] First-century Egypt belonged to the Mediterranean.

Egyptian beliefs also traveled. As Greece and Rome redesigned their afterlives in the fourth century, Egypt's hopeful divinities participated, when they were anthropomorphic. Marking a fundamental revolution in the afterlife, immortality broke loose from the mummified body. In Egypt itself, that break is marked by the disappearance of canopic jars and the shoddy mummification of the Roman period, the image of the person replacing the preserved body in importance. Proliferating after 333 BCE, Isis cults spread through Greece to Rome and beyond to the Danube, Spain, and Britain, scattering as evidence the occasional temple, scarabs, amulets, faithful ushabtis, and, more rarely, mummy.[70]

In Gaul, homemade *ushabtis* and amulets scrambled the hieroglyphics, showing that neither the maker nor the buyer could read the Egyptian script, though both trusted its efficacy. Nîmes, now immortal for the term *denim* (de Nîmes), once had a temple of Isis and still boasts, along with its emblematic crocodile beneath a palm tree, the Tour Magne (c. 16 BCE) modeled on the lighthouse of Alexandria. There a Roman legion settled, granted lands after service in Egypt, and the legionnaires brought along customs and beliefs they did not want to leave behind. Ushabtis have turned up in Orange and Avignon, not far from the palace of the popes.

Traveling through the Mediterranean to control the afterlife, Isis and Osiris absorbed preexisting regional imagery and magical practices and lost some of their own.[71] Apuleius was an initiate and priest of Isis; his underworld offers opportunities for worship, but the Field of Reeds has vanished for him. His goddess gleams in darkness through subterranean Elysian Fields. Syncretism was already visible in Herodotus (485–424 BCE). Ignoring zoomorphic deities, he identified Isis and Osiris with Demeter and Dionysus, assimilating pantheons. Specifying which animals were sacred to which gods, he regarded as trespassing on the domain of the sacred. In Rome, temples to Isis and Serapis were destroyed in 53 BCE, rebuilt in 43 BCE, and so popular they required regulation in 21 BCE.[72] In an aristocratic Roman household related by marriage to Nero, Osiris's image was placed among the Roman *lares*, or household gods. At the same period, Nero embalmed his murdered wife Poppaea with spices in "the style of the eastern kings."[73] In Ovid and in Apuleius, Isis is a heroine, performing a sex-change in Ovid and restoring a donkey to human form in Apuleius. The zoomorphic gods were not so readily received.

Alexander the Great had consulted the bull god Apis and the oracle of Amun to confirm his divinity (331 BCE). His successors the Ptolemies turned Apis the bull god into Serapis, a human image combining Apis and Osiris, whose worship they promoted.[74] Religious stelae represent Augustus performing sacrifice to animals, although as emperor he claimed to scorn it.[75] By the turn of the eras (first century BCE into CE), contempt for gods in animal form emerges, increasingly vicious as Egypt subsided into a Roman province, until it contaminated the mummy's immortality.

Commemorating Cleopatra and Antony's defeat by Octavian, Virgil set against Neptune, Venus, and Minerva, Egypt's "monstrous gods of every form and barking Anubis": "omnigenumque deum monstra et latrator

Anubis" (*Aeneid*, VIII, 698).[76] The Alexandrian Jew who wrote the Wisdom of Solomon (c. 38 CE [30 BCE-70 CE]) sneered that the Egyptians accepted "as gods those animals that even their enemies despised; they were deceived like foolish infants." Nor did they even choose animals wisely: "most foolish . . . they worship even the most hateful animals, which are worse than all others when judged by their lack of intelligence; and even as animals they are not so beautiful in appearance that one would desire them" (WS 12.24; 15.14, 18–19). A little later, Paul (fl. 50–64 CE) pitied those who exchanged "the glory of the immortal God for images resembling a mortal human being or birds or four-footed animals or reptiles" (Rom. 1:23, c. 60 CE). Egyptians and Greeks were equally wrongheaded to a Jew turned Christian. Plutarch (46–post 119) inveighed against the animal cults (*De Iside et Osiride*). Cicero anticipated Juvenal's hostility to "demented" Egypt: "Who does not know the custom of the Egyptians? Their minds are infected with degraded superstitions. . . ."[77] For Juvenal (60–100 CE) eternal life was more than counterbalanced by an anthropocentric aversion to gods in animal shapes: "Who knows not, O Bithynian Volusius, what monsters demented Egypt worships?" (Satire XV, ll.1–2). They prefer crocodiles, ibis, long-tailed apes, cats, and dogs to Diana.

Egyptians flaunted animal worship as a sign of cultural distinctiveness and national identity. The second-century satirist Lucian (c. 125–c. 192) mounted a sort of defense. In Hades, Egyptians were better preserved than other people because of their embalming.[78] In *Parliament of the Gods* (*Thea Ekklesia*), Momus mocks the Egyptian dog and bull gods for their barks and snorts, accompanied by ibis and crocodiles, but Zeus defends their mystic significance.[79] So, too, in the *Dialogues of the Sea-Gods* (*Enalioi Dialogoi*), the South Wind is troubled by Hermes' "giv[ing] up his own fine face for that of a dog." Io, once a heifer, has changed back to a woman in Egypt to become Isis, but Hermes, her guide, has turned dog-faced Anubis. The West Wind accepts cultural differences among the gods, "Let's not be inquisitive. He knows his business better than we do."[80] Lucian's contemporary, Apuleius (c. 125–c.180) apologizes to readers of his *Golden Ass* "put off by the Egyptian story-telling convention which allows humans to be changed into animals and . . . restored."[81] He does not mention gods' looking like animals.

By the third century CE, Cassio Dio links the absurdity of animal worship with mummification, tinged with resentment at the mummy's claim to overcome death. Octavian, centuries earlier, he affirms, stirred up his troops before Actium: Egyptians "worship reptiles and beasts as gods [and] embalm their own bodies to give them the semblance of immortality."[82] Their immortality is only seeming. By this time, Christianity was flourishing alongside Jews, Greco-Roman pagan philosophers, and traditional Egyptian beliefs. Egyptians were early adopters of Christianity, the inventors of monasticism and the original hermits, and the old creed anticipated the new in first promulgating the golden rule.[83]

Neither Christianity nor Islam cost Egyptians their immortality or their bodies, now to be resurrected entire and whole. Well before the modern religions to which Egyptians converted, Egypt had developed an afterlife that fulfilled pharaoh's wishes, consoled the living and the dying in their separation, promised reunions, integrated morality with a life to come, attempted to control minds and behavior by promises of afterlife rewards and punishments, and generated considerable anxiety to accompany its promises. "May existence always follow death!" say the late Ptolemaic "Instructions of Ankhsheshonq."[84]

Among the features that mark these conceptions as very early is their thorough embodiment. Body and soul are separable, but souls depend on the body. The body in turn is dependent on a technology of preservation (all mummification continues to be fascinating). The initial challenge to afterlife ascents is personal complaints of others against the dead, rather than a judicial process between the gods and the heart. Formal judicial process develops when others besides pharaoh and his closest associates make the ascent. The Pyramid Texts testify to a well-established system of judicial accusation, appeal, and arrest that becomes more formalized in the later Coffin Texts and Books of Going Forth by Day. The court or open space of accusation in the presence of local authorities comes to resemble a court of justice where elevated judges preside. Annihilation awaits the decay of the body, as the promise to Pepi I intimates: "[H]e will not decay, he will not rot, he will not be ended."[85] Burning terrified, for it turned those burned "into ones who do not exist."[86] That in the earliest texts pharaoh ascends to the stars, avoiding the land of the dead, discloses the early, abhorrent realm overlaid by later conceptions, reintegrated by judicial punishment. Among the dead, life was reversed: instead of excreting urine, one drank it, in darkness, not light. The realm of the gods was sunlight, and to that realm this god the mummy aspired.

The Books of Going Forth by Day guided through dangers reversing this life before a life like this one could be attained.

According to puzzled Greeks, conscious of their own aversion to looking at or touching the dead, Egyptians kept the dead as mummies in their houses and used them as security for debts.[87] Even the famed Scythian practice of eating the dead seemed preferable. For Egyptians death continued as controllable as the Nile, at once predictable and challenging, requiring expertise, technological skill, and more than a little magic. As Sobek the crocodile god murmurs in the Pyramid Texts, "I have come to my waterways which are in the bank of the flood of the Great Inundation, to the place of contentment, green of fields . . . green the herbage. . . ."[88] Another Nile at flood, death is a life-giving danger to be traversed by the boat of the sun, with a map certified by the scribes.

RESISTANCE IN SUMER AND BABYLON

Empathy with the body; social panic and grave goods; resisting death and intensifying its terrors; absence of morality; independence of legal codes; improving conditions for the dead; the transformations of Gilgamesh; the death of the city

Their contemporaries in Sumer and Babylon were not so fortunate. Their river at flood made the deluge that wiped out all mankind, save one family and some craftsmen.[89] Death was grim for kings, gods, and people. Sumer and Babylon embraced the rotting body underground that the Egyptian system deliberately prevented. Adepts of legal codes for this life, they failed to provide the justice that Egyptians looked for in the next, but they also imposed no judicial challenges to overcome. Morality and law remained independent of death. Yet they did not leave death altogether unimproved and hopeless. They invented, oddly and desperately, some hope for the man with many sons, and they looked to their gods and their families for clear water. Sumerians also took excellent care of dead infants, the best on record, comparable only to the Mesoamerican festival of *muertecitos*.[90] If Egypt imagined death as a continuation of life, Sumer and Babylon imagined the dead as if they were alive, thirsty, deprived of light, requiring the ritual care of the living.[91] Dreadful as death was, annihilation was worse.

To mark the contrast with Egypt, we look first at Sumerian afterlife representations, for their horror of the body and the state of the dead, the absence of explicit moral considerations regarding the dead, and the consolations they proposed for themselves in community solidarity, both before and after death. Then we turn to the great Babylonian/Akkadian poem *Gilgamesh*, derived from Sumerian sources and legend, and its desperate, failed challenge to death's inevitability. The song of mortality salience, *Gilgamesh* was revised by its later editors from individualist epic into corporate statement, adding in a twelfth tablet the best promises about the afterlife that Sumerian culture had produced. While Assyriologists are often unhappy about that appendage, it haunted the composer Bohuslav Martinů (1890–1959), whose choral *Epic of Gilgamesh* (1954–55) concludes with that tablet's vision of the state of the dead, Christianized or modernized only slightly, and perhaps unconsciously.

In Sumer, Babylon, and Assyria, death's definitive rupture lacked Egypt's pleasures and consolations. Even the gods of the underworld sat in the dark, lamenting their bitter bread and brackish water. Their theodicies were cheerless. "A Sufferer and a Friend in Babylon" finds the world as unjust and corrupt as the Egyptian, but makes no promises of justice in the next world. "People fill the storehouse of the wicked with gold, / While they steal a beggar's bowl." The gods permit behavior humans disapprove, deception and oppression, but no one understands why: "The way of your divine patrons is beyond human understanding . . . Though one may witness the will of one's divine patrons, / No one can understand it." All the sufferer can do is plead for a change of heart now, at once, soon: "May the divine patrons, who abandoned me, / Now have mercy on me . . . May Shamash, the good shepherd, / Once again shepherd his people as he should."[92] As in ancient Israel, when Sumerians and Babylonians attributed justice to their gods, they expected it in this life.[93] Their vision of the afterlife promised no atonement for injustice suffered in this world, no intervention by Ra, Thoth, or Isis. At best, the gods of the netherworld might allow the dead fresh food.[94]

Compared to Egypt, what strikes modern readers about Sumerian (c. 2100 BCE) and later Babylonian afterlives (c. 1750 BCE and later) is their unrelieved misery. So Alexander Heidel exclaims, "total annihilation would have been an incomparably better lot."[95] Yet there are no hideous torments like those in Christian, Muslim, or Buddhist hells. No Greek vultures rend livers, no rocks roll endlessly downhill. No Egyptian monster gapes to swallow the heavy-souled sinner. As with the Egyptians first and Christians later, those who improve afterlife prospects traditionally—and strategically—taint the promise with penalties. (Penalty-free heavens triumph only in the twentieth century.) The source of Heidel's dismay is the way the Mesopotamian afterlife empathizes with the dead.

The dead, lamenting, lie down, "never to rise again, never to rise again, never to rise again," the refrain insists. On a road from which no one returns, the dead reach a land of darkness, where the water is brackish and bread bitter; they feed on clay and dust. Bodies turn verminous and vile; the worm seizes them, crawls through their nostrils, and drops out; genitals dissolve into slime.[96] In a "Lament for Ur" around 2000 BCE, the city chokes with corpses, and "The flesh of the dead, like lard left in the sun, melts from their bodies."[97] Sumerians observed what happens to corpses in their marshy, riverine terrain—corpses they made no fruitless attempt to mummify—and they represented the afterlife in terms of what it would be like to be a corpse put underground, yet retaining some consciousness under the earth. They thought themselves into a body thrust out of the sunlight into the dark, immobile but conscious as they themselves were conscious. Death corrupts the body and deprives the person of everything the living desire. Heidel senses that this afterlife is very close to being buried alive and feeling oneself rot.

Death as life's inescapable antithesis Sumerians made central to their poetry. Egyptians showed what they valued by what they took with them into the next life; the Sumerians by what death took from them. Poem after poem takes up the lament: "Ninjiczida's Journey to the Netherworld," "The Death of Bilgameš," "The Death of Ur-Namma," "Bilgameš, Enkidu, and the Netherworld," "Dumuzid's Dream," "*Balbale* to Ninĝišida," "An *ululumama* to Suen for Ibbi-Suen," "A *šir-namursaĝa* to Inana for Iddin-Dagan," "A *šir-namšub* to Utu," and "The Descent of Inana."[98] Inana herself, goddess of love and war, descends from heaven to the world of the dead, passes through the seven gates, where she is stripped of her crown, her necklace, her breast adornments, her ring, her lapis measuring rod and line (insignia of power), and her robe. Death equalizes. Naked, mere body, the goddess hangs on a hook on the wall in the palace of Ereshkigal, goddess of death: dead meat. Revived by flies' bringing life-giving water and plant, she cannot leave her hook without a replacement. The rhythmic chant, mind-numbingly repeated by netherworld demons, ends in a chilling threat—death never lets go: " 'Who has ever ascended from the Underworld, has ascended unscathed from the Underworld? If Inana is to ascend from the Underworld, let her provide a substitute for herself.'"[99]

Taking away everything in which life recognizes itself, death's demons silhouette Sumerian self-concept and values. Not every dead Sumerian possessed a lapis measuring rod and line to give up, but the living knew the value of what the demons lack. Leveling death takes away what life enjoys: light, children, wives, gifts (celebration, family, sociality), sex, drink, fish, and garlic. The demons "know no food, know no drink, eat no flour offering and drink no libation. They accept no pleasant gifts. They never enjoy the pleasures of the marital embrace, never have any sweet children to kiss. They tear away the wife from a man's embrace. They snatch the son from a man's knee. They make the bride leave the house of her father-in-law."[100]

Bodily pleasures include the social bonds created by accepting gifts and the multi-generational ties of family, recognizing both men's and women's point of view. In "Dumuzid's Dream" the demons "who do not enjoy a wife's embraces, who never kiss dear little children" suffer missed culinary moments: "They never chew sharp-tasting garlic, . . . eat no fish, . . . eat no leeks."[101] So in the wilderness that would become death to them, resentful Hebrew slaves long for the Egypt they escaped: they want fish, cucumbers, melons, garlic, onions, and leeks (Num. 11:5). A land without fish and garlic is a land of the dead.

Although two Sumerian poems turn their dying kings (Bilgameš, Ur-Namma) into judges in the underworld, neither king is at all pleased with his assignment. Pharaoh, it will be remembered, had been promised precisely that becoming king among the dead would not happen to him. Advised not to go to the grave with his heart "knotted in anger" ("Death of Bilgameš"), the sighing, lamenting Bilgameš goes to the grave accompanied by human sacrifices, his wives and his "entourage."[102] Ur-Namma carries rich grave goods for the gods, not himself. The gifts he brings will not return to him the life he once led (a common assumption about grave goods), but, like the presents brought by petitioners to living kings, will persuade the gods under the earth to receive him kindly rather than threateningly.[103]

As actual grave goods, Ur-Namma's luxurious gifts to the gods of the underworld made a rich hoard: a bow with quiver and arrows, an artful dagger, a multicolored leather hip bag (Nergal); a spear, a leather bag for a saddle-hook, a lion-headed mace, a shield, a battle-axe (Gilgamesh); a bowl filled with oil, a long-fleeced robe (Ereshkigal); a sheep, a golden scepter (Dumuzid); a golden ring, cornelian jewelry (Namtar, fate); a lapis-handled box, a silver hair clasp adorned with lapis, a comb (Hušbišag, Namtar's wife); a golden-wheeled chariot, donkeys, horses (Ningišzida, the serpent, lord of the tree of life); a lapis seal, a gold and silver toggle with a bison's head (Dimpimekug); a headdress with alabaster ear pieces, a stylus, a line and measuring rod (Ninazimua, the scribe and wife of Ningišzida).[104]

Giving gifts to living kings is rational. Lavishing gifts on a dead king so he may conciliate the gods underground seems less so. Social panic motivates such generosity. In the poem, at the death of Ur-Namma, the world shatters. Cities are in ruins, canals broken, building projects halted; fertility ceases, in grass and cows. Moments of succession are dangerous, the people exposed and vulnerable. Magical thinking gives gifts to stave off pending disaster.

As judges in the underworld, neither Bilgameš nor Ur-Namma assesses the lived morality of the dead. No particular moral behaviors are demanded, no judicial process imposed on the dead, as in Egyptian guide books. Sumerians did not lack for laws. They first codified their moral behavior as laws under Ur-Namma (2112–2095 BCE; later texts allude to Urukagina's code, c. 2350 BCE), but law does not transfer to the dead. Addressing homicide, rape, adultery, slave marriage, divorce, false witness, fugitive slaves, physical injuries to noses, bones, teeth, slave women who curse and strike, misappropriated property,[105] law is a realm of disputes and settlements, of cases and resolutions, of conditions and consequences, if/when—then, rather than ultimate justice. It concerns the living, not the dead. As divine surrogate, the king is responsible for justice in this life, not the next.

Most tellingly, the next world is not even exploited for curses against those who tamper with the stelae bearing the laws and the name of the king. Lipit-Ishtar (reigned 1934–25) concluded with two columns of curses against anyone who alters his image or his name, but the curses all happen in this life—obliteration, childlessness, ruined cities, a land without a king. In Babylonian texts that shifts, slightly. The Babylonian Hammurabi's code (c. 1750 BCE) multiplies columns of curses—rebellion, obliteration, famine, darkness, sudden death, blotted out memory, life force spilled like water, no children for him or his people, rivers dried up, carbuncles breaking out on his body. One faint line lost somewhere in the middle looks to the next world—his ghost will lack water.[106] Lacking water means no children supply it. If Sumerians did not link their laws with the next world at all, the Babylonians also failed to take much advantage of an invisible world. Life's common disasters, war, disease, climate variability, insurrection, were evil enough. The next world did not figure as a useful threat, and not because it was too far off, as Aphra Behn's African hero Oroonoko thought (1689 CE).

As to Egyptian-style reunions with loved ones, Ur-Namma recognizes Bilgameš in the netherworld, but not his own family. In a recently discovered fragment, Bilgameš is promised that his mother, sister, and friend Enkidu are waiting for him and will come to him, but the promise has as yet appeared nowhere else, down the social scale:

> Your mother, your sister, your *siblings*,
> Your precious friend, your little brother,
> Your friend Enkidu, the young man your companion [await
>   you]. . . .
> From the sister's house the sister will come to you,
> From the *sibling's* house the *sibling* will come to you,
> Your own one will come to you, your precious one will come to
>   you.[107]

Yet Sumerians were not willing to let the next world remain so grim, so demystified. Valuing fertility and social solidarity within the city state, they improved the condition of some of the dead, not as in Egypt according to vice and virtue, loyalty to the gods or blasphemous defiance, but according to how fertile one had been and how one died. Sacrifices and libations for the dead reaffirmed the bonds across generations between the living and the dead, fostering communally supportive behaviors. Lipit-Ishtar, in the prologue to his laws, proudly claimed, "I made the father support his children. I made the child support his father. I made the father stand by his children. I made the child stand by his father."[108] Social bonds were crucial to Sumerian afterlife success. Only the living can make good their wishes for the dead: "May good beer never cease in your libation tube."[109]

Apart from a few elegies for named individuals, the only surviving Sumerian poem that promises happiness for common people in the underworld, "Bilgameš, Enkidu and the Netherworld" (*BEN*) spread widely. Often copied, it was excerpted, translated, and, when the Old Babylonian *Gilgamesh* was revised into the Standard Version, appended as a disconnected, but essential Twelfth Tablet.[110] In "Bilgameš, Enkidu and the Netherworld" death remains loathsome. The body crawls with vermin; what was once lovingly touched now disgusts. As in Egypt, the customs of the dead reverse those of the living. The dead have no oils, perfumes, sandals, games, no love or hate for wife and child. Yet even as social distinctions vanish, this afterlife builds a graded hierarchy resembling, as Dina Katz observes, a subterranean city-state.[111] How a person fares depends on how many sons he leaves behind, how he died, and whether anyone performs funerary rites for him. Starting from one son, then two sons, up to seven, the dead rise from weeping and sitting on bricks to yoking asses and ploughing, until the last, the man with seven sons, sits as with the gods giving judgment. With five sons, a man is as happy as a scribe in the palace of a prince.[112] Death is answered with a construction—built brick by brick—that proposes social solidarity, responsibility, and fecundity as a way of warding off loss.

Marking the sociality of such beliefs, their role in sustaining intergenerational solidarity, one version from the city of Girsu links the poem with funerary rites for mother and father. Told that his parents drink muddy water, Bilgameš resolves "O my father and my mother, I will have you drink clear water!" At the "Bank of Bilgameš" the rulers of Girsu performed the rites for their ancestors.[113] In moralized contexts, the father does not appear without the mother: both parents are fully recognized.[114]

Not all fates in the poem are fortunate. The infertile weep, male and female for unconsummated marriages: he weeps over a phallic rope, she weeps over a flat reed mat. The useless eunuch mourns propped against a wall, a dead stick; the childless woman, a defective pot. The man who has no funerary offerings survives on scraps and crumbs in the street. The abandoned dead are the scavenging homeless of the city of the dead.[115] Unexpectedly, the most purely pleasurable fate belongs to stillborn infants or children who did not long survive. "They play at a table of silver and gold, laden with honey and ghee." Placed almost at the end of the poem, dead children, women's interests, assume a socio-cultural importance deleted in the Greco-Roman literary tradition. (Plato dismisses dead infants, Virgil lets them keep crying.)

Two lines later the poem ends abruptly in annihilation by fire. The last, terrifying place goes to the man not to be found—whose soul has disappeared, who no longer exists at all: "'Did you see him who was set on fire?'/ 'I did not see him. His spirit is not about. His smoke went up to the sky.'"[116] Lost in the emptiness of the air, the soul vanishes, a fate worse, it seems, than weeping underground. Underlining the arbitrariness of the sign, other systems will prefer burning to burial, but the Sumerians, like the Egyptians, seem to have abhorred it. It annihilated the body on which even the miserable existence of ghosts depended.

There is little moral assessment here; no assignment of places on the basis of virtue or vice, scant insistence on obedience to the god, none on violation of their shrines. Although gods are often said to be principally moralists, the Sumerian gods were not.[117] Of some sixty-six surviving manuscripts of "Bilgameš," only three refer to behaviors we would regard as moral, two from Ur and one of unknown provenance now in a private Norwegian collection. The morality they propose is familial or divine: relations with parents or one's god (the fifth and third of the Ten Commandments given to Abraham of Ur's descendants). The man who did not respect the word of his father and mother never gets enough water; the man cursed by his mother and father is deprived of an heir and his ghost roams; the man who made light of the name of his god has a ghost that eats bitter bread, drinks bitter water.[118] A single manuscript concerns itself with the "one who cheated a god and swore an oath": in what survives, he is at the top where water libations are offered; another, at the place of sighs of his father and mother, is afflicted by Amorites he cannot push off or charge down.[119]

Rewards are few, but the principal punishments seem to be regret, hunger, thirst, and memories of pain. The man eaten by a lion "cries out 'oh my hands, oh my legs.'"[120] Searching for a moral lesson, one learns it is better not to be eaten by a lion. Bodies should be whole and entire, or they will miss their parts forever. It is wonderful to have five sons, even better to have seven, but only heartbreakingly sad to have none. The little explicit moralizing that does appear regulates familial relationships, affirming morality's evolutionary foundation in social solidarity, but also testifying to a continuing struggle between generations when childhood is left behind.[121]

Like burial, the Sumerian afterlife hinges on the dependence of the dead on the living, those to whom they gave birth and those who will care for them after death. No one can bury himself, and no one can provide herself funerary offerings, pouring beer in the libation tube. For such assistance, the dead must rely on the good will of those they leave behind. More than a contract between those who are living, those who are dead, and those who are yet to be born, fertility and social bonds constitute happiness in life and provide whatever protection there is in death and whatever morality there is in a Sumerian afterlife.

Taking up the Sumerian tales, the imperial Babylonians made matters worse, death grimmer and the gods and men more helpless. Nowhere is the process clearer than in the evolution of *Gilgamesh*. Translating and reworking existing shorter Sumerian poems about the adventures and death of the eponymous hero-king and underworld judge Bilgameš, the Babylonian *Gilgamesh* has a textual history that extends over a thousand years, beginning around 1700 BCE, seeing considerable activity in the period 1200–1000 BCE, and fixed by 700 BCE. In the Old Babylonian Version (OBV) the impossible attempt to elude death and find immortality constitutes the long falling action of the adventures of a pair of heroes, two-thirds god Gilgamesh and the natural man Enkidu, who together have overcome every other challenge that gods or monsters present.

Much more than the simple fusion of scattered poems that Jack Goody suggests,[122] the first or Old Babylonian *Gilgamesh* poet put an existing Sumerian hero whose adventures were scattered through many poems, into a new, unified action in which he tried, and failed, to escape death. Sumerian Bilgameš had risked death in his combat with Huwawa (Akkadian "Humbaba"); he had given advice to his servant Enkidu about visiting the netherworld; he had found Ziusudra who survived the flood; he had defeated the bull of heaven and Aga of Kish, and he had died.[123] Death angered him, but no poem centered on an attempt to escape death or to find eternal life.[124] That, however, was precisely the futile exploit the Babylonian author invented for his hero. Over time, other scribes added additional adventures.[125] The last hand, probably the named author Sin-leqi-unninni, reshaped the opening and ending into the twelve-tablet

Standard Babylonian Version (SBV or SV).[126] Doing so, he created a ring poem that accepted death's inevitability and dangled from it afterlife expectations, the pendant twelfth tablet.

In one variant of ring structure, the beginning of a poem is echoed at the end, and then a second ending follows. Mary Douglas calls the second ending a "latch," setting "the text as a whole in a larger context, less parochial, more humanist, or even metaphysical."[127] The most familiar example is the biblical book Ecclesiastes. "Vanity of vanities, all is vanity, saith the Preacher," in chapters 1 and 12, shutting down his circuit from unsatisfying life to death. Then another voice enters. A scribe adds an inconsistent, but pious conclusion lamenting the making of long books and advising the reader to fear God and keep his commandments. The disturbing work closed in a ring, another voice enters with a consolatory, conformist purpose. The *Gilgamesh* Twelfth-Tablet latch scandalizes the literary sensibilities of many modern readers, but for Babylonians it closed death down.

Akkadian literature made more of death, and liked it even less, than did the Sumerian originals of the flood story and Inana's descent to the land of the dead. In both languages, the flood occurs shortly after the creation of man. The surviving Sumerian fragments do not say whether the Sumerian gods created men to do their work for them, digging canals and irrigating the lands, as the tired Babylonian gods do (and as the Lord does in Genesis, making a garden for the man to till and keep, not Him). The Sumerian gods hope men will build brick cities, and four gods create "the black headed people" and the animals to multiply everywhere. That benign opening contrasts markedly with the Babylonian version.

In Babylon's *Atrahasis* human life originates in death. The gods murder one of their own, and his blood is mixed with clay, molded by the goddess Nintu. When the flood is over, and Nintu has hung her lapis jewels in the sky, a rainbow to remember the episode, the gods determine, still intent on population control, that one-third of women shall give birth unsuccessfully and others will have their babies snatched from their laps.[128] The conclusion of the Sumerian flood story is missing, so we cannot know if it too ended by highlighting women's roles, but the distress of childbearing is not its physical pain (as in Genesis), but its losses, the deaths of children. Those losses must be explained as an arbitrary act of the gods themselves, so unnatural and so wrong is it to fail at the birth. Dead gods and dead children bracket the Babylonian flood story.

As Dina Katz observes, Babylonians' richer detail of the underworld made it even more disagreeable.[129] Sumerian Inana's descent from heaven was unpleasant, but she traveled to the otherworld beyond the mountain. Babylonian Ishtar descended into a subterranean grave, where even the grave goods decayed, the beer turned muddy, and the water soured.[130] Inana had gone "On the road where traveling is one-way only," but Ishtar arrives "To the house where those who enter are deprived of light." Conditions worsen, reproducing the body's return to earth, imagining a body in the ground filling with dust, its mouth filling up with clay: "Where dust is their food, clay their bread./They see no light, they dwell in darkness,/ They are clothed like birds, with feathers." Darkness and helplessness settle upon the inhabitants, winged, but not for Egyptian journeys to the stars. The dead become dangerous, cannibals of the living. Ishtar threatens to smash the gates: "I shall raise up the dead and they shall eat the living;/ The dead shall outnumber the living." Ereshkigal, the goddess of death, feels sorry for herself and the aborted families she creates: "I eat clay for bread, I drink muddy water for beer./ I have to weep for young men forced to abandon sweethearts./ I have to weep for girls wrenched from their lovers' laps./ For the infant child I have to weep, expelled before its time."[131] In the underworld, gods and men, goddesses and women suffer alike. Even the presiding goddess wishes she were elsewhere, otherwise engaged. This darkening perspective motivates the resistance of Gilgamesh.

As his original auditors doubtless expected, the Old Babylonian Gilgamesh failed both himself and us in his quest for immortality. The text took off. Traveling up through Turkey and over to Palestine (where a copy was found in Megiddo[132]), it was translated into many languages, perhaps adapted for dramatic presentation,[133] re-worked by the traditional author Sin-leqi-unninni (probably between 1200 and 1000 BCE), and stabilized by the eighth century, Homer's and Hesiod's time, as the Twelve Tablet or Standard Version (SV, sometimes SBV for Standard Babylonian Version to differentiate it from OBV, the Old Babylonian Version).[134] Multiple copies were recovered from Ashurbanipal's palace in Nineveh (destroyed 612 BCE), and every currently available fragment of the epic has been translated and sketched and commented in A.R. George's heroic *The Babylonian Gilgamesh Epic* (2 vols. 2003). Copies later than the seventh century follow those made, as the tablets say, for Ashurbanipal, "king of the world." The latest copy carrying a date is from about 130 BCE, when the Ptolemies ruled Egypt, the Hasmoneans Judea, and the Romans Greece.

The narrative casts a long shadow over Homer's *Odyssey* and the biblical Genesis. To *Gilgamesh* we almost certainly owe the kind of hero Odysseus is, a traveling, tale-telling hero who learns the manners of men and visits the land of the dead, where so many other western adventurers follow him. Genesis is shot through with memories of the Mesopotamian literary tradition. Knowing a woman makes a man like a god in seven days of love-making. She introduces him to clothing and beer. A wily serpent cheats mankind of eternal youth and knows the secret of the tree of life.[135] A flood sent by the gods to destroy mankind ends with birds, a sweet-smelling sacrifice, a goddess hanging the rainbow in the sky as a memorial, and a few survivors collected by the forewarned builder of an ark.[136] Gods differ, but the early history of mankind is made of borrowed, retold episodes.

After Alexander's Greeks swept through the near east in the fourth century BCE, cuneiform literature began to lose its regional political and cultural dominance, a story Assyriologists have just begun to popularize.[137] Berossus's *Babyloniaca* (early 3rd cent. BCE) represented Babylonian history and culture to the Greek conquerors. Only fragments survive.[138] The last cuneiform inscriptions date from the first century CE. At the end of the second-century CE Lucian of Samosata sent Menippus to Babylon to investigate the underworld, but Gilgamesh and all the ancient regional gods had disappeared: Lucian knew nothing of them. His afterlife, like his language, is Greek. Sumerian and Babylonian literature had been buried by—and in—Greco-Roman, Jewish, and Arabian tales, to disappear for almost two thousand years until the nineteenth-century excavations brilliantly related in David Damrosch's *The Buried Book* (2007).

Now that it has become our book and almost always a composite, *Gilgamesh* has even more variants than it had already acquired three thousand years ago. Modern redactors cannot bear to let go bits earlier Babylonian editors dropped, and sometimes reject what they added in Babylon. Specifically, mortality salience lurking behind the curtain, they cannot bear to omit Siduri's advice on how to live in the face of death, and they have little use for the futile afterlife consolations of the Twelfth Tablet. Thus an eleven-tablet *Gilgamesh* triumphs, a new text for new readers.

Gilgamesh initially accepts death as inescapable, attacking Humbaba, "whose breath is death":

> Who is there, my friend, that can climb to the sky?
> Only the gods have [dwelled] forever in sunlight.
> As for man, his days are numbered,
> Whatever he may do, it is but wind.[139]

Fame is the hero's recompense: "If I fall, I should have made my name" (George, I, 201, tab. iv, l. 148). Both Gilgamesh and Enkidu know death, expect death, so as the plot twists to escape death, it seeks to escape something they both know has always been already there, waiting.

Represented not as an inevitable natural phenomenon, but as the gods' arbitrary will in response to an irresistible cause, death comes from outside—in a dream. For killing the bull of heaven someone must die, Enkidu dreams, and the gods choose Enkidu. Raging against death, Enkidu curses his life, his name, and the harlot, to annihilation. From the triumphal door brought from Humbaba's cedar forest, of any king or god, "May he remove my name and set up his own!" (George, I, 637, vii, 63). Only the description of his funeral, his statue, the mourning of Gilgamesh and the city reconciles him to having lived, if he must die. As with Sinuhe, fantasying being present at one's own funeral is evidently very ancient. Enkidu moves toward acceptance, sensing the imminence of his own death. But then he tells another dream, a dream of death that seems to be what kills him, in twelve days, the number of solar months: "The day he saw the dream [his *strength*] was exhausted" (George, I, 647, vii, 254).

That dream terrifies. Powerless, suffocating, dragged into darkness, Enkidu trembles sick at heart. Threatening disembowelment and ripping flesh, the lion claws and eagle talons of an Anzu-bird-faced creature seize him by the hair, "capsize [him] like a raft," trample him "[l]ike a mighty wild bull," turn him "into a dove ... [binding his] arms like (the wings of) a bird." (George, I, 643–45, vii, 169–183). A dove caught in the Anzu-bird's apotropaic talons, the warrior's mighty arms shrink to helpless, flightless wings. As in so many victory stelae, he is led captive to the house of Irkalla:

> to the house which those who enter cannot leave,
> on the journey whose way cannot be retraced;

> to the house whose residents are deprived of light,
> where dust is their sustenance, their food clay.
> They are clad like birds in coats of feathers,
> And they cannot see light but dwell in darkness.
> On the door [and bolt the dust lies thick,]
> On the House [(of Dust) a deathly quiet is poured.]
>
> (George I, 645, vii, 185–92)

Here useless crowns are heaped up, abandoned. Souls clothed with feathers, like birds, enact the "flight" of the soul or breath from the body; soul as *ba* or a bird occurs in Egypt and Greece, but here it does not fly.[140] Dead kings, purification priests sit with Etana, the king of Kish who flew to the heavens, now imprisoned in the dark, Shakkan, the god of the wild herds among whom Enkidu was raised, and Ereshkigal, Queen of Earth. Beletseri, her scribe, holds a tablet, raises her head, looks at Enkidu, and says, "Who brought this man?" In most translations, Enkidu awakes in terror, because nothing can be made of the remaining fragments. But the scene goes on, the fragments themselves terrifying:

> Before her [i.e., Ereshkigal] was squatting [Bēlet]-sēri, the scribe
>   of the Netherworld,
>   Holding [a tablet] and reading aloud in her presence.
> [She raised] her head, she saw me:
>   "[Who was] it fetched this man here?
> [Who was it] brought [*this fellow*] here?
>   [. . . .] made ready,
>   [. . . .] tomb.'"
> A short lacuna.
> '[. . . .] me,
>   [. . . .] Ereškigal.
>   [. . . .] the deluge.'
> Another short lacuna
> '[. . . . I] saw his person.' A longer lacuna . . . about thirty lines.
>
> (George, I, 645–47, vii, 204–21)

When the text resumes, Enkidu is speaking to Gilgamesh in the present, no longer of the dream.

The realm is female, ruled by the Queen of Earth, ordered by her scribe, also a woman, as in a queen's household. When Belet-seri looks up from her tablet (an item later associated with judgment or fate), she creates a moment of encounter sidestepped by Ur-Namma, when he gave the great feast and gifts to the gods assembled. George suggests Belet-seri's question and Enkidu's terror mark his having arrived in this realm without the expected gifts to placate the gods (II, 852n209–10). Nothing good happens here. Within the poem proper, this is the only description of the realm of the dead. Whether or not the OBV contained anything comparable is, at present, impossible to say. That tablet is dust indeed.

If the dream is indeed a Middle Babylonian or later addition (post 1400 BCE), death has again been made more fearsome, undoing the first dream's acceptance. George is certain Enkidu told Gilgamesh more about the ways of the underworld. Leaning on the line about seeing someone's "person," he suggests Enkidu might have seen famous individuals as Odysseus and Aeneas do on their later trips (George, I, 52, 483). But whatever Enkidu told Gilgamesh, it was not reassuring to either. No compensation to make death worthwhile has been promised, nothing to reconcile either man to the fate awaiting them both, a fate once so blithely dared for the sake of a name.

In the OBV, the moral of the story belongs to Siduri, goddess of taverns, the alewife. Hers is a curiously unheroic moral that links the individual to generation and the generations. Šamaš, the sun god, had warned Gilgamesh he would not find the life he seeks, and Gilgamesh cried out only for the light of the sun. There is more to life than light, Siduri assures Gilgamesh. Death she attributes to the gods' selfishness, and she advises a life of pleasure that is not solitary, but social. Eat, drink, and be merry, but also dance and play in fresh clothes, with a clean head, hold a child by the hand and embrace a wife. Feasts suppose guests; dancing and playing take partners; child and wife promise deep entanglement with another, even to the linking of bodies and generations:

> O Gilgameš, where are you wandering?
> You cannot find the life that you seek:
>   when the gods created mankind,
>   for mankind they established death,
>   life they kept for themselves.

> You, Gilgameš, let your belly be full,
>> keep enjoying yourself, day and night!
> Every day make merry,
>> dance and play day and night!
> Let your clothes be clean!
>> Let your head be washed, may you be bathed in water!
> Gaze on the little one who holds your hand!
>> Let a wife enjoy your repeated embrace!
> Such is the destiny [*of mortal men,*]
>
> (George, I, 279, OBV col.iii, 1–14).

As in Ecclesiastes (though neither the Harper nor St. Paul), recommended pleasures entail creating another generation and embed the dying in continuing life, if not precisely his own. There is no recuperation of work (as in Ecclesiastes, "Whatsoever thy hand findeth to do, do it with thy might; for there is no *work*, nor device, nor knowledge, nor wisdom, in the grave, whither thou goest" [9:10, KJV, emphasis added]). Only the privileged can dance day *and* night. Yet this demotic and accessible ideology finds no one alone in her pleasures, but deeply engaged with others in activities that strengthen social bonds.

The Standard Version (SV) does something quite surprising and almost always obscured in the composite texts prepared for modern readers. It shifts the moral of the poem from private to public, transferred from a goddess to an immortal man, the goddess feminized and disempowered. Creating a corporate, communal text out of an individualist, heroic poem, the SV replaces Siduri as the poem's moralist with Ūta-napišti, adds episodes (n. 125 below), and imposes the ring structure. As George observes, Gilgamesh brings back from his travels "the profound wisdom that underpins the proper, divinely ordained basis of human government and society" (I, 445). That wisdom is of course patriarchal. Elevating the city over the king, the permanent over the transitory, the poem glimpses the realm of the dead and threatens the living with invasion by the dead, but it also puts death in its place when the poem ends in the Twelfth Tablet. That tablet looks beyond the king to the people of the city and promises the continued care of the dead by the living, in a gesture to the community, to the city and its people. Yet it also concludes with a threat, reminding the living what will befall them if they fail to make good connections in life. There is danger in isolation in death.

Transferring as well as transforming his moral from private pleasures to public duties, the author of the SV erased Siduri's life-affirming advice and reduced her beyond recognition. Modern readers do not know that, because modern translations cannot bear to let her go. Once the poem's dominatrix moralist, she is still, for us, its heart. In the SV, however, the goddess at the sea's edge who challenged Gilgamesh and whose face he saw, now veils her face, frightened at his coming, and locks herself in her house. Once free-thinking and self-expressing, with an interest in supplying feasts with beer, Siduri turns into a veiled, timid exponent of hopelessness. She is not entirely silent, but she no longer advises and is not even certain about Gilgamesh's next move. Rather than giving counsel we all should follow, she underestimates Gilgamesh's prowess. No one, she advises, crosses this ocean to the Waters of Death except Shamash, but there is a boatman: "if [it may be] done, cross with him,/ if it may not be done, turn around (and go) back!" (George, I, 683–85, x, 81–84). Siduri has turned GPS, only a signaler of directions to the hero, and she is not even right about those.

Siduri's life-affirming simple pleasures, Ūta-napišti replaces with a philosophic moral that recognizes the hierarchy of kings and fools, the king's responsibilities to the gods (George, I, 445), and death's dominance over life. Death, Ūta-napišti assures Gilgamesh, is inevitable "both for Gilgamesh and for a fool" (Dalley, Tablet X, 107). In life the fool has dregs and rubbish, the king butter and advice. Death is equal, life is not. Ūta-napišti's fragmentary phrases, the gods "Sin and Bel," "the temples of the gods," "the holy shrines" (Dalley, 108), suggest the king has more to do than feast and play with his wife and child. When Ūta-napišti concludes with the impermanence of all things and the invisible power of Death, his imagery abandons individual desire for social and corporate relationships, houses, families, brothers:

> You are exhausting [*yourself* with] ceaseless toil,
> you are filling your sinews with pain,
>   bringing nearer the end of your life. [n. lit. 'your distant days']
> Man is one whose progeny is snapped off like a reed in the
>   canebrake:
>   the comely young man, the pretty young woman,
>   *all [too soon in]* their very [*prime*] death abducts (them).

No one sees death,
> no one sees the face [of death,]
>
> no one [hears] the voice of death:
> (yet) savage death is the one who hacks man down.
>
> At some time we build a household,
> at some time we start a family,
> at some time the brothers divide,
> at some time feuds arise in *the land.*
>
> At some time the river rose (and) brought the flood,
> the mayfly floating on the river.
>
> Its countenance was gazing on the face of the sun,
> then all of a sudden nothing was there!
>
> The abducted and the dead, how alike they are!
> They cannot draw the picture of death.
> The dead do not greet man in the land.
> [alt. mss. reading: Mortal man is imprisoned. . . .]
>
> (George, I, 697, x, 298–318).

Death has gained in power and significance, but it is also part of human corporate activity, building houses, filling them, inheriting them, disputing over them in feuds. If Siduri looked to life, Ūta-napišti meditates on death, elusive and inescapable.

In what remains of the poem, Ūta-napišti tells Gilgamesh the story of the flood that destroyed mankind and mocks him with a test. If Gilgamesh can stay awake seven days, immortality is his. Gilgamesh fails, and Ūta-napišti's wife proposes a consolation prize. Gilgamesh is advised to dive for a magic plant of eternal youth. (Otherwise unattested in Sumerian and Babylonian literature, the magic plant resembles the Soma that keeps the Vedic gods immortal and young.[141]) At last succeeding, he resolves to take the plant back to Uruk to test on an old man, but he loses it to a serpent. (Some readings find Gilgamesh at last selfless rather than merely cautious when he plans to share.) As Gilgamesh bathes at a pool, a snake steals the magic plant, confirming the subtlety of snakes, explaining their long lives with shiny youthful skins, and inaugurating their ability to trick mankind out of what humans most desire. All that remains for Gilgamesh is to return to contemplate his city, and so he does. The poem concludes as it began, addressed now to Ur-shanabi rather than the reader, affirming the grandeur of the city, its dimensions and its orchards, its temple and its clay-pits, within which the life of the people continues under the gaze of the king.

> Go up on to the wall of Uruk, [Ur-shanabi,] and walk around,
> Inspect the foundation platform and scrutinize the brickwork!
>   Testify that its bricks are baked bricks,
> And that the Seven Counsellors must have laid its foundations!
> One square mile is city, one square mile is orchards, one square
>   mile is claypits,
>   as well as the open ground of Ishtar's temple.
> Three square miles and the open ground comprise Uruk.
>
> (Dalley, 120, 50)

The city holds its people, the orchards feed them, the clay-pits supply a technology of bricks and pottery, the temple climbs to the divine, and the narrative ends naming the city. Gilgamesh alive, repeats these lines to Ur-shanabi, knowing he cannot escape death, praising his living city.

Then the editor adds the Twelfth Tablet, a version of "Bilgameš, Enkidu, and the Netherworld," despised by Assyriologists but loved by at least one modern composer and the culture that created the poem. George, who dislikes the Twelfth Tablet, is exceptionally eloquent on Gilgamesh's last lines: "For the Babylonians the city was the one institution without which civilization was impossible. It was also eternal, built by the gods and inhabited by men, more ancient than memory and enduring into an unknown future. Uruk, vast in expanse and manifestly ancient, is a symbol of the archetypal Babylonian city. The fourfold division . . . is pregnant with meaning . . . the four areas of activity that most preoccupy human life on earth. The city proper . . . denotes the built-up areas, the domestic dwellings where men establish their households and raise their families; the date-groves . . . represent with their archetypal crop the agricultural activity and produce that nourish the human race; the clay-pits . . ., whence came the clay for making mud bricks and modeling rough terracotta figurines and plaques, symbolize man's creativity as builder and craftsman; and the great temple precinct of Ishtar stands for man's spiritual and intellectual endeavours. These four activities express the whole of human life: procreation, food production, manufacturing and mental activity. All are enclosed within the great city's walls. . . . [G]aze on the city, consider the generations that surround you and learn that human life, in all its activities, is collective and not individual" (I, 527).

There George prefers the poem to end: open-ended, eternal, the proud hero and his city evading the closure that the poem describes for all. The Norton Critical Edition ends at the eleventh tablet, omitting any reference to the twelfth. N.K. Sandars disagreed; she thought Gilgamesh should die, like Beowulf, so her justly popular translation ends with another Sumerian poem, "The Death of Bilgameš," that no Babylonian before her ever thought to attach to the end of the poem.

The Babylonian scribes who created a ring poem had in view the purpose George teases from the last lines on the city walls, and they achieved it by translating, altering, and appending the second half of the Sumerian "Bilgameš, Enkidu, and the Netherworld." The infamously problematic Twelfth Tablet violates every Aristotelian narrative rule and makes modern critics shudder, but it ensures that we no longer take Gilgamesh's tale as applying only to an individual, but to all the men of the city who die.

At the bottom of Tablet XI an anguished catchline comes from nowhere and another poem: "If only I had left the *pukku* in the carpenter's house today!" (Dalley, 120, XII, co. vi; George, I, 725, 729, XII, 1: "Today, had I only left the ball in the carpenter's workshop!"). From that abrupt turn, the Twelfth Tablet dangles. The poem turns from the exceptional hero to the situation of the ordinary inhabitants of the city, telling them what their deaths will be like, what they can do to improve their situation under the ground, and what will happen to them if they fail to leave behind anyone to make offerings for their dead spirits. At its simplest, the poem argues that if Gilgamesh cannot escape death, who are you to complain? Live all you can, said Siduri, but that advice is now gone. In *BEN* and as added here, an imagined afterlife finally does what popular conceptions say they do—it provides comfort in the face of anguish, tells the individual what to do and what to expect, and unites the community in death and around the dead. It was also thought efficacious. A surviving eighth-century copy of the tablet explains that it was copied for use at the funerals of a king who had died on the battlefield, one of the categories of dead it names.

The Twelfth Tablet is an Aristotelian catastrophe. It fits neither as an ending nor as a continuation of the action of the poem. Scandalously, Enkidu, whose death motivates the poem just ended, is alive again; his relationship to Gilgamesh changes from friend to servant, and he does not die, but is captured by the earth when he goes looking for Gilgamesh's *pukku*. Absurdly, Gilgamesh advises him on how to behave in the netherworld so as to be able to emerge from it: no oil, no sandals, no games, no embracing the wife you love or beating the child you hate, i.e., act dead. Where does this knowledge come from? Ancient Sumer, where Gilgamesh has long been an underworld deity, but not the poem the auditor has just heard, except for a brief allusion by Ninsun, "[Will he] not dwell in the Land-of-No-Return with Ningišzida?" (George, I, 581, iii, 106).[142]

Even worse, the continuity was salvageable. The author/editor could have made his point by beginning at a later moment in *BEN*. This narrative disaster need not have happened. The meddling scribes could simply have begun from the moment a god lets Enkidu up out of the ground to tell Gilgamesh what death is like. In that alternate structure, Gilgamesh, still mourning, returns to his city, boasts of it, seeks the gods' help, and learns from the risen Enkidu about the death Enkidu has found. No awkwardness, no discontinuity, and the audience learn about death, just as they do from the discontinuous tablet now before them. The join between the poems would be seamless, and the episode would continue the action. Instead, the join occurs so as to violate every narrative expectation.

It is possible that late Babylonian editors were simply very stupid and did not understand the literary effect of their addition. It is more probable, as the translation's alterations of the original suggest, that they knew what they were doing. The awkwardness of the join allows the redactor to deliver his tablet on death with no danger that it will be mistaken for a continuation of the narrative. With a continuous narrative, the story remains focused on Gilgamesh, whose last move is not toward his city, but from his city back to mourning. Gilgamesh also changes from a man defeated by death, like other men, to a shaman-priest who can bring the dead up, with the gods' help. Given Gilgamesh's prominent role throughout the period in exorcisms and the netherworld—as judge, boatman, figurine—that would have been an easy move to make (George, I, 132–35). Instead, as appended, the Twelfth Tablet starts over. Gilgamesh is left as a living hero overlooking a living city, but that city is juxtaposed with the city underground that needs offerings from the city of the living. The ring structure seems to exist for two reasons: to shift attention from the hero to the city and to make the tablet dangle. By adding an appendage to the ring, the scribes made certain their auditors recognized the abruptness of the turn away from the principal narrative to the concerns of the city's inhabitants, understood though not named in the salute to the city.

The catch line itself carries significant emotional weight: "If only I had left the *pukku* in the carpenter's house today!" (Dalley, 120). The line creates suspense and evokes longing and loss, the eternal "if only" that would have changed everything. George's translation begins "Today," creating the tension of immediacy, the now, breaking into the reader's present. The pendant Tablet makes twelve, not an insignificant number in the ancient Middle East suggesting that the flood story may have been added to make a seven- or ten-tablet OBV into eleven, to which a twelfth could be added. Eleven has never counted for much, lying between the meaningful 10, the number of digits, and 12, the number of lunar months and of double-hours of the path of the sun that Gilgamesh traverses (George, I, 495; 671, ix, 82). Although the tablet is often dismissed as merely a translation of the Sumerian original, there are slight but significant alterations, especially at the end.

Those alterations to the Sumerian original comfort, reconcile, and warn those who attended to the story of Gilgamesh and Enkidu. As in *BEN*, once the pair finish sitting and weeping, the rewards begin for the man with two sons. The father of one still weeps, but the father of two eats bread, and the father of five enters the palace like a scribe, as of right. Yet the children disappear from their prominent place in the Sumerian ending. One hopes they have been moved to an earlier position in lost lines, but, as with Siduri's veiling, they may have been removed by a society interested less in women's investments than in manly ideology.

In the Sumerian original, the man killed in battle does *not* have his father and mother hold his head, while his wife weeps.[143] That negative is unimaginable. No society known to us fails to reinforce the desirability of young men's dying on behalf of the state. The society that produced Tablet XII "corrects" the error, providing the man killed in battle with his father and mother to honor him, as well as his weeping wife. He is then contrasted with the man whose corpse lies abandoned in open country, on the plain (George, I, 735, xii, 150). To be left to the dogs and birds was common for those who fell on the losing side in battle, their bodies unrecovered. Finally, the last line warns against isolation in death with an abruptness equal to the Sumerian poem's soul going up in smoke.

Rather than fearing fire, however, this poem fears solitude and demands relationships:

> "Did you see the one who [died] a natural death?" [lit. "the death of his god"] "I [saw (him).]
> He lies drinking clear water on the bed of the [gods]."
> "Did you see the one who was killed in battle?" "I [saw (him).]
> His father and mother honour his memory [lit. hold up his head] and his wife [weeps] over [(him).]"
> "Did you see the one whose corpse was left lying in the open countryside?" "I saw (him).
> His ghost does not lie at rest in the Netherworld."
> "Did you see the one whose ghost has no provider [providers in some mss] of funerary offerings?" "I saw (him).
> He eats the scrapings from the pot (and) crusts of bread that are thrown away in the street."
>
> (George, I, 735, xii, 146–53)

Unlike the Egyptians, judged by their deeds, swearing their innocence, these ghosts are measured only by how they died, how many descendants they left, and whether those descendants supply them. No higher-order, abstract system intervenes between the dead, their offerings, and their gods. Morality, the be-all and end-all of afterlives from the modern point of view, remains conspicuously absent. Only at two points are there intimations of better company: the man who dies "the death of his god" has clear water and a bed, perhaps with his god, just as the man with seven sons sits as with the gods giving judgment. These motifs, being with god and giving judgment, appear in the psalms, and are often read as anticipations of blissful afterlives. They may be relics of these most hopeful instants in Mesopotamia; certainly, they are equally undeveloped.

Engaging descendants and forbears, the system reinforces an incentive to "be fruitful and multiply" even in unpropitious or dangerous times. Curiously, it also defies the gods who sought to diminish the human population in the flood and who denied humankind immortality, keeping that for themselves. Human fertility becomes creative resistance to the gods' plan to silence humanity and abort its (re)productivity. Embracing mortal pleasures, human beings subvert the gods' imposition of mortality.

Sumerians felt death's horrors, but not for their own deaths. Elegies for Nannaya (him) and Nawirtum (her) wish them clear water and light and the gods' pity, but Nannaya's progeny will multiply and beer fill his libation tube. What horrified, was the death of the city. Then storm and fire and enemies turned the ziggurat to a ruined mound, husbands abandoned wives and mothers their children, and the corpses piled in the streets. "How long will the brickwork strain its eyes upwards in tears and lamentations?"[144] The laments for the destroyed cities of Sumer, for Urim, Nibru, Unug, and Larsam, time makes only more painful.

Although ancient Mesopotamia may have had its skeptics, "the fool who has said in his heart" that there is no afterlife, neither the Sumerian poems nor their Babylonian successors imagine such skeptics, nor do they punish them. They do divert the Euphrates over body, entourage, and grave goods in the "Death of Bilgameš," hiding the tomb from violators, a problem when grave goods are rich and the poor not superstitious.[145] Their demystified accounts of death and its putrefying processes are rational, real, and depressing enough to satisfy any empiricist who credited only the evidence of her senses. No skeptic scavenges among the outcasts unless she should have been hardy enough to forbid funeral offerings or so unpleasant as to alienate his offspring.

As libretto for *The Epic of Gilgamesh*, Bohuslav Martinů chose Ūtanapišti over Siduri for his choruses, and allowed the soprano only to ask Gilgamesh a question.[146] Friendship, death, and rising from the dead are the moments Martinů isolates. Calling on Ea to let Enkidu up, the music swells, eager, hopeful, expansive, edgy. But as Gilgamesh asks after the man who died suddenly, who rests on his bed, drinking cool water; the wife weeping for the man who died honorably; the restless spirits of the unburied, Enkidu answers only "I saw him." Modally based orchestral themes, long-spanned rhythmic ostinatos, and phrases chanted by a bass soloist on a single note: the living already know as much as the dead will tell them.[147] Gilgamesh's last question he never asked before—not of the isolated soul of Babylon or the annihilated soul of Sumer, but a spirit unknown to either, a gift from Egyptian or later inventions: "the spirit . . . for ever in torment." Sumerians wept their infertility or groaned their loss of limbs or groveled for scraps, but torment? For ever? These are the gift of the Christian tradition. Enkidu saw him, too, and the once percussive music does not protest, but subsides.

Babylonians and Egyptians shared practices that strengthen a culture through the threat death represents. They democratized death rites and afterlife beliefs, mastering death's rupture through recourse to survivors and to magic. Both dramatized the dependence of the dead on the living and identified the soul's fate with the body's. Burning the body destroyed the soul. Ashurbanipal forced his Elamite captives to grind up the bones of their ancestors.[148] The differences are more striking. The Babylonians embraced the body's mortification, neglected moralizing rewards and punishments, and had minimalist expectations for cuisine—clear water and rarely beer, rather than roast meats. Their grave goods were not for their own use, but to propitiate the gods. The Egyptian promises of self-delighting food, drink, play, and justice were simply not on offer, nor would they be until Virgil. Plato, privileging justice, dropped the food and drink as insufficiently philosophic. Virgil brought back feasts and war games. Most significantly, in Sumer and Babylon, as in Greece, moral and legal codes functioned independently of afterlife beliefs. That independence underlies the striking innovation of Israel-Judah, erasing any afterlife benefits in favor of life lived by a God-given legal code.

JERUSALEM AND ATHENS: JEWS, GREEKS, AND ROMANS

Dismal popular systems; the mysteries' improvements; philosophers and poets remodel popular beliefs in Greece and Rome; theological reform in Judea erases communication with the dead; paradoxical emergence of eternal life

In both Judea and Greece, the earliest surviving literary afterlives resemble the dismal pit of Sumer and Babylon, shades huddled together in the mindless dark. Both traditions send a few great heroes somewhere else—Hercules to Olympus, in-laws of gods to the Blessed Isles; Enoch and Elijah to walk with God or be whirled up by his chariot.[149] But no such destinations were posited for ordinary people, no Field of Reeds where justice was done and life continued. Conditions could have been worse. No one eats excrement upside down, as once in Egypt; nor is anyone annihilated or swallowed by a waiting monster. In Greece, a vague judgment occurs somewhere in the middle distance, and a few traditional offenders against the gods are tortured in ingenious, hideous ways. In Israel, the drowsing dead rouse themselves to mock great fallen kings joining them amidst the worms. There is nothing to look forward to, and no gods to keep company.

In Greece, Homer and Hesiod disseminated popular beliefs, and some philosophers, most influentially Plato, irritably recast Homer to improve the afterlife's social and moral effectiveness. Determined to liberate others from the fear of death, some, including Epicurus, denied there was any afterlife at all. From the fourth to the first century BCE, philosophers quarreled and poets invented, while mystery cults spread from east to west, including Isis's. Two thousand years after the Pyramid Texts, Greeks and Romans laid purely psychic claims to the bodily-based, technologically grounded immortality of the Egyptians. Greek immortal souls survived burning, retained their rages, if they died angry, fled to Hades guided by Hermes, and remained accessible at their burial or dying sites to receive libations or hear prayers, in the spooky action-at-a-distance the dead are so skilled in. In sum, the dead both went away and stayed around, as they do.

Greek multiplicity, philosophic free play, and self-conscious modification for didactic and moral purposes (e.g., Aristophanes, Plato, Lucian) anticipate modern literary and cinematic afterlives. Coexisting with traditional received beliefs, ancient or contemporaneous, such texts are fictions in which no one believes and which no one disbelieves. They do not represent reality, explain the unknown, or provide the truth. Instead, they play with what might be or what ought to be, self-consciously exploiting the residual familiarity of traditional views to generate new possibilities more satisfying to the philosophic or artistic or moral imagination. These afterlives instruct the living in how they should think about life and how little they know about death. The afterlife is invented, denied, mused over, elaborated, or mocked. Death is imbricated in life, and only the scientific materialists who deny any afterlife exists (e.g., Lucretius) are seriously concerned about empirical truth.

In Judea, something even more interesting happened. Other peoples' promising, integrated afterlives were rejected, and a lively commerce with the dead eliminated by determined theologians on ideological grounds.[150] That the Mesopotamian tradition had not moralized its afterlives simplified rejection. Paradoxically, this profoundly theistic move indicates why godless, atheistic societies need not undergo moral collapse in the absence of an afterlife promising rewards and threatening punishments. All that is required is a powerful alternative ideology. Judaism created (or was created by) such an ideology in the law of Moses, an all-encompassing moral system that governed the living, not the dead, and was predicated on the people's release from the social death of slavery in Egypt.

Fusing family, obedience, prosperity, life, and light, the law pushed death, disobedience, suffering, childlessness, and other evils into the dark. The binary thinking that divided animals into clean and unclean, men into circumcised and uncircumcised, God's image into male and female, was not insensitive to the binary living/dead. Separate as day and night were life and death, good and evil, light and dark. On the side of life, good, and light was the law: I set before you "this day life and good, and death and evil;. . . . [C]hoose life" (Deut. 30:15, 19, KJV). God guaranteed the law and life. With death he had nothing to do.[151] Afterlife there was none, apart from drowsing in the dark with other corpses.

Yet from this tradition emerges a promise of eternal life that has shaped western thinking for two thousand years: how did that happen? Within a few hundred years of the Torah's completion (c. 450–400 BCE), that law-defined community, deprived of the national independence promised in the founding traditions, faced persecution, division, and annihilation not for disobeying God's laws, but for obeying them (c. 175 BCE).[152] Judea's prophets had correctly foretold the destruction of a disobedient people and the restoration of an obedient one. That had happened already: the Temple destroyed in 587/86 BCE was rebuilt c. 515 BCE. God had once set things right and would again. If this world was awry, he would not leave his people without succor. About what would happen when God intervened again, opinion differed. He might be content with the people's obedience to the law and leave things as they were. He might restore the throne of David and the nation's independence (promised in the prophets); he might institute a universal reign of justice (promised in the prophets), with life restored even to the righteous dead (promised in the writings, Dan. 12:2–3). When one victim, crucified for preaching the approaching kingdom of God, appeared alive after his death in Jerusalem, many believed that his return as Lord was imminent (Dan. 7:13), and they began to wait, eagerly.

SILENCING THE DEAD: JUDEA ACT 1/ACT 2: MY DEAD BODIES SHALL ARISE

The cult of the dead in ancient Judea suppressed by religious reformers from the seventh century BCE; emergence of a doctrine of resurrection by the second century BCE; vestiges and extirpation of older beliefs; condition of the dead; moral and textual consequences of afterlife obliteration

Ancient Israel supplies the only known example of a society-wide, religiously motivated erasure of afterlife beliefs. In the modern era, from the eighteenth to the twentieth centuries, in France, Mexico, and Russia, the afterlife suffered collateral damage when proponents of secular ideologies attacked established religions and their imbrication in structures of power. New truth targeted an older, compensatory belief to discredit it. When God died, his afterlife usually went with him, chased away as deceptive folly by Marx, Freud, and Christopher Hitchens. The religious assault on the afterlife was equally ideological. It monopolized writing and elicited no articulate defense. Stamped out were local variants of the mummy's quasi-divine status as "this god" and the divinatory powers that raised Enkidu. Afterlife extirpation purified the universal monotheism developing in seventh-century BCE Judah. The Bible preserves the struggle over afterlife's erasure and its sudden re-appearance in a new concept, resurrection.

"Preposterous piffle, utterly absurd." So might bluster many modern Jews and Christians who believe in an afterlife and are firmly persuaded that such a promise is made in the Bible or in the Old Testament as well as the New. Once in place, belief can be read into passages where it is initially absent, as confirmation bias guarantees. The OT promises "life" at every turn. One need only insert a bracketed [eternal] to establish the eternal life Christianity prided itself on initiating when Jesus rose. Yet if eternal life were already there, how could Jesus have "abolished death, and ... brought life and immortality to light," as the New Testament proclaims? (2 Tim. 1:10).[153] Before he turned from persecuting to proselytizing for Jesus, how could Paul be sure death reigned, yet as a Pharisee already believe in "resurrection" (Acts 23:6, 23:8)?

Jesus rose not only from the dead but also in mid-first-century Judaism. Eternal life had come to be expected, but it was not there yet. The book of Daniel, the latest book received as Hebrew scripture, was written

c. 165 BCE during an ultimately successful revolutionary upheaval against pagan Greek overlords. It promised one "like the son of Man" who would receive an everlasting dominion never to pass away (7:13, KJV). Terrible end times climaxed in resurrection, the only moment the Jewish Bible promises a life after this one:

> And at that time shall Michael stand up, the great prince which standeth for the children of thy people: and there shall be a time of trouble, such as never was since there was a nation even to that same time: and at that time thy people shall be delivered, every one that shall be found written in the book. *And many of them that sleep in the dust of the earth shall awake, some to everlasting life, and some to shame and everlasting contempt.* And they that be wise shall shine as the brightness of the firmament; and they that turn many to righteousness as the stars for ever and ever.
>
> (Dan. 12.1–3, KJV, emphasis added)

Before this surreptitious emergence of the shiny new promise of resurrection, cached among the Writings in the last division of the Jewish Bible, the Jewish Bible records in the Torah and Prophets (c. 650–250 BCE) the struggle against traditional Canaanite afterlife beliefs and the rupture of the old communication with the dead.

Gilgamesh was still being copied in the seventh century BCE beside Tigris and Euphrates, two great rivers girding Eden in Genesis, when Jerusalem's rising religious orthodoxy prohibited and marginalized a lively commerce with the dead and the ancestors. In 621 BCE (a decade before Ashurbanipal's library was buried, with its multiple editions of *Gilgamesh*), a "book of the law" was discovered in the Temple at Jerusalem—the core of Deuteronomy, now the last book of the Torah or Pentateuch (the five books with which every Bible begins), but the first of the five to be received or written. Its authenticity certified by the prophetess Huldah (2 Kings 22:13–20), the text continued Hezekiah's reforms (715–687/6 BCE) and motivated a new series of reforms under Josiah (640–09 BCE).[154] The material accretion of statues and images in and around the Temple was done away with, and mediums and their afterlife contacts went, too (2 Kings 23:24; Deut. 18:10–14).

The historic importance of the Temple discovery of the first of the Books of Moses can scarcely be overstated.[155] It made the religion of Judea a religion of the book just before the eternal kingdom promised to David's son Solomon, the Temple builder (2 Sam. 7:2–16), was annihilated forever. Only the book found in the Temple, and Cyrus the Persian's intervention, prevented YHWH from going the way of the gods of "Hamath and Arpad. Where are the gods of Sepharvaim, Hena, and Ivvah?" (2 Kings 18:33–34). Where, indeed. Within a generation of the book's claim to authority, Jerusalem was conquered by the Babylonians under Nebuchadnezzar, 597 BCE. Ten years later, Jewish resistance prompted the Babylonians to destroy the Temple and city walls and deport Jerusalem's leading inhabitants to Babylon (587 BCE). The prophet Jeremiah urged submission and is last seen being carried toward Egypt, challenged by women who sulk that nothing bad had happened as long as they served cakes to the Queen of Heaven (Jer. 44:15–30). Fifty years later the Babylonian Exile ended (538 BCE). Cyrus the Persian, antiquity's great exponent of imperial toleration, permitted Jews to return to Jerusalem and rebuild the Temple and city walls. As to the ark holding the stone tablets inscribed with the Ten Commandments, some Greek-speaking Jews wondered what had happened to it when the Temple was destroyed. As they told the story, on that flight toward Egypt, Jeremiah had carried the ark and the tent to the mount of God and sealed them in a cave (2 Macc. 2:1–8). Under the Hasmoneans, straddling Greek and Roman rule (c. 163 BCE–63 BCE), Jews enjoyed their single century of independence before 1948 and the establishment of a modern Jewish state. Never again would a king of Davidic descent occupy the throne of Judea, but no one knew that yet.

The prophetic and Deuteronomist reading of history emerged re-energized, revitalized, and re-motivated by the cycle of Babylonian destruction and Persian restoration to Jerusalem. As the city fell, Jeremiah prophesied that the people would return in seventy years.[156] They made it back two decades ahead of schedule, armed with a book written before the event, Deuteronomy, assuring them that prosperity hinged on loyalty to YHWH. In the half millennium during (597/87–538 BCE) and after the Babylonian exile (538 BCE–70 CE), the Torah was compiled, the prophets collected, edited, and added to, the psalms and other writings accumulated until the Hebrew canon was closed shortly after the Temple was destroyed—again, this time by Romans—in 70 CE, during the rise of Christianity.

What these events mean for the afterlife is that the Bible was compiled by a religious orthodoxy hostile to communication with the dead out of older texts that contained traces of the earlier popular cult. The Hebrew Bible bubbles with Babylonian afterlife imagery and knows something of Egyptian practices, but the god-filled underworld of Babylon has vanished, replaced by a generic pit, *sheol*, into which the spirits of all the dead pass. There, under the earth, the dead lie, finding no justice, raising no prayers, enjoying no pleasures, communing with no god. As Karel van der Toorn argues, this dim, dreary account emerged from a full-scale attack on an earlier family religion that cared for the dead as in the cults of Babylon and Assyria.[157] Modern scholars who attempt to read resurrection into texts before Daniel can never be entirely sure whether they have found an early reference to the later concept or a late reference to an earlier cult of the dead.[158]

Storm and sky gods, like Baal, Zeus, Ishtar, and YHWH, were always differentiated from the gods of the dead, as far apart as the heavens and the grave. (Sun gods differ, since they pass half the day in a netherworld.[159]) The Bible knows the architecture of the afterlife, the gates and halls familiar from Egyptian and Babylonian texts: "Have the gates of death been opened unto thee? Or hast thou seen the doors of the shadow of death?" (Job 38:17, KJV), God asks Job. No underworld pantheon ever appears inside those gates, but in Hebrew grammar a few shades flit past of earlier conceptions. *Sheol*, the place where the dead go, is a feminine noun in Hebrew and cognate with Shuwela, the goddess of death, a Syrian variant of Ereshkigal.[160] *Mot*, past tense of the Hebrew verb to die, is also the name of the Ugaritic god of death, who defeats Baal and is then defeated by him. Hebrew "death," מות, *maret*, can also be written *mot*.[161] So when death and *sheol* are personified, as they often are in the biblical text, they verge on the gods of death known to neighboring peoples. There is, however, no mythology associated with them, no history, no character. They have been emptied of personality. They do not speak. They certainly do not judge.

So too the Bible presents YHWH as possessed of absolute dominion over death and the dead, a characteristic that contrasts him with Baal, his principal pre-exilic competitor in the Elijah sequence for the people's affections. Like YHWH a warrior sky god, Baal was a son of El, chief god of the Canaanite pantheon (identified by Isra-*el* with YHWH, Exod. 6:3) who displaced his father El (by contrast, YHWH absorbs El). As a dying and reviving vegetation god, Baal's adventure with death resembles Ishtar's and Dumuzi's (or Tammuz, Ezek. 8:14). In Ugaritic myth, Baal, swallowed up by Mot, the God of Death, descends to the underworld, like

Ishtar. His sister (remembering Ishtar and perhaps Isis) threatens Mot, and Baal is resurrected to the cry, "Baal lives!" In later combat he defeats Mot, but cannot destroy him.[162] For his festival, Baal arrives in his house (temple) from the netherworld on the third day.[163] Rising on the third day reminds Christians of Jesus, but ancient Israelites know such revivals are pagan, not of YHWH. The prophet Hosea mocks enthusiasm for a third-day rising and healing (Hosea 6:2) in a passage early Christians never cite as a proof text.[164]

In Hosea's contemptuous eighth-century account, the people of Israel, returning to the Lord, mingle knowledge of the Lord's power with expectations of being revived with Baal: "Come, let us return to the LORD; for it is he who has torn, and he will heal us; he has struck down, and he will bind us up. *After two days, he will revive us; on the third day, he will raise us up, that we may live before him*. Let us know, let us press on to know the LORD; his appearing is as sure as the dawn; he will come to us like the showers, like the spring rains that water the earth" (Hosea 6:1–3, emphasis added). To this mélange of power, fertility cult, and natural cycles, Hosea expostulates, "What shall I do with you, O Ephraim? What shall I do with you, O Judah?" (Hosea 6:4).

That Christian exegesis failed to cite the passage as a proof text suggests that early and late Christian interpreters still understood Hosea's passage as critical. Interpreting YHWH as a vegetation deity offended him. The Gospels prefer for Jesus's resurrection the unnatural "sign of the prophet Jonah," belched from the belly of a fish after three days (Jon. 1:17, Matt. 12:38). Whether Hosea or Jonah is the passage Paul has in mind when he says Christ rose in three days, "according to the scriptures" (1. Cor. 15:4), he avoids quoting any scriptural passage.

YHWH rejects cyclical compromises. Mocking third-day revivalism (Hosea 6:1–4), Hosea sets YHWH over death, undefeated: "O death, I will be thy plagues; o grave, I will be thy destruction" (Hosea 13:14, KJV). Like Baal, YHWH destroys Leviathan, sea monsters and dragons (Ps. 74:13–14; Isa. 27:1), but if he ever submits to a contest with death, it is he who swallows death, not the other way around: "He will swallow up death in victory" (Isa. 25:8, KJV). That seems merely a joyous metaphor, echoed by Paul who quotes liberally when passages suit him (1 Cor. 15:54, 15:55), but it figures death in terms derived from Canaanite myths. Death was organic, a giant maw that swallows up the living, and insatiable (Hab. 2:5, Prov. 30:16).

In Proverbs, murderous robbers identify themselves with death as they prey upon the living: "Let us swallow them up alive as the grave; and whole, as those that go down into the pit" (Prov. 1:12, KJV). The grave and the pit, where the body meets the worm, are devouring mouths. They swallow bodies whole, corpses entire (a view consistent with resurrection of the whole body, when that view developed). But the only gods found there are the dead themselves.

For ancient Israel did have, rather than an erased pantheon of underworld gods, a lively commerce with the dead themselves as divinities. Israel shared its material culture with the surrounding Canaanite groups and, before the Babylonian exile, practiced, if the Bible is to be believed and as excavations indicate, a highly syncretic religion that accommodated grave goods, mediums, male temple prostitutes, and Asherah, the Queen of Heaven. Her popular images have been identified by modern archeologists as YHWH's wife.[165] Before Josiah's reforms, the Temple itself housed goods consecrated to Baal and the host of heaven (2 Kings 23:4–15). The dead were fed by the living, regarded as "divine beings" in a form of ancestor worship associated with household gods (like those Rachel carried away from Laban, Gen. 31:30, and Jacob buried, Gen. 35:2–4. A narrative of appropriation and repudiation, Rachel sits on those gods while she claims to be menstruating, a humiliating situation for gods. Jacob curses with death anyone with whom they are found, and Rachel dies shortly thereafter.) Rattles and bracelets were buried with infants, and scarabs with young and old.[166]

The dead were also consulted about the future. Before the exile, the art of divining seems to have been shared between prophets and necromancers ("dead diviners": *necro-*: "dead"; *-mancy*, "mantis": diviner, prophet). Like Babylon's divining priests, necromancers consulted the dead relative to future events. The prophetic tradition, from the eighth century, regards such divination as problematic, but not false. The Bible preserves the paradigmatic story (set c. 1000 BCE) of the wise woman of Endor who conflates the religion of Israel and traditional necromancy when she calls up a dead prophet, Samuel, to prophesy Saul's future (I Sam. 28, 31). Saul, Samuel says, will die in battle the next day, the host of Israel defeated by Philistines, and so it happens: "to morrow shalt thou and thy sons be with me" (1 Sam. 28:19, KJV). Marking the competition between the living god and the dead as authoritative consultants, the woman's activity has been prohibited on pain of death by Saul (and will be prohibited in legislation recorded in Leviticus, Exodus, and Deuteronomy, Lev. 20:6, 27; Ex. 22:18 [Tanakh Ex. 22:17]; Deut. 18:11–14). But she is no false prophet and produces no false prophecy: her method works.[167]

Everyone knew what ghosts sounded like—they twittered from underground (Isa. 8:19–22; 29:4). Mediums mumbled, and like many ancient peoples, Israel addressed the dead as gods, ancestors, to be fed, propitiated, and consulted.[168] The eighth-century prophet Isaiah of Jerusalem, complicit in Hezekiah's reforms, disliked mediums and their clients, regarded them as consulting alternative gods in the dead, and prophesied for them darkness without dawn (Isa. 8:19–22). He knows very well what the dead sound like—they "chirp and mutter" (Isa. 8:19)—and whence they speak: "from the earth . . . from low in the dust . . . from the ground like the voice of a ghost" (Isa. 29:4). The mediums' advocates, arguing for consulting the dead, call the dead "gods," a conventional designation shared with Sumer, Babylon, and Egypt's mummies.[169] "[S]hould not a people consult their gods, the dead on behalf of the living, for teaching and instruction?'" the benighted Israelites ask, to Isaiah's horror (Isa. 8:19–20; Tanakh: "a people may inquire of its divine beings—of the dead on behalf of the living—for instruction and message"[170]). The translators of the KJV twist the knife in their version: "should not a people seek unto their God, for the living to the dead?" The dead become the singular God whom the people seek or look to. The locution occurs in 1 Samuel. When the woman of Endor calls up the dead, she sees "gods ascending" (KJV) or "a divine being" coming up, revealed to be Samuel (1 Sam. 28:13).

Neither Isaiah nor the author of 1 Samuel denies that the dead speak, mutter, and respond to consultations. The dead do those things, but the living should not ask them to do so. After the exile, in Trito-Isaiah, consulting the dead is as abhorrent as sacrificing to idols or eating swine's flesh. This people "sacrifice in gardens . . . sit inside tombs, and spend the night in secret places; [and] eat swine's flesh" (Isa. 65:3–4). The Chronicler rewrote Saul's story, probably in the fourth century BCE. Saul, who in Samuel sought the woman only because the Lord was not answering him, died because he consulted a medium: "moreover, he had consulted a medium, seeking guidance, and did not seek guidance from the LORD. Therefore the LORD put him to death and turned the kingdom over to David son of Jesse" (1 Chron. 10:13–14). Had Saul not consulted the medium, he might have won the battle and Jonathan ruled after him.

Food offerings were made to the dead, but not of the tenth sanctified to the Lord (Deut. 26:14). The dead might be fed, or at least have food given to them, but such offerings to the dead were to be separated from offerings to YHWH. Kindness to the dead over time migrates from making offerings to performing burials. Jesus, son of Sirach (Sirach, c. 200–180 BCE) counsels kindness to the dead, and mourning with those who mourn ("Give graciously to all the living; do not withhold kindness even from the dead" [7:33]), but he also uses offerings to the dead to define futility: "good things poured out upon a mouth that is closed are like offerings upon a grave" (Sirach 30:18). The simile suggests that such offerings continued to be made. He also cautions against mourning the dead more than two days, "Do not forget, there is no coming back; you do the dead no good, and you injure yourself' (Sirach 38:21). In Tobit, burying abandoned, executed bodies is an exceptionally pious act that endangers the hero (Tobit 1:17–19). Burial is also a duty to parents (6:15, 12:12, 14:12–13). Tobit advises his son, "Place your bread on the grave of the righteous" (4:17). Today, stones are placed.

Death itself was defiling, dead bodies polluting. Priests of the Lord are forbidden to approach the dead, except for their nearest blood relatives (father, mother, son, daughter, brother, and virgin sister). The high priest is forbidden to approach corpses even of his mother or father (Lev. 21:1–4, 21:11). Hence in Luke's parable of the good Samaritan the priest and the Levite avoid the injured man, who looks dead (Luke 10:30–32). Animals that die of themselves are not to be eaten, though they may be sold or given away to foreigners in the community (Deut. 14:21). The dead are separated from the living, cut off, and more especially cut off from the priestly class. They are also cut off from YHWH.

When the dead go underground, out of the sun, they disappear from YHWH's sight. Job knows the gloomy pit under the ground, *sheol*, where kings and slaves, the wicked and the weary, lie down together, as if they had never been. "For now I should have lain still and been quiet . . . With kings and counselors of the earth which built desolate palaces for themselves . . . as an hidden untimely birth I had not been, as infants which never saw light" (Job 3:13–16, KJV). Death releases from trouble, but provides no access to God or to wisdom. In death, God loses sight of man.

"For now shall I sleep in the dust; and thou shalt seek me in the morning, but I shall not be" (Job 7:21, KJV). In the dust or the pit (Ps. 143:7, Ps. 28.1) the dead are silent, neither praising nor remembering God. Only the living praise a living God (Isa. 38:18-19). "The dead do not praise the LORD, nor do any that go down into silence" (Ps. 115:17). "In death there is no remembrance of you; in Sheol who can give you praise?" (Psalm 6:5; KJV: "For in death there is no remembrance of thee: in the grave who shall give thee thanks?").

Indeed, the worshipper sometimes seems to be putting God on notice. If he dies, he leaves God's presence, and where then will God be? God loses his audience: "Wilt thou shew wonders to the dead? Shall the dead arise and praise thee? Selah. Shall thy loving kindness be declared in the grave, or thy faithfulness in destruction? Shall thy wonders be known in the dark? And thy righteousness in the land of forgetfulness?" (Ps. 88:10-12, KJV). To receive prayer and praise, God must keep his people alive. He depends on them as much as they on him.[171] Unlike the legal prohibitions, such views show real defeat for cults of the dead, divinities of the dead, rituals for the dead, and mediations through the dead. At the very least, they indicate at the heart of the Jahwist tradition, within piety itself, a repudiation of any hopefulness about what lies beyond death.

Neither Egyptian virtues nor Sumerian sons give anyone anything to look forward to after death. In the story of Saul, Samuel, and the woman of Endor, there is no privilege associated with having been the Lord's favored prophet: Saul and his sons join Samuel tomorrow. Death does not distinguish the beloved prophet from the rejected king. There is no reward for virtuous Samuel, no punishment for naughty Saul. The bones of Elisha may bring a dead man back to life, but Elisha remains just bones (2 Kings 13:20-21). When the child he begot in adultery on Bathsheba dies, David stops praying, rises, and orders dinner, explaining to his astonished servants: "Why should I fast? Can I bring him back again? I shall go to him, but he will not return to me" (2 Sam. 12:23). To suffering Job, God promises no otherworldly compensations from the whirlwind. Like the model Sumerian god of "A man and his god" (ETCSL t.5.2.4), he restores Job's goods and family in this life. Justice is nowhere if not here.

That justice's absence is one of Ecclesiastes' concerns. The race is not to the swift, he reminds us. "Time and chance" happen to all men caught, like animals, in the snare of an evil time (Cf. "Elegy for Nawirtum": "Upon the fledgling overstepping its nest, a net has . . .".[172]). The spirit returns to God that gave it, but who knows whether the spirit of man goes up and of beasts goes down? The same fate happens to all (Eccles. 3:19–21; 9:2–6). The best advice is that Siduri gave to Gilgamesh and Egyptians harped:

> Go thy way, eat thy bread with joy, and drink thy wine with a merry heart; for God now accepteth thy works. Let thy garments be always white; and let thy head lack no ointment. Live joyfully with the wife whom thou lovest all the days of the life of thy vanity, which he hath given thee under the sun, all the days of thy vanity: for that is thy portion in this life, and in thy labour which thou takest under the sun. Whatsover thy hand findeth to do, do it with thy might; for there is no work, nor device, nor knowledge, nor wisdom, in the grave, whither thou goest.
> (Eccles. 9:7–10, KJV)

The spirit returns to God who gave it, but there is no place there. Jesus, son of Sirach, sees the spirit's departing, but not to anywhere: "Do not forget, there is no coming back. . . . Remember his fate, for yours is like it; yesterday it was his, and today it is yours. When the dead is at rest, let his remembrance rest too, and be comforted for him when his spirit has departed" (Sirach, 38:21–23). As the wise woman of Tekoa observes, "We must all die; we are like water spilled on the ground, which cannot be gathered up" (2 Sam. 14:14). Such is the fate of the faithful.

As to Israel's enemies, the dead stir to greet them, but only to celebrate the powerlessness of their rotting bodies: "Sheol beneath is stirred up to meet you when you come; it rouses the shades to greet you. . . . 'You too have become as weak as we! You have become like us!' Your pomp is brought down to Sheol . . . maggots are the bed beneath you, and worms are your covering" (Isa. 14:9–11). Death is the only punishment, and it is punishment enough.

The OT has been scoured for possible references to an afterlife and occasionally emended to create such references when beliefs changed. Even the Masoretic text punctuates the question out of Ecclesiastes' query about the spirits of beasts' going down and men upward.[173] A few psalms suggest a refuge in God that seems to go beyond the usual clear expectation that the speaker hopes for safety right now, in time. Psalm 49 mocks those who seek to take their goods with them into the grave and concludes with the cheerful promise that the rich "will go to the company of their ancestors, who will never again see the light. Mortals cannot abide in their pomp; they are like the animals that perish" (Ps. 49:19–20). Like Ecclesiastes, the psalm assures its auditor that "the wise, they die; fool and dolt perish together." Yet one verse seems to promise being with God and escaping the grave. Death shepherds fools to Sheol (replacing God as shepherd), "But God will ransom my soul from the power of Sheol, for he will receive me" (Ps. 49:15; Tanakh: But God will redeem my life from the clutches of Sheol, for He will take me"). Being "received" by God recurs in Psalm 73: "You guide me with your counsel, and afterward you will receive me with honor [alt. to glory]" (Ps. 73:24; Tanakh, "You guided me by Your counsel and led me toward honor"; a note designates as unacceptable the common alternate reading, "And afterward receive me with glory"). Whether these phrases look forward to immortality, or back to the Mesopotamian protection by one's God in the afterlife, or refer to this life only, is uncertain.[174]

The afterlife has not been sought in dietary prohibitions, but the rejection of other peoples' immortal longings may explain the cryptic prohibition "thou shalt not seethe a kid in his mother's milk" (Ex. 23:19, 34:26, Deut. 14:21, KJV). Maimonides was confident it referred to some pagan practice, but biblical scholars have not located any such pagan rite in Canaan.[175] A possible origin is the Greek mysteries, where imagery of a kid and milk fulfilled the serpent's promise to Eve: "Tush, you shall not surely die. For God doth know that in the day ye eat thereof, ye shall be as gods" (Gen. 3:4–5, Tyndale's translation). Inscribed gold leaves found in grave mounds from fifth-century-BCE southern Italy associate a kid falling into milk with attaining immortality, becoming a god instead of a mortal. One leaf promises "happy and blessed one, god will you be instead of a mortal. Kid I fell in the milk." Another assures the dead man: "A god you have become from a man. Kid you fell in the milk."[176] The prohibition appears in Exodus not with the dietary laws but with sacrifice, amid the blood, fat, and first fruits brought to the Lord. In Deuteronomy, it ends the dietary rules, but follows death, namely the prohibition on eating animals that die of themselves, which may be sold or given to aliens. Prohibiting magical attempts at immortality would be consistent with the text's attitudes towards divining and the dead. The Orphic tablets say nothing about boiling or mothers, and the geographic and cultural distance between biblical prohibitions and golden burial hopes has no visible bridges. A coincidence in search of evidence, the tablets supply, unlike other interpretations, "a *Sitz im Leben* which really fits the passage."[177]

Whatever shadowy vision of the grave ancient Israel entertained, it imagined no rewards or punishments in another life. That absence had repercussions producing discomfort—and sometimes detestation—in modern readers. God often threatens his stiff-necked people with destruction, disaster, and famines in which mothers eat their own children and other people's. In both versions of the Ten Commandments God insists that he punishes children for the crimes of their parents to three and four generations (Ex. 20:5–6; Deut. 5:9). "Suffer, little children!" some readers gasp, Christopher Hitchens repeatedly.[178] They are equally outraged when God answers Job's anguish with mocking questions. Out of a whirlwind, no less, like the one that swept away Elijah, Leviathan's creator affirms his own unimaginable, murderous power. Who does he think he is—God?

If we think to remember that there is no afterlife, God's behavior—and morality—make better sense. With this world the only one, justice must be done here and, if not now, in the next few generations. The prophetic tradition begins not with the suffering of the innocent, as Job might lead us to expect, but with the complacence of the guilty, the serene happiness of the selfish. That tradition originates in the desire to punish those who enjoy doing wrongs they do not recognize, to pierce the self-satisfaction of the always justified self. Put more positively, prophecy demands social justice. Making that demand does not, as we well know, create social justice. It does not even make social injustice uncomfortable for the socially unjust, but it registers the concept. Israel was not the only society to moralize,[179] but hers is a large collection of texts frequently reprinted.

In the eighth century (c. 750 BCE), the prophet Amos created a meme. The day of the Lord would be a day of wrath, the *dies irae* of every Christian requiem. The events that justified Amos came later: the exile of the northern kingdom Israel from Samaria (721 BCE) and, after Deuteronomy's publication (621 BCE), the exile of the southern kingdom Judah (597 BCE). Outside any prophetic lineage, a herdsman and pruner of sycamore trees (7:14), Amos, like Israel, knows the day of the Lord as a day desired, a festival of lights and rejoicing. Amos turns it into a day of dread. That day he who forms the mountains and creates the winds (Amos 4:13) will bring wailing upon the highways and the vineyards: "Woe unto you that desire the day of the LORD! To what end is it for you? The day of the LORD is darkness and not light. As if a man did flee from a lion and a bear met him; . . . Shall not the day of the LORD be darkness, and not light? Even very dark, and no brightness in it" (Amos 5:18–20, KJV).

Amos's day of the Lord turns into the spectacular Christian day(s) of judgment in Revelation, but Amos is not imagining the end of the world. He attacks the rich who lie upon ivory beds and couches, who follow the advice of Siduri and Ecclesiastes. They eat the lambs from the flock, chant songs, drink wine, anoint themselves—and think about the poor and needy only to sell them for a pair of shoes (Amos 6:4–6, 2:6–8). Required is justice to the poor and before God: "Seek good, and not evil, that you may live. . . . Hate evil, and love good, and establish judgment in the gate . . . Let justice roll down like waters, and righteousness as an ever-flowing stream" (Amos 5:14, 15, 24). This great motif runs through the prophets—like water, as a mighty stream. Warfare, famine, captivity, earthquake, the uncontrollable evils of human life are in God's hands, not man's.

Such prophetic threatening has given the Hebrew Bible a bad reputation, its just but angry God well traded in for the softer, merciful, loving Jesus of the NT. Readers forget that the OT God lets wicked and just alike sleep in the grave, while the forgiving NT God thrusts most believers and all nonbelievers into eternal hellfire. The angry God gets over it; the merciful one bears a grudge that lasts forever. Both meet the demand for ultimate justice, collective or individual. The day the Lord returns, justice, now deferred or partial, will be complete. Israel (the northern kingdom) earned its destruction (721 BCE) by cultic infidelity, and Judah did not turn in time to ward off the consequences of violated law (597/587 BCE). Whenever justice is enacted in this world, the Lord has returned and made it happen, and that includes the destruction of his own temple.

Such collective justice is individualized in vengeance exacted on the children. Other-worldly postmortem punishments are unnecessary when what one loves best is threatened in this life. Punished after death is the only part of a person that survives death—her children. The prosperity of the wicked is illusory. Justice will be done in the next generation, or the next, but it will come. The threat is exceptionally canny. It exploits natural fears for one's children, and it knows that unseen terrors are more dreadful than almost any that actually occur. The ancients found this threat as unbearable as do moderns.

Challenged by Ezekiel and Jeremiah, the argument is significantly absent from Job, though it still appears later than might be expected. Herodotus reports that Croesus was defeated by Cyrus as retribution for the misdeed of a usurping ancestor five generations earlier.[180] As late as the first century CE, the offspring of the ungodly are "evil . . . accursed" in the Wisdom of Solomon (3:12–13). Yet for all the arguments Job's friends make to justify his suffering, they neglect the surest and most obvious explanation, if this rule were operational. Job's boils and dead children must be his father's or great-grandfather's fault, something they did that he knows nothing about and had nothing to do with. He is atoning for someone else's guilt. That folk karma crosses no one's mind. Ezekiel's and Jeremiah's rejection of the concept prevailed. They opposed what they called a proverb (not a phrase in the law): "The fathers have eaten sour grapes, and the children's teeth are set on edge" (Ezekiel 18:2, KJV; Jer. 31:29–30). Each person, they insist, is to live or die by his own righteousness or wickedness.

Yet why would any culture consent to so little in the way of an afterlife and persist in the erasure for so long? Israel in Egypt ought to have been well acquainted with the benefits an afterlife could offer. Both Jacob and Joseph were embalmed in the Egyptian fashion (Gen. 50:2, 26). Scarabs have turned up in Israelite burials. If Egyptians, Sumerians, and Babylonians could invent a better afterlife, take the initiative and improve their lot underground, why did Israel show so little imagination and urgency about death? Ultimately, Judah patched together bodily resurrection to judgment (Daniel) and the Greeks' immortal soul (Wisdom of Solomon), a process repeated in Christianity. Yet from a self-absorbed modern perspective, how did they love and serve a God who did not provide eternal life, who let them molder in the ground? What, to put it bluntly, was in it for them?

The skeptical Ecclesiastes gives one answer. "[W]henever a man does eat and drink and get enjoyment out of all his wealth, it is a gift of God" (Eccl. 3:13, Tanakh). God gives life and puts himself in the minds and hearts of men. That is enough. But God also gave something else to join the generations of the living. God gave the law, and men made the Torah, and a woman certified the first volume.

Some modern Christians and Jews find the law an intolerable burden, about as attractive as punishing children for the crimes of their grandparents. Martin Nilsson calls it "fetters [fastened] on the whole of man's life."[181] Kafka's parable shows a door that any man can enter, a door always open for him, but Kafka's hapless hero does not enter. The Psalms tell another story: "Blessed is the man [whose] delight is in the law of the LORD; and in his law doth he meditate day and night" (Ps. 1:1-2, KJV). The law provides meaning—all action takes place under the eye of God, the creator and ultimate repository of value. It defines and promises justice, and it establishes an eternal community across the generations. In the *Shema*, Deuteronomy expresses both communal belief ("our") and individual allegiance ("thy," singular): "Hear, O Israel: The LORD our God is one LORD: And thou shalt love the LORD thy God with all thine heart, and with all thy soul, and with all thy might." The next verses penetrate the heart, cross the generations, infiltrate daily life, and mark time, the house, the body: "And these words, which I command thee this day shall be in thine heart: And thou shalt teach them diligently unto thy children, and shalt talk of them when thou sittest in thine house, and when thou walkest by the way, and when thou liest down, and when thou risest up. And thou shalt bind them for a sign upon thine hand, and they shall be as frontlets between thine eyes, And thou shalt write them upon the posts of thy house and on thy gates" (Deut. 6:4-9, KJV). In Deuteronomy's fiction of origin, individual and communal identities are linked in the moment when the Lord frees the people from the social death of slavery in Egypt to life in a land promised. In Deuteronomy's reforming reality "these words" constitute a communal ideology that overcomes death and time, extending back to Moses and forward into future uncertainties. It also takes a form, law, not associated with afterlife mythology in Mesopotamia.

Within the law is the cosmos; outside annihilating isolation. Like Hammurabi's ratios in the epilogue to his much earlier code, Deuteronomy promises fourteen verses of blessings on kine and store (Deut. 28:1-14) and fifty-three of curses on crops, bodies, and the land: blight, famine, invasion, siege, cannibalism, defeat, exile. Common vicissitudes in the ancient world, reviving in our own, death or enslavement to one's enemies might seem the worst of punishments, or eating one's newborn baby (Deut. 28:55-57). The Deuteronomist knows something still worse. The last curse of Deuteronomy is solitude: "And the LORD shall bring thee into Egypt again with ships, by the way whereof I spake unto thee,

Thou shalt see it no more again: and there ye shall be sold unto your enemies for bondmen and bondwomen, and no man shall buy *you*" (Deut. 28:68, KJV). A slave whom no one will buy: such a person has no place between heaven and earth. He is a wandering ghost that has not yet died.

This new role for the law is realized in the structure of the Torah, and its dramatic situation. The five books of Moses place at their center three books that are principally law (Exodus, Leviticus, Numbers) and end with a book that recapitulates the law (Deuteronomy). At the heart is Leviticus, a book that at once remembers the temple and rejects narrative for holiness consecrated to the Lord. Laws are justified by the Lord and enslavement in Egypt: "Thou shalt love [the stranger] as thyself, for you were strangers in the land of Egypt: I am the Lord your God" (Lev. 19:34, KJV). The liberating narrative is retold in Deuteronomy.

On the way to the law, death is situated as the consequence of the first act of disobedience, in the beginning. Unique in representing death as humanity's own fault, the Jewish Bible never again refers to the story of Adam and Eve, their expulsion and death's arrival.[182] The prohibitions that matter come through Moses. Yet as prologue to the law, Eve and Adam perch as paradigm. They bring death and other evils—pain in childbirth, wifely subordination, clothing, and agricultural tillage—on themselves, and their descendants, through their own action. More ominously, but also comically, if the Lord utters a prohibition, it will be transgressed. On the side of obedience lie life and good, on the other death and evil, and God over all. Traditional Near Eastern thought had supplied an afterlife without explicit morality. Ancient Jewish thought, embracing explicit morality, the law, as all-encompassing, could let the afterlife go.

Only when history jeopardized the correlation between life and the law did afterlife as resurrection develop. "[B]lessings shall come upon you and overtake you, if you obey the LORD your God . . . Blessed shall be your basket and your kneading bowl. Blessed shall you be when you come in, and blessed shall you be when you go out" (Deut. 28:2–6). History broke the link between blessings and obedience and forged a new link with martyrdom. When obeying the law meant incurring death in the persecutions of Antiochus Epiphanes IV, the door opened to resurrection.

ACT 2: MY DEAD BODIES SHALL ARISE *(ISA. 26:19)*

Resurrection as necessary for Christianity's emergence; origins within Judaism; the problem of Mark

"Don't say afterlives make nothing happen. . . ."

When an afterlife emerges in Judaism, it arrives as a solution to the problem of martyrdom almost five hundred years after the ancestral ghosts were quieted. It takes two forms, only the first of which enters the Tanakh: a resurrected body, raised by God at the end time (Daniel c. 165 BCE), and an immortal soul, borrowed from the Greeks (Wisdom of Solomon c. 30 BCE–70 CE; Philo, c. 20 BCE–45 CE). The new afterlife promise responds not to innocent suffering like Job's, but to suffering chosen specifically on behalf of the good and God, for obeying the law. In violation of the fundamental promise of Deuteronomy, suffering is incurred not for covenant breaking, but for covenant keeping. God promised life to those who obeyed him; now obedience means being killed for God. Where then was the life he promised? Confirming that the concept has been added to an already complete interpretation of life, resurrection belongs not to the ordinary cycle of life and death and law, but to a unique transformative moment at the end of this world and instauration of another. As Abraham Neuman puts it, "[The idea of immortality] in Judaism arose not to appease man but to vindicate God."[183]

Without that development, Jesus could never have been raised from the dead. Or, if he had been, no other Jews would have believed it.

Resurrection to life begins as a single verse at the end of Daniel, a writing not included among "the law and the prophets," as Jesus refers to the scriptures, but fundamental to Jesus's expectations of the coming son of Man.[184] In Matthew, Mark, and Luke, Daniel's vision of "one like a son of man coming with the clouds of heaven" (7:13) appears often (Matt. 24:30, 26:64; Mark 13:26; 14:62; Luke 21:27). Ostensibly in Babylon during the exile (597/87–538 BCE), Daniel allegorizes Jewish suffering and resistance under the Hellenizing Seleucids in the period just before the Maccabees purified the temple in 164 BCE.

Moral tales of obedience and resistance find martyrdom thwarted by divine intervention. Daniel and his friends observe the dietary laws and worship only God. His three friends are tossed into a fiery furnace, he into the lions' den. They are saved and their persecutors destroyed, incinerated or ripped apart by lions. Those inspiring stories yield to mysterious visions that describe political struggles through 165 BCE with miraculous precision and then lose the thread, when prediction replaces coded history. Telling Daniel what will happen at the end time, one in human form predicts a happy ending for those who endure: "There shall be a time of anguish, such as has never occurred since nations first came into existence. But at that time your people shall be delivered, everyone who is found written in the book. *Many of those who sleep in the dust of the earth shall awake, some to everlasting life, and some to shame and everlasting contempt.* Those who are wise shall shine like the brightness of the sky, and those who lead many to righteousness, like the stars forever and ever" (Dan. 12:1–3, emphasis added). This awakening is not universal: "Many. . .who sleep," not all. The promise of life to the faithful now includes those who do not survive the lion's mouth.[185]

About forty years later, a Jewish historical account of the period, written in Greek, makes resurrection a current expectation (2 Maccabees, outside the Jewish canon, c. 124 BCE; Catholic and Orthodox canon, Protestant Apocrypha). Of seven brothers tortured by Antiochus, three and their mother insist martyrdom ensures their resurrection. The third brother introduces this new idea as well established (emphases added): "You accursed wretch, you dismiss us from this present life, but the King of the universe will *raise us up* to an everlasting renewal of life, *because we have died for his laws*" (2 Macc. 7:9). The fourth repeats his hope, adding his persecutors' exclusion from life: "One cannot but choose to die at the hands of mortals and to cherish the hope God gives of being *raised again* by him. But for you *there will be no resurrection to life!*" (2 Macc. 7:14). The fifth promises retribution in this life against the persecutors' children: "Keep on, and see how his mighty power will torture *you and your descendants*" (2 Macc. 7:17). No resurrection to torture has yet been imagined; it is God's promise of life that continues.

The sixth assures the tyrant the brothers are dying for their own sins, but the seventh, urged by his mother, also identifies the brothers as suffering for the nation, not unlike Isaiah's suffering servant. His mother gives to get back: she trusts the Creator "will in his mercy give life and breath back to you again, since you now forget yourselves *for the sake of his laws*"

(2 Macc. 7:23). She urges her seventh to "Accept death, so that in God's mercy *I may get you back again* along with your brothers" (2 Macc. 7:29, emphases added). Having "drunk of ever-flowing life under God's covenant" (2 Macc. 7:36), the brothers will "bring to an end the wrath of the Almighty that has justly fallen on our whole nation" (2 Macc. 7:39). Woven together are resurrection to life and breath for the law-keepers, reconciliation between an angered God and his people, and punishment for the wicked here and now and their progeny in the future. Daniel's resurrection to "shame and contempt" (not fire and pain), may point, Greenspoon suggests, to Hellenizing Jews who preferred new Greek practices to the fathers' law.[186] A century later, introducing the very different Greek concept of an immortal soul "in the hand of God," the Wisdom of Solomon (30 BCE–50/70 CE; canonicity like 2 Macc.) also connects the immortality of the righteous with their suffering at the hands of the wicked (1.14–5).

Stunningly, however, the older, traditional view has been not just abandoned, but turned actively evil. Absence of belief now belongs to the wicked, motivates malevolence, and engenders persecution. Wrenched into a twist worthy of Nietzsche and mingled with classical lyric motifs, Ecclesiastes' beautiful language of evanescence turns casually cruel. The turn has been italicized:

> For we were born by mere chance, and hereafter we shall be as though we had never been. . . . Our name will be forgotten in time, and no one will remember our works; our life will pass away like the traces of a cloud, and be scattered like mist. . . . Come, therefore, let us enjoy the good things that exist, and make use of the creation to the full as in youth. . . . Let us crown ourselves with rosebuds before they wither. Let none of us fail to share in our revelry; everywhere let us leave signs of enjoyment, *because this is our portion, and this our lot. Let us oppress the righteous poor man; let us not spare the widow* or regard the gray hairs of the aged. But *let our might be our law of right*, for what is weak proves itself to be useless. . . . (WS 2:1–11, emphasis added)

These first-century Leopolds and Loebs are motivated by the hatred and contempt the righteous express towards them, opposing their actions, reproaching them for sins against the law. Suggesting a civil war within Judaism, the young are pitted against the old, Hellenistic (and Ecclesiastes') imagery against morality, but in service of a concept that is not traditional.[187] What follows eerily anticipates Mark's passion sequence:

"Let us lie in wait for the righteous man . . . he avoids our ways as unclean; he calls the last end of the righteous happy, and boasts that God is his father . . . let us test what will happen at the end of his life; for if the righteous man is God's child, he will help him, and will deliver him from the hand of his adversaries. Let us test him with insult and torture, so that we may find out how gentle he is, and make trial of his forbearance. Let us condemn him to a shameful death, for, according to what he says, he will be protected" (WS 2:12–20).

Isaiah's suffering servant echoes here, along with the language cast at Jesus on the cross, the mockery and whipping at the trial. What is to be believed about the afterlife has become a locus of ideological struggle.

The final judgment imagined by WS pits the dead righteous against the living ungodly. The ungodly quake, finally understanding their error, and vanish like thistledown, a light frost, smoke, a guest who stays only a day (WS 4:16; 5:2–14; cf. 4:18–19). The righteous, whose "hope is full of immortality," receive a crown, a diadem, and reign forever in the shelter of the Lord's arm as he destroys his enemies (WS 3:4, 7–9; 5:15–23). Notably absent are the fiery pits and eternal tortures that play such a conspicuous part in New Testament promises. Those appear in 4 Maccabees and 2 Esdras 9:12, writings contemporaneous with the Gospels (c. 50–125 CE and after 70 CE, respectively). Outside of Egypt and India, the history of hell is just beginning.[188]

WS's debts to contemporary Greek thought are transparent. Still obscure—and contested—is how Israel developed its concept of resurrection, the event in which Christianity originates. The concept, a body raised from the grave, life and breath restored, at the end of time, nineteenth-century scholarship attributed to Persian Zoroastrianism, as do McDannell and Lang's *Heaven: A History* and Alan Segal's *Life After Death*.[189] More recent scholarship argues that the concept proceeds from a repurposing and reinterpreting, a metamorphosis, of the revival and restoration prophecies in the exilic prophets.[190] A later analogy might be the repurposing of Isaiah and the Psalms to produce a crucified Messiah in Jesus of Nazareth.[191]

Certainly, there was contact with Persian culture from the sixth century, attested in Cyrus's decree of 538 BCE, loan words, Esther's name (Astarte) and Persian setting (c. 4th cent. BCE). When Daniel was written (2nd cent. BCE), Zoroastrianism was, like Judaism, gathering up its old traditions against the Hellenizing pressure of Alexander's successors. The surviving Zoroastrian documents are, however, later than the biblical texts, so there is no evidence of resurrection in Persian thought that pre-dates its appearance in Jewish thought. (Nor does it appear in Plutarch [45–125 CE]'s account of Zoroastrianism in *On Isis and Osiris*.) Zoroastrian influence remains perfectly possible, even likely, but so far not demonstrable. Had Alexander the Great not burned the greater library at Persepolis, our information would be better.[192]

What is clear is that a resurrection first appears in the prophets Ezekiel and Deutero-Isaiah, allegorizing the revival of the whole Israelite community, lost in exile. It refers not to raising individuals at an end time but to reviving an entire community here and soon. Cognate with the miracles of the ninth-century prophets Elijah and Elisha (and Jesus in the NT, excepting his own), resurrection is to this life here, not an eternal life elsewhere. Elijah and Elisha resurrect newly dead children; Ezekiel performs on a field of very dry bones in a valley, fleshless relics of ancient battle.

"Can these bones live?" asks the Lord, and commands Ezekiel to prophesy to the bones. "[A] noise, a rattling, and the bones came together, bone to its bone," with sinews and flesh, but no breath. "Prophesy to the breath," and the bodies stand on their feet, living, "the whole house of Israel" (37:1–11). The two-stage process recapitulates Adam's creation from clay and breath. The Lord explicates his allegory: "I am going to open your graves, and bring you up from your graves, O my people; and I will bring you back to the land of Israel" (Ezek. 37:22). Nor is the prophecy complete until Israel and Judah reunite, the dispersed gather from among the nations, a Davidic king is installed, land and sanctuary restored, and the ordinances and statutes observed faithfully, forever (Ezek. 37:21–28). By the second century, in Dead Sea fragments from Daniel's time, Ezekiel had been reinterpreted as promising an individual resurrection.[193] Now, for everyone, at the Last Judgment, "rattling bones together fly/ From the four corners of the sky" (John Dryden, *To the Pious Memory of . . . Mrs. Anne Killigrew*, 1685).

Celebrating the end of exile after 538 BCE, Isaiah also sees a community revive.[194] Israel's enemies will die, says Isaiah, but Israel will live: "Thy dead men shall live, together with my dead body shall they arise. Awake and sing, ye that dwell in the dust: for thy dew is as the dew of herbs, and the earth shall cast out the dead" (KJV, Isa. 26:19; NRSV: "Your dead shall live, their corpses shall rise. O dwellers in the dust, awake and sing for joy! For your dew is a radiant dew, and the earth will give birth to those long dead," literally, "birth to the shades." Tanakh: "Oh, let Your dead revive!/ Let corpses [grammar of Heb. unclear] arise!/ Awake and shout for joy, / You who dwell in the dust!—For Your dew is like the dew on fresh growth;/ You make the land of the shades 'come to life' [meaning of Heb. uncertain]"). Her enemies, however, are done for: "They are dead, they shall not live; they are deceased, they shall not rise: therefore hast thou visited and destroyed them, and made all their memory to perish" (26:14; NRSV suggests the fate of the wicked is the usual lot: "The dead do not live; shades do not rise—because you have punished and destroyed them, and wiped out all memory of them"). Isaiah may be adapting cyclical Baalist imagery (as Day proposes), or anticipating Christian resurrection (as Greenspoon argues), but celebrated is miraculously restored communal life after suffering, in particular the suffering of an innocent servant (Isa. 49, 50:4–11, 52:13–15, 53). The New Testament alludes to these revival passages in the opened graves that give up their dead saints in Matthew (Matt. 27:52–53).

The resurrection of Jesus was read by his early followers not as the solitary salvific act of the son of God on behalf of individuals, but as the first act in the arrival of the kingdom of God, when he would return to restore the community. Jesus himself, if Mark has it right, after being baptized by John preached repentance, for "The time is fulfilled, and the kingdom of God is at hand" (Mark 1:15, KJV). These words had many meanings then, and they have even more now, but they indicate that Jesus expected God's kingdom soon, perhaps restoring the (Davidic) kingdom to Israel, perhaps drawing the gentile nations under his wing (in Paul's later interpretation and the story of the Syro-Phoenician woman). Whether the man named Joshua from Nazareth expected his own crucifixion to bring that kingdom, any more than John's beheading, is uncertain. That crucifixion, according to the Gospels written by the next generation of believers, disconcerted his first followers. Their belief was redirected or reconfirmed when he appeared alive to them, raised from the dead.

The New Testament narratives (Gospels and Acts) and Josephus make very clear that Jewish opinion around 30 CE, and certainly by 90 CE, when the Gospels were written, divided over eternal life. Resurrection distinguished skeptical Sadducees from believing Pharisees, Essenes, and followers of Judas the Galilaean.[195] Writing in Greek to a Greco-Roman audience, Josephus attributes belief in an immortal soul, followed by resurrection "in the revolution of the ages," to three of four Jewish philosophies. Only the Sadducees, a priestly minority party, believe soul dies with the body, a strict Torah reading they shared with the Samaritan priestly party.[196] Without counting Christians, the ratio suggests that resurrection had already carried the day, especially when Jews frequently named their children "Anastasia/us/os," risen/raised up.[197] Among the views Josephus attributes to the Pharisees are rewards and punishments "under the earth," as in Virgil's *Aeneid*, and eternal imprisonment for the wicked (no tortures described).[198] As in WS, the souls of righteous men are "allotted the most holy place in heaven, whence in the revolution of the ages, they return to find in chaste bodies a new habitation."[199] Return to a "new habitation" has been taken for metempsychosis, but the same verb is used for resurrection in 2 Macc. 7:9. Imagined is soul restored from heaven to body on the revived and reanimated earth sung by the prophets.

For the earliest Christian writer, resurrection was fundamental, well understood, and known to be contentious. At his arrest, according to Acts, Paul could appeal to Pharisees for support, claiming to be a Pharisee, a son of Pharisees, and "on trial concerning the hope of the resurrection of the dead" (Acts 23:6, c. 90 CE). His device worked: the gathered, accusing Jews began quarreling with each other. To his Corinthian congregation, happy to be Christ's for this life only, Paul struggled to explain that the dead must rise or the Corinthians' faith is vain: "If in this life only we have hope in Christ, we are of all men most miserable" (1 Cor. 15:19). For Paul, Jesus is the "first fruits of them that slept," of the dead. Paul expects Jesus's return in his own lifetime to restore the kingdom of God, to rouse the sleeping dead, and to transform earthly bodies into spiritual ones (Cor. 15; 1 Thess. 4:13–18). Jesus' form is "a life-giving spirit" (1 Cor. 15:45, "quickening," KJV), appearing to many: "[H]e appeared to Cephas, then to the twelve. Then he appeared to more than five hundred brothers and sisters at one time, most of whom are still alive, though some have died [lit. fallen asleep]. Then he appeared to James, then to all the apostles. Last of all, as to one untimely born, he appeared also to me" (1 Cor. 15:5–8). Though Paul never met Jesus in this world, experiencing the risen Jesus has taught him what to expect, however undefined life in that future world remains, beyond judging the angels and rejoicing with the prophets.

The Gospels' view of resurrection is similarly disembodied twenty to fifty years later (c. 70–100 CE). Jesus opposes, McDannell and Lang suggest, a current embodied view of resurrection as Israel restored on earth to its vine and fig trees, deriving from prophetic visions of return from exile.[200] In the Synoptic Gospels (Matthew, Mark, Luke), the Sadducees quiz Jesus about a widow's seven husbands: to which will she married "in the resurrection"? (Luke 20:27–40; Matt. 22:23–33; Mark 12:18–27). The raised, alas, neither marry nor are given in marriage. To be raised from the dead is to be alive right now, in the present, as a continuous spirit: "And as for the dead being raised, have you not read in the book of Moses, in the story about the bush, how God said to him, 'I am the God of Abraham, the God of Isaac, and the God of Jacob'? He is God not of the dead, but of the living" (Mark 12:26–27). Abraham and Isaac are in some way now alive, to God but not to us, their state unspecified.

In Luke Jesus adds that resurrection is not for everyone, and he does not seem to imagine resurrection to damnation: "they which shall be accounted worthy to obtain that world, and the resurrection from the dead, neither marry nor are given in marriage. Neither can they die any more: for they are equal unto the angels; and are the children of God being the children of the resurrection" (Luke 20:35–36 KJV). As to the resurrected Jesus, he is and is not fully embodied: he eats (Luke 24:41–43) and his wounds can be fingered (John 20:27; Luke 24:40). In neither case is anyone said actually to touch the wounds offered. He also passes through walls (John 20:19, 26), disappears instantaneously (Luke 24:31), and cannot be recognized by his most devoted followers, Mary Magdalene (John 20:14–15) or the disciples en route to Emmaus (Luke 24:13–35).

The Gospel of John makes "eternal life" its dominant theme and permits no one to question it. The inquisitive, mocking Sadducees vanish. Meticulous on how to obtain eternal life—believe in Jesus, drink his blood, eat his body—it describes that state not at all, anticipating whatever illumination is needed in Jesus's imminent return. A verbal construct, eternal life is an unconsidered, unanalyzed desire embedded within a preaching practice. The beloved disciple unique to John who was expected still to be alive when Jesus returned, has recently died—and the Gospel carefully explains that Jesus did not say that disciple would not die, but only "if I will that he tarry until I come," a distinction some may find without much difference (John 21:23). In Matthew, the graves open at Jesus's resurrection, Isaiah's earth ejecting its dead. In Revelation, the martyred dead in heaven, under the throne, await the end of this world and the instauration of a new. "He which testifieth these things saith, Surely I come quickly. Amen. Even so, come, Lord Jesus" (Rev. 22:20, KJV).

Within the NT, the concept of resurrection is fluid: what is resurrected, what the state is like, when it will be. Nowhere is that fluidity more striking than in the contrast between the miracles of resurrection Jesus performs, modeled on Elijah and Elisha, and the meaning of his own resurrection, augury of the end. Jesus's revivals of Lazarus, Jairus's daughter, and others anticipate his resurrection, yet those individuals are returned to life on this earth, not to a renovated world. While modern theologians insist on the difference between "resuscitation" and "resurrection," the Gospels' Greek makes no such distinction. It uses the same word for Jesus's rising as for his raisings.[201] That failure to distinguish makes perfect sense if those Jesus has restored to life are Christ's at his coming (1 Cor. 15:23), whether they are dead or alive (1 Thess. 4:16–17), and if his coming is imminent.

On a preexisting belief in resurrection, Christianity depends—or once depended. Thus it has long troubled scholars that the earliest of the Gospels, Mark, not only recounts no post-resurrection appearances by Jesus, but also fails to attest anyone's belief in the resurrection. The resurrection is announced to some women, who say nothing to anyone. Written c. 70 CE, plundered as a source by Luke and Matthew (80–90 CE; the holy ghost as plagiaries), the earliest manuscripts of Mark end when three women find Jesus's tomb empty on the third day and flee terrified from a young man clothed in white. He tells them, "Be not affrighted: Ye seek Jesus of Nazareth, which was crucified: he is risen; he is not here: behold the place where they laid him. But go your way, tell his disciples and Peter that he goeth before you into Galilee: there shall ye see him, as he said unto you" (Mark 16:6–7). The women go out, fast enough, amazed and trembling, but they tell no one, "for they were afraid" (Mark 16:8). And there Mark stops.

That ending has puzzled interpreters for centuries, including dissatisfied early Christians who pasted on resurrection appearances filched from other gospels (16:9–20).[202] Mark, however, knew exactly what he has doing. What he did not realize was that by simultaneously and accidentally creating the literary genre "gospel" (literally, "good news") as a biography of Jesus, he would obscure his intention. Mark's narrative opens, "The beginning of the gospel of Jesus Christ, the Son of God" (1:1). Mark's own text is not "the gospel," but its "beginning": an account of what led up to the gospel, the good news, that is, the resurrection. For Mark, as for Paul, beheaded before any "gospels" were written, the good news/gospel is that "he is risen" and "ye shall see him." Mark's favored literary device has long been recognized as the intercalated episode, in which one episode is set inside another: the death of John the Baptist inside the sending out of the disciples, the woman with the issue inside the raising of Jairus's daughter, and many others. Mark's narrative is itself an intercalated episode within the gospel of Resurrection.

Luke, Matthew, and John understood. None begins his book by referring to the "gospel." Instead, they add new openings to Mark (birth stories in Matthew and Luke, a hymn to the Word in John) and resurrection appearances at the end. Mark stops when the "beginning" ends and the gospel arrives.

In time, the expectation of Jesus's imminent return dies away (2 Peter, c. 150 CE), to revive where it began, at the margins, in every generation. What remains in place of the restored kingdom is the relationship with Jesus established through the gospels and the tradition they preserved. Supplements to an existing faith, written within it, the gospels and epistles constitute an ideology for living in end times that do not end. They are always with us, criticizing the ordinary ways we live now. The Corinthians knew what they were about when they were contented with Jesus's message for this life only—it was enough, all they really needed.

When Paul's living spirit fuses with the immortal Greek "soul" of which WS spoke so confidently, there will be generated a new concept, the resurrection "of the body." The scriptures lack the phrase, for Jesus's resurrection is of the dead, whole persons. Soul and body become independent entities in scholastic thought.[203] Once body and soul separate, soul requires disposal. In the Catholic tradition, soul lives with God (or burns in purgatory or hell) while the body sleeps, awaiting resurrection and reunion with soul at the Last Judgment. Protestants, annihilating purgatory, were forced to decide whether the soul slept unconscious until the resurrection to Judgment at the last day, as scripture suggested, or was judged twice, once at death and again at the Last Judgment in the body. Calvin solved the problem of double judgments with God's foreknowledge.

All this travels far from the Wisdom of Solomon, but shared is the immortality that brings one to God and confidence in justice: "The beginning of wisdom is the most sincere desire for instruction, and concern for instruction is love of her, and love of her is the keeping of her laws, and giving heed to her laws is assurance of immortality, and immortality brings one near to God" (WS 6.17-19). The move to immortality is very easy to make—only one term needs to be inserted between the laws that always brought one near to God and God. "Immortality" often meant merely long life, one not ended prematurely.[204] Long life was always God's gift, and now it lasts longer. Seemingly inevitable, the move astonishes only in that it was not there from the beginning. But it is also clear that the move remains unnecessary.

Whether or not justice is administered to individuals in a next life, what matters is that God is there, standing behind justice and standing for justice. Should God depart, no one need notice. The community still stands if God is constructed, as Deuteronomy and Jeremiah tell us he should be, from within, from the circumcised heart. Immortality is perhaps a useless distraction, intervening between the laws of life and the God who gave both.

GREEKS BEARING GIFTS ONTO ROMAN ROADS

Dismal afterlife origins in Homer and Hesiod, improved without moralizing in the mysteries, popularly moralized in Aristophanes, philosophically in Plato, and contested in a stew of possibilities and purposes, Aristotle, Epicurus, Stoics; then the Romans: Lucretius, Cicero, Virgil: clearance, roundabout, and highway.

The Greeks did nothing so original as the Jews, save in one respect. Israel knew the fool who said in his heart, "there is no God." Greece knew a philosopher who said to anyone who cared to listen, "there is no afterlife." Epicurus's is a late fourth-century contesting of common opinion (Epicurus, 341–270 BCE), powerfully restated under the Roman republic by Lucretius (c. 96-55 BCE) in *De Rerum Natura*. Jews had found a new truth. Transforming the structure of their traditional afterlife, they left *sheol* and *mot* unimproved behind, and leaped up to God, claiming a new life on or above the earth, propelled by prophetic imagery of rebirth. Among the Greeks, only Hercules joined the gods in such an ascent.

The Greeks made their improvements underground, retaining the original grim structure, but brightening it in the mysteries. Pre-Socratic philosophers turned death over, mulling possibilities. Socrates took no interest in death; Plato did. Plato multiplied afterlives, inspiring, useful, and moral, if implausible to such natural philosophers as Aristotle and Epicurus. Greece and Rome make visible a tradition of self-conscious afterlife improvement that leaves belief behind, except for the materialist afterlife deniers. The afterlife was then what it wants to become in our own time: the crown of a coherent understanding of life's meanings and purposes within a public space.

By the sixth century BCE, the mysteries had redeemed the initiated from the dismal *sheol*-like murk in Homer and Hesiod (eighth century BCE) to a blissful afterlife, while everyone else endured the expected miry darkness. The mysteries required only initiation into a new group identity, no moralizing, reciting of virtues, or rejecting of vices. Justice for the pre-Socratic philosophers and Socrates remains an affair of this life. Popular culture wanted more. Aristophanes (450–388 BCE) shows wrongdoers punished in the other world for violating moral rules in this. Exploiting that fluid popular space, Plato (428–348 BCE) rejected Homer's afterlife and probably Socrates's. Entertaining multiple possible afterlives in a half dozen dialogues, he seals his *Republic* with a well policed and psychologically astute afterlife. Aristotle rejected Homer and Plato on the afterlife, but made no issue of it. Describing the process of death, he considered what a "soul" might be, as if facts spoke for themselves. So many afterlives facilitated, in the name of truth and science, Epicurus's and Lucretius's disputing all afterlife threats and blandishments. Virgil, stifling his early Lucretian sympathies, challenges Plato (as well as Homer) with a syncretic afterlife epitomizing his own literary and politico-ideological ambitions. How they handle metempsychosis is the clue to their differences. In this trajectory, the afterlife turns from grim inevitability, imagined through the body, into popular consolation, improving literature, tool of ideology, and, for Lucretius, derided police-procedural fiction. As in our own time, what comes after does not erase what came before, but coexists with it, casting doubts on certainties, and creating certainty to combat doubts' multitudes.

Homer and Hesiod provide the earliest Greek accounts of the afterlife, even as they jockey for position as Greece's earliest author.[205] No more satisfying than Israel's *sheol* or Gilgamesh's netherworld, their eighth-century accounts are roughly contemporaneous with Amos, Isaiah, and the Standard Version of *Gilgamesh*. Greeks practiced both burial (*Antigone*, *The Libation Bearers*) and burning (*Iliad*, *Odyssey*), alien to the bodily based immortality of Egypt and Sumer. They made offerings to their dead and celebrated their return at the festival of the Anthesteria.[206] In Hesiod's genealogy of the gods, Death is the fatherless child of Night, the pitiless, iron god hateful even to the immortals, deathless gods, *a-thanatoi* (*Theogony*, ll. 212, 758–66, 807–10).[207] Several hundred years later, Aristotle approvingly quotes Sappho: even the gods hate death, she explains, because they did not choose it for themselves. Between them, Hesiod and Homer assemble the architecture of the classical afterlife that philosophers challenge.

In Hesiod's *Theogony* only defeated divinities, not dead humans, appear. Tartarus, the source and limits of earth, sea, and skies, lies a nine days' fall from earth, among the dank, distressful things "which even the gods hate" (*Theogony*, ll. 720, 807–10). Cerberus the fifty-headed dog guards the marble gates, fawns on arrivals and devours those who try to escape (*Theo.* 311, 767–74). Hades and Persephone rule (*Theo.* 767–74, 912) beneath the earth (*Theo.* 455), with Styx (*Theo.* 775), duplicating the original "Chasm" or chaotic void, terrible and dark (*Theo.* 736f.). Punishing semi-divine beings, Zeus hurled Menoetius into Erebus, for his defiance (*Theo.* 515), and attached Prometheus to a pillar, an eagle feasting on his ever-growing liver, until Hercules released him (*Theo.* 520–34). The Titans plunged down after their epic battle with Zeus (*Theo.* 729), and Medusa, the mortal Gorgon, is the first to die and descend.

Geographically distinct, lying to the sunny west, are the blessed isles, reminiscent of the immortal Ūta-napišti's dwelling across the waters from the garden of the gods. Of the demigods or heroes who fought at Thebes or Troy, death took some, but others Zeus sent to "the Islands of the Blessed beside deep-eddying Ocean—happy heroes, for whom the grain-giving field bears honey-sweet fruit flourishing three times a year" (Hesiod, *Works and Days*, 166–73).

As to justice, for men there is none to be found among the shades. The justice Hesiod expects happens in this world. Sometimes Zeus's justice, like YHWH's, destroys a whole city, through famine or pestilence, war, shipwreck or infertility (*WD*, 238–47). Everywhere, immortal guardians watch, advise, judge (*WD*, 248–73). To the just they give wealth (*WD*, 280); to evildoers, loss (*WD*, 320–34). Giving is good, but grabbing gives death (*WD*, 356). Hesiod's iron age inverts justice. Men will not honor their parents for their rearing, and violence triumphs: "Their hands will be their justice, and one man will destroy the other's city" (*WD*, 187–89). Justice is an affair between living men, and funerals are unlucky.

Hesiod's details supplement the vaguer, internally contradictory geography of Homer's afterlife. The *Iliad* does not agree with the *Odyssey*, nor the *Odyssey* with itself. The *Odyssey* cobbles four inconsistent sources, Hesiod's pleasant western island, now excluding heroes and restricted to relatives of gods (Book 4), a cold, gloomy land to the far north for equal, mindless, insubstantial shades (Book 11), a setting for hideous tortures of men who offended the gods (Book 11), a place where Hermes leads twittering, bat-like shades who tell their stories on arrival to those already there, greeting and greeted (Book 24). Only the last returns in Plato.

The *Iliad* sends many heroes to "*Pluto's* gloomy reign" (I,3), where "Infernal *Pluto* sways the Shades below" (XV,213).[208] As in Hesiod, but not the *Odyssey*, Tartarus lies "Low in the dark . . . With burning Chains fix'd to the Brazen Floors,/And lock'd by Hell's inexorable Doors;/As deep beneath th'Infernal Centre hurl'd,/As from the Center to th'Æthereal World" (VIII, 16–20; Virgil recycles that geographical detail, *Aeneid* VI, 577–79). An almost bottomless pit, the living plunge towards it, but no mortal inhabitant is seen inside it. Zeus threatens only other gods with sun-less, wind-less confinement there.

The *Odyssey's* land of the dead is not under the earth, but at the world's end. So the Sumerians located their afterlife sometimes underground, sometimes in the mountains. Across the waters, it is far to the north, dark, bleak, and cold, but located where Odysseus, like Gilgamesh before him, by skillful sailing can reach it. The blessed western islands, snow free, with balmy breezes, ruled by Rhadamanthus, Homer allows only to Menelaos, not as a hero but as a son-in-law of Zeus (*Odyssey*, 4). Menelaos teases classical scholars, since, like Hesiod's heroes (and Ūta-napišti), he seems to be promised an escape from death, but he is not referred to again. Everyone else, including Odysseus, goes to Erebus, darkness (Book 11).

No one rots or crawls with vermin among Odysseus's shades. Burning prevents that, but unlike Enkidu and Gilgamesh, Odysseus cannot embrace his mother, his origin, when he finds her unexpectedly among the dead. Anticleia explains: once human bodies burn to ash, they become substance-less, life-longing, blood-desiring shades. Only blood, the life, enables them to communicate with the living.

By contrast, Book 24 supposes talkative shades recognizing each other and telling their stories on arrival among the dead. Contradicting the conditions of Book 11, that supposition lets Homer re-tell Penelope's shroud trick and the suitors' slaughter as a shorter set piece, for an abbreviated evening's entertainment. The condition of the dead bends to the artist's desire to interpolate an (extractable) episode. As to justice, the virtuous mingle with the vicious. Achilles and Ajax are no better off than Eriphyle, who betrayed her husband, and Iocaste, who bedded her son and hanged herself. The great heroes seem more miserable in the dark than the wicked women, boasting their identities to Odysseus. Odysseus assures Achilles he must be a king among the dead, Ur-Namma's and Gilgamesh's fate and the one Pharaoh hoped to avoid. Achilles treats Odysseus's assurance with contempt. He would abandon himself to see the sunlight in a line Plato strikes from the poem: "I would rather be slave to a hired man than reign as king of the dead" (11). Dead men thrill at news of their sons; dead women boast of their sons, but no one expects to see them or be nurtured by them, not even Agamemnon, thirsting for revenge, not libations.

Justice appears only as a panorama suddenly materializing in front of Odysseus, punishments for crimes against the gods, not men, contradicting the geography already established.. Odysseus has been standing on the seashore before a trench filled with the blood of a sacrifice, the dead slurping the blood to speak. Now abruptly and inexplicably, judgment and tortures unfold before his eyes. That awkwardly joined set piece elaborates Hesiod's tortures and introduces piety to Homer's otherwise morality-free zone. At a distance Minos is seen judging, a king among the dead, like Gilgamesh and Ur-Namma. Whom or what he judges is not revealed. Odysseus sees Hesiod's Prometheus covered by vultures, not released by Hercules; Ixion is on his wheel; Sisyphus toils up his hill. Except for Tityos's rape of Zeus's mistress, the tortures are unexplained. In the traditional tales that Homer does not repeat, these malefactors committed offences against the gods, not against their fellow men. Under the earth, the gods see to justice only for themselves, as in a few Sumerian fragments (p. 55 above).

Human justice is still done only in the world. So Agamemnon enquires after his son Orestes, for justice on his murdering wife and her lover. Their punishment will be only death, like Agamemnon's. (Surely no husband ever deserved murder more than Agamemnon? May his rage continue forever, its own helpless punishment.) So, too, the suitors, the youth of Ithaca, will die, slaughtered with a mighty bow like that of Hercules, stained with blood, Odysseus's last interview. Fleeing the whispering dead, Odysseus fears that the netherworld will seize him (as Enkidu was seized)—that Persephone will send up the gorgon's head to fix him, forever.[209] No translation catches the sense of release better than Pope's, or perhaps Broome's, where the ominous shrouds let us go and the reader leans into the wind:

> Swift o'er the waves we fly; the fresh'ning gales
> Sing thro' the shrouds, and stretch the swelling sails.
>
> (Pope, XI, 793–94)

The Greeks began brightening their gloomy dead through the mysteries and philosophic schemes just as Judea was breaking off communication with her dead. A sixth-century Hymn to Demeter, mother of Persephone, is the first textual evidence for the mysteries' improvements: "Blessed is he of men on earth who has beheld them, whereas he that is uninitiated in the rites, or he that has had no part in them, never *enjoys a similar lot* down in the musty dark when he is dead" (emphasis added).[210] The pre-Socratic philosophers considered death as part of natural processes. Anaximander (c. 610–c. 547 BCE) had proposed that "Things of necessity are resolved at death into the same elements out of which they had their birth; for they do justice and make recompense to one another according to the ordinances of time" (Guthrie, 222–23). For Herakleitos (c. 540–480 BCE), death is momentary stasis within constant change, "the way up and down" (fr. 69, Guthrie 252) that is life: "Fire lives the death of air, and air lives the death of fire; water lives the death of earth, earth that of water" (fr. 25, Guthrie, 252). "All things we see when awake are death" (fr. 64, Guthrie 226), and most obscurely of all: "Immortal mortals, mortal immortals, living the death of the one, dying the life of the other" (fr. 67,

Guthrie, 228), "The living and the dead are the same" (fr. 78, Guthrie, 229). Whatever death is, it cannot be left alone but enters every process and transformation. More immediately comprehensible, but no more descriptive: "when men die there awaits them what they do not expect or think" (Guthrie, 229).[211]

Aeschylus (525–456 BCE) and Pindar (c. 522–c.438 BCE) split the Homeric difference between darkness and light in the fifth century. In *The Libation Bearers/Choephoroe*, Orestes and Electra pour libations to Agamemnon, calling up his spirit's anger. Like Homer's Agamemnon and Ajax, his fury still works under the ground, at his burial place. In *Persians* desperate mages arouse Darius from Hades only to hear their doom. Pindar, by contrast, embroiders Hesiod's and Homer's happier state in the Second Olympian Ode (476 BCE). Justice is done under the earth, lawless spirits are punished, souls transmigrate through states of being, and those tested three times waft off to the Islands of the Blessed, where Peleus, Cadmus, and at last Achilles are to be found, released from Homer's dark.[212]

Sophocles (496–406 BCE) and Euripides (484–406 BCE) supply no consoling images of a life beyond death. Oedipus is content to feel the sun's rays for the last time, as he moves into the invisible other world of tombless darkness (*Oedipus at Colonnus*). Antigone expects her father, mother, and brother to welcome her to Persephone's mansions, but beyond recognition there is no gladness in the dark, even for one performing the burial obligation (*Antigone*). A fragment from *Triptolemus* endorses the mysteries, but the uninitiated share Oedipus's and Antigone's fates: "Thrice blessed are those mortals who have seen these rites and thus enter into Hades: for them alone there is life, for the others all is misery." Sophocles helped introduce the cult of Asclepius, god of healing, to Athens in 420 BCE, suggesting more interest in this life than the next. [213]

That surviving tragedies neglect the mysteries' consolations marks the mysteries' limits. Euripides wonders, "Who knows if life be death, and death be thought life in the other world?" (Guthrie, 237). Echoing Herakleitos, the question supposes a way of thinking death quite remote from Homer. Death has become a concept to turn over, to play with, not to accept as a given. By this time, the afterlife has acquired a history, sign of an important topic without immediate urgency. Herodotus (484–430/20 BCE) charges his countrymen with intellectual theft for claiming as their own Egyptian ideas of a transmigrating and immortal soul (Burkert and others credit India, not Egypt). But he declines to finger the plagiarists: "I know their names but do not write them."[214]

Greek unwillingness to be left in the dark emerges most clearly in the works of Aristophanes (445–385/75 BCE) and Plato (428–348 BCE). Treating what is evidently now the traditional mythology no more solemnly than Lucian in 125 CE or Offenbach in 1870, Aristophanes mocks mystery initiations (*The Clouds*) and revisits the realm of Persephone and Hades, after Hercules, to adjudicate the claims to literary excellence of Aeschylus, Sophocles, and Euripides (*The Frogs*, 405 BCE). He unveils a terrain stocked with clichés, Charon and Cerberus, Echidna and Gorgon, where popular culture has at last imposed human justice on Homer's afterlife. Visibly for the first time, wrongdoers are punished for traditionally serious crimes against humankind (betrayal of guests, abuse of parents), but also for bad taste and cheating a prostitute. Mystery initiates rejoice in a happy region, without claiming any particular merits or superior virtue. Buried in filth, in streams of dung, are

> Whoso has wronged the stranger here on earth,
> Or robbed his boylove of the promised pay,
> Or swinged his mother, or profanely smitten
> His father's cheek, or sworn an oath forsworn,
> Or copied out a speech of Morsimus.

Meanwhile, beyond the mire, are flute music, brilliant light, myrtle groves, and blissful throngs of men and women clapping their hands for joy, "[t]he happy mystic bands."[215] When Dionysus leaves Euripides behind and takes Aeschylus, he cites Euripides on death as representative nonsense: "Who knows if death be life, and life be death,/And breath be mutton broth, and sleep a sheepskin?" (433). Comedy makes visible the repairs popular culture had made to the traditional darkness of Homer and Hesiod, still glooming the tragic poets. Brought to light, the mysteries promise bliss in imagery Virgil adopts. Second-century Roman emperors Hadrian and Marcus Aurelius had themselves initiated.

Among the philosophers, the soul and its migrations after death became a lively topic, a homunculus miniaturizing entire philosophic projects. For the natural philosophers, Democritus, Aristotle, Epicurus, and some sophists, the gods retreated, the soul dispersed, and the afterlife vanished. To Plato, as to Aristophanes (attacking sophists in *The Clouds*) and the Stoics, such accounts were intolerable. In Plato, the afterlife evolves from the *Apology*, which may approach what Socrates actually thought, through multiple rational defenses of the soul's immortality in *Gorgias, Phaedo, Phaedrus*, to the *Republic*. There Plato chooses to end his account of justice in this world by imagining a visit to the next in "The Myth of Er."

Facing death in the *Apology*, Socrates recognizes annihilation as a possibility, but argues for the immortality of the soul and the safety of the good soul. Fantasying a chatty, discursive reunion underground with the great spirits of antiquity, he improves Homer along the lines of *Odyssey*, Book 24. Thereafter, Plato persistently invents. *Gorgias* expects judgment and requires that souls be naked, lest justice be perverted; *Phaedo* imagines the soul released from the prison of the body, and *Phaedrus* borrows terms from the mysteries.[216] Reincarnation, an "ancient doctrine," carries no moral weight, but proves immortality; souls reborn from other souls in Hades must continue to exist. Souls heavy with corporeal stain will be reborn as appropriate animals.[217] In *Phaedrus* the soul is immortal because self-moving. Originally winged, fallen from heaven, it cycles for ten thousand years before returning to heaven and regaining its wings.[218] Of his hypotheses, Plato observes, it is "not fitting to say something like this is true, but fit to say something ought to be like it" (*Phaedo*, 114de). In *The Republic* he does it all: concocts a cosmology, administers justice, teaches how to choose like a philosopher, and satirizes the choices people actually make, exposing their hopelessly habit-driven, non-philosophical selves. Plato's object is not truth, but to form philosophers, and he prepares his ground in the *Republic* by attacking the popular imagery purveyed by the poets.

Plato disliked Homer's representation of a dreary, gloomy afterlife where virtuous, just souls squeaked in the gloom among nefarious malefactors and booby heroes. He objects not to the truth or falsity of doctrine, but its utility. Free men must not fear death, and the better such passages are as poetry, the worse they are as example. The poets must submit:

> The poets must be told to speak well of that other world. The gloomy descriptions they now give must be forbidden, not only as untrue, but as injurious to our future warriors. We shall strike out all lines like these:

> I would rather be on earth as the hired servant of another, in the house of a landless man with little to live on, than be king over all the dead; [Achilles, *Odyssey* xi]
>
> Or these:
>
> Alack, there is, then, even in the house of Death a spirit or a shade; but the wits dwell in it no more. [Achilles, *Iliad*, xxiii]
>
> We shall ask Homer and the poets in general not to mind if we cross out all passages of this sort. If most people enjoy them as good poetry, that is all the more reason for keeping them from children or grown men who are to be free. . . .[219]

Shuddery references to "loathsome Styx" and "infernal spirits" must also vanish.

Plato practiced what the *Republic* preaches: he always spoke well of "that other world." Aestheticized, that world projects a glorious vision of the harmony of the cosmos. Totalized, it comprehends all beings from birth to death and around again within a self-sustaining system with no way out, not even for the popular festival of the returning dead at the Anthesteria. Although his afterlife offers justice, rewards for the good, punishments for the evil, retribution is not Plato's principal objective, but right thinking and right choices.

The Myth of Er is not a necessary ending to the *Republic*. Socrates has just persuaded his interlocutor that this world punishes the wicked and makes prosperous the good, a view as traditional as Hesiod or Deuteronomy or the Buddha (or philosophical optimism or evolutionary psychology). Justice has been affirmed as the order of things. The Myth of Er rivets that affirmation. External judgments impose rewards and punishments, while people's own judgments determine their future lives, beyond reward and punishment.

Er's is a "mythos," a deliberately fictive account of a vision of the next world that reveals what ought to be true. Er dies, but his body does not change. For ten days, his people wait. Then placed on the funeral pyre, he revives from his near-death experience to tell what he saw in the land of the dead. The genre is still popular. Er's report could not be further from the dank and drear Hades of Hesiod or Homer or the busy Charon and barking Cerberus of Aristophanes. Only the mysteries leave traces.

Rapt by the radiant beauty of the cosmos, Er sees the spindle on which the universe turns and hears the music of the spheres. Moving up, not down, he finds himself in a meadow where souls are gathering, returned from their thousand-year journey above—in the beauties of a paradise, their good actions and justice rewarded—or their thousand-year journey below, where they expiated their evil deeds ten times over, in physical tortures. While Er had much to say "concerning infants who die at birth or live but a short time," Socrates found them "not worthy of mention."[220] (Other Greeks paid dead infants attention: at the Anthesteria, little wine jugs, painted with scenes of food offerings, were placed in their graves, along with toys and playthings, "to make up for what [they] had missed."[221])

Some evils too heinous for atonement incur eternal punishment. A tyrant, scourged with thorns a thousand years, approaches the light only to be pulled back down into the darkness, disappearing forever. Murder is added to the usual crimes of dishonoring gods or parents. Judges dispatch souls up to paradise or down to torture, but the traditional judges Minos, Aeacus, and Rhadamanthus named in *Gorgias* (523e), are not named here. Plato demythologizes. Judgment is only a stage in what interests him more—thinking philosophically.

After their thousand years of bliss or woe, souls choose another life. In *Phaedrus* and *Phaedo*, metempsychosis, the soul's change of place, is part of matter's endless, mindless transmutations. In *Phaedrus* the wingless soul grasps anything solid. In Ovid's demoralized account of Pythagoras, the soul recycles itself, like all other things, unconsciously:

> Thus all things are but alter'd, nothing dies;
> And here and there th' unbodied spirit flies,
> By time, or force, or sickness dispossess'd,
> And lodges where it lights, in man or beast;
> Or hunts without, till ready limbs it find,
> And actuates those according to their kind;
> From tenement to tenement is toss'd;
> The soul is still the same, the figure only lost.
>
> (Dryden, ll. 239–46)[222]

Moralized, metempsychosis assigns the soul a new place based on the cumulative character of earlier actions. Earlier Socrates explains that the good enjoy all blessings "save perhaps for some suffering entailed by offences in a former life."[223] In the seductive new Platonic twist, what one becomes is one's own choice, a rational, philosophic, self-expressive, and conscious move.

Scattered before the souls are the "lives of all living creatures, [and] all conditions of men," taken from the lap of Lachesis, daughter of necessity, mingling beauty, riches, power, sickness, poverty, good, and evil. Socrates advises the wise to calculate what the choice will do to the soul: "calling a life worse or better according as it leads to the soul becoming more unjust or more just. All else he will leave out of account" (Cornford, 356). Responsibility removes from heaven to the self: whatever happens in one's next life, one chose it. "Heaven is blameless" (Cornford, 355).

Having explained how we should choose, Plato shows what we do choose. Er's story concludes with the sad or comical choices people actually make. An anonymous good man, having snatched despotism, howls as he realizes what evils he will bring on himself and others. Choices reflect frustrated desires and old habits. Atalanta, seeing the prizes to be won, becomes a male athlete, recognized at last, caught by other apples. The artisan who made the Trojan horse turns craftswoman, eager to explore crafts forbidden him as a man. Orpheus becomes a swan from pure misogyny; hating women, he will not be born of one. The singing creatures become human. Ajax becomes a lion, Agamemnon an eagle, apt emblems for heroes, ominous for men.

Choices across the species barrier surely liberate. Another consciousness, another mode of being surprises and delights: to be a fly, a snake, a butterfly, to see through a thousand eyes, to glide, to flutter. And to forget Socrates' lesson: a beast is no longer a man, possessed of reason, responsible to harmony, capable of justice. Ajax and Agamemnon are heroically brawny and brainless. Thersites did better turning ape. Crafty Odysseus chooses a humble private life, neither inspiring nor brutish, but with access to virtue. Plato has imagined an afterlife that has nothing to do with death. The condition of his Er is emblematic. Er was not dead, but alive, and the message he brings back from the dead is for the living soul.

Other philosophical schools were equally impatient of Aristophanes' mythology and Plato's. For Aristotle the soul is the form of the body; empirically it requires heat. In death, bodies cool down and lose their form. Theoretically either all souls, animal and human, survive, or none do. If all dogs go to heaven, so does everything else. If they don't, no one does. For Stoics and Epicureans, the body resolves to its material components, for Epicureans atoms, for Stoics fire. Epicurean atoms separate, recombine; the soul disperses; self and personality end.

For Stoics, an immortal spark within human beings returns to the primordial Mind-Fire that ultimately constitutes all things. For some, souls live on in the upper air until the final conflagration destroys the world and begins it anew. This earliest view Cleanthes taught, and Marcus Aurelius may have held. For the Stoic Chrysippus, only just souls preserve their identities; the bad are reabsorbed at once. Others held that all souls are at once reabsorbed, and still others that there is a period of purgation, as Virgil suggests, before the soul rejoins the primordial fire.[224] Meditating on death, Marcus Aurelius moves from Epicurean dispersion to Stoic transmutation, briefly regrets the absence of rebirth for the most virtuous souls, but acquiesces in Nature's ceaseless renewal and the uncertainty of what comes after death, insensibility or another life.[225] No such hesitation marks the Epicureans. The soul is as mortal as the body, they have no doubt, and they will prove it to you. Nowhere did the contest among these differing views engage itself more fiercely than in Rome. They had intellectual gladiators there. Romans, staging a battle to the death over how to live, fought it out in the afterlife.

ROMAN ROADS: LUCRETIUS'S CLEARANCE, CICERO'S ROUNDABOUT, AND VIRGIL'S HIGHWAY

In Rome, the conflict played out between philosopher-poets Lucretius (c. 96–55 BCE) and Virgil (c. 70–19 BCE). Cicero (c. 106–43 BCE) mediated with prejudice. Rome had a dazzling variety of hopes and customs relating to the dead, reaching out to other cultures to import Isis or Osiris or to secure initiation into the Eleusinian mysteries. The neighboring Etruscans celebrated a banquet of the dead atop their cineraria. Roman funerary practice often supposed a shadow life in and near the tomb, where survivors came to share meals at Parentalia, the main festival for the dead ancestors, 13–21 February. In May at Lemuria graves were again visited for a meal for kinless hungry ghosts, and at Rosalia, flowers were laid.[226] Some expected to mingle with the earth as flowers; others anticipated reunions with husbands, children, friends.[227] Ovid observed in the *Fasti* 2.547–56 that spirits turn nasty if neglected.[228] Some Romans were not in their tombs at all (NF NS NC, non fui non sum non curo), but others insisted on continuing to drink, and pipes sent down libations. From Narbonne in southern Gaul, Lucius Runnius Pollo still claims, "I drink continuously all the more eagerly in this monument of mine because I must sleep and remain here forever."[229] The logic of simultaneous sleeping and drinking need not be pressed, but Lucretius sneers at those for whom death is endless thirst.

Amidst all these possibilities, Cicero and Virgil gang up against Lucretius's Epicurean skepticism. Through fictive afterlives that materialism derides as illogical, narcissistic folly, they enforce a commitment to public life from which the Epicurean withdraws. Who won? Cicero lost, but Lucretius and Virgil continue to make powerful claims on the imagination, whether to the sense of reality, or the obligation to aspire.

In his six-book philosophical poem, *De Rerum Natura (On the Nature of Things/DRN*, c. 55 BCE), Lucretius (c. 96–55), a poet of the Republic, denied every afterlife myth with Epicurus as his muse. Venus reigned as goddess, mother of the Aeneadae, fertility, and love (I.1), instigator of the natural processes through which men and animals come into being. All things, Lucretius held, are made of atoms, combining and recombining in the void; the gods exist but are indifferent to man; the highest good is the study of natural causes—the nature of things—disdaining ambition's tormented pursuits of power, wealth, fame. Death is mere dispersal of atoms, nothing to fear.

Cicero (c. 106–43 BCE), pleader, consul, author, *novus homo* ambitious of power and fame, wanted something better than dispersal for souls of manly virtue. His brother admired Lucretius's work; Cicero shied tactfully off. He detested Epicureans' cocky withdrawal from public affairs and rewrote Plato's *Republic* for Rome, replacing Er's myth with Scipio's dream.[230] He ended murdered on Mark Antony's orders, his head and hands set up in the Forum where he often spoke. Point to Lucretius.

Virgil (c. 70–19 BCE), child of civil war, shifted allegiance from Epicurean withdrawal to heroic action as the favored poet of Augustus. A decade after Cicero's murder, Augustus destroyed Mark Antony, Cleopatra, and Caesarion, Julius Caesar's son. Echoing Lucretius in his early eclogues and georgics, Virgil turns apostate in the *Aeneid*.[231] His friend Horace (65–8 BCE) called himself "good for a laugh, a hog from Epicurus's herd" (*Epistles* I. 4, l.16) and disclaimed addressing Caesar or painting bristling war (*Sat.* 2.1). Those grander topics Virgil yearned after in his pastorals (*Eclogue* 6) and seized in the *Aeneid*. In Book 6 Aeneas travels through the underworld at the center of Virgil's challenge to Greek epic hegemony and Epicurean ideology. Dazzlingly, Virgil synthesizes popular traditions, psychological interpretation, rational adjustments to traditional views, poetic revisioning, philosophical seriousness, historical highlights, and political commentary. No afterlife quite covers the bases the way Virgil's does, and without the challenge presented by Lucretius and the Epicureans, Virgil might not have been so thorough. Going well beyond Plato, he provides an afterlife Christians could find comfortable and correct in most points, saving the gods. When Dante chose Virgil for his guide, he chose the poet who had already mapped the underworld and transformed it into an ethical, philosophical, historical, and political space.

More surprising now than Lucretius's system is that Cicero and Virgil felt impelled to answer it and to erect an alternative. Epicurus's thirty-six volumes of writings had not yet been mislaid by the Christian tradition, nor had Plato and Aristotle acquired their subsequent dominance within that tradition. NF NS NC was inscribed on tombs, to be collected among Latin inscriptions and disparaged by modern Christian scholars.[232] If popular superstition maintained its hold, so did popular skepticism, the "practical atheism" Plato attributed to most people.[233] One public-spirited Epicurean of the second century CE, Diogenes of Oinoanda, inscribed his Epicurean tenets in thousands of words on an 80-foot wall in the center of his obscure town in Asia Minor, southwestern Turkey.[234] Cicero's brash Epicurean Velleius often leads off dialogues, the better to be disputed later (speaking first, Cicero knew, was a disadvantage). "[A]s is usual with that school," Cicero sighs, "Velleius," the Epicurean spokesman, always displays "no lack of confidence."[235] In the second century CE, even the Stoic Marcus Aurelius never managed to shake off the suspicion that chance and atoms might rule. He could not determine whether he would be transmuted by death or dispersed and returned to atoms, to be recombined.

The simplicity and logic of Epicurean atomism were seductive. In death things clearly break apart, creating new life, as maggots wriggle out of a corpse. Easier to challenge was the atomist doctrine of creation by atoms' combining. From Cicero through Savonarola to Thomas Creech, Lucretius's seventeenth-century translator, that idea seemed patently ridiculous: "An Opinion so absurd, that even the bare mentioning of it confutes it."[236] Like most of Epicurus, Lucretius was mislaid in the Christian era, but the Renaissance saw *DRN* rise. Atomic theory had the same exhilarating effect on early natural scientists that it had had on Lucretius himself, awed by his sense of piercing through "the walls of the world" to ultimate reality. Stephen Greenblatt's *The Swerve*, the story of Lucretius's recovery, testifies to Lucretius's enduring power to liberate. Of his views on death—the absurdity of concern for burial, the futility of life spent half asleep, the vacancy of the period before one's birth, as after death—many were transmitted, less scandalously, in Pliny's *Natural History*, Book 7, chap. LV, "Man." Telling tales of souls' travel outside the body, Pliny mocks a future life, but without the sting of Lucretius's insistence that the soul dies, just like the body. Lucretius jabs the unthinkable in the eye:

> What has this bugbear, death, to frighten man,
> If souls can die as well as bodies can?
>
> (Dryden, ll. 1–2; *DRN* III.830–31: Nil igitur mors est ad nos neque pertinet hilum, quandoquidem natura animi mortalis habetur.)

So dangerous was the idea of a dead soul that Dante literally put a lid on it.

Cicero Dante places with the virtuous pagans, Lucretius he does not know, but Epicurus "and his followers"—who make the soul die with the body—he places in gaping tombs that will be sealed at the Last Judgment, their bodies joining their souls beyond the last death (*Inferno*, x. 14–15: "con Epicuro tutt'i suoi seguaci,/ che l'anima col corpo morta fanno"). They will spend eternity buried alive.

At Dante's threat, Lucretius laughs. Death ends the third book of *DRN*, the midpoint of Lucretius's six, where Homer and later Virgil also set their *katabasis*. Lucretius knows that he does not know what "soul" is. It ought not to be immortal, since coupling an immortal with a mortal thing defies logic (*DRN* III, 800–805). It is palpably bodily, sickening and fretting and recovering along with the body. Soul and body make the self that death annihilates by separating them, each dying its own death:

> we are only we
> While souls and bodies in one frame agree.

Should the dance of atoms reconstitute that body, bringing precisely those atoms back together, that body is a different self. You, cloned, would not be you. (Nor would your mind running on another computer be you, somewhere in the cloud.) Identity requires memory of the union of body and soul. Death creates "a gaping space ... where memory lies dead" (ll. 17–26, 38–39, 47; *DRN* III, 839–42, 847–51, 860). Should soul migrate from one body to another, its animating a new body creates a new being with no connection to the earlier embodied self. Body is dominant over soul, yet it is soul that is conscious of the bodily self. We feel no concern for those preexisting selves (Lucretius does not address Shirley MacLaine or Pythagoras). This life, then, is the only one any self has. It should be improved by natural study and frank pleasures (W. B. Yeats thought Dryden's translation of Book 4, on love, the finest description of sexual intercourse ever written). The common pursuits of wealth, honor, and power are better avoided for learning and simple "undisturb'd delight" (Dryden, "Beginning of the Second Book," l. 21). Disengaged and uninvolved, one regards from afar, on shore, ships caught in tempests at sea, or troops on the march, engaged in "the brutal business of the war" (Dryden, "Beginning of the First Book," l. 41). Death is nothing to fear, but part of a necessary and natural cycle. Life is something given to us, through which we pass, and then it passes on to others:

> All things, like thee, have time to rise and rot,
> And from each other's ruin are begot,
> For life is not confin'd to him or thee;
> 'Tis giv'n to all for use, to none for property.
>
> (ll. 171–75; *DRN* III, 964–71)

The Etruscan banquet of the dead, the Roman funerary meals among the graves at Parentalia and Lemuria, Lucretius recognizes as the living remembering the dead, and his personified Nature appropriates. She tells us, clinging to life, that life is a feast and feasting has rules. Guests never stay forever, nor gracious guests too long. Henry Fielding praised the "good supper" he had in Lisbon when he said farewell to his life and his readers in *A Journal of a Voyage to Lisbon* (1754). Dryden makes Nature's speech on limits a challenge to limits. Her cornucopia and his couplet overflow:

> For if thy life were pleasant heretofore,
> If all the bounteous blessings, I could give,
> Thou hast enjoy'd; if thou hast known to live,

> And pleasure not leak'd thro' thee like a sieve;
> Why dost thou not give thanks as at a plenteous feast,
> Cramm'd to the throat with life, and rise and take thy rest?
>
> (Dryden, III, 126–31)

So much has Nature given us, that Dryden's usual five-beat, ten-syllable couplet spills over to a third line—sign both of nature's generosity, overwhelming the couplet, and our leakiness, dribbling over. The next couplet thrusts in two extra syllables and crams a trochee down our throats: the lines are longer than they should be, a pair of six-beat, twelve-syllable Alexandrines. The heroic couplet, overstuffed, bursts with life's good things in every dimension.

Life is given to all for use, but Lucretius's ground is the privileged individualism of the body. The body is within a community, but it no longer needs that community in its death: burial does nothing for the dead. The embodied mind, its memories, insights, and activity, understands and should not be perturbed by its own always pending dissolution. Empathic identification with the body underground or abandoned above ground, Lucretius understands as psychological process. Dryden's rhymes make utterly contemptible such concern for "[t]he lifeless lump uncoupled from the mind" (Dryden, III, 10). Anyone trembling

> That after death his mould'ring limbs shall rot,
> Or flames, or jaws of beasts devour his mass,
> Know he's an unsincere, unthinking ass . . .
> The fool is to his own cast offals kind.
>
> (Dryden, III, 50–55)

Bodily empathy makes traditional funerary customs equally horrifying: embalming is "to be at once preserv'd and chok'd"; tombs asphyxiate; sculptures crush, Dryden's baroque addition: "Or crowded in a tomb to be oppress'd/ With monumental marble on thy breast?" (Dryden, III, 71, 74–75). Dante anticipated that one.

Plato detested poets' "dismal tales" (Dryden, III,. 183) as terrorizing. Lucretius understands their psychological resonance, but overthrows them as simply false. Gone is the elaborate stage set of the afterlife, the tortures, flames, and rivers that Hesiod displayed, popular tradition elaborated, and Aristophanes parodied. Those underground torture chambers do not exist and never have:

> As for the Dog, the Furies, and their snakes,
> The gloomy caverns, and the burning lakes,
> And all the vain infernal trumpery,
> They neither are, nor were, nor e'er can be.
>
> (Dryden, III, 221–24)

The familiar punishments Lucretius decodes as allegory. The rock impending over Tantalus's head is fear of chance or the irrational punishments of imaginary gods (Dryden's embellishment). Tityus's nine-acre, regrowing liver stabbed by vultures is anyone tormented by passion, regrowing in his vitals. Rolling that stone, Sisyphus is an unsuccessful politician, sweating to please the crowd, straining to secure his place. The fifty foolish virgins carrying water in sieves embody unfulfilled desire, hopelessly questing new pleasures, aimlessly seeking satisfaction.

Yet without post-mortem torture chambers, how is morality to be enforced? Plato argues metaphysics and myth: retribution works itself out in this life's justice, and a thousand-year torture chamber lies down and off to the left. Lucretius responds with social institutions. Positive law, the actual arrangements men make, enforces behavior through penalties inflicted on the bodies of wrongdoers:

> But here on earth the guilty have in view
> The mighty pains to mighty mischiefs due;
> Racks, prisons, poisons, the Tarpeian rock,
> Stripes, hangmen, pitch, and suffocating smoke.
>
> (Dryden, III, 226–29)

A surviving precept of Epicurus observes that until the guilty are dead—when they know nothing—they cannot know that they will not be caught.[237] Fear of detection dogs them always, making life the hell others anticipate. For Lucretius, the guilty project their fears forward into eternity's imagined afterlives.

Yet if our lives are merely a point between a past we did not experience and a future that stretches to eternity without us, what did our being here mean? Curiously, Lucretius never considers an afterlife a source of hope. Unlike Pliny, he does not even ridicule consolatory folly.[238] Those we most admire have died before us: how should we be exempt?

> Consider Ancus great and good is dead;
> Ancus, thy better far, was born to die,
> And thou, dost thou bewail mortality?
>
> (Dryden, III, 236–39)

This argument even Lucretius's admirers rarely repeat, though perhaps better than any other it reconciles us to our own mortality. After Ancus follow Xerxes, Scipio Africanus, Homer, Democritus, and finally the master. Here alone Lucretius names Epicurus, invoked in every book. Naming the name, Lucretius presents a sign of the thought that enabled his own. Why should we be alive when those who created our lives' meanings are dead? Why begrudge the only thing we share with them? Most of us are half dead anyway, lives snored or trafficked away in trivialities and twittering.

For Lucretius, life's project is to understand life, to "study Nature well, and Nature's laws" (Dryden, III, 296), to search for the causes of things. Analyst of endless desire, he recognizes—and sketches—the motor of human insatiability that made Rome a great city, rich, prosperous, crammed with poor people and slaves, wealth and corruption, law and crime. While others crave the thick of things, the Epicurean condemns participation in favor of contemplation, withdrawal from the pursuits that animate the common run of men, in favor of philosophic enlightenment. Superstition and fear vanish before Epicurus and reason. Lucretius dedicates his poem to Venus, the "delight of humankind, and gods," parent of Rome, who breeds all things born, bringing life wherever life exists. To the goddess of love, he brings a devotion that loves life back ("Beginning of the First Book," ll. 1–6). All the meaning anyone needs is found looking through the cosmos to what the world is, understanding one's momentary part in the continuously recombining whole.

Yet for all his brilliance, Lucretius continues to terrify some readers, beginning with Cicero. He shows why we should not fear death—and we agree. He shows traditional tales are fables—and we learn more about human psychology. He shows that the desire for eternal life is part of human insatiability and discontent of spirit, never contented with the present, always desiring the absent—and we understand ourselves better for it. He spiritedly mocks the identification with the body that underlies funerary ritual and afterlife imaginings. But I am not sure we change; I do not think desire ceases; it may even increase under Lucretius's ministrations. Certainly the terror of the open vowel, long, lonely, unending, has never echoed more powerfully than in Dryden's last lines.[239] Nor has the "length of death" ever seemed longer than that assonance makes it. These lines end Dryden's translation as the thought ends Lucretius's Book III; but who ever read them without turning the page to see, surely, if there is not just a little more?

> Nor, by the longest life we can attain,
> One moment from the length of death we gain,
> For all behind belongs to his eternal reign.
> When once the Fates have cut the mortal thread,
> The man as much to all intents is dead
> Who dies today, and will as long be so,
> As he who died a thousand years ago.

Cicero could not bear it, and he was not one for silence. In 54 BCE he replied to his brother Quintus's praise for *DRN* carefully: "The poetry of Lucretius is, *as you say* in your letter, rich in brilliant genius, yet highly artistic" (emphasis added).[240] That compliment accommodated to someone else's praise, Cicero never repeats, and he never again names Lucretius.[241] Cicero claimed—in both voices in one dialogue—to prefer to go wrong with Plato than right with anyone else. In his *Tusculan Disputations* "A," unlike Socrates, considers death evil, but asked if he fears Cerberus and Acheron, "A" sneers. He fears no three-headed dogs in hell; nobody believes such things.[242] His opponent "M" then jeers those famous philosophers who preen themselves on discovering the falsity of what nobody believes. They also fail to address what people do fear about death—ceasing to exist or the suffering that may accompany death. Cicero almost certainly has Lucretius in view, and his poisonous point is sharp.

Self-consciously Romanizing Plato's myth of Er to end his own *Republic*, Cicero aimed a *Dream of Scipio* against Epicureans' deriding the immortal soul as incredible fables.[243] As a dream, Cicero's lacks the reality claim of Er's near-death experience, but appropriates the liminal space between this world and the other. Less egalitarian, more historical, aggressively heroic, it adopts the perspective of a privileged spectator far above the earth, viewing the Milky Way, mapping the cosmos. Personal and familial identities, the city and the heavens confirm each other, simultaneously aggrandizing and diminishing individuals.

After a long day's journey and an evening's conversation about his grandfather Scipio Africanus (237–183 BCE), victor in the second Punic War, the younger Scipio Aemilianus Africanus (185–129 BCE) dreams his grandfather, resembling his bust, speaking.[244] He learns his own history: that the Carthage his grandfather defeated under Hannibal, he himself will burn to the ground, triumphing in the third Punic War. He will save Rome from the Gracchi and die assassinated. Reunited with his father Paulus, Scipio embraces and kisses him, not eluded by a shade. They share a vision of the cosmos, giant stars and Milky Way, the earth barely visible, the spheres making music, the stars returning upon themselves in the cosmic year. Among the stars, looking down at earth, Scipio learns that his immortal soul derives from the eternal fires of the constellations, much as we are now told that we are made of stardust. City-preserving souls come from and return to heaven. Small as the earth is, across its banded zones the inhabitants forget or never learn of each other: Scipio's fame will not reach the Ganges.

From Plato's *Phaedrus* Cicero argues soul's immortality from its motion. Since soul makes body move, soul is god to the body and so immortal. Souls given to sensual pursuits and pleasures are tossed to and fro (like Epicurean atoms) for ages of banishment before they return heavenward. Punitively, Epicurean "hog[s]" grovel, close to earth, denied the sublime vision granted Scipio, preserver of his country. Cicero had not yet learned that they also escape the assassination of a Scipio or a Cicero.

Like Cicero, Virgil knew nonexistence would never do. Seventeen years old when Lucretius died, Virgil knew Lucretius's poem well. Bernard Knox calls Virgil a "devotee" of Epicurean philosophy; Philip Hardie has shown how Lucretius permeates not only the deliberately Epicurean *Eclogues* and *Georgics*, but also the anti-Epicurean *Aeneid*. Henri Bergson saw Lucretius's phrases playing everywhere in Augustan literature, though least in Horace, a softer avowed Epicurean.[245] Virgil's second Georgic sounds the distinctive Lucretian note—ambitious to search out nature's laws while indifferent to fortune or fate. Desired are natural knowledge and "a soft secure inglorious life."[246] The first book of the *Aeneid* ends with Iopas's Epicurean song celebrating natural knowledge and the origins of things. Twenty-seven when Cicero was assassinated, Virgil matured during the murderous chaos of Rome's republic-destroying civil wars. Stability imposed by Augustus, Virgil shifted to the active engagement represented in Cicero's *Dream of Scipio*. When Aeneas, puzzlingly, leaves the underworld through the gate of false dreams after hearing a history of Rome, Virgil gestures to Cicero's *Dream of Scipio* as well as Ennius's "Dream of Homer."[247]

Aeneas's underworld travel occurs at the poem's center. It is the pivot where the action turns, the womb from which the history of Rome emerges, spilling over the limits of Aeneas's era into the living present of Virgil, Augustus, and the already dead Marcellus, once Augustus's heir. On it, Virgil lavishes reason, invention and philosophy to transform Homer's infantine afterlife into a powerful machine of Roman propaganda and ideology.

The surest sign of cognitive control, Virgil's afterlife can be mapped.[248] At entry crowd the causes of death: sickness, grief, famine, war, and strife. Beyond looms the great elm of terrifying dreams and premonitions. (Scipio's dream predicted assassination by his relations.) Aeneas boats with Charon over the river to Cerberus, walks past the Mourning Lovers and the Warriors, where the road forks left to Tartarus and right to the Fields of the Blessed. The direction "to the right, to the sacred meadows and groves of Persephone" occurs in mystery initiation texts from Thuroi, associated with the kid in the milk.[249] Making no blood sacrifice or first-fruits offering, Aeneas bears a sacred golden bough to Persephone's groves. Otherwise, Virgil's afterlife is thoroughly rationalized. Like Odysseus, Aeneas draws his sword to slash at terrifying chimeras, but he is advised by the Sibyl to put up his useless sword, for these are only phantoms. Bodiless shades no longer shy from weapons they cannot feel. Longing for burial (Odysseus's Elpenor) is mathematized and motivated (Aeneas's Palinurus). The unburied must wander a hundred years before finally resting in the underworld. R. G. Austin finds no source for Virgil's hundred-year figure. The round number arousing and allaying anxiety over the body may be the poet's invention.[250]

Twitting the enlightened, Virgil makes a place for every belief Cicero and Lucretius scorned. The Sibyl throws a sop to Cerberus as the erstwhile

Epicurean loads up "the Dog, the Furies, and their snakes,/The gloomy caverns, and the burning lakes,/And all the vain infernal trumpery." Not one item is left out of the familiar catalogue.

As Aeneas makes his way through the underworld, every encounter transforms and intensifies a Homeric moment. Homer's parade of beautiful women, mothers of heroes and lovers of gods, becomes a domain of lovelorn, passionate victims of their own intense sexual desires, Virgil's Fields of Mourning. There Dido mimes the hero Ajax's fury (and Cleopatra's defeat). As Odysseus's dead Greek heroes followed the famous women, so Aeneas next encounters gender-segregated warriors. Mutilated Deiphobus reimagines Agamemnon's murder, victims of guilty sisters (Helen and Clytemnestra), who abandoned one man and took another. In Tartarus's torture chamber, Virgil shows off: Tityos's vultures celebrate Rome's superior grisliness. Homer's vultures flock in a long shot over the recumbent body. Virgil moves into the body cavity where a single vulture gropes, beak and talons inside pulling at the liver (6.595–600).

Aeneas meets Anchises, his father, the goal and end of his journey, inverting Odysseus's unexpected, unwished encounter with Anticleia, his mother, at his beginning. Homer's bodily pathos recurs in the parent's elusive shade. Virgil's narrative then turns: a philosophical statement on the nature of being flows effortlessly into history and the present. Odysseus's story of Achilles' son becomes the pageant of Aeneas's descendants. Odysseus's encounter with Hercules augurs his personal destiny, the terrible bow he will wield against the suitors. Virgil's stories about the dead become the story of the future, not as in Homer the heroic individual's future, but the state's.

Virgil's new metaphysic makes space for more than Homeric imitation and popular folklore. Improving on the mysteries, he inscribes justice from multiple perspectives. Entering the underworld, Aeneas encounters the untimely dead: wailing infants, those unjustly condemned in human courts, and suicides. The children are remembered, but not consoled. The silent condemned are judged again by Minos. The suicides echo Achilles: they long for poverty and hard labor if only they could view the sun again ("nunc et pauperiem et duros perferre labores!" 6.437). Rethinking Plato's orders, Virgil does not strike the line but reassigns it. No longer Achilles' experience as best of the dead, aching for the life thrown away now persuades against suicide, a hostility shared with Cicero (and Plautus).[251]

Cultivating death's terrors, unlike Cicero, Virgil amplifies Plato's retributive punishments and casts a slyly sardonic glance at Lucretius's prisons.

Homer's and Hesiod's Tartarus, yawning twice as far below the earth as earth from the sky (*Aeneid* 6.577–79), Virgil turns into a gigantic prison, specialized as a place of punishment. Racks and wheels and iron scourges, groans, lashes, and dragging chains echo dismally, too horrid for description. No longer restricted to god-defying heroes, punishment strikes crimes in Rome, against one's fellow men, in a list far longer than Plato's. Yet most of the crimes Virgil enumerates are not punishable by law. Lucretius's "Racks, prisons, poisons, the Tarpeian rock" could not touch them.

Adding to Homer, Virgil catalogues the usual god-defying suspects: the Titans, Salmoneus, twin sons of Aloeus, Tityos, the Lapithae Ixion and Pirithous, with a rock hanging over their heads, and forbidden laden tables. To them he adds behaviors Romans wanted to control: those who hated their brothers, struck their fathers, defrauded a client, failed to share wealth with relatives (huge numbers of those); those slain for adultery, those who warred against their own country and betrayed their lords. Some sold their country for gold, others foisted a tyrant on the people, some passed or repealed laws for money, others raped their daughters (6.608–24). A sociology of the city and a glancing rebuttal of Lucretius, most of these acts, antisocial though they are, are not crimes amenable to law. No legal sanction punishes those who fail to share wealth with relatives or hate their brothers, and men killed for adultery are already dead.[252] Implicitly, Virgil addresses Lucretius's criticism that all we need is law, by pointing to behaviors, moving from wrong to unimaginably monstrous, "immane nefas" (6.624), that the law does not address. Justice for these wrongs takes place only in another world.

Virgil also encourages specific good behaviors. Leaving tortures behind, Aeneas and the sibyl arrive at the realm of reward, the "Blissful Groves" ("Fortunatorum Nemorum," 6.639) or "Elysium" (6. 744). A sun and stars appear. Wrestling, games, grappling, dancing, and singing occupy the happy, while Orpheus plays his lyre amid traces of his mysteries. Horses browse, unyoked for a while from the nearby chariots, lances stuck in the earth. Nor is feasting forgotten, and a chant rises within a fragrant laurel grove. Enjoying these happy exercises of the body are Trojan ancestors and those whose behaviors deserve praise and should provoke emulation: men who suffered wounds for their country (they did not need even to die); holy priests, poets worthy Apollo; those who discovered truths useful to mankind, and those who served their fellows through acts of beneficence. Warfare, religion, song, science, arts, philosophy, and service: all support the state and its purposes among the famed and the anonymous. The freedom of movement characteristic of earlier afterlives finds spaces worth moving through, groves, meadows, streams (6.672–75). In just such terrain Dante places his virtuous pagans, including the Muslims Averroes and Avicenna.

So superior in design is Virgil's underworld that it induces critics to fault its arrangements: why is Dido not among the suicides? Why is Sychaeus, her husband, with her in the field of mourning lovers, since he died beloved and faithful to the end? Why are the Trojan warriors not among those who incurred wounds for their country in Elysium with Teucer's line? Spatial fluidity characterized Homer's and other afterlives. Once across the river, shades not tied down to tortures could be found anywhere. Outside the rarely visited court of Hades and Persephone, the geography recapitulated the random gathering of shades at the brink, tumbling pell-mell from life. When Virgil imposes order on his underworld, moments that violate the design stand out. The text systematizes traditional received ideas, integrating them with grander concepts, reshaping the present to control the future, too successfully. A tribute to the rationalizing impulse the text creates in the reader, the reader arriving from the future demands more rigor.

Once Aeneas meets Anchises and the shade flits thrice through the living arms that would embrace it, the Homeric underworld, with its moralized Platonic additions, is finished. Poor Anticleia explained no more than the soul's flying as the body burns to ash. Anchises explains the nature of the universe, in terms of the Stoic doctrine of *anima mundi*, the world spirit or mind from which all things come, to which all things go, and in which all things participate. Transposing Anticleia's pathetic vision of a wasted, weakened soul fleeing the fire, Anchises rears before the mind's eye a vision of the universe as fire.

> Know, first, that heav'n and earth's compacted frame,
> And flowing waters, and the starry flame,
> And both the radiant lights, one common soul

Inspires and feeds, and animates the whole.
This active mind, infus'd thro' all the space,
Unites and mingles with the mighty mass.
Hence men and beasts the breath of life obtain,
And birds of air, and monsters of the main.
Th'ethereal vigor is in all the same,
And every soul is fill'd with equal flame.

(Dryden, 6. 980–89)

Father for mother and philosophical transcendence for acceptance of common fate: Virgil systematically trades up elements. Against Lucretius's atoms, swerving in the void, Virgil raises a philosophic alternative in Stoic-Ciceronian fire that consumes those atoms, denies their difference, and subtends them.

With philosophy transcending the popular fables he has just retold, Virgil launches into Roman history, politics, and purpose. Nothing could be further from Epicurean withdrawal than this energetic account. Rejected are the seductive ethics of contemplative disengagement for an ideology of action in history, the progress of the Roman art of empire. From Aeneas's earliest descendants through Augustus himself, from Romulus and Numa to the tragic civil war between Caesar and Pompey, Virgil rewrites Cicero's history of Rome and its heroes to end in his own present, with Marcellus. The dead heir of Augustus and Livia is wept as Aeneas weeps when he sees the story of Troy on Dido's walls, "sunt lacrimae rerum et mentem mortalia tangunt" (1.462; [here too] are tears for things and mortal sufferings touch the mind).

Cicero's Scipio had been advised that the Ganges will never hear his name, nor the rising or the setting sun. Fame lasts barely a year in mortal minds, and Cicero recalls Lucretius's evocation of the eons before one's birth, "of what importance is it to you to be talked of by those who are born after you, when you were never mentioned by those who lived before you."[253] Cicero, for once, is judged too modest. To Augustus Virgil promises an empire and fame past Africans and Indians, "Garamantas et Indos" (6.794), beyond the stars and solar year of Scipio's dream (6.795–96). Left far behind is Epicurean contempt for public life. Fame is desirable, widespread, and as enduring as the imperial justification Virgil creates for Rome and every Latin-reading empire since:

> tu regere imperio populos, Romane, memento
> (hae tibi erunt artes) pacique imponere morem,
> parcere subiectis et debellare superbos.
> 6.851–53
>> (You rule by command the peoples, Roman, remember /(these will be your arts) peace and custom to impose,/ to spare the subjugated and to break the proud.)

This Pax Romana, the imperial credo, the civilizing mission rejects utterly the Lucretius who mocked sweating Sisyphus as the active politician of the Roman republic.

Not content with reversing values, Virgil jabs at what Lucretius explicitly valued. Virgil's attack on Ancus has puzzled numerous commentators, who suspect Virgil may have confused one king or Ancus with another.[254] Ancus, the fourth king of Rome, is routinely praised, his paternity questioned, by Cicero (*Republic* II, xviii, 33, p.141). Horace linked Ancus with Numa, as a casualty of death like ourselves. The Forum may see you now, but you will have to go where Numa and Ancus have gone: "ire tamen restat Numa quo devenit et Ancus" (*Epistles* I.6.27). In Lucretius, Ancus holds a privileged position: he begins the list of worthy dead that Epicurus will end. As a public, political character he is followed by the doomed, unnamed Xerxes who paved the seas to his own destruction, and so figures ironically, and then by the "son of the Scipios," thunderbolt of Carthage, as predictable as those who follow him: Homer, Democritus, and Epicurus. The praise of Ancus is generous:

> Consider Ancus great and good is dead;
> Ancus, thy better far, was born to die,
> And thou, dost thou bewail mortality?
>
> (Dryden, 236–39)

As rare as Lucretius's praise is Virgil's condemnation. Uniquely among the Roman fathers, he charges "bragging Ancus" with panting after the popularity Lucretius scorns in Sisyphus:

> Whom Ancus follows, with a fawning air,
> But vain within, and proudly popular.
>
> (Dryden, 6.1115–16)

quem iuxta sequitur iactantior Ancus,
nunc quoque iam nimium gaudens popularibus auris.

(6.815–16)

Virgil mocks in Epicurean satiric terms, as vain, petty, and would-be popular, a figure the Epicureans Lucretius and Horace conspicuously and persistently praise. Ancus, Cicero notes, had divided among the citizens the lands he conquered. He also made the forests of the sea coast, his conquests, public property.[255] Respect for public things clung to his memory. There may be some other secret reason for Virgil's unique depreciation of a Roman father, but the jab marks Virgil's contesting Lucretius's history and Ancus's public donations, before there was a republic, before Augustus's principate. Perhaps only Horace, another Epicurean, would have noticed.

With Virgil, the afterlife has acquired the characteristics and structure that Christianity will absorb when its time comes, in less than a century. Augustus, son of a God (the deified Julius Caesar), will restore the golden age ("Augustus Caesar, Divi genus, aurea condet/saecula" 6.792–93). Suicides chastised, infants in limbo, punishment, reward, purgation, and rebirth of souls: all eventually enter Christian doctrines and fantasies. Revelation's heavenly city is remote from Virgil's pastoral fields, nor does Virgil envision the destruction of his Rome, "Babylon, that great city" that rules the world from her seven hills (Rev. 17.5, 9, 18). Yet Virgil maps the underworld that later medieval writers will revisit, as they follow his trajectory through myth to transcendence.[256] Dante knew whom he needed for a guide.

Did Virgil believe any of it? Of an afterlife so clearly constructed from others' bits and pieces, one should probably follow one of Virgil's sources. To repeat Plato's observation in *Phaedo*, it is "not fitting to say something like this is true, but fit to say something ought to be like it" (114de). Facing the dead Marcellus, Virgil has only an "unavailing gift" (Dryden, 6. 1226), "inani/ munere" (6.885–86), less than the "tristi munere" Catullus offered his brother (*Carmen*, 101). The monsters and chimeras flocking the entry to the underworld fade before this unborn image of a man already dead. So, too, to John Jortin's dismay, Aeneas leaves the underworld through the gate of false dreams.

An episode commenced by invoking the gods to "let me tell what I have heard" and reveal the secrets of the depths (6.264–67) shifts from represented action to mere dream, and a false dream rather than a true one. As Edward Gibbon observed before he became Rome's historian, many think the ivory gate wrecks Book 6: "the common opinion, that by six unlucky lines, Virgil is destroying the beautiful System, which it had cost him eight hundred to raise. [Jortin] explains too this preposterous conduct, by the usual expedient of the Poet's Epicureism. I only differ from him in attributing to haste and indiscretion, what he considers as the result of design."[257] Tactfully, the skeptical Gibbon lets the cleric Jortin conclude Virgil at heart an Epicurean. As to others' belief in Virgil's system, a modern student of Roman death and burial finds echoes only in poetic epitaphs, not in prose or funerary art.[258] Like Lucretius, propagandizing for the study of nature as Virgil for civic action, Virgil seems to care enough about truth as matter of fact to mark his vision false, even though it has told many truths.

Lightly presented here, running across several millennia, is the human imagination working over and developing its conceptions of what happens after death, responding to social change, generating new ideologies in reimagined spaces of the dead. Most of the work is anonymous, and much of it popular, but from Homer to Virgil the luck of literary survivals lets us see purposeful bricolage in action. Justice, long absent, is vigorously stitched in, and such imaginary afterlives as Plato's and Virgil's are manifestly intended to shape the behavior of the living, regardless of the dead. Seventeenth- and eighteenth-century thinkers, wriggling free of a thousand years of Christian hegemony, blamed priests for successful mind control; they did not think to blame their beloved poets and philosophers.

Of two enlightenment revolutions in the afterlife, one followed Lucretius and denied an afterlife on rationalist, materialist principles, a position associated with David Hume, Edward Gibbon, and some deists. The second revolution is perhaps more interesting: the afterlife was undermined from within by the desire to improve it, to create a happier and better future state than was currently on offer, even in Christianity. When an afterlife is predicated upon its being empirical fact, as the Christian afterlife is, can it both change and remain true at the same time?

That afterlives originate in the human mind and serve social purposes is, of course, no proof of their falsity, any more than religion's origins and development disprove God. Any God worth believing can surely oversee the evolution of appropriately worshipful creatures, and countless other beings both indifferent and inimical to man, as He informs Job. So, too, the Christian's delayed *parousia* demands a concept of progressive revelation. The world having not come to its promised end, God adapts and is adapted to changes in human psychology and society, taking on the ideal configuration of the changing human face. (Or, with Christopher Hitchens, its diabolism.) In the British enlightenment, the afterlife came to originate in the mind, serve social purposes, and reflect the human image, all without disturbing orthodoxy. A good God, his benevolence unchallenged, would not give people false ideas.

Before eternity takes this final twist, however, let us follow Scipio's gaze towards the Ganges. What afterlife or lives could he expect there? Related but alternative logics flourish in a vast, cyclically generating and self-destroying cosmos, where no eternity is permanent, except the flame of a blown-out candle.

3

TOURING ASIAN AFTERLIVES: ETERNAL IMPERMANENCE

In the dazzling diversity of Asian afterlives, traces appear of an undifferentiated underworld like that of Sumer or Greece (India, China, Japan), as well as diligent efforts to improve its living conditions (China). The dead depart, but some spirits do not go far enough away, troubling the neighborhood; others, the ancestors, must be fed and maintained to secure their help (India, China), and come and go for festivals (China, Japan). Heaven contends with spirits and gods for hegemony, and hell develops late, unnecessary when spirits watch or supplemental when elaborate codes order social relationships (Hindu dharma, Confucian rites and way of heaven). Rebirth is regarded as essential for morality, or discounted as mythology.[1] Hells police the isolated, piercing egotism, creating anxiety about death and salvation. Eastward lie many sumptuous heavens, interactive tombs,[2] and horrific hells, as well as nirvana and nothing at all.

To speak of "the afterlife," however, is often to commit a category error. Neither heavens nor hells are eternal, when they exist. Nor is death a terminus. Ancestors remain nearby. After death, one may wander on (*samsara*). Rebirth creates a before and after for the self—or no-self (Buddhism). Birth continues, death repeats. Moralized as karma, rebirth makes individuals as responsible for the past as for their immediate future, and the futures that follow their deaths. In perhaps the ultimate cautionary tale—or tribute to human dissatisfaction—rebirth once invented, had then to be prevented.

These afterlives, their texts, and their relationships can only be sketched here, but they enlarge our repertoire of afterlife imaginings as well as the cosmos, within and without. Tracing such afterlife-shaping concepts as ancestors, rebirth, karma from their Vedic origins in India through Buddhism, Jainism, and Hinduism, the chapter picks up Confucianism, Daoism, and new varieties of Buddhism in China, stares awestruck at Tibet, and on to Japan, ending with two encounters between Buddhism and the Christian west, a seventeenth-century dispute and a twentieth-century fiction.

Jews, Christians, and Muslims have, ostensibly, one God and the overlapping books that make them, in the Qur'anic phrase, "peoples of the Book." Hindus alone have the *Rig* and three other *Vedas*, the *Brahmanas*, the *Upanishads*, the *Puranas*, the *Ramayana*, and the *Mahabharata*, the last fifteen times longer than the Christian Bible, written over a six-hundred year period with no single, authorized version.[3] The *Ramayana*, which to western eyes seems a romance with the poetic authority of Homer, lays claim as it concludes to the religious authority of the *Vedas* (c. 1700–300 BCE).[4] We expect different philosophical schools to come and go, but the gods also keep changing, emerging from nowhere like Shiva or declining into irrelevance like Brahma and Indra.[5] "Hindu" is a foreign neologism for "those across the Indus," whatever they may happen to believe, whenever.[6] (Religions coextensive with their region lack names, until a missionary religion—Buddhism, Christianity, Islam—arrives, providing followers with an identity that transcends such conventional forms of identity as region, family, tribe, language. The new name enables a transition from one social order, polity, or people to another.) At least the Hindu canon is confined to one language, Sanskrit, and there is some agreement as to what it contains.

Buddhism proceeds otherwise. Not the story of a god or gods, but of a teaching (*dharma*) and its practices, Buddhist canons flourish in at least four additional languages, Pali, Burmese, Chinese, and Tibetan, as well as Sanskrit.[7] The new Fo Guang Shan library in Yangzhou, China, has a 100,000-volume collection of Buddhist scriptures.[8] The Chinese canon includes the world's oldest printed book, 868 CE, the *"Diamond-Cutter" Perfection of Wisdom Sutra*.[9] The Tibetan *Book of the Dead* (the *Bardo Todrol* or Liberation by Hearing), in the West perhaps the single most famous Buddhist text, but only one item in a vast Tibetan canon, appeared as late as the fourteenth century. Texts are revered, chanted, preserved, copied, and multiplied, and every new school has produced new writings and privileged some texts over others. Originating in northeast India (near Patna) in the fifth or sixth century BCE and flourishing in India until the thirteenth century CE, Buddhism traveled west, north, and east through Afghanistan (the Buddhas of Bamiyan) to China, Mongolia, and Tibet, Vietnam, Korea, and Japan, as well as south and east to Sri Lanka, Myanmar, Thailand, Cambodia, Laos, and Indonesia. Traveling, it accommodated the systems of thought it encountered, integrating gods and spirits, reshaping its own philosophical positions.

In China, before Buddhism arrived in the first century CE, there flourished alongside popular religion's restless spirits and "unruly gods,"[10] multiple philosophical schools that, preferring cosmology to theology and present rites to afterlives, had no afterlife rewards and punishments to enforce morality or console survivors. The descendants kept the watchful eyes of their ancestors open, to reward or punish the living, not the dead. Heaven looked down from above and validated the order of which it formed part, without being a person, a creator, or a place to take up residence. It rewarded the living with life, and took life away, like Confucius's favorite disciple, but paid no attention to the dead.[11] The world teemed with spirits consulted in divinations or creating havoc requiring divination, and those matters required specialists in divination. Heaven, earth, and man in between: death participated in the natural order controlled by rites and custom, for Confucius and Mencius.

Laozi and Zhuangzi, texts or authors later venerated by Daoists, with their canon of 1500 works,[12] probed death's natural terrors, but imagined no alternative, apart from staying alive as "immortals." Immortality became for the first time a serious scientific pursuit, a search for methods of not dying at all. An anecdote from *The Analects of the Warring States* catches that openness to multiple possibilities, a strong preference for life, and acceptance of others' deaths, but not one's own. The widow of the Duke of Qin wanted her lover from Wei buried alive with her when she died. He attempted to dissuade her: she did not believe in an afterlife, so his being with her would do her no good. If there were an afterlife, however, her husband the Duke would not be pleased to see her arrive with her lover.[13] At the turn of the eras, Daoism and Buddhism promoted other worlds, while Confucian thought periodically reestablished its hegemony and wrinkled its nose at popular superstition.

Because a continuous literary tradition extends from the earliest *Veda* (the *Rig Veda*, a collection of hymns c. 1700–1000 BCE) to the *Mahabharata* and *Puranas* and because Hinduism dominates the subcontinent where all three first appeared, "Hinduism" is often misunderstood as the elder tradition, from which Buddhism emerges. That privilege belongs, however, not to Hinduism, but to Vedic religion and its descendant Brahmanism, so called for its administration by priests, Brahmins, and their ritual texts, the *Brahmanas* (800–500 BCE). That evolving religious practice generated its own internal questioning in the early *Upanishads* (600–400 BCE, others 200 BCE–100 CE).[14] Buddhism and Hinduism emerge dialectically relative to that tradition and each other, gripping the fundamental doctrines (dharma) that displaced the Vedic world of the fathers: self (or not, in Buddhism), rebirth, karma, and release (*moksha*).

Nor do Buddhism and Hinduism exhaust Indian religious traditions. Of at least six groups with which the Buddha and his followers competed for ideological dominance, one survives as the Jains. Another periodically revives, the afterlife-denying materialism of Ajita Kesakambalin.[15] Jains, too, seek liberation from karma. Their last (twenty-fourth) teacher the Mahavira was contemporaneous with the Buddha (sixth or fifth century BCE), their penultimate Parsva several hundred years earlier, and their teachings are suspected of links with the Indus Valley civilization (c. 2300–1750 BCE), antedating the *Vedas* (c. 1700–300 BCE). Regional indigenous traditions, animist and shamanist, include those subsequently developed in Tibetan Bon and Japanese Shinto.[16] Buddhism reached Tibet in the seventh century CE and Japan, through Korea, in the sixth.[17] Hindu-Buddhist syncretism marks southeast Asia, where Hindu Angkor Watt abuts Buddhist Angkor Thom.[18]

Islam and Christianity enter India within their first centuries of existence, by way of trade and missionaries, joined by Parsis (Zoroastrians, traditionally settling in western India in 937 CE) and Jews. A Christian missionary reaches China from Persia about 658 CE.[19] In southeast Asia, Muslim traders spread Islam, ultimately displacing Buddhism and Hinduism in Indonesia and Java, except for Bali. In India, Muslim conquests have been blamed for the disappearance of Buddhism in the thirteenth century, their monasteries and libraries denied elite patronage and destroyed as pagan, not of the Book. (Islamic painting absorbs Buddhist influence in the seventeenth century, and Buddhism returns to India in the late nineteenth century, compounded by the twentieth-century Tibetan diaspora.[20]) Guru Nanak founded Sikhism in the sixteenth century, a way to the one God that combines karma and samsara with grace: "There is no Hindu or Muslim, so whose path shall I follow? I shall follow the path of God." All this makes for a heady afterlife mix.

If Judaism, Christianity, and Islam once supposed a single resurrection and a singular God ruling one eternity in one closed universe, so multiple rebirths and divinities, innumerable eons and uncountable world systems populate eastern traditions. To Christianity's one Incarnation, Vishnu has ten avatars, embodiments, or incarnations, sometimes including the Buddha.[21] If there was once one Gotama gathering disciples in Magahdi, there are now thousands upon thousands of Buddhas in innumerable Buddha-fields throughout universes that expand and contract but are neither created nor extinguished.[22] If the east multiplies, it also subtracts: the self (Sanskrit *ātman*) may be everything or nothing, emptiness or Buddha nature or Ātman, the absolute. Western deities punish violations of their own laws, here or hereafter. In the east, cause and effect is still more inexorable. Past actions play themselves out, and their consequences punish and reward the perpetrators in this life and lives to come. "We are not punished *for* our actions, but *by* our actions," a modern adherent explains. Suffering or prosperity in this life is the ripening of karma from past lives, and so is love, those miraculous inexplicable attachments that suddenly appear.

As in the Christian Bible, any assertion can be contradicted. Enlightenment is possible only now, in this life, yet funeral rites guide the dead to Buddhahood and enlightenment. Nor is release always sought: rebirth is sometimes desired, and not every tradition supposes rebirth. Confucians "pay their respects to the spirits of their ancestors" and reverence the order of things in the heavens and earth. They "never discuss whether there is life after death," or so it seemed to a Japanese Zen-Buddhist Christian convert in the early seventeenth century.[23]

BIRTHING KARMIC REBIRTH AND *ĀTMAN*

If a historical question vexes the eastern afterlife, it is the birth of rebirth: Who did it? Where did it come from? As obscure and sought after as resurrection's origins in Christianity and Judaism, ethicized rebirth appears in the earliest *Upanishads* time enough to be taken as a fundamental description of life's process by Hindus, Jains, Buddhists, and to be disputed by others, but no one knows yet quite how it got there. Gananath Obeyesekere proposes that rebirth was an element in Indian tribal religions "ethicized" as karma.[24] Wendy Doniger objects that "tribal sources" merely name an unknown. Equally mysterious is how Upanishadic rebirth turned into the Buddhist canon's five realms of existence: hells, hungry ghosts, animals (*ashuras*, or angry demons, later make a sixth), humans, and gods.

The earliest texts, the hymns of the *Rig Veda* (1700–1000), send the souls of those rewarded to the world of the fathers, with shade, lovely women, Soma, honey, and butter. There Yama presides, the first man to die, now a god (*RV* 10.135.1; 10.14; 10.154.1). Traces appear of a dreaded house of clay, like Enkidu's nightmare in *Gilgamesh* (*RV* 7.89), and a pit, darkness, for demons, but not for human sinners (*RV* 7.104).[25] Some Indologists suggest that the original afterlife was the house of clay, the undifferentiated underground analogous to Ereshkigal's domain, the place of bodies, the pit.[26] The pit is said to be sacred to the ancestors, but it is also a place where the hymnist wishes demons, sorcerers, and his enemies crushed, burned, and thrust down into darkness (*RV* 7.104). As the fathers moved into the light, the pit darkened for those who gave Brahmins lame cows.[27]

Intimations of automatic, continuous rebirth within the clan appear.[28] An injunction to the dead to take root in the plants with your limbs (*RV* 10.16.3) suggests a later Upanishadic description of how rebirth happens. Falling from the world of the fathers (its merit/karma consumed), the soul returns in rain to plants; the plants eaten become semen, and the semen emitted, the soul is reborn (*Chāndogya Upanishad* [*CU*] 5.10.1–10).[29] Several hymns urge taking bodies and reaching descendants, but in the other world, not this one. The fire (Agni) releases the body to the fathers and descendants: "Set him free again to go to the fathers, Agni, when he has been offered as an oblation in you and wanders with the sacrificial drink. *Let him reach his own descendants, dressing himself in a life-span. O knower of creatures, let him join with a body*" (*RV* 10.16.5, Doniger pp. 49–50). *RV* 10.14.8 urges "Leaving behind all imperfections, go back home again; merge with a glorious body." Since the deceased is off to the fathers, the body should be with them, not on earth, but a new body has been imagined, and later rituals will make new bodies to secure rebirth.[30]

If these rebirth intimations are not Borgesian traces, antecedents created by what followed them, they are very faint, and they are not moralized. In tribal societies from south India to the Inuit, dead ancestors return to their kin group in new births. Often the ancestor reborn can be identified, and grandfathers have a penchant for reappearing in grandsons.[31] Such rebirths have no moral component. Nor does attaining the Vedic world of the fathers. That destination depends not on morality, but its close cousin, correct ritual actions (*karma*) conducted by Brahmins and performed by male heirs that secure a place with the ancestors, linking the generations.[32] The community strengthened, the body is dispersed: the eye to the sun, breath to the wind, limbs to the plants, all else to sky, earth, or water (*RV* 10.16.3).[33] Often equated with drinking soma or enjoying a long, vigorous life of 100 years, immortality is achieved "through offspring" (*RV* 2.33.1; 4.4.10; 6.7.3).[34]

In the *Vedas*, Sanskrit *karma* means "action" and refers to the rites or sacrifices performed to secure life's—and death's—good things. Properly performed, Vedic rituals (karma) produce the desired results without the intervention of any god. When karma extends beyond ritual to other actions, Patrick Olivelle argues, the autonomy it possessed as rites transfers to the autonomy of one's (other) actions' consequences.[35] Karma, good and bad, accrues as merit or demerit, first as sacrifices, then as deeds. It becomes the consequences that actions produce through time, or "the residual effect of past actions."[36] Originally material accretions to a self that burn up in another life, karma remains a fruitful concept. Past actions, disconnected from a self, accumulate, like plastic detritus in the ocean or white privilege. Whatever the origins and however transmitted, the *Upanishads* treat their knowledge of rebirth as new, the hidden answer to a question posed in Vedic terms. They also discover death.

Death rises to startling prominence in the earliest *Upanishad*, the *Bṛhadāraṇyaka* [*BU*, c. 600–500 BCE[37]]. Its first song identifies the Vedic sacrificial horse with the cosmos, but in the second, death rules, creates, becomes the horse and the fire: "In the beginning there was nothing here at all. Death alone covered this completely, as did hunger, for what is hunger but death?"(*BU* 1.2.1). Death creates a body, copulates with speech, gives birth to the world, eats all, and dies, his corpse bloating, his mind thinking, desiring to become an offering. The horse and the fire are death. This knowledge "averts repeated death" (*BU* 1.2.4–7).[38] As Doniger and others emphasize, repeated death, intrinsically undesirable, precedes the theorization of rebirth.[39] What the text overcomes, however, is skepticism about rebirth, not re-death.

A miracle of editorial suturing in three parts, separated by lineages of Brahmins (2.6, 4.6, 6.5, pp. 75, 131, 163–65), the *BU* presents death, breath, and the cosmos (part 1); centers on rebirth, karma, and the absolute (part 2); and ends in practice: the routes the dead self follows and practical instructions about birth and sex (part 3), including what to eat to have a "learned and famous son" or, surprisingly, "a learned daughter who will live out her full life span" (6.4.17–18, p. 159). Moving from death to birth, from cosmos to intimacy, the text ends eagerly collaborating with the desire for offspring that it has already advised giving up to avoid re-death and rebirth. This is not a fault. Although it is logically inconsistent, it is comprehensive.

In the pivotal passage in the second part, the new doctrine of karma (action) is introduced as a secret, partially disclosed. Equally remarkable, the secret answers a question couched precisely in the terms of *Rig Veda* 10.16.3. What happens to "the person" after the body's cosmic dispersal at death? Ārtabhāga asks Yājñavalkya, the Brahmin, "tell me—when a man has died, and his speech disappears into fire, his breath into the wind, his sight into the sun, his mind into the moon, his hearing into the quarters, his physical body into the earth, his self (*ātman*) into space, the hair of his body into plants, the hair of his head into trees, and his blood and semen into water—what then happens to that person?" Yājñavalkya recognizes the canonical terms, and he has the answer, but the answer cannot be openly disclosed: " 'My friend, we cannot talk about this in public. Take my hand, . . . let's go and discuss this in private.' So they left and talked about it." Fortunately, someone overheard, so the narrator discloses the secret. They talked only about "action," they praised only "action," and Yājñavalkya said, "A man turns into something good by good action and into something bad by bad action" (3.2.13, p. 81). This secret will be unfolded, but first skepticism must be overcome. Rebirth, they say, is not possible.

A song likens a dead man to an uprooted tree. Cut down, a tree may grow again from the root (as Job knew), or a man from a seed before he dies (when he begets a son), but an uprooted tree will not grow again: "Once he's born, he can't be born again./ Who, I ask will beget him again?" (*BU* 3.9.28 p. 103). One later answer is himself, for his wife becomes his mother when she bears him a son.[40] That possibility has already been dismissed: it happens before he dies. No guaranteed automatic re-begetting seems to be on offer. Yet "Perception, bliss, *brahman*" belong to those who know how to answer this unanswerable question, how to be born again.

The key is *brahman*. Death dismembers a man, and a dismembered man created the cosmos (*RV* 10.90). Dismembered in death, all parts dispersed, what remains is the ungraspable, essential self (ātman). Self is perception, self is—or can be—*brahman*. It is like this: at death, the self (ātman) knocks down the body and stretches out, like a caterpillar from the tip of one leaf to another. A desiring self follows its character into a new life. A self without desire is *brahman* and is not reborn. In *brahman* there is no perception, no diversity, no difference of good or bad, no desire for sons or wealth, no outside, no inside, just self, *brahman*.[41] Those who reach *brahman* are not reborn, and it is a state also attainable in this life, before death. The absolute puts an end to rebirth—and re-death.

To establish these points, questions and answers resume—but now the king challenges the Brahmin and drives him to the heart of the mystery. The "other world" intersects with this world in the world of dreams (4.3.9, p. 113). Stacked one upon another are the world of the ancestors, the world of the Gandharvas, the worlds of gods-by-rites and gods-by-birth, the world of Prajāpati, the creator, and finally of *brahman*, each hundreds of times more blissful than the one before (4.3.20–32, pp. 115–19). The Brahmin claims to have reached the end, but then the king forces him to address the process of dying, and the Brahmin, hunted home, tells all, tells of karma and those who return and those who do not return (4.3.34–4.4.24; p. 119–27).

The secret sentence is repeated, "A man turns into something good by good action and into something bad by bad action" (4.4.5, p. 121). A new distinction is added: the man who desires "returns/ back to this world,/ back to action" while the man who is unattached, without desires, is *brahman*, "and to *brahman* he goes" (4.4.6, p. 121). *Brahman* is attainable in this world, when desires are banished: "Then a mortal becomes immortal, / and attains *brahman* in this world" (4.4.7, p. 121).[42]

In the third part, the fundamental practical question—where does the person go after death?—is answered. Two new paths, one of knowledge, the other of sacrifice, lead from the Vedic funeral fires, and a dismal third way leads where one would not wish to go (6.2.2, 6.2.15–16, pp. 145–49). The person who knows, enters the flame passes to the day, the waxing moon, the sun, the world of the gods, the lightning, and on to *brahman*—and never comes back. Others who have made sacrifices, given gifts, and even practiced austerities enter the smoke. They pass to the waning moon, the world of the fathers, the moon where the gods feed on them, and thence into wind, rain, and back to earth, into the fires of a man and a woman, to circle around again and again. Those ignorant of the paths, who neither know nor give, become "worms, insects, and snakes" (6.2.16).[43] The secret was not entirely secret: a verse quoted from the *Rig Veda* tells of two paths: "Two paths mortals have, I've heard:/ the paths to fathers and to gods" (6.2.2).[44] What the verse did not tell was the way beyond the gods to *brahman* or back to the fathers. Nor did it threaten anyone with being reborn as a worm or snake.

The equally ancient *Chāndogya Upanishad* names what foods people become for rebirth: "rice and barley, plants and trees, sesame and beans, from which it is extremely difficult to get out" (5.10.6, p. 237). Eaten, they become semen, and deposited come into being again, without reference to *BU*'s more poetic fires of man and woman. Shifting the path to the gods from the middle to the end of the narrative, the last stop before *brahman* (*CU* 4.15.5, p. 227, versus *BU* 6.2.15), it ranks austerity (associated with the fourth life stage, renunciation) with knowledge as leading to the path of gods and *brahman* (*CU* 5.10.1, p. 237). In *BU*, austerity was classed with sacrifice and gift-giving that led to rebirth (*BU* 6.2.16, p. 149). *CU* also threatens. Good behavior leads to a good womb—Brahmin, Kshatriya, or Vaishya—bad to "a foul womb, like that of a dog, a pig, or an outcaste woman" (*CU* 5.10.7, p. 237).

The *Kaushītaki Upanishad* simplifies the process and sends everyone at once to the moon. Those who can answer the moon's question pass on and through; the rest come back from the moon in rain, as "a worm, an insect, a fish, a bird, a lion, a boar, a rhinoceros, a tiger, a man or some other creature—each in accordance with his actions and knowledge" (1.2, p. 327). Beyond the moon, a man passes worlds of many gods, shakes off his good and bad deeds onto relatives (those he likes get the good, those he dislikes the bad), and passes onto Brahman, the real, where he is greeted by nymphs and flowers and food and sweet scents, and engages another metaphysical disquisition that enables him to remain. There are no hells. To be reborn in a stinking womb, as a pig, a dog, an outcast, or as a mite, born and dying (*CU*), or as a worm or snake (*BU*) suffices for discipline. Nor does everyone want to go beyond the moon. *Chandogya Upanishad* holds out the hope of being reborn in a better womb than one experienced this time round (*CU* 5.10.7, p. 237).

Those who mocked rebirth in *BU* reappear in the *Katha Upanishad*, along with "joyless worlds," otherwise undescribed. A boy worries that the dry, barren cattle his father is sacrificing are worse than useless: " 'Joyless' are the worlds called, /to which a man goes/ who gives them as gifts" (*KathaU* 1.3, p. 375). Visiting Death, however, the boy does not ask about the relationship between cattle and worlds, but whether anything at all awaits after death. Some say after death there is nothing, and some say there is something. Those who say, "This is the world; there is no other," fall into death's power again and again, or so Death claims (*KaU* 2.6, p. 383).[45] Such materialists or annihilationists, in Hinduism the Charvaka school, appear also in Buddhist texts in the person of Ajita Kesakambalin, who insists: "There is no such thing as this world or the next.... A human being is built up of the four elements. When he dies, the earthy in him returns.... to the earth, the fluid to the water, the heat to the fire, the windy to the air, and his faculties pass into space."[46]

The *Katha Upanishad* also demonstrates, more elegantly than the *BU*'s delightful third part, the way the tradition synthesizes contradictory elements, in this case sacrifice and the self as equally sources of immortality. Ritual comes first: the fire sacrifice. The "foundation" of all, hidden in the "cave of the heart," it leads "to an endless world" (1.14, p. 377). Performing this sacrifice three times—and it will now be named for the boy Naciketas—overcomes "birth and death" (1.17, p. 377) and the performer "rejoices in heaven" (1.18, p. 379). At this point, all should be over, but then philosophy begins. Having reached heaven and immortality through the fire sacrifice, Naciketas asks, bizarrely, what happens to a man when he is dead: " 'He exists,' say some, others, 'He exists not' " (1.20, p. 379). Even more bizarrely, Death pleads that "even the gods of old" had doubts about this question—though he has just promised that through the sacrifice Naciketas has thrust the "fetters of death" aside and arrived in heaven (1.18). Pressed, he explains the self and the knowledge that leads to the "unborn and eternal, primeval and everlasting" "grandeur of the self"

(2.18, 20, pp. 385–87). The self escapes from samsara, which now first means "round of rebirth" (3.7, p. 389; p. 607n).

Two or three things happen here. On the one hand, the fire sacrifice evidently no longer suffices. Heaven is no longer enough; the sacrifice no longer answers every question. On the other, the fire sacrifice is given pride of place within the newer philosophical orientation: it comes first. The boy rejects the temptations of pleasures and wealth and sons and ever-so-long life, all transient, in favor of the new, secret knowledge of self (1.26–2.11; 3–4, pp. 379–403). The sacrificial and the philosophical systems interweave, strengthening each other, much as the way to *brahman* includes the world of the fathers and earlier heavens as it passes by.

What is this self? Unfamiliar as the absolute *brahman* or *ātman* within, we know it from the structure of consciousness and the relationship between consciousness and speech, Upanishadic obsessions. It is caught in the body, but like bodiless wind, rain-cloud and lightning, it rises up without a body (*CU* 8.12.2, p. 285). It is what sees with the sight, smells with the sense of smell, "The one who is aware: 'Let me say this'—that is the self; the faculty of speech enables him to speak" (8.12.4, p. 285), and it thinks with the mind. "[T]hat is *brahman*; that is the immortal; that is the self (*ātman*)" (*CU* 8.14, p. 287). It is also the ultimate origin: "In the beginning this world was the self (*ātman*), one alone, and there was no other being at all that blinked an eye. He thought to himself: 'Let me create the worlds'" (*Aitareya Upanishad* 1.1, p. 317). Ungraspable and indescribable, it nevertheless is; it is that. Afterlife enquiries lead into the self, beyond which there is nothing. Meanwhile, heavens exist, and a strange propensity for unintentional entries.

HEAVENS, HELLS, HINDUISM, AND ESCAPE HATCHES

Encouraging charity, sacrifice, and knowledge, threatening vile rebirths, the early Upanishads imagine no hells, many heavens, and release through renunciation. Hells emerge belatedly linked with dharma in the *Ramayana* and *Mahabharata*, epics separate from the Vedic tradition but claiming authority with it in Hinduism. The *Ramayana*, 200 BCE–200 CE, knows nothing of samsara and *moksha* (liberation), but attends to modeling dharma in its hero and its heaven, with reward more prominent than punishment. [47] Dharma, in Buddhism the term for doctrine or teaching, in Hinduism is duty, the duty specific to one's caste (*varna*), gender, occupation, circumstances, life stage (*ashrama*: youth who studies, householder who gains wealth and children, forest dweller who downsizes, and renouncer [*samnyasa*] who dies alive, giving up everything to seek liberation). As the web of rules and expectations that govern social life, dharma is relational, situating the person relative to others. "Everyone has a svadharma, a proper dharma, a pattern of life incumbent upon him or her that will ensure his or her welfare after death. But . . . one's svadharma is not individual or personal."[48] One's dharma is the right thing to do in any given situation, the right way to act and to be depending on one's identity, age, gender, occupation, *varnashramadharma*.

The *Ramayana*'s Yama judges in his kingdom (judging others' performance of dharma is his dharma), and everyone eats the fruit of his own actions (karma). Malefactors are ripped and boiled and burned and shredded, but however dire their situation, their misdeeds are not reported. By contrast, what constitutes good, and elicits reward, is clearly modeled. Beneficent actions—giving cattle, sharing rice, bestowing dwellings—are reciprocated.[49] A wily skeptic contests the usefulness of feeding the ancestors, implicitly challenges rebirth, and explicitly derides a world to come: "at death [everyone's] lot is annihilation just the same." Jabáli the Brahman's adharma is "at variance with righteousness."[50]

Compensating for the *Ramayana*'s omission, the *Mahabharata* explains heavens, hells, karma, and rebirth, much as Odysseus's mother explains the flight of the soul. Yudhishthira's descent to hell is anticipated discursively in the dying Bhishma's answering Yudhishthira's questions (*Book Twelve. Peace. Volume Three. The Book of Liberation*, literally *Mokṣadharma*). Both Odysseus and Yudhishthira are shocked by what they find: a relative unexpectedly dead and relatives unexpectedly in hell. The outcome is better for Yudhishthira's relatives than Odysseus's. Embodying dharma, Yudhishthira refuses to leave hell without his relations—a determination that releases them all from this dismal illusion. Like Homer's tortures, the hells are already conventional set pieces: rivers of boiling water, forests of sword leaves, ground sprouting razors, trees with thorns for impaling, and corpses with their entrails scattered. (A Jain variant has a river with waves like razors.[51])

Once Yudhishthira refuses to go to heaven and leave his people behind, the system is explained to him. Good kings on their deaths visit hell to burn away their bad karma and then ascend to heaven. Bad kings go first to heaven, burn up their good karma, and then fall away into hell. Neither heaven nor hell is permanent, and eventually both are reborn according to their karma on arrival. Yudhishthira and his went to heaven and beyond, to the world "beyond which there is nothing."[52] They did not come back: *moksha* unsought. Like the routes of the dead in the *BU*, the *Mahabharata's* account of rebirth, heavens, and hells is a minor episode relative to the cosmic metaphysics at its didactic and spiritual center, the *Bhagavad Gita* (Song of God) where, linking dharma and *bhakti* (devotion to a god), death and the self split and fuse.

The great war that will destroy two related clans about to begin, Arjuna the archer realizes he cannot bear to kill his relatives and turns to his charioteer, the god Krishna disguised, to withdraw. Arjuna would rather die than kill. *Ahimsa*, doing no harm, protecting others' dharma: surely these are absolute moral values. When men die in battle, their families, their familial law (dharma), and their dead, the ancestors, die again: "When the ritual offerings of rice and water fail, their Fathers fall degraded" (1.42).[53] Hell waits for violated dharma. Krishna persuades Arjuna that his duty as a warrior, a Kshatriya, is to kill. That is his *varnadharma*, caste duty, his righteousness, honor, virtue.

Krishna's complex and beautiful arguments begin from the self, eternal and undying, and end in vision: the god Krishna's self as the destroyer of worlds, all-consuming time. As the self occupies a changing body from childhood through adulthood to old age, so it finds a new body after death. Men lying dead on the battlefield do not die; only the impermanent, unreal body dies. The eternal self drops the body like old clothes and takes up another. Equally sure is the death of those born, and the birth of those dead: one should not grieve for what cannot be prevented (2.11–30). Far from hell, heaven opens to welcome the warrior who finds a battle unsought: "It is heaven's gate thrown wide" (2.32).

The battle suspended, Krishna takes Arjuna along many paths to self-realization and transcendence. The final vision is not self, but other. From Krishna, the worlds unroll, the origin of gods and sages, without beginning, the source of everything that is (10: "The divine splendor"). Beginning in beauty, vision ends in terror, as the infinite cosmic body of the god draws the world into its fiery jaws, consuming all beings. Arjuna cries out, "Who are you?" as he sees the men he knows on the battlefield disappear into the burning mouth. The answer, as it flashed into Robert Oppenheimer's mind, witnessing the first atomic bomb: "I am become Death, the destroyer of worlds" (11.32). The men waiting to join battle are dead already, Krishna tells Arjuna; even without your participation, they will all die. After many turns, the creating death of the *BU* reappears, more startling than ever. Death, like the self, is everything and nothing.

Once they were discovered—and Arjuna knows them—Hinduism did not give up its hells. They multiply, complicate, and systematize, perhaps in competition with Buddhism, but they also take an odd, perhaps unique turn, after a predictable, rationalizing development. The *Puranas* (300–1500 CE) explain, as the *Ramayana* does not, what misdeeds are to be punished.[54]

The *Markandeya Purana* (c. 300 CE) condemns not giving food or umbrellas, killing a cow or a father, destroying a pond. It sends perpetrators to hells named Terrible, Great Terrible, Darkness, Cutting-off, Unsupported, Sword-leaf-forest, and Hot-pot.[55] Bowker counts 6 to 28 hells with 144 sections beneath the seventh or lowest world, where punishments fit crimes. In that Sword-leaf-forest, leaves are swords that slice those who needlessly cut down trees or kill camels.[56] Other Sword-leaf-forests entice lovers to slice themselves climbing up and down a tree to a wheedling beloved.[57]

Especially in pluralistic societies, ritual rules require more reinforcement than moral rules (so the Ten Commandments start from four anomalous ritual commands: no other gods but me, no idols, no naming, keeping the Sabbath, while the remaining six appear wherever prohibitions are found). The gravest acts offend against ritual: the killer of a cow precedes in atrocity the killer of a Brahmin, who precedes killers of women, children and the old (*Agni Purana*, 1200–1500 CE). Crows rip out through the anus the intestines of men who have urinated in front of a cow, Brahmin, the sun, or fire (*Vamana Purana*, 300–1000 CE). A Muslim or Buddhist neighbor might not regard such acts as wrong. "Snatching" is a word translators of the *Puranas* often use to describe disapproved activities relative to others' wives, wealth, or mustard.[58] Cycling between heavens and hells gains a malevolent twist. Those in heavens see those in hells and know that they will fall when their merit has burned up. Those in hells see those in heavens, envy their happiness, and rejoice to see them fall.⁵⁹ Yama acquires a fanged assistant, his scribe Citragupta, determined that malefactors get what they deserve.

Yet the *Puranas* also emphasize escape, extending compassion beyond the family to strangers and insisting on the efficacy of new rituals over old. Yudhishthira's story is twice retold, of kings Vipashchit (*Markandeya Purana*, 300 CE) and Mahīratha (*Padma Purana*, 1000–1400 CE). Each time, the king bestows his merit on strangers, releasing them as he ascends to the highest heaven, beyond even meditating saints. In the *Padma Purana*, performing only Vedic rituals dooms a son's otherwise virtuous father to ten rebirths as an animal before he rises to hungry ghost, familiar Buddhist realms of rebirth. Fortunately, the son can help by observing Puranic rituals, especially the "full-moon day of Vaiśākha," of which the benefits last a thousand years. That month's "full-moon day" preserved king Mahīratha from punishment for sensual enjoyments and enabled him to release sufferers from hell. Merely watching other devotees perform such worship for a month saves a particularly vile sinner, the lapsed Brahmin Dhaneśvara, from the hell Citragupta insists he deserves. When Dhaneśvara is cast into a fiery hell, it suddenly cools. So puzzled are the wardens of hell by this undeserved escape that before being transported to another world, he is treated to what seems a Buddhist-influenced spectacle: seven named hells, of six sections each, forty-two in total but multiplied to eighty-four by the distinction between deliberate and non-deliberate actions.⁶⁰

Devotion to a god also comes to promise release or a heaven, like that awaiting Yudhishthira in the *Mahabharata*. Devotional Hinduism, implicit in Rama's divinity and explicit in the *Gita*, develops from about the third century CE. Ascent to the highest heaven, not to return, once limited to those who know the Vedas and those who practice austerities, now figures as an alternative for the devout, with heavens peculiar to Shiva (called Kailāsa), or Vishnu (Vaikuṇṭha), appropriated for their devotees.⁶¹ Daneśvara escaped from hell by idly watching other devotees worship. So, too, Shiva's heaven has been achieved even by hunters and dog-cookers who accidentally perform a Shiva-worshiping ritual.⁶² A Buddhist frog has the same kind of luck—smacked on the head while hearing a chant, he awakes in a marvelous heaven, wondering how he got there.⁶³

Success hinges on a well-spent last moment, albeit accidental. While the *Ramayana* and *Mahabharata* lay out death practices, the *Bhagavata*

Purana addresses a very specific question: "what . . . should be done by a person about to die?"[64] Death is to be prepared for, and the meaningful ending is intentional. Concentration delivers a renouncer to ātman, beyond rebirth, beyond perception, merged with the absolute. A good death, farewells made, food and drink given up, attention focused on the god or rebirth to come, takes others dying where they wish to go. Within a year, the soul will have found another body.

Accidental salvation stretches the boundaries when people—or frogs—are saved without trying. But there is an even odder twist, and it may be unique to Hinduism: the salvation by an unintended accident of the deliberately vicious in the act of committing a crime.

Jesus and the Buddha cherished the vicious, but salvation hinged on belief for Jesus and attention for the Buddha. That frog was listening to the dharma (doctrine). Reform is usually expected as a quid pro quo of salvation. But Shiva's heaven is particularly partial to "unreformed sinners." A bibulous, fornicating, dicing thief climbs on a Shiva lingam to steal a temple bell, the bell rings, and at once he is carried triumphantly to heaven.[65] Well might he wonder how he got there. Someone will explain that he had worshiped Shiva by ringing the bell and embracing the lingam. The story attests Shiva's power and accessibility, as well as the doctrine that all souls of all sentient beings will ultimately be saved, whatever their beliefs. But surely this story takes that view too far, much too far?

An implication of dharma, attributed to Gandhi, is that "Everything you do is insignificant, but you have to do it."[66] Contrariwise, if you have done it, it signifies. It counts in the accumulation of karma.

JAINS, BRIEFLY

Like Hindus, Jains are called "eternalists" in Buddhist scriptures. The *jiva*, self or soul, is as eternal and uncreated as the world itself. Rid of karma, understood as material particles created by clogging actions and emotions, the soul rises liberated above the five heavens to the top of the universe with the great ford-makers, or *tirthankara*, and other enlightened souls, omniscient, blissful, potentially infinite in number. Its materiality suggesting an early origin, Jain karma is adhesive: it clings to the *jiva* or soul like dust to a damp cloth.[67] There is no creator god who intervenes in human affairs, though many gods are equally part of the uncreated, eternal cosmos that turns like a wheel through endless eons. In those turnings, the truth of Jain practice dies out and must be brought back by a ford-maker, who teaches once again how to ford the ocean of rebirth. Mahavira ("great hero," a title like Buddha "awakened" or Christ "anointed") was the twenty-fourth. Until liberation, the soul migrates through heavens of the gods, animals, at least seven hells, plants, water, earth, air and fire, laypeople, and, in one variant, women. The sky-clad Dvigimbara Jains argue that since female ascetics cannot go naked ("sky clad") as ascetics must to achieve liberation, women can achieve liberation only after they are reborn as male. The white [cloth]-clad Shvetembara suppose male and female ascetics equally capable of liberation, but not laypeople, who accumulate merit and prevent as much influx of karma as possible. The eighteenth Shvetembara ford-maker was a woman, Malli, reborn in that form as punishment for performing more asceticism than had been agreed upon. Her Dvigimbara equivalent is male.[68]

Rebirth is immediate: the soul leaps "like a monkey" from one body to the next.[69] Although the soul moves fast, dying may take an idiosyncratic elongation—or once did. Some devout Jains have practiced death by fasting (*sallekhana*). Simultaneously they cleanse the body of karma and concentrate the mind while awaiting death to achieve liberation or a desired rebirth. Buddhist scriptures record strenuous disapproval of the practice. Today this deliberate and intentional death is uncommon as a Jain practice, but it has become a secular choice for those otherwise unable to end their lives. An after-death ritual practiced by the Shvemtabara, the *Antaraya Karma Puja*, reduces the hindrance karma of the dead so as to promote a better rebirth.[70] Inconsistent with immediate rebirth, the practice lets survivors participate in the death to help, for one last time. Beyond rebirth, the liberated soul rises unobstructed. Liberation is possible only from a human body; many gods in the heavens await rebirth in human form to achieve liberation. Hell-beings have longer to wait, since they must work their way up through animals.

And there are the plants: Jains retain the Vedic and Upanishadic integration of plants into the totality of life processes and rebirth. To plants they attribute consciousness, in their timely germination and their potential rebirth as sacred trees before a human birth.[71] Like the other religions originating in India, Jainism condemns harm to other living things. Doing no harm, *ahimsa*, the Jains take further than any other sect, extending the principle to gnats, ants, and worms, and even to root vegetables, since eating the root destroys the plant. Jain monastics often wear face masks to prevent accidentally destroying a tiny life form. From a Jain friend Gandhi learned nonviolence.

Like Death in the *Katha Upanishad*, Jains faced challenges from materialists who disputed the soul's existence. The legendary King Prasenajit scoffed that no soul emerged from the cauldron containing a criminal sealed in to die and that no soul could be found when another criminal was chopped to pieces in search of it. The monk Keshin explained: the soul was like the sound of a drum, which can be heard outside a sealed house, and chopping up the body to find soul was like chopping wood to find fire.[72] Unlike Hindus, Jains are not simple eternalists: the soul both is and is not eternal. Asked if the soul was eternal, the Mahavira said, "Yes, Jamali, the soul does not cease to exist." Asked if the soul was not eternal, the Mahavira said, "Yes, Jamali, from a hellish creature it becomes an animal, from an animal man, from man a god."[73] To such questions about existence, the Buddha answered not at all.

BUDDHISM, ONE AND MANY

Though sometimes he answered too much: did the Tathāgata still exist after he died and entered nirvana? He would not be reborn, but *was* he still? Somewhere, something? When one is talking "afterlives," that is a pretty basic question to which one might reasonably expect a clear response. "It is inept to say of him—of the Uttermost Person, the Supernal Person, the Attainer of the Supernal—that after dying the Tathāgata is, or is not, or both is and is not, or neither is nor is not . . ."[74] The problem is the question's phrasing; it is "inept," but we are not told how to ask it right. When we insist on an answer, we demonstrate precisely the clinging, craving desire that the Buddha existed—or exists—or both or neither or—to move us beyond. Buddhism both erases and generates afterlives. When it contracts to its own dharma (doctrine or teaching), the afterlife empties out, vanished. When it contemplates the sufferings of sentient beings caught in *samsara*, its starting point, it finds way upon way to rescue them. The means range from immediate enlightenment to innumerable worlds of Buddhas and bodhisattvas—and Buddhist schools.

Buddhism defines dharma as doctrine or teaching, devaluing the bio-cultural social order in favor of insight into the "universal law of becoming and passing away."[75] It denies the existence of that essential self, Ātman, that joined the eternal (Hindu) or rose to solitary bliss among other solitudes (Jain). Buddhism erased the self for "no-self." No essential, unchanging, independently subsisting entity inside us constitutes us. This sleight of mind privileges the flickering impressions and memories that were all Hume found when he looked inward, searching for self, consciousness, identity (and should cheer Daniel Dennett, unless he objects to being scooped).[76] Nor, argues the second century CE Mahāyāna philosopher Nāgārjuna, is there a ground elsewhere, outside us, in something else: every existent depends on other non-self-subsisting entities. (The obvious analogy is language: words have no absolute meaning in themselves but only relative to other words, and what relationship has language to reality?) Nothing exists of itself; everything is empty of self-existence.[77] With no self, there is equally no other, neither outside nor inside, only interdependence, relatedness, and awareness.[78]

This emptiness complicates afterlives and their status. In nirvana (Sanskrit "extinction" or "extinguished," like a candle flame), one passes beyond rebirth, beyond the five realms of existence, beyond death, into a state the Buddhist canon takes pains to differentiate from annihilation or extinction. "[T]here is an unborn, unbecome, unmade, unconditioned [that enables] escape from the born, become, made, and conditioned."[79]

In the origin story, the young man who would become the enlightened one, the Buddha, dismayed by birth, sickness, old age, and death, sought to achieve release by traditional Indian ascetic practices, as did his contemporary "Nigaṇṭha Nātaputta," as Mahavira the Jain is called in the Pali canon. For the Buddha-to-be, painful practices did not succeed. One day, under the Bodhi tree, enlightenment came, and the young man entered nirvana, an indescribable state in which desire and craving and clinging cease. He understood that life is suffering. The first human sound is a wailing cry, the last a rattle. Suffering arises from craving, craving can be ended, and there is a path that leads to the end of craving. These four noble truths enclose the Eightfold Path in the fourth. For the next twenty years, he taught the way to liberation he had found to others, and then he died, entering *parinirvana*, beyond the cycle of rebirth. He left behind the *dhamma* (in Pali, *dharma* in Sanskrit) to bind and guide his followers, his funeral to be conducted by the laity, and they also to erect *stupas* for his ashes so that those who worshipped there could achieve liberation.

As an afterlife, this is not much. Nirvana sweeps away some of the most gorgeous afterlife webs ever spun. Wandering through lifetimes, the path ends where the atheist-materialist begins, nowhere much at all. As Ajita Kesakambalin put it, the body returned to its four elements, "while his faculties went into space."[80] Nirvana or space, the names differ, but the situation seems much the same. Why bother? One answer, though not the attainment, is simple: the objective is enlightenment in this life. Once enlightened, one clings neither to self/non-self nor to desire/dread of rebirth. How one occupies one's world is transformed.[81] Another answer is that all beings exist in dependence on others, born, made, conditioned. That web of causation extends indefinitely, through "all the heavenly and human beings and the asuras of the entire world, . . . the thousand-millionfold lands."[82] The world one occupies is transformed. Buddhism is, as it happens, its own expanding and contracting cosmos, and much of the action is in the afterlives.

Siddhartha Gautama (his personal name in Sanskrit), the Buddha or "the enlightened," "the awakened," spoke Magadhi, an Indo-Aryan language related to Sanskrit. His teachings were transmitted orally, with quarrels over what constituted the canon and the true teachings emerging within seventy years of his death.[83] His traditional dates are sixth century, the Buddha, 563–483, and the Mahavira, 599–527; recent scholarship moves their lives into the fifth century, 463–383 BCE and 499–427 BCE, a century closer to Buddhist scriptures (Jain scriptures date from c. 496 CE.).[84] In the first century BCE, the teachings that reach back to the historical Siddatha Gotama (his personal name in Pali) were committed to writing in Pali in Ceylon. Called the *Tripitaka* (Three Pitakas or Baskets), the Pali canon of the Theravada tradition was fixed by the fifth century CE in some fifty-six volumes. The baskets are the *Vinaya Pitaka* or disciplinary rules of the monastic order, the *Sutta Pitaka* or discourses and sayings of the Buddha in five collections (*Long Discourses, Mid-Length Discourses, Additional,*

Miscellaneous and Small), and the *Abhidhamma Pitaka* or philosophical discourses, concerning the doctrines of the schools.[85]

Theravada Buddhists, who accept only the Pali canon, flourish from Sri Lanka to Laos and Cambodia. Sometimes designated Southern Buddhism, their practice is directed towards attaining enlightenment as a monk or nun, becoming an *arhat*, like the Buddha himself in his lifetime. Nirvana achieved, the *arhat* passes out of reach, again like the Buddha himself, but not as a Buddha, or with him. The Buddha was an *arhat*, but there is only one Buddha, at any one time. When the doctrine declines and enlightenment becomes difficult or impossible, then Maitreya, the Buddha-to-come, will restore it. There is a great gulf fixed between the Buddha and *arhats*, as between the master and disciples, but they end in the same situation.

Mahāyāna, or Northern, Buddhism has larger canons (sutras composed between the first and sixteenth centuries CE in India, Central Asia, China, Tibet) and different objectives. Every sentient being is ultimately capable of the goal, becoming a Buddha. Some take the bodhisattva vow to help others attain Buddhahood, a process taking lifetimes.[86] The bodhisattva becomes both an object of worship and a path for laity as well as monks to follow. Initially, Mahāyāna sutras were probably midrashic—filling gaps, answering questions left by the canonical texts.[87] By the seventh century CE, those who venerated bodhisattvas and aimed at Buddhahood called their orientation "Mahāyāna" ("greater [mahā] vehicle [yāna]") and denigrated those who rejected their innovations as "Hīnayāna" ("defective" or "lesser [hīna]" "vehicle [yāna]"). Monks who sought only their own enlightenment were selfish; better to attempt the bodhisattva path to help others, so the claim went once the schools separated. Mahāyāna schools extend from China, Tibet, and Vietnam to Korea and Japan, sometimes subdivided into Northern Buddhism—Tibet, Mongolia, Bali—and Eastern—China, Vietnam, Korea, and Japan.[88]

Both persuasions once flourished in the same monasteries in India, as a visiting Chinese Mahāyānist reported at the end of the seventh century CE. Monks followed the same discipline and rules, but "Those who worship the Bodhisattvas and read the Mahāyāna *Sūtras* are called the 'Mahāyānists,' while those who do not perform these are called the Hīnayānists."[89] The orientation once termed "defective" by their opponents is now designated

"Theravada," from another early school. Mahāyānists have not been the only ones to call names. C. F. Rhys Davids calls the bodhisattava a "Bîrana weed," choking out the path of self-training with "a gorgeous hierarchy of mythological wonder-workers."[90]

Buddhist dharma jolted the afterlife. The goal was to end rebirth, but the Buddha's disciples wanted to know what had become of their dead. Naming names, the Buddha tells: one has attained arahantship; sister Nandâ has "become an inheritor of the highest heavens, there to pass entirely away, thence never to return"; another has become a *Sakadâgâmin* who on his first return to this world will make an end of sorrow. Fifty have reached sister Nanda's level, ninety Sakadâgâmins, and five hundred arahants.[91] One female follower is outraged that she has been reborn in a higher heaven than three male disciples, two of whom vow to imitate her and try harder. These impressive success rates the Buddha and his followers occasionally contrasted with those of other teachers.

Buddhist rebirth tilts towards better things, from the beginning. The Buddha advises aspiration. In the order of discourse, bad rebirth precedes good: those who do not do well will be "reborn into some unhappy state of suffering or woe." Those who do well are "reborn into some happy state in heaven."[92] That order seems to emphasize bad outcomes, except that they are rapidly left behind for better and better worlds. Attention continues moving upwards as the heavens multiply, ascending *deva* realms, regions of lights and gods Radiant, Luminous, Cool, All-seeing. Heavens ascend from the pleasant, familiar heavens of desire, through many heavens of form, to heavens of formlessness that correspond to states of meditation. Except for the very highest of heavens from which one passes to nirvana without return, no heaven is permanent. The limit for the returning highest heavens is eighty-four thousand eons, a mere nine million years for the lowest.[93] There are heavens beyond heavens to try for, and something beyond even that.

A serene death is one of the five rewards of a good life.[94] Rich, respected, confident, anxiety-free, the person dying concentrates in the last moments on where to go next. As in the *Upanishads*, one may aim for strictly socio-economic improvement. The Buddha sympathetically counsels how to achieve a better material rebirth, but he also suggests one might look a little higher. The virtuous dying householder, concentrating his attention with serenity in dying, may aspire to be reborn as a wealthy Brahmin or noble or householder. Holding the thought "fixed, firmly established, and expand[ing] it . . . conduces to rebirth within that range." Or he may look higher, where *devas* in the realm of "the four kings of the firmament are long-lived, splendid in appearance and lead a blissful existence." Or he may spiral upwards to "the Three-and-Thirty gods, the Yama, the Tusita, the Nimmanarati, the Paranimmita-vasavatti gods, or [among] the gods of the Brahma world."[95] Beyond the Brahma world are other heavens of formlessness, from which nirvana can be achieved without rebirth.

Looking down, Buddhism also looks in. Hells' external tortures are internal torments. They threaten from outside and goad from within, but they are not eternal. In the *Long Discourses*, frequent terms for bad rebirths are "the waste, the woeful way, the downfall, the constant round [of transmigration.]" [96] In the *Middle Length Discourses* the familiar "five destinations" appear: hell, animal, hungry ghost, human, gods.[97] The bad would seem to outnumber the good, if we did not already know how many realms of gods there are.

With proper guidance, even the most undeserving can escape punishment and win the heaven most desired. That is one moral of the *Dhānañjāni Sutta: Sutta 97*. Another moral is that the most undeserving have potential beyond what they desire. The Buddha's disciple Sāriputta deftly leads the misbehaving brahmin Dhānañjāni from hell's pains to the Brahma world, an amazing accomplishment for which the Buddha gently chides his disciple.

Healthy and happy, Dhānañjāni plundered Brahmin households and the king; Sāriputta warned him uselessly about hell. Dying, Dhānañjāni asks the master to visit him "out of compassion." Arrived, Sāriputta asks if Dhānañjāni has the symptoms of a good death—decreasing pains—but he does not. His increasingly painful feelings resemble hell tortures: a strong man splitting my head with a sharp sword, a tough leather strap being tightened around my head, violent winds carving up my belly like a butcher an ox, violent burning as if I were being roasted over hot coals. From that hell Dhānañjāni already feels, Sāriputta leads him out, asking which is better, hell or the animal realm? Animal or ghost? Ghost or human? Human or . . .? In four questions with obvious answers Dhānañjāni is out of his own hell and into the realms of the gods, where after seven questions about which god realm is better (Yama or Tusita? etc.),

Sāriputta decides to leave Dhānañjāni in the Brahma-world, since "these brahmins are devoted to the Brahma-world." Sāriputta establishes Dhānañjāni in "the inferior Brahma-world" and goes his way "while there was still more to be done." For that the Buddha chides. Dhānañjāni had the potential to move beyond the Brahma world toward enlightenment, but now he "has died and has reappeared in the Brahma-world."[98]

Comical and endearing, the sutta takes the student through the levels, reveals the importance of the moment of dying, in which Dhānañjāni is able to reverse a lifetime of misdeeds, sneers at brahmins' contentment with the "inferior" Brahma-world (the highest heaven in non-Buddhist contexts), and marks the familiar pains of sickness as one source of hell's tortures. Penal codes are another source of hell tortures. Sadistic hellish tortures imagined for the dead derive, after all, from sadistic tortures inflicted on living bodies.

The peculiar horrors of the *Bālapaṇḍita Sutta (Fools and Wise Men)* 129, in the *Middle Length Discourses*, derive from the penal system feared by the guilty. The living fool sees what is done by kings to robbers, and realizes he too deserves such punishments. They are grisly indeed: "flogged with whips, beaten with canes, beaten with clubs, having his hands cut off, his feet cut off, his hands and feet cut off; his ears cut off, his nose cut off, his ears and nose cut off; having him subjected to the 'porridge pot,' to the 'polished-shell shave,' to the 'Rāhu's mouth,' to the 'fiery wreath,' to the 'flaming hand,' to the 'blades of grass,' to the 'bark dress,' to the 'antelope,' to the 'meat hooks,' to the 'coins,' to the 'lye pickling,' to the 'pivoting pin,' to the 'rolled up palliasse,' and then splashed with boiling oil, thrown to be devoured by dogs, impaled alive on stakes, and his head cut off with a sword."[99] The fool knows he deserves such treatment now, and fears it after he dies, tormenting himself while he lives, as Lucretius assures us fools do. Ultimately, the poor fool is reborn into a poor human condition, outcast, scavenger, destitute, deformed, ugly, with none of life's good things. Doing amiss, he dies and goes to hell once again, "the complete perfection of the fool's grade."

For the wise man, the outcome is pleasant: the seven treasures and four successes of "a Wheel-turning Monarch." The seven treasures are the wheel-treasure, which rolls triumphing over the whole earth; the elephant-treasure, a flying white elephant for the king to ride; the horse-treasure, a flying white horse with a raven-black head; the jewel-treasure, a glowing beryl; the woman-treasure, a perfect human beauty, eager to serve, sweet in speech, with warm limbs in cool weather and cool limbs in warm weather, chaste, breathing lotus and exuding sandalwood; the steward-treasure, who produces gold whenever it is wanted; and the counsellor-treasure, who governs on the king's behalf. Indeed, the wheel-turning monarch has nothing to do except preside over the world, fly his horse or his elephant and be adored. Beautiful, long-lived, with a good digestion, he is loved by Brahmins and householders, so he orders his charioteer to drive more slowly so that they may look at him longer, as they have requested. The wise man who enjoys this heaven will be reborn in a noble or rich household, where he will enjoy his beauty and other good things, "clothes, vehicles, garlands, scents, and unguents." He will act well and be reborn in another heaven when he dies.[100]

The wise man evidently has other things than enlightenment in view. Repurposing and expanding *Sutta* 129's account of hell, the *Devadūta Sutta (The Divine Messengers): Sutta* 130 trades in the wheel-turning monarch's pleasures for the Buddha's own enlightenment narrative and insists on personal responsibility. When the "wardens of hell" bring the worst of the dead before him, King Yama, fallen far from the Vedic realm of the fathers, catechizes them one by one about the "divine messengers." Have they seen an infant fouled in its excrement (birth), a hideous old man or woman (age), an adult fouled in excrement (sickness), a prisoner tortured (with details verbatim from Sutta 129), and a corpse one to three days old, "dead, bloated, livid, and oozing with matter" (death)? Repeated after every question is a reminder. "[T]his evil action of yours was not done by your mother or your father, or by your brother or your sister, or by your friends and companions, or by your kinsmen and relatives, or by recluses and brahmins, or by gods: this evil action was done by you yourself, and you yourself will experience its result."[101] The English cadence could be mistaken for Deuteronomy. From 130.10–16, the text is identical with Sutta 129.10–16, but at 130.17, instead of tracking off to the animal realm, hells keep flaming, externally and internally.

In the Great Hell, flames surge from wall to wall; the sufferer attempts escape through an opening door that closes as he reaches it. The eastern door finally lets him out into a new series of named hells: Excrement, Hot Embers, Simbali Trees, Wood of Sword-leaf Trees, then into a caustic river. Dragged out, he is force-fed hot metal balls (a common feature in hungry ghost scrolls) and molten copper for drink, and then thrown back into the Great Hell. At the end of each torture, "he feels painful, racking, piercing feelings." Proceeding torture by torture through the sutra, not by horrific excerpts, that repetition, "painful, racking, piercing feelings," creates inwardness. The physical descriptions transform themselves into accounts of inner states, like a very long and unpleasant anxiety attack. Or a very bad dream: more than anyone else King Yama wants out and to learn the Dhamma. (Awakening is possible, the very last lines assure us.)

Later texts systematize and moralize the hells—and are given more privileged positions in the canon. The *Mahāvastu* introduces the *Vinaya-pitaka*, the first basket containing the rules for monastics and tells its hells three times.[102] A venerable old man visits hell and then all the "other worlds," from animals to eight levels of heavenly devas. The hells are laid out systematically: 8 great hells have 16 secondary hells, making 136. The first telling names the hells, describes the tortures, and explains that the sufferers "do not die, because they are upheld by karma." The second description shrinks to a schematic, and the final repetition expands, moralizing the hells, fitting specific acts to appropriate tortures.

The acts condemned are principally violence against other sentient beings, both human and animal, though hostile thoughts and anger are condemned to the same hatchet-cutting hell as warring kings, thieves, and soldiers. Swords and daggers grow on the hands of those who urged war against villages, and now they slice each other up. (Frequently pictured, such images inspired Saigyō's twelfth-century poetic sequence.[103]) Among the darker paradoxes is being shredded from neck to hip for preparing instruments of torture. Mountains crush those who crushed lice with their fingernails or smashed worms or bludgeoned living creatures to death. Monkeys, rats, serpents, bees, scorpions, centipedes, wild animals, sheep: all are avenged in named hells. These crimes reach out to catch ordinary people—who would not crush the head of a scorpion?

In the other realms, the hungry ghosts have their thin necks and huge bellies, their bald and repulsive heads. They feed on excrement and phlegm and pus, longing for rice and water, never obtaining them. The beast level is rarely represented visually, its problems ignorance, asociality, and violence better laid out in words: "They knew neither mother nor father, neither brother nor sister, neither teacher nor teacher's pupil, neither friend nor kinsman. They devoured one another and drank one another's blood. They slew and strangled one another. From darkness they passed into darkness. . . ." The *ashuras*, or angry demons, as a sixth level mark the text as late. They are appropriately huge, angry, and hideous. Skipping the human level, the text passes to the devas, the heavens, and runs through the levels, each more beautiful than the last. But none is permanent—except those remote heavens in which an *arhat* can achieve full Buddhahood.

That gesture indicates Mahāyāna inflection, and with Mahāyāna, even the highest aspiration ascends. The goal is no longer to be an *arhat*, liberated, but to be a buddha. Once there was only one; in Mahāyāna there are many. As the *Lotus Sutra* has it, the Buddha preaches various doctrines that fit the needs of diverse living beings, but concludes, "At all times I think to myself: / How can I cause living beings/ to gain entry into the unsurpassed way/ and quickly acquire the body of a Buddha?"[104]

The *Lotus Sutra* is among the most influential Mahāyāna texts, the basis of several Chinese and Japanese schools, Tiantai (China, Vietnam), Tendai (Japan), Cheontae (Korea), and Nichiren (Japan). It may have originated in Central Asia or India in a regional dialect, but first appears in Chinese translation, 255 CE.[105] It rebalances Mahāyāna emptiness, skill in means, and the bodhisattva way.

Of emptiness the principal philosopher is Nāgārjuna (c. 150–250 CE, south India). The corollary of non-self, emptiness registers the nonexistence of essences or substance, of anything pertaining to "I" or ego, of any ultimate ground. As Westerhoff points out, Hume was perfectly comfortable with a non-self that acted as if it thought it were a self, but for Nāgārjuna that illusion interferes with the apprehension of reality, of Buddha nature, and one mind.[106] He wants to correct cognition: that is hard. There is no difference between samsara and nirvana, Nāgārjuna declared. The world, "a web of fluxing, interdependent, baseless phenomena," is "empty of inherent nature," but relational. "Unconditioned" nirvana contrasts with "conditioned" samsara as the same field traversed by insight and by ignorance.[107] Samsara becomes as ungraspable as nirvana has always been. Later, Pure Land advocates claimed Nāgārjuna as an authority.[108] One of them, challenged as to why anyone should follow the path if samsara and nirvana were the same, replied that if the questioner found samsara satisfying, he should stay there; if he did not, he could return to pursue the path.

"Emptiness" the *Lotus Sutra* carries concealed within it. "Skill in means," skillful means or expedient means, it obtrudes: the Buddha adapts his teaching to the level of his hearers. It follows that there are two categories of truth: ultimate and conventional (or provisional). A teaching may be not "true" but only "provisional," suitable to a student at a certain level and abandoned as the student increases in proficiency. Ultimate truth dissolves conventional teaching. Which truth is ultimate and which conventional will, in turn, divide schools.[109]

Merely reciting or copying the *Lotus Sutra* leads to salvation, the *Lotus Sutra* assures its auditors and readers. It discloses vast Buddha lands, Buddhas, bodhisattvas, Brahma gods, dragon kings, *gandharva* and *garuda* kings, *arhats*, nuns. Inclusive and generous, it knows nothing of hell, except for those who slander the sutra itself. They are reborn in the lowest hell or as a scabby dog with oozing sores. No horrific details are offered about hell, though if a sutra-slanderer should be reborn human, he will be ugly and have bad breath and odor. People he gives medicines to will die. The sutra skips supernatural hungry ghost and *ashura* realms for animal sufferings in those who cut off their "buddha-seeds."[110] Promising "peace in this life, good rebirth in the afterlife," it assures its listeners that whatever their spiritual capacity, the Buddha fits each: "It is like the rain falling from that great cloud upon all the plants and trees, thickets and groves, and medicinal herbs. Each, depending upon its species and nature, receives its full share of moistening and is enabled to sprout and grow."[111] Yet amidst all this burgeoning, the ultimate is emptiness, separation from desire, extinction of grasping:

> The Thus Come One knows that this is the Law of one form, one flavor, namely, the form of emancipation, the form of separation, the form of extinction, the form of ultimate nirvana, of constant tranquility and extinction, which in the end finds its destination in emptiness. The Buddha understands all this. But because he can see the desires that are in the minds of living beings, he guides and protects them, and for this reason does not immediately preach to them the wisdom that embraces all species.[112]

Emancipation, separation, extinction, nirvana, tranquility, extinction: Divide six into two sets of three: emancipation, separation, extinction.

Nirvana, tranquility, extinction. Nirvana is emancipation; separation is tranquility. Divide six into three sets of two: emancipation, separation. Extinction, nirvana. Tranquitility, extinction. The end is emptiness. Emptiness is entering the body of a Buddha. What happened to flying elephants? Or copying the sutra?

With its gorgeous evocation of worlds, the *Lotus Sutra* supplies the phrase and the narrative that erases its own structure, but accommodates every reading: the story of the burning house and the doctrine of expedient means. A father sees his children at play in a house on fire; he offers them a goat-cart, deer-cart, ox-cart, anything they want to get them out of the house. They run eagerly out, but there are no little carts: instead he gives each a huge jewel-laden carriage.[113] Was he lying? Was he deceiving them? Or was he using "skillful means" to save them? The father is the Buddha or the dharma; the burning house is this world, the little carts other Buddhist vehicles (the *arhat*, voice hearer or disciple, who heard the words of a Buddha and attained nirvana; the pratyeka-buddha or solitary buddha who awakened by his own efforts, often practicing in the forest; the bodhisattva who sets out to become a perfect buddha and to awaken others[114]). The single jewel-laden vehicle is Buddhahood, and what then is the truth of Buddhism? Is it a jeweled carriage or extinction or emptiness beyond jeweled carriages? All or none? Or some?

The question is inept. With no ending and no beginning, there can be no middle, as Nāgārjuna says.[115]

CHINA BEFORE BUDDHISM

Entering China about 60 CE, Buddhism encountered ancestors, spirits, popular gods, proto-Daoist Way[s], the Confucian *Tian* or Heaven, and as destination for the dead, the Yellow Springs. Established, entrenched, competitive, vital, each was intertwined with ritual and divinatory practices and staked out alternative approaches to death while blurring boundaries with borrowings. There was no trace of a moralized afterlife with rewards and punishments to be enjoyed after death or any certain method to live again—though ancestors could die again. Buddhism offered something quite new: karmic rebirth, a moralized opportunity to possess another life. As philosophically fertile as India in the Buddha's time, the fifth to third centuries BCE had been in China the period of "100 Schools," of Confucius, Mencius, Mozi (Mo Di), Zhuangzi (Chuang Tzu), Laozi (Lao Tze, "Old Master"), succeeded in the first century CE by the rationalist Wang Chong. The Yellow Springs will be familiar: an ancient, subterranean underworld without reward, without punishment, to which all the dead depart and where they are reunited, and so carry insignia of rank for recognition.

Exiling his mother in 721 BCE for her attempt to seize power, a ruler vowed they would meet again only in the Yellow Springs. A loving couple commit suicide, going together to the Yellow Springs. Even the skeptical Wang Chong (27–97 CE) accepted the Yellow Springs as a destination. A tomb was a disagreeable "hole dug underground beside the Yellow Springs."[116] Of the dead, a Han poet wrote that they lie "asleep below the Yellow Springs, never to awake in a thousand years."[117] A "Land of Darkness," presided over by a grim queen of the earth, the Yellow Springs persisted,[118] but Han and later tombs show there came to be considerable activity underground—dancing, music, visits. Above ground there were earnest efforts not to die at all, to live very long, to be immortal.

Ancestor worship did not, however, abet any of those goals, except protecting longevity. Ancestors, while in some sense alive, have no lives of their own. Characteristic of ancestor worship is vagueness about where precisely the ancestors are or who they were (as they recede in time) and what they are doing. They have a place in the calendar and the rituals that honor them, but they also have new names, not those of the persons they were when alive, that fix them in the ritual system of invocation and sacrifice. They are also vulnerable, as in the *Gita*. They depend on their descendants not only for existence—no descendant, no ancestor—but also for sustenance. If they are not fed, they die again. Abandoned, hungry, they may trouble other families.[119]

The Shang dynasty (c. 1200–1045 BCE), its oracle bones' inscriptions the earliest writing in east Asia, had no netherworld gods, but ancestors for twenty-one generations (from us to Chaucer) confirmed their claim on political power. The ancestors were consulted over the ruler's own health, safety, and ritual correctness. The ancestresses—and to qualify one had to be both the wife of a king who was the son of a king and the mother of a king—were asked only for progeny and received less auspicious name days. Other gods, of rain, lightning, sun, and moon, received prayers over such crucial public matters as rain, insects, and harvests.[120] Shang ancestor worship began with grandparents. Dying parents grieved or relieved their offspring, but did not become ancestors until after their son's death, and only if he had a male child.

As a system for binding generations, and ensuring that there be generations and male privilege, a better could scarcely be devised. Ancestors protect and empower, but they also depend. The descendants whom they produce and for whom they provide continue to be responsible for them and their well-being. When the Zhou overthrew the Shang, inadvertently demonstrating (Keightley observes) the Shang ancestors' failure to protect their clan, the Zhou did not do away with ancestor worship, but reformed it, as if they understood its appeal and utility. Royals would have seven generations of ancestors to revere and commoners two—parents and grandparents.

The watchful eye of the ancestors also policed. In a text probably from the Western Zhou (1027–771 BCE), a Shang ruler threatens that his people's own ancestors will punish them for their refusal to cooperate with him: "Our former rulers [his ancestors] will restrain your ancestors and fathers (so that) your ancestors and fathers will reject you, and not save you from death.... Your ancestors and fathers urgently report to my High Rulers, saying, 'Execute great punishments on our descendants.'"[121] Such ancestors were very much living presences, however remote and depersonalized they might be as the ladder of generations rose out of sight. A lament from the *Shih Ching (Book of Songs*, c. 600 BCE) puts the ancestors' failure to protect where an Egyptian, Babylonian, or Israelite deplores the inscrutability of his god: "The fourth month was summer weather;/ The sixth month, blistering heat./ Have our ancestors no compassion/ That they can bear to see us suffer?"[122]

Many more poems celebrate the blessings bestowed by the ancestors, pleased with the food and drink offered them at banquets, when someone played the ancestor receiving the offerings. Whatever external controls the ancestors exercised, they were less powerful than the internal controls created by the awareness of their presence. The Han practiced visualization techniques during sacrifices. Imagining the home, the voice, the aimless conversation of the dead made them present.[123] Such techniques suggested that the ancestors were summoned up by the mind and revered in the name tablet. They did not reside in the tablet or cluster in some void waiting to be called, as Zhu Xi put it (twelfth century CE).[124] But the ancestors had nothing to say about what it was like being dead.

Nor did Confucianism address that question directly, though proto-Daoism considered it. Both fitted death into the natural or social order, though proto-Daoists often tweaked the nose of Confucian social order. These antithetical traditions, subversive and orderly, mystical and harmonious, play back and forth against each other, sometimes bitterly opposed, often mutually appreciative and understood as comprehending different registers of action and meaning. By 86 BCE Confucius and Laozi were thought to be contemporaries, with Laozi about twenty years older than Confucius (traditional dates 551–479 BCE). Confucius's "Conversations," the Chinese title of the *Analects*, assumed their present form about a hundred years after his death.[125] Confucius's reality seems certain, but the archives official who vanished after giving a 5000 character book, the *Dao de Jing*, to the Keeper of the Pass has largely been abandoned as an identity.[126] Given, however, that the name "Laozi" means "old [lao] master [zi]," we can safely say it could have been written by no other, whoever he was. The other principal proto-Daoist text is the *Zhuangzi* (*Chuang Tzu*) by Zhuangzi (Chuang Tzu), that is, Master Zhuang, a century later, between 370 and 301 BCE, the time of Confucius's disciple Mencius in the Warring States period.

Confucius declined inquiries about that world of spirits in favor of the way (*dao*) of this world under heaven (*tian*). In the Christian West, heaven is the abode of an anthropomorphic God and his saints, while the godless and amoral "way of the world," from Bunyan's Mr. Worldly Wiseman to Congreve's *Way of the World*, is its antithesis. Heaven for Confucius is neither anthropocentric nor an abode. It is the order of nature, comprehending the progress of the seasons, the movements of celestial bodies, the proper functioning of states, kingdoms, families, the life spans of living beings. Heaven and earth, with man in between, proceed by rule. Obeying the rules and rituals established in the past secures the prosperity of the present. "Tend carefully to death rites, and pay reverence to those long departed, and the people will in the end be rich in virtue." As to the spirits of the dead and death itself, those Confucius deftly sidestepped: "When you don't yet understand life, how can you understand death?"[127]

Insisting on reverence for the long dead and fidelity to the rituals, Confucian tradition relegated to folklore traditional animist, oracular afterlife practices and beliefs, scoffing at superstition, yet without the hostility with which Deuteronomists quashed the dead in ancient Israel or Wang Chong expostulated in the first century CE against ghosts, revenants, and communication with the dead.[128] Insofar as Confucius addressed spirits, they were a force for good: "Bounteous indeed is the moral force of the ghosts and spirits."[129] There remained intense empathy with bodies of the dead and graves of the ancestors: a soul remained in the body after death. Confucius hearing a report of burned bones responded with horror to the pain the dead must have suffered, and he wept when he learned his father's tomb had been damaged in a flood.[130] Such stories about Confucius, like those about the Buddha, come from long after Confucius himself and evidence the attitudes his admirers attributed to him and presumably shared.

At death for Confucius the two souls that make up the living person separate and change their names. The *po*, renamed *gui*, remains with the body, and the *hun* or spirit, renamed *shen*, departs to "a condition of glorious brightness."[131] To the *hun* the ritual of calling back the dead is addressed: if the *hun* does not return, the person dies.[132] In the *Book of Rites (Li chi)*, Confucius explains that " 'ghost' means the *po* that remains underground after death, but the spirit, or *hun*, flies on high to become a divine being. 'Once this opposition is established,' the Master continued, 'two kinds of rituals are framed in accordance and (different) sacrifices are regulated.' "[133] Burning fat and scented wood for the *shen* brings to mind the ancestors. Grain, liver, delicacies, and liquor for the *gui*, or animal spirit, remind people to love one another and cultivate good feelings for those around them. The rituals stabilize the present and join present to past. Beyond the rituals, the rules for mourning, and his feeling for the *po*'s vulnerability, Confucius does not go. A powerful ideational structure imbricated with ritual actions requires no afterlife to enforce morality, and rituals console survivors. Confucian forms coordinated the family, the state, the heavens, and the individual for the sake of this world, which includes all others.

The early proto-Daoist texts, the *Dao de Jing* and *Zhuangzi*, punctured Confucian social order in favor of a natural order equally accepting of death but contemptuous of ritual, convention, and common sense. *Dao* means "way," a favorite term of Confucius for the proper functioning of society under Heaven (*Tian*). The Daoist Way is, by contrast, paradoxical, inexplicable, elusive. Slippery and stimulating, it presses against and slips past meaning. The *Dao de Jing* begins by defining its terms:

> The Tao that can be spoken is not the eternal Tao;
> The name that can be named is not the eternal name.
> The Nameless is the origin of Heaven and Earth,
> The Named is the mother of all things. [134]

Parsing such sentences can occupy—and has—many lifetimes. The *Dao de Jing* speaks often of death, of the spirits made harmless by the Dao's hegemony (#60), of the dead as stiff and strong, the new born pliant, weak, and superior (#76), of the people, who do not fear death and lightly lose their lives (#74, 75). Long life is desirable (#55, 59), death inevitable, caused by desire for life. One section (#50) anticipates the invulnerability of Daoist immortals and has also been read from a Buddhist perspective as passing beyond life and death into non-being:

> Man comes in to life and goes out to death.
> Three out of ten are companions of life.
> Three out of ten are companions of death.
> And three out of ten in their lives lead from activity to death.
> And for what reason?
> Because of man's intensive striving after life.
>
> I have heard that one who is a good preserver of his life will not
>   meet tigers or wild buffaloes,
> And in fighting will not try to escape from weapons of war.
> The wild buffalo cannot butt its horns against him,
> The tiger cannot fasten its claws in him,
> And weapons of war cannot thrust their blades into him.
> And for what reason?
> Because in him there is no room for death.[135]

Striving after life leads to death, but a good preserver of life is invulnerable to death. How is one to leave no room for death without striving intensely after life? That is the secret of the immortals, who make their first literary appearance in *Zhuangzi*. Their lives are collected in *Liexian Zhuan* (*Collected Biographies of Immortals*, ed. Lu Xiang, c. 79–8 BCE), and their mysterious diet informs the macrobiotic instructions found in manuscripts in tombs.[136]

For the Confucian whose Way is something to be followed, a path, the Daoist tangles the mind. More teasing and less portentous than Laozi, Zhuangzi challenges the transparency of language, the medium we live in: "Words exist because of meaning; once you've gotten the meaning, you can forget the words. Where can I find a man who has forgotten words so I can have a word with him?"[137] Irreverent, yet profound, Zhuangzi also challenges the rites and even the nature of death.

Correct mourning rituals, the central concern of the Confucian *Book of Rites*, the *Zhuangzi* violates shockingly in multiple anecdotes. Zhuangzi's wife dies, and he is found beside her corpse singing and drumming a tub. He explains to his horrified friend that his wife's progress from nothing to nothing is merely "the order of things pass[ing] on": "I looked back to her beginning and the time before she was born. . . . In the midst of the jumble of wonder and mystery a change took place and she had a spirit. Another change and she had a body. Another change and she was born. Now there's been another change and she's dead. It's just like the progression of the four seasons, spring, summer, fall, winter."[138] Death belongs. "[I]f I think well of my life, for the same reason I must think well of my death."[139] Rather than devaluing or de-terrorizing death by making it nothing, in the Lucretian mode, Zhuangzi gives death a positive, if momentary, value. Going further, he considers the condition of being dead as potentially superior to being alive.

Playing with that paradoxical possibility, Zhuangzi turns over many metaphors. Death might be a way back to the home of one's youth, a captivity better than the freedom one has lost (Lady Li), a situation one would not trade for a kingdom, or so a skull tells him. Traveling, Zhuangzi sees a clean skull beside the road and asks it what it did wrong to lie unburied and exposed, supposing three types of evil deeds, or perhaps just cold and hunger, or perhaps just time. He uses the skull for a pillow that night, and the skull appears in a dream full of contempt for Zhuangzi's foolish living ideas. "Among the dead there are no rulers above, no subjects below, and no chores of the four seasons. With nothing to do, our springs and autumns are as endless as heaven and earth. A king facing south on his throne could have no more happiness than this." Zhuangzi does not buy it: if the Clerk of Destinies re-fleshed him, surely the skull would want to return to parents, family, home? The skull wrinkles his fleshless brow and seems to say no, "Why would I throw away more happiness than that of a king on a throne and take on the troubles of a human being again?"[140] The skull's account of death is very dead: there is no secret or hidden life in it. To the skull's question, a medical text has a quick answer in another question and answer: "What is the most valuable thing under Heaven? Life."[141]

The opportunity to be re-fleshed by the Clerk of Destinies was not entirely theoretical. In 297 BCE, three years after his death, a man was returned to life after an appeal to "the Director of the Life-mandate" initiated by his patron, the general Xi Wu.[142] The resurrection account turned up in a tomb dating before 206 BCE, too late for the historical Zhuangzi (370–301 BCE), but not for additions to the original text. Under such circumstances, the skull's rejection becomes more considered, emphatic, and paradoxical. There is no violation of common sense. That belongs to the earliest literary portrayal of an immortal old flying man, perhaps a popular belief, perhaps a poet's invention elaborating Laozi's "one. . . . good preserver of his life." Zhuangzi unleashes the fantastic immortals of later religion, art, and story and deadly practical research.

Ying-shih Yü cites Zhuangzi's first chapter as the earliest description of ascetic, reclusive, "otherworldly" immortals: "Far away on the mountain of Gu Ye there lived a spiritual man. His flesh and skin were like ice and snow. His manner was elegant and graceful as that of a maiden. He did not eat any of the five grains, but inhaled the wind and drank the dew. He rode on clouds, drove along the flying dragons, and thus rambled beyond the four seas."[143] The person reporting this phenomenon finds it "insane and refuse[s] to believe it."

His companion scolds him for his misunderstanding: "This man, with this virtue of his, is about to embrace the ten thousand things and roll them into one. . . . There is nothing that can harm this man. Though flood waters pile up to the sky, he will not drown. Though a great drought melts metal and stone and scorches the earth and hills, he will not be burned. . . . Why should he consent to bother about mere things?"[144]

The response slides smoothly from the challenge to such a person's existence (repeated by Wang Chong in the first century CE, "The Spuriousness of the Tao"[145]) to a defense of his abandoning his Confucian social responsibilities. Similarly, the three friends, of whom two sang to the third's corpse, had prized joining with others without joining with others, leaving earth below: "Who can climb up to heaven and wander in the mists, roam the infinite, and forget life forever and forever?"[146] While Confucians, Legalists, and Mohists left it alone, other proto-Daoists scrambled after real immortality. *Immortality* sometimes meant merely "longevity," but it also slid beyond longevity to not dying at all.

The boundary is difficult to police: a quest for "immortality" becomes mere "longevity" when someone dies. Not dying was sought through diet, breathing, herbs, elixirs, yogic practices, alchemical researches, and magical practices to bypass death. More than one Han emperor lost his life taking poisonous elixirs, including cinnabar, that promised to lengthen what they ended. In the Six Dynasties period (220–589), Daoist texts propose three to twenty-one ways to make cinnabar edible.[147] Living long, becoming a spirit, freeing oneself from form (as his friends sing Sanghu has done in *Zhuangzi*), traveling magically through the cosmos appear in the medical literature of the age: "Long life is generated through storing and accumulating. As for the increasing of this life, above one observes in the Heavens, and below one distributes to the Earth. He who is capable will invariably become a spirit. He will therefore be able to be liberated from his form. He who clarifies the great way travels and traverses the clouds."[148]

This world adjoined another, rich in paradises, immortals, elixirs of immortality. It enjoyed isles of the blessed and Mt. Penglai, where peaches ripen once in three thousand years. With a bureaucratic netherworld and thirty-two heavens, there were occasional ascents to heaven by daylight, and, more rarely, a resurrection. The Yellow Emperor departed for heaven on a dragon's back, accompanied by a harem of seventy. A prince who died in 122 BCE took his household including dogs and cocks. In 7 BCE a humble official named Tang Gongfang took his wife, family, animals, and house (daubed with immortality ointment) in his translation into another existence. The *Canon of Immortality (Xian Jing)* explained that persons of high rank could escape death, but lower ranking persons had to die, shedding their bodies like cicadas.[149] The empty tomb—clothing folded up, no body—was a popular motif.[150]

The desire for an existence elsewhere just like this one had long been expressed in tombs. Underground, a bureaucracy saw to the etiquette and administration of death, while activities, entertainments, visits, and paradises flourished, for those who could afford them. Among the entertainments was reading. In jade headrests, on bamboo slips, people carried with them their favorite texts, ranging from copies of *Laozi* in a concubine's tomb (c. 233–202 BCE) to medical texts instructing in proper diet and care of the yin (penis), and hopeful tales of other people's resurrections.[151] These dead now share their reading, adding texts unknown before the excavation of the tombs. (Had the Greeks done the same, we might have Sappho.) Writing tools—ink stones, ink, and brushes—also appear, as if official duties, Jessica Rawson suggests, or poetry were to continue in the tomb.[152]

From Neolithic times (c. 4000 BCE) the Chinese had buried their dead with utensils and food. Dragons, tigers, and constellations later represented the cosmos.[153] They invented coffins, and the *I Ching* comments on the change. From the Shang through the early Han (third century BCE), they took others with them. Human sacrifices numbering 166 at the highest to 5 at the lowest, accompanied important deceased persons. Some persons sacrificed had their own coffins near the center; others lay at the periphery without coffins. Some had their own burial goods; others were mutilated. Attendance, but also protection: tombs of fallen Qin rulers were promptly vandalized.[154]

The persistence of human sacrifice down to the third century BCE, diminishing from the fourth century,[155] suggests an unwillingness to send powerful dead below alone or, given the advance planning such tombs required, the unwillingness of the living to descend without such company as they were accustomed to. In the fifth century BCE, the first tomb found with apertures for the *po* to circulate surrounded its marquis with eight women in coffins in his chamber, and thirteen in another chamber. He would not be lonely, or bored, with such companionship. Perhaps they shared the gold vessels for food under his coffin.[156] There would always be someone there, someone he already knew.

In the Eastern Zhou (771–256 BCE), terrestrial deities appear who might be underworld deities: Lord of the Earth, Master of the Place, God of Posthumous Journey, God of Life-Mandate, and deities to manage dangerous ghosts who died unnaturally.[157] Tombs acquired beds, tables and lamps, often of better quality than the traditional ritual offerings.[158] From about the fifth century BCE, what Wu Hung calls "the happy home," and

Jessica Rawson "a new view of the universe," begins to appear. Tombs represent a cosmic environment, the immortal paradise (from early Han), and comfortable living spaces—as if "the tomb builders provided all the answers they knew to questions about the afterlife."[159] Enjoying musical instruments, elaborate foodstuffs, and doors and windows, the *po* soul moves about.

Inscriptions from Han tombs record nearly twenty kinds of subterranean officials who govern the netherworld in general and tombs specifically.[160] In 168 BCE, the Household Assistant from the family of the Marquis of Dai wrote to the *langzhong* in charge of the dead with a "list of mortuary objects" to be forwarded to "the Lord of the Grave (Zhusang Jun)." Three tiers communicate: the Household Assistant in this world, "the Assistant in charge of funeral goods" in the next who receives the complete list of goods to transmit to his superior, "the Lord Administrator of funeral goods."[161] Functionaries addressed those of their own rank, so a town's Assistant Magistrate addressed the "Underworld Assistant." Sometimes the deceased reported his death himself to the underworld Lord (Dixia Zhu).[162] The officials were often historical figures, transplanted to another life. As in other bureaucracies, there is error: and this bureaucracy corrects it. When Xi Wu declared that Dan had been summoned too early, "he was not yet fated to die," the mistake was rectified, after three years.[163]

Coordinating this world and the next, as he consolidated China, the Emperor Wu (r. 141–87 BCE) cobbled together spirit worlds.[164] Confucius had been dead about three hundred years when the emperor declared Confucianism the official doctrine of the state.[165] He modeled his palace and gardens on a Daoist paradise.[166] When a *fang shih*, or diviner, told him that T'ai i was the supreme celestial deity, he established the worship of T'ai i (Grand One) at his capital in 113 BCE.[167] He sought elixirs of immortality, sending ships in quest of the blessed isles. Disappointed by a Daoist practitioner who died before he delivered the promised elixir, he executed the next two practitioners before they failed him.

As the emperor intervened to shape heaven, Heaven became more interventionist.[168] In the *Huai-nan tzu*, ante 139 BCE, fusing Confucian, legalist, and Daoist materials, Heaven, acting in this world (the only one, multileveled), punishes the unjust, as earthly sovereigns do, while it rewards the virtuous by saving them from death.[169] That responsibility had been the ancestors', not heaven's, the family's, not the state's. Wang Chong criticizes the concept, in the first century CE.[170] Others criticized Heaven's justice when the wise and good suffered untimely deaths and misfortunes.[171] A monotheistic problem that dualism solves and polytheism avoids, dubious events became Heaven's will, rather than the outcome of a contest between ancestors and families or the meddling of spirits of the heavens, winds, stars, mountains, water, death, and the grave. Meanwhile some thirty-six thousand demons were required by ordinance to keep away from tombs, their names listed and persons described for 320.[172]

Gorgeous as were the tombs, hopeful the medical texts, orderly the rituals, with misty blessed isles circled by immortals, not everyone was reconciled to loss, or imagined a destination for the vanished spirit even so certain as the Yellow Springs. So Cai Yong (132–192 CE) lamented Lady Ma:

> She is gone, never to return,
> Sinking into the great darkness.
> O! Alas!
> Her table and mat are set out in vain;
> Her curtains and screens are put up to no purpose.
> Such things are still here,
> But we don't see their owner.
>
> The qi[173] of her hun soul whirls and drifts.
> Where can we settle her spirit?
> Upon what can her sons (now) depend?
> And to what can her daughters draw near?[174]

NEW DIRECTIONS IN CHINA: PURE LAND AND CH'AN

When Buddhism reached China after 60 CE, its missionaries proceeding north through Gandhara and Afghanistan and then east, the Buddha was taken for a western barbarian flying immortal, able to bring good fortune. Its key concepts were translated at first in Daoist terms.[175] It seemed clear that when Laozi disappeared, he had gone south and become known as "Buddha." Daoist metaphysics led Wang Fu (90?–165?), the Confucian political thinker, to complain that "Scholars nowadays like to talk about matters concerning vacuity and nonbeing."[176] The Buddhist variants emptiness and non-self proved equally stimulating.

In the first millennium CE, Buddhism and Daoism, John Lagerwey suggests, "run each other ragged and wear each other smooth in a complex process involving debate, plagiarism, appropriation, revelation, and synthesis" until "a relatively harmonious cohabitation" of Buddhism, Daoism, popular religion, and Confucianism emerges in the Tang (618–907).[177] Daniel Overmyer places the emergence of Daoism proper between the second and fifth centuries CE.[178] The timing suggests provocation by Buddhist competition, and the Taoist Canon charts the absorption of Buddhist ideas and images, though Buddhists never conquered the tombs. Among the dead in a sixth-century CE sarcophagus, Daoist deities fly, wings sprouting from their shoulders, dragons drawing chariots through the sky, female deities drawn by tigers, hares running through hillsides, jeweled flowers, musical processions. Scenes of nature, deities, immortals, dragons, clouds, and flying: Daoist paradises liberated the dead.[179] Choice was not always necessary. In the garden scenery of one spacious Tang tomb appear both a Buddhist monastery and Daoist temple.[180] Buddhism's progress was slow, but it slid into and filled out existing conceptual lacunae as it competed with established systems of thought, simultaneously recognizable and revolutionary.

The stunning possibility of rebirth, of living again in this world after death, struck a chord among seekers of premortem immortality, although to others it seemed simply incredible, like the immortal in *Zhuangzi*: "The Buddhists say that after a man dies he will be reborn. I do not believe in the truth of these words. . . . "[181] Among third-to-fourth-century CE Daoists, one earthly immortal, a Mr. Puoshi, preferred to remain among worldly pleasures rather than ascend to heaven.[182] With rebirth, one died, but one could get this world back, and better, with diligent last-moment concentration.

Explaining rebirth, Buddhism gained an immortal soul. Hui-yüan (fourth century CE) described that immortal spirit as "an extremely subtle, immaterial and everlasting principle in man" that leaps from one body to another like flame on firewood, the emotions keeping it in existence, indestructible.[183] To a context already accustomed to precise and careful administrative calibrations in the netherworld bureaucracy, Buddhism brought a thoroughly systematized other-worldly cosmology for heavens above and hells below.

Hells were an innovation. Five Daoist underworld gods became Ten Yama Kings, with scribes, wardens, in ten courts for eighteen hells or eighty-four thousand.[184] Chinese dynasties had struggled, risen, and fallen without a punitive underworld to secure the moral order. A cosmology defined by Heaven, Earth, and Water had no obvious place for "hell." The word devised was "Earth Prison": a tomb with no visiting privileges. The threats of the Daoist *T'ai-p'ing ching* (Scripture of Great Peace, second century CE) use penal and judicial terminology, but are nothing to the sword-leaf forests of the Pali canon or Genshin's later *Ōjōyōshū*. Death itself is the initial punishment, incurred by the acts themselves, not by Heaven's intervention, and responsibility is one's own:

> If a man commits evils unceasingly, his name will then be entered into the Register of Death. He will be summoned to the Underworld Government . . . where his body is to be kept. Alas! When can he ever get out? His soul will be imprisoned and his doings in life will be questioned. If his words are found to be inconsistent, he will be subject to further imprisonment and torture. His soul is surely going to suffer a great deal. But who is to blame?[185]

Daoist hells flourish after about 400 CE, keeping up with Buddhism. Texts that treat the Nine Realms of Darkness always explain how to escape the Department of the Long Night.[186] Ultimately, the netherworld was inserted among the deities of the lower body parts.[187]

In China, the dominance of Mahāyāna seems in retrospect inevitable. Daoism had already come under attack from Confucians for its preference of the recluse over the socially committed actor. As early as the *Zhuangzi* the immortals' withdrawal requires defense. The Daoist *Scripture of Great Peace* ranks those who sought to "transcend this world with . . . family" above those who seek only "personal salvation."[188] So Mahāyānists charged those they called "Hīnayāna" with selfishness. Of the two principal Buddhist orientations originating in China, Ch'an (Zen in Japan) and Amitābha's Pure Land, the latter overflows with compassion for living beings, the former aims at awakening—the Buddha nature, the one mind, the original enlightenment within all sentient beings.

Every Buddha, and many a bodhisattva, has a Buddha field, realms of influence, or, more narrowly, a Pure Land. The bodhisattva Maitreya, the Buddha-to-come, resides in Tusita Heaven (Tosotsuten, highly valued in Tibet and in Japan by the Shingon sect). The bodhisattva Kannon has Fudaraku, across the sea. Śākyamuni himself preaches the Lotus Sutra eternally in Sacred Eagle, or Vultures', Peak.[189] Sukhāvatī (blissful land), lying billions of worlds away in the western quarter of the universe, is the Pure Land of Amitāyus (infinite or eternal life) or Amitābha (infinite or immeasurable light) Buddha, in Japan *Amida*, in China *Amituo*.[190]

Developing in the same period as Hindu *bhakti*, devotion to a Buddha reshapes Buddhist cosmology from vertical heavens to lateral Pure Lands, extending in the ten directions, as the heavens collapse into the six realms, displaced as destination. Creating non-returners, Pure Lands shift the devotee's focus at death from liberation or heaven to rebirth in a Pure Land, where enlightenment will be attained in the future. Those who choose Maitreya will return with him to find their enlightenment then. Most Pure Land sutras originated in India, but the three regarded as fundamental to Amitābha's Pure Land were combined, and one was written, in China.[191]

Amitābha's Pure Land desires the salvation of all sentient beings (usually no animals reside in a Pure Land, but there are exceptions[192]). Created by the fulfillment of the bodhisattva Dharmakāra's vows (forty-eight altogether), Sukhāvatī forever prevents the devotee's falling into the lower realms (vow 2). To be reborn there, mindfulness suffices, if the dying call on Amitābha's name ten times (vow 18). (Excepted are those who commit one of the five great crimes: murder of father, mother, or *arhat*, injury to a buddha, schism in the order [*sangha*].) The Buddha and his retinue welcome the dying devotee (vow 19), and sincere desire to be reborn in Amitābha's Pure Land will be fulfilled (vow 20).[193] The eighteenth vow underlies the recitation of the *nenbutsu* (*nembutsu*) to achieve salvation, literally "thought" + "Buddha," or "mindfulness of the Buddha." Elaborate deathbed practices enabled the dying to recite serenely "*Nāmo 'mitābhāya Buddhāya*,' 'Honor to Amitābha Buddha' " ten times while thinking of Amitābha, hopeful for that hierarchy-inverting vision.[194] It sounds very simple. Nāgārjuna described devotion as the "easy practice" to become a non-returner, but reaching the Pure

Land demanded strenuous meditation and visualization techniques.[195] A moment's distraction could lose everything. So in medieval Japan Shinran's daughter feared that his death showed he had not reached the Pure Land, but others reassured her.[196]

If compassion for others and their eventual enlightenment sustains Pure Land, present enlightenment animates the Ch'an meditation school. China's agile, impudent ninth-century CE *Platform Sutra* mocks Pure Land devotees and misguided interpreters of other sutras who anticipate enlightenment (*bodhi*) in a Pure Land: "To search for Bodhi somewhere beyond this world/ Is like looking for a rabbit with antlers."[197] Enlightenment is possible only now, in this world, from a human body, and it is this moment only that instantiates transcendence. Insight may be gained by strenuous sitting meditation (*zazen*, Japan) or walking meditation, or at a blow in a sudden cognitive shift (the koans). Buddha-nature is common to all. The project is to realize that nature, to become a Buddha now: "Without depending on words and letters/ Pointing directly to the human mind;/ Seeing the innate nature, one becomes a Buddha."[198] The realization cannot be taught; it can only be performed. The afterlife evaporates: mist, dew, sparkle. Buddhahood achieved, there is no rebirth to fear or to desire.

Pure Land looks to Amitābha Buddha "without," Ch'an to Buddha-nature "within."[199] China treated the antithetical emphases as complementary. Suggesting the vicissitudes of schools, in Japan's Soto Zen, the Zen practitioner in the funeral service performs the Buddhahood of the dead. A torch draws in the air a circle, symbol of enlightenment and emptiness; the monk says, "The cages of life and death are but phantom relations. When these phantom relations perish, [one] returns to the source. One morning: wind and moon. One morning: perishing. . . . The late [person's name] took refuge in the Great Ascetic [the Buddha], converged on the place beyond knowledge [enlightenment], and marched through the gateway to perfect nirvana. . . . Where the red fire burns through the body, there sprouts a lotus, blossoming within the flames."[200]

Not everyone went to a Pure Land or achieved Buddhahood now, or attempted to do so. In stories China's other-worlds preserved an incorrigible this-worldliness. Probably ninth century or later, the assessor of "T'ai Tsung in Hell" exploits his lowly position in the court of the dead, and his wits, to improve his status above ground, in this life, where happiness is found, or not at all. His next-world job serves as stepping stone to greater prosperity in this, and he keeps both jobs.²⁰¹ The worlds of the dead and the living are simultaneous, parts of a whole where actions in one produce effects in the other.

Arrived at the court of the dead, worried but still arrogant, the fratricidal emperor T'ai Tsung humiliates Lord Yama as "only sector-leader of a parcel of demons."²⁰² Yama slinks off, leaving the case to a low-level underworld functionary, the assessor Ts'ui Tzu-yü. In a mortifying failure of etiquette, the emperor is left waiting. Anxious, Ts'ui Tzu-yü nevertheless outwits his master (who expects something for nothing, as the oblivious powerful always do). To escape death by justifying his actions, the emperor need only explain that a sage ruler will murder his brothers and imprison his father (as this emperor had done) to save a kingdom. The consequence: the emperor gives the functionary a much finer post above ground, returns to life himself for ten years (he'd asked only for five days), and promotes the copying of the *Great Cloud Sutra*. A wily bureaucrat triumphs over a scary emperor and secures a harmonious outcome for every one, including the cosmos, where the sutras multiply.

TIBET: A VERY BRIEF GUIDE TO READING THE *BOOK OF THE DEAD*

> The relatives and friends surrounding us in this life
> Are like a gathering of shoppers at a market. . . .
> When the market closes, the shoppers will disperse.
> —*Tibetan Book of the Dead*²⁰³

Buddhism reached Tibet in the seventh century from China and developed a vast canon under Indian influence. Saluted in George Saunders' *Lincoln in the Bardo* (2016), the *Book of the Dead* or *Bardo Thos-grol Chen-mo* (Great Liberation by Hearing in the Intermediate States) first appears in the fourteenth century, revealed as a long-hidden eighth-century text.²⁰⁴ The Tibetan tradition possesses a rare self-consciousness that the rites of the dead serve the living, that the book of the dead guides life.²⁰⁵ That consciousness is explicit in the title: Liberation by Hearing.

It is also explicit in the text: the living are enjoined to read the book three times a day, to read it aloud, and to read it in public places.[206] The dead have up to forty-nine days before rebirth to achieve the liberation the living also seek. When the book is read to the dead, who hears it? It is not only the dead who listen.

Entering the text as a general reader is not easy. There is no substitute for an informed guide through a complex philosophical and meditative tradition so different from our own. A barista in Chicago, eying the orange cover of the complete translation, with the Dalai Lama's own introduction and generous apparatus, lamented having tried and given up. This remarkable edition, for such readers, is best grasped, as Swift would say, by the tail: starting from the end and working back, from the popular play "A Masked Drama of Rebirth," a Tibetan *Everyman* (chap. 13), through the "Aspirational Prayers" (chap. 12) to "The Great Liberation by Hearing" (chap. 11). The terms once familiar, the reader can start again from the dazzling beginning.

The opening, it must be confessed, is seductive. Mortality salience surfaces at once. In the daily verses of the preliminary practice (chap. 1, "Natural Liberation of the Nature of Mind . . ."), consciousness of death excites the practitioner to persevere, to "start . . . with the reflection on death" as the way to completion. Ten similes represent the world of phenomena we live in, some beautiful, some requiring explication: selfless, empty, free from conceptual elaboration, illusion, mirage, dream, reflected image, celestial city, echo, reflection of the moon in water, bubble, optical illusion, intangible emanation. There is a truth to be realized, but we are caught in cyclic existence, overwhelmed by our past actions, and need to be saved from the "six-dimensional city," the familiar six realms of rebirth.

The truth to be realized is the non-dual Buddha nature of mind. "Just to recognize this is enough! If you recognize this brilliant essence of your own conscious awareness to be the Buddha [nature], then to gaze into intrinsic awareness is to abide in the enlightened intention of all the buddhas" (231).

Looking for Buddha-nature elsewhere than in the mind is futile. People who look "to something else, above and beyond [mind],/Resemble someone who has already found an elephant, but is out looking for its tracks [elsewhere]" (51). For those of us taken with that elephant, "A Masked Drama of Rebirth" is a "skillful means" leading to the "Aspirational Prayers" and "The Great Liberation by Hearing."

The "Aspirational Prayers" draw the reader into the solitude and terror of death. Sent into a great wilderness, alone, driven by past actions, buffeted by cause and effect, with no firm ground, "I roam in cyclic existence" (310–12). Existential anxiety is soothed by the helps that surround and enclose the dying, buddhas, bodhisattvas, and reassuring knowledge provided in the recitation itself.

"The Great Liberation by Hearing" is the "skillful means which liberates yogins of average ability during the intermediate states" (225) of dying, reality, and rebirth. Superior practitioners, recognizing the inner radiance, are liberated in the first state, at the moment of death. Most dead are confused, uncertain, terrified by the lights and sounds arising, panicked, and enter the second intermediate state, reality. Still identifying as bodies, they realize they are dead when they try to speak to the living, who cannot perceive them. From within the consciousness and past actions of the dead, phantasmagoric apparitions arise, lights, sounds, the peaceful deities emerging, but the dead may turn away, "[a]lthough it is impossible not to be liberated by [the successful recognition of] this [introduction]" (243). At any moment, liberation is possible, the text exhorts and counsels.

The wrathful deities arise from the power of evil past actions and "habitual tendencies." Yama Dharmarāja will appear, vast and terrifying, but his forms "have no material substance. Emptiness cannot be harmed by emptiness." "Your body is a mental body, formed of habitual tendencies. Therefore, even if you are slain and cut into pieces, you will not die. You are [in reality] a natural form of emptiness, so there is no need to be afraid" (268). To achieve liberation, the dead must recognize their own emptiness and radiance. Finally, the unliberated dead enter the third intermediate state of rebirth, longing for a new body and finding their way home into cyclic existence.

"The Great Liberation by Hearing" begins with the greatest of all "Aspirational Prayers." Death manifests its power to unify survivors, strengthening the community that comes together in the shadow of the word, extending concern to all beings, in a series of wishes unlikely to be fulfilled, but worth wishing, though they may be achievable only by the dead, as Zhuangzi suspected:

> May all sentient beings be endowed with happiness!
> May they all be separated from suffering and its causes!
> May they be endowed with joy, free from suffering!
> May they abide in equanimity, free from attraction and aversion!
> (220).

Wishing does not make it so, but it makes us feel for a moment as though it might be so. And for the instant of recitation, it is so; words displace reality.

As to the future state, in the play *Masked Drama of Rebirth* wrongdoer Lakṣanāraka is chagrined to discover that, unlike the phenomenal world, the hells are real. He had been certain that once his body decayed and his mind vanished, there would be nothing left to go to any hells, and he laughed at those who feared them. Fierce Yama Dharmarāja cannot save him from the consequences of his past actions. Yet no one wants sufferings to last forever. The play ends with a well-doing householder rewarded and a final prayer: "May the hells be exhausted and emptied!" (333).

JAPAN'S DIALECTICS AND THREE INTONATIONS OF PURE LAND

In Japan, Buddhism officially arrives with a gift of sutras from a Korean principate in the mid-sixth century, shortly before Japanese literature begins with two collections of historic, mythological tales, the *Kojiki*, (Record of Ancient Matters, 711–12), commissioned by the Empress Genmei, and the *Nihon shoki* or *Nihongi* (Chronicles of Japan, 720), dedicated to her daughter Empress Gensho (both ruling empresses). The *Nihongi* recounts the contested arrival of Buddhism to a land that already possessed "180 Gods [*kami*] of Heaven and Earth," "yin and yang" and four other worlds, several of Chinese origin.[207]

A seventh-century widow wishes for her dead spouse a "heavenly land of long life," the Daoist-inflected *tenjukoku*.[208] The *Nihongi* and *Kojiki* allude to an "eternal land" across the seas of *Toko-yo no kuni* (the land of the ancestors or gods). Its waves lap the shores of Ise, and fragrant fruits flourish out of season as on Mt. Penglai. Below the ground is *Ne no kuni*, the root country, a netherworld to which the rude storm god Susanoo is expelled and where he belatedly takes up residence after his marriage. Although being sent down is a punishment, there is nothing disagreeable about his new terrain. Roots in the earth suggest life and growth, whether vegetation or ancestors. More aversive is the familiar land of darkness, the land of Yomi, written with the Chinese characters for "Yellow Springs."[209]

That quiet Chinese place has become a scene of horror and a powerful pollution taboo. A thwarted Orpheus, the deity-kami Izanagi meant to rescue his dead sister-spouse Izanami from death, but she had eaten among the dead. Lighting a torch, he saw her—rotting, maggot-ridden, eaten. Horrified, he flees, she pursues, and he seals her in her dark cave, Yomi, with a rock, like a hillside burial. Izanami screams that she will destroy one thousand human grasses a day; Izanagi replies that he will have fifteen hundred born. Cleansing himself from this pollution, Izanagi bathes; from his right eye comes the sun goddess Amaterasu, his left the moon, and his nose that ill-behaved storm god.[210] Some commentators identify Susanoo's *Ne no kuni* with Yomi, and Susanoo wails because he wants to follow his mother Izanami to "the Nether Land."[211] But he never meets her, and the connotations of the spaces differ. Susanoo never rots, nor is he associated with others rotting. Izanami becomes Yömö-tu-opo-kämi, Great deity of Yomi, but no one visits her, even when they draw near the "yellow springs."[212]

When the *Nihongi* laments a king's death in battle, two undifferentiated entities follow antithetical trajectories. Both are "he," but one disappears into air, space; the other sinks downward to darkness, like Lady Ma. The dead king "passed upwards and was lost in the infinite. Like flowing water, he returns not again, but remains at rest in the dark dwelling."[213] "Lost in the infinite" is less positive than the *shen's* movement upward to divinity, brightness. Up, down, and fluidity in between: that was all even a king could expect.

Japan had flourished with no ethicized afterlife, no retribution beyond the grave, no underworld gods threatening the dead. Izanami sealed in her cave threatens the living, not the dead. From his *Ne no kuni*, Susanoo threatens no one. Underground, he disappears from the *Nihongi*. In the

Kojiki, his daughter's lover, who has already been killed twice, outwits him, making off with his bow, sword of life, and daughter. He shouts good advice after them, and all is well. *Kami*, or spirits, inhabited places, objects, and persons: earth, rivers, mountains, wind, sun, moon, trees, rocks, gods, fire, and certain people, living or dead. They could be helpful, vengeful, or indifferent, and they required placating and solicitation. Digging into the earth was particularly disturbing to them and demanded propitiation. Court and local officials oversaw the appropriate rites, and the *Nihongi* recounts opposition by such officials to a new *kami* (Buddha) arrived from Korea.

The spirits compete and collaborate with Buddhism into the present, with the *Kojiki* and the *Nihongi* laying out alternate perspectives. The *Kojiki* ignores Buddhism to tell of creation, history, and the *kami*. The *Nihongi* integrates systems, but also describes their conflict. Chinese yin and yang appear unseparated before creation, and the word *Shinto* when an emperor succeeds who "believed in the Law of Buddha and reverenced the Way of the Gods, [*Shinto*]," the first instance of the term.[214] The new kami's opponents represented their opposition as loyalty to the indigenous gods against a powerful foreign import.

That conflict has periodically re-entered Japanese politics in the form of revivals of "authentic" Shinto and hostility to Buddhism, extending to destruction of temples and artifacts as late as the nineteenth century. The political implications have made scholars cautious. No separate, unbroken lineage of pre-Buddhist indigenous practices exists, as the word "Shinto" seems to imply and as the State Shinto of the Meiji era insisted. "Shinto" has a clear referent, the way of the kami, but that way has a history intertwined with Buddhism, power, and politics, sometimes collaborating, sometimes coopting or coopted, and sometimes hostile.

The Buddha arrived as a gold and copper statue, with three sutras in 552 CE, according to the *Nihongi*.[215] The *Golden Splendor Sutra* (Sanskrit *Svuarṇa prabhāsa sutra*, Japanese *Konkōmyō saishōō kyō*) was early among the most popular at court, frequently read and lectured on, with one hundred copies sent to the provinces.[216] In 577 CE, more books and six Buddhists disembarked as gifts from Korea (Pèkché)—an ascetic, a meditator, a nun, a mantra-reciter, a maker of images, and an architect.[217] By 606 CE, Buddhist rites had been incorporated in imperial funerals.[218] By 640 CE, the *Larger Pureland Sutra* had been explicated at court, and

Buddhism remained a court monopoly, forbidden to be taught to common folk.[219] According to the *Nihongi*, the "wonderful" new doctrine had been recommended as "most excellent [but] hard to explain and hard to comprehend." It led "to a full appreciation of the highest wisdom,... every prayer... fulfilled." Others, defending the interests of the gods already on the premises, attributed an epidemic to wrath at the new kami.[220] Sutras were read when emperors were ill, but they worked less well than praying to the four directions, Chinese style, when rain was wanted.[221]

Folded into existing practices and beliefs, competing with kami and claiming them as adherents or predecessors, Buddhism brought a detailed, moralized account of what happened—or could happen—after death. Three moments are especially instructive about that afterlife's trajectory into the living, dying present: Genshin's tenth-century *Ōjōyōshū*, Fukansai Habian's seventeenth-century *Myōtei Mondō*, and Natsume Sōseki's twentieth-century *I Am a Cat*. Written by a Tendai monk, the *Ōjōyōshū* (985) is a Buddhist treatise that makes startlingly vivid to its readers or auditors the reality of the lives to come after death and shows them how to secure rebirth in Amida's Pure Land. Enormously influential, it inspired paintings, poems, and, a century after the author's death, two Buddhist schools that still command numerous adherents, Hōnen's Jōdo-shū (Pure Land School) and Shinran's Jōdo Shin-shū (True Pure Land School).

The second, *Myōtei Mondō* (1605), had no influence whatever. Written by a Zen-Buddhist Christian convert, it was not available in complete form until the late-twentieth century (1972). A dialogue between two Japanese nuns, Myōshū a Buddhist and Yūtei turned Christian, it attacked the afterlife accounts and belief systems of twelve Buddhist schools, Confucianism, and Shinto to promote the Christian afterlife. If *Myōtei Mondō* produced any Christian converts, they vanished in the Shogunate's efforts to stamp out Christianity, after 1614. Habian himself abandoned Christianity in 1608. What Habian shows is the desire for a ground denied by Buddhist philosophical speculation, and he turns that speculation against the beliefs Genshin had made so immediate and so vivid. As to Natsume Sōseki, enthusiast of Swift's *Gulliver's Travels* and Sterne's *Tristram Shandy*, *I Am a Cat* (1905–1911) is just a novel narrated by a cat up to the cat's last-moment thought. After Habian's dissolving all possible belief, Sōseki's cat illustrates the persistence of belief that does not need belief, when "afterlife" as an empirical phenomenon is irrelevant, or just not the point.

Written in six months following the funeral of his widowed mother (983 CE), revisiting a town he had not seen for thirty years, Genshin's *Ōjōyōshū* (985 CE) takes the shape of a sutra as it moves away from "the unclean world" to the Pure Land "in the West ten thousand hundred millions lands away."[222] As a monk of the Tendai order, established at Mt. Hiei near Kyoto in 805 CE, Genshin (942–1071) privileged the *Lotus Sutra* and rigorous meditation and contemplation techniques to realize the one Buddha mind and nature,[223] but he was also sympathetic to Amida's Pure Land. The Pure Land enabled those who could not achieve enlightenment through meditation in this world to do so in another. The *Ōjōyōshū* intends to help simple people escape the *Lotus Sutra*'s "burning house" through "the one gate of Nembutsu."[224]

Unlike Hōnen (1133–1212, Jōdo-shū) and Shinran (1173–1263, Jōdo Shin-shū or Shin), whom his work inspired, Genshin regarded as intrinsic to the nembutsu recognition through deep meditation of one's innate enlightenment, "self-insight," but not everyone was capable of that.[225] His allegiance to contemplative meditation is clear in the structure of his work, with seven of ten parts given to how to practice nembutsu. Like the *Lotus Sutra*, he adapts the dharma to all capacities, from country people at a funeral to an elite brotherhood formed to practice the nembutsu together and to assist each other in dying.[226]

Genshin begins with a campaign of terror: a blistering attack on sensory attachment to this world. Japan even more than China, with its reclusive immortals, seems to have lacked an indigenous renunciant tradition like India's. Localities were required, the *Nihongi* reports, to contribute ten religious a year to monastic purposes. Nuns signed on before monks—whether coerced or seizing an escape from life's usual offers. Giving up this world was a Buddhist innovation, at odds with ordinary mortal pleasures and intimacy with the kami that peopled the world unseen. The *Ōjōyōshū* works hard to generate revulsion at this world and longing for another. Disrupting a sutra's correct order from bad to better and better, hells take more pages than the other five realms combined (hungry ghosts, beasts, *ashuras*, humans, heavens), and nothing improves within the six realms. The Pure Land itself is only half again as long as the hells.

Collected from Buddhist sutras, the eight hells from Repetition to No Interval inflict relentless physical suffering. The human realm, traditionally a privileged position for hearing the dharma en route to the heavens or enlightenment, disgusts (with impurity), suffers (age, death, sickness), and vanishes (impermanent). Genshin counts our bones—360—and sets the viscera rotting. Eighty-thousand worms crawl through cavities and orifices; the corpse bloats, pus oozes, birds and dogs feed on the remains. The body is a stinking mass of corruption that suffers innumerable agonies from birth to death—and withal so brief, impermanent and fleeting.

The heavens are agonizing to leave, the psychological suffering worse than hell pains, to lose bliss. Even the Daoist flying immortal, the hermit "who rides on the wind, sits on the clouds and flies about feely enjoying himself," and sees "seven times the birth of a new world," must ultimately face death—and traverse the six realms if he did "not desire the way of the Hotoke [Buddha]."[227]

With Amida's Pure Land, Genshin proposes what seems a real other place to desire. Welcomed by the bodhisattvas Kwannon and Daiseishi descending, beholding Amida, arriving from a grass hut to a lotus seat, held safely in Kwannon's arms, freed from fear of falling into the three evil realms: the devotee arrives where Nāgārjuna himself wished to go: "I, therefore, do nothing but offer my life to Mida and desire to enter the Pure Land."[228] In the Pure Land, one sees the Buddha and recites the scriptures, converses and meditates among jewels, beautiful clothes (that do not require mending, sewing, or cleaning), fragrances, flowers, and food with "sweet and sour" taste as the heart desires it.[229] From millennium-later perspectives, there are notable absences: friends, family, intellectual activity alternate to the Buddhistic, famous people (as in Dante). In this exquisite space, their absence is not felt.

Apart from its emphasis on food, fragrance, wild ducks, and lotus ponds, Amida's Pure Land differs from Christian paradises principally in that it includes the idea of progress beyond the Pure Land to enlightenment. The final pleasure of Pure Land is "Pleasures of Making Progress in the Way of the Buddha."[230] That progress may take *kalpas*, but it is part of the understanding of the place. (As a unit of measurement, a *kalpa* is the time it takes a granite mountain to disappear when a butterfly's wing brushes it once every three years.) Christians have nowhere else to go and nothing more to achieve once they reach their blissful abode. Those who reach Amida's Pure Land are "non-returners," but another goal awaits. The impermanence of the goal underlies what has seemed a contradiction in Genshin.

Genshin prefers (Tendai) contemplative nembutsu to (Pure Land) invocation nembutsu, and he subordinates nembutsu to "immediate realization of Buddhahood" in *Kanjin ryaku yōshū (Essentials of Self-insight)*.[231] Nembutsu achieves the Pure Land, but only contemplative practices lead beyond to Buddhahood. As an epigraph to the *Ōjōyōshū* has it, "I was seeking the way of Buddha all through the night but it was really to find my own heart."[232] Nembutsu seeks and finds the Buddha. "My own heart" remains to be found.

That seeking engages visualization meditations of stunning complexity, laid out with careful instructions. Contemplating the Buddha-marks, the practitioner is told that they cannot be seen and then what he will see and accomplish when he does see what cannot be seen: "The fleshy topknot: There is no one who can actually see this. It appears high and round like a heavenly parasol. Those who wish to contemplate it in detail should contemplate like this: Above this topknot is a great aureola of a thousand colors. Each color produces eighty-four thousand apparition-Buddhas. Above the topknot of each apparition-Buddha there is also an aureola. The various rays follow one upon another reaching to the countless worlds of the ten regions. Moreover, in the ten regions there are apparition-Bodhisattvas who descend like clouds and surround the apparition-Buddhas.... Those who rejoice in this mark will annul one hundred billion *kalpas* of extremely heavy bad karma and will not fall into the three evil paths."[233]

Genshin also codified deathbed practices that endure to the present. Mindfulness at death was the key opening the door to the desired Buddha land. The dying person was advised to "hold a five-colored cord fastened to a Buddha image, visualize Amida's coming, and chant the *nembutsu*, . . . so as to generate the all-important 'last thought' that would ensure birth in his Pure Land."[234] Holding the cord communicated following the Buddha, the chant filled the mouth and ears with Buddha, the color and image the eyes, the cord the touch. Sick and dying persons were reminded of their good deeds to assist them in concentrating on the Buddha, and the last thought at the moment of death enabled a joyous transit to the Pure Land, with Amida descending to lead the dying there.

After 1680, the first two parts of the *Ōjōyōshū* were frequently printed alone in illustrated editions, without the practical instructions.[235] Those parts address only two doctrinal points. Evidently the view is common, and Genshin holds it dangerous, that the world continues to exist, but people don't. Genshin is earnest against a heresy that holds the four great elements (earth, wind, fire, water) to be permanent and the body impermanent, for it dies and dissolves into the four great elements. (Ajita's) illiterate, illusory position misunderstands "the real nature of things" and the complex activity within the four elements.[236] Buddhism aims for the annihilation of annihilation, not annihilation, and that can be confusing. As Genshin quotes the *Daikyō*, "All work is impermanent. This is the law of life and annihilation. To end the annihilation of life and annihilation, such calm annihilation is true happiness."[237]

Nāgārjuna is quoted every few pages, a poem, an aperçu. Whether authentic or midrashic, the citations mark what Nāgārjuna meant to Genshin. Where Nāgārjuna is, the Void cannot be far behind. Genshin supposes someone asking, "It is easy to understand the teachings about Impurity, Suffering and Impermanency and that every phenomenon which appears to us has a noumenon back of it, but what is meant by the Void?"

The answer is to think it "like a dream and a vision." There follows a long story of a man trying to keep silent while asleep but finally his dream becomes too real and he cries out. Most people live the dream of vain thoughts and look upon things in the Void as though they were real—and never wake up.[238] Understanding the Void is essential to Buddhahood, as Amida himself explains: "Knowing that all phenomena are like a flash of lightning, let them decide upon the way of the Bodhisattva, achieve the various virtues, obtain a fixed mind and attain Buddhahood! If they understand that the nature of all phenomena is voidness and that there is no ego, and if they seek eagerly after the pure Buddha land, they shall certainly obtain a land like this."[239] Or as Nāgārjuna is quoted immediately after: "The law of all existence is Impermanency and of a Non-ego Principle. It is like the moonlight upon the water, like the sparkle of a dew drop, or a flash of lighting. There is no law which can be called a Law."[240]

The fame of Genshin's text was compounded by its inspiring first artists and then Hōnen (1133–1212) and his disciple Shinran (1173–1263). In their reforms, Genshin's subtleties and complications drop away, along with his methods of veneration and visualization. Hōnen took his epigraph from Genshin: "Among causes of rebirth, nembutsu is fundamental" and privileged recitation over meditative nembutsu. Recitation was the only needful action.[241] Shinran emphasized the Buddha's compassion and the devotee's dependence on "other power" rather than "self power," implicitly denigrating Genshin's demanding meditative and contemplative practices. In turn, nembutsu practice inspired Nicheren (1222–1282), founder of the Nichiren school, who insisted on the primacy of the Lotus Sutra and an easy "self-power" practice to Buddhahood. He recommended chanting the formula *Namu myō-hō ren-ge-kyō*, "Honor to the *Lotus Sutra* of the True *Dharma*" and contemplating a wooden plaque inscribed with the formula.[242] Valuing visuals, and auguring his work's influence on artists, Genshin began the tradition of illustrating his work. He portrayed not a hell or even a hungry ghost, but Amida and the bodhisattvas welcoming the dying.[243]

Pure Land has been credited or charged with smoothing the way for Christianity in both Japan and Korea.[244] Sir Charles Eliot, an eminent Victorian, refused to call it Buddhism, and western scholars have traditionally been more interested in other Buddhist schools. While the Bibliothèque nationale de France has a few studies of Pure Land, almost all written in English, it has many more studies of Zen, written in French. Fujita Kōtatsu has compassion for "an understandable lack of interest in a tradition superficially resembling Western monotheism."[245]

It is surprising, then, to be told by a seventeenth-century ex–Zen Buddhist monk that there is no afterlife in Pure Land. The monks know better—something else—and are just not telling. A fictional widow, comforted for the death of her husband by a promised Pure Land reunion on a lotus flower, realizes she has been deceived. The promise is, in every sense, empty: "[T]he heart of Buddhist teaching is that neither the gods nor buddhas, nor Hell nor the Land of Ultimate Bliss, actually exist outside our minds. Now I realize why the monks used to say to me somewhat dismissively: 'Now listen Myōshū. Hell and the Land of Ultimate Bliss, and the gods and buddhas are not what you think they are. But since enlightenment is difficult to attain just you go on sitting there chanting the *nenbutsu*.' "[246] Myōshū feels betrayed by "skillful means."

Fukansai Habian (1565–1621, a.k.a. Fabian Fucan) spent twenty years as a Christian convert and lay brother, assisting the Jesuit mission in Japan with an adapted, romanized *Heike monogatari*, aggressive Christian proselytizing in public debates, and the *Myōtei Mondō* (*Myōtei Dialogues* [1605]). The title blends the names of Myōshū, a Buddhist, and Yūtei, a Christian, who search for an afterlife through eight Buddhist schools (Kusha, Jōjitsu,

Risshū, Hossō, Sanron, Kegon, Tendai, Shingon), plus Zen and Pure Land for ten, and Ikkō and Nicheren for twelve. Kusha, Jōjitsu, and Risshū belong to the "superficial" and "shallow" Hīnayāna, the others to the "profound" Mahāyāna (68). Shinto and Confucianism (with Daoism) follow. Finally, Yūtei shows Christianity's superior afterlife and logic.

Habian left the Jesuits around 1608, before Christianity was outlawed in 1614. He complained of their arrogance and failure to ordain Japanese; they alleged in private correspondence that he had gone off with a lay sister. Jesuits ordained only one Japanese, not Habian, and most diocesan clergy were ordained after he left the order.[247] In 1620 he published *Deus Destroyed (Ha Daiusu)*, attacking Christianity from a Buddhist perspective, and he probably died the next year. Akutagawa Ryūnosuke (1892–1927) called him "a genius" and wrote a new section for *Ha Daiusu* in the story "Lucifer" (1918).[248] Others have called him an "auto-didact," as if he learned about Buddhism and other systems while reading on his own for the Jesuits. James Baskind has shown his intimate knowledge of a Rinzai Zen koan manual from Daitokuji monastery,[249] so that derogatory term misleads. What is clear, and perhaps creates the "auto-didact" impression, is that Habian kicked over what he had been taught (up to the age of eighteen, when he converted) and set up his own unguided reason against the subtle teachings of the schools.

What Habian found—and then gave up—in Christianity was a ground for truth. He wanted truth that existed outside the mind, real, solid, empirical. In the *Dialogues*, he delights in scientific accounts of earth's circumference, eclipses, the moon's changes and light, or geographical accounts of the Khyber Pass. When he attacks a Buddhist school, tale, or doctrine, he often begins by contrasting a Buddhist myth with some discovery brought "by Christianity." The same authority he attributed to western science, he gave, for a time, to Christian theological doctrines, especially its afterlife. The rational soul, *anima rationalis*, not faith, grounded Christian immortality,[250] and he treated Confucian silence about the afterlife with unusual—for him—respect. Rejecting Christianity, he rejected not its concept of the afterlife, but the truth of its concept. Resurrection and ascent to heaven sound "quite splendid," but in a faith perverse from its roots, all must be "devilish illusion, magical trickery."[251]

In that translation from *Deus Destroyed*, Habian sounds angry, like someone who has been cheated of something he wanted and realizes he has been played. To end the *Dialogues* he had expressed a pious hope: "But this I have done as a prayer that I may be accepted into Heaven in the next life" (194). When he jeers at the nonexistence of the Christian afterlife in *Deus Destroyed*, he does not reassert any Buddhist afterlife against it. The next life remains an illusion. The arguments of the *Dialogues* stand.

Habian could motivate a study in liminality—discourses suddenly intersect and a paradigm lurches. Comic, biting, a satirist, he insists on the dualisms others are intent on overcoming. He learned to write from the *Heike monogatari* of the "evanescence of this fleeting world . . . the clarity of the autumn moon rising in the clear night sky . . . hidden by dawn in scattered clouds." Myōshū quotes "the Buddha's words, 'All conditioned phenomena are like a dream, a phantom, a bubble, a shadow' [which] if it were not for the question of the next life, said it all." She recounts the advice of that deceptive priest, whose advice does not after all seem so bad, when he advises the young widow not to kill herself: "It would be very unfortunate for he [sic] who has gone before you. They say . . . that 'the seed of buddhahood arises from a connection.' If you make this the seed of your awakening, change your appearance and chant the *nenbutsu* to bring constant consolation to his spirit, in the end you will be born on the same lotus flower as him [in the Pure Land] and your conjugal vows will be fulfilled both in this world and the next" (56). Habian has a gift for scenes, the Gojō area of Kyoto: "[A]mong the mansions with their high, crested gates I found a hut with a rough door made from a single piece of wood, and next to it was the kind of brushwood fence you find in mountain villages. It was a truly desolate, rustic scene. Since it was late autumn, the lonely atmosphere was more pronounced than elsewhere, with withered creeper leaves and morning glories in the garden, and on a worn grassy path of which only a part remained stood a lone child facing in the opposite direction."

For Habian, the inwardness of Buddhism is its fatal flaw. To become enlightened is to realize one is inherently a buddha and that hells and lands of ultimate bliss are nowhere other than "in our minds"(105). If existence comes from and returns to and is the void, and enlightenment is (the apprehension of) that knowledge-process, then apprehension itself, but not apprehension *of* anything, is the there there. Habian takes the key Buddhist terms for approximating ultimate reality and takes them where annihilationist heretics do: to nothing at all.

"Thusness," "void," "emptiness," "one mind," "nothingness," "buddha-nature," "buddha-hood," "no self," "extinction," "original state": Yūtei finds not the phenomenology of enlightenment, but nonexistence. What the Buddha "was enlightened about [is] 'ultimate emptiness,' which in the final analysis means that neither the exalted person of the 'Buddha' himself nor inferior 'sentient beings' such as us actually exist. Enlightenment is realizing where Heaven and Hell really are. Anyone who becomes enlightened in this fashion is called a buddha. That's the essence of the Dharma: nothing more" (66). Karma and the four noble truths disappear: "we ourselves, this self that we believe exists, does not in truth exist. It teaches that the real does not exist" (80). "[O]nce you have understood essential nothingness. . . . it's all just doctrine in the end" (120).

Jan Westerhoff, though he does not have Habian in mind, considers denying the reality of the real "misleading."[252] It is not that "the real" does not exist; it is that what we perceive is not the real, and the real is not what we perceive. Modern physics supplies an analogy that would please the de-converted Habian: we and the chairs we sit on dissolve into atoms that are mostly void, atoms keep disintegrating into other bits and pieces, but still we sit on chairs.

Habian has no time for hell terrors, or the other realms. Buddhism always distinguishes the "provisional and the true. The provisional asserts that temporarily on the surface the Buddha, Hell, and Heaven all exist; the true . . . states that Hell and Heaven have no real existence" (67–68). Such states arise merely in the mind: "The mind of man sometimes suffers and hell arises; sometimes there is sorrow and [the hell of] hungry ghosts arises; but with no-thought and no-mind the fruits of the Buddha are manifest" (93). The intimacy of the dharma does not seduce him: "Generally speaking, in Buddhism nothing is said to be divorced from our body. This is what Kukai meant when he said: 'The Buddhist Dharma is nowhere remote. It is in our mind; it is close to us. Thusness is nowhere external. If not within our body, where can it be found?' " (89)

Nirvana is nowhere. Enlightenment "means to understand that since empty buddha-nature does not exist, fundamentally no one is born and no one dies . . . The underlying meaning is that when we die, sentient beings return to this Void; they become nothing" (26–27). Wanted is self that survives death: "without self . . . when each one of us dies . . . he is just absorbed into the void of thusness" (73). Myōshū thought there were buddhas residing in pure lands of ultimate bliss, but disappointingly it seems it just all leads "to enlightenment" (86). Yūtei rebukes those who want to speak of "Buddhisms": Hīnayāna, Mahāyāna, Zen, Pure Land, eight schools or twelve, "in the final analysis, it's 'all the same Buddhism . . .' " (70).

Habian ends the Buddhist discussion with Pure Land, from a Christian perspective the most challenging of Buddhist schools for its similar promises. The structure he imposes signifies: he first denies Pure Land rebirth—it is emptiness again. He then revives his earlier technique of setting an empirical fact against a Buddhist mythos, but this time to conclude rather than introduce. Scorning Pure Land cosmology, he mocks its adherents. Having distinguished "immediate" and "imminent" rebirth, Yūtei quotes Pure Land theorists who identify Pure Land rebirth with awakening or enlightenment. If one remembers Genshin and his careful, intentional planning of our dying, Habian's account of the last moment is quietly devastating. "[A]t the moment of death the *nenbutsu* practitioner experiences the same nothingness to which those in other schools have already become awakened" (122).

From this erasure, Habian returns to science: he wants something that really exists. Amida and his land to the west "ten trillion Buddha lands away" do not. The universe is not flat and has no east and west. The story is all just Lord Śākaymuni "at his tricks again" (123–24). Worse and worse, the chanters drive everyone else out of their minds: 'So Pure Land adherents ring their bells, shake their heads, and chant '*namu Amidabutsu, namu Amidabutsu*' without a thought for anyone else in the neighborhood, and when they really get going to an outsider it sounds just like the 'heave-ho' you hear as men pull up their boats from the sea. It would seem that to make people chant the *nenbutsu* like that is designed to bring them to a state of no-mind" (126).

Habian is respectful of Confucianism, less so of Daoism, and Shinto he deconstructs as an allegory of yin and yang, sexually, historically, ethnographically, and politically—a tour de force. What draws Habian to Christianity is a rational soul that exists eternally and will not fall from heaven: "[T]ransmigration does not exist, even if you might wish it did," Yūtei says, referring to but not mentioning hell (181). The Christian paradise receives less detail than Pure Land paradises usually do, and Myōshū is shocked only by the exclusion of animals, since Buddhism teaches the "fifty-two species" have "the same nature as man" (173). Rejecting Christianity, Habian derides eternal damnation for a persimmon: "the all-merciful, all compassionate Deus! Him only shall you call all-merciful and all-compassionate who sweeps away suffering and grants joy!"[253] The one who does that, however, is never named.

Relative to the afterlife, once Habian leaves Christianity, there is no indication that he holds any position other than Myōshū's before Yūtei's exposition of Christianity. Myōshū, asked to explain what she thinks about the afterlife, does not know what survives and suspects it must be nothing at all: "All we know is that by reciting the *nenbutsu* one achieves salvation, but I have no idea what survives or what shape it takes. But from what they tell me, they proclaim the existence of Hell and Paradise in the afterlife but only as an expedient truth, so what kind of thing really survives to experience either suffering or pleasure? Since human bodies are composed of the five elements, earth, water, fire, wind, and air, they combine while we live, but after death if cremated they become ashes and if buried they turn into earth. Water returns to water and fire to fire and all is dispersed, so if I am pressed to say what it is that survives to experience suffering or pleasure, I would have to say nothing" (173). Genshin deplored that position, six hundred years earlier.

Six hundred years earlier still, Wang Chong (27–97 CE) would not have disagreed: "When a fire is extinguished, its light does not shine any more, and when a man dies, his intellect does not perceive any more. The nature of both is the same.... What is the difference between a sick man about to die and a light about to go out?"[254] Nirvana means "extinguished" or "quenched," like a flame,[255] and no concept has ever been more difficult to explain. To it the Trinity doesn't hold a candle—blown out. It is in fact more difficult to comprehend something's simply being gone than it is to understand it as having gone elsewhere. Subtracting agency does not come easily to our species. From the *Rig Veda* to Myōshū, the parts dispersed go somewhere else. David Hume reduced causation to correlation and expected his own extinction, but even he offered the compliment that if there is such a thing as soul that survives the death of the body, "The Metempsychosis is ... the only system of this kind that philosophy can hearken to."[256]

Rebirth engages the double perspective that life stops (forever) and that it goes on (eternally), that the individual is one body and many minds, that life is eternally desirable and that eternal dying is detestable. Eternalists, like Hindus, Muslims, Plato, and Christians, split the life/death binary with the Annihilationists, like Wang Chong, Ajita Kesakambalin, Samuel's woman of Tekoa, and Lucretius (who admitted metempsychosis as a possibility, but only as not self). Buddhists hold out a middle way. But how can there be a middle way between life and death, surely the ultimate either/or dualism, that turns a self into an object?

The middle way abjures that dualism of which we ever experience only half—mind in body—for a network of interdependent processes and relationships. If there is no there there—no substantial existence—, there is also no not there not there—no nonexistence. When a character dies at the end of a book, is there finality, or is there a pattern of relationships established within, through, and beyond the book, between characters and readers, characters and writer, writer and readers?

To illustrate, the last word and a long quotation belong to Natsume Sōseki, revisiting a poem by Hume's contemporary Thomas Gray, "On the Death of a Favorite Cat Drowned in a Bowl of Goldfishes." The cat was Horace Walpole's tabby, Selima; the bowl was a Chinese vase, and Sōseki introduced eighteenth-century English literature to Japan. Sōseki's reworking of Gray's satiro-comical poem profits from Sterne's precise physical detail in *Tristram Shandy*. Sōseki's novel *I Am a Cat* is narrated by the cat, who has no name. The cat falls into a deep clay jar holding water and cannot get out; it struggles, suffers, relaxes, and gives way. Similar situations afflict sentient beings with two legs.

Sōseki's passage reproduces almost as physical experience the Buddha's ancient perception that life is suffering, that attachment and desire are the cause of suffering, that it is possible to end suffering, that letting go is the way to enlightenment, and that enlightenment is concentrated letting go. Passing from dualism to non-differentiation, the last-moment thought to secure a good rebirth—and none after that—is the *nembutsu*, the meditation on Amida. The translation is Aiko Ito and Graeme Wilson, until Elizabeth Porcu steps in at the last six sentences. It is an unconscionably long quotation. It repays slow, very slow reading.

> When I came again to myself I found I was floating in water. Because I was also in pain I clawed at what seemed its cause, but scratching water had no effect except to result in my immediate submersion. I struck out

desperately for the surface by kicking with my hind-legs and scrabbling with my fore-paws. This action eventually produced a sort of scraping sound and, as I managed to thrust my head just clear of the water, I saw that I'd fallen in a big clay jar against whose side my claws had scraped. All through the summer this jar had contained a thick growth of water-hollyhocks, but in the early autumn the crows had descended first to eat the plants and then to bathe in the water. In the end their splashing about and the heat of the sun had so lowered the water level that the crows found it difficult either to bathe or to drink, and they had stopped coming. . . .

From the water's surface to the lip of the jar, it measures some five inches. However much I stretch my paws I cannot reach the lip. And the water gives no purchase for a jump. If I do nothing, I just sink. If I flounder around, my claws scrabble on the clay sides but the only result is that scraping sound. It's true that when I claw at the jar I do seem to rise a little in the water but, as soon as my claws scrape down the clay, I slide back deep below the surface. This is so painful that I immediately start scrabbling again until I break surface and can breathe. But it's a very tiring business, and my strength is going. I become impatient with my ill success, but my legs are growing sluggish. In the end I can hardly tell whether I am scratching the jar in order to sink or am sinking to induce more scratching.

While this was going on and despite the constant pain, I found myself reasoning that I'm only in agony because I want to escape from the jar. Now, much as I'd like to get out, it's obvious that I can't: my extended front leg is scarcely three inches long and even if I could hoist my body with its outstretched fore-paws up above the surface, I still could never hook my claws over the rim. Accordingly, since it's blindingly clear that I can't get out, it's equally clear that it's senseless to persist in my efforts to do so. Only my own senseless persistence is causing my ghastly suffering. How very stupid. How very, very stupid deliberately to prolong the agonies of this torture.

"I'd better stop. I just don't care what happens next. I've had quite enough, thank you, of this clutching, clawing, scratching, scraping, scrabbling endless struggle against nature." The decision made, I give up and relax: first my fore-paws, then my hind-legs, then my head and tail.

Gradually I begin to feel at ease. I can no longer tell whether I'm suffering or feeling grateful. It isn't even clear whether I'm drowning in water or lolling in some comfy room. And it really doesn't matter. It does not matter where I am or what I'm doing. I simply feel increasingly at ease. No, I can't actually say that I feel at ease, either. I feel that I've cut away the sun and moon, they pull at me no longer; I've pulverized both Heaven and Earth, and I'm drifting off and away into some unknown endlessness of peace. [shift of translations] I die. I die and gain peace. Peace cannot be gained without dying. Namu Amida Butsu, Namu Amida Butsu. Thank you! Thank you![257]

Are we or are we not all drowning cats?

Ito and Wilson translate the very last words more accurately, "thankfully, thankfully," but doing so loses the English cliché even as it represents the process of the sense more "fully."

Will this cat be reborn in Amida's Pure Land? Surely that question is inept.

The last-moment thought is less about where you are going, than where you already are.

4

PURSUING HAPPINESS: HOW THE ENLIGHTENMENT INVENTED AN AFTERLIFE TO WISH FOR

"Do'st think we shall know one another in the next world, Cariola?"
—JOHN WEBSTER, *DUCHESS OF MALFI*

Hope springs eternal in the human breast:
Man never Is, but always To be blest . . .
What future bliss, he gives not thee to know,
But gives that Hope to be thy blessing now.

Lo! the poor Indian, whose untutored mind
Sees God in clouds, or hears him in the wind;
His soul proud Science never taught to stray
Far as the solar walk, or milky way;
Yet simple Nature to his hope has given,
Behind the cloud-topped hill, an humbler heaven. . . .;
Where slaves once more their native land behold,
No fiends torment, no Christians thirst for gold! . . .
But thinks, admitted to that equal sky,
His faithful dog shall bear him company.
Go, wiser thou!. . . .

—Alexander Pope, *Essay on Man*

On future expectations

There is a sweet enthusiastic melancholy that sometimes steals upon the soul—even thought itself is for a while suspended, and every scene in nature seems to wear an image of the mind. How delightful are the sensations at such a time! though felt, they cannot be described; it is a kind of anticipation of those pleasures we are taught to expect hereafter: the soul seems intirely abstracted from every earthly idea, wrapped up in the contemplation of future happiness. Ask yourself in one of these moments, what there is in this world that is worth a thought; and you will answer nothing: its greatest sublunary pleasure is but as a dream, and vanishes like a shadow; this should convince us more than any thing, that there is a future state: our souls were formed to taste higher delights, more refined sensations than anything in this life can excite; and something from within tells us we shall one day enjoy them—else why these ideas—why these expectations—of what use would be those noble sentiments, with which the mind is sometimes impressed; if we were only to act an insignificant part for a few years in this life, and then sink into nothing? No, there must be a future state, and that immortal!

—"Reflections by a Lady," *London Magazine*, 1778

[T]he hoary atheist who has studied away his soul, has elaborated his theory of annihilation from whole libraries, and given up one life to discover there is no other.

—Sydney Smith, *Six sermons preached in Charlotte Chapel, Edinburgh*, 1800

It is easy to conceive that infinite art is necessary to give an account of what we do not absolutely know anything, and of which, by the nature of the subject itself, we never can know any thing.

—*Encyclopedia Britannica*, "Metaphysics," 1771

By the turn of the Anglophone twentieth century, the afterlife could be anything one wished it to be. George Bernard Shaw visited hell and fantasied heaven for the "Don Juan in Hell Interlude" in *Man and Superman*

(1903). In hell, all the beautiful people amuse themselves talking of love and beauty and art and morality, and poor Don Juan, sent down for murder, is bored to death. Heaven or hell is a matter of taste, like classical concerts or racetracks. Most people prefer the racetrack, though many suffer through classical concerts because they think they ought to. Heaven, for most people, is a colossal bore. They are satisfied with amusements that Don Juan finds unbearably—hellishly—tedious. Eventually, like Mozart, Nietzsche, and a few nameless dowdy women, he heads up to heaven to contribute what he can to the self-actualizing progress of the human species. Shaw's is a back-seat-driving socialist heaven that seeks to collaborate with history. Heaven remains the goal, for motivated and moving folk, and, unlike hell, there are no crowds. Wagner is in hell.

Within the decade, Mark Twain offered the readers of the 1908 Christmas issue of *Harper's* magazine a two-part "Extract from Captain Stormfield's Visit to Heaven." Heaven, Capt. Stormfield discovered to his surprise, is gazillions of miles away, a large-scale replica of the worlds below it, containing every conscious being that ever was, from eight-legged blue things to serial killers and Arabs. Our solar system is a flyspeck, and earth a wart; Satan is more accessible than the patriarchs; people are rewarded on the basis of their potential, not their achievements, and no one is excluded or punished. As to the Deity, he is way off somewhere, and no one seems to ask after him, though he is much respected. It is a deist heaven, on Christian principles of love, mercy, and inclusiveness, and people spend their time learning and touring and hoping to spot celebrities, like Adam or Esau or the more accessible Charles II or Captain Kidd the pirate.

Clearly, one of the pleasures of making up one's own afterlife is to do as Dante did, and Shaw does—put your favorites where you think they belong and your enemies where they get what they deserve. Twain figures his enemies will be so upset by finding everyone in heaven that he need not impose any further vengeance. Twain and Shaw empty Christian forms of theological content to serve newer ideologies, as Aristophanes, Plato, and Virgil restitched classical folklore and philosophy. In Shaw's and Twain's heavens (did you notice?) no one sees God, the climax of Christian eschatology. God has gone away, but he has left his afterlife behind.

Yet how did the Christian afterlife loose its hold? And how, letting go, did it reframe the way people thought about their lives, so that Twain and Shaw, mocking the old Christian afterlife imagery and expectations, use their new versions still to articulate what they value most deeply? The next world was transformed by the forces revolutionizing this one: the intellectual, material, commercial, and imperial growth that set in after the 1720s, removing resignation to traditional limits, imposing capitalism's deep disciplinary effects, diminishing the secular power of the church, shifting political power from an irresponsible court to an answerable parliament.[1] Newton's intelligently designed universe undergirded confidence in the continuing progress of human knowledge; Locke's psychological and epistemological revolutions motivated enquiries into the sociable human mind that turned God into an aspect of man's newly benevolent nature.[2] Alexander Pope sneered in the 1740s at the tendency to "Make God man's image, man the final cause," forgetful that he had modeled the process a decade earlier in his *Essay on Man:* "Know then thyself, presume not God to scan;/ The proper study of Mankind is Man." A kinder, gentler, more benevolent God argued for the fulfillment, not the vanity, of human wishes, and the insatiable human desiring mocked by satirists and Epicureans, pitied by Buddhists and Stoics, became proof positive of human immortality.

These changes were not the work of skeptics, but of clerics pushed along by religious laypeople, often women unencumbered by responsibility to theological orthodoxy (like Elizabeth Phelps's *The Gates Ajar* [1870] a century later irritated Twain into inspiration[3]). Some changes came from below, popular culture moving into mainstream theological acceptance, as the dead are put back in contact with the living and the realm of the dead opens to include friends and family, a paganism unimagined even by Peter Gay. More startlingly, the cleric-wit Laurence Sterne turned the Christian heaven into a place for literary play as if it were pagan Elysium or Hades. Adam Smith discovered the psychological structures that underlie afterlives' invention, though he did not recognize that he had done so. He also reframed the Christian afterlife as a place where human potential frustrated in life, is fulfilled, anticipating Twain's heaven by a century. Shifting its grip on the afterlife, Christianity found others grabbing hold, too.

What we today call "afterlife" was for the eighteenth century the future state toward which human life moved. When Samuel Johnson defines the adjective "future" in the *Dictionary* (1755), he uses *the* definite, not *an* indefinite, article to designate what all come to: "That which will be hereafter; to come; as, the *future* state." In Johnson's *Dictionary*, what seems a simple definition is sometimes a tendentious assertion. Christianity's future state was firmly in place, but no topic was more bruited or debated than "*a* future state," threading its way through poems, plays, sermons, novels, histories, disquisitions, discourses. Samuel Bowden felt obliged to prefer "hereafter" over "here" in his essay on health: "Next to the peace and welfare of our minds, our connection with a future state, and our happiness hereafter, there is nothing of greater importance than our health...."[4] A future state illustrated the progress of grammar, as when George Harris attacked using apostrophes with a participle: 'I had almost forgot to mention another Instance in which *s* is used as an Abbreviation, without the least Pretense for it: for Example, *The Doctrine of a future STATE's being universally taught*.'[5] When Samuel Johnson expressed a preference for an eternity of torment over annihilation, his anxious interlocutor thought he gave too much credence to annihilation's possibility.[6]

The future state that most people expected altered beyond recognition over the century. No one noticed. The raptures of a God-centered heaven and the terrors of eternal punishment for the wicked some pushed gently aside in favor of progress that never ends, happiness that always increases, and human relationships that fulfill and sustain without disappointment forever and ever. Theorists moved God from the center of the afterlife experience and replaced him with their friends and relations; they challenged the perpetuity of hell, and they insisted that human nature required an afterlife to fulfill human wishes, the better to accommodate human desire. God's nature guaranteed the innovations, his benevolence demanding better treatment for creatures he had once threatened with damnation. With effort, perseverance, and passion they created for themselves—and us—what Roy Porter describes as "a basically secular life with the comforts of religion superadded."[7] They remodeled our mansion in the sky to suit the new occupants.

So thorough was their work that even Porter forgets that religion once offered much more than comfort. It fostered guilty terrors, scrupulous anxiety, fear of eternal tortures, certainty of damnation, and complex metaphysical disquisitions, still visible in James Boswell's dreams and Samuel Johnson's and William Cowper's waking hours. As late as 1757, David Hume could smile in the penultimate paragraph of his *Natural History of Religion*: "The comfortable views, exhibited by the belief of futurity, are ravishing and delightful. But how quickly vanish on the appearance of its terrors, which keep a more firm and durable possession of the human mind?" Boswell embodies the contest. His first, horrific memory, he wrote Rousseau in 1764, was of eternal punishment, an idea he owed to his Calvinist mother. But at eight, about 1748, he acquired a tutor who promised after this life happiness, knowledge, meetings with the great men of the past and one's friends. The tutor was a product of what D. P. Walker memorably called "the decline of hell," a decline that in turn provoked reaction.

Methodists and evangelicals sought to restore the traditional discomforts of religion. Others regarded desire and aspiration as signs of absence, not proofs of presence. Skeptics wondered with David Hume where the dead of all the universe's planetary systems would be housed.[8] It was too late, however, altogether to undo the complacency of a prosperous people who expected the next life to deliver even more happiness than they enjoyed in this. The men and women of the eighteenth century put in place the afterlife their grandchildren debunked, Marx as the opiate of the people and Freud as an illusion he hoped had no future.

Death itself was called into question, twice. For the first time since *Gilgamesh*—or the gospels—men challenged death's inevitability. A member of the English House of Commons assured the public in 1700 that it was no longer necessary to die. His book was burned, but he wasn't. Christ's having died on the cross, John Asgill argued, was indeed a full and complete sacrifice—men and women could now go directly to heaven without needing to pass through death.[9] Within a hundred years, a secular thinker posited that the progress of mind would soon make dying unnecessary. If, William Godwin argued towards the end of *Political Justice* (1793), people could overcome sleep and stay cheerful, death (and sexual generation) would end. No longer would human inquiry have to start all over again every thirty years.

Unlike Asgill, Godwin was somewhat embarrassed to make the claim. His chapter title provides no clue ("Of the Objection to this System from the Principle of Population"), while Asgill's book flaunts his. Godwin also invoked a prestigious source at several removes—Benjamin Franklin, as retold by Dr. Richard Price and confirmed by Price's nephew. Conjecturing sublimely, Godwin reports, Franklin once affirmed that mind would "one day become omnipotent over matter." And if mind could rule over matter, why not that mind tangled in us over that matter that somehow also composes us?[10] Franklin's and Godwin's intellectual heirs still ask that question, and Godwin's improbable project engages many thinkers today.[11] Asgill has no takers.

A successful lawyer as brash and full of projects as his fellow bankrupt Defoe or any of Swift's "moderns," Asgill was expelled from two Houses of Commons, first the Irish, then the English, for asserting his "Whym ... at a time when the rest of Mankind are so deeply engaged in Secular Affairs." What got him into trouble was not his attack on death, "this Custom of the World to die," but his scriptural argument.[12] "Custom it self, without a Reason for it is an Argument only to Fools": Asgill observed that Jesus had promised "that Man by him may live for ever," and then added, dangerously, "And this is that Magnetick which hath drawn the World after him." That phrase was the first the Commons challenged in 1707.[13] It turned revelation's eternal life from a divine truth into a human motive and a mechanical device, working of necessity, deforming will. That move Asgill did not intend. His aim was God's truth, not his own. If it is only my idea, it will "sink, and fall, and die; But if it be his that I think 'tis, it will kindle it self like a Firebrand from one to another, till it hath set the World in Arms against Death."[14]

Alas, the world only waited for Asgill to die. The year after the book appeared (1701), the director of *Nouvelles de la République des Lettres* queried from France, "They say that Mr. Asgill the immortal man is dead; try to find out and if he is please let me know, it's a piece of news worth printing."[15] Taking Asgill's question seriously, Henry Grove explained in a funeral sermon (1727) why God had not simply abolished death on his first incarnation.[16] Debtors' prison saw Asgill die (1738), and there is no record of his last words. The outmoded custom of the world to die continues.

Neither Asgill nor Godwin meditates on afterlife—since the one requirement for reaching the afterlife is to die. Godwin readied himself for departure by proposing monuments to great men in an *Essay on Sepulchres*.[17] Unlike Godwin's compensatory fame, Asgill's enthusiasm for eternal life before death seems quaint and a little absurd. Still, he answered anew a question Protestants had been struggling with for two hundred years and that deists' indifference to detail laid to rest.

When did the afterlife start? At death, or at the resurrection to the Last Judgment? Catholic souls had long arrived at hell, purgatory, or heaven to await their resurrected bodies.[18] Purgatory sixteenth-century Protestants had expunged as unattested in scripture, but scripture did not say what happened when the body died. Jewish scripture, as Isaac Watts observed, had no concept of a soul separate from the body or "person." Early Christians did not expect to wait long before the general resurrection at Christ's return.[19] John Jortin mildly lamented, "The intermediate state between death and the resurrection is a subject of inquiry, upon which the scriptures have not said so much as one would wish."[20] With scripture indecisive, even Luther and Calvin had disagreed.

For Luther, souls slept or died until the Last Judgment. Calvin, like God, knew they went at once to heaven or hell, but God alone knew who went where. His God knew the final disposition of souls before they were born, circumventing the Lutheran problem that scripture does not mention two judgments, so how can a soul be assigned a place without a judgment? Others argued an intermediate state, not fully heaven or hell, but very close, until the Last Judgment.[21] Isaac Newton knew the soul slept until resurrection; Isaac Watts insisted on an intermediate state; Daniel Defoe's Robinson Crusoe reported seeing no intermediate state in his heavenly vision.[22] Real questions to which people needed answers, the *Athenian Oracle* and other papers obliged, with a steady diet of explanations.[23] Edward Young's wandering Protestant soul flitted about the cosmos while the body slept, playfully undetermined but awake, until it rejoined its body:

> The Body thus renew'd, the conscious Soul,
> Which has *perhaps* been flutt'ring near the Pole,
> *Or* midst the burning Planets wond'ring stray'd,
> *Or* hover'd o'er, where her pale Corps was laid;
> *Or* rather coasted on her final State,
> And Fear'd, or Wish'd for her appointed Fate:
> This Soul returning with a constant Flame,
> Now Weds for ever her Immortal Frame.[24] (italics added)

Questions about where or when troubled deists not at all. Many confidently affirmed expectations of immortality, some probably to avoid imputations of atheism, others as part of their creed.[25] In English deism's founding document, Edward, Lord Herbert of Cherbury's (1583–1648)

De Veritate (Paris, 1624), future rewards and punishments appear among the five "Common Notions," along with a supreme creator-being, divine providence, gratitude expressed through prayer, and the immortality of the soul.[26] Charles Blount claimed immortality in his *Religio Laici* (1783), replying to Dryden's (1782). When John Wilmot, Earl of Rochester, translated Seneca's "After death nothing is, and nothing death," Blount found self-contradiction: Rochester's "mighty Genius is a most sufficient Argument of its own Immortality." Anthony Collins died (1729) with hopeful expectations on his lips, according to reports: "I am told that his dying words were to this effect, 'I have endeavoured to serve true Religion and my Country, and I hope that I shall go to a place where I shall find others that have done the same.'"[27] Benjamin Franklin's epitaph (written at the ripe age of twenty-two) promised he would appear in "In a new/And more beautiful edition/Corrected and Amended/By/The Author."[28] Voltaire, not ruling immortality altogether out when Boswell came inquiring in 1764, said, "it may be, but he knows nothing of it."[29] Tom Paine assured the world (1795) that "I believe in one God, and no more; and I hope for happiness beyond this life."[30] Equally hopeful were Matthew Tindal, Thomas Chubb, Thomas Morgan, and Joseph Reed.[31]

Tougher John Toland expected "never to be the same Toland more,"[32] and Dr. Samuel Garth's bedside manner was legendary. He comforted a dying actress panicked over her sins by telling her "to rest contented [for] upon his honour there was neither a God nor future State."[33] Henry St. John, Lord Bolingbroke (pub. 1754) reduced theism's tenets to a supreme being, a moral order, and a created world. A future state reason could neither affirm nor deny, as some Christian apologists also argued.[34] (If a future state could not be proved from nature or reason, it followed that the only access to immortality was through revelation, annihilating deist pretentions to immortality.[35]) Still, Bolingbroke disliked Lucretius's bumptious certainty that the soul was mortal and considered that, on balance, he would rather be immortal than not: "[H]aving tasted existence, I might abhor nonentity."[36] Let Lucretius parse the probability of abhorring one's own nonentity.

Even the first avowed English atheist had immortal hopes: "For my part I firmly wish for such a future state, and though I cannot firmly believe it, I am resolved to live as if such a state were to ensue" (1782).[37] Bishop Butler in 1736 revived the soul as [butter]fly, noting the analogy with the

"Change of Worms into Flies, and the vast Enlargement of their locomotive Powers by such Change."[38] The most scandalous French materialist made the bishop's metaphor prettier, more sentimental, and less maggoty. Julien Offray de la Mettrie (*La Homme Machine*, 1747) smiled at a caterpillar's lamenting his fate amidst the scattered skins of his peers, unable to imagine metamorphosis. Existence after death was no more imaginable to living machine-men than becoming a butterfly to a caterpillar, but equally natural and, implicitly, happy.[39] (A Margaret Atwood heroine observes that butterflies die.[40]) If deists and atheists had such hopes, Christians would not be far behind. Christianity had already improved the afterlife by creating one, as 2 Timothy said, quoted again and again: Jesus had "brought life and immortality to light" (2 Tim. 1.10, KJV).

Deists thought they had their afterlife from reason and nature, but Dryden knew better. If Aristotle had been unable to demonstrate the soul's immortality, Charles Blount had not reached it by pure ratiocination: " 'Tis revelation what thou think'st discourse."[41] Dryden had in mind, alas, not deism's unconscious appropriation of scripture, but the tradition that Noah's descendants had handed down an afterlife after the flood. By the 1770s, what Dryden should have meant is in common circulation, in Francis Blackburne (1772) and a dialogue of the dead between Mr. Hume and Dr. Dodd (1778). Bishop William Warburton's *Divine Legation of Moses Demonstrated* (1738–41) contributed by advancing the view, controversial to some, not all, that the Jews had neither needed nor had a future state since they were under the direct care of divinity. Christian redesign pushed beyond deism on two fronts: a heated, controversial, conspicuous attack on hell's eternal punishments, and a stealth enlargement of the pleasures of heaven that displaced God and welcomed the family.

People noticed the attack on hell. During the civil wars, the digger Gerard Winstanley and Cromwell's chaplain Jeremiah White had challenged perpetual torments, anticipated by Fukansai Habian.[42] Their antithesis, Charles II of the barren wife he would not divorce and twelve ennobled bastards, assured a future bishop, "he was no atheist, but he could not think God would make a man miserable, only for taking a little pleasure out of the way."[43] Charles's poet laureate John Dryden endorsed Origen's heretical hope that even the devil would finally be saved in the preface to *Absalom and Achitophel* (1681), but spoke of "everlasting punishments" in *Religio Laici* (1682) where the topic carried its full theological freight. Dryden's friend and theological consultant, John Tillotson, archbishop of Canterbury, regarded questioning eternal torments as improper for public discussion (1690) but thought God was not required to impose eternal punishment; he could remit, if he would.[44] In Aphra Behn's *Oroonoko* (1688), a lying Christian swears by "eternal torment in the world to come" should he violate the oath he does not intend to keep.[45] John Locke's *Reasonableness of Christianity* (1695) gave the wicked only death, not eternal torture, and readers noticed the omission, often disapprovingly.[46] In *Robinson Crusoe* (1719), Friday, under Crusoe's Christian instruction, concludes that the devil too will at last be saved. "*Well, well*, says he, mighty affectionately, *that well; so you, I, Devil, all wicked, all preserve, repent, God pardon all.*" Crusoe is dumbfounded, and Defoe never attempts to give him a better argument, though he expostulates in Crusoe's *Serious Reflections*.[47]

Against such growing, grudging resistance, Sir William Dawes, baronet, preaching before King William in 1701 devoted a sermon to *The true meaning of the Eternity of Hell Torments*. There would be no mere annihilation for the wicked; they were to suffer. Nor was hell merely banishment from God's presence; it meant active infliction of pain. Nor would there ever be any release: the wicked would not be punished for a time and then annihilated, but punished forever and ever eternally. Dawes's five sermons between 1699 and 1701 addressed the certainty, greatness, eternity, true meaning, and objections (answered) to eternal hell-torments, a topic the future archbishop of York considered pressing, so many objections having been raised against hell's eternal tortures. Dawes' careful, lucid, dispassionate reasoning did not staunch the opposition. It overflowed into happiness for all.

A passionate protest against Dawesian orthodoxy, Thomas Burnet's posthumously published *De statu mortuorum et resurgentium tractatus* (1720) found three translators as "Concerning the State of Departed Souls," Matthias Earbery, answering the heresies in notes (1727), Thomas Foxton (1729) and the redoubtable John Dennis (1730, 1733, 1739).[48] Tertullian and other church fathers had ranked watching the tortures of the damned high among the pleasures of the blessed in heaven. Burnet (1635?–1715) rejected such pleasures in the name of man and God: "Human Nature abhors the very Name of eternal Punishments which sets before our Eyes a Spectacle of insatiable, implacable Revenge; and this for no Manner of Profit or Hopes of Amendment . . . Reason, the Nature of God, and the Nature of Things, cry out loudly against it. . . ." For Burnet, "the Nature of God" opposed a doctrine the New Testament endorsed. Abraham tells Dives he can have no cooling water in hell (Luke 16.19–31). Burnet demanded "some commodious Explication of the divine Passages, that both human Rights and divine may not at once be violated. . . ."[49]

Answering Burnet's call, numerous divines explicated away eternal punishments, finding "eternal" a word of multiple significations and variable duration, while others testily restored the obvious reading.[50] In 1739 Edmund Curll sent the work again into the world with a brash new title, proclaiming *Hell Torments Not Eternal. Argumentatively Proved, from the Attribute of Divine Mercy*. God could not be less good than men thought themselves to be, who dreaded seeing friends and acquaintances in the pit.

The good headed for another place. As Peter Walmsley observes of the immensely popular *Practical Discourse Concerning Death* (1689, 23 editions by 1739), William Sherlock "tells his reader that 'We are traveling to Heaven,' never stopping to explore other options."[51] When Sherlock explored "other options," fewer readers followed. *A Discourse concerning the Happiness of Good Men, and the Punishment of the Wicked in the Next World* (1704) reached only a fourth edition by 1726; *A Practical Discourse Concerning a Future Judgment* (1692) reached only a tenth by 1731. Evidently the word *punishment* in the title could cut even Sherlock's editions by 75 percent, while *judgment* reduced them 50 percent.

In the 1730s, Alexander Pope twitted the saints lolling on painted chapel ceilings and the smooth sermons that "never mention Hell to ears polite." His ladies laugh at hell and gush, "But ah, how charming if there's no such place."[52] The Swiss deist Marie Huber, happy to see even the devils in heaven, thought hell useless: "Everyone is persuaded, that he himself is not of the number of the Wicked, whose Portion shall be in the Lake of Fire and Brimstone."[53] Catherine Trotter Cockburn's niece read Huber enthusiastically, incurring a gentle check from her aunt (1744), pleased by the idea "of the whole creation being happy at last," but uneasy over equal happiness for the wicked and the virtuous.[54]

Even Samuel Johnson closed an *Adventurer* (#107, 1753) with the observation that involuntary errors, would not be held against the dead at their judgment: "what is beyond we can only conjecture. . . . [yet] we can repose with comfort [on] the care of Providence, whose eye takes in the whole of things, and under whose direction all involuntary errors will terminate in happiness."[55] Fred Parker finds Johnson's last line "a fragile, almost perfunctory gesture, too close to a conventionally pious signing-off to function as the true conclusion of such a substantial essay."[56] Not recognizing the hopeful assertion of happiness as a new gesture, he regards it as the tired old one it has since become. He also fails to notice Johnson's implicit exception for voluntary errors. They presumably "terminate" in the opposite of happiness, misery, and suggest Johnson's (unfulfilled) demands upon himself.

By the late 1730s, eternal happiness was breaking out all over. Le Clerc's letter to Bayle, published in the *Life* (1734), insisted that God subjected even the "impenitent" only to "moderate punishments, before he puts them in possession of eternal happiness."[57] Pierre Cuppé's "new system," translated in 1743, promised to do away with hell once and for all, insisting *That All Men shall be Saved, Or, Made Finally Happy* (full title: *Heaven Open to All Men. Or, A Theological Treatise, in which, Without unsettling the Practice of Religion, Is Solidly Prov'd, By Scripture and Reason, That All Men shall be Saved, Or, Made Finally Happy.*)[58] A minister formerly in Virginia promptly denounced it as "atheistical."[59] That "foolish book" was embraced by "our debauchees" above the Gospel, grumbled L.T.K. in the *Gentleman's Magazine* a decade later.[60]

David Hartley (1705–57) turned the desire for happiness into its "probability," equally derivable from computation and from scripture. The second volume of his *Observations on Man, His Frame, His Duty and His Expectations* (1749) proudly announced the ultimate end of eternal hellfire and torture, though not without great punishments for the wicked until then: "Sect. V. Of the final Happiness of all Mankind in some distant future State. *It is probable from Reason, that all Mankind will be made happy ultimately, 419–25. . . . from the Scriptures. . . . 426–437.*" Reason and computation precede Scripture, which both crowns the end and comes in second, attached to the real proofs. Neither the world nor Hartley was yet prepared for an easy happy ending, however.

Hartley's preface reassured his readers that the wicked would be very severely punished in the next world: "I do most firmly believe, upon the Authority of the Scriptures, that the future Punishment of the Wicked will be exceedingly great both in Degree and Duration, i.e. infinite and eternal, in that real practical Sense to which alone our Conceptions extend."[61]

Others annihilated hell and the wicked, reserving happiness for the good. Word spread north, to Scotland. Alexander Robertson of Struan rejoiced over the death of one malevolent neighbor and stamped on his "native Dirt," expecting gleefully that he was where "Proud LUCIFER takes Care of thee." But by 1752 even he had had "A Morning Thought":

> I fear no Torments in a future State,
> For God is ever good as he is great:
> It were a Cruelty in God to give
> Eternal Pain to him he made to live.
> Annihilation then must be their Lot,
> Who live in Wickedness, and are forgot.
> Tho' this new System may be counted odd,
> 'Tis all intended to the Praise of God.[62]

The flattest verses God has ever received, Robertson sums up seventy years of theological debate and still finds the conclusion, endearingly, "new" and "odd."

Justice, the divine attribute supporting eternal punishment, was becoming something always already there in this life, as it had been for Socrates, Plato, and the Old Testament, and something people took charge of themselves. The failures of justice in this life had been—and remain—a powerful argument for the next. In the 1680s, one doctor of divinity required God to administer justice to keep His job description. If there were no judgment, argued Dr. Anthony Horneck, there was no God. A God who did not judge was imperfect and therefore no God at all.[63] The ill distribution of justice in this life demanded another where retribution and recompense would have their place. "[V]irtue," Dryden observed, "is generally unhappy in this world, and vice fortunate: so that 'tis hope of futurity alone that makes this life tolerable, in expectation of a better" (1685).[64] The prosperity of the wicked beyond any social control makes this life "[in]tolerable." That unhappy conclusion suggests a sense of powerlessness relative to life's distributions.

Such powerlessness fades in the next century, after two political revolutions strengthening parliament relative to the monarchy (1689, 1714), the epistemological triumphs of empiricism (1665, 1672, 1687, et seq), and economic innovations ranging from Gregory King's demographics to the

Bank of England (1694), the national debt, and the first stock bubbles (1720). The uncontrollable, God-given hazards of agriculture were challenged by the manipulable, human-driven hazards of rapidly expanding commerce. Satirists and reformers, "projectors," addressed the endemic injustices of a complex social order (sometimes, like Jonathan Swift, they were the same person). The epic project updating *Paradise Lost* declared "Happiness! Our being's end and aim!" affirmed "An honest man's the noblest work of God," challenged "The right divine of kings to govern wrong," and insisted, over and over, that "Whatever is is right" (1733–34, Pope, *Essay on Man*, IV, 1, 248; I, 294, IV, 394). Meanwhile, the poet's other works found fault almost everywhere.

By the 1740s, philosophers as various as Catherine Trotter Cockburn, David Hume, and Lord Bolingbroke, Pope's "guide, philosopher, and friend," objected to the constant linkage of virtue and misery, vice and happiness. Hume and Cockburn agreed that happiness favored virtue in this life, and Bolingbroke objected, as did Cockburn, to whining about "[t]he imaginary unjust distribution of good and evil."[65] Anticipating the philosophers, Alexander Pope made a distinction Adam Smith echoed: If virtue lacked "a Coach and Six" (1734), perhaps virtue had not been engaged in coach-and-six-getting practices: "'But sometimes Virtue starves while Vice is fed.'/ What then? Is the reward of Virtue bread?" (*Essay on Man*, IV, 170, 149–50). Smith explains: Virtue receives the reward appropriate to it—love and esteem—but we tend to wish it honors, riches, etc., the rewards properly speaking of business and industry, not virtue.[66] Smith's course in natural theology at Glasgow taught that God intends human happiness in this life, and his *Theory of Moral Sentiments* (1759) reaffirmed the view, restricting God's intention to "mankind, as well as all other rational creatures."[67]

In perhaps the most subversive of all his moves, David Hume suggested that as much justice as was to be found in this life established the limits for the justice to be expected from God. To suppose otherwise was to go beyond the evidence available.[68] It is easy to overlook what Hume suggests—that the amoral, unjust world in which we live shows us the face of God. From him we can expect no better than he has already given. If what we see of this world is what we get in heaven, mind the gap. Such a view erases hope from futurity, but returns justice to this world as responsibility. It is also what God told Job about himself from the whirlwind.

Justice had become something one should do something about. As Philip Almond suggests, imaginary reforms in the afterlife precede reforms in the worldly judicial system, and play dialectically back and forth.[69] *The Adventurer* opined in 1752 that eternal punishment and the gibbet were equally useful, and one does not want to get rid of either.[70] Eternal punishment Henry Fielding (1707–1754) thought undeniably scriptural, but diabolical.[71] As a novelist, he reformed the afterlife in the 1740s. In the 1750s as a magistrate, he proposed a parallel reform in this world's penal system. Fielding's *Journey from This World to the Next* (1743) kept the Bottomless Pit, but sent no one into it, though a thousand years earlier it swallowed the perpetrators of a massacre. Hanged felons expecting hell's worst, Fielding's Elysium welcomes at once to eternal happiness. A decade later, as Westminster magistrate, Fielding proposed concealing Tyburn's entrance to eternity. Hangings should be hidden inside Newgate to diminish the festival visibility of punishment. Like his Bottomless Pit, the threat remained, but out of sight.[72]

Rigorous proponents of both eternal punishment and the gallows found themselves insensibly shrinking both. Hanging a man for robbing another of a small sum which the man robbed can well spare, setting one man's life, his all, against a pittance, Jeremiah Seed (1700–1747) knew was out of proportion. Still, it was necessary to counter crime, which "tends to render Property, and what is valuable in this Life, precarious, and to subvert the Peace of Society." So he limited the numbers of the eternally condemned: "It may be likewise presumed, that the Number of the Damned will bear no more Proportion to that of the Blessed throughout the whole Creation; than a Workhouse or a Prison does to the whole Extent of a large Kingdom."[73] Tidily reversing the biblical expectation that many are called, and few chosen, Seed also exchanges the broad and narrow ways. The saved have moved into a comfortable majority. By the 1760s, punishments in the future life had to be justified as not contrary to Christianity, but a necessary sanction in a "well-policied state."[74] Hell never goes away, but its conditions are contested. Of the century's principal religious visionaries, John Wesley's "Methodist poison" was accused of reviving hell's terrors,[75] while Emmanuel Swedenborg's "comfortable views" horrified Wesley.[76]

Emmanuel Swedenborg's visionary tracts began turning up in London in Latin after his vision there in 1745, with translations from 1769. Swedish baron and scientist, Swedenborg (1688–1772) published works on metallurgy, geology, and trips to heaven that appear regularly in the libraries of members of the Royal Society and the universities.[77] Having talked to a hundred thousand or so dead, he reported that the dead retained their governing passions, a body and senses, occupying beautiful houses and mansions and streets. Dead, they found themselves "living men as before, and in a similar state of mind (for immediately after death every one's state of life is the same as when he left this world, but is successively and gradually changed either for heaven or hell) they were affected with a new kind of joy at their being alive, and said that they could scarce believe their senses; and yet wondered at their former hebetude and blindness with respect to a future state. . . ."[78] Conjugal love flourished, with God arranging childfree marriages (251). Death takes nothing away but thoughtless matter; all vital power belongs to the spirit, which already in the body is joined with the world of spirits, though most remain unaware of their society (288, 303). William Blake briefly joined the Swedenborgian Church of the New Jerusalem in 1789, and Swedenborg's mystical analogies and correspondences are lovingly treated in McDannell and Lang.[79] As to hell, the evil choose to go there, as the good choose to go to heaven. The wicked would not enjoy heaven, argued John Norris's discourses and Philip Doddridge's sermons long before, quoted by Laurence Sterne in his.[80] To the sneer that heaven would be hopelessly dull, just like church, the authorized response was that the complainant would never have a chance to find out.

Passionate revivalist for hell, John Wesley was frantic to dissociate his orthodox views from Swedenborg's "brainsick" visions, with which his Methodists were often unkindly linked.[81] Worst for Wesley is hell's decline in Swedenborg: "For, first, he quenches the unquenchable fire. He assures us there is no fire there: only he allows that the governor of it, the Devil, sometimes orders the spirits that behave ill, to be 'laid on a bed of hot ashes.' And, secondly, he informs you, that all the damned enjoy their favourite pleasures. He that delights in filth, is to have his filth; yea, and his harlot too! Now how dreadful a tendency must this have, in such an age and nation as this?"[82] Hell quenched, the new benevolism extends to the next world, sympathetically averse to tortures, eternal or quotidien.

Hell revives as mercy's oil spreads, but within a fundamentally altered discursive context that includes sentimental softening, derisive scoffing, parodic play, and paralyzing terrors. By 1791 the evangelical Hannah More was struggling to restore hell, original sin, damnation, and judgment and to disabuse her contemporaries of their "unwarranted assurance of salvation," their illusion that held "every body to be in a safe state."[83] The "decline of hell" had been noted, and deplored.

IMPROVING HEAVEN: ABANDONING THEOCENTRISM FOR KNOWLEDGE AND SELF-KNOWLEDGE

While hell drew the attention as heaven opened to "all men," heaven cautiously, surreptitiously began to give men and women more of what they wanted from this life in the next. Swedenborg had his converts after 1750, but the significant action took place within orthodoxy itself, protected by the extremes of Swedenborgianism and Methodism. The afterlife laid claim to self-consciousness, human relationships, reunions with loved ones, including dead children, and self-directed, intellectual activity. One by one, these arrive to take their place as if they had never been absent. Ultimately, human desire (craving) becomes in itself proof of heaven. Always a physical place, heaven's reality was now confirmed by the human mind. The century snaps shut when Adam Smith turns the next world into a psychological projection from this one.

At the close of the seventeenth century, heaven's raptures were intense and beyond description, everyone agreed. The available imagery was largely biblical—songs, music, angels, light, divine presence, crowns, glory. Poets saw their dead mounting, flying, carried or greeted by angels, and almost heard the heavenly choir warbling or swelling in anthems of praise, but then the brightness of the vision hid them from sight.[84] Milton, discoursing on his blindness, limns heaven as light, ambrosial odors, song, and language (*Paradise Lost*, Book 3). That the glories of heaven were to the living as the beauties of the earth to a blind man was a common trope in sermons. God and death were the oculist that would open human sight to the utterly unimaginable.[85]

These ecstasies focused on the soul's encounter with God and ended in that encounter. The rapt soul, lost in contemplation of the ineffable beatific vision, joined the company of angels and "just men made perfect," whoever they might be. Bunyan sees Christian and Hopeful disappear into the New Jerusalem, newly dressed and blending into the singing throngs (*The Pilgrim's Progress*, 1678). In the glory of God human memories vanish into an eternal moment. When Christiana and her four sons—and their wives—follow some years later in Part Two (1684), she dreams of her husband on the other side of the river, but not of his arriving to greet her. She goes to meet the Prince. Peleg Morris, lolling in Jesus's embrace, lives "for ever on his numerous Charms."[86] The experience of heaven was worshipful and contemplative, God-centered, human-relations erasing, atemporally transcendent, and closed to human sight. Thomas Emlyn, preaching his first sermon after his wife's death in 1701, rivets the living dead in a vision of eternal stasis before God, Dante simplified, de-intellectualized, made purely amorous: "*Where* Infinite Beauty unveils its face to open view, Where it amazes, ravishes, and overcomes *Myriads* of attentive Spectators; Its attractive *Charms*, draw and fasten all their Eyes, so that they never look off from that *amiable Object; they always behold him:* Where they need no Books of *Devotion* to warm their Hearts; One view of his *ineffable Glory* is instead of a thousand Arguments, and wraps them up in the flames of ardent admiring love."[87] Such visions never disappear, but they recede in favor of visions in a newer style that accommodate the progress of science and the primacy of human relationships and, especially, self-consciousness and self-knowledge.

The new glories of science and progressive knowledge were the first element added to the traditional Christian afterlife. Unlike the cosmic visions of Plato, Cicero, and Virgil, where knowledge was revealed complete, these visions emphasized the progressive unfolding of continuing knowledge to the individual (later fundamental to Swedenborg). In the late seventeenth century, the delights of increased natural knowledge in the next world still count for less than the resolution of troubling theological questions. By the first decades of the eighteenth century, theological agonizing has been replaced by more general intellectual curiosity about the cosmos to be gratified in the next world. In such thinkers as Thomas Burnet and Sir Isaac Newton, the older theology-first pattern still holds, while the more popular and accessible *Micrographia* (1665) of Robert Hooke points out another direction, moving from theology to natural knowledge. Moving into the next world, science for the first time realized its own potential for infinite progress.

Theorizing in *Sacred Theory of the Earth* (1681) that the flood caused the present irregular, mountainous, malformed world, Thomas Burnet maintained that at the millennium the initial perfect, egg-shaped world of Paradise would be restored. Burnet had biblical warrant in Isaiah, set to music in Handel's *Messiah*, 1742. When the valleys will be exalted, the mountains made low, the crooked straight, and the rough places plane, the world will again be round and smooth as an egg. Burnet's blessed will spend their time in "'Devotion and Contemplation', the 'publick devotions' being very splendid and sometimes culminating in a visible appearance of Christ in the sky." The questions to which they long for answers will include whether Satan and the souls in hell can hope for salvation.[88] Although Burnet gloried in "being exalted above all the Planets . . . view[ing] the boundless Ocean of the Universe, and innumerable Globes of Worlds, floating along the vast Stream of the Sky, each fill'd with its proper Inhabitants," he was more concerned with the fate of sinful souls in the afterlife. He challenged eternal punishment, as we have seen, and demanded a better "Explication of the divine Passages."[89]

So, too, Newton's discoveries turned him from natural philosophy to theology, to the study of the prophecies of Daniel and the structure of the tabernacle as a model for the universe.[90] A mortalist who held that the soul dies or sleeps until the trumpet sounds for the Last Judgment, Newton argued the sleep would seem only an instant. He also suspected the awakening was coming sooner than anyone anticipated. Eliminating the only biblical evidence against mortalism, Newton noted that Dives and Lazarus was a parable and re-pointed Christ's words on the cross to the Good Thief, "I say to you today you shall be with me in paradise" (Luke 23:43; Dives 16:19–31). Usually read as a promise that the thief and Jesus will be in paradise today, the statement Newton observed makes better sense pointed as "I say to you today." Jesus himself, after all, would not be in paradise for more than a month (forty-four days), according to the same gospel author (Acts 1:3, 9–11). Anti-mortalists often argued that deferring judgment until the resurrection put it too far off to deter bad behavior. Surely God would forget about misdeeds in all that time, the hypothetical atheist reassured himself.[91] Newton, however, had evidence that the last trump would soon sound.

The book of Daniel promised that at the end time "knowledge shall be increased." When had knowledge ever increased as much as the late seventeenth century, crowned with Newton's own *Principia Mathematica* (1687) and *Opticks* (1672, 1704)? If the structure of the universe had been revealed to Newton, as it had been, then the end foretold in Daniel was near: "seal the book, even to the time of the end: many shall run to and fro, and knowledge shall be increased" (Dan. 12:4). Taking the application personally, Newton turned back to the book and set about decoding Daniel.[92] Intellectual progress led Newton back to specific theological questions to which he sought another key, like the one he had discovered for the cosmos.

By contrast, Robert Hooke's *Micrographia* (1665) adapted a biblical metaphor to abandon biblical for natural, secular knowledge. Newton's antithesis, Hooke's concern is this world, not the next, and he makes an equally startling claim for the progress of knowledge. Human efforts will re-create paradise. Telescopes revealed new worlds at a distance; microscopes things near but hitherto invisible. On every scale, he observed, "*there is a new visible World discovered to the understanding. By this means the Heavens are open'd, and a vast number of new Stars, and new Motions, and new Productions appear in them, to which all the antient Astronomers were utterly Strangers . . .*" Then, in a very curious metaphor, he proposes reversing the curse of Adam and the sin of Eve by humanity's own intellectual efforts. "*And as at first, mankind fell by tasting of the forbidden Tree of Knowledge, so we, their Posterity, may be in part restor'd by the same way, not only by beholding and contemplating, but by tasting too those fruits of Natural knowledge, that were never yet forbidden.*"[93] Re-enacting the steps of the fall—behold, contemplate, taste, [share]—man achieves his own salvation by his own actions via "natural knowledge." Such knowledge is ethically neutral: it is not the moral knowledge of good and evil once forbidden. The biblical metaphor leaves theology behind as man remakes his own paradise.

In the afterlife, Hooke's progressive knowledge was most influentially elaborated by Joseph Addison, as Jacob Sider Jost observes.[94] In periodical essays in *The Tatler, Spectator,* and *Guardian* (1709–1714), Addison and Richard Steele pursued immortality. Mingling moral and intellectual improvement, Addison (1711) proposed "the perpetual Progress" of the soul to "the Perfection of its Nature, without ever arriving at a Period in it." This unfinishable business continues from this life into the next, ever in motion, ever drawing nearer to Godhead. In endless "Accessions" as the Soul adds "Virtue to Virtue, and Knowledge to Knowledge," it ever more closely resembles God himself, without quite ever becoming God, "like one of those Mathematical Lines that may draw nearer to another for all Eternity, without a Possibility of touching it."[95] Both the metaphor and perpetual progress resonated.

Swedenborg developed a similar image in his *Divine Providence*, 1764. As man becomes more and more conjoined to the Lord, his conjunction nearer, his wisdom and happiness greater, he himself becomes at once more his own and the Lord's. Beilby Porteus, the Bishop of Chester, admired Addison on the "*perpetual progress of the soul towards perfection*" as late as 1783,[96] and the 1793 *English Review* preferred Porteus and Addison to a less gifted writer on the future state: "We could not avoid the recollection of Bishop Porteus's more persuasive eloquence on this animating subject. Nor could we help recurring to the beautiful papers of Addison on the restless nature and progressive advancement of the powers and faculties of man in the scale of perfection."[97] God, it may not be noticed, has slipped from view as man advances, like the moon at midday.

In Thomas Tickell and Henry Grove, frequent contributors to *The Spectator*, Addison found writers ecstatic before the "spacious firmament on high" and its role in the afterlife. Henry Grove (1684–1738), a dissenting minister Samuel Johnson esteemed, Elizabeth Singer Rowe's biographer, rejoiced in the possibilities for understanding the natural world created by an eternity of investigation. Passionate for new discoveries, the devout Grove inadvertently transforms whole-souled worship into a balancing act, hierarchy into equilibrium. When he finally collapses in awe before his God, Grove has just been extracting from His brain His cosmic plans. Tonson, the bookseller, included Grove's *Spectator* #635 (1714) in his Addisonian compilation *Evidences of the Christian Religion* (1730).[98]

Hearing no hymns sounding among the spheres, Grove moves through the stars as rapidly as Milton's angels (or Twain's Stormfield racing comets). A later writer will affirm technically that the new body acquired in death is not subject to gravity, "we shall transport ourselves from one world to another, with a celerity perhaps equal to that of light."[99] To all the scientific questions with which God had taunted Job from the whirlwind, about things he did not know and never could know, Grove expects answers:

> [I]t pleases me to think that I who know so small a portion of the Works of the Creator, and with slow and painful Steps creep up and down on the Surface of this Globe, shall ere long shoot away with the Swiftness of Imagination, trace out the hidden Springs of Nature's Operations, be able to keep pace with the heavenly Bodies in the Rapidity of their Carreer [sic], be a Spectator of the long Chain of Events in the natural and moral Worlds, visit the several Apartments of the Creation, know how they are furnished and how inhabited, comprehend the Order and measure the Magnitudes, and Distances of those Orbs, which to us seem disposed without any regular Design, and set all in the same Circle, observe the Dependance of the Parts of each System, and (if our Minds are big enough to grasp the Theory) of the several Systems upon one another, from whence results the Harmony of the Universe. In Eternity a great deal may be done of this kind.[100]

Indeed, a great deal may be done in eternity. Grove turns to God only after his explorations of the cosmic system are accomplished, acknowledging God as the greatest joy, though now indistinctly known. Grove wants natural knowledge, and when he collapses in rapture before the divine presence, he has just been picking God's brain. He has been seeing what God sees, not seeing God:

> All created Glories will fade and die away in his Presence. Perhaps it will be my Happiness *to compare the World with the fair Exemplar of it in the divine Mind*; perhaps *to view the original Plan of those wise Designs* that have been executing in a long Succession of Ages. Thus employed in finding out his Works, and contemplating their Author! how shall I fall prostrate and adoring, my Body swallowed up in the Immensity of Matter, my Mind in the Infinitude of his Perfections! [emphasis added].[101]

Being swallowed up, ordinarily the first event on arriving in heaven, is deferred by Grove for some time. The resurrection is curiously out of sight, his "Body" confounded with "the Immensity of Matter."

Characteristically, women authors often advance innovations, including the progress of mind, before their male counterparts. Mary, Lady Chudleigh in 1710 had already promised Sophia, the electress of Brunswick, that in the future state, "Knowledge, in all Probability, will be everlastingly progressive." Noting that clouds are made of water, "the liquid Plains of Air," she too expects to range "thro' all the Realms on High," "Where something new would still delight,/ Something my Knowledge still improve."[102] Joseph Boyse in Dublin in 1724, discoursing on the *Four Last Things: Death, Judgment, Heaven and Hell*, anticipated Twain's pleasures in meeting the inhabitants of other worlds, perfecting "our souls in rational and intellectual powers . . . [and enjoying] the most vigorous Exercise of those perfected Powers on the most noble and agreeable Objects." Unluckily for contemporary prejudices against Irishmen, he also observes that progress in knowledge will at last become easy, no longer tedious and disappointing.[103] Bishop Butler hoped to increase his acquaintance from human beings to "other Orders of virtuous Creatures, in that future State."[104]

Scientists enlisted. Joseph Priestley saw evidence for a future state in the positive circumstances of this one: "things are evidently in a progress to a better state. There is some reason, therefore, to expect that this *melioration* will go on without limits."[105] Charles Bonnet promised that "our eyes will then unite in themselves the qualities of microscopes and telescopes," and Newton smile at his own accomplishments as if they were those of a child.[106] Humphry Davy's *Consolations in Travel* (1830) features strange tubular creatures who exceed us in knowledge, and so on to Twain and his eight-legged blue creatures. As William Kenrick has it in 1759, science is Jacob's ladder, "Reaching, its foot on earth, to heav'n."[107]

Not only did the soul progress in knowledge and towards perfection, but the soul's progress itself argued for the existence of a future state. If this progressively improving being simply fell unfinished into annihilation, what, Addison asked, was the point? "Are such Abilities made for no Purpose? . . . can we believe a thinking Being, that is in a perpetual Progress of Improvements, and traveling on from Perfection to Perfection, after having just looked abroad into the Works of its Creator, and made a few Discoveries of his infinite Goodness, Wisdom and Power, must perish at her first setting out, and in the very beginning of her Enquiries?"[108] As Eliza Haywood explained, in *The Female Spectator* (1745–46), whether a future state offered two places, one happy and the other miserable, or "a Multiplicity of Worlds" to travel through, everyone agreed "from the Nature of God, and the Nature of our own Ideas, this Spot we now inhabit is but the first Stage the Soul has to make in her eternal Progress."[109] Henry Home, Lord Kames, agreeing that human improvement knew "no assignable limits," proposed that even abstracting from revelation, "there is great probability, that the progress begun in this life will be completed in some future state."[110] The *Gentleman's Magazine* affirmed in 1800, "this *constant* progression towards perfection, is a strong argument for futurity."[111] If God's justice continued to require a compensatory, retributory future state, man's nature and desires began to put in a stronger claim.

If God is good and great and just, he will not have created a useless, frustrated, unhappy creature. Addison found evidence for immortality in the soul's hopes and feelings: "its Passions and Sentiments, as particularly from its Love of Existence, its Horrour of Annihilation, and its Hopes of Immortality."[112] The hope itself was evidence. Benjamin Martin concluded "with certainty" a future state, "from natural inclination and desire of immortality and an unavoidable concern for what is to come hereafter, implanted in all men." Man was "designed for a better and more worthy State of Life, than the best he can enjoy in this World."[113] David Hartley swelled the chorus, arguing from the desire for immortality and the horror of annihilation: "All other Appetites and Inclinations have adequate Objects prepared for them: It cannot therefore be supposed, that this Sum total of them all should go ungratified."[114]

As the ill distribution of justice in this world required another, more just world to come, so the ill-adaptation of man to this world meant that there had to be another to which he was better suited. William Kenrick (1729/30–1779) anticipated John Stuart Mill's complaints, that man sacrifices "ease, health, and life . . . to pursuits that are of no use to him merely as an animal; but, on the contrary, serve to promote the intellectual perfection of his species; hence [these are] apparently intended for the enjoyment of a state of existence, to which those faculties are adapted." "[C]ertainty of a future state" is ours.[115] Catherine Macaulay Graham (1731–91) invoked the powers of imagination, ranging over past and future, which could so easily have been spared "if they had not been necessary principles of knowledge and action, to render man capable of a more enlarged and more uninterrupted happiness in a future state of existence." Otherwise, "those faculties of the mind, . . . on a state of positive mortality seem to have been given as a curse, rather than a blessing...."[116] *The British Apollo* may have put it best, as early as 1740. Asked what proof there was of a future state from "reason or the nature of the thing?" the oracle replied firmly, "We may gather the immortality of the soul, from our very desire of an immortal state.... [I]f we shall not enjoy that immortality we so earnestly pant after, we, tho' the noblest workmanship of the Almighty Artificer, *are of all* creatures *the most miserable.* For if the soul perisheth with the body, what has our Creator done, but tortur'd us with desires that shall never be satisfy'd; rack'd us with wishes that have no foundation, and tantaliz'd reason with fruitless longings."[117] St. Paul (1 Cor. 15:19: If the dead are not resurrected, "we are of all men most miserable") merges with a psychology he never imagined, and God's morality demands human immortality.

Samuel Johnson concurred. His *Adventurer* #120 feels the psychological pains suffered in this life, tentatively opens to the gratifications of the next, and feeds the illusory expectation that whatever is will someday be right:

> It is scarcely to be imagined, that INFINITE BENEVOLENCE would create a being capable of enjoying so much more than is here to be enjoyed, and qualified by nature to prolong pain by remembrance and anticipate it by terror, if he was not designed for something nobler and better than a state, in which many of his faculties can serve only for his torment, in which he is to be importuned by desires that never can be satisfied, to feel many evils which he had no power to avoid, and to fear many which he shall never feel: there will surely come a time, when every capacity of happiness shall be filled, and none shall be wretched but by his own fault.[118]

"[W]hen every capacity of happiness shall be filled" flutters briefly above human wretchedness.

A few skeptics declined to sign on to the argument that wishing made it so, regarding the wish as grounded in an insight into God's purposes that they were unwilling to claim. So Aaron Hill (1685–1750) was willing to leave the future life "among the SECRET 'THINGS which belong unto GOD;' having, in this Case, no sufficient Foundation on which may be built any thing more certain than Conjecture, which may perhaps, afford Means of wishing, but none of proving."[119] William Kenrick also acknowledged that wishing does not make it so, "Whate'er in hope be heaven's intent,/ This is, my friend, no argument." Unlike Hill, he did not rest there, but moved to a peculiarly unattractive version of the butterfly argument:

> T'is here his fate
> To winter his aurelia state;
> In time to burst his cell design'd,
> And leave his clay-cold case behind;
> Flutt'ring on angel wings, to rise
> A bright papilio to the skies![120]

Voltaire replied to Boswell's argument from wishing, that Boswell might wish to be King of Europe, but it was "not probable."[121]

Although England's first atheist, Matthew Turner affirmed merely skepticism, not rejection, of the amiable possibility of eternal life, he did hold Priestley's syllogism of wishes "inadmissible or inconclusive." Priestley proposed, as item 27, "A wish produced by nature is evidence of the thing wished for, but a future state is wished for, therefore there is evidence of a future state."[122] The atheist was not convinced. Ultimately, desire breaks loose from God, and in his notes to *Hellas* (1822) Percy Shelley affirms of the "inextinguishable thirst for immortality" that the mind is its own, but also its only, evidence: "this desire itself must remain the strongest and *the only* presumption that eternity is the inheritance of every thinking being"[123] (emphasis added).

Human wishes had once been highly suspect in affairs of the afterlife. The Commons had reacted with horror, hostility, and expulsion to Asgill's suggestion that Jesus's promise of eternal life was the "Magnetick which hath drawn the World after him."[124] John Boys recognized the sensual appeal of the ancients' Elysium by contrast with the "spiritual" gratifications of the true afterlife (1661). Sir Robert Howard warned in 1694 that heathen priestcraft had made the next world resemble this, so as to control men's minds, a practice continued by the church of Rome to this day: "*the Notions they taught concerning the* Other World *were made sutable to what is seen and familiar to us in this that they might be more easy for Mens Digestion.*"[125] Muslims in particular indulged their alleged sensuality in "Turkish Pleasures" and "impure delights."[126] In Montesquieu's *Persian Letters* (1722), a dead Muslim woman enjoys multiple delightfully fulfilling sensuous experiences (Letter 141). The episode is the most original in the volume.

As late as 1734, Pope sympathizes with the Indian who expects to be restored to the life of which Christians have deprived him (epigraph above). The Indian hunts freely in eternal fields, his dog by his side, his liberty restored. What Pope allowed, and praised, in the Indian, he mocked in the desiring, bibulous Christian: "Go, like the Indian, in another life/ Expect thy dog, thy bottle, and thy wife. . . ." (*Essay on Man*, IV, 177–78). The bottle lets us know how much to disapprove, but is the wife as unlikely and unsuitable for heaven as the dog? An Anglican dean in 1871, cited by McDannell and Lang, perhaps remembered Pope when he condemned a soothing novelistic afterlife as "worthy rather of a Red Indian's expectation, than of a Christian's."[127] The attractive promise of eternal life comes second in Gibbon's list of five causes for Christianity's success in spreading through the Roman empire.[128] What changes is orthodox acceptance of wishes.

At his most advanced, Addison had suggested, and Tickell reformulated as a "maxim," complete gratification of desire: "*Our Happiness in this World proceeds from the Suppression of our Desires, but in the next World from the Gratification of them.*"[129] Yet Addison still had desires he knew would not be gratified because they would no longer be desires, for example, hankering after literary immortality, "when his Body is mixed with the common Mass of Matter, and his Soul *retired into the World of Spirits*" (emphasis added).[130] Immortality still means losing individuality and human ambitions to achieve perfect happiness. Clerics pushed further.

Edward Young's *Night Thoughts*, repudiating the tentativeness of Pope's *Essay on Man*, demanded wishes be fulfilled without specifying which.[131] Others turned the restless, endless, dissatisfied desiring mocked by Lucretius and Juvenal, cured by the Buddha, into a source of happiness in the next world. Such dissatisfaction is often assumed to be a new discovery owing to capitalism. It is a very old discovery attributable to leisure and hierarchical divisions of labor. What is new to capitalism, and the eighteenth century, is the positive revaluation of insatiability. By 1783, the bishop of Chester thought it unreasonable that we should "be for ever in search of happiness, without arriving at it, either in this world or the next." So he supposed the soul was assured, through God's moral perfections, of "another state of existence, where it will find that satisfaction it looks for here in vain; and where hope will at length be swallowed up in enjoyment."[132] It remained for Hugh Blair, Presbyterian divine, friend of David Hume, tossed and gored (but also admired) by Samuel Johnson, to note the conflict between repose and activity, God and progress, perfect, immobile content and the actual conditions of human happiness.

Blair shifts heaven towards the human need for activity, rejecting for the next world the end of our wishes and the perfect enjoyment of repose (the exhausted laborer's desire). "Our enjoyment consists in pursuit, not attainment. Attainment is with us, for most part, the grave of pleasure. Had we no object to excite fresh activity, and to impel us to new toils, human life would quickly stagnate in melancholy indolence."[133] Restlessness, dissatisfaction, insatiability, familiar satiric objects throughout the centuries, the basic psychology of consumer capitalism: these evidence futurity's active blessings. Blair has turned Johnson's "hunger of imagination that preys incessantly upon life" into a proof of eternity and the character of its happiness.

INVITING THE FAMILY AND FRIENDS

Yet certain gratifications remain unnamed by Addison, blanks unfilled by Young: reunions with friends and loved ones, children or spouses. The *Spectator* prized the male friendships hinted by the *Odyssey*'s afterlife, but did not notice familial ones. Addison rejoiced that Achilles appears with Patroclus, delighted that friends continue to know each other in the next world (*Od.* 11.576, IX, 412; *Tatler* # 154), but he praised Fenelon for his account of the inner raptures of the blessed, not their relationships with others.[134]

The period lacked no concern for dead children. Fathers and mothers lamented dead infants and older children in verse and diaries. Steele turns a one-month old drowned in a cold-water bath into a guardian spirit overlooking others' welfare, living out the time he would have lived.[135] Happy to be dead, he remembers his mother only as "a fine young Lady," but he communicates with Mr. Tatler, not with any members of his own family. Addison ignores the fate of dead infants in his assessment of Virgil's *Aeneid*, Book 6 (*Tatler*, 1710, #154). Although he echoes Milton's "Millions of spiritual Creatures walk the Earth/Unseen," this world and the next do not communicate. A novel's heroine from 1757 explains why: "There can be no Certainty that we shall know one another in a future State."[136]

An afterlife without friends, relations, and beloved now seems unimaginable. Dante found Beatrice. Yet she turns away from him to the vision that then swallows Dante up too. Revelation-instructed Protestants absorbed in worshiping God in a theocentric heaven neither look for their friends on arrival nor concern themselves with their still living friends below. As the best-selling William Sherlock put late seventeenth-century orthodoxy, "Good Men will have no Friends, no Relations in the other World, but those who are truly good, who are Members of the same Mystical Body of Christ, the Children of God."[137]

In 1727, Jonathan Swift entertained no hopes as his friend Stella (Esther Johnson) lay dying. The dean of St. Patrick's lamented to his friend Alexander Pope, "I have often wished that God almighty would be so easy to the weakness of mankind, as to let old friends be acquainted in another state; and if I were to write an utopia for heaven, that would be one of my schemes. This wildness you must allow for, because I am giddy and deaf."[138] As a priest condoling the bereaved, Swift suggested no consolations for loss except loving less and never promised that loved ones would be restored to sight or consciousness by a loving, commiserating God. A generation later, when Henry Fielding's Mr. Allworthy fantasies meeting his dead wife never again to part in *Tom Jones* (1749), some neighbors suspect his sanity and sincerity, others his religion (Bk I, chap. 2).

Yet as Stella lay dying, a widowed female dissenter, Elizabeth Singer Rowe, was writing Swift's utopia. As Lady Chudleigh anticipated Addison and Mary Astell corrected John Norris, paralleling love of our neighbor with love of God, Rowe created an afterlife as visionary, and more influential, than Swedenborg's. What she called "Fairy-Tale" in 1728 would be adopted as orthodoxy by Anglican and dissenting divines in the 1760s, scriptural warrants duly found.

In *Friendship in Death: Twenty Letters from the Dead to the Living*, Elizabeth Singer Rowe (1674–1737) confidently answered—in fiction— the intensely painful questions believing Christians barely dared ask themselves in 1728. Will we see our loved ones again? Will we know them in the next world? Are we present to them in this? Are they still with us, though departed? What of my dead child? Is my child saved or damned or lost forever? Will I see my baby again? All but the last, which (childless) she does not consider, Rowe wipes away. We will see our dead, and they watch us now; human love animates the heavens, and a dead child is happier than if he had lived. Rowe's curious text answered every question, soothed every loss, and addressed every desire, except that for reunions with dead children. That demand she left to the fathers of young dead daughters.

Published anonymously in 1728, the year after Stella died, with a bearded scholarly male as frontispiece, Rowe's book reached a second edition within the year, and "almost sixty" editions by 1800.[139] A well-known poet, she concealed her authorship through several editions. A volume of verses as "Philomela" had appeared in 1696, and in 1720 Alexander Pope affixed "On the Death of Mr. Thomas Rowe" (as "Upon the Death of Her Husband" by Mrs. Elizabeth Singer), to the second edition of his *Eloisa to Abelard*. Her biographer observes that the *Bibliothèque Britannique* in its account of *Friendship in Death* "were not only ignorant of her name but mistook even the sex of the writer."[140] Its last edition, before its late twentieth-century revival as a woman's text, was 1808.[141] Victorians did not require Rowe's reassurance: her work had been done.

Comical and classical letters from the dead to the living had long been popular.[142] Rowe's abandon Elysium and Hades for the Christian heaven. Eight of her twenty letters embrace heavenly amorous passions. A lover weaving garlands awaits the death of his beloved; another looks forward to reunion with his wife. A young woman confides to a female friend that she has taken up with her living friend's dead, golden-lute-strumming brother, "your charming Brother, gay as a Cherubim." Love unrequited or unspoken on earth blossoms: "Hope and languishing Expectation are no more, and all Desire is lost in full and compleat Fruition" (37–38). As Peter Walmsley observes, Milton's angels are Rowe's source for human lovers who "embrace with a pleasure more intense than earthly coupling: 'union of pure with pure/Desiring.'"[143] "[T]he Almighty" is deferred to the third letter, from a child to his mother. Only in the seventh and fifteenth letters does divine vision, ultimately beyond description, outrank reunions with loved ones. A dead husband assures his wife that reunion with him will be "much the smallest Blessing of this Place" (45). Two letters undertake the stellar and scientific explorations enjoyed by Rowe's biographer-to-be, Henry Grove.

Missing from Rowe (as from that later visionary Emanuel Swedenborg) are reunions with dead children, although the third letter features a dead child. Rather than promising reunion, however, Rowe reproduces the inscriptions on infant tombstones. The child is happier than the grieving parents left behind. Now far advanced in knowledge and wisdom, the child advises his mother to stop mourning. He is no longer the lost bouncing baby the mother would reclaim.[144]

Before Rowe, Queen Anne had been consoled for the death of William, Duke of Gloucester, her last surviving, eleven-year-old child, by Mary, Lady Chudleigh and Edward Young. Chudleigh royally peoples heaven: the child recognizes Charles I, his grandfather the martyr; Mary Stuart, Queen of Scots; and his aunt Mary II, "the fair *Maria*": "All these the lovely Youth carest,/And welcomed him to their eternal Rest." Chudleigh promised herself reunion with her dead mother-in-law, and the enjoyment of "new . . . unexperienced Charms" not in divine, but "in her Mother's, and her Daughter's Arms," her body laid in "long Tranquility" beside "their dear Relicks."[145] Marking a gender difference, Young carefully defers meetings to the Last Judgment, when orthodox theology allows them, and limits the encounters to Charles I and Anne's spouse and children. Young's *Poem on the Last Day*, named in Rowe's dedication of *Friendship in Death*, sees Queen Anne sailing beyond the third heaven, until the "Heaven of Heavens" opens and angels receive her.[146] The judge of all compares her grandfather Charles I's "Scarlet of a circling Wound" with his own wounds, while Anne gathers the nuclear family:

> a Female Face,
> Her Consort by; around them smiling move,
> The Beauteous Blossoms of their fruitful Love;
> Known of their Parents, they their Parents know;
> Their Bosoms with a double Transport glow;
> Blest in themselves, but more than blest to find
> All they hold dear in Equal Blessing joyn'd.[147]

After Rowe, dead children begin to meet their parents sooner than the last day. In the *Gentleman's Magazine*, 1731, L. H. expects to sleep until the Last Judgment in the grave beside his dead eleven-year-old daughter, "like a bridegroom beside his bride," but he also hopes to be greeted by her when he dies: "Do you with Heav'nly Raptures meet my Ghost/On th'utmost limits of that happy Coast: /Let me receive Increase of Joy from you! / Till then, my little Saint, *Adieu, Adieu.*" In 1736, M.A. promised a bereft mother, "There, thou shalt meet thy much lamented *son*" who had known only the pleasant morn of life.[148] In 1743, Henry Fielding rapturously embraced his dead six-year-old daughter in *Journey from This World to the Next*, a context carefully classical, not Christian. Such statements were sufficiently rare that in 1775 William Giles reprinted L.H.'s poem in *A Collection of Poems on Divine and Moral Subjects, selected from various authors*. Giles found also "A father's soliloquy over his dead child":

> ... bear me swiftly to my only child!
> And thou dear babe! With tending angels wait
> To hail me welcome to thy blest estate;
> Rush to my arms—soft whisper—"I am thine,"
> And lead me to the GOD who made thee mine![149]

Giles seems to have been actively seeking such poems, in which mourning fathers furnish a genre later associated with women. Charles Dickens, looking for material to recommend to mourning friends, found only Fielding's episode and embellished it. The daughter Fielding embraces Dickens describes as making a wreath for her dead daddy at the moment she is found. Boswell's daughter Veronica performed a service neither Fielding nor Dickens imagined. Asked by her father what she would do if she were to die and go to heaven and see her father shut out in the bleak wastes beyond the heavenly city, she said she would go to God and ask him to let her father in. Boswell was greatly relieved.[150]

Whether friends would know each other in heaven remained controversial, finding its tipping point and turning over into theological orthodoxy only in the 1760s. Rowe ended her volume with the devastating *Thoughts on Death Translated from the Moral Essays of the Messieurs du Port Royal*, unidentified as Pierre Nicole's (published 1671–78). For Walmsley, Nicole marks a "startlingly different" view of the afterlife contrasted self-consciously with Rowe's own.[151] Another interpretation is possible. Nicole explains why Rowe wrote her book: what she felt and what she sought to allay by writing. He lays out the agony of separation and the necessary dependence of the self on others ripped apart by death.

Nicole catches the imbrication of self (soul) and other. Self is annihilated when its other vanishes, its propensity for love unsupported. When the soul loses what it loved, "[S]he loses all, finds nothing, all sinks under her, all vanishes, and disappears for ever. . . . 'Tis a terrible Fall of the Soul, by a sudden Removal of all its Supports; . . . 'tis an infinite Void, by the Annihilation of all that fill'd it . . . 'tis a dreadful Desolation, by the Want of all Consolation; 'tis a cruel Rupture, which violently rends the Soul from every Object of its Love."[152] Human souls are not made to be alone. The soul always needs some "foreign Support. It was form'd to know and love, but finding nothing within sufficient to satisfy these Inclinations, it is forced with some other Objects to fill the Void it finds in it self."[153] For Nicole as for Rowe, divine love makes up all losses, but Rowe reaches out, restoring those lost.

In his *Complaint: or, Night Thoughts* (1742–46), Edward Young approaches Rowe's "fairy tale" communication with the dead. In interrogatives, he hopes for "hovering shades . . . their silent, soft address, / Their posthumous advice, and pious prayer?"[154] Such intimations authorized Samuel Johnson's careful wishes for his dead wife's attentions and presence in 1752: "*if* thou hast ordained the souls of the dead to minister to the living" (emphasis added).[155] When Rowe died, she assured several friends she would see them in heaven, and hoped to be the first to greet the countess on her arrival, but said nothing of meeting her husband or her father, under whose stone she asked to be buried.[156]

E. Derek Taylor has brilliantly laid out how complex and ambiguous a destination is the heaven in Samuel Richardson's *Clarissa* (1747–48). Wavering between an afterlife that was all beatific vision and one where friends knew each other, Sarah Chapone badgered Richardson as to what doctrine he held, and Richardson did not answer. Although he had twice printed Rowe's *Friendship in Death* in the 1740s, Richardson's novel craftily intimates both that God is all in all and that individuals meet again never to part. Clarissa withdraws from the world to die, creating from strangers a community of virtuous souls. The "just men made perfect" one meets in heaven are not the people one has known and loved in this life. Yet again, Clarissa writes of meetings beyond the grave in what become, once she dies, her letters from the dead to the living.[157]

Eliza Haywood in her *History of Jemmy and Jenny Jessamy* (1753), urging deaths be accepted with "perfect resignation to the decrees of providence," is more willing than Richardson to entertain "a wild idea." The dead may do what Rowe's do, watch us now and wait for us, planning to meet us on our arrival: "though it may seem perhaps a wild idea, in supposing a possibility that he may be still a witness of our actions, be pleased at our remembrance of him; and, at the hour of our dissolution, even be appointed our conductor to the celestial mansions...."[158] In these careful formulations, the dead themselves are not represented as the goal. The reunion is not the end; the dead merely lead the way further in to heaven, like Dante's Beatrice. Still, they are encountered first, and the narrative stops with the reunion.

Uncertainty prevailed alongside hope. Samuel Johnson assured readers of the *Idler* (1759) that "Reason" stops "at the grave." That did not, however, prevent him from hoping that the living might still be the objects of "attention and kindness of those who . . . are now receiving their reward."[159] In *Rasselas* (1759), Nekayah looks no further beyond the grave than to see her beloved Pekuah again and to "enjoy [her] friendship."[160] Yet when Boswell asked about the future state in 1772, Johnson would not go beyond Henry More and scripture. He affirmed no certainty about future relationships, except that everyone talked of it: "Then, Sir, they talk of meeting our relations: but then all relationship is dissolved; and we shall have no regard for one person more than another, but for their real value. However, we shall either have the satisfaction of meeting our friends, or be satisfied without meeting them."[161]

By 1772, when "they" were all talking of "meeting our relations," two secular and two clerical writers had founded their arguments on three separate faculties of the human mind: the passions and affections, self-knowledge through others, and memory. The secular pair were Richard and Elizabeth Griffith, publishing their own courtship letters, and the female character led.

Richard and Elizabeth Griffith's Frances spoke first, for the passions. In the Griffiths' popular, flatly titled *A Series of Genuine Letters between Henry and Frances* (1757, 1761, 1770, 1786), Frances knows "there can be no Certainty that we shall know one another in a future State." She is not, however, willing to rest in uncertainties, especially with Addison's argument from progress in hand. Using God's nature to displace God, she argues that passions must retain their human objects. Just as God's goodness requires that his creatures have eternal life, so his wisdom requires that we continue to enjoy our passions in the next life. Those passions and attractions attach themselves not to God, but to the persons who elicited those emotions: "I think it is arraigning the Wisdom of the Almighty, to imagine that he should form us with Passions, and Attractions *for each other*, (which more frequently produce Misery, than Happiness, in this Life) and let those strongest, noblest Faculties of the Soul perish with the Body in the Grave. No——it cannot be; they were ordained to answer higher Ends, to make the everlasting Happiness of his Creatures, and will exist to all Eternity" (emphasis added). Judgment requires memory, and memory engages affections: "Besides, we are taught to believe, that we must render an Account of our past Lives. Sure 'Love is the informing, active Fire, that kindles up the Mass;' and is it not the highest Absurdity to suppose, that, when in a State of Perfection, we shall remember the Effects, but forget the Cause?—"[162] The "higher ends," "everlasting happiness," "the Cause" ought to be divinity itself. Instead, passion for "each other" displaces the divine. Both Frances and her Henry are willing to take her argument for good divinity. The original ending of the novel, Henry's five letters challenging eternal punishments vanish in the second edition, but Frances's arguments stand. Two divines supply, within the decade, the scriptural evidence Frances neglected.

In 1766, the Anglican William Dodd (1729–1777) insisted that we would know our loved ones in the next world, *Mutual Knowledge in a future State; Offered as an Argument of Consolation under the Loss of Friends*. Other funeral sermons, including Isaac Watts' *Death and Heaven* forty years earlier, had expressed the hope that friends would know one another; Tillotson had affirmed it in passing.[163] Bunyan's Great-heart hoped it in the gynocentric second part of *Pilgrim's Progress*, but Dodd asserted the position as if it were proved and made it focal. The sermon had all the conviction communicated by repeating oneself: Dodd had already made the argument in *The Visitor*, 1764, reprinted from *The Ledger*, 1760–61.[164] The next year, 1767, the dissenter Richard Price (1723–1791, Godwin's authority against death, Edmund Burke's nemesis-to-be) chimed in with his third dissertation *On the Reasons for expecting that virtuous Men shall meet after Death in a State of Happiness*. The Anglican Dodd scooped the dissenter Price, and his popular *Reflections on Death* (1763) reached over a dozen editions and the Americas by 1806, including a handsome illustrated edition in 1796. Price's work earned him four editions by 1777 and the lifelong friendship of the Earl of Shelburne, who sought him out for consolation after the death of his wife.[165] The coincidence does not, perhaps, rank with Newton's and Leibniz's simultaneous discovery of the calculus, but it too is a creative convergence.

Hanged for forgery and nicknamed the "macaroni parson," William Dodd is best known for eliciting Samuel Johnson's most famous quip: when a man knows he is to be hanged in a fortnight, it concentrates the mind wonderfully.[166] Yet before he pointed a tale, Dodd introduced alterity and a profounder psychology to the afterlife. In *Reflections upon Death* (1763), Dodd, hoping for the balmy consolation of again meeting friends, and his redeemer, looked forward to "union with thyself, and with my friends."[167] In the funeral sermon, abandoning all caution, Dodd assures his auditors of "The certainty, the glorious and transporting certainty, that we shall meet again and enjoy those beloved friends, who have got the start of us in the course of life, and are first happily admitted to our Father's house." *Clarissa* may have been in his ear: Jesus spoke of "*my* father's house" (emphasis added). The phrase "our Father's house" evokes Clarissa's duplicitous letter to Lovelace, promising that he may, if he behaves, see her at "her Father's house." "Expectations," stronger than "hopes," become "*realities*": "to pass an eternity in consummate reciprocations of affection. . . . which the fear and pain of parting nevermore shall interrupt! these are the expectations,—nay, I ought to say more,— These are the great, the interesting *realities*, which every true believer hath before his eyes: . . ."[168] Life is defined in a distinctly non-theocentric way: "What is life, but the enjoyment of those we love?" God and Jesus are doubtless included among "those we love," but they do not seem to be Dodd's principal referent.

For his text, Dodd takes a strong, comical misreading of 2 Samuel 12:23. Shrugging off his prayers and demanding his dinner when Bathsheba's son dies, David explains to his perplexed courtiers that the time to plead with God is over: "I will go to him, but he will not return to me."[169] For Dodd, this passage can only be consolatory. The alternate, ironic reading is simply unacceptable, a caustic where Dodd insists on "balm." The New Testament Abraham knows Dives and Lazarus; Jesus promises company to the thief on the cross.

The most interesting aspect of Dodd's argument is psychological. We must know our friends again because personal consciousness is defined through knowledge of others. Unless we know them, we cannot know ourselves: "[D]eprived of his consciousness to which mutual knowledge is inseparably joined . . . he would if I may so express myself, cease to be himself; he would become another person. So that if we retain personal identity in a future state . . . we must retain mutual knowledge."[170] Bunyan's Great-heart had argued a Cartesian position: self-knowledge is self-sufficient. "Do they think they know themselves then? Or that they shall rejoice to see themselves in that bliss? And if they think they shall know and do these; why not know others, and rejoice in their welfare also?"[171] Dodd reverses that dependence. Personal identity and social relations, self and other, silently take priority over the experience of God.

Dodd refigures the contemporaneous debate between self and others, instantiated in Jean-Jacques Rousseau's vehement rejection of others' influence and Adam Smith's careful analysis of others as fundamental to self-formation, and morality in particular. Dror Wahrman sees Dodd's relational self as losing ground even in Smith's own formulation of the "man within." It is time to revisit it.[172] For Smith, others are the mirror through which we come to self-understanding. That self-understanding includes an otherness-within, a division into two persons, one of whom judges, the other is judged, by standards we derive from others, who alone enable us to see ourselves.[173]

Richard Price escaped hanging, but not hanging up: Edmund Burke turned him into Hugh Peters *redivivus* in 1790.[174] Treading more cautiously than Dodd or Elizabeth Griffith, Price was more passionately convinced that the afterlife gave life meaning. Without a future state, a "chill or damp" falls over every action and friendship. With it every enjoyment "receive[s] an additional relish." Even "the face of nature" shines more brightly.[175] Memory and consciousness, without Griffith's reference to passions or Dodd's identity through others, form the basis of his confidence. Jesus's promise to prepare a place for his disciples is inconsistent with their dispersal "into different parts of the universe, and scarcely leaves us any room to doubt on the present question . . . Shall we be together with Christ, and yet not with one another? . . . Being in the same happy state with our present virtuous friends, and relatives, will they not be accessible to us? And if accessible, shall we not fly to them, and mingle hearts and souls again?"

(331–32). When these mingled souls will look towards God, Price does not say. Price imagines St. Paul looking among his Thessalonian converts as the dead rise, rather than to Christ. The dead have, inadvertently, been made an end in themselves.

For Price, these reunions—of friend with friend, parent with child, husband with wife, master with family—make "one of the most agreeable circumstances in the future state of felicity. It has a tendency to render the contemplation of another world much more delightful." It would be unfair to focus on the theocentric heaven as a delight-free zone. Price's insistence on his own desires, so infuriating to Burke in another context, marks the shape of things to come. "The hope of [reunion] rises up unavoidably in our minds, and has generally, if not always, accompanied the belief of a future existence" (334). Those reunited will joy in the common danger escaped— "our friends preserved amidst the dismal wreck"—while the eternal hellfire of the wicked rages on. "[T]he future everlasting rejection and extermination of all that work iniquity" (337–39): Hell Price has every which way. "Rejection and extermination" suggest annihilation. Hellfire may be "everlasting" even if the doomed sinners in it are not.

Retaining hell and insisting that reunion is for "virtuous," "good men" contributed to Price's being taken more seriously than Dodd. Dodd's funeral sermon the *Critical Review* faulted for "extravagant Encomiums" on Dodd's dead patron, the bishop of St. David's, and similar excess in his doctrine. Dodd breached "the limits which revelation prescribes." Dodd had gushed:

> How eligible, in this world, must be that future world, that *kingdom of universal reception*, to which every pilgrim below is unerringly directed, and at which every pilgrim must undoubtedly arrive! Not a friend left behind, but we shall one day welcome thither: not a friend left behind, but shall one day *glad our expecting eyes*, and add by his arrival augmentation to our bliss!

(Dodd had been less sanguine about despairing poor men who reviled their wives and did not attend church. To them he offered only what consolation he "*dar'd* to offer."[176]) The reviewer observed that this "very comfortable doctrine" was not one on which we can "in every case, depend."

Admission was limited to those qualified for bliss. "Were the mansions of happiness open to all, were every pilgrim indiscriminately admitted, heaven itself would become a scene of confusion, and the habitation of the just *a den of thieves.*"[177] Did the *Critical* reviewer remember this remark a decade later when Dodd was hanged, thief and forger?

Happily for him, Dodd had confidence in his salvation as he faced the hangman. Thanking Samuel Johnson for his assistance, Dodd anticipated welcoming Johnson to the "realms of bliss" and greeting him there, having arrived earlier: "And admitted, as I trust I shall be, to the realms of bliss before you, I shall hail *your* arrival there with transport, and rejoice to acknowledge that you was my Comforter, my Advocate, and my *Friend!* GOD *be ever* with *you.*"[178] It is perhaps churlish to suspect that Dodd was reminding Johnson that he, too, would die, sooner or later, or to consider how little Johnson would appreciate such a reminder, but neither Johnson nor Boswell entered any cavils at Dodd's theology.

For Dodd's and Price's desires, John Jortin had found better biblical arguments, but his sermons appeared posthumously only in 1771. Urged to publish, he demurred, "let them sleep until I sleep."[179] Eternal punishment he psychologized, leaving the wicked to their consciences. Terrible and perhaps eternal, hell's worst punishments are self-reproach for having given up happiness, forced "perpetually [to] converse with the worst of companions, even with his own uneasy thoughts."[180] For Jortin as for Price, seeing one's friends again depends on their virtues and temperament, which might shut out Dr. Dodd: "The righteous will there converse with the best and the wisest beings and, as they may reasonably hope, with those whom they loved here below *for their good qualities*" (emphasis added). God shifts from God to first friend, descending from object of vision to model of equal friendship:

> Our Saviour had his friends when he dwelt here; and when he saw them deeply afflicted at the thoughts of losing him, . . . he . . . applied a suitable consolation. I only go, says he, to prepare a place for you, that where I am, there ye may be also. He says not to them, as a just Master, ye shall be happy; but he says, as an affectionate Friend, you shall be where I am, along with me; intimating *possibly* that such alliances are immortal, and that Death, which breaks all other bonds, dissolves not the union between *virtuous* minds (emphasis added).[181]

Jortin's "possibly" shows less certainty about future friendships than Watts, Dodd, or Price possessed, but his scriptural argument is bolder, more leveling. Going beyond them in speculation and forgetting contemplation of divinity, he regrets that occupations are not revealed to us. Since we will be like angels, however, we may "have the care of other creatures in other worlds committed to" us. The works of God visible and invisible will entertain without exhaustion (Grove need not collapse, Boyse's easy learning triumphs). We may have new senses in a new life, and there will of course be inequality among the blessed.

As prominent clerics promoted their own "reasonable hopes," the laity chimed in, emboldened by claims they had long made in advance of their instructors. In the Richardson circle, in 1749, Catherine Talbot endorsed eternal sociability: "The more connections we make here . . . the more friends we shall have to rejoice with hereafter in a permanent state of felicity."[182] William Mickle at last published his *Voltaire in the Shades* (1770), written, he claimed, at twenty (c. 1754) when he was furious against the deist "sophistry that would destroy the dearest hope of his heart, the hope of yet meeting the deceased friend in another and better state of existence."[183]

By the 1780s, later writers interpret the careful Young as justifying reunions with loved ones. So "Clementina" in *Letters Religious and Moral* (1786), floats imaginatively upwards: "The departure of our beloved relatives and friends . . . invites our thoughts to those heavenly regions, where we hope they are ascended, and breathes a consolatory expectation of a reunion with them in the realms of bliss if so happy to choose, and persevere in the same virtuous path. Dr. Young judiciously observes . . ." In 1788, G. Wright, collecting *Pleasing Reflections on Life and Manners . . . Principally selected from Fugitive Publications*, found that in death the blessed "renew those ancient connections with virtuous friends, which had been dissolved here below by death." "[T]he happiness of a future state" once concluded in God or angels, divine or scientific visions. Now it ends with no more separations: "[N]o revolutions of nature shall ever be able to part us more!—Such is the society and blessedness of the saints above."[184]

In less pious precincts, Goethe's Werther had shot himself in anticipation of joining his beloved Charlotte in heaven (Goethe, 1749–1832; *Sorrows of Young Werther* 1774). Rousseau demanded reunions in death for himself in the *Confessions* (1782) and his Julie and St. Preux in *Nouvelle Eloise* (1759), making explicit what his admired Richardson a decade earlier had fudged, and been harried for fudging. The *Critical* reviewer must have trembled for heaven: everyone seemed flooding in, on Dodd's open-access pass.

By 1790, Hugh Blair and Richard Polwhele claimed reunions after death for Christians, turning Rowe and Young from hopeful speculation to doctrine. The most popular preacher of the century—and the early part of the next—Hugh Blair (1718–1800) proposed reunion as the principal consolation for those grieved by a friend's loss: "let [the mourner] turn for relief to the prospect of a future meeting in a happier world. This is indeed the chief soother of affliction; the most powerful balm of the bleeding heart. . . . Until this season of *re-union* arrive, no principle of religion discourages our holding correspondence of affection with them by means of faith and hope" (emphasis added).[185] Until the 1780s, the "reunion" celebrated in the future state had been that of soul and body at the resurrection (a usage unnoticed in the *OED*). Hugh Blair changed the referent.[186]

In 1807, the *Critical Review* declared Blair's sermons to be, except for the *Spectator*, "the most popular work in the English language." Blair, eminent Presbyterian preacher, first Regius Professor of Rhetoric and Belles Lettres at the University of Edinburgh, tenant and friend of David Hume, defender of Ossian from "that barbarian Samuel Johnson's" skepticism, owed his sermons' publication to Johnson. Johnson admired the sample the bookseller showed him after the bookseller had already declined what became Blair's first volume in 1777. When the sermons succeeded, Johnson preened himself on his part in bringing them forward.[187] They earned Blair more than 2,000 pounds, his publisher increasing his copyright payment with every volume and making later cash gifts.[188] To put that sum in perspective, Johnson was paid 1,500 pounds for the *Dictionary*, from which he had to pay copyists, paper, and ink. Blair's only expense for his sermons was considerably less paper and ink.

From the first volume (1777) through the second (1780) and third (1790), Blair's confidence about reunions mounted, from "Our imperfect knowledge of a future state" (Sermon 4, 1777) to the certain reunions with "ancient and beloved friends" ("On Death," 1780) that constitute "The Happiness of a Future State" (1780): "re-union with those with whom our happiest days were spent; whose joys and sorrows once were ours; and from whom, after we shall have landed on the peaceful shore where they dwell, no revolutions of nature shall ever be able to part us more!—Such is the society of the blessed above. Of such are the multitude composed who *stand before the throne*" (255). "The throne" puts God at the edge of the picture, just out of the frame, reordering a society otherwise taken up entirely with itself. In 1790, Blair discovers scriptural warrant for his hopes. "On the sacrament of the lord's supper" (Sermon 15) reads a passage in Matthew (26:29) as a promise that Jesus and his disciples will meet on the other side, a promise only Matthew makes. In Mark, Matthew's source, Jesus tells his disciples he will again drink of the vine only in his Father's kingdom. Matthew adds "with you" to Mark 14:25: "I tell you, I will never again drink of this fruit of the vine until that day when I drink it new *with you* in my Father's kingdom." Blair likes his Savior the better for this promise: "in how amiable a light does our Saviour appear here, looking forward to a future reunion with those beloved friends, whom he was now leaving, as to a circumstance which should increase both his own felicity and theirs, when they met again in a happier world!" He is glad to generalize from Jesus and his disciples to confirm "what has always been a favourite hope of good men; that friends shall know and recognize each other, and renew their former connections, in a future state of existence." Indeed, death would be too bitter "if no support were to be ministered by religious hopes . . . If there were no voice to whisper to our spirits, that hereafter we, and those whom we love, shall meet again in a more blissful land?"[189] Blair, like Fielding, L.H., and the philosopher in *Rasselas*, had suffered the loss of a daughter, his twenty-year-old only child, in 1769, and "retired 'for some time from social intercourse and professional labour.'"[190] He returns, having ministered to himself, reading consolation to the world.

Blair was distinguished and Presbyterian, Richard Polwhele (1760–1838) a prolific Anglican cleric. Each represents an established church now offering unquestioning confidence in gospel warrant for heavenly reunions. An early admirer of Catherine Macaulay, Polwhele later became a scourge of Jacobin feminist writers in *The Unsex'd Females* (1798), where Christ and the Devil square off as Hannah More and Mary Wollstonecraft. Enemy of French revolutionaries, contributor to the *Anti-Jacobin Review* (1799–1805), careless topographer of Devon, he turned heavenly reunion into an argument for Christianity against anticlerical revolutionaries.

A few years later, he would win a prize, and come to two editions, for demonstrating the immediacy of the afterlife to the satisfaction of the Church Union Society in *An Essay on the Evidence from Scripture that the Soul, immediately after the Death of the Body, is not in a state of Sleep or Insensibility; but of Happiness or Misery: and on the Moral Uses of that Doctrine* (1818, 1820). With equal confidence in invisible evidence, his earlier "On the reunion with our friends in a future state," Discourse X of his 1791 *Discourses on Different Subjects*, affirmed that the gospels promised reunions, and reunions demonstrated Christianity's superiority to other religions and philosophies, including the religion of nature. The gospel "confirm[s] the fondest wishes of the mourner . . . That we shall be restored to the friend whose separation from us is the cause of our grief, is the strongest of all consolatory arguments. To be assured of this was the great, the fervent longing of unenlightened nature. And this fervent longing had its full satisfaction in Christianity."[191] Blair and Polwhele say nothing of infants, but they neither exclude them, nor offer the old advice not to mourn. If children are not exactly what most people understand by "friends," that distinction is not drawn.

HEAVEN FICTIONALIZED

While devotional writers were refitting the afterlife, it remained for a clergyman-novelist to turn the Christian afterlife, like the classical, into a site of literary fantasy, familiar now in *New Yorker* cartoons or, at our outset, Twain and Shaw. Popular since Aristophanes and Lucian, who used their own afterlives, Christian-era satirical commentaries and dialogues of the dead took place in the classical afterlife, not the Christian. Quevedo's *Sueños* name Jupiter, Pluto, Mercury, though his own hell was the one he had in mind.[192] Such exceptions as Erasmus's *Julius Exclusus* and Dante's broadly satirical *Inferno* skewered politico-theological problems. Wishful reformers still kept to Elysium, not addressing Heaven. In 1742, when Henry Fielding remodeled the afterlife in his *Journey from this World to the Next*, his motives were Christian, his terrain classical.[193] Even freer thinkers, rewarded, kept to classical geography. Quevedo Jr. moved Tindal, Collins, Locke, and the Puritans "from Hades to the pleasantest meadow in Elysium" in 1743.[194] Mickle put "Voltaire in the Shades" in 1770, and the anonymous *Philosophical and Religious Dialogue in the Shades between Mr. Hume and Dr. Dodd* (1778) took place outside Elysium's borders, where Hume was held up by a severe enquirer long enough to meet Dodd dying the next year (1776, 1777). In 1762, in the sixth volume of *Tristram Shandy*, Laurence Sterne redrew heaven's gate to accommodate modern sensibilities. He made no apology and incurred no reproach: readers loved it and critics applauded.

Sterne's incursion, the century's most significant after Elizabeth Singer Rowe's, has long been hiding in plain sight.[195] When Yorick dies in the first volume (1759), the parsons are cautious. Parson Sterne has his parson Yorick express hope but no certainty about meeting his friend Eugenius beyond the grave: "*if* it was their fate to meet hereafter,—he would thank him again and again" (vol. 1, chap. 12). A black page marks where Yorick lies dead. Two years later (1762) Sterne grew bolder, not about meetings but about regulating heaven's conduct. Two angels in the Christian heaven delete a violation of the commandment against taking the Lord's name in vain in favor of beloved Uncle Toby. In passing, Sterne invents the phrase "the recording angel," appearing most recently in Tony Kushner's *Angels in America: I*.[196]

The transit from earth to heaven has rarely seemed more natural or inevitable or easy. Heaven's rules bend to benevolence. An officer named LeFever lies dying, his child with him, and the hapless, benignant Uncle Toby swears, "by G——, he shall not die!" Up in heaven the angels are agitated, one blushes, another weeps over Toby's criminal words: "—The ACCUSING SPIRIT which flew up to heaven's chancery with the oath, blush'd as he gave it in;—and the RECORDING ANGEL as he wrote it down, dropp'd a tear upon the word, and blotted it out for ever" (vol. 6, chap. 8). A recording angel could be presumed from the Book of Life, though this is his first public appearance. The "accusing spirit" adapts the "adversary" (Hebrew *Satan*) of the Book of Job, who accuses mankind to God. Job's accuser is cynical; Sterne's is not. Versified by Jane Timbury (1787), parodied by James Gillray in *The Accusing Spirit which Flew up to Heaven's Chancery with the Oath* (1791), the scene offered no excuses.[197]

No "fairy tale," Heaven is an accessible, fallible place where accidents happen, spirits regret their roles, and angels mess up their papers. Unlike Fielding, Sterne claims the apparatus of the real Christian heaven for sentiment and comedy. God remains out of view, but Sterne has a cleric's confidence—or Swedenborg's—in his knowledge of how things work. And his readers had no problem with it. Sterne shocked contemporaries with his bawdy innuendos and his own sermons published as by his fictional character Parson Yorick. This scene spoke to their sense of divine judgment and the heavenly sphere. Even Samuel Johnson would probably have included Toby's cry among the "involuntary errors" that still terminate in happiness.

It remained for heaven to let everyone in, as Dodd hoped and Twain would insist after 1900. A deist led the way, Joseph Reed in *Saint Peter's Lodge: A Serio-Comi-Legendary Tale* (1786), dedicated without permission to the prince of Wales. A blithe defense of reason, reformation, and universal salvation, the poem attacks in passing Byron's bête-noir, the Athanasian creed, "*that* Creed, From which I wish our Church were freed," and the pillorying of old Peter Annet "for making too *free* with the *Pentateuch*" (3n). A new trinity of authorities, Locke, Newton, and Pope, are singled out for preferring reason and a moral life to faith (4), and "Dan Gay," a.k.a. John, is credited for the moral-without-a-moral. In *Religio Medici* (1643) Sir Thomas Browne thought several St. Peters needed, each religion to turn the key for his own kind. St. Peter kept Erasmus's Pope Julius out of heaven, and Milton blew him away with other Catholic trumpery. Now, in the Christian heaven, one napping St. Peter serves for all: Jews and Muslims, Catholics and Calvinists, Chinese and Negros.

For Reed, theological difference is still a problem: his ghosts quarrel over religion, and each sect needs its own sector of heaven to prevent civil war. Coming down the road to St. Peter's lodge, all the souls have passports, issuer unidentified. "Made immortal," they do not naturally possess immortality. Chatting happily until religion enters the conversation, they fall to blows, which, since they are ghosts, do no harm. But "new-made fellowship takes wing." St. Peter explains the geography of heaven: "To each Religion, every Sect / A sep'rate bound'ry we select; / For, should they meet, eternal squabble / Would render Heaven a second *Babel*." Catholics join Jesuits; a Puritan seeks Calvin, "this murderous Snake," admitted only by Servetus's entreaty; a Mahometan arrives, whose "bill of fare of bliss eternal/ Is false, voluptuous, and carnal," and whose region is shaped like a crescent, extensive yet compact, "You'll reach it in an hour at most, Sir, / And join the Shade of your *Impostor*." There follow a Quaker, an Anabaptist, with two Sabbaths and full dipped baptism; a Methodist who hanged himself to avoid committing adultery; then a flock of Pagans, Wild-Indians, Negros, Tartars, and finally an adherent of "no Sect or godly Class" (35). St. Peter wonders how the last obtained his document. As in Coetzee's *Elizabeth Costello*, there was an "examination" at which he made "This brief, yet honest declaration," trusting "Man's great CREATOR, SIRE, and FRIEND," "doing Good, and shunning ill," holding all men "my Brethren to the Grave." St. Peter, thrilled, embraces him and gives him full run of paradise, for following reason and not the priest. He alone is invited to "Range thro' these Realms, whose space immense is,/ And view, in rapture lost your senses, /The countless wonders Heaven has wrought,/ So far surpassing human thought." St. Peter's final request is that the deist come to visit him every now and then, "You'll find me constantly at home. . . . If I had judg'd like you, my fate / Had ne'er confin'd me to this Gate."

Young's *Poem on the Last Day* had put Turk, Jew, Christian, and pagan happily together before the throne for the Last Judgment, but Young avoided saying what happens to the non-Christians.[198] It looks well for them all, but a few lines on we learn that Caiaphas and Judas are also hopeful, though a little worried. Pope's prayer was universal. In Reed, the deist's explicitly Christian heaven widens, Twain's way, by the rule of Christian charity, to include non-Christians.

We have arrived, and it looks just like home, what we always expected to find in the next world. As Keith Thomas and Jacob Sider Jost suggest, filling in the next life's activities creates a world that resembles more and more the world one leaves, as does the self one takes to it. This stealth revolution depended for success on its not being noticed that anything much was changing even as the ground shifted. The inhabitants of Kansas woke up in Oz, and they declared that things had always been just so.

POLITICAL IMPLICATIONS AND CORRELATIONS— A MIGHTY PAUCITY

Although the correlations are not rigid, Whigs and women tended to improve the afterlife more diligently than Tories, to reshape it to meet human desire (as did John Asgill, Joseph Addison, Mary, Lady Chudleigh,

Isaac Watts, Elizabeth Singer Rowe, Henry Fielding, and Joseph Reed). It was a lady who assured Boswell, disconsolate at going to a world where there was no Shakespeare, that the first thing he would "meet" in the next world was a fine copy of the complete works. Neither Boswell nor Johnson demurred; indeed "Johnson smiled benignantly at this."[199]

Tories were either more skeptical (like Henry St. John, Lord Bolingbroke, David Hume [who thought himself a "sceptical whig"], and Edward Gibbon) or more conservative (like Jonathan Swift and Hannah More), or more inclusive (like Alexander Pope and Samuel Johnson). Whigs were also deists (Toland, Collins, Reed), Socinians (Locke, Newton), and Other (Shaftesbury); they were more pious than some Tories (Defoe relative to Swift), and less pious (Fielding relative to Richardson and Johnson). Methodists, Swedenborgians, and Moravians present no clear political affiliations. Of Dodd, Price, and Jortin, Price was the most "whiggish," intent on putting things right both in this world and the next. Dodd, the fashionable "macaroni preacher," had been equally active in charitable initiatives. Even these approximations break down in the generation of political radicals: the dissenting Price provoked the orthodox Burke in politics, but they did not disagree about an afterlife. The heretical but devout materialist Unitarian Joseph Priestley, the deist Tom Paine, and the Anglican Mary Wollstonecraft all held to an afterlife against her spouse the atheist immaterialist William Godwin, and his atheist son-in-law Percy Bysshe Shelley. Politics does not predict afterlife views, though a dedication to self-styled "progressive" politics may carry over to improving the afterlife or dissolving death, as with Asgill, Price, or Godwin.

Correlated with afterlife liberalization is the church's waning coercive power. Spectacular hells, like spectacular executions, flourish in periods that seek to reinforce their police. Hells diminish as policing, external and internal, improves. As hell lapsed and heaven accommodated human desire, in this world occasional conformity bills could not be maintained, convocation lost its power to sit, agitation against the Thirty-Nine Articles and Athanasian creed proceeded apace. Parliament passed a Jewish Naturalization Act (1753) and proposed toleration for Catholics (1780). Both incurred violent popular opposition: A Jew was murdered during anti-Semitic press campaigns in 1753–54, and London burned again in the anti-Catholic Gordon riots of 1780. The Naturalization Act was repealed, Catholic toleration abandoned for a generation. Peter Annet, at seventy, stood in the pillory for mocking Moses. Meanwhile, the first atheist declared himself. Shifting and changing, the afterlife kept pace with other social values, not, except for Swedenborg and Abraham Tucker,[200] as innovations or discoveries, but as rereadings of the biblical text that disclosed an overlooked truth. Such progressive revelations gave the afterlife a new lease on life, and religion a new hold on people, at precisely the moment when "ideology" replaced "theology" as a master discourse (Destutt de Tracy's "philosophy of mind," 1796), and established religions endured the massive assault of the French Revolution. Religion rebounded strengthened, but never again had the universe of discourse to itself.

TAKING OVER THE OTHER SIDE: ADAM SMITH REMODELS FOR PHILOSOPHERS

If those who believed in an afterlife made it fit new desires, what of those who did not believe? The year 1786, when Reed's tale appeared, was also the year of Robert Burns's Kilmarnock edition. In poems he suppressed, Burns declared his disbelief. Poems he published mocked the devil and the religious, including himself, and built comforting, homely afterlives for others. "The Devil and Dr. Hornbook" tells a preposterous lying tale "as true's the Deil's in hell/ Or Dublin city."[201] Shelley recast the line in *Peter Bell the Third* where "Hell is a city much like London" (Part the Third, I, 1 [1819]), echoed more euphoniously by Shaw, "Hell is a city much like Seville" ("Don Juan in Hell Interlude"). The devil is certainly in Dublin city; whether he is in hell is a question.

Hume's "comfortable" doctrine Burns early dismissed, unpublished. A "Song" expects a poor, obscure life "till down my weary bones I lay in everlasting slumber O." An epitaph buries the Laird of Boghead: "But if such as he in Heav'n may be, /Then welcome, hail! damnation." By contrast, his father's friend need not snatch at afterlife hopes: "An honest man here lies at rest, /As e'er God with his image blest. . . . If there's another world, he lives in bliss;/ If there is none, he made the best of this."[202] Versified psalms Burns could publish. He juxtaposes Psalm 1, where good men prosper and the wicked are doomed, with Psalm 90, where God's power brings all men from nothing and returns them to nothing: "Thou layest them with all their cares/ In everlasting sleep." Psalm 90 has the last word.

Burns's published doctrine becomes very comfortable indeed. With his Scottish country upbringing and public humiliations for fornication, he remembers the punitive Scots afterlife to tease God with His benevolence. Two poems written "in the prospect of Death" require God to forgive Burns's sins since He created the "Passions wild and strong" that led to them. "No other plea I have,/ But, *Thou art good;* and Goodness still / Delighteth to forgive" ("A Prayer, in the Prospect of Death," 1786). The next year, "Stanzas on the same Occasion" (1787) faced, terrified, "an Angry GOD, /And . . . his sin-avenging rod." Burns reminds God that Burns's sins are His responsibility. God controls the sea and tempest, so He ought to be able to "aid me with Thy help, *Omnipotence Divine!*" If Burns sins more, God's help needs stepping up. The sinned against is responsible for the sinning, for forgiving it, and for the sinner's sinning on.

Burns glides easily between heaven, hell, and no afterlife at all, a feat now so familiar as to be unappreciated. The afterlife-dismissing poems circulated in many manuscripts, cautiously, tactfully, but not silently. Burns claimed never to have altered a word in a poem except once, for "Dr. Blair," still supporting Scots poets after Ossian (and persuading Burns not to publish *The Jolly Beggars: A Cantata*).[203] Yet Burns happily creates the new traditional heaven for his rustic family in "The Cotter's Saturday Night," after Blair's own heart. God invisible, the trusting family sing together, hopeful

> That thus they all shall meet in future days,
> There, ever bask in uncreated rays,
> No more to sigh or shed the bitter tear,
> Together hymning their Creator's praise,
> In such society, yet still more dear;
> While circling Time moves round in an eternal sphere.
>
> (139–44)

In that last line, Burns is at a great distance from his finally happy family, but he does not let on. His skepticism quiet, others are consoled, but Time moves on; it neither watches nor cares. Wordsworth's "Rolled round in earth's diurnal course" originates here, "with rocks and stones and trees" ("A Slumber Did My Spirit Seal"). It remains for a writer Burns admired to theorize the transition Burns's poems have already made.

Adam Smith did it. It is odd, but pleasant, at this date in time to add something new to what our world owes Adam Smith (1723–1790), friend and acolyte of David Hume, subscriber to Burns's poems, author of *The Wealth of Nations* (1776), critic of empire and the slavery that subjects magnanimous black "heroes . . . to wretches . . . whose levity, brutality, and baseness, so justly expose them to the contempt of the vanquished."[204] In 1790, revising his 1759 *Theory of Moral Sentiments (TMS)*, Smith repudiated the theocentric heaven with which this chapter began as violating "all our moral sentiments." Feeling strongly, he repeated the phrase: once was not enough. He evicted the priests from heaven and made room for anti-theist philosophers, like the unnamed Hume. Situating the afterlife in the human mind and desires, like many of his contemporaries, he undermined its reality, as they did not. Nor did Smith deny the afterlife outright, any more than the deity. In the Platonic, Christian, enlightenment traditions, he redefines what ought to be true. God elided, his afterlife is free from fear. "All our moral sentiments" are gratified in the reward of persons and accomplishments Smith values. Most poignantly, even unrealized human potential is recognized and rewarded in heaven.

In 1759, God's looming judgment in the afterlife was more real than people's actual experiences of others' deaths, their intuitive irrational sympathy with the dead. In the first edition's first chapter (*TMS*, 1759) Smith analyzes the projection into the bodies of the dead that underlies all afterlife inventions (and that Lucretius had ridiculed). "[T]his illusion of the imagination" Smith called it. We pity the dead for being trapped underground in the dark, forgotten by their friends, bereft of all they loved. We lodge, Smith says, "if I may be allowed to say so, our own living souls in their inanimated bodies, and thence conceiv[e] what would be our own emotions in this case."[205] Unlike Hume, Smith forgives such errors: they are how the mind works, not how it ought to work. Smith's "sympathy," those dead bodies make clear, goes beyond pity to irresistible bodily identification, a new meaning that Bence Nanay describes as "a very simple, visceral, quasi-automatic imaginative process."[206] In Smith, that relation to others precedes self-formation.

Yet what should concern us about the dead is not what makes us shudder, but their actual predicament: "that awful futurity which awaits them." Our friends' future judgment alone concerns them and ought alone to concern us. The afterlife and natural human feeling contradict each other. Over retribution, they come together, climaxed by a dark and dismal account of the Atonement.

Against Hume's utilitarian account of justice, Smith insisted that the demand for retribution precedes any rational concern for justice as the support of society. Smith called the utilitarian view refined and plausible, but secondary. The impulse precedes it. Our moral sentiments so demand justice that we pursue it beyond the grave, where it is useless for society: "the example of . . . punishment there cannot serve to deter the rest of mankind, who see it not, who know it not, from being guilty of the like practices here."[207] We want murder avenged, the widow and orphan compensated as an immediate desire, not a utilitarian rationalization. Like identifying with corpses, the demand for justice or retribution is immediate, visceral, and irrational. Utility—and reason—have nothing to do with it. In 1790, Smith closes that discussion with the (inaccurate) observation that every religion or superstition the world has known has featured a Tartarus for punishment, an Elysium for reward.[208]

The curious, ill-fitting climax of this discussion had been from 1759 the Atonement. Man's unworthiness before God merits, Smith feels, only punishment. Some atonement must be made for human failings. Happily, "[t]he doctrines of revelation coincide . . . with those original anticipations of nature": "the most dreadful atonement has been paid for our manifold transgressions and iniquities."[209] Hume had remarked (1757) how believers' terrors overwhelmed their hopes in that futurity Smith designated "awful" (1759). The atonement figures for Smith as "dreadful" but necessary to overcome human unworthiness before God. By 1767 he had begun tampering with the language until in 1790 the discussion vanished as a change of "no great moment." Human nature demands justice, whether as Virgilian geography or Christian doctrine.

In a review of *The Look of Silence* on the killings of Indonesian communists, Anthony Lane quotes a victim's mother, "In the afterlife, their victims will take revenge." He concludes, "What's unnerving is not how rare that ancient sentiment sounds, in a documentary, but how badly you want it to be true."[210]

In 1761 (*TMS* second edition), a still orthodox Smith defended God and his afterlife from the unpublished but devastating contempt of Hume's essay "On the Immortality of the Soul," printed, but withdrawn from publication in 1755 (published posthumously in 1777).[211] A benevolent deity's leaving unclear something so important as eternal rewards and punishments Hume called cruel, iniquitous, and unjust, "a barbarous deceit."[212] This was strong language from the famously good-tempered "bon David." Smith in 1761 felt compelled to answer that slur. If we had all the information we will ultimately possess about the next world, he argues, we would be unable to carry on the business of society in this world. The more important world to come would erase consideration of this.[213]

In 1790, Smith admits for the first time the "melancholy ... suspicion of a fatherless world," but he prefers the joy-giving conviction that the world is conducted by "universal benevolence," desiring "the greatest possible quantity of happiness" for all the universe's "inhabitants," the "great Judge," "the author of Nature" in place.[214] That happiness includes another life to compensate for such brutal injustices as that inflicted on Jean Calas at Toulouse in 1762, broken on the wheel and burned to death, as a Protestant accused by Catholics of murdering his convert son.[215] (Smith had been in Toulouse 1764–65, when Voltaire was agitating the reversal of the court's sentence, achieved in 1765.)

Rooted in human nature, an afterlife promotes lofty ideas of human dignity, cheers us against death, consoles us in distress, and sees to justice (no punishment mentioned). Our happiness in this life often depends upon it (as Dryden observed a century earlier). Smith's, however, promises justice beyond any earlier dreamed of. He imagines righting the wrong of unrealized potential. Smith is improving, massively, a hint Thomas Gray gave in his *Elegy Wrote in a Country Churchyard* (1751). Mark Twain followed a hundred years later.[216] Looking at the graves of the nameless and illiterate, Gray muses on what might have been, what unused gifts lie buried around him,

> Perhaps in this neglected spot is laid
> Some heart once pregnant with celestial fire;
> Hands, that the rod of empire might have sway'd,
> Or waked to ecstasy the living lyre:

> But Knowledge to their eyes her ample page,
> Rich with the spoils of time, did ne'er unroll;
> Chill Penury repress'd their noble rage,
> And froze the genial current of the soul . . .
>
> Some village-Hampden, that with dauntless breast
> The little tyrant of his fields withstood,
> Some mute inglorious Milton here may rest,
> Some Cromwell, guiltless of his country's blood."[217]

In Smith's heaven, that "celestial fire" is recognized, rewarded, and elevated. The unrealized potential of marginalized individuals receives a reward that the marginalized individual did not even dare imagine. There

> the owner of those humble talents and virtues which, from being *depressed by fortune*, had, *in this life, no opportunity of displaying themselves; which were unknown, not only to the public, but which he himself could scarce be sure that he possessed*, and for which *even the man within the breast could scarce venture to afford him any distinct and clear testimony*; where that *modest, silent, and unknown merit*, will be placed upon a level, and *sometimes above those* who, in this world, had enjoyed the highest reputation, and who, from the advantage of their situation, had been enabled to perform the most splendid and dazzling actions . . .

The "humble hope and expectation" of afterlife, "deeply rooted in human nature," does other good things, but this is the climax and the lengthiest of its merits. Of course, those who dazzled in this life may be disappointed to find others more dazzling, but that, as Smith objects of Hume, is matter of reflection, not intuition.

Then abruptly Smith subverts the vision in a move as devastating as Virgil's sortie by the gate of false dreams. This afterlife stitched to one's most secret desires, pregnant with social implications, turns, slipping from "venerable" to "comfortable" to "flattering," and stumbles over "doubt." Reality checks and withdraws, emphases added:

> That there is [such] a world to come . . . is a doctrine, in every respect so *venerable*, so *comfortable* to the weakness, so *flattering* to the grandeur of

human nature, that the virtuous man who has the *misfortune to doubt* of it, cannot possibly avoid wishing most earnestly and anxiously to believe it.[218]

The "virtuous man" is left merely "wishing . . . to believe." Surely Smith sprained his soul as that sentence twists round to collapse, bringing human wishes and their vanity down with it.

Most commentators on the passage call it encomiastic because even unbelievers would wish to believe.[219] That the structure of the sentence quite unnecessarily pulls belief out from under any afterlife is politely ignored. The virtuous man doubting and wishing can only be Smith. Smith had called Hume the most perfectly virtuous man he had ever known, as Plato called Socrates (*Phaedo*), but he had also described Hume's cheerfully approaching death without afterlife expectations (to very bad press in his letter to Strahan, 9 November 1776). Reading Lucian's dialogues, Hume supposed bargaining (unsuccessfully) with Charon to stay for a last revision of his works or until the reigning superstition ended. Hume also lacked "lofty ideas of [human] dignity." He did not think "every stupid clown, that ever existed" should have eternal life.[220] Stranded outside Elysium in the 1778 *Dialogue between Mr. Hume and Dr. Dodd*, Hume was by his own account nowhere at all. Yet once Smith made the afterlife into a wish, he promptly remodeled it on Virgilian principles to welcome David Hume.

The traditional theocentric afterlife, Smith asserts, violates "all our moral sentiments."[221] Smith evicts monks and priests better to accommodate warriors, heroes, and philosophers. He does not name Hume, but he does quote Voltaire. Rewarding the monkish, priestly life of devoted contemplation is as corrupt as a monarch's preference for courtiers' present flattery over "faithful and active service" in distant fields. As the Bastille and Europe's greatest monarchy fell, France's church lands were confiscated, and Edmund Burke defended monkish contemplation, Smith attacks a French bishop who a half-century earlier (d. 1742) told his military congregation that monks reached heaven at once and warriors might not attain it at all.

"[M]onks and friars" Smith does not include among "those to whom our natural sense of praise-worthiness forces us to ascribe the highest merit and most exalted virtue." Such virtue Smith had ascribed to Hume, and here it fits out a Virgilian Elysium: heroes, statesmen, lawgivers, poets, philosophers, those who invent, improve, or excel in life-promoting arts (of subsistence, convenience, or ornament), protectors, instructors, benefactors of mankind. For such is the afterlife made. Privileging the "devout and contemplative virtues" only makes the afterlife risible, especially to those who lack a turn for the devout virtues. The chapter ends citing Voltaire in a footnote, mocking theists' burning Plato, Homer, Cicero.[222] Hume smiles. Hume's preference for soldiers over clerics he had made conspicuous in "Of National Characters." Soldiers are brave, open, and conversable; clergy guarded grimacing hypocrites. And he was a philosopher himself, with little turn for the "devout virtues."

On Hume's behalf, Smith simultaneously doubts the afterlife and transforms it better to suit the doubter's wishes. Unlike the afterlife reformers of the 1760s, Smith did not speak of reunions, but the last words he is reported to have addressed to friends supposed them: "I believe we must adjourn this meeting to some other place." A variant does not suppose reunion: "I love your company, gentlemen, but I believe I must leave you to go to another world."[223] Destroying his papers before his death suggests an acceptance of mortality rarely found in writers. Perhaps sensitive to Hume's triumphant and Smith's sidling withdrawal, Adam Ferguson's reported last words in 1816 were "There *is* another world!"[224]

Arrived is that moment when, if you believe in the afterlife, you can change it to suit. And if you don't believe in an afterlife, you can change it to suit. How you change it will show what you value and whose clichés dominate your thinking. Smith is an index, not an influence, his revolution unremarked in the turbulent 1790s. When a wishful Christian heaven reappears, occasioning a literary quarrel that would once have taken place on the banks of Styx or in Elysium, politics has replaced theology as the topic that gets an author and his printer into trouble. Asgill is safe.

VISIONS OF JUDGMENT: SOUTHEY AND BYRON, A CODA

A Vision of Judgment (1821) promises mankind's Last Judgment, but Robert Southey had more important matters to put in heptameter. George III had died in 1819, and Southey celebrates his pre-resurrection arrival at heaven's gate and triumphant passing through. It had been over a century (1714) since a beloved, if controversial, English monarch had died. The first two Georges inspired no major poets in their moving on (1727, 1760). In music, Handel's Zadok the priest celebrated the coronation of the new king, not the destination of the old (1727). Edward Young's Queen Anne had sailed into the third heaven in the dedication to his *Vision of the Last Judgment* (1713), but Southey stops George III on the way in to celebrate monarch and nation.

Political and nationalist self-congratulation replaces the customary pious salute to the monarch's salvation. As in Lucian, Plato, Fielding, or Young, celebrities gather. George III reconciles not with his God but with George Washington. Rising from hell to accuse him, Junius and Wilkes slink back down, abashed, silent. British genius stands around or wanders through: Bacon and Edmund Burke, Shakespeare and Warren Hastings. Edward Young's *Vision of the Last Judgment* (1713) had toyed with seeing the great ones of the past, but "Alas! A nearer Care your Soul demands,/ *Caesar* Un-noted in your Presence stands." More confident souls have more time for celebrities.

Along with Southey's roll call of British worthies, the eighteenth-century's new terms are firmly in place. Hell overcome, Dante's gate is rewritten as heaven's: " 'This is the Gate of Bliss,' it said: 'through me is the passage/ To the City of God, the abode of beatified Spirits./ Weariness is not there, nor change nor sorrow nor parting; /Time hath no place therein, nor evil. Ye who would enter, /Drink of the Well of Life, and put away all that is earthly' "(Sect. IV, The Gate of Heaven). Dante's gate, created by justice, power, wisdom, and love for eternity, says, "Through me is the way into the sorrowing city . . . into eternal sorrow . . . among the lost people." To be put away, left behind, by those who entered was hope. (PER ME SI VA NELLA CITTÀ DOLENTE,/ PER ME SI VA NELL' ETERNO DOLORE,/ PER ME SI VA TRA LA PERDUTA GENTE./ GIUSTIZIA MOSSE IL MIO ALTO FATTORE:/ FECEMI LA DIVINA POTESTATE,/ LA SOMMA SAPIENZA E 'L PRIMO AMORE./ DINANZI A ME NON FUOR COSE CREATE/ SE NON ETTERNE, E IO ETTERNA DURO./ LASCIATE OGNI SPERANZA, VOI CH'ENTRATE. *Inferno*, III, 1–9).[225]

Nor will the reader of this chapter be surprised that Southey's vision ends in a section called "The Meeting." And who is met? Surely God or Jesus? The reader knows better: who but George's daughter Amelia, the popular princess whose early death had saddened a public. It is, frankly, a little depressing to think that this, this is where the intellectual movement traced in this chapter has been tending, but the reader may as well know the worst:

> He hath recovered her now: all, all, that was lost, is restored him;—
> Hour of perfect bliss that o'erpays all earthly affliction.
> They are met where Change is not known, nor Sorrow, nor Parting;
> Death is subdued, and the Grave, which conquers all, hath been conquered.
>
> When I beheld them meet, the desire of my soul overcame me;
> And when with harp and voice the loud hosannas of welcome
> Filled the rejoicing sky, as the happy company entered
> Through the everlasting Gates, I, too pressed forward to enter;
> But the weight of the body withheld me. . . .[226]

The Christian heaven still surpasses Greco-Roman afterlives—meeting wishes, gratifying desires, fostering reunions, uniting the nation, enabling readers to cope with death and to confront life. Yet another father has been led into heaven by his daughter. Southey has been called, "blasphemous" by a modern critic, but neither Southey nor his readers in his own time regarded this fulfillment of political and social desire as anything but fitting, George Gordon, Lord Byron, and his printer's supporters excepted.[227]

Their problem was not Southey's presuming to read the mind of God, but his politics and his preface, which condemned "the Satanic school" of poets and their works as unsuitable for maidens and children. Annoyed by Southey's slur and his politics, Byron riposted in *The Vision of Judgement* (1822). Allowing George III to slip into heaven, if that is where he wants to be, Byron gives the occasion a politico-theological turn, attacking the Athanasian creed, opposing eternal damnation, and enlisting St. Peter on the side of Catholic emancipation. George III's opposition to emancipation rouses the impetuous old saint to a fury against this "royal Bedlam bigot": "Ere heaven shall ope her portals to this Guelph, / While I am guard, may I be damned myself!" (stanzas 49, 50). Although the heavens fill with Americans and Scots and French massacred by George, his ministers, and his generals, the two witnesses called, Wilkes and Junius, decline to testify against him now—they had their say under the sun. Like Shelley in *Peter Bell the Third* (1819), Byron pinches his denouement from Pope's *Dunciad* (1728, 1742). Taking off Wordsworth, Shelley had sent Pope's great yawn on another errand of universal stupefaction. Byron's Southey reads from his works. Heavenly and hellish hosts scatter at the third line, and St. Peter knocks him down at the fifth. Like Pope's divers, Southey sinks, but his rotten, hollow works float. Meanwhile, in the uproar, the old blind king slips into heaven and starts practicing his psalm. Heaven is open to all men, even kings. It is also open to all literary purposes.

Byron was a little nervous about his poem. His usual publisher Murray refused it, and Byron took pains over a preface that named virtuous antecedents, Quevedo, Fielding, Swift, for jocular treatments of the afterlife.[228] Like everyone else he forgot Sterne, whose phrase "recording angel" appears in his third stanza. When the government moved against the printer, Byron was abroad, and dead before the verdict was delivered. But the indictment charged no one with blasphemy. Instead, the malicious intent was "to injure, defame, disgrace, and vilify, the memory, reputation, and character of his late Majesty King George the Third, the Father of our Sovereign Lord the now King. . . . [and] to cause it to be believed that his said late Majesty was a bad King, guilty of misrule, and a protector of tyrants, and that his death was unlamented and unregretted even by those who attended his burial. . . ."[229] It goes on, and Byron's "impiety" was noted, but that was not the focus of the charge.

The afterlife revolutions had already happened by the time Byron makes his contribution, and Byron could have gone further in fulfilling his own wishes. In 1806, he had written in a private letter that in heaven everyone is divorced, and loves around.[230] Such sentiments Swedenborg and Blake might have recognized as the flippant version of their own imaginings of amorous freedom. Revolutions in the afterlife are peculiar in their invisibility, for no one wants the situation ever to have been different from what the revolution achieves. Whatever one believes in the present instant ought to be eternally true. No one laments the loss of a theocentric heaven which, after all, need not be lost. It is still there for anyone who desires it.

5

WANDÂFURU RAIFU, OR *AFTERLIFE* INVENTIONS AND VARIATIONS

In ancient China, which we have never seen, the wife of a drowned man expressed her unbearable grief in a poem we still read.

—HIRAGA GENNAI, *ROOTLESS WEEDS*

The Poet scarce introduces a single Person, who doth not suggest some useful Precept to his Reader, and designs his Description of the Dead for the Amendment of the Living.

—JOSEPH ADDISON, *TATLER*

> At death, you break up: the bits that were you
> Start speeding away from each other for ever
> With no one to see. It's only oblivion, true:
> We had it before, but then it was going to end,
> And was all the time merging with a unique endeavor
> To bring to bloom the million-petalled flower
> Of being here. Next time you can't pretend
> There'll be anything else.
>
> —Philip Larkin, "The Old Fools"

Joseph Addison imagined "Futurity" as a foreign country he was certain one day to visit—and therefore very curious about, with none of Hamlet's dread of the "undiscovered country."[1] Like other vacation travels, its pleasures swelled in anticipation. Yet what if there is no hereafter? Who visits a foreign country she does not believe exists? In the grave, Jonathan Swift rolls his empty eye sockets at Sir Thomas More. Gulliver chatted up the dead, but did not visit their dwellings. The afterlife's nonexistence once accepted, the skeptic's project becomes Addison's—an ideological construction that uses the other side of death to address living needs and desires. Skeptics, freed from the obligation to combat conventional belief, now take their turn on the playgrounds of eternity.

From Lucretius to Shelley, afterlife deniers did not visit otherworldly heavens, though they mocked hell with pleasure. Human deaths, others' and their own, participated in the cycles of the cosmos, rolled round with "rocks and stones and trees" or splashed with dizzying radiance an infinite moment against the dome of light: "Worlds on worlds are rolling ever, from creation to decay." Their modern descendants invoke infinite galaxies expanding endlessly or collapsing and exploding, recurrently: our own bodies, and all that lives, made of stardust.[2] Temple Grandin, the autistic specialist in animal consciousness, asked if she believed in God or an afterlife, replied, "I have a poster on my wall of the Hubble Deep Field, which shows hundreds of galaxies out in outer space. When I think about those big issues, I just think about that Hubble space poster."[3] W. H. Auden had reservations about being "astraddle/ An ever expanding saddle,"[4] but the old four-walled heavens, mirroring human faces, excluding beetles, have been too small for several centuries. The Asian cosmos has more room, about the right distance away. Anti-afterlife genres flourish. In Jim Crace's *Being Dead*, corpses rot; in Julian Barnes' *Nothing to Be Frightened Of*, the lights go out. In *Salmagundi*, Nadine Gordimer's "Afterlife" savages other people's hopes. A. N. Wilson puts it precisely: "Life After Death: A Fate Worse than Death."[5] As for reunions with one's dead, the living who want their dead back, want them here, beside them now, returned again to the lives they lived, not deferred to some undisclosed future location.

At the turn into the twentieth century, debunking other people's afterlives still preoccupied most skeptics, in spite of Shaw's and Twain's demonstrations that a visit to heaven or hell offers theist, deist, atheist, socialist, or Christian an opportunity to limn ideals and pose problems. Mid-century saw the post-traumatic stress disorder of the absurd. So many deaths, too many deaths for imagination to house: "Vladimir: Where are all these corpses from? Estragon: These skeletons."[6] Heidegger and Adorno faced off over death as a limit, and Levinas declared death impossible: so much death balked thinking beyond it. Time heals all wounds, erases memories, like kudzu. With the collapse of "godless communism" in the 1980s, a political inhibition on western atheism lifted, freeing skeptical discourse to be at once more dogmatic and more playful.[7]

By the time the twentieth century passed, un-mourned, away, the afterlife had become almost as interesting to those who did not believe in it, as to those hopeful for evidence from trips to heaven and back. Against Kevin and Alex Malarkey's *The Boy Who Came Back from Heaven*, Richard Sigmund's *My Time in Heaven*, or Gordon Macdonald's *Glimpses of Heaven*, all in a row on a rack at Chicago O'Hare, August 2013, important names in contemporary literary fiction—and film—have visited or approached or sniffed at eternal life: Milan Kundera and J. M. Coetzee, Steve Stern and George Saunders, Spike Jonze and Hirokazu Kore-eda.[8] Kore-eda. Kore-eda Hirokazu in Japanese naming order.

Three Americans, one European, one South African, and one Japanese: their afterlives have almost nothing in common and little to do with each other. Yet in each case the afterlife as a conceit opens into the heart of ideology, commandeering death to define what really matters, and in each case the author ends with or leaves behind a woman, young, middle-aged, or old, through whom life continues. (Some tropes have very long afterlives.) Privileging afterlife fantasies, they look through death, nuzzling it en passant, sucking up its power. They know death as life's ancient partner, pattern maker. Such fantasies turn artists at once most idiosyncratic and most representative, in themselves, their work, and the culture from which they come.

Americans obsess over American materialism, popular culture, and staying alive in Spike Jonze's film *Being John Malkovich* (1999), George Saunders' story "commcomm" from *In Persuasion Nation* (2006), and Steve Stern's novel, *The Frozen Rabbi* (2010). South African J. M. Coetzee in *Elizabeth Costello* (2003) and European Milan Kundera in *Immortality* (1990) layer literary afterlives, caught between annihilation and self-assertion, ashamed to believe anything at all, determined to write themselves out of being into Being, for a moment or until overwhelmed by otherness. In his film *Wandâfuru Raifu* (1998, English title *Afterlife*) Japan's Hirokazu Kore-eda goes further. His afterlife conceit reaches out from the characters in the film to ensnare the film's viewers, whether they like it—or the film—or not.

An improbable afterlife movie, given Hollywood's abundance, Spike Jonze and Charlie Kaufman's satiric *Being John Malkovich* (1999) enacts, even more decisively than Steve Stern's *Frozen Rabbi*, the modern American dream of living forever. William Godwin, it will be remembered, attributed his hope for staying alive eternally to the quintessential American, Benjamin Franklin. Sending up celebrity culture with its many pleasures and manageable pains, Jonze's film proposes reincarnation without death for a privileged few, yet simultaneously celebrates the self's autonomy and mortality in its own body. Death can be evaded forever, in serial displacements. Whether that evasion is desirable is a question the viewer must answer for herself as she ponders Jonze and Kaufman's twist on the traditional Hollywood afterlife-movie denouement.

Most American afterlife movies allow characters to come back to life and start their romance all over again, whatever the afterlife conceit. Frank Capra's *It's a Wonderful Life* (1946) tries the rule: Capra sends the hero into his nonexistence, from which he returns to resume a re-valued married life. The afterlife may feature clouds, airplanes, and heavenly bureaucrats making mistakes about who dies in *Here Comes Mr. Jordan* (Alexander Hall, 1941), remade as *Heaven Can Wait* (Warren Beatty, 1978). In Kafka, such an error would neither be rectifiable nor admitted. Since these are American movies, the functionaries scramble to rectify those errors to ensure customer satisfaction. There may be a lurid hell, borrowing Dante's frozen heads, with a glossy, kitschy heaven, as in *What Dreams May Come* (1998), designed for admirers of the art of Thomas Kinkade or Claude Monet. In *Defending Your Life* (Albert Brooks, 1991), heaven is a resort where transient residents enjoy plush hotel suites, golf courses and entertainment centers, with all-you-can-eat sundae buffets. Bulimics gorge without purging since there is no danger of gaining weight. *Wristcutters: A Love Story* (Goran Dukic, 2007) designs an afterlife exclusively for suicides, featuring a dreary road trip, depressed Russian families, and a miserable job at Kamikaze Pizza. *Cabin in the Sky* (Vicente Minnelli, 1943) is only a dream of heaven's gate and hell's minions, but a dream with Duke Ellington, Louis Armstrong, and Ethel Waters' telling Lena Horne, "Honey, everything you've got, I've got, and more of it."

Most of these films address significant political, economic, or moral issues, as Capra does, and each ends with true love starting up all over again. The suicides stir in adjoining hospital beds in *Wristcutters: A Love Story* or meet after the ball game in *Heaven Can Wait* or meet as children in *What Dreams May Come* or go together to the next stage in *Defending Your Life*. (The un-American source for *Wristcutters*, Israeli Etgar Keret's "Kneller's Happy Campers," separates the incipient lovers, sending the girl back into the world, leaving the guy waiting for her, hopeful, a little changed, but still alone and trapped.[9]) Excursions to the afterlife are temporary; the marriage plot is eternal, bringing characters back to life and love. Sometimes the marriage plot links the living and the dead or the dead and the not yet born, as in *The Lovely Bones* (Peter Jackson, 2009) or *Made in Heaven* (Alan Rudolph, 1987). Whatever their merits as films, and some have considerable merit, their ideological grounding is firmly in the terrain of Bill and Judy Guggenheim's remaindered *Hello from Heaven! A New Field of Research—After-Death Communication—Confirms That Life and Love Are Eternal* (Bantam, 1996), especially the love part. As in Robert Redford's *All Is Lost*, in Hollywood nothing is ever lost.

Like other Hollywood afterlife films, Charlie Kaufman and Spike Jonze's *Being John Malkovich* proposes love and reproduction as the ultimate value, but love and reproduction line up with mortality against an eternal life that comes at the cost of losing one's body and sharing one's consciousness. The film is a favorite of philosophers of the self and aesthetics, medical theorists, and Levinas-inflected theologians, all more concerned with self than the film's "bizarre immortality," which is noticed and passed by.[10] *BJM* satirizes every contemporary meaning-making cliché, both inward looking, such as self-actualization, psychoanalysis, artistic self-expression, and gender identity, and outward facing, such as celebrity culture (*John Malkovich*), artistic success, and true love (*Being* [a]). What else is there? The desire to live forever, of course, is here too (*Being* [b]). The secret wisdom of the film is that we are always filled with others' voices and too much self is dangerous. Whether we would live forever at the film's price is a question the film's commentators do not address.

In *BJM*, eternal life no longer condemns to the condition of Swift's ghastly, ever-aging, never-dying Struldbrggs (*Gulliver's Travels*, Book 3). Long, long ago on the seventh-and-a-half floor of a New York City office building (so not *that* long ago), a nineteenth-century captain of industry discovered or invented a portal that allows him to occupy a new body when that body reaches forty-four years of age.[11] This evasion of death has a downside in eternal middle-age and shape-shifting. One never again has a youthful body, and one loses one's own. The self that is one's body vanishes forever. Christians' new spiritualized bodies at the resurrection were once thirty-three, Jesus's age when he rose again.[12] That body was closer to its prime. Still, at eighty-eight, there is much to be said for shifting out of an eighty-eight-year-old body and slithering down a slippery canal into someone else's forty-four-year-old (only forty-four!) brain and body, taking it over and adapting it to suit oneself.

An actor's tour de force, the real-live John Malkovich plays John Malkovich (real-person/actor) as Malkovich, Richard III (very badly), and Uncle Vanya; then John Malkovich as occupied by Craig Schwartz (i.e., John Cusack), the failed puppeteer who finds the portal, and finally John Malkovich as occupied by Mr. Lester (i.e., Orson Bean), Craig Schwartz's boss, himself occupied by the nineteenth-century captain of industry and master of the portal. Until the portal closes at forty-four, anyone can enter for fifteen minutes and see the world through Malkovich's eyes, Malkovich prowling the fridge for leftovers, ordering towels by phone, showering. Then the visitor is ejected on to the New Jersey turnpike (with an excellent view of the twin towers of the World Trade Center). The first paying visitor to Malkovich calls himself "a sad pathetic fat man" who wants to escape from himself into anyone else. Maxine (Catherine Keener), a coworker with whom Schwartz has fallen in love, takes the man's money and sneers, like the viewer, at someone who wants not to be himself. Lotte (Cameron Diaz), Schwartz's wife, discovers her true masculinity in her passage through Malkovich and demands a sex-change operation, though ultimately she prefers lesbian love to sexual reassignment.

Having established that celebrity, wealth, and success inside someone else produce more happiness than obscurity and failure in one's own person, the film ends with a coda "nine years later" that juxtaposes the promise of renewed life and the mortal life that will be disrupted by that promise. In the coda, Malkovich's body is occupied by Lester, yet he retains something of Malkovich's inner life. He has won the woman Mr. Lester futilely desired (the triumph of love), but he also offers Malkovich's friend, balding Charlie Sheen, a chance at eternal life through Emily, the new portal. Admiring the photos of Emily on his wall, Malkovich murmurs, "Isn't she lovely?" Love and friendship thrive in immortality; self takes a hit, but Lester-Malkovich seems delighted at the prospect of becoming a woman, and that desire is more recognizably Malkovich's than Lester's. Would the viewer follow him, into Emily?

From Malkovich's admiration, the film moves to nine-year-old Emily, at a pool with her happy, laughing, loving, mortal mothers, Lotte and Maxine. Emily, conceived while Lotte was inside Malkovich, is the new portal, but she already has a voice inside her that she does not hear. Schwartz, the puppeteer, has been shunted into the new portal and trapped in Emily's subconscious. (The film does not specify when portals become available for visits—post-puberty, perhaps?) Gazing at her mothers, Emily ignores the puppeteer's despairing voice inside her, saying "look away, look away." Then she goes for a swim, moving effortlessly under water, in another medium, controlling her body and her breathing, through all the credits. Antithetical to the puppet's "dance of despair and desolation" with which the film begins, Emily moves freely, autonomously in the world of the dying, careless of the new realm without death. Any other voice inside her is subject to her.

Yet at forty-four, whatever she has become, Emily will be taken over by "Malkovich," able at last really to be (inside) a woman, along with whoever wants to join him. He has invited Charlie Sheen, but Flo will surely come, and what of Lotte, who knew Lester, and Maxine, who knew Malkovich? The viewer who regards that prospect with dread has rejected immortality for the sake of the self's autonomy. If an unsuspecting Emily is taken over as Malkovich was, first by Schwartz and then by Lester, the prospect chills. But what if Emily is complicit, alerted by her mothers and their friend[s]? She gains multiple minds absent from her experience heretofore; she acquires immortality through the next portal. Yet what would the viewer wish? Would s/he go into Emily in order not to die? The viewer who thrills at the prospect, gleeful, embraces new life and new experiences, endless new selves and involutions. The viewer who shudders holds fast to his body as himself. The film's Möbius strip of modernity keeps both sides in play.

Viewers may approve or abhor the film's promised reincarnation, but as they are in no danger of experiencing it, its interest is suggestive rather than doctrinal. It evidently allows more persistence of self than other systems of reincarnation. Yet the puppeteer's presence in Emily intimates the falsity of any antithesis between an autonomous and an other-filled self. Malkovich persists in the invasions of Malkovich, self and other. The multiple discourses through which moderns make meaning, literature, psychoanalysis, media, instantiate the multiple selves made of other voices—cultural, historical, familial—that swim through us. Robert Pogue Harrison calls it *The Dominion of the Dead*.[13] To some of these voices, we attend; others we ignore, and of many, we are not conscious. Those in the nightly queue enjoy Malkovich as virtual-reality entertainment, rather than personal transformation. Moviegoers, of course, have paid good money (but less than $200) for ninety minutes to be with John Malkovich being other people inside John Malkovich. Selves are all very well and good, but they need others.

Nowhere is that clearer than the stunning scene in which John Malkovich enters his own portal. Suspicious of his strange stalker girlfriend Maxine, he breaks into the queue to his brain, pushing to the head of the line, and crawls in. Beyond the dark, lies an elegant dining room, red velvet and black tie, where the chanteuse on the piano, the waiter at the table, the woman shrugging her décolletage, the dwarf entering the room, the men at another table, the words on the menu, the words issuing from the waiter's mouth—everything and everyone is Malkovich Malkovich. Tall, short, fat, thin, male, female, bent, bespectacled, tattooed, or bereted, a tour de force of identity in difference, everyone looks like Malkovich. Malkovich is all that is written, and Malkovich is all anyone says, or sings, angrily, happily, perplexedly, smugly, seductively. It is the film's visit to hell: nothing but self, inescapable, omnipresent, all otherness metamorphosed into one's own shape. The boundaries between self and other disappear, but there is no liberation. This is what happens when it's "all about me." How can we adjust ourselves in the mirror of the other when all the others are us? By contrast, Malkovichian renewal cycles through other bodies and other experiences. The film's final argument, its final image, is not transcendence but immersion in an alien medium with others' voices already inside us. Whichever version of mortality or immortality the viewer of *BJM* prefers, its immortality is of this world, and we are invited to recognize the other voices that compose us and enable us to enjoy, or suffer, who we are—from Emily Dickinson and Heloise and Abelard to Elijah the chimp, named, as our precursor, for the Precursor.

In American fictions, dying verges on the unconstitutional: the first guarantee of the *Declaration of Independence* is life. (The third is, of course, happiness as befits a 1770s document.) As the reluctant, resistant Lazar Malkin of Steve Stern's "Lazar Malkin Enters Heaven" screamed at the angel of death, "There ain't no world but this!"[14] Why then meddle with angels of death, imaginary beings who make dying more interesting, more companionable, and much more mysterious? Unlike *BJM*, Stern's novel *The Frozen Rabbi* remembers the desire for transcendence and takes off a real, if not realistic, immortality project: the cryogenics movement. (Don DeLillo's *Zero K* [2016] is another recent entry.) Stern has noticed that businesses that offer immortality by freezing bodies and thawing them had better initiate their processes only after human immortality has been achieved. Otherwise, the resurrected dead will just—like butterflies—have to die all over again. Perhaps that is why Eugene O'Neill's Lazarus laughed.

Long interested in very old voices, Stern inverts the body-mind relationships of *BJM* and injects a young mind into an old body. Better put, the young mind takes on the carapace of the old to be at one with itself and others. As to the afterlife, the desire for transcendence becomes desire as transcendence, and the most fervent imaginings of another world pale against the realities of this perishing one. Yet it is those fervent imaginings that give perishing reality its comedy, beauty, value.

Rabbi ben Zephyr (son of the west wind),[15] frozen while meditating out of his body beside a flooding pond in the late nineteenth century, preserved by diligence and guile in his block of ice, defrosts during a power failure in Memphis, Tennessee, in the late 1990s. Introduced to modern culture through the glories of afternoon television, he soon becomes an entrepreneur of enlightenment, offering seminars in Zen Judaism and promoting himself on billboards with the slogan "Feel good in yourself is the whole of the law."[16] His young mentor Bernie Karp, given to spontaneous out-of-body experiences in biology class (cf. *Calvin and Hobbes*), seeks esoteric, ancient traditions, to the amused contempt of the Rabbi, content with the fleshpots of Memphis. His reading-inspired search for frozen liver having led to the bottom of the family freezer and the discovery of a frozen rabbi, a frozen liver, indeed, Bernie Karp yearns for mystical transcendence, the wisdom of the ages, words of "alternative worlds." The thawed Rabbi assures him that this life, in America, is Paradise, Gan

Eydn (*FR* 52, 48, 177, 182). The history of the rabbi's preservation and passage to America suggests that, at least comparatively, he has it right.

Bernie, however, longs for the wisdom that the rabbi happily trades for modernity. With some impatience, the rabbi regales him with the tree of life and its rotten branches, the kabbalistic concepts of "intensity and cleaving," and the "tzimtzum, God's retreat from His own universe. Like a landlord, disgusted with the tenants who had trashed his premises, rather than evict them [Isaiah 5:1–10, Matthew 21:33–46, Mark 12:1–12, and Luke 20:9–19], he exits slamming the door. The noise of his withdrawal is the big bang, the shevirah, behind which the whole house of cards collapsed, the dust from the rubble rising to heaven where it caused the Lord to sneeze" (52). Then there are the intersecting other realms of demons and dybbuks, some of whom want to "complete the mitzvot they'd left unfinished on earth," all that "unfinished business" Americans fret about. Others trick souls on their "posthumous journey toward Kingdom Come: They turned the laws of reincarnation, the gilgul, helter-skelter, giving false direction to souls already bewildered by the mapless thoroughfares of the afterlife" (53). Bernie tingles with desire; the rabbi barely keeps awake: " 'It's from below that the yester horeh, the yearning,' revealed Eliezer, suppressing a yawn, 'brings about the completion above' " (53).

Yearning for the above also brings about invention below. Revisiting Asgill's ambitions, one of Bernie's forebears attempts to harness aerodynamics to enable "a wholesale exodus of the Jews ... to make aliyah to the Upper Yeshiva without having to die" (98). The thrashing blades attached to the interior rafters of his house do not open the way to paradise, but do produce a cooling breeze in the room. In America, the house of a rich man on Fifth Avenue is "the hekhalot, the very corridors of heaven as described in the *Seder Gan Eyden*, though the book had failed to do the place justice" (196). Without the *Seder Gan Eyden*, the house on Fifth Avenue exhibits merely the meticulously rendered opulence of the gilded age, on view in Edith Wharton or the Frick. The *Seder Gan Eyden* introduces a form of desire that cannot be touched, that whistles us beyond the material to the ineffable. Yet reality, the passages suggest, has its points. To that house on Fifth Avenue, many are called, but few are chosen.

In *The Frozen Rabbi*, the afterlife is the terrain of literature and imagination. Death when it comes is definitive. As the rabbi observes, "There ain't no path; there's only the end of the road. What you call the path, it's just messing around" (342). "Messing around" is both rabbinical wisdom and sex, as Rabbi ben Zephyr teaches. The fiction tantalizes with its evocation of possible other worlds but does not venture there. It settles for the shared experience of this loving, dying, babbling, growing world of babies and nightingales and finds its consummation in the trivial, transcendent little death that takes people, for a few moments, out of themselves while into someone else. For all its fond, comic evocation of the bloated materialism of American life, the novel ends in ascetic circumstances, and with a shift to a young woman's point of view, Stern's dubious heroine Lou Ella. It is she who finally sees "the harum-scarum rooftops of the shtetls of Paradise [and hears] from a playpen somewhere back on earth the warbling of her baby sister in the tongue of nightingales, whose language Lou understood perfectly" (370). So the head argues for what goes on in our bodies. Stern's old discourses of the afterlife once linked this world through endless curiosity with a next, elaborating, layering, querying, testing, mirroring, but not reflecting this world. Now that old discourse mirrors its own longing, itself an obscure object of desire.

Not all American writers stay so determinedly in this world as Kaufman and Jonze or Stern. George Saunders' *In Persuasion Nation* has a bleaker, sourer take on American life than his peers, and in "commcomm," the final story of that collection, Saunders engineers an escape that is not escapist. The premise of much of Saunders' oeuvre is that love, men's fears for those they love, and their efforts to protect them bring disaster on themselves and hapless others. Evil is a by-product of our best, most intimate motives. Goodness recognizes the claims of others. The story asks what to do with the body of a long dead stranger, defunct for a century or more. The easy, obvious answers—try to identify him and bury him with honor or send him to a museum for study—are complicated by the fact that the body's finding will derail a perishing community's last hopes for survival. Work on a facility to replace a closing air base will be suspended indefinitely if the archeologists are called in. Reminding readers that the unhappiness our culture suppresses—be happy; get therapy; take a pill—is in fact inevitable and pervasive, Saunders renews the puzzling Buddhist perception that life is suffering.

The story "commcomm" supposes two sorts of dead people: one sort do not know they are dead.[17] The position is logical enough: death is unknowable, the dead can know nothing, so they cannot know they are dead. Murdered by addled, home-invading Latvian crackheads, the narrator's parents stay in their house with their son. They reenact their murder nightly or revisit pleasant memories in the warmth of a lamp. By day, they sit slack-jawed, like the demented in nursing homes, or they move objects in panicked rages, like the subway ghost in *Ghost* (Jerry Zucker, 1990). Their eventual fate, if they never learn they are dead, is to tear at each other like ravening birds, Homer's vultures turning on each other. The other dead, also murdered, know they are dead and have a single opportunity to appear as apparitions with a message to the living before they disappear.[18] These dead soon know everything.

The story is named for the narrator's work at his air base's department of "community communications." The base is closing, people are losing jobs or must relocate, a child dies of cancer, a wife is immobilized by a stroke, a husband learns his child is not his own, shops go out of business: painful banalities of every day as communities wither. The dead suspended in this world by the longing and guilt of the living are immensely relieved to learn they are dead; they vanish into little gulps of light (like *Ghost* again or the radiances of the bardo). The dead, it seems, should not be held hostage by the living. Death recognized is embraced. Those privileged to reappear as apparitions, the evangelical Giff and the unnamed narrator, know they are dead, perhaps because no one else knows enough to keep them in the world. The dead teach others to die. Visiting ended, the dead Giff and narrator speed forward into a cosmic merging as sorrows rise from countless small despairs, around and below them. The dead and the reader take the place of God, hearing prayers that bear upwards, into the air, the innumerable, trivial, agonizing sorrows of the world:

> Snow passes through us, gulls pass through us. Tens of towns, hundreds of towns stream by below, and we hear their prayers, grievances, their million signals of loss. Secret doubts shoot up like tracers, we sample them as we fly through: a woman with a too-big nose, a man who hasn't closed a sale in months, a kid who's worn the same stained shirt three days straight, two sisters worried about a third who keeps saying she wants to die. All this time we grow in size, in love, the distinction between Giff and me diminishing, and my last thought before we join something I can only describe as Nothing-Is-Excluded is, Giff, Giff, please explain, what made you come back for me?[19]

At "nothing-is-excluded" consciousness merges. This afterlife is not much to look forward to. Knowledge increases, but not happiness. Self vanishes. The pain of the world permeates consciousness; the apotheosis of empathy makes nothing happen, but extends the horizon of concern, the web of imaginary connection. Neglected children, men losing their self-respect and ability to protect their families, terrors of the mirror: it is enough to make one feel sorry for God. Christian and Buddhist thought merge in this transit of insignificant lives. Giff had been a grape-juice-drinking Passion re-enactor. The agony endured by the Man of Sorrows takes its place not as a unique event suffered by God, but as an emblem of thousands crucified, millions tortured, and not one able to look back upon a life without pain. Still, love shoots through, pain's reciprocal. Compassion suffers with, not alone.

If American writers thrum the next life to make us cling more wholeheartedly to this one or to move more compassionately within it, J. M. Coetzee in *Elizabeth Costello* (2003) and Milan Kundera in *Immortality* (1990) invite us to think more deeply about what being in this one signifies. Their principal characters are writers, Elizabeth Costello and the narrator Kundera, and their afterlives are literary genres, the Kafkaesque parable and the dialogue of the dead. Literature protects them from the problem of belief, and the afterlives they affirm are only the texts they craft for themselves and their readers. Such afterlives might seem to be "just literature," and indeed they are, for Kundera and Coetzee dread the extinction of literature more than their own or the world's. Science's promised un-day looms, Costello lectures, when "all trace of [books and authors] will be liquidated from the master catalogue. After which it will be as if they had never existed."[20] Meanwhile literature is both life and afterlife.

The modern afterlife has long been as you like it; it aims to please. Predictably, for him, Coetzee sends his protagonist Elizabeth Costello to an afterlife she did not want, does not desire, out of a writer she does not care for, Kafka. Restoring judgment at the end of a life, Coetzee turns his afterlife into a demand for a "statement of . . . belief," a "confession," and brings his protagonist to ground (194, 209). There she must engage what she believes and what she does, "who she is," trailing after, like a lost, hopeful dog. Coetzee uses his afterlife as Temple Grandin her Hubble space poster: to address really big questions. Beyond death, at the gate— or a gate—separating the writer from eternal light, Coetzee subjects his protagonist to a final, meandering, inconclusive—what conclusion could there be?—interrogation of the self, by the self, on behalf of the self, somewhat resentful of others, who do not figure in the self's construction. Rather than interacting with others in this liminal space, Costello ponders trying to secure a typewriter, to take up novel writing again and to wait for voices to call.

Only two chapters in *Elizabeth Costello* were written exclusively for the novel: "Lesson 7 Eros" and "Lesson 8 At the Gate": love and death, divinity and judgment, reality's last things. Discussions of how and what to write, from narrative realism to the postscript's rewritten Hofmannsthal, each chapter appeared elsewhere before being corralled. In "Eros," Costello meditates on gods, goddesses, and their intercourse with men and women. Some of her conclusions are familiar: death gives life urgency and intensity (189; Ūta-napišti lacked both), all beings are called by love (192), the gods are indifferent to us (from Hölderlin [188], rather than Epicurus, who appears near Newton and Nietzsche in the atoms' whirlwind [192]). Sometimes a vision opens, a pattern unfolds, then closes again (192). There are some quaint reversals. The gods do not hate death (as Sappho and Hesiod thought); they are infinitely curious about it, but timorous, and so they sniff around human beings, whom they dare not abandon (189). As to finality, the novel abhors it, like death. The last "Lesson 8 At the Gate" is the last chapter, since the chapters are called "lessons," but it is not the end of the novel. Beyond the lessons lies a "Postscript: Letter of Elizabeth, Lady Chandos," signed "Elizabeth C." Dirk Klopper suggests the "postscript" is written by "Elizabeth C[ostello]," signing her work as the names rhyme across four centuries.[21] Elizabeth Costello made her name as a novelist by rewriting Joyce's *Ulysses* from Molly Bloom's point of view, as *The House on Eccles Street*, evoking Coetzee's *Foe*, *Robinson Crusoe* with a female perspective. Professional rewriters, at least one of them, perhaps both, rewrite Hofmannsthal.

The surroundings at the gate are unappealing—a dusty, dreary piazza reminiscent of Tennessee Williams' *Camino Real* or the tentative outpost of Coetzee's own *Waiting for the Barbarians*. The functionaries are not helpful caseworkers, angels, demons, or bodhisattvas, but Kafka's indifferent bureaucrats. The judges, caricatured, monstrous, severe, mock the petitioner they examine. The writer is allowed a glimpse through the gate, but sees only a bright light, that disappoints: "the light is not unimaginable at all. It is merely brilliant, more brilliant perhaps than the varieties of light she has known hitherto, but not of another order, not more brilliant than, say, a magnesium flash sustained endlessly" (196). The episode sits oddly near the end of the novel not because it introduces allegory (the "lessons" and lectures of which the novel is assembled have accustomed the reader to radical discontinuities), but because of the problem Elizabeth Costello has with her statement of belief. In lesson after lesson, she has maintained the cruelty of humans to animals; she has argued that representing evil re-creates it in ways that are damaging for the writer and reader, so certain forms of evil should not be represented. Lecture after lecture—and this is now number eight—has told us what Elizabeth Costello believes. Nothing should be simpler than for her to submit Lessons 3 and 4, published earlier with replies from Peter Singer and Wendy Doniger, among others, and be on her way. Granted she has wavered, no longer certain what she thinks at the end of Lesson 6 (181), desiring a third way, a synthesis that does not come, over the representation of evil.

This woman of opinions, whom Coetzee has created for her opinions, now disengages from opinions, contemptuously designating them "opinions and prejudices, no different in kind from what are commonly called beliefs" (200). Pushing them away as alien to her ideal self, she insists, against all the evidence the reader has read through, that she has no beliefs. She rejects belief as an impediment to her calling and claims merely to represent voices that come through her, voices of murderers and victims. Without seeming to notice, she renounces her earlier attack on Paul West for his contaminating representation of evil: the scribe of the "invisible" has no moral responsibilities except to the voices.

Revising her statement, having been advised that the judges will be satisfied with passion, Costello tells a story of the death and resurrection of frogs as a river dries up and floods. It is a beautiful story, for which she incurs a dreadful judgment. Her judge says she believes, as a storyteller, in the "spirit of life." Odysseus sacrificed a black ram at the shore of Hades, a live ram, black blood spilling, ghosts hovering: she has wondered if that would be a "good enough" story for her judges (211). Now she is justly appalled by her own banality: "*She believed in life:* will she take that as the last word on her, her epitaph? Her whole inclination is to protest: *Vapid!*" (219). Intellectual snobbery writhes as it sees through itself. She might feel less shame had she chosen an allegory of tapeworms or maggots or the liver fluke, but she did not. She chose frogs, the only endearing plague in Egypt: "And the river shall bring forth frogs abundantly, and they shall go up and come into thine house and into thy bedchamber, and upon thy bed, and into the house of thy servants, and upon thy people, and into thine ovens, and into thy kneading troughs" (Exodus 8.3, KJV). In their little fingers stretching and ending in balls of mucus, she takes pleasure, finds joy.

Still worse, she is asked of the effect of her second statement on her first: does she repudiate it, reconsider it, revise it? "Has she changed her story?" (220). A Humean subject, she knows herself as constantly changing and indescribably constant. She has nothing but contempt for personal memory: "breez[ing] through one's hearing with anecdotes from one's childhood . . . every petitioner [taking] up autobiography, and the court stenographer [washed away] in streams of free association" (223). So she characterizes herself in Lacanian terms, filched from Rimbaud: "*I am an other.*" Had she quoted Alexander Pope, she might have caught her own difficult relationship to other animals:

> Our depths who fathoms, or our shallows finds,
> Quick whirls, and shifting eddies, of our minds? . . .
> On human actions reason tho' you can,
> It may be reason, but it is not man:
> His Principle of action once explore,
> That instant 'tis his Principle no more.
> Like following life thro' creatures you dissect,
> You lose it in the moment you detect.[22]

Her judges want to pin her down, but all she will do is affirm and not affirm and separate herself from affirmation and denial. They ask, " 'Do you speak for yourself?' 'Yes. No, emphatically no. Yes and no. Both. . . . I am not confused' " (221). Her judge cannot resist the joke, "But who is it who is not confused?" and the bench collapse in helpless laughter.

"*Fidelities*" is the word that comes to Elizabeth Costello to save her from the embarrassment of belief (disbelief does not embarrass). As she turns it over, she has a vision of the other side of the gate, the side she is trying to reach—a mangy dog sleeping against the gate and "a desert of sand and stone, to infinity" (224). Cerberus and Shelley meet as Costello rejects the palindrome GOD-DOG as too literary. There is nothing to guard as Ozymandias's sands stretch far away. She has no vocation for whatever lies beyond the gate: light, a mangy dog guarding nothing, gods who no longer believe in people. If the dog is Cerberus, there seems no one for him to prevent leaving. If the dog is Argo, he awaits someone to recognize. The love of the divine for mortals was the subject of the previous lesson "Eros," but the gate evokes no desire. It is, like death, merely a barrier. Costello has no curiosity about, invests no imagination in where she is presumably meant to go. Her beliefs, concerns, and quotations—fidelities—lie all this side of the gate. Convinced of her difference, she asks the functionary at the gate if he sees many people like her, in her special situation, and he replies, in the last words of the chapter, "All the time . . . We see people like you all the time" (225). This is not the answer she wanted, but the rest is silence.

What looks a generous, universalizing gesture "All the time . . . people like you all the time," could in these literate days mean merely how many writers line up at the gate. Nor does the novel *Elizabeth Costello* end there. Coetzee backs off from his imagined afterlife—surely the end?—to demand salvation through writing from the overwhelming pressure of sensory experience: a world burgeoning with too many frogs. Turning the page, the reader passes beyond Costello, beyond her rewriting Joyce and Coetzee's rewriting Kafka, to one or both of them rewriting Hofmannsthal. The gate's dreary, arid vision abuts the flourishing excess of Hugo von Hofmannsthal's *Letter of Lord Chandos to Sir Francis Bacon, This 22 August, A.D. 1603* (1902). Hofmannsthal's eloquent Lord Chandos will write no more, he has lost his words, he tells Bacon.[23] The world brims with the wordless ecstasy of being: cart tracks winding over a hill, a stunted apple tree, a beetle. Now and then, something opens, beyond words; Lord Chandos prefers experience to words.

Fullness, presence, love, everything means: Costello/Coetzee's equally eloquent Elizabeth, Lady Chandos cannot bear it. Out of the rush of experienced, wordless revelation she cries to be saved from her raptures and his revelations and infinite presences. "Drowning, we write out of our separate fates. Save us" (230). What saves is the writer's craft, a work of this world, not the next: "Yet he writes to you, as I write to you, who are known above all men to select your words and set them in place and build your judgements as a mason builds a wall with bricks" (230). "[A]s a mason builds a wall with bricks": to last, to keep in, to keep out, to hide, to protect, to house, inanimate words. Words cannot express the experience of the inexpressible, but words evoke both the experience and the inexpressible if they be properly "set in place . . . as a mason builds a wall." Costello likened her belief in her books to the belief of a "carpenter . . . in a sturdy table, or a cooper in a stout barrel" (208). With words, tentative, repetitive, circling, Elizabeth expresses unspeakable feelings called up only through words. She demands that words in turn control, compose, confound that experience that they alone have permitted the reader to share or to comprehend. "Save us." Can words "save"? Salvation once referred to a final judgment before God, at the gate, anticipated by Hofmannsthal's Chandos. The novel's structure rejects the afterlife as its ending, as an ending. A textbook supplement, the "postscript" asserts the essential problem of the relation between experience and language, and, repudiating afterlife, returns to a dying, duplicated world of words. As Sir Richard Steele observed, a lady's letter seldom expresses her mind until the postscript. As renaissance letter, as Hofmannsthal letter, as Costello doubling, as Coetzee doubling, as piece already published, this "after writing" precedes the novel it comes after many times over. All the action, all the writing, is this side of the gate.

"Only the light soul hangs in the air," says a Polish woman to the newly arrived Elizabeth Costello, as she smokes, luxuriating in laughter at the idea that there is only one gate to the next world (*EC*, 213–14). Milan Kundera's *Immortality* (1990) is playful—a toccata of immortalities.[24] The immortality the title has in mind is fame, the survival after death of the name that identifies a person. For "major" immortality, many people recognize the name; in "minor" immortality, only a domestic circle knows the name, and in "ridiculous" immortality, ludicrous death makes an anecdote: Tycho Brahe of a burst bladder, "Kundera" fearing (hoping) he might copy Musil and collapse while lifting weights. What ought to survive as evidence of life is the art produced by "immortals," dead men whose names we know. Those dead men, however, here Hemingway and Goethe, hanging somewhere in the air, discover to their dismay that no one any longer reads their works. The works have been displaced by biography, interest in the author's person, a shift that delights Kundera's characters Paul and Bernard. (Blame Hume, and his "My Own Life.") Even "major" immortality moves toward the erased "master catalogue" that Elizabeth Costello fantasied and dreaded.

Traditional Christian immortality had nothing to do with fame, and the anonymous afterlives of immortal souls, Christian or other, have no place in Kundera. His characters toy from time to time with traditional afterlife concepts as if to signal their transition to other modes of immortality. Invited in a dream by an interplanetary visitor to decide whether she and her husband wish the next life to reunite them, the heroine Agnès affirms that she and her husband (Paul) desire never to meet again. Samuel Johnson observed that couples would meet again in heaven or divine wisdom would determine that it was better they not meet. Happiness followed in either case. For Agnès, Johnson's afterlife is a dream and science fiction, and it is to be settled as she likes. If not in a next life, why tomorrow? The afterlife fantasy illuminates Agnès's relation to her marriage and sets her on a path to another life, in this world.

Another traditional afterlife fantasy, the dialogue of the dead is revived between Goethe and Hemingway as each complains of what is made of him by the hostility of his admirers. Disembodied voices, in the air, nowhere, Hemingway complains of female schoolteachers, Goethe of the schoolmaster's rod. Devoted critics and biographers root for trash, snorting and grunting in self-delight at the discoveries they expose. Hemingway cringes. He at least was spared the ubiquitous camera Kundera knows and Agnès dreads: "in the end one single stare will be instituted that will not leave us for a moment, will follow us in the street, in the woods, at the doctor's, on the operating table, in bed; pictures of our life, down to the last detail, will be filed away to be used at any time, in court proceedings or in the interest of public curiosity. . . . The eye is everywhere. The lens is everywhere"(29, 30). (These videotapes of our lives Kore-eda's *Afterlife* tucks away in storage.) That eye has always belonged to an author's power over characters, though authors may choose from time to time to blink, to look away, to conceal.

Immortality's lightest joke about immortality is Goethe's denying that authors are "in" their works while Kundera diligently writes himself as "Kundera" into his novel as the author of his novel so as to be inescapably "in" the work. Laura, Agnès's sister, demands "the only real life: to live in the thoughts of another. Otherwise I am the living dead" (156). At the center of the fiction, the greatest of the immortals present in the work,

Goethe, explains to the denser Hemingway that dead authors cannot be found in their works at all, since they no longer exist. If they cannot be found in their own, can they be found in someone else's? And in what sense were "they" ever there at all?

> And I'll tell you something else. I am not even present in my books. He who doesn't exist cannot be present. [Hemingway calls that too philosophical. Goethe explains:] Forget for a moment that you're an American and exercise your brain: he who doesn't exist cannot be present. Is that so complicated? The instant I died I vanished from everywhere, totally. I even vanished from my books. Those books exist in the world without me. Nobody will ever find me in them. Because you cannot find someone who does not exist. (214)

Goethe's argument suggests that Kundera will be "in" his novel until he dies. After that, readers will find "Kundera" there, but not Kundera, who is and is not "Kundera." Writing himself "in" beside Goethe and Hemingway, no more really there than they are, Kundera expects eventually to be as absent, or as present, as Goethe and Hemingway in their immortalities and in his book. The conceit gains its charm from "Kundera"'s being so much less interesting a character than Agnès, his heroine,[25] and indeed he gives the last gesture of the novel to her.

While the immortality the title has in mind is fame, the immortality the text has in mind is less articulate. Gestures, ideas, moments, images, impressions, experiences, feelings (memes) pass from person to person. In the text an initial gesture, the wave of an old woman at a swimming pool, arouses in the author/narrator an "immense, inexplicable nostalgia" (7). From that woman's gesture, the author/narrator creates the character Agnès and passes the gesture from character to character. Goethe's "Wayfarer's Night Song II" passes between Agnès and her father:

> On all hilltops
> There is peace,
> In all tree-tops
> Hardly a breath.
> Birds in the woods are silent.

Just wait, soon
you too will rest.

(Wandrers Nachtlied II)
Über allen Gipfeln
Ist Ruh,
In allen Wipfeln
Spürest du
Kaum einen Hauch;
Die Vögelein schweigen im Walde.
Warte nur, balde
Ruhest du auch. (26–27)

Not unlike Robert Frost's "Stopping by woods on a snowy evening," peace, silence, a stilled moment imply death, but also triangulate an intensely experienced awareness of the instant's fragility. Of this poem, the author/narrator considers that its purpose is not to astonish, "but to make one moment of existence unforgettable and worthy of unbearable nostalgia" (27), like the vanished moment of the old woman's gesture.

"Homo sentimentalis" is the novel's central section (the fourth of seven). Sentimental man Kundera defines not as "a man with feelings (for we all have feelings), but as a man who has raised feelings to a category of value" (194). Yet the man of sentiment shifts quickly to "inexplicable indifference" when the performance is over (195). As François Ricard observes, Agnès opposes living to being. In living there is no happiness, "carrying one's hurting self through the world." In being rests deep, silent happiness: "Being: becoming a fountain, a fountain on which the universe falls like warm rain." In such a moment, Ricard continues, self is erased, the peace of Goethe's poem descends, and there is "no more world, no more laughter or love, no more paths or exile. And no more novel."[26] In His will is our peace. That is not, however, where Kundera ends things. The novel ends not with rest, not with being, but with the active, painful, restless yearning that the novel claims as its origin and that the author now hands off to the reader. A "moment of... unbearable nostalgia" impelled the novelist into invention, and the novel ends as it creates another such moment. The kind of experience that set the novel off, once private, often described, is at last forced on the reader.

Early in the novel, Agnès is horrified by the ugliness of the life around her, and she imagines going to a florist, as Virginia Woolf's Mrs. Dalloway actually did. She will buy "a forget-me-not, a single forget-me-not. . . . She would go out into the street holding the flower before her eyes, staring at it tenaciously so as to see only that single beautiful blue point, to see it as the last thing she wanted to preserve for herself from a world she had ceased to love" (21). The aestheticized moment shuts out other people much as the novel's characters persistently withdraw from husbands, lovers, sisters, jobs, life. Unlike Mrs. Dalloway, Agnès never buys her flower, and she dies in a freakish auto accident reported early in the novel on the radio. After her death, to that early moment of longing for beauty the novel returns. To celebrate his novel's conclusion, the author/narrator revisits the health club where the idea was born. Emerging from this place of origin, the novel impossibly allegedly already finished, "Kundera" concludes:

> The cars were honking their horns, and I heard the shouts of angry people. It was in such circumstances that Agnès longed to buy a forget-me-not, a single forget-me-not stem; she longed to hold it before her eyes as a last, scarcely visible trace of beauty. (345)

A forget-me-not is a tiny, undistinguished, almost-wild flower, blue or white (the name is the same in French, though the "ne-m'oubliez-pas" can also be called "mouse's ear"); Agnès wants a blue one. Circling back to a moment long before Agnès's accidental death, this evocation of an episode that never happened produces "unbearable nostalgia" for what is passed and passing. Goethe's poetic effect the novel partly achieves, "to make one moment of existence unforgettable and worthy of unbearable nostalgia" (27). Kundera absorbs Goethe, with uncredited assistance from Virginia Woolf. The page offers up to remain with us as if we saw it something we never saw, that the novel never represented, the forget-me-not "before her eyes." "Kundera" recalls a moment of longing that he invented (and never fulfilled) in which the object, the flower, obscures the longing that is his actual subject, making the longing "scarcely visible." Inventing Agnès's longing, inventing Agnès, "Kundera" creates that momentary stillness in the midst of chaos, and they share the "forget-me-not." "Kundera" also recognizes that after we put the book down, his exquisite moment with

Agnès and her forget-me-not will be forgotten. Still, the pair hold her un-held flower toward us.

Kundera's sleight of immortality makes the merely imagined more real, more memorable, more provocative of deep emotion, than the real. That is, it does what literature always aspires to, though with a meta layer more than usual, created by putting the "author" into the work. An artificial memory has been created for us, reminding us that the literary project is always to make words become experiences, then memories. A work that does not live in the thoughts of others, through the metempsychosis of reading, is, as Laura says, "the living dead." As John Dryden mocked modern playwriting plagiarists, they make love to their predecessors the Egyptian way, and "join the dead living to the living dead."

Kundera and Coetzee situate the self before death vis-a-vis literature—what an author does, why he does it, what claims a reader has on the writer. Unlike Coetzee's astringent, thick self-examination, Kundera's mille-feuille of immortalities privileges the ephemeral moment in its passing. The Japanese, specialists of the "floating world," have a phrase for that aesthetic, *mono no aware*—sensitivity to the ephemeral, to the pathos of things in their passing. It is a feeling, an emotion, a value, and an aesthetic (*mono:* things, *aware:* sensitivity, sadness, pathos). It is more evident in Kundera than in Kore-eda, where it is ostinato, not theme.

Kundera's trick of handing off his remembered (invented) moment to his reader, Hirokazu Kore-eda's film *Wandâfuru Raifu* (1998, English title *Afterlife*) multiplies through a dozen filmed characters, who in turn transmit the impulse to the film's viewers. Asking its characters for a memory, the film elicits the autobiography Coetzee's Elizabeth Costello despised: "breez[ing] through one's hearing with anecdotes from one's childhood . . . the court stenographer [washed away] in streams of free association" (223). It then requires that the memory selected be filmed. Just as self discovers its core to itself, that twist reveals a social construction of self as imbricated with others. Like burial, movie making depends on other people. Filming the memory reveals, as Kore-eda put it, that "the self is not just something internal."[27]

Kore-eda's invention, the film's peculiar afterlife conceit, is very simple: the dead are invited to choose a single memory to take with them into eternity and given several days to make the choice. No one knows what eternity is like, but one will be there with/in one's memory. The memory is filmed collaboratively, the film screened, and the dead vanish into eternity, taking the memory with them, leaving behind the archived film, as well as the workers who continue making others' memories into film, unless they decide to choose a memory, too.

The film's is perhaps the most valuable afterlife invention since the demise of the real ones. It models the insignificant and unimportant and passing moment as sources of value, and it impels its viewers quite irresistibly to perform the self-evaluation that death is famous for inspiring. A young American, defending the film from attack, observed that "It isn't often a movie changes the way you think about your life." This movie's imitation of an action provokes imitation of its action, soliciting judgment about the value, meaning, or futility of one's own life and, inferentially, others' and those modeled in the multiplex.

A documentary filmmaker making only his second feature film, Koreeda interviewed some five hundred ordinary Japanese and asked them for not their "best" or "happiest" memory (as reviewers often describe it), but the "most important."[28] Those documented memories, interwoven with actual memories of cast members and invented memories and relationships, represent lives and moments of exemplary ordinariness. A bell's tinkly sound, an afternoon on a bench, the smell of cold, the glint of light on a bus pass: nothing much, nothing unavailable to anyone. No one remembers a Nobel Prize or dating John Malkovich.

The film looks like no American idea of heaven or Japanese image of the Pure Land: no heavenly birds sing, no celestial music sounds, no fragrances waft through the radiant light, no bejeweled streams pass by beautiful flowers springing up, or trees covered with bells.[29] In the opening shot, figures emerge through mist into an exquisitely defined geometrical space and then materialize into a *wabi-sabi* aesthetic: the imperfect, rough, marred, unfinished, unpolished of a drab institutional building. (*Wabi*, rustic, like Yūtei's small fenced house among the mansions, *sabi*, withered, like the morning glories and creepers in autumn, in Habian's description.) Nature's greens are muted, snow turns to slush; browns, beiges, dark blues, indigo, Kyoto colors. Paint peels, dust-motes hang in the air, the bath rusts, a fuse blows when hairdryers are turned on simultaneously on filming day. Nothing glossy, no techno-orientalist, glitzy nineties Tokyo of *Lost in Translation* (2003), no lurid Technicolor impressionist heaven (*What Dreams May Come*, 1998), no evocation of high-status glamor (*Being John Malkovich*, 1999; Albert Brooks' *Defending Your Life*, 1991): the space is as democratic as the memories and the camera.

That camera is egalitarian, participatory, and doubled (when one cinematographer and his crew film another cinematographer and his crew filming scenes in the film).[30] As Timothy Iles observes, the camera establishes itself immediately as a participant in the scene.[31] It walks upstairs behind two characters chatting in the opening shot, stands shoulder to shoulder with the case workers while the week's tasks are assigned, moves around among the people waiting to be called at their seated level, looks at the employee calling names from their position. Interviewing, the camera occupies the interviewer's chair, at first cutting rapidly from person to person for exposition of the film's project, then spending more time with the interviewees as they recount their memories.[32] From time to time, the camera just stops.

The camera lingers, paused on long shots down vacant halls with peeling paint. It gazes at a name tag hanging from a doorframe. It watches a garden in which nothing is happening. It looks at a lamp in the moonlight. It considers the snow.[33] In continuous speech, the camera jumps just a little, a tiny cut, to remind viewers the camera is there. Medium shots, straight on or from slightly below, dominate; figures walk to the edge of their frame, wheel just in time or walk out of range and return. The mise-en-scène is down-at-heels and technologically challenged (that blown fuse, a rotary phone, film reels). Three times the screen goes black, as if there has been an ending, a Mizoguchi or Ozu episode, and three times the film resumes.

What Kore-eda's deliberate intermittent slowness permits, and other techniques prevent, is introspection. When the camera stops and gazes down an empty hallway for what seems a long, long time, viewers may squirm—why is this camera stopped, why is nothing happening? Jarringly, (non-Japanese) audiences are invited to look at the play of light and shadow within an unfamiliar aesthetic. The film's project has, however, given viewers an idea. One young viewer reported finding the movie so boring that he just started running through his memories, searching for his own moment.

Those moments validate lives that might be called unlived, within a reassessment of twentieth-century Japanese social and political history, an homage to Japanese (and American) filmmaking, and a valorization of Japanese aesthetic and cultural traditions. The first person interviewed wants only to forget, not to remember, and chooses a dark room where he hid as a child. The second fingers a problem with the setup that Americans might think peculiarly American: "just one?" The huge (to a child) rice balls a kimono-clad woman remembers making with her family in a bamboo grove appeared at a specific historical moment. The Great Kantō earthquake (1923) took 140,000 lives and set off riots massacring Koreans and Korean-Japanese; the woman also remembers the "false rumors" about the Koreans.[34] WW II is death and defeat (1945). An old soldier remembers surrendering hopefully to the Americans, cadging a cigarette and upping his demands from salted rice to chicken. Beyond lie the salary men, sex workers, and rebellious youth of postwar prosperity and the Disneyland invasion, but the memories are always simple. An old man's suicide attempt at twenty, thwarted by silvery-blue light glinting on the railroad tracks; a valley girl's day at Disneyland with friends traded in for a moment with her head in her mother's lap. (Shiori, the counselor, told her she was the thirteenth teenager to choose Disneyland this year.)

Lying with one's head in one's mother's lap is a moment to which "happy" or "best" scarcely applies.[35] The moment is suffused with feeling, but the significant emotion is surely not "happiest," or "best," or even "important." The girl says she does not in fact remember the moment very well. Such a moment, however, Yosa Buson (1716-1784) chose to end his linked song sequence "Spring Breeze on the Kema Embankment" ("Shunpu Batei Kyoku," 1777), with a gesture to another poet, Taigi (1707–1771):

> Perhaps you know this hokku by Taigi, now dead:
> Home for three days,
> she sleeps again beside
> her widowed mother[36]

Sleep, death, impermanence: only the poets are conscious of this moment as it passes, and one of them is now gone, too. The film preserves as it parodies such typical motifs. Cherry blossoms are pink paper; an allusion to the moon is not understood, but the privileged art form is film, from Ozu's tatami shots through a recitation of American movies, to a title from Frank Capra. "Wandâfuru raifu" is "wonderful life," and the film nudges its viewers away from grand gestures towards small wonders belonging only to one person, often in solitude, to what gives a life value. Film is also the film's pivot.

Requiring that the memory be filmed pulls the viewer out of the self into relation with others. Some viewers object, strenuously, to this objectification of a private delight. They prefer to hug their memory in secret, to themselves. There are also videotapes, one for every year of a person's life, supplied to those who find choosing difficult, like Watanabe, the well-dressed salaryman, who wants "evidence of life." Why not just spot the moment on the tape and replay it, select your memory and go? Why enlist a film crew to stage and reenact the memory, especially when someone else will have to act your part if you are old and the memory when you were young?

Visually contrasted with film (a contrast occasionally elided in critical commentary on the film[37]), the videotapes, on cassettes, are grainy and pixilated, objective security-camera records of a life, from an undefined point of view, Agnès's dread realized. Viewers of their own lives are cautioned that the videos will not correspond to their memory of an event. "What really happened" as recorded on the video is external to memory. By definition precisely not what memory recalls, video is an alien medium of capture. To watch in solitude an external record of one's own life, to push the button at a particular point, and to vanish is to be a passive consumer of someone else's point of view, controlled by surveillance camera. Such a life is recognized, not remembered: it is not one's own.

Filming reveals aspects of memory we are ordinarily unconscious of—its selectiveness, its forgetfulness, its constructed-ness. A woman finds her fiancé on a bridge after the war. Knowing there must have been hundreds of people in the road, on that bridge, she remembers seeing only the man she had been certain would return alive. In her memory, they were alone, just the two of them. Characters filming their memories are troubled as memory's uncertainty presses itself upon them. How did the elderly woman hold the handkerchief when she was a little girl dancing in a red dress? Instructing another little girl, distressed, she cannot remember. The schoolboy on the bus the day before the last day of school, when summer stretches all possibility yet untouched, was his cap on or off? Puzzled, the middle-aged man he became sinks into a seat, meditative, solemn, as taped traffic sounds evoke a vanished self and moment.

Filming the memories reveals the nature of memory as nothing else can: that memory is contingent, constructed, and fallible, the mind's creation.

Obscured by the medium itself, filming also means that someone is always watching, the most powerful (internal and external) form of social control. The memory one chooses must be a memory one is willing to share and to reenact before others. Foucault would disapprove. (It is easy to imagine the film crew's initial eagerness to film exhibitionist scenes and their subsequent, "you're the thirteenth person this month to choose. . . .") The film's plotting reenacts the imbrication with others demanded in filmmaking by way of two thwarted love triangles that intersect in the last third of the film: Watanabe, Mochizuki, and Kyoko, two men and a woman; Mochizuki, Kyoko, and Shiori, a man and two women.

Imitative desire saves Watanabe, the best-dressed of the week's dead. Searching his "so so" prosperous life on seventy videotapes for "evidence of life" and a worthy memory, Watanabe revisits his ambitious youth, when he wanted to make a difference, followed by his arranged marriage and windowed corner office. Wielding binoculars hidden in his clear desk, he gazes into the distance, always looking elsewhere. Watching his tapes with his counselor, the young and very handsome Mochizuki, killed just before the end of World War II, Watanabe realizes what Mochizuki does not suspect he knows—that Mochizuki was the dead fiancé whose grave Watanabe's wife visited annually. Seeing his life and marriage through other eyes, the eyes of someone denied both and whose life would have meant for Watanabe another life, at least another wife, enables Watanabe to re-value a life, self, and relationship he despised as nothing special, a promise unfulfilled. Someone's finding his domestic life worth watching makes worthwhile that life's having been lived.

Mochizuki, when he learns that Watanabe knew, rejects Watanabe's interpretation of his silence. Mochizuki experiences himself as isolated, detached, disconnected from others. His coworker, Shiori, a young woman with a crush on him, has watched him watching Watanabe's tapes and teased him about Kyoko. She insists he is involved without even knowing it, speaking for both herself and Kyoko, and she tracks down Kyoko's memory film among the stored-away reels. The elderly Kyoko and a young Mochizuki in uniform share an autumnal park bench. Then, on Kyoko's videotapes, they locate the precise moment she chose, in the same park, on the same bench that Watanabe chose. Poor Watanabe has set off into eternity with a woman who did not choose him, who chose someone else, in the same place, at another time. He was right to have been a little jealous all those years and has been cuckolded for eternity. Yet Mochizuki has figured in the ultimate happiness of both wife and husband, once as beloved memory, once as catalyst.

That recognition of imbrication enables him to choose, to Shiori's chagrin, a memory of himself alone on the same park bench in the filming studio, filmed by his coworkers' being filmed waving good-bye to him. Instead of reciprocal recognition, Kore-eda unobtrusively proposes *La Ronde*. Every person chosen chooses someone else to be with forever, a cosmic cuckolding to embitter the moral that it may (have to) be enough to be part of someone else's happiness.

And what of those who do not choose? This afterlife depends on those who reject nirvana's elusive promise: all those filmmakers and caseworkers. The harried workers resemble hapless, exasperated bodhisattvas, without their selfless motives. They each have personal reasons of their own for declining to move on, yet they do assist others. Their motives vary: attachment and responsibility to a living child (Kawashima), lack of attachment to anyone (Mochizuki), terror of abandonment (Shiori), responsibility "for [one's own] life" (Iseya), or the pleasures of music, go, and work (Nakamura, the station chief) or of conversation, elegant bronzes, and Earl Grey tea (Sugie). The numerous filmmakers who suddenly appear to create the films evidently stay around to continue making movies.

Like all those filmmakers who have refused to choose, Shiori continues entangled with others, who will forget her when they choose their own memories. Father-less, bereft, she makes a quietly feminist move from girl-with-a-crush to young woman-with-work and purpose. She has advised the teenage girl that her memory has been used before, listened silently as her male colleagues talk about their earliest memories, tried out in the bath the suggestion that immersion can reduce anxiety and restore the womb's security, moved in solitude through a populous city that does not see her, showed Mochizuki what he had meant to Kyoko in his absence, and suffered his loss. With Mochizuki gone, Shiori emerges as a counselor in her own right. If a protagonist had to be designated, it is this solitary young woman at the margins who moves to the center, filled with anticipation, awaiting her first client's entrance, as the film ends. Kore-eda concludes not with disappearing selves, but with the on-going work of making movies of the lives and stories and moments of others. Shiori looks toward a door about to be opened by a new, never before seen or encountered person entering eternity.

From this afterlife religion has been removed, but it perhaps requires a Japanese Buddhist context to be imagined in the first place. (Granted, Kore-eda has said that the initial idea for the film came while transcribing some television footage in an editing room, "when I had an odd sensation: what if after you die you sat in front of a TV monitor watching endless images from your own life?"[38]) The absence of hell and everyone's ending up here surprises Iseya, a lanky, smirking, spiky-haired youth in leather pants and purple-ruffed shirt, who finds fault with the concept (Why memory? Boring) and refuses to choose. The Japanese began satirizing hell in the eighteenth century (having acquired it only in the sixth century CE). Hiraga Gennai's *Rootless Weeds* (1763) parodies hell's expansion by shady real-estate dealers, while contemporaneous prints show the boiling torture cauldrons covered with spiderwebs, the demons playing cards, and Enma picking his nose—nobody has arrived in hell in so long. Hellish imagery remains current, as in the lurid cult film *Jigoku (Hell*, 1960). In the film, the next stage remains as obscure as nirvana or enlightenment. No one knows what it is like, but here it is achieved by attachment to one memory/thought, and detachment from all others.

Comically, benignly, the film turns a traditional Buddhist preparation for death into going to the movies. In the Pure Land Buddhism that developed in the Heian period (794–1185), the monk Genshin codified the procedures to follow to be reborn in the "pure land" of Amida Buddha. Once there one's own Buddhahood was assured. Concentration at the last moment on Amida Buddha was essential: a stray or mistaken thought could send one to an evil realm of rebirth. So one looked at an image of the Buddha, visualized the Buddha, and chanted the *nenbutsu*. In a secular modern context, what activity better promotes absolute concentration than watching a movie of one self? Staring at a screen in the dark, one disappears into the film, which remains other. The "last-moment thought" is both outside and inside, like the Buddha. Such a death is available to any of us who choose in our last moments to think of what we loved, if our last moments permit our doing so.

Kore-eda's afterlife borrows death to validate a moment or sequence of insignificant moments. Yet he also instructs us in what matters, in what we should value, which he leaves—with perfect confidence—in our hands. We will not choose wrong. We look into ourselves for what we want to find right or lovely—loved—about our lives. Often we find others there, or dependence on others. If we look past ourselves to the filmmaker making our film and his own, we find ourselves, where we often are and like to be, at the movies.

These current afterlives are all in their ways didactic; they moralize the life of the present, though no more than any other fiction. What special brief are they looking to find by entertaining a world beyond the life of this one? These fictions juxtapose this teeming life with an immortality they simultaneously deny and invoke. Their purposes are various—Coetzee draws the writer into herself, into the final place of demands on responsibility and being; Kundera into a wry acceptance of immortality's passing; Stern into wondrous stories to be told while otherwise staying alive; Saunders into the pathos and pain of being. Kaufman and Jonze move from New York to California and dive into a pool. Kore-eda provokes his viewers into the life assessment of traditional judgmental afterlives and invites us to accept the insignificance of our passing by.

No one believes in the afterlife he considers. Coetzee's afterlife is too literary and allusive to be mistaken for an actual hypothesis, as Costello herself observes. Kundera and Stern are explicit—lest we be confused or tempted or doubt their anti-afterlife bona fides—that nothingness lies at the end of the road. Saunders may have a hankering after his vision of merging with all being, but it is doubtful that he believes in the adventures of his chatty staying and returning dead. The dead, of course, do stay and do return, as the Chinese poet Yiwu Liao observes, "I have had many dreams about people who have been dead a long time, but their souls are still among us."[39] Their souls are, as "John Malkovich" knows and Fukansai Habian complains, in our heads. Like Kundera's Agnès, they will disappear when we do.

No one is concerned that absence of belief in an afterlife encourages immorality or devalues life and deprives it of meaning. It is true that many of the behaviors endorsed in Kundera and Stern, Coetzee and Saunders, Jonze and Kore-eda would once have been regarded as desperately immoral. Fornication is pervasive, and Kundera and Jonze permit adultery. Would they concur with Samuel Scheffler's thought-experiment—that without the immortality or continuing existence of our species, moral valuation and meaning would cease? Certainly, they value life's on-going-ness, and the recurring trope of the young woman starting anew sustains Scheffler's argument. Yet for human valuing, the life that continues need not be human. It need not even be life. Elizabeth Costello should find in the disappearance of the human species the salvation of the animals, the gray whales, the frogs. Only the beetles need no assistance from human absence. Other beings may people other stars, but they are not required for Temple Grandin to experience awe before the stars.

Moral evaluation and meaning of course cease without people. As Emmanuel Levinas reinterprets Genesis 1–4, there was no good until the woman took the fruit and made humans able, unlike nature, to differentiate good and evil. Until there are no people, or other moral evaluators and meaning-makers, morality and meaning continue. Scheffler's apocalyptic thought-experiment impels him to a more impassioned and ingenious sense of global responsibility, not accidentally but inevitably. Thinking about what happens at death does that to people. As we elaborate what happens "after," we articulate our profoundest values and adjust how we fit in the cosmos. It is a universal phenomenon in every sense.

As for "wonderful life," that is what anti-afterlife ideology is all about. That is what embarrasses Elizabeth Costello, and Kore-eda puts in a foreign language, what Stern and Jonze possess and evokes Kundera's nostalgia. Even sardonic Philip Larkin pins Dante's multi-foliate rose, "million-petalled," between Lucretius and Epicurus's two oblivions, "being here" and not there. Yet denying the life to come and affirming the life that passes suppose considerable complacency about the way things are. Surely there are many people for whom life is not wonderful. Kore-eda knows some want only to forget. Saunders finds misery rising everywhere. Larkin describes old age as driveling and drooling, though not abandoned in a ditch, before and after his lament for atoms separating. The bumper sticker "Life happens" means nothing good.

It is possible to deny a life to come and disparage the life in place. As Samuel Beckett has it, "fuck life." His characters speak of dust and dead children, "the face in the ashes," and being gone.[40] Rockaby's recorded "Voice" calls up death: "rock her off/ stop her eyes/ fuck life/ stop her eyes/ rock her off/ rock her off." His Henry considers not heaven, but hell, in terms Addison and Steele would find familiar: "Ada, too, conversation with her, that was something, that's what hell will be like, small chat to the babbling of Lethe about the good old days when we wished we were dead. Price of margarine fifty years ago. And now. Price of blueband now!"[41] "The good old days when we wished we were dead": Kundera's nostalgia dogs even Beckett and his Henry "mad to talk." Beckett's women are old and sterile, the old trope recurring as antithesis. No suicides, though: old men, old women, mere mouths keep on. Keeping on, turning despair over and over, twisting it like a strand of hair, a rope of sand, a prayer, the nonsense syllables soothe, like any mantra, like a rosary told on beads of syllables.

So "That Time" ends, "not a sound only the old breath and the leaves turning and then suddenly this dust whole place suddenly full of dust when you opened your eyes from floor to ceiling nothing only dust and not a sound only what was it it said come and gone was that it something like that come and gone come and gone no one come and gone in no time gone in no time" (234). Narrative disintegrates to babble, but babbling the babble soothes. Repeated, varied, babbled syllables restore the soul. Try it. Read Beckett's last two lines aloud. Lexical associations make syntax unnecessary. Or "A Piece of Monologue": "The dead and gone. The dying and the going. From the word go. The word begone.... on all sides nowhere. Unutterably faint. The globe alone. Alone gone" (268). Globe gone. Keeping the words in play, vowels lengthening and shifting, reminds Coetzee's readers that words do not oppose experience but constitute their own. Beckett plays the lexemes of mortality salience like an organ toccata, touching every key. "Birth was the death of him" (263): the thought is dismal, the repetition consoling, the paradox inspiring, enlivening, the commonplace joyful and bitter. No spurned or spurning lover of "wandâfuru raifu" (the thing, not the movie), Beckett models that sad lover, angry at having been born, angrier at not being dead, angriest at having to die. It brings out the best in him. "Not I" knows, as the curtain falls, "hit on it in the end ... then back ... God is love ... tender mercies ... new every morning ... back in the field. ... April morning. ... face in the grass ... nothing but the larks. ... pick it up—" (223). Croak murmurs, pausing, in "Words and Music," "The face. The face. The face. The face." Music in the stage direction waxes *warmly sentimental, for about one minute* (131). Life is a miserable gig, but at least it does not last forever.

The desires and attachments that lead us to create other worlds because we want more of this do not cease with the knowledge that there is no other world. Such knowledge only increases the poignancy of longing, itself a form of pleasure. Tracing and erasing imaginary worlds speaks the unrequited love that all beings have for their world. There is community in the dark. "I will go to him, but he will not return to me."

NOTES

PREFACE

1. "Of Tragedy," *Essays Moral, Political, and Literary*, ed. Eugene F. Miller, rev. ed. (Indianapolis, IN: Liberty Classics, 1987), 222.
2. Letter to William Temple, 12 August 1775, *Letters of James Boswell, Addressed to the Rev. W. J. Temple* (London, 1857), 214.
3. Kelvin Tavarez once admitted such a hope.
4. 1598 E. Blount in Marlowe *Hero and Leander*, Ep. Ded. sig. Aiij, "The impression of the man, that hath beene deare vnto vs, liuing an *after life* in our memory, there putteth vs in mind of farther obsequies."
5. Or continuations: Bernard A. Drew's *Literary Afterlife* charts continuations of over three hundred literary works (Jefferson, NC: McFarland, 2009). The MLA Bibliography, March 2018, listed 1633 instances of the word *afterlife*, mostly in titles of studies of reputations, up from 593 in May 2010. Margaret Cavendish used "afterlife" for fame in 1662, *Plays Written by the Thrice Noble, Illustrious and Excellent Princess, the Lady Marchioness of Newcastle*, 111.
6. John Speed, *The History of Great Britaine Under the Conquests of ye Romans, Saxons, Danes and Normans. Their Originals, Manners, Warres, Coines & Seales: with ye Successions, Lives, acts & Issues of the English Monarchs from Iulius Caesar, to our most gracious Soueraigne King Iames* (London, 1611), 331. The OED's first reference is 1615, Sir Edward Hoby's account of the Sadducees' afterlife denial.
7. Denis the Carthusian (1402–1471), *Thus endeth the prologue of this book named. Cordyal. Whiche treteth of the four last and final things that ben to come . . .* (Westminster, England: Caxton, 1479).
8. Richard Allestree, *Eighteen Sermons whereof fifteen preached the King, the rest upon publick occasions* (London, 1669), 109, 187.

9. Gervase Babington, *A profitable Exposition of the Lords Prayer, by way of Questions and Answers for most playnnes: Together with many fruitfull applications to the life and Soule, as well for the terror of the dull and dead, as for the sweete comfort of the tender harted*. (London: 1588). It lies between George Turberville's translation of Mantuanus, *The Eglogs of the Poet B. Mantuan Carmelitan, Turned into English Verse, & set forth with the Argument to euery Egloge* (London: 1567) and Richard Verstegan (c. 1550–1640), *The Copy Of A Letter Lately Written By A Spanishe Gentleman, To His Freind In England: In refutation of sundry calumnies, there falsly bruited, and spred emonge the people* (Antwerp, 1589).
10. In A. Campbell (d. 1756), *Authenticity of Gospel-Hist. Justified"* (1759) I. x. preface. Among rare earlier uses is Thomas Adams, *The Deuills Banket described in foure Sermons* (London: 1614), 219: "Read in euery Starre, and let the Moone be your Candle to doe it, the prouident disposition of God, the eternitie of your afterlife."
11. *The Quest for Immortality: Science at the Frontiers of Aging* (New York: W. W. Norton, 2001), 27.
12. Keith Thomas, *The Ends of Life: Roads to Fulfillment in Early Modern England* (New York: Oxford University Press, 2009), 231.
13. 1945. The concept but not the phrase appears in Rodgers and Hammerstein's European source, Ferenc Molnár's *Liliom: A Legend in Seven Scenes and a Prologue* (1909) (New York: Boni and Liveright, 1921), 164–65. The phrase is deducible from Hume's "The Platonist" of human perfectibility: "The task, which can never be finished in time, will be the business of an eternity," Hume, *Essays Moral, Political, and Literary*, 158.
14. Philippe Ariès, *Western Attitudes toward Death from the Middle Ages to the Present*, trans. Patricia M. Ranum (Baltimore, MD: Johns Hopkins University Press, 1974).
15. *The Meanings of Death* (Cambridge, England: Cambridge University Press, 1991), 28.

1. CONCERNING THE PRESENT STATE OF LIFE AFTER DEATH

1. Rob Walker, "Things to Do in Cyberspace When You're Dead," *New York Times Magazine*, January 9, 2011, 31+.
2. *The Historie of the World: commonly called, The Naturall Historie of C. Plinius Secundus*, trans. Philemon Holland (London 1634), Book 7, chap. lv.
3. "If You Believe in the Hereafter, Which Kind of Immortality Would You Most Like to Have?" January 4, 2016. www.cbsnews.com/news/60-minutesvanity-fair-poll-the-afterlife.
4. For "old souls," see Tom Shroder, *Old Souls* (New York: Simon & Schuster, 1999).
5. Roper Center for Public Opinion Research, Cornell University, 2017. *https://ropercenter.cornell.edu/paradise-polled-americans-and-the-afterlife*.
6. *New York Times Book Review*, September 25, 2011, 33. *90 Minutes in Heaven* is now a minor motion picture, directed by Michael Polish, 2015. Curiously, the *NY Times* review begins, "Caveat emptor: '90 Minutes in Heaven' does not in fact depict a full hour and a half of the afterlife, as the travel-guide-like title might suggest." Nicolas Rapold, "'90 Minutes in Heaven,' Then a Long Road Back," *New York Times*, September 11, 2015, C8.

1. CONCERNING THE PRESENT STATE OF LIFE AFTER DEATH 293

7. *New York Times Book Review*, April 14, 2013, 20. On the paperback best-seller list, Eben Alexander's *Proof of Heaven* is no. 1 and Todd Burpo and Lynn Vincent's *Heaven Is for Real*, no. 6. Oddly, Samuel Parnia, insisting from the emergency room that one returns from these "true death" experiences, has not yet made his way to the lists, Samuel Parnia, *Erasing Death: The Science That Is Rewriting the Boundaries between Life and Death* (New York: Harper Collins, 2013).
8. I owe this reference to Anna Pasquin, at Mrs. London's, June 5, 2010. Kathryn Davis, "Lost," *Salmagundi*, 195-96 (Summer-Fall 2017), 201-05.
9. www.possibilian.com.
10. Robin Henig is confident that "belief in an afterlife is universal." Robin Henig, "Darwin's God," *New York Times Magazine*, March 4, 2007, 85; Ashley Montagu, *Immortality, Religion, and Morals* (New York: Hawthorn Books, 1971), 2, 18-36, supposes belief in immortality to be itself eternal. John Bowker, author of *The Meanings of Death* and general editor of *The Oxford Dictionary of World Religions* (New York: Oxford University Press, 1997), is better informed.
11. John Scheffer, *The History of Lapland* (Oxford, 1674), 35.
12. Ralph Harold Faulkingham, *Political Support in a Hausa Village* (Ann Arbor, Michigan: University Microfilms, 1971 [1972]), 116.
13. Brooks B. Hull and Frederick Bold, "Hell, Religion, and Cultural Change," *Journal of Institutional and Theoretical Economics (JITE)*, 150:3 (1994):455-57.
14. Adam Smith included an aversion to the extinction of the species as one of the basic human ends. "Self-preservation and the propagation of the species, are the great ends which Nature seems to have proposed in the formation of all animals. Mankind are endowed with a desire of those ends, and an aversion to the contrary; with a love of life, and a dread of dissolution; with a desire of the continuance and perpetuity of the species, and with an aversion to the thoughts of its intire extinction." Adam Smith, *The Theory of Moral Sentiments*, ed. D.D. Raphael and A.L. Macfie (Indianapolis, IN: Liberty Classics, 1976), II.i.5. 9, p. 77.
15. S. Jay Olshansky and Bruce A. Carnes, *The Quest for Immortality: Science at the Frontiers of Aging* (New York: W. W. Norton, 2001), 28.
16. *Future of an Illusion*, sec. III (New York: Classic House Books, 2009), 14-16. Freud describes death as "a return to inorganic lifelessness," 15, an odd way to think of a dissolving organic compound like the body.
17. Karl Marx, "Introduction," *The Critique of Hegel's "Philosophy of Right,"* trans. Annette Jolin and Joseph O'Malley (Cambridge, England: Cambridge University Press, 1970), 131.
18. Fyodor Dostoyevsky, *The Brothers Karamazov*, trans. Richard Pevear and Larissa Volokhonsky (San Francisco: North Point Press, 1990), 263.
19. So does the OED, not yet updated from 1885. The 1699 citation from Shaftesbury concerns God's providence, not his existence. Pierre Bayle defined atheism as the denial of providence and a future state, Jonathan Israel, *Radical Enlightenment*, 9, a usage echoed in David Hume's essay, "Of a Particular Providence and a Future State," *Philosophical Essays Concerning Human Understanding* (London, 1748).

20. Preface to *Sylvae*, John Dryden, *Works of John Dryden: Vol. 3 Poems 1685-92*, ed. Earl Miner (Berkeley: University of California Press, 1969), 11–12.
21. Quentin D. Atkinson and Patrick Bourrat, "Beliefs About God, the Afterlife and Morality Support the Role of Supernatural Policing in Human Cooperation," *Evolution and Human Behavior* 32 (2011): 42.
22. The "Baines" Note, as originally submitted, BL Harley MS.6848 ff.185–6. www.rey.prestel.co.uk/baines1.htm.
23. Catharine Trotter Cockburn, *Philosophical Writings*, ed. Patricia Sheridan (Peterborough, Ontario: Broadview Editions, 2006), 138, 142–43. Benjamin Beit-hallahmi, "Morality and Immorality among the Irreligious," in *Atheism and Secularity. Vol. 1: Issues, Concepts, and Definitions*, ed. Phil Zuckerman (Oxford: Praeger, 2010), 113–34.
24. "Reason will neither deny, nor affirm, that there is to be a future state: and the doctrine of rewards and punishments in it has so great a tendency to enforce civil laws, and to restrain the vices of men, that reason, who cannot decide for it on principles of natural theology, will not decide against it, on principles of good policy. Let this doctrine rest on the authority of revelation." Henry St. John, Viscount Bolingbroke, *Philosophical Works of the Late Right Honourable Henry St. John, Lord Viscount Bolingbroke*, 5 vo, ed. David Mallett (London, 1754), V, 32. See also I, 268; IV, 64, 288.
25. *Covent-Garden Journal*, #11, *The Covent-Garden Journal and A Plan of the Universal Register-Office*, ed. Bertrand A. Goldgar (Middletown, CT: Wesleyan University Press, 1988), 80–81.
26. Simon Dickie, *Cruelty and Laughter: Forgotten Comic Literature and the Unsentimental Eighteenth Century* (Chicago: Chicago University Press, 2011), 177.
27. Two angels walking across the clouds, one pats the other on the back: "When you get a chance, remember to ask God the meaning of life—it's a riot." Zachary Kanin, *New Yorker*, June 22, 2015, 31.
28. Sheldon Solomon, Jeff Greenberg, and Tom Pyszczynski, *Worm at the Core: On the Role of Death in Life* (New York: Random House, 2015). For examples of cross-cultural effects, Kim-Pong Tam, Chi-Yue Chiu, and Ivy Yee-Man Lau, "Terror Management among Chinese: Worldview Defence and Intergroup Bias in Resource Allocation," *Asian Journal of Social Psychology* 10 (2007): 93–102; Ryutaro Wakimoto, "Mortality Salience Effects on Modesty and Relative Self-effacement," *Asian Journal of Social Psychology* 9 (2006): 176–83. Critics of Terror Management Theory offer alternative evolutionary explanations for the observed phenomena, e.g., Lee A. Kirkpatrick and Carlos David Navarrete, "Reports of My Death Anxiety Have Been Greatly Exaggerated: A Critique of Terror Management Theory from an Evolutionary Perspective," *Psychological Inquiry* 17:4 (2006): 288–98.
29. Phyllis Korkki, "Need Motivation? Declare a Deadline," *New York Times*, April 21, 2013, BU 9.
30. Mike Friedman, "Religious Fundamentalism and Responses to Mortality Salience: A Quantitative Text Analysis," *International Journal for the Psychology of Religion* 18:3 (2008): 216–37.
31. Lennart J. Renkema, Diederik A. Stapel, Nico W. Van Yperen, "Go with the Flow: Conforming to Others in the Face of Existential Threat," *European Journal of Social Psychology* 38:4 (2008): 747–56.

1. CONCERNING THE PRESENT STATE OF LIFE AFTER DEATH   295

32. Immo Fritsche and Eva Jonas, "Gender Conflict and Worldview Defence," *British Journal of Social Psychology* 44:4 (2005): 571–81.
33. Kim-Pong Tam, Chi-Yue Chiu, Ivy Yee-Man Lau, "Terror Management among Chinese: Worldview Defence and Intergroup Bias in Resource Allocation," *Asian Journal of Social Psychology* 10 (2007): 93–102.
34. Ryutaro Wakimoto, "Mortality Salience Effects on Modesty and Relative Self-effacement," *Asian Journal of Social Psychology* 9 (2006): 176–83.
35. David Hume, "Of Tragedy," *Essays Moral, Political, and Literary*, 216–17.
36. Roni Caryn Rabin, "Study Links Religion and Terminal Care," *New York Times*, March 18, 2009, A18. Quoting Holly G. Prigerson, senior author, "Religious Coping and Use of Intensive Life-Prolonging Care Near Death in Patients with Advanced Cancer," *JAMA*, March 19, 2009, 1140–1147. "To religious people, life is sacred and sanctified, . . . and there's a sense they feel it's their duty and obligation to stay alive as long as possible."
37. Frank J. Tipler, *The Physics of Immortality: Modern Cosmology, God and the Resurrection of the Dead* (New York: Doubleday, 1994), 225–26, 241–42. Hans Moravec, *Mind Children: The Future of Robot and Human Intelligence* (Cambridge, MA: Harvard University Press, 1988), 122–24. Quoted in Tipler, 225–26. John Leslie, *Immortality Defended* (Oxford: Blackwell, 2007). Jim Holt, "Eternity for Atheists," *New York Times Magazine*, July 29, 2007, 11–12.
38. Tatiana Schlossberg, "Black Bear Kills a Hiker in North Jersey," *New York Times*, September 23, 2014, A25.
39. Steven Millhauser's story of contagious suicidal exuberance takes the form of "A Report on Our Recent Troubles," submitted by a Committee, *Voices in the Night* (New York: Alfred A. Knopf, 2015), 86, 96–97.
40. Karen Dwyer and Marlina Davidson, 2012, cited in Joan Acocella, "I Can't Go On!" *The New Yorker*, August 3, 2015, 69.
41. Tom Pyszczynski, Jeff Greenberg, Sheldon Solomon, Molly Maxfield, "On the Unique Psychological Import of the Human Awareness of Mortality: Theme and Variations," *Psychological Inquiry* 17:4 (2006): 342.
42. Gilad Hirschberger and Tsachi Ein-Dor, "Does a Candy a Day Keep the Death Thoughts Away? The Terror Management Function of Eating," *Basic and Applied Social Psychology* 17:2 (2005): 179–86.
43. C. Nathan DeWall and Roy F. Baumeister, "From Terror to Joy: Automatic Turning to Positive Affective Information Following Mortality Salience," *Psychological Science* 18:11 (2007): 984–90. Summarized as "Mortal Thoughts," *Atlantic Monthly*, March 2008.
44. Samuel Scheffler, "The Importance of the Afterlife. Seriously," *New York Times*, Sept. 22, 2013, 1, 6, and Samuel Scheffler, *Death and the Afterlife* (New York: Oxford University Press, 2013). Scheffler argues that for consolation and purpose we require others' lives to continue after our own deaths, the immortality of our species. Certainly, the immortality of the species is meaningful and consolatory for those who deny a personal afterlife or metempsychosis. Scheffler underestimates, however, the elasticity and inventiveness of human identification, which does not confine itself to humans but readily extends to

other, nonhuman species, to the earth itself, or to solar space, as in Jan Zalasiewicz's *The Earth After Us: What Legacy Will Humans Leave in the Rocks?* (New York: Oxford University Press, 2008). Mortality salience tells against Scheffler, as does the current vogue for apocalyptic literature, which invigorates through the prospect of annihilation. Granted, most American apocalypses focus on a few survivors—*Snowpiercer* is down to two people and a polar bear—but others enjoy watching the asteroid make its way toward all of us, with Kirsten Dunst, in Lars van Trier's *Melancholia* (2011).

45. Quoted in Alec Wilkinson, "Finding the Words," *The New Yorker*, August 4, 2014, 50. *Gabriel: A Poem* (New York: Knopf, 2014), 3.

46. Edward B. Tylor theorized that the difference between a dead body and a living one, combined with the traces in dreams and visions, led to the concept of the soul among primitive men, enduring among modern ones. Edward B. Tylor, *Primitive Culture: Researches into the Development of Mythology, Philosophy, Religion, Art, and Custom*, (1871) (New York: Gordon Press, 1974), I, 387.

   Freud remarked the expectation that what goes returns in the child's "fort-da" game. Sigmund Freud, *Beyond the Pleasure Principle*, trans. James Strachey (New York: Liveright, 1950), 13–15.

47. David Hume, "On the Immortality of the Soul," *Essays Moral, Political, and Literary*, 597.

48. Emmanuel Levinas, *God, Death, and Time*, ed. Jacques Rolland, trans. Bettina Bergo (Stanford, CA: Stanford University Press, 2000), 9, 11.

49. *God, Death, and Time*, 47.

50. *God, Death, and Time*, 19.

51. Jennifer A. Kingson, "What Do Babies Know?" *New York Times*, April 23, 2013, D2.

52. Frans de Waal, *Primates and Philosophers: How Morality Evolved* (Princeton: Princeton University Press, 2006), 24.

53. Pascal Boyer analyzes these processes as separate systems active in the brain that respond inconsistently to a dead person: an intuitive psychological system (theory of mind plus), an animacy system, and a person-file system. Pascal Boyer, *Religion Explained: The Evolutionary Origins of Religious Thought* (New York: Basic Books, 2001), 217–20.

54. Robert Hertz, "A Contribution to the Study of the Collective Representation of Death" (1907) in *Death and the Right Hand*, trans. Rodney and Claudia Needham (Glencoe, IL: The Free Press, 1960), 70, 78.

55. Michael Shermer, *The Believing Brain* (New York: Henry Holt, 2011), 145.

56. Christophe Boesch and Hedwige Boesch-Achermann, *The Chimpanzees of the Taï Forest: Behavioural Ecology and Evolution* (Oxford: Oxford University Press, 2000), 248–51.

57. Iain Douglas-Hamilton, Shivani Bhalla, George Wittemyer, Fritz Vollrath, "Behavioural Reactions of Elephants towards a Dying and Deceased Matriarch," *Applied Animal Behaviour Science* 100:1–2 (2006): 87–102.

58. Charles Siebert, "Watching Whales Watching Us," *New York Times Magazine*, July 12, 2009, 31, 35.

59. Anne Zeller, "The Grieving Process in Non-human Primates," in *Coping with the Final Tragedy: Cultural Variation in Dying and Grieving*, ed. David R. Counts and Dorothy A. Counts (Amityville, NY: Baywood, 1991), 11–15.

60. Dora Biro, Tatyana Humle, Kathelijne Koops, Claudia Sousa, Misato Hayashi, and Tetsuro Matsuzawa, "Chimpanzee Mothers at Bossou, Guinea, Carry the Mummified Remains of Their Dead Infants," *Current Biology* 20:8 (April 27, 2010): R351-52.
61. Christophe Boesch, "Patterns of Chimpanzees' Intergroup Violence," *Human Morality and Sociality: Evolutionary and Comparative Perspectives*, ed. Henrik Høgh-Olesen (New York: Palgrave Macmillan, 2010), 139.
62. Boesch, "Patterns," 140-41.
63. Other cases report "unusual calls" or repeated "loud alarm calls." Boesch and Boesch-Achermann, *Chimpanzees*, 248, 250. Reporting the "wraah" call are Kazuhiko Hosaka, Akiko Matsumoto-oda, Michael A. Huffman, Kenji Kawanaka, "Reactions to Dead Bodies of Conspecifics by Wild Chimpanzees in the Mahale Mountains, Tanzania," *Reichorui kenkyu/Primate Research*, 16:1 (2000): 15.
64. In a similar case, a mother carried for two days her two-year-old son, his neck broken after falling from a tree. Just before she finally left the body, other females and juveniles returned to the body, made "soft 'hou' calls," and then left. Boesch and Boesch-Achermann, *Chimpanzees*, 250.
65. Geza Teleki, "Group Response to the Accidental Death of a Chimpanzee in Gombe National Park, Tanzania," *Folia Primatologica* 20 (1973): 81-94.
66. James R. Anderson, Alasdair Gillies, and Louise C. Lock, "Pan Thanatology," *Current Biology* 20:8 (April 27, 2010): R349-R351.
67. Boesch and Boesch-Achermann, *Chimpanzees*, 249.
68. Anderson, Gillies, and Lock, "Pan Thanatology," R349-R351.
69. Zeller, "Grieving Process," 7.
70. Jonathan Swift, "Verses on the Death of Dr. Swift," ll.228, 241-42. Jonathan Swift, *Swift Poetical Works*, ed. Herbert Davis (New York: Oxford University Press, 1967), 504.
71. Evincing some discomfort with that project is Osamu Nishitani, "The Wonderland of 'Immortality,' " *Contemporary Japanese Thought*, ed. Richard F. Calichman (New York: Columbia University Press, 2005), 136, 143.
72. "The Modern Life of Shidoken" (Furyu Shidoken Den, 1763), in *Early Modern Japanese Literature: An Anthology, 1600-1900*, ed. Haruo Shirane (New York: Columbia University Press, 2002), 492.
73. Michael S.A. Graziano, *Consciousness and the Social Brain* (New York: Oxford University Press, 2013), "Speculations on the Evolution of Awareness," *Journal of Cognitive Neuroscience*, 26:6 (2014): 1300-1304. Daniel C. Dennett, *Consciousness Explained* (Back Bay Books, 1992) and *From Bacteria to Bach and Back: The Evolution of Minds* (New York: W. W. Norton, 2017).
74. Peter Ramsden, "Alice in the Afterlife: A Glimpse in the Mirror," in *Coping with the Final Tragedy: Cultural Variation in Dying and Grieving*, ed. David R. Counts and Dorothy A. Counts (Amityville, NY: Baywood, 1991), 35.
75. Henri Chambert-Loir and Anthony Reid, eds. *The Potent Dead: Ancestors, Saints and Heroes in Contemporary Indonesia* (Honolulu, HI: University of Hawai'i Press, 2002), 77-78.
76. Erik Hornung, *The Ancient Egyptian Books of the Afterlife*, trans. David Lorton (Ithaca: Cornell University Press, 1999), 1, 5, 7, 9.

77. Ying-Shih Yü, "'O Soul, Come Back!' A Study in the Changing Conceptions of the Soul and Afterlife in Pre-Buddhist China," *Harvard Journal of Asian Studies* 47:2 (1987): 379; "Shen," *Oxford Dictionary of World Religions* (New York: Oxford University Press, 1997).
78. Douglas Palmer, *Neanderthal* (London: Macmillan, 2004), 124–25. Palmer dates the bin 300,000 years ago, as do Josep M. Parés, Alfredo Pérez-González, Arlo B. Weil, and Juan Luis Arsuaga, "On the Age of the Hominid Fossils at the Sima de los Huesos, Sierra de Atapuerca, Spain: Paleomagnetic Evidence," *American Journal of Physical Anthropology* 111:4 (2000): 451–461. More recently the skulls at the bottom of the 43-foot shaft have been dated to about 430,000 years ago, Sindya N. Bhanoo, "Ancient Skull Points to an Early Murder," *New York Times*, June 2, 2015, D2; Nohemi Sala, Juan Luis Arsuaga, Ana Pantoja-Pérez, Adrián Pablos, Ignacio Martínez, Rolf M. Quam, Asier Gómez-Olivencia, José María Bermúdez de Castro, and Eudald Carbonell, "Lethal Interpersonal Violence in the Middle Pleistocene," *PLoS One*, May 27, 2015. Zach Zorich, "A Place to Hide the Bodies," *Archaeology*, September/October 2015, 21. In 2015, DNA sequencing showed the two dozen individuals in Sima de los Huesos to be closely related to early Neanderthals. Gemma Tarlach, "Human Origins," *Discover*, July/August 2016, 40, confirming earlier morphological analysis, Juan Luis Arsuaga, Ignacio Martínez, Lee J. Arnold, Eudald Carbonell, et al. "Neandertal Roots: Cranial and Chronological Evidence from Sima de los Huesos," *Science* 344:6190 (2014):1358–363; Ewen Callaway, "Ancient DNA Pinpoints Dawn of Neanderthals," *Nature* 531:7594 (March 17, 2016):286.

    In 2013, an analogous cache of some 1,500 fossils representing 15 individuals identified as a new species *Homo naledi* was found in a South African cave. The fossils have not been dated, but disposal of corpses by a small-brained species has surprised the discoverers. Chris Springer, "The Many Mysteries of *Homo Naledi*," *eLife*, September 10, 2015. 4:e10627. Russ Juskalian, "Homo Naledi and the Chamber of Secrets," *Discover*, January/February 2016, 10–11.
79. Katerina Harvati and Terry Harrison, eds. *Neanderthals Revisited: New Approaches and Perspectives* (Dordrecht, Netherlands: Springer, 2006), 321–22; João Zilhão, "The Emergence of Ornaments and Art: An Archaeological Perspective on the Origins of Behavioral Modernity," *Journal of Archaeological Research*, 15:1 (March 2007):1–54.
80. Paul Mellars, *The Neanderthal Legacy: An Archeological Perspective from Western Europe* (Princeton: Princeton University Press, 1996), 379–380; Ian Tattersal, *The Last Neanderthal*, rev. ed. (New York: Nevraumont, 1999), 168–69, plate 115.
81. Francesco d'Errico and Lucinda Backwell, "Earliest Evidence of Personal Ornaments Associated with Burial: The *Conus* shells from Border Cave," *Journal of Human Evolution* 93 (April 2016): 91–108.
82. Andrew Curry, "The World's First Temple?" *Smithsonian*, November 2008, 54–60.
83. Thomas A. Kselman, *Death and the Afterlife in Modern France* (Princeton: Princeton University Press, 1993), 52. Home-baked cakes are still placed on graves in Russian Orthodox circles. Joshua Yaffa, "The Double Sting," *New Yorker*, July 27, 2015, 47.
84. Kumiko Kakehashi, *So Sad to Fall in Battle: Based on General Tadamichi Kuribayashi's Letters from Iwo Jima* (New York: Ballantine Books, 2007), 94.

1. CONCERNING THE PRESENT STATE OF LIFE AFTER DEATH   299

85. V. Gordon Childe, "Directional Changes in Funerary Practices During 50,000 Years," *Man* 45 (January/February 1945): 13–19.
86. Donna C. Kurtz and John Boardman, *Greek Burial Customs* (Ithaca, NY: Cornell University Press, 1971), 203–17.
87. John Boardman, ed. *Oxford History of Classical Art* (New York: Oxford University Press, 1993), 19.
88. Fredrik Hiebert and Pierre Cambon, *Afghanistan: Hidden Treasures from the National Museum, Kabul* (Washington, DC: National Geographic Society, 2008).
89. Bernard Sellato, "Castrated Dead: The Making of Un-ancestors among the Aoheng, and Some Considerations on Death and Ancestors in Borneo," in *The Potent Dead*, 10–11.
90. As in Steve Stern's *Frozen Rabbi* (New York: Workman, 2010).
91. *Verses on the Death of Dr. Swift, D.S. P.D,*. with the epigraph, "Dans l'adversité de nos meilleurs amis nous trouvons quelque chose, qui ne nous deplaist pas. (In the Adversity of our best Friends, we find something that doth not displease us." *Swift Poetical Works*, ed. Herbert Davis (London: Oxford University Press, 1967), 496.
92. The *Ten Canoes* is the product of collaboration among a (dead) anthropologist, a filmmaker, a prominent aboriginal actor (who provides the film's voice-over), and a community. Louise Hamby, "Thomson Times and *Ten Canoes* (de Heer and Djigirr, 2006)," *Studies in Australasian Cinema* 1:2 (2007): 127–46; Therese Davis, "Remembering Our Ancestors: Cross-cultural Collaboration and the Mediation of Aboriginal Culture and History in *Ten Canoes* (Rolf de Heer, 2006)," *Studies in Australasian Cinema* 1:1 (2007), 5–14; James Bell, "The Way It Was," *Sight and Sound* 17:6 (2007): 34–37. The title derives from a photograph made by the anthropologist Donald Thomson in 1935–37 of ten canoes, each with a single canoeist, crossing a reed swamp. The actors in the film apportioned parts according to their descent from the canoeists in the photograph. Cf. Mircea Eliade, *From Primitivism to Zen: A Thematic Sourcebook* (New York: Harper and Row, 1967), 186.
93. Frans de Waal, *Primates and Philosophers* (Princeton: Princeton University Press, 2006); Neil Levy, *What Makes Us Moral? Crossing the Boundaries of Biology* (Oxford: Oneworld, 2004); David Sloan Wilson, *Darwin's Cathedral: Evolution, Religion and the Nature of Society* (Chicago: University of Chicago Press, 2002); Dean Hamer, *The God Gene: How Faith is Hardwired into Our Genes* (New York: Doubleday, 2003); Michael Ruse, *Taking Darwin Seriously: A Naturalistic Approach to Philosophy*, 2nd ed. (Amherst, MA: Prometheus Books, 1998); Jane Maienschein and Michael Ruse, eds., *Biology and the Foundation of Ethics* (Cambridge, England: Cambridge University Press, 1999); Dennis L. Krebs, *The Origins of Morality* (New York: Oxford University Press, 2011); Christopher Boehm, *Moral Origins: The Evolution of Virtue, Altruism, and Shame* (New York: Basic Books, 2012).
94. De Waal, *Primates and Philosophers*, 29, 29–36, 42–49, 69–73, 172.
95. Adam Smith, *Theory of Moral Sentiments*, I.i.i.3, p. 10. Bence Nanay, "Adam Smith's Concept of Sympathy and Its Contemporary Interpretations," *The Philosophy of Adam Smith: Adam Smith Review, volume 5: Essays commemorating the 250th anniversary of The Theory of Moral Sentiments*, ed. Vivienne Brown and Samuel Fleischacker (New York: Routledge, 2010), 85–105.

96. De Waal, *Primates and Philosophers*, 18, 42–44.
97. Frans de Waal, YouTube TED Talk.
98. Boesch, "Patterns," 142–46.
99. Dennis L. Krebs, *The Origins of Morality* (2011); "Born Bad? Evaluating the Case against the Evolution of Morality," in *Human Morality and Sociality: Evolutionary and Comparative Perspectives*, ed. Henrik Høgh-Olesen (New York: Palgrave Macmillan, 2010), 13–30.
100. "Shen," *Oxford Dictionary of World Religions* (1997).

2. IMPERMANENT ETERNITIES: EGYPT, SUMER, AND BABYLON, ANCIENT ISRAEL, GREECE, AND ROME

1. A. R. George, trans., *The Babylonian Gilgamesh Epic*, 2 vols. (Oxford: Oxford University Press, 2003) I, 279. Most quotations from *Gilgamesh* will be from this edition, as less generally available and enabling comparison with other translations.
2. Muhammad Abdel Haleem, "Life and Beyond in the Qur'an," in *Beyond Death: Theological and Philosophical Reflections on Life After Death*, ed. Dan Cohn-Sherbok and Christopher Lewis (New York: St Martin's Press, 1995), 66–79.
3. Tractate Sanhedrin, m10.1–2; Part VI, chap. 11, *The Talmud: The Steinsaltz Edition*, vol. 20 (New York: Random House, 1999), 83.
4. The resurrection is not forever: another death precedes entry into the purely spiritual, unbodied world to come. Moses Maimonides, *Moses Maimonides' Treatise on Resurrection*, trans. Fred Rosner (New York: KTAV, 1982), 25, 33.
5. Dan Cohn-Sherbok, "The Jewish Doctrine of Hell," in *Beyond Death: Theological and Philosophical Reflections on Life After Death*, ed. Dan Cohn-Sherbok and Christopher Lewis, 54–65. Claudia Setzer assures readers that Jews once did believe in an afterlife, however unlikely that now seems. "Resurrection of the Dead as Symbol and Strategy," *Journal of the American Academy of Religion*, 69: 1 (2001): 65–101. The joke was repeated on Terry Gross's *Fresh Air* in 2011.
6. But concealed or forgot earlier anti-iconic movements. Yuval Yekutieli argues that the first regional evidence of a theological reformation, specifically the "Aniconic Reformation" of the Early Bronze Age, appears in the latter Chalcolithic period (post 4200 BCE) in the southern Levant. A cache of hidden icons wrapped in bloodstained cloth occupies a cave adjacent to twenty-one murdered bodies in the Judean desert. Icons and significant sculpture in the region disappearing in the immediately subsequent Bronze period, Yekutieli hypothesizes that iconoclasts moved against images and those who cherished them already in prehistoric polytheism. Image making revives in later periods, but the prohibition of images is enshrined in the Decalogue. "Solving a 6000-Year-Old Murder Mystery," Greenberg Middle East Lecture Series, Skidmore College, Saratoga Springs, NY, Oct. 9, 2016.
7. François Lenormant, *Chaldean Magic*, ed. [William Ricketts Cooper], (London: S. Bagster, 1878); Christopher A. Faraone and Dirk Obbink, *Magika Hiera: Ancient Greek Magic & Religion* (New York: Oxford University Press, 1997); Martin P. Nilsson, *Greek*

2. IMPERMANENT ETERNITIES 301

Folk Religion 1940 (Philadelphia: University of Pennsylvania Press, 1961); David Ogden, *Greek and Roman Necromancy* (Princeton: Princeton University Press, 2001); David Ogden, *Magic, Witchcraft and Ghosts in the Greek and Roman Worlds: A Sourcebook* (New York: Oxford University Press, 2002); Paul Mirecki and Marvin Meyer, eds. *Magic and Ritual in the Ancient World* (Leiden: Brill, 2002); Joseph Naveh and Shaul Shaked, *Amulets and Magic Bowls: Aramaic Incantations of Late Antiquity* (Jerusalem: Magnes, 1985); Richard N. Longenecker, ed. *Life in the Face of Death: The Resurrection Message of the New Testament* (Grand Rapids, MI: William B. Eerdmans, 1998).

8. Salima Ikram, *Death and Burial in Ancient Egypt* (London: Pearson Education, 2003), ix.
9. Taking 3500 BCE, the first grave goods, as a starting point and 400 CE, the empowerment of Christianity, as end point. If texts make the basis, there are 2,750 years between the first Egyptian texts and the last mummies, so Christianity will catch up in 850 years (2,000–100= 1,900 years).
10. "Briefly Noted: *The Rise and Fall of Ancient Egypt*," *The New Yorker*, June 6, 2011, 81. Others date the Middle Kingdom 2125–1773 BCE: these are matters for experts to disagree on.
11. A fine short account of changes in burial practices, styles, texts, and quality of mummification is John Taylor, "Before the Portraits: Burial Practices in Pharaonic Egypt," 9–13, in *Ancient Faces: Mummy Portraits in Roman Egypt* (Metropolitan Museum of Art Publications), ed. Susan Walker (New York: Routledge, 2000). See also Jan Assmann, *Death and Salvation in Ancient Egypt*, trans. David Lorton (Ithaca: Cornell University Press, 2005); Wolfram Grajetzki, *Burial Customs in Ancient Egypt: Life in Death for Rich and Poor* (London: Duckworth, 2003); Erik Hornung, *The Ancient Egyptian Books of the Afterlife*, trans. David Lorton (Ithaca: Cornell University Press, 1999); Salima Ikram, *Death and Burial in Ancient Egypt* (London: Pearson Education, 2003); Salima Ikram and Aidan Dodson, *The Mummy in Ancient Egypt: Equipping the Dead for Eternity* (London: Thames and Hudson, 1998); Ian Shaw, *Exploring Ancient Egypt* (New York: Oxford University Press, 2003); John H. Taylor, *Death and the Afterlife in Ancient Egypt* (Chicago: University of Chicago Press, 2001); Peter Ucko and Timothy Champion, ed. *The Wisdom of Egypt: Changing Visions through the Ages* (London: UCL Press, 2003); Toby Wilkinson, *The Rise and Fall of Ancient Egypt* (New York: Random House, 2011).
12. John Lanchester, "Money Talks," *The New Yorker*, August 4, 2014, 30–33. The first reference to a Nilometer is said to be 3050 BCE, on the Palermo Stone. Toby A. H. Wilkinson, *Royal Annals of Ancient Egypt: The Palermo Stone and Its Associated Fragments* (London: Kegan Paul International, 2000), 23, 95. Zaraza Friedman dates the Palermo Stone to 2480 BCE, "Nilometer," *Encyclopedia of the History of Science, Technology, and Medicine in Non-Western Cultures*, ed. Helaine Selin (New York: Springer, Dordrecht, 2008).
13. Alan F. Segal, *Life After Death* (New York: Doubleday, 2004), 31–33, emphasizes security. Emphasizing insecurity and threat is Toby Wilkinson, *The Rise and Fall of Ancient Egypt*, 107–09, cf. 47. Literary remains describe the insecurity of the peasant's life, his grain attacked by snakes, mice, thieves, and tax collectors, his body beaten, his family scattered. William Kelly Simpson, ed. *The Literature of Ancient Egypt* (New Haven: Yale University Press, 1973), 344.

14. P. M. Vermeersch, et al. "A Middle Palaeolithic Burial of a Modern Human at Taramsa Hill, Egypt," *Antiquity* 72 (1998): 475. I owe this reference to John Taylor's kind response to an inquiry.
15. John Taylor, "Before the Portraits: Burial Practices in Pharaonic Egypt," 9–13; *Death and the Afterlife in Ancient Egypt* (Chicago: University of Chicago Press, 2001), 13–16, 46; Ian Shaw, *Exploring Ancient Egypt* (Oxford University Press, 2003), 7, 15.
16. S. G. F. Brandon, *The Judgment of the Dead: The Idea of Life after Death in the Major Religions* (New York: Scribner's, 1967), 37; Taylor, *Death and Afterlife*, 16–21.
17. V. Gordon Childe, "Directional Changes in Funerary Practices During 50,000 Years," *Man* 45 (Jan./Feb. 1945): 16.
18. Wilkinson, *Rise and Fall*, 57, 75–78.
19. Werner Forman and Stephen Quirke, *Hieroglyphs and the Afterlife in Ancient Egypt* (Norman: University of Oklahoma Press, 1996), 51, 187.
20. Wilkinson, *Rise and Fall*, 145, 173.
21. Forman and Quirke, *Hieroglyphs and the Afterlife*, 149, 157, 165–67. Wilkinson, *Rise and Fall*, 402, 434.
22. S. G. F. Brandon criticizes the democratization argument, *Judgment*, 21. William J. Murnane points out that the Pyramid Texts sent the pharaoh to the stars and the sun-god, while the texts for commoners sent them to Osiris in the netherworld. Later the two divinities and realms are conflated. "Taking It with You: The Problem of Death and Afterlife in Ancient Egypt," in *Death and Afterlife: Perspectives of World Religions*, ed. Hiroshi Obayashi, (London: Praeger, 1992), 42. For gendered burials at a later period, see Wolfram Grajetzki, *Tomb Treasures of the Late Middle Kingdom: The Archaeology of Female Burials* (Philadelphia: University of Pennsylvania, 2014).
23. Ikram, *Death and Burial*, 21.
24. Miriam Lichtheim, *Ancient Egyptian Literature*, 3 vols. (Berkeley: University of California Press, 1973–80), I: 230. William Kelly Simpson, ed. *Literature of Ancient Egypt*, 67–68.
25. Wilkinson, *Rise and Fall*, 126–27; Forman and Quirke, *Hieroglyphs*, 63–73.
26. S. G. F. Brandon, *Judgment*, 27–28; Forman and Quirke, 120–22.
27. Erik Hornung, *The Ancient Egyptian Books of the Afterlife*, 90, 83.
28. Forman and Quirke, *Hieroglyphs*, 158; Wilkinson, *Rise and Fall*, 425–27.
29. *Persian Wars*, II.86–87 in *Herodotus*, trans. A. D. Godley, 4 vols. (Cambridge, MA: Harvard University Press, 1921–25), I, 370–73.
30. Hugh Bowden, *Mystery Cults of the Ancient World* (Princeton: Princeton University Press, 2010), 160.
31. John Boardman, ed. *Oxford History of Classical Art* (New York: Oxford University Press, 1993), 361. Susan Walker, ed. *Ancient Faces: Mummy Portraits in Roman Egypt*, 24.
32. National Museum of Ireland, Dublin. Funeral shroud, 1911.442; Mummy, 1911.440.
33. Ikram and Dodson, *The Mummy in Ancient Egypt*, 50, 282; Forman and Quirke, 167.
34. Alan K. Bowman, *Egypt after the Pharaohs 332BC–AD642* (Berkeley: University of California Press, 1986), 186; Forman and Quirke, *Hieroglyphs*, 172.
35. Bowman, *Egypt after the Pharaohs*, 193, 188–92.
36. Lucie Duff Gordon, *Letters from Egypt*, quoted in Bowman, 166.

37. At Chicago's Field Museum, June 2012–2013, an exhibit called "Images of the Afterlife" used mummies, forensic science, and CT scans to reconstruct portrait busts of the dead. The dead faces are beautiful, their features based on averages, the biological criterion for beauty.
38. Edwin Yamauchi, "Life, Death, and the Afterlife in the Ancient Near East," in Richard N. Longenecker, ed. *Life in the Face of Death*, 26
39. Forman and Quirke, *Hieroglyphs*, 56.
40. James P. Allen, trans, *Ancient Egyptian Pyramid Texts* (Atlanta, GA: Society of Biblical Literature, 2005), 23–66. Hereafter parenthetically in text. In Susan Brind Morrow's recent translation of the first Pyramid Text, *The Dawning Moon of the Mind: Unlocking the Pyramid Texts* (New York: Farrar, Straus and Giroux, 2015), this negative subtext is no longer visible.
41. Allen, *Ancient Egyptian Pyramid Texts*, Unis, #169, 46; #19, 19; #147, 31; Teti, #204, 83; Pepi I, #32, 106; #333, 130; rotting #337, #480, pp. 133, 165; guilt, #342, #352, #356, #443, pp. 134–35, 138–39, 150.
42. Brandon, *Judgment of the Dead*, 27.
43. Frans L. Roes, "The Size of Societies, Stratification, and Belief in High Gods Supportive of Human Morality," *Politics and the Life Sciences* 14:1 (1995): 73–77; Frans L. Roes and Michel Raymond, "Belief in Moralizing Gods," *Evolution and Human Behavior* 24:2 (2003): 126–35; Ara Norenzayan, "Why We Believe: Religion as a Human Universal" in *Human Morality and Sociality: Evolutionary and Comparative Perspectives*, Henrik ec. Høgh-Olesen (New York: Palgrave Macmillan, 2010), 65; John Snarey, "The Natural Environment's Impact upon Religious Ethics: A Cross-Cultural Study," *Journal for the Scientific Study of Religion* 35:2 (1996): 85–96.
44. Victor H. Matthews and Don C. Benjamin, *Old Testament Parallels: Laws and Stories from the Ancient Near East*, rev. ed. (New York: Paulist Press, 1997), 208–14.
45. "A Farmer and the Courts," with versions from 2258–2052 BCE and 2134–1786 BCE, Matthews, *Old Testament Parallels*, 222, 215, 219. The dead sucked the breast of lactating Isis. Allen, *Pyramid Texts*, p.20, #30.
46. *The Secrets of Tomb 10A: Egypt 2000 B.C.*, exhibit, Museum of Fine Arts, Boston, Jan-May 2010.
47. Edwin Yamauchi, "Life, Death, and the Afterlife in the Ancient Near East," in Longenecker, *Life in the Face of Death*, 25.
48. Ikram, *Death and Burial*, 128–31.
49. Forman and Quirke, *Hieroglyphs and the Afterlife*, 72.
50. Ikram, *Death and Burial*, 43–44.
51. Matthews, *Old Testament Parallels*, 206–07.
52. Egyptian legal edicts and stelae date from the thirteenth-fourteenth century BCE, and the earliest Egyptian legal code from 700 BCE. Russ VerSteeg, "The Machinery of Law in Pharaonic Egypt: Organization, Courts and Judges on the Ancient Nile," *Cardozo Journal of International and Comparative Law* 9 (2001): 109. Contemporaneous with late Mesopotamian stelae were the Edict of Horemheb (c. 1323–1295 BCE) and the Nauri Decree of Seti I (c. 1294–1279), in stone, in Nubia. As in Mesopotamia, the rules collected on stelae bear only a tangential relation to the extensive remains of lawsuits, contracts, and other records that demonstrate a lively legal system, VerSteeg, 107–09.

53. Wilkinson, *Rise and Fall*, 134; Taylor, *Death and the Afterlife*, 117, 123.
54. Yamauchi, "Life, Death, and the Afterlife," 28.
55. Ikram, *Death and Burial*, 130.
56. Field museum wall text, 2013.
57. Ogden Goelet, Jr. "A New 'Robbery' Papyrus: Rochester MAG 51.346.1," *Journal of Egyptian Arcaheology* 82 (1996): 107–27; T. E. Peet, *The Great Tomb Robberies of the Twentieth Egyptian Dynasty* (Oxford, 1930).
58. Ikram, *Death and Burial*, 196–200.
59. Jean Capart, Alan Henderson Gardiner, and Baudouin van de Walle, "New Light on the Ramesside Tomb Robberies," *Journal of Egyptian Archaeology* 22:2 (1936): 188, 173.
60. Harco Willems, "Crime, Cult and Capital Punishment (Mo'alla inscription 8)," *Journal of Egyptian Archaeology*, 76 (1990): 27–54.
61. Jan Assmann, "When Justice Fails: Jurisdiction and Imprecation in Ancient Egypt and the Near East," *The Journal of Egyptian Archaeology* 78 (1992): 149–62; Henri Sottas, *La Preservation de la Propriété Funéraire dans l'ancienne Egypte* (Paris, 1913). Assmann finds a profound change in the New Kingdom apprehension of divine intervention, 155.
62. Capart, Gardiner, and van de Walle, "New Light on the Ramesside Tomb Robberies," 171–72.
63. Mansour El-Noubi, "A Harper's Song from the Tomb of Roma-Roy at Thebes (TT 283)," *Studien zur Altägptischen Kultur* 25 (1998): 254, "heretical"; Edward F. Wente, "Egyptian 'Make-Merry' Songs Reconsidered," *Journal of Near Eastern Studies* 21:2 (1962): 122, "dubious."
64. Miriam Lichtheim, "The Songs of the Harpers," *Journal of Near Eastern Studies* 4:3 (1945): 178–212.
65. Brandon, *Judgment*, 26; Lichtheim, "Songs of the Harpers," *JNES*, 191-2; Simpson, *Literature of Ancient Egypt*, 307.
66. Bowman, *Egypt after the Pharaohs*, 187. The text is printed in full in Lichtheim, *Ancient Egyptian Literature*, III, 59–65.
67. Lichtheim, *Ancient Egyptian Literature* III,22, 54n, 58–59.
68. Wilkinson, *Rise and Fall*, 474–75.
69. East along the Mediterranean littoral, about the same period, a priest of Bel at Apamea-on-Orontes headed an Epicurean school, suggesting that priesthood and philosophy were compatible. Stephanie Dalley, *Legacy of Mesopotamia* (New York: Oxford University Press, 1998), 118.
70. Sarolta A. Takács, *Isis and Serapis in the Roman World* (Leiden: E. J. Brill, 1995), 29, 5, 124-5, 189–91; Robert Turcan, *The Cults of the Roman Empire*, trans. Antonia Nevill (Oxford: Blackwell, 1997), 75–78, 84, 95, 101–03; J. M. C. Toynbee, *Death and Burial in the Roman World* (Ithaca: Cornell University Press, 1971), 41–42; Françoise, Dunand, *Le culte d'Isis dans le basin oriental de la Mediterranée*, 3 vols. Leiden, 1973.
71. Malcolm Drew Donalson, *The Cult of Isis in the Roman Empire: Isis Invicta* (Lewiston, New York: E. Mellen, 2003), 115–19, 167.
72. Benjamin Isaac, *The Invention of Racism in Classical Antiquity* (Princeton: Princeton University Press, 2004), 358. Isaac blends zoomorphic and anthropormorphic gods in his discussion of hostility to animal cults and fails to take into account the popularity outside

2. IMPERMANENT ETERNITIES   305

Egypt of Egyptian cults, 369. Molly Swetnam-Burland, *Egypt in Italy: Visions of Egypt in Roman Imperial Culture* (Cambridge, England: Cambridge University Press, 2015), 4, 170–72.

73. Tacitus, *Annals*, 16.6; Maureen Carroll, *Spirits of the Dead: Roman Funerary Commemoration in Western Europe* (New York: Oxford University Press, 2006), 164; Toynbee, *Death and Burial*, 41.
74. Wilkinson, *Rise and Fall*, 442.
75. Bowman, *Egypt After the Pharaohs*, 170.
76. The description of Cleopatra in that Virgilian scene catches her self-representation as Isis without naming the goddess Isis. Ovid, in contrast to Virgil, presents a much more Romanized and integrated Isis in his *Amores* and *Metamorphoses*. Vassiliki Panoussi, "Isis at a Roman Wedding: Ritual and Ethnicity in Ovid's *Metamporphoses 9*," David H. Porter Classical World Lecture, Skidmore College, April 7, 2015.
77. "Aegyptiorum morem quis ignorat? Quorum inbutae mentes pravitatis erroribus" *Tusculan Disputations*, 5.78; in Isaac, *Invention of Racism*, 357.
78. Lucian, "Menippus or Descent to Hades," in *Lucian*, ed. A. M. Harmon. Loeb Classical Library (1925) (Cambridge, MA: Harvard University Press, 1953) IV, 97.
79. Bowman, *Egypt After the Pharaohs*, 178–79.
80. "Dialogues of the Sea Gods," *Lucian*, VII, 219.
81. *The Golden Ass of Apuleius*, trans. Robert Graves (New York: Farrar, Straus, and Young, 1954), vi.
82. Isaac, *Invention of Racism*, 359.
83. "A Farmer and the Courts" Matthews, *Old Testament Parallels*, 219. More accurately rendered in Lichtheim, *Ancient Egyptian Literature*, I, 174: "'A good deed is remembered./ This is the precept:/ Do to the doer to make him do./ It is thanking a man for what he does,/Parrying a blow before it strikes." In James B. Pritchard's version, "Now this is the command: 'Do to the doer to cause that he do.' That is thanking him for what he may do." *Ancient Near Eastern Texts Relating to the Old Testament*, 3rd ed. (Princeton, NJ: Princeton University Press, 1969), 408.
84. Miriam Lichtheim, *Ancient Egyptian Literature*, III, 167.
85. Allen, *Pyramid Texts* 337, 133.
86. Assmann, "When Justice Fails," 154.
87. Lucian, " On funerals," IV, 127–29, and 128n.
88. R[aymond] O. Faulkner, *The Ancient Egyptian Pyramid Texts* (Stilwell, KS: Digireads.com, 2007), 99; Allen, *Pyramid Texts*, #222, 60.
89. Assyriologists now regard the Mesopotamian (and its biblical derivative) flood story as having an historical basis in catastrophic floods in the alluvial plain, as rivers changed their directions. A. R. George, *The Babylonian Gilgamesh Epic: Introduction, Critical Edition and Cuneiform Texts*, 2 vols. (Oxford: Oxford University Press, 2003), I, 509, cited in text as George; Steven W. Cole and Hermann Gasche, "Levees, Floods, and the River Network of Northern Babylonia: 2000–1500 and 1000–500 BC—A Preliminary Report," in Johannes Renger, ed. *Babylon. Focus Mesopotamischer Geschichte* (Saabrucken, 1999), CDOG 2, 87–110; Irving Finkel, *The Ark Before Noah: Decoding the Story of the Flood*. (London: Hodder and Stoughton, 2014). For the environmental implications of ancient

Mesopotamian literature, see Stephanie Dalley, "Ancient Mesopotamian Literature and the Environment," in *A Global History of Literature and the Environment*, ed. John Parham (Cambridge, England: Cambridge University Press, 2017), 21–36.

90. Anticipating modern Mexico's Day of the Dead festivities, indigenous Mexican peoples celebrated two festivals for the dead, Miccailhuitontli, or Fiesta de los Muertecitos, for the infant dead and Xocotlhuetzi, or Fiesta Grande de los Muertos, for adults. In 1579, the Dominican Diego Durán was perturbed by the fact that on All Saints Day, the Indians made their offerings "for the dead children, that this is what they had done from antiquity, and that they retained this custom." On All Souls Day, they made offerings "for the grown-ups." Claudio Lomnitz, *Death and the Idea of Mexico* (New York: Zone Books, 2005), 116. The Romans imagined children at play, though Virgil does not, and an Ethiopic apocalypse of Peter gives aborted infants a guardian angel and a place of delight. Danuta Shanzer, "Voices and Bodies: The Afterlife of the Unborn," *Numen* 56 (2009): 330, 340–41. Al-Sara'i's *Paths of Paradise / Nahj al-faradis* (Herat, 1466) sends children who died prematurely to the Heavenly Paradise of Abraham, where they climb trees, peep at their visitor Muhammad, and play games inside and outdoors. *Jerusalem 1000–1400 Every People under Heaven*. Metropolitan Museum, NYC, October 2016–Jan. 8, 2017.

91. Jean Bottéro, *Mesopotamia: Writing, Reasoning, and the Gods*, trans. Zainub Bahrani and Marc Van De Mieroop (Chicago: University of Chicago Press, 1992), 268–86. Caitlín E. Barrett, "Was Dust Their Food and Clay Their Bread? Grave Goods, the Mesopotamian Afterlife, and the Liminal Role of Inana/Ishtar," *JANER* 7:3 (2007): 7–65.

92. Matthews, *Old Testament Parallels*, 223–28. This late theodicy dates from about 1000 BCE, the oldest copies from Ashurbanipal's library, 668–626 BCE, and the most recent from the Persian period, fifth century, a period extending from Amos, c750 BCE, to a post-exilic Job.

93. "*Adab* to Nergal for Šu-ilišu," "*Adab* to Bau for Išme-Dagan," "*Balbale* to Ninĝišida," "A *tigi* to Enki for Ur-Ninurta," "An *ululumama* to Suen for Ibbi-Suen," "A *šir-namursaĝa* to Inana for Iddin-Dagan," "A *šir-namšub* to Utu," in Jeremy Black, Graham Cunningham, Eleanor Robson, Gábor Zólyomi, *The Literature of Ancient Sumer* (Oxford: Oxford University Press, 2004), 160,252, 271, 273–74, 266, 259–61. website www.etcsl.orinst.ox.ac.uk.

94. "An Elegy on the Death of Nannaya," *Electronic Text Corpus of Sumerian Literature (ETCSL), http://www.etcsl.orinst.ox.ac.uk*, t5.5.2. 88–98.

95. Alexander Heidel, *The Gilgamesh Epic and Old Testament Parallels* (Chicago: University of Chicago Press, 1949), 193.

96. "Death of Bilgameš," other details from "The Descent of Inana," "Death of Ur-Namma," "Bilgameš, Enkidu and the Netherworld," ETCSL. The last three appear in Black, Cunningham, Robson, Zólyomi, *The Literature of Ancient Sumer*, 65–76, 56–62, 31–40.

97. Matthews, *Old Testament Parallels*, 236.

98. Black, *Literature of Ancient Sumer*. The Romanization differs in ETCSL, as do the translations, but the numbers for the relevant poems are: "Ninjiczida's Journey to the Netherworld," 1.7.3.; "The Death of Bilgameš," 1.8.1.3; "The Death of Ur-Namma," 2.4.1.1.; "Bilgameš, Enkidu, and the Netherworld," 1.8.1.4; "Dumuzid's Dream," 1.4.3.; "*Balbale* to Ninĝišida," 4.19.1; "An *ululumama* to Suen for Ibbi-Suen," 2.4.5.4; "A *šir-namursaĝa*

to Inana for Iddin-Dagan," 2.5.3.4; "A šir-namšub to Utu," 4.32.e; the great creation-flood poem, 1.7.4; and "The Descent of Inana," 1.4.1.

99. "Inana's Descent to the Underworld," in Black, *The Literature of Ancient Sumer*, 73.
100. "Inana's Descent," Black, *Literature of Ancient Sumer*, 73–74, 76n., 295–305.
101. "Dumuzid's Dream," Black, *Literature of Ancient Sumer*, 80.
102. George, I, 15. Graves with human retinues interred have been found at Ur, Kish, and Susa. Klaas Spronk, *Beatific Afterlife in Ancient Israel and in the Ancient Near East* (Kevelaer: Butzon und Bercker, 1986), 107.
103. For other instances, George, I, 487–89; II, 900n19.
104. "Death of Ur-Namma," ETCSL c.2.4.1.1. Bilgameš also brings gifts for the gods, not himself: "audience-gifts for Ereškigala. He set out their gifts for Namtar. He set out their surprises for Dimpikug. He set out their presents for Neti. He set out their presents for Ninĝišzida and Dumuzid. He. . . . the audience-gifts for Enki, Ninki, Enmul, Ninmul, Endukuga, Nindukuga, Enindašuruma, Nindašuruma, Enmu-utula, En-me-šara, the maternal and paternal ancestors of Enlil; for Šul-pa-e, the lord of the table, for Sumugan and Ninḫursaĝa, for the Anuna gods of the Holy Mound, for the Great Princes of the Holy Mound, for the dead en priests, the dead lagar priests, the dead lumaḫ priests, the dead nindiĝir priestesses, and the dead gudug, the linen-clad and. . . . priests," http://etcsl.orinst.ox.ac.uk/cgi-bin/etcsl.cgi.
105. Martha Tobi Roth, *Law Collections from Mesopotamia and Asia Minor*, 2nd ed. Writings from the Ancient World, vol. 6, Society of Biblical Literature (Atlanta: Scholars Press, 1997), 13–22.
106. Martha Tobi Roth, *Law Collections from Mesopotamia and Asia Minor*, 34–35, 136–40. The Sumerian laws also curse, but only for this life, 39.
107. George, I, 141–42.
108. Roth, *Law Collections*, 25. Cf. 44.
109. "An Elegy on the Death of Nannaya," c.5.5.2, ETCSL.orinst.ox.ac.uk.
110. *BEN* is probably not the name of *BEN* in Sumerian. The poem begins not with Enkidu and death, but with a tree of Inana's, infested by an Anzu-bird, a serpent, and a phantom maiden, elements associated with the dead. These Bilgameš evicts for her, cutting down the tree to make furniture for her and a pukku and stick for himself. The netherworld part of the story begins when Bilgameš loses his pukku, and Enkidu his servant volunteers to fetch it. The Sumerian poem puts the netherworld into relation with creation, the gods, and the motif of the great tree that links the world of the gods and the netherworld.
111. Dina Katz, *The Image of the Netherworld in the Sumerian Sources* (Bethesda, MD: CDL Press, 2003), 109. Katz points out that when Enkidu goes down to the underworld to fetch Gilgamesh's ball and head-severing bat, Gilgamesh advises him to behave like a non-socialized, de-socialized corpse (the advice of Siduri reversed). That way, the dead won't notice him, and he'll be able to come back. Enkidu ignores the advice—he is alive, and cannot act as if he is dead—and so he is trapped.
112. Black, "Gilgameš, Enkidu, and the Netherworld," *Literature of Ancient Sumer*, 37–38.
113. A. R. George, *The Epic of Gilgamesh* (New York: Penguin, 2000), 177, 190–91; II, 777. Including his mother in the ancestral line, Bilgameš repeats three times "my father and my mother."

114. "The message of Lu-dijira to his mother," extravagantly beautiful, makes the praise of the good woman in Proverbs seem like blame by comparison. *ETCSL, t.5.5.1.*
115. Scavenging was a shameful activity of the destitute to be performed after nightfall. An old Babylonian—not Sumerian—proverb had it that "the widow scavenges evenings on the road for something to eat." Falkowitz, 1980, proverb 3.19, quoted in Karel van der Toorn, *Family Religion in Babylonia, Ugarit, and Israel: Continuity and Changes in the Forms of Religious Life* (Leiden: E. J. Brill, 1996), 30.
116. Black, "Gilgameš, Enkidu, and the Netherworld," *Literature of Ancient Sumer*, 39.
117. Blakey Vermeule, *Why Do We Care about Literary Characters?* (Baltimore: Johns Hopkins University Press, 2010), 146: "The most ancient and universal experience of God is that he is a moralist, and this experience supersedes all abstract ideas about him. Gods and spirits may be omniscient, but in practice, they are mainly interested in moral questions." Citing Pascal Boyer, *Religion Explained: The Evolutionary Origins of Religious Thought* (New York: Basic Books, 2001), 158.
118. George, number of mss, II, 745–48; locations, II, 985–86; moral lines, II, 776. Gregory Shushan cites Dina Katz, *Image of the Netherworld*, 2003; Jerrold S. Cooper, "The Fate of Mankind: Death and Afterlife in Ancient Mesopotamian Religion," in Hiroshi Obayashi, ed. *Death and Afterlife: Perspectives of World Religions*, 1992; and Jean Bottéro, "Les inscriptions cuneiforms funéraires," 1982, as regarding BEN as "heterodox" since its view of the afterlife is not as uniformly cheerless as scholars represent the Mesopotamian afterlife. He does not point out that most copies of BEN do not contain the moral injunctions regarding parents, tending to confirm Katz's and Cooper's views. Nor are those lines in the *Gilgamesh* Twelfth Tablet, which he does not discuss. Shushan, *Conceptions of the Afterlife in Early Civilizations: Universalism, Constructivism, and Near-Death Experience*. Foreword, Gavin Flood (London: Continuum International, 2009), 73, 83.
119. George, II, 777.
120. Black, "GEN," *Literature of Ancient Sumer*, 40n287; George, Penguin, 188; II, 775.
121. Roth, *Law Collections*, 25, 44, 113, 120.
122. *The Novel*, ed. Franco Moretti, 2 vols. (Princeton: Princeton University Press, 2006), I, 8.
123. The surviving Sumerian poems about Bilgameš: Bilgameš and Huwawa; Bilgameš, Enkidu, and the Netherworld; The Death of Bilgameš (which mentions his trip to Ziusudra); Bilgameš and the Bull of Heaven; Bilgameš and the Aga of Kish; Bilgameš and Huwawa is an episode in the original Old Babylonian version; Bilgameš and the Bull of Heaven first appears in a middle Babylonian version. The visit to Ziusudra is recast in the OBV and given a new purpose—to escape death, rather than to restore the rites before the flood. Bilgameš and the Aga of Kish is not used at all.
124. A. R. George argues that the quest for immortality "was in fact well known in the Sumerian literary tradition" (I, 19), but no surviving Sumerian poem makes such a quest its topic. George's argument hinges on a Babylonian "poem of early rulers" that contains the line, "where now is Gilgamesh, who sought life like Ziusudra?" The tablet is twelfth century, later than the OBV, and George considers it a Sumerian composition extant in Babylonian copies, I, 99, 96. Bilgameš's visit to Ziusudra is clear in "The Death of Bilgameš," but he sought not to obtain eternal life but to restore the rites from before the flood and

2. IMPERMANENT ETERNITIES 309

he succeeded—he brought the forgotten rituals back. The gods recall this achievement as they discuss Bilgameš's imminent and inevitable death in a dream. (Other kings claim to have restored the rites, as well.) In a version from Me-Turan, Segment F, ll. 116–30, the flood explains the origins of death: afterwards no one, except Ziusudra the survivor, would live forever. For the difficulties of Sumerian translation and this poem in particular, see Niek Veldhuis, "The Solution of the Dream: A New Interpretation of Bilgameš' Death," *Journal of Cuneiform Studies* 53 (2001): 133–48. The text in its fragments appears on the ETCSL website: http://etcsl.orinst.ox.ac.uk/cgi-bin/etcsl.cgi.

125. Relatively little of the Old Babylonian version survives, but it did not have the ring structure that has reached us. Stephanie Dalley translates four surviving OBV tablets in her *Myths from Mesopotamia: Creation, The Flood, Gilgamesh, and Others* (Oxford: Oxford University Press, 2000), cited in text as Dalley. In his astonishing 2 volumes, A. R. George translates all the fragments currently extant, produces a hybrid text of the SBV in English and Akkadian, and provides sketches—and some photographs—of the tablets themselves.

Its opening line supplied by the colophon on subsequent tablets ("Surpassing all other kings," a line that now follows the prologue in the SBV), the surviving OBV text begins with Gilgamesh's dreaming about Enkidu before he meets him, Enkidu's domestication through seven days of sex with a harlot and her introducing him to civilization through clothing and beer. Enkidu and Gilgamesh struggle against each other, as Enkidu keeps Gilgamesh out of a new bride's bed before her husband, and they then join together to combat Humbaba, protector of the cedar forest, embodiment of wilderness. Missing tablets must describe Enkidu's death and Gilgamesh's mourning, since in what survives, Gilgamesh meets Shamash and Siduri after Enkidu's death as he seeks immortality, and he destroys the stones Sur-sunabu depends upon to carry him across the waters of death to Ūta-napišti, the one man granted immortality by the gods. Sur-sunabu orders Gilgamesh to cut poles so as to pole across the waters to Ūta-napišti. There the tablets break off again, and the end of the poem is missing.

In addition to the prologue, episodes missing in the OBV are Enkidu's dream, his death, his funeral, and Gilgamesh's mourning, as well as the episode of Ishtar and the Bull of Heaven that in the SBV precipitates Enkidu's death. Missing is all of the present ending: the visit to Ūta-napišti, the story of the flood, the sleep test, the quest for and loss of the magic plant of youth, and the return to the city and the Twelfth Tablet.

126. Sin-leqi-unninni is named in a Neo-Assyrian authors' list as author; the series of Gilgamesh is from his mouth. George, I, 28. He is variously identified as a magician and a diviner priest and was regarded as an ancestor by cult-singers, I, 29. A late Babylonian king list makes him a contemporary of King Gilgamesh, I, 29, the poet as ancient as the hero. In George's view, Sin-leqi-unninni is not the author of the OBV but of a MB version, I, 30, who, in what George calls a "bold" suggestion, recast the OBV into an eleven-tablet version with prologue and reprising epilogue, I, 32, with Tablet 12 a "prose appendix" that turns a hero story into "a somber meditation on the doom of man," I, 33. George finds the OBV version more energetic, young, ambitious, the SBV more meditative and modern.

127. Douglas, *Thinking in Circles: An Essay in Ring Composition* (New Haven: Yale University Press, 2007), 126.
128. Dalley, *Myths from Mesopotamia*, 34–35. These features may be attested in Sumerian poems that have not survived.
129. Katz, *The Image of the Netherworld*, xvi–xvii. The ETCSL translations place the "underworld" "below" the earth, but that may be simply contagious expectation.
130. Katz, *Image of the Netherworld*, 109, 218, 238. Between "Inana's Descent" and "GEN," however, the Sumerian afterlife goes underground.
131. "The Descent of Ishtar to the Underworld," in Stephanie Dalley, ed. *Myths from Mesopotamia*, 155–56. The lines about the dead eating the living do not appear or are not preserved in the Sumerian "Gilgameš and the Bull of Heaven." http://etcsl.orinst.ox.ac.uk/cgi-bin/etcsl.cgi.
132. It has been dated from the fifteenth or fourteenth century BCE, but George queries the dates. I, 26, 339–47.
133. In a remarkable parable of the difficulties of this scholarship, for those who actually engage it: an Elamite tablet was presented as a dramatized version of *Gilgamesh* in 1990. That identification was demolished by another scholar, and yet another scholar has identified the same tablet as a private letter, viz., "Epic of Gilgamesh or Economic Tablet from Persepolis? Neither one nor the other." George, I, 24n67.
134. A. R. George's two volumes supplant earlier scholarship on the epic's development, even as they promise scholars that more work needs to be done. Sin-leqi-unninni may be either the author of the OBV or the editor of the SBV. George inclines to the latter, but there is as yet no determining evidence. George, I, 30–31. The classic account of the development of the *Gilgamesh* epic has been Jeffrey H. Tigay, *The Evolution of the Gilgamesh Epic* (Philadelphia: University of Pennsylvania Press, 1982). Gary Beckman extends and advances Tigay's account relative to recent findings and provides exceptionally useful charts indicating what parts of the epic appear in which manuscripts, "Gilgamesh in Hatti," *Hittite Studies in Honor of Harry A. Hoffner Jr.*, ed. Gary Beckman, Richard Beal, and Gregory MacMahon (Winona Lake, IN: Eisenbrauns, 2003).
135. Susan Brind Morrow observes that the Egyptian words for "snake" and "life" are the same, "The snake is the life in the tree of life." *The Dawning Moon of the Mind: Unlocking the Pyramid Texts*, 45.
136. The means of transmission remain unclear, but the Genesis stories obviously borrow whole cloth from the earlier Sumerian/Babylonian tales—plot lines, motifs, narrative elements—while changing fundamentally the meaning of the stories to conform to Hebrew/Israelite theology. Stephanie Dalley, et al., *The Legacy of Mesopotamia*, 57–83. Ronald A. Veenker, "Gilgamesh and the Magic Plant," *The Biblical Archaeologist* 44:4 (Autumn 1981): 199–205, makes the especially delicate point that in the Gilgamesh flood story, a person who will be drowned closes the ark for Ūta-napišti, whereas in the Biblical J narrative, YHWH himself closes the ark. In the Babylonian Atrahasis version, Atrahasis closes the ark himself, and if the Atrahasis version had been the source, it seems logical that Noah could have shut his own ark. Instead, the Jahwist makes God responsible and does not impugn God's justice in making Noah depend on a doomed sinner. For the

2. IMPERMANENT ETERNITIES 311

relationship between *Gilgamesh* and the Greeks, see Walter Burkert, *Babylon, Memphis, Persepolis: Eastern Contexts of Greek Culture* (Cambridge, MA: Harvard University Press, 2004), 21–48; M. L. West, *The East Face of Helicon: West Asiatic Elements in Greek Poetry and Myth* (Oxford: Clarendon, 1997); George, I, 55–59.

137. Stephanie Dalley, ed. *The Legacy of Mesopotamia* (Oxford: Oxford University Press, 1998). M. J. Geller. "The Last Wedge," *ZA* 87 (1997), 43–95. Darius I's stele commemorated the first Suez Canal's opening in 497 BCE in cuneiform and hieroglyphics; Sumerian and Babylonian learning survive into Greek magical papyri and the origins of Stoicism, succumbing to Christian, Muslim, and Zoroastrian hostility. *Legacy*, 166, 169.

138. Stanley Mayer Burstein, *The Babyloniaca of Berossus* (Malibu, CA: Undena, 1978).

139. George, I, 201, OBV col.iv, 140-43; cf. Dalley, Tablet 3, column iv, 144.

140. "[F]ly up to the sky and live with them [the gods], cause your wings to grow with your feathers on your head and your feathers on your arms," Faulkner, *Pyramid Texts*, 282.

141. John Bowker, *The Meanings of Death* (Cambridge, England: Cambridge University Press, 1991), 154; Ronald A. Veenker, "Gilgamesh and the Magic Plant," *The Biblical Archaeologist* 44:4 (Autumn 1981): 199–205; Jerrold S. Cooper, "The Fate of Mankind: Death and Afterlife in Ancient Mesopotamian Religion," in Hiroshi Obayashi, ed. *Death and Afterlife: Perspectives of World Religions* (London: Praeger, 1992), 31n6.

142. Asking Shamash to protect Gilgamesh as he goes against Humbaba, Ninsun questions the sun god over a series of inconsistent fates, including that promised Bilgameš in the "Death of Bilgameš":

O Šamaš, will Gilgameš not . . . the gods?
Will he not share the heavens with you?
Will he not *share* a scepter with the moon?
Will he not become wise with Ea *of* the Apsû?
Will he not rule the black-headed race with Irnina?
[Will he] not dwell in the Land-of-No-Return with Ningišzida?", Tablet III.
   ll. 101–106; George I, 581.

143. "Did [you see] the man fallen in battle?" "I saw him.]" "How does he [fare?]"
"His father and mother could not hold his head, his wife weeps." George, II, 776.
Of the emendation on the Twelfth Tablet, George observes: "The Akkadian follows a tradition in which the first verb is not negated. Both the legible Sumerian manuscripts have a clear negative . . .; the Nippur sources are broken at the crucial point" II, 904n149.

144. "The Lament for Nibru," 181–183. ETCSL, t. 2.2.4.

145. A similar security for the grave may be imagined for Enkidu in some fragmentary lines from Tablet VIII, ll. 207–10; George, I, 490.

146. Recorded by the BBC Symphony Orchestra, 1996, Jiří Bělohlávek conducting. BBC Music, vol. 4, no. 11.

147. Barry Brenesal, *Fanfare: The Magazine for Serious Record Collectors* 31:4 (Mar/Apr 2008), 168. Theodore Ziolkowski, *Gilgamesh Among Us: Modern Encounters with the Ancient Epic* (Ithaca, New York: Cornell University Press, 2012), 71–77.

148. *Relief of the Capture and Decapitation of the Elamite King*, upper left register, British Museum, 124801a, *From Assyria to Iberia at the Dawn of the Classical Age*, Metropolitan Museum, Nov. 2014. For bones, Cooper, "Fate of Mankind,"27–28.
149. Hercules, with Hebe on Olympus in Homer and Hesiod, is the classical prototype for afterlife ascents. Walter Burkert, *Greek Religion*, trans. John Raffan (Cambridge, MA: Harvard University Press, 1985), 198, 211, 427n40, n41, 433n40.
150. Karel van der Toorn, *Family Religion in Babylonia, Ugarit, and Israel*, 208, 354–62.
151. Wisdom of Solomon addresses the problem death creates in Genesis: it had never been God's intention for man to choose death, WS 1:13–15; 2:23.
152. The Torah was assembled during and after the exile 597/87 BCE–538 BCE, achieving something like its modern form about 450 or 400 BCE. The prophets were collected by about 250 BCE, forming Jesus' "Law and the Prophets." Resurrection first appears in Jewish writing during the Maccabean rebellion against Antiochus Epiphanus IV in Daniel, c. 165 BCE (canonized c. 100 CE as part of the Writings), the Christian deutero-canonical books Maccabees, and outside the Bible in some Dead Sea fragments, especially Enochic literature. John F. Hobbins, "Resurrection in the Daniel Tradition and Other Writings at Qumran," in *The Book of Daniel: Composition and Reception*, ed. John J. Collins and Peter Flint (Leiden: Brill, 2001), II, 395–420.
153. Unless otherwise specified, biblical quotations are from the NRSV, *HarperCollins Study Bible*. KJV designates the King James Version, 1611.
154. The earliest reforms referred to by the Deuteronomist under Asa concern only idols, male temple prostitutes, and an image of Asherah, made by the Queen Mother. 1 Kings 15.12–13, ca. 913–873 BCE.
155. It has, however, been doubted. Philip R. Davies, "Spurious Attribution in the Hebrew Bible," in *The Invention of Sacred Tradition*, ed. James R. Lewis and Olav Hammer (Cambridge, England: Cambridge University Press, 2007), argues that Deuteronomy is post-exilic, Ezra nonexistent and his and Nehemiah's story a late fiction composed during the fifth century BCE to prove that Deuteronomy preceded the exile and had been endorsed by a righteous king, 267, 273–74. At issue is not the importance of the Deuteronomists' book but its timing. Timo Veijola, "The Deuteronomistic Roots of Judaism," in *Sefer Moshe: The Moshe Weinfeld Jubilee Volume, Studies in the Bible and the Ancient Near East, Qumran, and Post-Biblical Judaism*, ed. Chaim Cohen, Avi Hurvitz, and Shalom M. Paul (Winona Lake, IN: Eisenbrauns, 2004), 459–78. For a hostile account of the Deuteronomists' work as obscuring the authentic religion of ancient, pre-exilic, pre-textual Israel and Judah, see *Religious Diversity in Ancient Israel and Judah*, ed. Francesca Stavrakopoulou and John Barton (London: T & T Clark, 2010).
156. Van der Toorn suggests that Jeremiah's father Hilkiah may have been the same Hilkiah who took the book of the law to king Josiah, and his uncle Shallum may have been the same Shallum who had been the husband of the widow Huldah, the prophetess who verified the book of the law, *Family Religion*, 370.
157. Karel van der Toorn, *Family Religion*, 225–29. T. J. Lewis, *Cults of the Dead in Ancient Israel and Ugarit*, HSM 39 (Atlanta, GA: Scholars, 1989).

158. Leonard J. Greenspoon, "The Origin of the Idea of Resurrection" in *Traditions in Transformation: Turning Points in Biblical Faith*, ed. Baruch Halpern and Jon D. Levenson (Winona Lake, IN: Eisenbrauns, 1981), 247–322.
159. For Šamaš in nocturnal divination in Babylon, Piotr Steinkeller, "Of Stars and Men: The Conceptual and Mythological Setup of Babylonian Extispicy," *Biblical and Oriental Essays in Memory of William L. Moran*, ed. Agustinus Gianto, Biblica et Orientalia 48. (Rome: Editrice Pontificio Istituto Biblico, 2005), 24–45.
160. Rachel S. Hallote, *Death, Burial, and Afterlife in the Biblical World* (Chicago: Ivan Dee, 2001), 113.
161. Klaas Spronk, *Beatific Afterlife*, 231 and n3; Nicholas J. Tromp, *Primitive Conceptions of Death and the Nether World in the Old Testament*, Biblica et Orientalia 21 (Rome: Gregorian and Biblical Press, 1969), 99–100; John Barclay Burns, "The Mythology of Death in the Old Testament," *Scottish Journal of Theology* 26: 3(1973): 327–40.
162. Michael David Coogan, trans. and ed. *Stories from Ancient Canaan* (Philadelphia: Westminster Press, 1978), 112–13; Oxford Study Bible, *59; J. C. L. Gibson, *Canaanite Myths and Legends* (New York: T & T Clark International, c. 2004), "Baal and Mot."
163. Spronk, *Beatific Afterlife*, 169–70, 276. Cf. John Day, "Resurrection Imagery from Baal to the Book of Daniel," in *Congress Volume: Cambridge 1995. Supplements to Vetus Testamentum* ed. J. A. Emerton (Leiden: Brill, 1997), LXVI, 128–9.
164. Later Christians sometimes do: Greenspoon, "Origin of the Idea of Resurrection," 307–09. Cf. James S. Ackerman, "Satire and Symbolism in the Song of Jonah," *Traditions in Transformation*, 220.
165. William G. Dever, *Did God Have a Wife? Archaeology and Folk Religion in Ancient Israel* (Grand Rapids, MI: W. B. Eerdmans, 2005); John Day, *Yahweh and the Gods and Goddesses of Canaan* (Sheffield, England: Sheffield Academic Press, 2000); Tilde Binger, *Asherah: Goddesses in Ugarit, Israel and the Old Testament* (Sheffield, England: Sheffield Academic Press, 1997); Richard J. Pettey, *Asherah: Goddess of Israel* (New York: Peter Lang, 1990). Phyllis A. Bird, "The End of the Male Cult Prostitute: A Literary-Historical and Sociological Analysis of Hebrew QĀDĀŠ-QĔDĒŠÎM" in *Congress Volume: Cambridge 1995. Supplements to Vetus Testamentum*, ed. J. A. Emerton (Leiden: Brill, 1997), LXVI, 37–80.
166. Elizabeth Bloch-Smith, *Judahite Burial Practices and Beliefs about the Dead* (Sheffield: JSOT Press, 1992), 133, 140–42.
167. Van der Toorn suggests that Saul's outlawing mediums may not be an anachronism, but a move by Saul against family religion and its cult of the dead, *Family Religion*, 318.
168. Elizabeth Bloch-Smith, *Judahite Burial Practices*, 109–32; Francesca Stavrakopoulou and John Barton, ed. *Religious Diversity in Ancient Israel and Judah* (London: T & T Clark, 2010); Theodore J. Lewis, *Cults of the Dead in Ancient Israel and Ugarit*, HSM 39 (Atlanta: Scholars Press, 1989); Barry M. Gittlen, ed. *Sacred Time, Sacred Place: Archaeology and the Religion of Israel* (Winona Lake, IN: Eisenbrauns, 2002); Saul M. Olyan, *Biblical Mourning: Ritual and Social Dimensions* (New York: Oxford University Press, 2004); *Household and Family Religion in Antiquity* (Oxford: Blackwell, 2008).
169. Karel van der Toorn, *Family Religion*, 48–65, 125.

170. *Tanakh: The Holy Scriptures, The New JPS Translation According to the Traditional Hebrew Text* (Philadelphia: Jewish Publication Society, 1985).
171. Karel van der Toorn finds the same bargaining with one's gods in Old Babylonian texts, *Family Religion*, 140. So Abraham barters over Sodom, Genesis 18.22–33.
172. ETCSL translation t.5.5.3.
173. Klaas Spronk, *Beatific Afterlife*, 11, 13–24. Cf. K. A. D. Smelik, "The Witch of Endor: I Samuel 28 in Rabbinic and Christian Exegesis Till 800 AD," *Vigiliae Christianae* 33 (1979): 160–79.
174. Klaas Spronk, *Beatific Afterlife*, 75, 109; Jean Bottéro, "Les inscriptions cuneiforms funéraires" in Gherardo Gnoli and Jean-Pierre Vernant, ed. *La mort, les morts dans les sociétés anciennes* (Cambridge, England: Cambridge University Press, 1982), 392–403.
175. Stefan Schorch, " 'A Young Goat in Its Mother's Milk'? Understanding an Ancient Prohibition," *Vetus Testamentum* 60 (2010): 120; Jacob Milgrom, *Leviticus 1–16: A New Translation with Introduction and Commentary* (New York: Doubleday, 1991), 737–38; Burkert, *Greek Religion*, 295; Robert Ratner and Bruce Zuckerman, " 'A Kid in Milk'? New Photographs of 'KTU' 1.23, line 14*," *Hebrew Union College Annual* 57 (1986): 15–60; Calum M. Carmichael, "On Separating Life and Death: An Explanation of Some Biblical Laws," *Harvard Theological Review* 69: 1–2 (1976): 1–7.
176. Fritz Graf and Sarah Iles Johnston, *Ritual Texts for the Afterlife: Orpheus and the Bacchic Gold Tablets* (New York: Routledge, 2007), #3, 9; #5, 13; #26 a, b, 37; Walter Burkert, *Greek Religion*, 295; Günther Zuntz, *Persephone: Three Essays on Religion and Thought in Magna Graecia* (Oxford: Clarendon, 1971), 323–27, 277–86; Arthur Bernard Cook, *Zeus, a Study in Ancient Religion: Vol. 1: Zeus God of the Bright Sky* (1914–40) (New York: Biblo and Tannen, 1964), I, 676–8.
177. Stefan Schorch, 120. Wisdom of Solomon, c. 30 BCE-50/70 CE, connects grief for dead children with idolatry and "secret rites and initiations," WS 14.15.
178. Christopher Hitchens, *God Is Not Great: How Religion Poisons Everything* (New York: Hachette, 2007), 99, 217–28: "Is Religion Child Abuse?"
179. Sumerian kings insisted on their care of the widow and the orphan, their protection of the poor against the strong, e.g., "A Praise Poem for Išme-Dagan," ETCSL, t.2.5.4.01.
180. Herodotus, *Persian Wars*, I.91, Loeb, 116–17.
181. Martin P. Nilsson, *Greek Folk Religion*, 107. Blurred deliberately in this discussion is the distinction between Torah or the Law as icon and Torah as particular rules and regulations. For a discussion of the distinction and the relationship, see John J. Collins, *The Invention of Judaism: Torah and Jewish Identity from Deuteronomy to Paul* (Berkeley: University of California Press, 2017).
182. Eden as the garden of the Lord appears in Isaiah 51:3 and Ezekiel 36:35; 28:13, but there is no reference to the narrative of the trees, death, and curses on Adam, Eve, and serpent. Sirach (200–180 BCE) knows the story but breaks the Genesis narrative's link between death and knowledge (Sirach 16:30–17:11). Paul thematizes the first Adam's bringing death, enabling Augustine's original sin, I Cor. 15.45.
183. Abraham A. Neuman, "A Jewish Viewpoint," in *In Search of God and Immortality*, ed. F. Lyman Windolph (Boston, MA: Beacon, 1961), 5.

184. James D. G. Dunn, "The Danielic Son of Man in the New Testament," in *The Book of Daniel: Composition and Reception*, ed. John J. Collins and Peter Flint (Leiden: Brill, 2001), II, 528–49.
185. Greg Goswell, "Resurrection in the Book of Daniel," *Restoration Quarterly* 55:3 (2013): 139–51.
186. Leonard J. Greenspoon, "The Origin of the Idea of Resurrection," *Traditions in Transformation*, 319–20.
187. John J. Collins, *The Invention of Judaism: Torah and Jewish Identity from Deuteronomy to Paul* (Berkeley: University of California Press, 2017), 125, 128–29.
188. Alan E. Bernstein, *The Formation of Hell: Death and Retribution in the Ancient and Early Christian World* (Ithaca, NY: Cornell University Press, 1993); Alice K. Turner, *History of Hell* (New York: Harcourt Brace, 1993), 12–15; E. A. Wallis Budge, *The Egyptian Heaven and Hell* (1925) (New York: AMS, 1976); R. O. Faulkner, trans. *The Ancient Egyptian Book of the Dead*, ed. Carol Andrews (Austin: University of Texas Press, 1990); Jens Braarvig, "The Buddhist Hell: An Early Instance of the Idea?" *Numen* 56 (2009): 254–81.
189. Colleen McDannell and Bernhard Lang, *Heaven:A History*, 12; Alan F. Segal, *Life After Death* (New York: Doubleday, 2004), 183, 200.
190. Baruch Halpern and Jon D. Levenson, ed. *Traditions in Transformation: Turning Points in Biblical Faith*; Klaas Spronk, *Beatific Afterlife in Ancient Israel and in the Ancient Near East*, 57–59, 125, 294–96, 171; Daniel I. Block, "Beyond the Grave: Ezekiel's Vision of Death and Afterlife," *Society for Biblical Research* 2 (1992): 113–141; Philip C. Schmitz, "The Grammar of Resurrection in Isaiah 26:19a-c," *Journal of Biblical Literature* 122:1 (2003): 145–49; Jon D. Levenson, *Resurrection and the Restoration of Israel: The Ultimate Victory of the God of Life* (New Haven, CT: Yale University Press, 2006); *The Book of Daniel: Composition and Reception*, ed. John J. Collins and Peter Flint (Leiden: Brill, 2001), 2 vols.; Jan N. Bremmer, "The Resurrection between Zarathustra and Jonathan Z. Smith," *Nederlands theologisch tijdschrift* 50:2 (1996): 97; Michael Stauberg, "A Name for All and No One: Zoroaster as a Figure of Authorization and a Screen of Ascription," in *The Invention of Sacred Tradition*, ed. James R. Lewis and Olav Hammer (Cambridge, England: Cambridge University Press, 2007): 177–98.
191. The gospel of Luke explains that when Jesus appeared to the disciples after his death, he took them through the scriptures (now the Christian Old Testament) and pointed out the applicable passages (Luke 24:27). The "suffering servant" passages in Isaiah (42:1–4; 50:4–9; 52:13–53:12) now predict a Messiah, rather than recording the sufferings of faithful Israel. Psalm 22 provides Jesus's last words on the cross and the gambling for his garment. In Acts, the disciple Philip interprets a puzzling passage from Isaiah (Isaiah 53:6–8) for a high-ranking eunuch of Queen Candace of Ethiopia, founding the Ethiopian church (8:26–39).
192. Walter Burkert, *Babylon, Memphis, Persepolis*, 101.
193. Fragment 4Q385, Jan N. Bremmer, "The Resurrection between Zarathustra and Jonathan Z. Smith," *Nederlands theologisch tijdschrift* 50:2 (1996): 92–93; Stephen Goranson, "The Exclusion of Ephraim in Rev. 7:4–8 and Essene Polemic against Pharisees," *Dead Sea Discoveries* 2:1 (1995): 84–85.

316   2. IMPERMANENT ETERNITIES

194. Isaiah combines texts by and about the eighth-century prophet Isaiah of Jerusalem, by a sixth-century celebrant of Judah's imminent return from exile (Deutero- or Second Isaiah), and by writers struggling with the return (Trito-Isaiah). Mingled texts promise doom and marvel at restoration. Second Isaiah calls Cyrus the Persian "the Lord's messiah" (Isaiah 45:1; cf. 44:28, 45:13) and hears the voice calling for the road in the wilderness to be made straight for the Lord's—and the people's—return. There will be no wanderings as in the first wilderness of Exodus (Isaiah 40:2): "A voice cries out, in the wilderness prepare the way of the Lord, make straight in the desert a highway for our God." Re-punctuated to put the voice, rather than the way, in the wilderness, a "voice cries out in the wilderness, prepare the way," the verse identifies John the Baptist's preparing the way for Jesus, as lord (Mark 1:3; Matt. 3:2).

195. Flavius Josephus, *Jewish Antiquities*, XVIII.11–25, in *Josephus*, trans. Louis H. Feldman (Cambridge, MA: Harvard University Press, 1965), IX, 9–23.

196. James D. Purvis, "The Samaritan Problem: A Case Study in Jewish Sectarianism in the Roman Era," in *Traditions in Transformation*, 339.

197. Jan N. Bremmer, "Resurrection between Zarathustra and Smith," 91n10, citing P. W. Van der Horst, *Ancient Jewish Epitaphs* (1991), 117.

198. *Jewish Wars*, ii.119–166. *Josephus*, II, 369–87.

199. *Jewish Wars*, iii.374, *Josephus*, II, 681.

200. McDannell and Lang, *Heaven: A History*, 25–26.

201. Regina Janes, "Why the Daughter of Herodias Must Dance (Mark 6:14–29)," *JSNT* 28:4 (2006): 446–48.

202. Donald A. Hagner, "Gospel, Kingdom, and Resurrection in the Synoptic Gospels," in Longenecker, *Life in the Face of Death*, 112–13.

203. Udo Thiel, *The Early Modern Subject: Self-Consciousness and Personal Identity from Descartes to Hume* (New York: Oxford University Press, 2011), 138, 35–36, 18–30.

204. Prods Oktor Skjærvø, "Zarathustra: A Revolutionary Monotheist?" in Beate Pongratz-Leisten, ed. *Reconsidering the Concept of Revolutionary Monotheism* (Winona Lake, IN: Eisenbrauns, 2011), 345.

205. Burkert gives Homer priority, suggesting that Hesiod's reference to lying muses criticizes Homer's depictions of the gods, *Greek Religion*, 246.

206. H. W. Parke, *Festivals of the Athenians* (Ithaca: Cornell University Press, 1977), 116.

207. Hesiod, *Theogony, Works and Days, Testimonia*, trans. Glenn W. Most (Cambridge, MA: Harvard University Press, 2006).

208. Alexander Pope, *The Iliad*, 2 vols., ed. Maynard Mack (New Haven, CT: Yale University Press, 1967), I, 82; II, 205; I, 395–96.

209. The Greeks associated severed heads with immobility, the instant between a fight or flight response. Regina Janes, *Losing Our Heads* (New York: New York University Press, 2005), 25.

210. "To Demeter," ll. 478–482. *Homeric Hymns, Apocrypha, Lives*, ed. Martin L. West (Cambridge, MA: Harvard University Press, 2003), 68–71. Hugh Bowden, *Mystery Cults of the Ancient World* (Princeton: Princeton University Press, 2010); Walter Burkert, *Ancient Mystery Cults* (Cambridge, MA: Harvard University Press, 1987) and *Greek Religion*,

2. IMPERMANENT ETERNITIES   317

          199, 296–97; *Babylon, Memphis, Persepolis*, 74–79, W. K. C. Guthrie, *Orpheus and Greek Religion* (London: Methuen, 1935), 148–54; Parke, *Festivals of the Athenians*, 70; Michael Pollan, *The Botany of Desire* (New York: Random House, 2001), 147.
211. Hans-Georg Gadamer, *The Beginning of Knowledge*, trans. Rod Coltman (New York: Continuum, 2002), scrutinizes these inscrutable passages, 28, 31–2, 46, 49, 54, 60–64, 71–72.
212. "Second Olympian Ode," ll. 57–80, Pindar, *The Odes of Pindar, including the Principal Fragments*, trans. Sir John Sandys (1915) (Cambridge, MA: Harvard University Press, 1989), 22–27.
213. Burkert, *Greek Religion*, 289, 460n36, c 38. Parke, *Festivals*, 135, 63–64.
214. Herodotus, II.123, pp. 424–25.
215. *Aristophanes*, trans. Benjamin Bickley Rogers, 3 vols. (New York: G. P. Putnam's Sons, 1924), II, 311.
216. *Gorgias*, 523a-527e, Plato, *Gorgias, Menexenus, Protagoras*, ed. Malcolm Schofield, trans. Tom Griffith (Cambridge, England: Cambridge University Press, 2010), 109–13. "They could see beauty shining, when with the divine chorus they beheld the blessed sight and vision . . . we went through the initiations which it is right to call the most blessed, which we celebrated in complete wholeness . . ., seeing, as *mystai* and *epoptai*, entire and whole . . . and happy visions in pure light." 250b-c, *Phaedrus*, trans. Robin Waterfield (New York: Oxford World's Classics, 2002), p. 215; *Phaedo*, 82e, trans. David Gallop (Oxford: Clarendon, 1975).
217. *Phaedo*, 70cd, 81c-82d. Pythagorean materiality resembles Jain karma.
218. *Phaedrus*, trans. Robin Waterfield, 245c-246e, 249ac; Fred D. Miller Jr. "The Platonic Soul," in Hugh H. Benson, *A Companion to Plato* (Oxford: Blackwell, 2006), 278–93; Hugh Bowden, *Mystery Cults of the Ancient World*, 143.
219. Plato, *The Republic of Plato*, ed. Francis MacDonald Cornford (New York: Oxford University Press, 1974) II. 383-87, p. 76.
220. Cornford, *Republic of Plato*, X.614, p. 352.
221. Burkert, *Greek Religion*, 237–38.
222. "Of the Pythagorean Philosophy: From Ovid's *Metamorphoses, Book xv*," *Fables*, 1700.
223. Cornford, *Republic of Plato*, X.612, p. 347.
224. Maxwell Staniforth, "Introduction," *Meditations of Marcus Aurelius* (New York: Penguin, 1979), 15–16.
225. Marcus Aurelius, *Meditations*, II.3, pp. 54–55; V.13, pp 83–84; VI. 24, p. 96; VII. 21, p. 110; VIII. 25, 58, pp. 126, 134; X.7, p. 153; XI. 3, p. 166; XII.5, 21, pp. 181, 183.
226. Hanne Sigismund Nielsen, "The Value of Epithets in Pagan and Christian Epitaphs," in Suzanne Dixon, ed. *Childhood, Class and Kin in the Roman World* (New York: Routledge, 2001), 91, 173. Alison Sheridan, ed. *Heaven and Hell and Other Worlds of the Dead* (Edinburgh: NMS, 2000), 143.
227. Maureen Carroll, *Spirits of the Dead*, 4.
228. Betty Rose Nagle, trans. *Ovid's Fasti: Roman Holidays* (Bloomington, IN: Indiana University Press, 1995), 72. Her lines correspond to the Latin.

318 2. IMPERMANENT ETERNITIES

229. CIL xii.5102/ILS 8154. Maureen Carroll, *Spirits of the Dead*, 4.
230. The only afterlife vision in Roman literature before Virgil's, Cyril Bailey, *Religion in Virgil* (Oxford: Clarendon, 1935), 266.
231. Monica Gale, "Lucretius and Previous Poetic Traditions" in Stuart Gillespie and Philip Hardie, ed., *The Cambridge Companion to Lucretius* (Cambridge, Eng. : Cambridge University Press, 2007) 114–15. "Epicurean apostate": J. D. Minyard, *Lucretius and the Late Republic* (Leiden: E.J. Brill, 1985), 65.
232. Maureen Carroll insists seven examples from CIL and ILS are not typical, compared to expectations of mixing with the earth as flowers or reunion with surviving children, husbands, wives, friends. *Spirits of the Dead*, 4. Mingling with earth as flowers is more consistent with Epicurean sentiments than with familial reunions.
233. *Leg.* 948c. Burkert, *Greek Religion*, 315. "Most people fear" and "say" the soul is destroyed at death with the body, *Phaedo* 77e, 80d.
234. John Bodel calls Oenoanda [sic], a Hellenistic city strangely remarkable for ostentatious inscriptions. *Epigraphic Evidence: Ancient History from Inscriptions* (New York: Routledge, 2001), 14. More recent excavations estimate the wall was originally 12-feet high and 200 feet long, containing about 25,000 words. It has been damaged by earthquakes and recycling of its blocks for other uses. Eric A. Powell, "In Search of a Philosopher's Stone, *Archaeology*, July, August 2015, 34–37. Images at www.archaeology.org/philosopher and Martin Ferguson Smith, "In Praise of the Simple Life: A New Fragment of Diogenes of Oinoanda," *Anatolian Studies* 54 (2004): 35–46.
235. Marcus Tullius Cicero, *De Natura Deorum/On the Nature of the Gods*, Liberty Fund online, sect. viii. Marcus Tullius Cicero, *Brutus, On the Nature of the Gods, On Divination, On Duties*, trans. Hubert M. Poteat (Chicago: University of Chicago Press, 1950), sec. 8, p. 185.
236. Thomas Creech, trans., *Titus Lucretius Carus, Of the Nature of Things: In six books* (London, 1722), Preface, n.p.; Cicero, *On the Nature of the Gods*, sec. 21, p. 199; Savonarola, Stephen Greenblatt, *The Swerve: How the World Became Modern* (New York: W.W. Norton, 2011), 220.
237. Epicurus, *Vatican Sayings*, #7; *Principal Doctrines* #35. www.epicurus.net. *Letters, Principal Doctrines, and Vatican Sayings*, ed. Russel M. Geer (Indianapolis, IN: Bobbs-Merrill, 1964), 64, 66.
238. Cf. David Armstrong, ed., *Vergil, Philodemus, and the Augustans* (Austin, TX: University of Texas Press, 2004), 13–14, 19.
239. Alexander Pope, reworking Dryden's lines, made them more succinct but did away with their longing as well: "The blest today is as completely so, As who began a thousand years ago" (*Essay on Man*, I, 75–76). Dryden, incidentally, claimed not to believe a word of what Lucretius had to say about the mortality of the soul. As poet laureate, he Englished the best bits, on death, sex, philosophic indifference, and Venus, in 1685, post-Creech. He also made Lucretius more aggressively atheistic than he is in Latin. Lucretius liberates, even those who have converted, like Dryden, from radical Protestantism to Anglicanism to Catholicism, perhaps especially those.
240. On Feb. 11, Greenblatt specifies, *The Swerve*, 51.

241. Eve Adler, *Vergil's Empire: Political Thought in the* Aeneid (New York: Rowman and Littlefield, 2003), 44–45; Leah Kronenberg, "Mezentius the Epicurean," *Transactions of the American Philological Association* 135 (2005): 416n41. E. J. Kenney, ed. *Lucretius De Rerum Natura Book III* (Cambridge, England: Cambridge University Press, 1971), 8, 226.
242. *Tusculan Disputations*, trans. J.E. King (London: William Heinemann, 1927), I. xvii. 39–40, p. 47; I.xxi.48–49, p. 59; *Tusc. Disp.* I.vi.10–12, p. 15.
243. Macrobius, *Commentary on the Dream of Scipio*, trans. William Harris Stahl (New York: Columbia University Press, 1952), 81–83.
244. John Pollini, "Ritualizing Death in Republican Rome: Memory, Religion, Class Struggle, and the Wax Ancestral Mask Tradition's Origin and Influence on Veristic Portraiture," in Nicola Laneri, ed. *Performing Death: Social Analyses of Funerary Traditions in the Ancient Near East and Mediterranean*. Oriental Institute Seminars No. 3 (Chicago: Oriental Institute of the University of Chicago, 2007).
245. Virgil, *The Aeneid*, trans. Robert Fagles, intro. Bernard Knox (New York: Viking, 2006), 6. Henri Bergson, *The Philosophy of Poetry: The Genius of Lucretius*, trans. Wade Baskin (New York: Philosophical Library, 1959), 28–35. Philip Hardie, *Lucretian Receptions*, 180–228.
246. Dryden, 2 *Georgics*, 673–737; Virgil, *Georgics* II, 475–512.
247. Hardie, *Lucretian Receptions*, 147–48 and *Virgil's Aeneid: Cosmos and Imperium* (Oxford: Clarendon, 1986), 76–83; Peter Aicher, "Ennius' Dream of Homer," *The American Journal of Philology*, 110:2 (1989): 227–232; Emma Gee discusses Virgil's use of Cicero's poetry, "Cicero's Poetry," *Cambridge Companion to Cicero*, ed. Catherine Steel (Cambridge, England: Cambridge University Press, 2013), 95–101.
248. Sadly, the uncredited uterine map in Turner's *History of Hell*, 38, has it wrong, misplacing the two gates of dreams, the crossroads that separates Tartarus from the gated way to the Elysian Fields, and much else. Cf. Andrew Feldherr, "Putting Dido on the Map: Genre and Geography in Vergil's Underworld," *Arethusa* 32 (1999): 85–122. P. Vergili Maronis, *Aeneoidos Liber Sextus*, ed. with commentary, R. G. Austin (Oxford: Clarendon, 1977), 48–58; 81, l. 132; 124, l. 295.
249. Burkert, *Babylon*, 81, Plate II B 2, from G. Pugliese Carratelli, *Le lamine d'oro orfiche. Istruzioni per il viaggio oltremondano degli iniziati greci* (Milan, 2001), 112f; Bowden, *Mystery Cults*, 150–51.
250. Austin, *Aeneoidos Liber Sextus*, 134, n.329.
251. Macrobius, *Commentary*, 141; Toynbee, *Death and Burial*, 34, 285n73.
252. It is possible those slain for adultery are the wives, but that creates an anomalous gender-switch in the middle of a list (and book, Feldherr, "Putting Dido," 103n46) that seems largely masculine. Some of the crimes are mentioned in legal codes or seem to have been punished when known. Tacitus reports a man thrown from the Tarpeian rock for incest with his daughter, but, like a later case of brother-sister incest, he views the charges as a lie trumped up to appropriate the victim's fortune or fiancée (*Ann.* 6.19). Filial impiety as the specific crime of beating a parent is "an ancient law of Servius Tullius [Festos 260L]," while defrauding clients is a violation mentioned in the 12 Tables. Austin, *Aeneoidos Liber Sextus*, 194, l.609. The Lex Julia of 18 BCE, the year after Virgil died, empowered husbands to kill the male adulterer as well as the wife. Austin, 195, l. 612.

253. *De Re Publica, De Legibus,* trans. Clinton Walker Keyes (London: William Heinemann, 1928), DRP, Book 6, sec. xxi, p. 277.
254. Austin, *Aeneoidos Liber Sextus,* 250–51, l.815; Agnes Kirsopp Michels "Lucretius and the Sixth Book of the *Aeneid,*" *American Journal of Philology* 65 (1944): 135–48.
255. Cicero, *De Re Publica, De legibus,* Book 2, sec. xviii, pp. 140–41.
256. Jan M. Ziolkowski and Michael C. J. Putnam, ed. *The Virgilian Tradition: The First Fifteen Hundred Years* (New Haven: Yale University Press, 2008).
257. Edward Gibbon, *Critical Observations on the Sixth Book of the Aeneid* (1770) (London, 1794), 54.
258. Toynbee, *Death and Burial,* 37. Citing Cumont, *Lux Perpetua,* 73n7.

3. TOURING ASIAN AFTERLIVES: ETERNAL IMPERMANENCE

1. Tomomi Ito, " 'Dhamma' Study and Practice in Contemporary Thai Buddhism: Thoughts of Buddhadasa Bhikku," *Southeast Asia: History and Culture* 1997:26 (1997): 113–36.
2. Jonathan Hay, "Seeing through Dead Eyes: How Early Tang Tombs Staged the Afterlife," *Anthropology and Aesthetics* 57/8 (2010): 16–54.
3. Wendy Doniger, *The Hindus: An Alternative History* (New York: Penguin, 2009), 262–63.
4. "This epic, which promotes long life, grants good fortune and destroys sin, is equal to the Veda and should be recited by the wise to men of faith." Chap. 111, *The Ramayana of Valmiki,* trans. Hari Prasad Shastri. Vol. 3: *Yuddha Kanda, Uttara Kanda* (London: Shanti Sadan, 1959), 637.
5. Some scholars identify a proto-Śiva in an Indus Valley seal; others deny the identification. Doris Srinivasan, "Unhinging Śiva from the Indus Valley Civilization," *Journal of the Royal Asiatic Society of Great Britain and Ireland* 116:1 (1984): 77–89; "The So-Called Proto-Śiva Seal from Mohenjo-Daro: An Iconological Assessment," *Archives of Asian Art* 29 (1975): 47–58; Yan Y. Dhyansky, "The Indus Valley Origin of a Yoga Practice," *Artibus Asiae* 48: 1/2(1987): 89–108.
6. Doniger, *Hindus,* 24–28.
7. Peter Harvey, ed. *Buddhism* (New York: Continuum, 2001), 2; *An Introduction to Buddhism: Teachings, History and Practices,* 2nd ed. (New York: Cambridge University Press, 2013), 459–62. See also Ulrich Pagel, "The Sacred Writings of Buddhism," in Peter Harvey, *Buddhism,* 29–63.
8. Ian Johnson, "Is a Buddhist Group Changing China, or Is China Changing It?" *New York Times,* 25 June 2017, [1,] 16.
9. Harvey, *Introduction to Buddhism,* 307.
10. Meir Shahar and Robert P. Weller, ed. *Unruly Gods: Divinity and Society in China* (Honolulu: University of Hawai'i Press, 1996).
11. Lee Dian Rainey, *Confucius and Confucianism: The Essentials* (Malden, MA: Wiley-Blackwell, 2010), 60.
12. Kristofer Schipper and Franciscus Verellen, *The Taoist Canon: A Historical Companion to the Daozang,* 3 vols. (University of Chicago Press, 2004), I, 2.

13. Rainey, *Confucius*, 58.
14. Patrick Olivelle, ed., trans. *Early Upaniṣads* (New York: Oxford University Press, 1998), 12–13; Wendy Doniger, *On Hinduism*, provides a chronology of Hinduism's texts (New York: Oxford University Press, 2014), xviii-xx.
15. The six are frequently listed together. *Cūlasāropama Sutta: Sutta 30: The Shorter Discourse on the Simile of the Heartwood; Mahāsaccaka Sutta: Sutta 36, The Greater Discourse to Saccaka; Mahāsakuludāyi Sutta: Sutta 77; The Greater Discourse to Sakuludāyin, The Middle Length Discourses of the Buddha (A New Translation of the Majjhima Nikāya)*, trans. Bhikku Ñāṇamoli and Bhikku Bodhi (Boston: Wisdom, 1995), 291, 343, 630–31.
16. John Breen and Mark Teeuwen, ed., *Shinto in History: Ways of the Kami* (Richmond, VA: Curzon, 2000).
17. Harvey, *Buddhism*, 18, 21.
18. Harvey, *Introduction to Buddhism*, 200.
19. Nicholas Standaert, ed. *Handbook of Christianity in China* (Leiden: Brill, 2001), I, 18.
20. Harvey, *Introduction to Buddhism*, 398–401.
21. John Clifford Holt, *The Buddhist Visnu: Religious Transformation, Politics and Culture* (New York: Columbia University Press, 2004), 14.
22. Rupert Gethin, "Cosmology and Meditation: From the Aggañña-Sutta to the Mahāyāna," *History of Religions* 36:3 (1997): 183.
23. Fukansai Habian in James Baskind and Richard Bowring, eds., *The Myōtei Dialogues: A Japanese Christian Critique of Native Traditions* (Leiden: Brill, 2016), 143.
24. "The Rebirth Eschatology and Its Transformations: A Contribution to the Sociology of Early Buddhism," in *Karma and Rebirth in Classical Indian Traditions*, ed. Wendy Doniger O'Flaherty (Berkeley: University of California Press, 1980), 137–64. Herman W. Tull argues that karma as sacrifice is ethicized in the *Brahmanas* and that its earliest appearance in the *Upaniṣads*, the *Bṛhadāraṇyaka*, retains the sense of rites properly performed: "one becomes good by good action and bad by bad [action]." *The Vedic Origins of Karma: Cosmos as Man in Ancient Indian Myth and Ritual* (Albany, NY: State University of New York Press, 1989), 104–06.
25. *The Rig Veda: An Anthology*, trans. Wendy Doniger O'Flaherty (NY: Penguin: 1981, 2000), 126, 92–95; Doniger, *Hindus*, 132–33; Cf. Henk W. Bodewitz, "Pits, Pitfalls and the Underworld in the Veda," *Indo-Iranian Journal*, 42: 3 (Jul 1999): 218.
26. Bodewitz, "Pits, Pitfalls and the Underworld in the Veda," 218; Rita Langer, *Buddhist Rituals of Death and Rebirth: Contemporary Sri Lankan Practice and its Origin* (New York: Routledge, 2007), 27–34; H. W. Bodewitz, "The Dark and Deep Underworld in the Veda," *JOAS* 122: 2 (Apr.–Jun., 2002): 213–223.
27. Bodewitz, "Dark and Deep," 215.
28. Michael Witzel, "Vedas and Upaniṣads," in *Blackwell Companion to Hinduism*, ed. Gavin Flood (Oxford: Blackwell, 2003), 84. He is more cautious elsewhere, viz., "The Earliest Form of the Idea of Rebirth in India," *Proceedings of the Thirty-First International Congress of Human Sciences in Asia and North Africa, Tokyo-Kyoto 1983*, ed. Tatsuro Yamamoto (Tokyo: Toho Gakkai, 1984), I, 145–46.

29. Patrick Olivelle, trans., *The Early Upaniṣads*, 237.
30. Doniger O'Flaherty, *Rig Veda*, 48, 44, 45n9. Stephanie W. Jamison and Joel P. Brereton see rebirth in a far-off heaven (10.56; 10.135) and caution against the temptation to "read back" in the Vedas (7.104). *The Rigveda: The Earliest Religious Poetry of India*, trans. Stephanie W. Jamison and Joel P. Brereton, 3 vols. (New York: Oxford University Press, 2014), III, 1466, 1620; II, 1016.
31. Gananath Obeyesekere, *Imagining Karma: Ethical Transformation in Amerindian, Buddhist and Greek Rebirth* (Berkeley: University of California Press, 2002), xiii.
32. Thomas J. Hopkins, "Hindu Views of Death and Afterlife," in Hiroshi Obayashi, ed., *Death and Afterlife: Perspectives of World Religions* (London: Praeger, 1992), 147–48.
33. Doniger O'Flaherty, *Rig Veda*, 49.
34. RV 4.4 Patrick Olivelle, "AMṚTĀ: Women and Indian Technologies of Immortality," *Journal of Indian Philosophy* 25:5 (1997): 431; Doniger O'Flaherty, *Rig Veda*, 206, 221.
35. Olivelle, *Early Upaniṣads*, intro. 20–21.
36. Olivelle, *Early Upaniṣads*, 519.
37. Dates for the Upanisads are correlated with dates for the Buddha. Michael Witzel proposes 500 BCE for the early Upanisads as "not impossible." "Tracing the Vedic Dialects," *Dialectes dans les Littératures Indo-aryennes* (Paris: College de France Institut de civilization indienne, 1989), 244–51.
38. Olivelle, *Early Upaniṣads*, 37–39.
39. Doniger, *On Hinduism*, 92; H. W. Bodewitz, "Redeath and its Relation to Rebirth and Release," *Studien zur Indologie und Iranistik* 20 (1996): 27–46.
40. Olivelle, "AMṚTĀ: Women and Indian Technologies of Immortality," 431.
41. Olivelle, *Early Upaniṣads*, 119–25, BU 4.4.1–24. *Brahman* is a term with sliding meanings: "a sacred utterance," the ritual formulas of the Vedas or the Veda, "formulation of truth," source of reality or the absolute, and so sometimes interchangeable with Ātman; Olivelle, 491n3.21.
42. "On this point there is the following verse," 121, otherwise unidentified. It appears in the final song in the *Katha U*, 6.14,403, Olivelle 4. 4.7,519, but the end of *Katha U* is thought to be later than *BU*.
43. Olivelle, *Early Upaniṣads*, BU, 149. CU, 5.3.7, 237.
44. RV 10.88.15, Olivelle, *Early Upaniṣads*, 527 n6.2, 2.
45. Olivelle, *Early Upaniṣads*, 383.
46. Doniger, *On Hinduism*, 45–48; #2 *Sāmañña-Phala Sutta [Fruits of the Life of a Recluse] Dialogues of the Buddha*, part 1 *[Digha Nikaya: Long Discourses of the Buddha]* Part 1, trans. T.W. Rhys David, in *Sacred Books of the Buddhists*, ed. F. Max Müller (1899), (London: Luzac, 1956), II, 73–74. Also "Annihilationists" in #1 *Brahma-Gâla Sutta, Sacred Books of the Buddhists [SBB]*, II, 46–49.
47. John Brockington, "The Concept of 'Dharma' in the *Rāmāyana*," *Journal of Indian Philosophy* 32:5/6 (2004): 660, 665.
48. James L. Fitzgerald, " 'Dharma' and its Translation in the 'Mahābhārata,' " *Journal of Indian Philosophy*, 32:5/6 (2004): 679; Patrick Olivelle, "The Renouncer Tradition," *Blackwell Companion to Hinduism*, ed. Gavin Flood (Oxford: Blackwell, 2003), 277–78; Patrick

Olivelle, *The Āśrama System: The History and Hermeneutics of a Religious Institution* (New York: Oxford University Press, 1993).
49. Vālmīki, *The Rāmāyana of Vālmīki*, trans. Hari Prasad Shastri, vol. 3: *Yuddha Kanda, Uttara Kanda* (London: Shanti Sadan, 1959). *Uttara Kanda*, chap. 21, p.431. Modern translations often cut these concluding books.
50. *Rāmāyana Book Two Ayodhyā by Valmīki*, trans. Sheldon L. Pollock (New York: New York University Press and JJC Foundation, 2005), 100.10–13, p. 551; 100.1, p. 549.
51. K. C. [Kailash Chand] Jain, *History of Jainism*, 3 vols. (New Delhi: D.K. Printworld 2010), I, 156.
52. Doniger, *On Hinduism*, 97. Karma, the soul, and death are among the instructions the dying Bhishma gives Yudhishthira after the battle. *Mahābhārata. Book Twelve. Peace. Volume Three. The Book of Liberation*, trans. Alexander Wynne (New York University Press and JJC Foundation, 2009), Sections 181, 187, pp. 87–89, 119–27.
53. *The Bhagavad Gita*, trans. Eknath Easwaran (Tomales, CA: Nilgiri Press, 2009).
54. Freda Matchett, "The Purāṇas," in Gavin Flood, ed. *Blackwell Companion to Hinduism*, 129–43; Wendy Doniger, ed. *Purāṇa Perennis: Reciprocity and Transformation in Hindu and Jaina Texts* (Albany, NY: State University of New York Press, 1993).
55. Wendy Doniger O'Flaherty, ed. *Textual Sources for the Study of Hinduism* (1988) (Chicago: University of Chicago Press, 1990), 116–23.
56. *Meanings of Death* (Cambridge, England: Cambridge University Press, 1991), 156.
57. "Genshin's Ojo Yoshu: Collected Essays on Birth into Paradise," trans. A. K. Reischauer, *Transactions of the Asiatic Society of Japan*. Second Series, Vol. 7 (1930): 32.
58. N. A. Deshpande, *The Padma-Purāṇa*, parts iii, vi, viii, in *Ancient Indian Mythology*, ed. D. P. Bhatt (Delhi: Motilal Banarsidass, 1991), vol. 41, 1166 (II.67, 95b–103b).
59. Doniger, *On Hinduism*, 98.
60. N. A. Deshpande, *The Padma-Purāṇa*, parts iii, vi, viii, in *Ancient Indian Mythology*, ed. D. P. Bhatt, vols. 44, 46 (Delhi: Motilal Banarsidass, 1991) vol. 44, p. 2117 (V.98.97–103), p.2128 (V. 100. 33–39), p. 2134 (V.102); vol. 46, pp. 2708–2712 (VIII.113–114).
61. Cornelia Dimmitt and J. A. B. van Buitenen, *Classical Hindu Mythology: A Reader in the Sanskrit Purāṇas* (Philadelphia: Temple University Press, 1978), 12.
62. Wendy Doniger, "The Scrapbook of Undeserved Salvation: The *Kedara Khanda* of the *Skanda Purana*," in *On Hinduism*, 237–45.
63. Allan A. Andrews, *The Teachings Essential for Rebirth: A Study of Genshin's Ōjōyōshū* (Tokyo: Sophia University, 1973), 4.
64. E. H. Rick Jarow, *Tales for the Dying: The Death Narrative of the Bhāgavata-Purāṇa* (Albany, NY: State University of New York Press, 2003), 6.
65. Doniger, *On Hinduism*, 239–40.
66. Vauhini Vara, "Bee-Brained: Inside the Competitive Indian-American Spelling Community," *Harper's Magazine*, May 2017, 60.
67. Paul Dundas, *The Jains* (London: Routledge, 1992), 83–86.
68. Jeffrey D. Long, *Jainism: An Introduction* (New York: I.B. Tauris, 2009), 18–19.
69. Dundas, *The Jains*, 88.
70. Dundas, *The Jains*, 155–56, 245n27.

71. Dundas, *The Jains*, 90–91.
72. Dundas, *The Jains*, 81. Cf. *Dialogues of the Buddha: translated from the Pali of the Digha Nikaya*, trans. T. W. and C. A. F. Rhys David, fifth ed. (London: Pali Text Society, 1966), 349.
73. Long, *Jainism*, 122.
74. E. A. Burtt, ed. *The Teachings of the Compassionate Buddha: Early Discourses, the Dhammapada and Later Basic Writings* (New York: New American Library, 1982), 92; Harvey, *Introduction to Buddhism*, 78–80, discusses such passages.
75. Paul Horsch, "From Creation Myth to World Law: The Early History of 'Dharma,' " trans. Jarrod L. Whitaker, *Journal of Indian Philosophy* 32:5/6 (2004): 438.
76. The similarity may be more than coincidence: Hume may have learned something of Buddhism from Jesuits he met in France. Alison Gopnik, "Could David Hume Have Known About Buddhism? Charles François Dolu, the Royal College of La Flèche, and the Global Jesuit Intellectual Network," *Hume Studies* 35.1 & 2 (2009): 5–28; revisited as "David Hume and the Buddha: How My Search for the Eastern Roots of the Western Enlightenment May Have Solved a Philosophical Mystery and Ended My Midlife Crisis," *The Atlantic*, October 2015, 96–110. Buddhism and Hume may see all the "there" that is there. For the view that "consciousness" or "awareness" is a distorted model deriving from the "attention" the brain pays to its own processes, see Michael S. A. Graziano, *Consciousness and the Social Brain* (New York: Oxford University Press, 2013); "Speculations on the Evolution of Awareness," *Journal of Cognitive Neuroscience*, 26:6 (2014): 1300–1304; Daniel C. Dennett, *Consciousness Explained* (New York: Back Bay Books, 1992); and *From Bacteria to Bach and Back: The Evolution of Minds* (W. W. Norton, 2017). The relationship between Dennett's views and Nāgārjuna's is discussed in Jan Westerhoff, *Nāgārjuna's Madhyamaka: A Philosophical Introduction* (Oxford: Oxford University Press, 2014), 208–10; the relationship to Hume, 156–157.
77. Paul Williams, *Mahāyāna Buddhism: The Doctrinal Foundations*, 2nd ed. (New York: Routledge, 2009), 86.
78. Daigan and Alicia Matsunaga, *The Buddhist Concept of Hell* (New York: Philosophical Library, 1971), 49–54.
79. *Udāna* 8:3/80, i.e., chap. 8, sutta 3 and the 80th vol of the PTS edition, quoted in *The Middle Length Discourses of the Buddha (A New Translation of the Majjhima Nikāya)*, trans. Bhikku Ñāṇamolí and Bhikku Bodhi (Boston, MA: Wisdom, 1995), 31. In rebirth of a non-self, the effects of action continue. As one practitioner puts it, one's life packs a suitcase and ships it ahead; someone else picks it up and lives its contents, one's "effects."
80. *Sāmañña-Phala Sutta [Fruits of the Life of a Recluse] Dialogues of the Buddha, part 1, [Digha Nikaya: Long Discourses of the Buddha]*, SBB, II, 73.
81. Rupert Gethin, "Cosmology and Meditation: From the Aggañña-Sutta to the Mahāyāna," *History of Religions* 36:3 (1997): 183–217 argues the interchangeability of cosmological and psychological states in the Pali canon.
82. *Lotus Sutra*, trans. Burton Watson (New York: Columbia University Press, 1993), 98.
83. Ulrich Pagel, "The Sacred Writings of Buddhism," in Harvey, ed. *Buddhism*, 33.
84. Long, *Jainism*, 34.

85. The sutras are collected in five groups or Agamas in Sanskrit: the Digha Nikaya, or long discourses; the Majjhima Nikaya, or medium-length discourses; the Anguttara Nikaya, or additional collection; the Samyutta Nikaya, or miscellaneous collection; the Khuddaka Nikaya, or small collection, which does not exist in Sanskrit, its items having separate names. A.A. G. Bennett, trans. *Long Discourses of the Buddha* (Bombay: Chetana, n.d.), 1, 3.
86. Occasionally excepted from universal salvation was the *icchantika*, "an irredeemable evildoer," and the Avici hell is sometimes referred to as eternal. Barbara Ambros, "Animals in Japanese Buddhism: The Third Path of Existence," *Religion Compass* 8:8 (2014): 255.
87. It has been argued that the Pali canon was open for a period, differing from monastery to monastery, but closed in response to new Mahāyāna texts. Joseph Walser and Sanchez Walsh, *Nāgārjuna in Context: Mahāyāna Buddhism and Early Indian Culture* (New York: Columbia University Press, 2012), 19.
88. Harvey, *An Introduction*, 6–7 map.
89. Paul Williams, *Mahāyāna Buddhism: The Doctrinal Foundations*, 2nd ed. (New York: Routledge, 2009), 5.
90. *Dialogues of the Buddha. [Digha Nikaya: Long Discourses of the Buddha]* Part 2, 5th ed. (1951), trans. T. W. and C. A. F. Rhys Davids, in *SBB* (London: Pali Text Society, 1966), III, 1.
91. "16. Mahâ Parinibbâna Suttanta/ Book of the Great Decrease," *Dialogues of the Buddha. [Digha Nikaya: Long Discourses of the Buddha]* Part 2, 5th ed. (1951), trans. T. W. and C. A. F. Rhys Davids, in SBB, vol. III, 98–99.
92. "16. Mahâ Parinibbâna Suttanta/ Book of the Great Decrease," III, 91.
93. Harvey, *Buddhism*, 96.
94. "16. Mahâ Parinibbâna Suttanta/ Book of the Great Decrease," 91. The five-fold losses of the wrongdoer householder: poverty through sloth, evil repute noised abroad; shy and confused in society he enters, full of anxiety at death, "and lastly, on the dissolution of the body, after death, he is reborn into some unhappy state of suffering or woe." The well-doing householder enjoys wealth through industry, good reports, confidence in company, dies without anxiety, "and lastly, on the dissolution of the body, after death, he is reborn into some happy state in heaven." The passage repeats in "33. Sangīti Suttanta [The Recital]," *Dialogues of the Buddha Part III*, (1921) *SBB*, IV, 226.
95 *Sangīti Suttanta, Dialogues of the Buddha. Part III, SBB*, IV, 240–41.
96. "15. Mahâ-Nidâna-Suttanta [The Great Discourse of Causation]," *Dialogues of the Buddha [Digha Nikaya: Long Discourses of the Buddha]* Part 2. 5th ed. (1951), trans. T. W. and C. A. F. Rhys Davids, in SBB, III, 51.
97. "Mahāsīhanāda Sutta: Sutta 12:35 -42 (The Greater Discourse on the Lion's Roar)," *Middle Length Discourses*, Ñāṇamoli and Bodhi, 169–72.
98. *Middle Length Discourses*, Ñāṇamolí and Bodhi, 791–797.
99. *Middle Length Discourses*, Ñāṇamolí and Bodhi, 1016–17. The same description appears in the "Mahādukkhakkhandha Sutta: Sutta 13:13–14 (The Greater Discourse on the Mass of Suffering)," 13, 13.14, p. 182, where the sufferers are plural "they" rather than "him," the individual fool.

100. "Sutta 129," *Middle Length Discourses*, 1023–27. The treasures of the wheel-turning monarch are listed without description in the "Brahmāyu Sutta: Sutta 91.5," *Middle Length Discourses*, 744.
101. "Devadūta Sutta (The Divine Messengers): Sutta 130," *Middle Length Discourses*, 1031–32.
102. A late compilation, the *Mahāvastu* is described as a Lokottaravāda text (Williams, *Mahāyāna Buddhism* 215, 20) and as a Mahāyāna-influenced text of a pre-Mahāyāna school (Harvey, *Buddhism*, 265).
103. Joseph T. Sorensen, "Poetic Sequence as Personal Salvation: Saigyō's Poems 'Upon Seeing Pictures of Hell,' " *Japanese Language and Literature*, 46:1 (2012): 1–45.
104. Chap. 16, "Life Span," *Lotus Sutra*, trans. Burton Watson, 232.
105. *Lotus Sutra*, ix. Harvey, *Introduction*, dates the translation 286 CE, 110.
106. Jan Westerhoff, *Nāgārjuna's Madhyamaka*, 157.
107. Harvey, *Introduction*, 120, 124–26, 96.
108. Kenneth K. Tanaka, *The Dawn of Chinese Pure Land Buddhist Doctrine: Ching-ying Hui-yüan's Commentary on the Visualization Sutra* (Albany, NY: State University of New York Press, 1990) 7, 10–12, 174–75.
109. Williams, *Mahāyāna Buddhism*, 86.
110. Chap. 3, "Simile and Parable," *Lotus Sutra*, 74.
111. Chap. 5, "Parable of the Medicinal Herbs," *Lotus Sutra*, 99.
112. "Medicinal Herbs," *Lotus Sutra*, 100.
113. "Simile and Parable," *Lotus Sutra*, 56–59.
114. Harvey, *Introduction*, 111.
115. *Nagarjuna: Buddhism's Most Important Philosopher*, trans. Richard H. Jones (New York: Jackson Square, 2010), 13.
116. Wu Hung, *The Art of the Yellow Springs: Understanding Chinese Tombs* (Honolulu, HI: University of Hawai'i Press, 2010), 7; Ying-shih Yü, " 'O Soul, Come Back!' A Study in the Changing Conceptions of the Soul and Afterlife in pre-Buddhist China," *HJAS* 47:2 (1987): 382, places the appearance of the Yellow Springs as a term in common use in the eighth century, the time of duke Zhuang.
117. Michael Loewe, *Faith, Myth and Reason in Han China* (1994, 1982) (Indianapolis, IN: Hackett, 2005), 34.
118. *Cambridge History of Ancient China*, ed. Michael Loewe and Edward L. Shaughnessy (Cambridge, England: Cambridge University Press, 1999), 719. It becomes "the Ninefold Springs" in T'ang Hsien-tsu (1550–1617), "Twenty-two Quatrains on Receiving the Obituary Notice for My Son Shih-ch'ü," *The Shorter Columbia Anthology of Traditional Chinese Literature*, ed. Victor H. Mair (New York: Columbia University Press, 2000), 139–40.
119. K. E. Brashier, *Ancestral Memory in Early China* (Cambridge, MA: Harvard University Press, 2011), 194.
120. David N. Keightley, "The Making of the Ancestors: Late Shang Religion and its Legacy," in *Religion and Chinese Society: Vol. I: Ancient and Medieval China*, ed. John Lagerwey (Hong Kong: Chinese University Press 2004), 7–8, 22, 27–28.
121. Keightley, "Ancestors," 35, 43.

122. Arthur Waley, trans., *The Book of Songs* (New York: Grove, 1960), #140. Cf. James Legge, trans. *The Chinese Classics: Vol. IV The She King* (Hong Kong: Hong Kong University Press, 1955), 357. Book V, Ode x, decade of Seaou Min, x. Sze yueh.
123. Brashier, *Ancestral Memory*, 209.
124. Brashier, *Ancestral Memory*, 215, 228.
125. *The Analects of Confucius*, trans. Burton Watson (New York: Columbia University Press, 2007), 5, 1.
126. Ssu-ma Ch'ien, now Sima Qian (145 or 135–86 BCE), in his *Records of the Historian*, the source on both Laozi and Zhuangzi, told the story of Laozi's being consulted by Confucius and described as a dragon. Wing-tsit Chan, trans., *The Way of Lao Tzu* (New York: Bobbs-Merrill, 1963), gives a clear account of the controversy over Laozi's existence and the dating of his book, 3–4, 35–53, 61–82.
127. Confucius, *Analects*, I.9, p. 17; XI.12, p. 73.
128. Michael Loewe, *Faith, Myth and Reason in Han China*, 27, 35, 110.
129. Fukansai Habian, in James Baskind and Richard Bowring, eds. *The Myōtei Dialogues: A Japanese Christian Critique of Native Traditions* (Leiden: Brill, 2016), 142 and n28.
130. Jie Shi, " 'My Tomb Will Be Opened in Eight Hundred Years': A New Way of Seeing the Afterlife in Six Dynasties China," *HJAS* 72:2 (2012): 219–20.
131. *Li Chi: Book of Rites*, trans. James Legge (1885), ed. Ch'u Chai and Winberg Chai (New Hyde Park, NY: University Books, 1967), II, 220, Book 21, chap. 1, sec. II, par. 1.
132. Ying-shih Yü, "O Soul Come Back," 365.
133. *Li Chi*, II, 221, Book 21, chap. 1, sec. II, par. 3.
134. Wing-tsit Chan, ed., *The Way of Lao Tzu*, 97. *Dao de jing* breaks down to Way (*dao*), Virtue (*de*, or a favor or good deed done some one), Essence (*jing*; or many other possible meanings).
135. Chang Chung-yuan, ed. *Tao: A New Way of Thinking* (New York: Harper and Row, 1975), 137–39.
136. Donald Harper, *Early Chinese Medical Literature: The Mawangdui Medical Manuscripts* (London: Kegan Paul International, 1998), 113–14.
137. Zhuangzi, *Zhuangzi: Basic Writings*, trans. Burton Watson (New York: Columbia University Press, 2003), 141, sec. 26, "External Things."
138. *Zhuangzi*, 115, sec. 18, "Supreme Happiness." Cf. pp. 80–82, sec. 6, "The Great and Venerable Teacher." Other mourning ritual violations concern Laozi and his disciple (47–48), friends singing in the presence of their friend's corpse (82), son for mother (84).
139. *Zhuangzi*, 76, sec. 6, "The Great and Venerable Teacher."
140. *Zhuangzi*, 116–18, sec. 18, "Supreme Happiness." Lieh Tzu addresses another found skull: "Only you and I know that you have never died and you have never lived. Are you really unhappy? Am I really enjoying myself?" 118.
141. Harper, *Chinese Medical Literature*, 399.
142. Donald Harper, "Resurrection in Warring States Popular Religion," *Taoist Resources* 5.2 (1994): 13–16, 20–21.
143. Ying-shih Yü, *Chinese History and Culture: Vol. 1: Sixth Century B.C.E. to Seventeenth Century* (New York: Columbia University Press, 2016), 26–27.

144. *Zhuangzi*, 27–28, sec. 1, "Free and Easy Wandering."
145. Kristofer Schipper and Franciscus Verellen, *The Taoist Canon: A Historical Companion to the* Daozang, 3 vols. (Chicago: University of Chicago Press, 2004), I, 7. Translated as "Taoist Untruths," *Lun-Hêng: Part I: Philosophical Essays of Wang Ch'ung*, trans. Alfred Forke, 2d ed. (New York: Paragon, 1962), I, 336.
146. Section 6, "The Great and Venerable Teacher," *Zhuangzi*, 82.
147. Stephen Little, *Realm of the Immortals: Daoism in the Arts of China* (Cleveland, OH: Cleveland Museum of Art, 1988), 4, *The Shenxian fuer danshi xingyao fa* and *Shangqing ji uzhen zhongjing neijue*, *Taoist Canon*, I, 100, 102.
148. Harper, *Chinese Medical Literature*, 398.
149. Wu Hung, *Art of the Yellow Springs*, 32.
150. Donald Harper, "Resurrection in Warring States Popular Religion," *Taoist Resources* 5:2 (1994): 21; Patricia Eichenbaum Karetzky, "A Scene of the Taoist Afterlife on a Sixth-Century Sarcophagus Discovered in Loyang," *Artibus Asiae*, 44:1 (1983): 11.
151. *Taoist Canon*, I, 57–58; Harper, *Chinese Medical Literature*, 399.
152. Jessica Rawson, "Eternal Palaces," 14.
153. Wu Hung, *The Art of the Yellow Springs*, 47. Cf. David N. Keightley, "Chinese Religions—The State of the Field Part I: Neolithic and Shang Periods," *Journal of Asian Studies* 54:1 (1995): 130.
154. Lothar von Falkenhausen, "Mortuary Behavior in Pre-Imperial Qin: A Religious Interpretation," 121–22, in Lagerwey, ed., *Religion and Chinese Society*.
155. Lothar von Falkenhausen, "Mortuary Behavior in Pre-Imperial Qin," 129.
156. Alain Thote, "Burial Practices as Seen in Rulers' Tombs of the Eastern Zhou Period," in *Religion and Chinese Society*, ed. Lagerwey, 90–91, 95.
157. Wu Hung, *Art of the Yellow Springs*, 33.
158. Thote, "Burial Practices," 96.
159. Wu Hung, *Art of the Yellow Springs*, 35, 55.
160. Wu Hung, *Art of the Yellow Springs*, 33.
161. Ying-shih Yü, *Chinese History and Culture*, I, 86; Anna Seidel, "Traces of Han Religion in Funeral Texts Found in Tombs," in *Dōkyō to shūkyō bunka* (Tokyo: Hirakaw Shuppansha, 1987), 25.
162. Ying-shih Yü, *Chinese History and Culture*, I, 87.
163. Donald Harper, "Resurrection in Warring States," 14; three years not just bureaucratic red tape, 21; Mu-chou Poo, "The Concept of Ghost in Ancient Chinese Religion," 177–78, in *Religion and Chinese Society*, ed. Lagerwey.
164. Rawson, "Eternal Palaces," 18–19.
165. Watson, *Analects*, 1, 2, 5, 6.
166. Jeongsoo Shin, "From Paradise to Garden: The Construction of Penglai and Xuanpu," *Journal of Daoist Studies* 4 (2011): 4.
167. Donald Harper, "Chinese Religions—The State of the Field Part I: Warring States, Ch'in, and Han Periods," *Journal of Asian Studies* 54:1 (1995): 155–56; Rawson, "Eternal Palaces," 19.
168. Jessica Rawson, "Eternal Palaces," 5.
169. Seidel, "Traces," 29.

170. Seidel, "Traces," 29. Translated as "On Reprimands," *Lun-Hêng*, I, 119–29.
171. Yün-Hua Jan, "The Chinese Understanding and Assimilation of Karma Doctrine," in Ronald W. Neufeldt, ed., *Karma & Rebirth: Post Classical Developments* (Albany, NY: State University of New York Press, 1986), 147.
172. *Taoist Canon*, I, 127–29; "Statute of the Dead Souls," attested 485 CE, Seidel, "Traces," 41.
173. *Qi*, or "vital energy," emerges in the cosmology of the fourth century BCE. "Qi permeates the entire cosmos. It is in constant movement and, when differentiated and individuated, all things in the world are formed." Yang-shih Yü, *Chinese History and Culture*, I, 10. Its two types, light and heavy, anticipate the yang and yin to come, and the *hun* and *po* souls in place.
174. Brashier, *Ancestral Memory*, 303.
175. Wu Hung, *Art of the Yellow Springs*, 56. Yün-Hua Jan, "The Chinese Understanding and Assimilation of Karma Doctrine," 145–68.
176. Ying-shih Yü, *Chinese History and Culture*, I, 144.
177. John Lagerwey, ed., *Religion and Chinese Society*, xiii.
178. Overmyer, "Chinese Religions—The State of the Field Part I: Intro.," *Journal of Asian Studies* 54:1 (1995): 127.
179. Patricia Eichenbaum Karetzky, "A Scene of the Taoist Afterlife on a Sixth-Century Sarcophagus Discovered in Loyang," *Artibus Asiae*, 44:1(1983): 6–7, 11.
180. Jonathan Hay, "Seeing Through Dead Eyes: How Early Tang Tombs Staged the Afterlife," *Anthropology and Aesthetics* 57/8 (2010): 36.
181. *Mou Tzu Li-huo*, trans. William Theodore de Bary et al., in *Buddhist Tradition in India, China and Japan* (New York: Vintage, 1969), 134, quoted in Yün-Hua Jan, "The Chinese Understanding and Assimilation of Karma Doctrine," *Karma & Rebirth*, 147.
182. Ying-shih Yü, *Chinese History and Culture*, I, 53n111.
183. E. Zurcher, *The Buddhist Conquest of China. The Spread and Adaptation of Buddhism in Early Medieval China* (Leiden: Brill, 1972), 239, 73; Kenneth K. S. Ch'en, *Buddhism in China: An Historical Survey* (Princeton, NJ: Princeton University Press, 1964), 111–12.
184. Stephen F. Teiser, *The Scripture on the Ten Kings and the Making of Purgatory in Medieval Chinese Buddhism* (Honolulu, HI: University of Hawai'i Press, 1994).
185. Ying-shih Yü, "O Soul, Come Back!" 390.
186. *Taoist Canon*, I, 223, 225, 199, 231.
187. Patrice Fava, "The Body of Laozi and the Course of a Taoist Journey through the Heavens," trans. Vivienne Lo, *Asian Medicine* 4 (2008): 526. *Taoist Canon* I, 544.
188. Ying-shih Yü, *Chinese History and Culture*, I, 41.
189. Jacqueline I. Stone and Mariko Namba Walter., ed. *Death and the Afterlife in Japanese Buddhism* (Honolulu, HI: University of Hawai'i Press, 2008), 6. Harvey, *Introduction*, 162–63, 174–75.
190. Harvey, *Introduction*, 173.
191. Kenneth K. Tanaka, *The Dawn of Chinese Pure Land Buddhist Doctrine: Ching-ying Hui-yüan's Commentary on the Visualization Sutra* (Albany, NY: State University of New York Press, 1990), 11–13 Paul Williams, *Mahāyāna Buddhism: The Doctrinal Foundations*, 2nd ed. (New York: Routledge, 2009), 238–43; Richard K. Payne and Kenneth K. Tanaka,

eds. *Approaching the Land of Bliss: Religious Praxis in the Cult of Amitābha*. Kuroda Institute Studies in East Asian Buddhism (Honolulu, HI: University of Hawai'i Press, 2004).

192. Barbara Ambros, "Animals in Japanese Buddhism: The Third Path of Existence," *Religion Compass* 8:8 (2014): 256.
193. Williams, *Mahāyāna Buddhism*, 240–41, from the *Longer Sukhavativyuha Sutra*.
194. Harvey, *Introduction*, 174.
195. Tanaka, *Dawn of Chinese Pure Land*, 12. Anything Nāgārjuna describes as easy....
196. James C. Dobbins, *Letters of the Nun Eshinni: Images of Pure Land Buddhism in Medieval Japan* (Honolulu, HI: University of Hawai'i Press, 2004), 27.
197. Heng Sure Bhikshu and Martin J. Verhoeven, trans., "The Platform Sutra of the Sixth Patriarch," *Religion East and West* 12 (2014): 19–20.
198. Saying attributed to Bodhidharma, legendary founder of Chan, in an 1108 text, Harvey, *Introduction*, 218.
199. Harvey, *Introduction*, 222.
200. William M. Bodiford, "Zen in the Art of Funerals: Ritual Salvation in Japanese Buddhism," *History of Religions* 32:2 (1992): 161–63.
201. Arthur Waley, *Ballads and Stories from Tun-Huang* (New York: Macmillan, 1960), 165–73, 261.
202. Waley, *Ballads*, 166. Yama does not seem to be accompanied as yet by Ten Kings; the awkward fit between one king of the dead and ten continues into the sixteenth century in Japan, where Haruko Wakabayashi finds the juxtaposition of motifs awkward as late as the Muromachi period (1336–1573). The motif of traveling back and forth between worlds is present in both. "Officials of the Afterworld: Ono no Takamura and the Ten Kings of Hell in the *Chikurinji engi* Illustrated Scrolls," *Japanese Journal of Religious Studies* 36: 2 (2009): 319–49.
203. *Tibetan Book of the Dead*, trans. Gyurme Dorje, Intro., the Dalai Lama (New York: Penguin, 2005), 337.
204. *Tibetan Book of the Dead*, xxxix-xlii; Georgios T. Halkias and Richard K. Payne, ed., *Luminous Bliss: A Religious History of Pure Land Literature in Tibet* (Honolulu, HI: University of Hawai'i Press, 2012), 146.
205. *Tibetan Book of the Dead*, xxxi. The claim is disputed in Bryan J. Cuevas and Jacqueline I. Stone, eds., *The Buddhist Dead: Practices, Discourses, Representations* (Honolulu, HI: University of Hawai'i Press, 2007), 4.
206. *Tibetan Book of the Dead*, 271.
207. *Nihongi: Chronicles of Japan from the Earliest Times to A.D. 697*, trans. W. G. Aston (1896) (London: George Allen & Unwin, 1956), II, Book xix, sec. 35, p. 67; I.i.1, p.1. Helen Hardacre observes that from the late fourth century Korean and Chinese artisans, many of whom were Buddhists, had immigrated to Japan. "State and Religion in Japan," *Nanzan Guide to Japanese Religions*, ed. Paul L. Swanson and Clark 'Chilson (Honolulu, HI: University of Hawai'i Press, 2006), 276.
208. *Tenjukoku*, a term not found in Buddhist scriptures, has been taken by some scholars to be a first Japanese reference to a Pure Land. Michael I. Como, *Shōtoku: Ethnicity, Ritual,*

and *Violence in the Japanese Buddhist Tradition* (Oxford: Oxford University Press, 2008), 34. Given "long life," Daoist influence seems possible, with "land," perhaps a Buddha-field evocation.

209. Jacqueline I. Stone and Mariko Namba Walter, eds., *Death and the Afterlife in Japanese Buddhism* (Honolulu, HI: University of Hawai'i Press, 2008), 3; Nelly Nauman, "Death and Afterlife in Early Japan," in Susanne Formanek and William R. LaFleur, eds., *Practicing the Afterlife: Perspectives from Japan* (Vienna: Der Österreichischen Akademie der Wissenschaften, 2004), 51–62.

210. *Nihongi*, I. 18–26, pp. 24–31. *Kojiki*, trans. Donald L. Philippi (Princeton, NJ: Princeton University Press, 1969), Book I, chap. 9–11, pp. 61–70.

211. *Nihongi*, I.22, p. 28; *Kojiki*, I.13.1–7, pp. 72–73.

212. *Kojiki*, I.10.16 and n.18, p. 66; *Nihongi*, II.xxv.43, p. 233; xix.11, p. 45.Genshin still uses the term, "Genshin's Ojo Yoshu," 60.

213. *Nihongi*, II.xix.47, p. 76.

214. *Nihongi*, II.xxi, p. 106.

215. *Nihongi*, II. xix.33, p. 65. Harvey, *Introduction*, gives the date as 538 CE, 226.

216. *Nihongi*, II, pp. 335, 346, 378, 408, 416—100 copies, 421.

217. *Nihongi*, II.xx, p. 95.

218. Stone, *Death and Afterlife*, 4; Matsumura Kazuo, "Ancient Japan and Religion," trans. Benjamin Dorman, in *Nanzan Guide to Japanese Religions*, 139.

219. *Nihongi*, II.xxiii.15, p. 170; Allan A. Andrews, *The Teachings Essential for Rebirth: A Study of Genshin's Ōjōyōshū* (Tokyo: Sophia University, 1973), 31.

220. Nihongi, II.xix.34–36, pp. 66–67.

221. Nihongi, II.xxix.57, p. 371; xxiv, p. 175. The "Mahāyāna sutra" was specified for rain.

222. "Genshin's Ojo Yoshu," 69.

223. Robert F. Rhodes, *Genshin's Ōjōyōshū and the Construction of Pure Land Discourse in Heian Japan* (Honolulu, HI: U of Hawaii Press, 2017), does not repeat the funeral story.

224. "Genshin's Ojo Yoshu," 27, 25.

225. Andrews, *Teachings Essential for Rebirth*, 41.

226. Andrews, *Teachings Essential for Rebirth*, 40.

227. "Genshin's Ojo Yoshu," 56.

228. "Genshin's Ojo Yoshu," 69. The Nāgārjuna quotations are not sourced by Reischauer or discussed by Andrews or Rhodes.

229. "Genshin's Ojo Yoshu," 62, 76.

230. "Genshin's Ojo Yoshu," 27.

231. Andrews, *Teachings Essential for Rebirth*, 89, 41. Rhodes concludes the text is a forgery, *Genshin's* Ōjōyōshū, 176–78.

232. "Genshin's Ojo Yoshu," 25.

233. Andrews, *Teachings Essential for Rebirth*, 57–58.

234. Jacqueline I. Stone, "The Secret Art of Dying: Esoteric Deathbed Practices in Heian Japan," in *The Buddhist Dead*, ed. Bryan J. Cuevas and Jacqueline I. Stone, 134–35. Isabella Tobiason first drew my attention to the importance of the last-moment thought.

235. "Genshin's Ojo Yoshu," 18.
236. "Genshin's Ojo Yoshu," 38.
237. "Genshin's Ojo Yoshu," 64.
238. "Genshin's Ojo Yoshu," 65–66.
239. "Genshin's Ojo Yoshu," 90.
240. "Genshin's Ojo Yoshu," 90.
241. Andrews, *Teachings Essential for Rebirth*, 74.
242. Harvey, *Introduction*, 233.
243. Andrews, *Teachings Essential for Rebirth*, 40.
244. Boudewijn Walraven, "The Other-worldly Counter-Discourse of *Yŏmbul pogwŏnmun*: An Eighteenth-century Pure Land Text," *Journal of Korean Religions* 6:1 (2015): 159–87.
245. Fujita Kōtatsu, "Pure Land Buddhism in India," trans. Taitetsu Unno, in James Foard, Michael Solomon, and Richard K. Payne, ed. *The Pure Land Tradition: History and Development*, Berkeley Buddhist Studies Series No. 3. (Berkeley, CA: Institute of Buddhist Studies, 1996), 3.
246. James Baskind and Richard Bowring, ed., *The Myōtei Dialogues: A Japanese Christian Critique of Native Traditions* (Leiden: Brill, 2016), 105. Subsequent citations from Habian parenthetically in text.
247. Joseph J. Spae, "The Catholic Church in Japan," https://nirc.nanzan-u.ac.jp/nfile/3065, 4.
248. Akutagawa Ryūnosuke, "Kirishitan Stories by Akutagawa Ryūnosuke," trans. Yoshiko and Andrew Dykstra, *Japanese Religions* 31: 1 (2006): 30–33.
249. Baskind and Bowring, *Myōtei Dialogues*, 10; Baskind, ibid., 28–29.
250. Kiri Paramore, "Early Japanese Christian Thought Reexamined: Confucian Ethics, Catholic Authority, and the Issue of Faith in the Scholastic Theories of Habian, Gomez, and Ricci," *Japanese Journal of Religious Studies*, 35:2 (2008): 231–62.
251. George Elison, *Deus Destroyed* (Cambridge, MA: Harvard University Press, 1973), 280.
252. Westerhoff, *Nāgārjuna's Madhyamaka*, 157.
253. Elison, *Deus Destroyed*, 271, 274–75.
254. *Lun-Hêng*, I, 196.
255. Harvey, *Introduction to Buddhism*, 73.
256. David Hume, "On the Immortality of the Soul," *Essays Moral, Political and Literary*, 603.
257. Sōseki Natsume, *I Am a Cat*, trans. Aiko Ito and Graeme Wilson (Rutland, VT: Tuttle, 2002), 469–70; Elisabetta Porcu, *Pure Land Buddhism in Modern Japanese Culture* (Leiden: Brill, 2008), 112.

4. PURSUING HAPPINESS: HOW THE ENLIGHTENMENT INVENTED AN AFTERLIFE TO WISH FOR

1. Brooks B. Hull and Frederick Bold, "Hell, Religion, and Cultural Change," *Journal of Institutional and Theoretical Economics (JITE)*, 150:3 (1994): 447–64. David Spadafora, "Secularization in British Thought, 1730–1789: Some Landmarks," in W. Warren Wagar, ed., *The Secular Mind: Transformations of Faith in Modern Europe* (New York: Holmes and

Meier, 1982), 35–56; David Spadafora, *The Idea of Progress in Eighteenth-Century Britain* (New Haven, CT: Yale University Press, 1990); Margaret C. Jacob, "Private Beliefs in Public Temples: The New Religiosity of the Eighteenth Century," *Social Research* 59:1 (1992): 59–84; Thomas L. Haskell, "Capitalism and the Origins of the Humanitarian Sensibility, Parts 1 and 2," *American Historical Review* 90:2, 3 (1985), 339–62, 547–57; Charles Wilson, *England's Apprenticeship, 1603–1763* (New York: Longman, 1984); M. J. Daunton, *Progress and Poverty: An Economic and Social History of Britain, 1700–1850* (New York: Oxford University Press, 1995); John Brewer and Roy Porter, ed., *Consumption and the World of Goods* (New York: Routledge, 1993); John Brewer and Susan Staves, eds., *Early Modern Conceptions of Property* (New York: Routledge, 1994); Ann Bermingham and John Brewer, eds., *The Consumption of Culture 1600–1800: Image, Object, Text* (New York: Routledge, 1995); John Brewer, *The Pleasures of Imagination* (New York: Farrar, Straus, and Giroux, 1997); Dror Wahrman, *The Making of the Modern Self* (New Haven, CT: Yale University Press, 2004), 198–217.

2. Raymond Martin and John Barresi, *Naturalization of the Soul: Self and Personal Identity in the Eighteenth Century* (London: Routledge, 2000); Edward J. Andrew, *Conscience and its Critics: Protestant Conscience, Enlightenment Reason, and Modern Subjectivity* (Toronto: University of Toronto Press, 2001).

3. Gregg Camfield, *Sentimental Twain: Samuel Clemens in the Maze of Moral Philosophy* (Philadelphia: University of Pennsylvania Press, 1994), 124. Camfield calls the original "Wakefield" story an "attack on the very concept of heaven," 64, and Twain took forty years from first inspiration in 1868 to publication in 1908, writing against Phelps in 1878–80. Far from attacking the "concept of heaven," however, Twain guts Christian imagery to renovate on deist lines.

4. Samuel Bowden, "An Essay on Health," *Poems on Various Subjects . . .* (Bath, 1754), 343.

5. *Observations Upon the English Language. In a Letter to a Friend* (London, 1752), 23. The sentence recurs often in grammar books, including A. [Anne] Fisher (1719?–1788), *A New Grammar, with Exercises of Bad English; or an Easy Guide to Speaking and Writing the English Language Properly and Correctly*, 3rd ed. (London, 1753), 116–17.

6. *Critical Review*, 64 (July 1787): 75–76; John Taylor, *A Letter to Samuel Johnson on the Subject of a Future State* (London, 1787), 6. Sir John Hawkins also saw fit to "put to rest the idle reports that [Johnson] dreaded annihilation." It was his savior he dreaded meeting. *The Life of Samuel Johnson, LL.D.*, ed. O M Brack Jr. (Athens, GA: University of Georgia Press, 2009), 340n.

7. Roy Porter, *English Society in the Eighteenth Century*, rev. ed. (New York: Penguin, 1990), 280.

8. David Hume, "On the Immortality of the Soul," *Essays Moral, Political, and Literary*, 597.

9. John Asgill, *An argument proving, that according to the Covenant of Eternal Life revealed in the Scriptures, Man may be translated from hence into that Eternal Life, without passing through Death, altho the Humane Nature of CHRIST himself could not be thus translated till he had passed through Death* ([London], 1700). Thomas Cathcart and Daniel Klein overlook these biological-immortality pioneers in theology and political theory, *Heidegger and a Hippo Walk through Those Pearly Gates* (New York: Viking, 2009), 186.

10. *Political Justice* (London, 1793), II, 862. Thomas Holcroft, the author of *Anna St. Ives*, also opposed death: "It is nonsense to say that we must all die; in the present erroneous system I suppose that I shall die, but why? Because I am a fool!" Peter H. Marshall, *William Godwin* (New Haven, CT: Yale University Press, 1984), 88. Godwin's view was much ridiculed, and his skepticism about the afterlife cost him the woman he proposed to the year after Mary Wollstonecraft's death, Marshall, 215, 218, 197–98.
11. Peter Thiel, PayPal's cofounder, promises, "The great unfinished task of the modern world is to turn death from a fact of life into a problem to be solved—a problem towards whose solution I hope to contribute in whatever way I can." Thomas Mallon, "Bookends," *New York Times Book Review*, June 21, 2015, 27. Ray Kurzweil plans to resurrect his father digitally, according to an NPR interview. In "The Singularity," immortality is achieved by uploading a digital version of oneself into machines that have acquired consciousness, Jaron Lanier, "The Spy Who Came in from the Cold 2.0," *Smithsonian*, January 2013, 26; John Gray, *The Immortalization Commission: Science and the Strange Quest to Cheat Death* (New York: Farrar, Straus & Giroux, 2011); Elmo Keep, "Life without End," *Smithsonian*, June 2017, 44–54.
12. John Asgill, *An argument proving, that according to the Covenant of Eternal Life revealed in the Scriptures, Man may be translated from hence into that Eternal Life*, 11.
13. *Mr. Asgill's Defence upon his Expulsion from the House of Commons of Great Britain in 1707. With an Introduction, and a Postscript* (London, 1712), 46, in *A Collection of Tracts Written by John Asgill Esq; From the Year 1700. To the Year 1715. Some relating to Divinity: And others to The History of the Monarchy, The Succession of the Crown, and Constitution of the Government of Great Britain* (London, 1715).
14. John Asgill, *An argument proving*, 3, 4. A lawyer, member of Irish and British parliaments, cofounder of the first land bank, proponent of a land title registry, apologist for the Hanoverian succession, Asgill wrote on poor relief and debt relief. He was active in corporations for employing the poor and the Orphans' Fund, but his Irish land work fell afoul of corruption charges. Richard Greaves, *Oxford DNB*.
15. Ann Thomson, *Bodies of Thought: Science, Religion, and the Soul in the Early Enlightenment* (New York: Oxford University Press, 2008), 144.
16. Henry Grove, *Death abolished by Jesus Christ: A Funeral Sermon for Mr. S[amuel] Mullins, who died at Taunton, in the seventeenth year of his age* (London, 1727). God could have done so, but death continues as a standing lesson and example of the evil of sin, which death extinguishes, 16–17. It serves for trial of Christian faith and grace, 19, and makes the final end more spectacular, "more glorious for the Redeemer," 21.
17. *Essay on Sepulchres: or, A Proposal for Erecting Some Memorial of the Illustrious Dead in All Ages on the Spot where their Remains have been Interred* (London, 1809).
18. In Erasmus's colloquy "The Funeral," the dying man expects to see the heavenly light, to be separated from his wife only in the body and only for a little while, and to rejoin his body at the last judgment. *Ten Colloquies* (New York: Bobbs-Merrill, 1957), 110–11; Jacques LeGoff, *The Birth of Purgatory* (Chicago: University of Chicago Press, 1986).
19. By the mid-second century, 2 Peter addresses the problem of the "delayed parousia" by explaining that "one day is with the Lord as a thousand years, and a thousand years as one

day" (2 Peter 3:8). The dead are described as "asleep" (2 Peter 3:4). Francis Blackburne attributes to Eusebius and Origen the abandonment of the view that the soul died and corrupted with the body, to await the resurrection. *An Historical View of the Controversy concerning an Intermediate State and the Separate Existence of the Soul between Death and the General Resurrection*, 2nd. ed. (London, 1772), 270. Watts, *The World to Come* (London, 1739), 63–65.

20. Francis Blackburne, *An Historical View of the Controversy concerning an Intermediate State*, 272.
21. B. W. Ball, *The Soul Sleepers: Christian Mortalism from Wycliffe to Priestley* (Cambridge, England: James Clarke, 2008); William M. Spellman, "Between Death and Judgment: Conflicting Views of the Afterlife in Late Seventeenth-Century English Eulogies," *Harvard Theological Review* 87:1 (1994): 49–65, especially 59–62 for soul and body.
22. Jeffrey R. Wigelsworth, "Samuel Clarke's Newtonian Soul," *Journal of the History of Ideas* 70:1 (Jan 2009): 48–52; [Defoe], *Serious Reflections during the Life and Surprising Adventures of Robinson Crusoe: with his Vision of the Angelick World. Written by Himself* (London, 1720), 50–51.
23. *Athenian Oracle* (London, 1703–04), 201; *New Athenian Oracle* (London, 1704), 17, 55, 82, 83.
24. Edward Young, *A Poem on the Last Day*, 2nd. ed. (Oxford, 1713), 26–27.
25. Christian apologists regarded denials of immortality as tantamount to declarations of atheism, Isabel St. John Bliss, "Young's *Night Thoughts* in Relation to Contemporary Christian Apologetics," *PMLA* 49:1 (1934): 37–66. It is difficult to find unambiguous denials of belief in an afterlife. David Berman argues that fideist arguments (only the gospel gives immortality) often masked atheism. "Deism, Immortality and the Art of Theological Lying," *Deism, Masonry, and the Enlightenment: Essays Honoring Alfred Owen Aldridge*, ed. Leo J. A. Lemay (Newark, DE: University of Delaware Press, 1987), 61–78. Translators of Seneca's chorus like Rochester certainly flirted with the concept. Among the readers who pushed Creech's translation of Lucretius (1682) to six editions by 1722, there must have been others like Aphra Behn, who found religion's arguments "feeble" and "routed," in her commendatory verses to Creech on his poem (1682), lines bowdlerized when printed ("To Mr Creech [under the name of Daphnis] on his Excellent Translation of Lucretius," stanza 2). Dryden and Lady Chudleigh demonstrate that orthodox believers could find Lucretius thrilling, but so might the unbeliever. Richard Foster Jones argues that the Royal Society's linguistic rules were meant to exclude enthusiastic atomists, and the silence of Edmund Halley on religious issues has long been taken as suggestive. "The Rhetoric of Science in England of the Mid-Seventeenth Century," in *Restoration and Eighteenth-Century Literature: Essays in Honor of Alan Dugald McKillop*, ed. Carroll Camden (Chicago: University of Chicago Press, 1963), 5–24. Certainly, apologetic writers were sure the world was teeming with atheists. Fielding directs an essay in the *Covent Garden Journal* against the demotic Robin Hood Society with its dialect-ridden denials of God. John Leland was not sure whether to believe deists' avowals of a future state: "since at other times they have thrown out suspicions against it, and represented it as a matter of uncertainty; and some of them have used their utmost efforts to invalidate the proofs which are brought for it." *The Advantage and Necessity of the Christian*

Revelation, shewn from the State of Religion in the Antient Heathen World: Especially with respect to the Knowledge and Worship of the One True God: A Rule of Moral Duty: and A State of Future Rewards and Punishments. To which is prefixed, A Preliminary Discourse on Natural and Revealed Religion, 2 vols. (London, 1764), Vol. II, part 3, chap. 1, p.297.

26. *The Tatler*, ed. Donald F. Bond, 3 vols. (Oxford: Clarendon, 1987), # 135. Feb. 18, 1710, II, 279.
27. Charles Blount, *Religio Laici, in a Letter to John Dryden* (London, 1683), 49–50, 95; John Wilmot, Earl of Rochester, *Letters of John Wilmot, Earl of Rochester*, ed. Jeremy Treglown (Chicago: University of Chicago Press, 1980), 234; Zachary Pearce, minister of St.-Martin's-in-the-Fields, reported on Collins, 1729, Jeffrey R. Wigelsworth, *Deism in Enlightenment England* (Manchester: Manchester University Press, 2009), 177.
28. *Works of Benjamin Franklin* (London, 1807), 141. His 1731 memorandum for the party of virtue concluded with belief in the immortality of the soul and God's rewards and punishments "either here or hereafter." *Autobiography of Benjamin Franklin* (Toronto: Ryerson Press, 1965), chap. vii, 90.
29. *Boswell on the Grand Tour—Germany and Switzerland 1764*, ed. Frederick A. Pottle (New York: McGraw-Hill, 1953), 294.
30. *Age of Reason, Life and Major Writings*, ed. Philip S. Foner (New York: Citadel, 1961), 464.
31. Wigelsworth, *Deism in Enlightenment England*, 176, 186. Matthew Tindal, *An Address to the Inhabitants [sic] of the two great cities of London and Westminster: in relation to a pastoral letter, said to be written by the Bishop of London* (London, 1728), 60, 65; *Christianity as Old as Creation* (London, 1730), 125, 417; Gordon Rupp, *Religion in England 1688–1791* (Oxford: Clarendon, 1986), 277.
32. Stephen H. Daniel, *John Toland: His Methods, Manners, and Mind* (Montreal: McGill-Queen's University Press, 1984), 13–14: "His spirit is join'd with its aithereal father/ From whom it originally proceeded, /His body yielding likewise to nature/ Is laid again in the Lap of its Mother. /But he's frequently to rise himself again,/ Yet never to be the same Toland more./ Born ye 30 of Novemb. 1670 [corrected from 1674 by Daniel]/ Dy'd the 11th of March 1722. / If you would know more of him/ Search his Writings." Daniel interprets "rising again" as being read, 62.
33. Ophelia Field, *The Kit-Cat Club: Friends Who Imagined a Nation* (London: Harper, 2008), 341.
34. Henry St. John, Viscount Bolingbroke, *A Letter, Occasion'd by one of Archbishop Tillotson's Sermons, Philosophical Works of the Late Right Honourable Henry St. John, Lord Viscount Bolingbroke*, 5 vols., ed. David Mallett (London, 1754), III, 257-58; *Fragment 42*, V, 322.
35. David Hume frequently used the fideist argument. Joseph Hallett's was answered by Henry Grove, *Some Thoughts Concerning the Proofs of a Future State, from Reason. Occasioned by a Discourse of the Revd. Mr. Joseph Hallett, junr. on the same Subject* (London, 1730).
36. Walter McIntosh Merrill, *From Statesman to Philosopher: A Study in Bolingbroke's Deism* (New York: Philosophical Library, 1949), 113–17, 134; Bolingbroke, *Works*, V, 492, 391–92.
37. [Matthew Turner], *Answer to Dr. Priestley's Letters to a Philosophical Unbeliever. Part I* (London, 1782), xxx. Preface and postscript signed "William Hammon."

38. Joseph Butler, *The Analogy of Religion, Natural and Revealed, to the Constitution and Course of Nature* [1736] (London, 1740), 18.
39. *Man a Machine*, ed. Gertrude Carman Bussey (La Salle, Ill: Open Court, 1012), 147. Joseph Priestley quotes the passage, *Disquisitions relating to Matter and Spirit. To which is added, The History of the Philosophical Doctrine concerning the Origin of the Soul, and the Nature of Matter; with its Influence on Christianity, especially with respect to the Doctrine of the Pre-existence of Christ* (London, 1777), 163.
40. *Lady Oracle* (Toronto: Seal Books, 1976), 106.
41. *Religio Laici*, 1682, l. 71. Francis Blackburne, *An Historical View of the Controversy concerning an Intermediate State*, 193. *A Philosophical and Religious Dialogue in the Shades between Mr. Hume and Dr. Dodd* (London, 1778), 32n.
42. D. P. Walker, *Decline of Hell* (Chicago: University of Chicago Press, 1964), 6, 67, 104, 107, 133; Philip C. Almond, *Heaven and Hell in Enlightenment England* (Cambridge, England: Cambridge University Press, 1994), 116–22, 145.
43. Gilbert Burnet, *A History of His Own Time*, 2 vols. (London, 1724), I, 61.
44. *A Sermon Preach'd before the Queen at White-hall, March 7, 1689/90* (London, 1690), 20, 12-13.
45. Aphra Behn, *Oroonoko, The Rover and Other Works*, ed. Janet Todd (New York: Penguin, 1992), 104.
46. J. V. to John Locke, 26 May 1697, *Electronic Enlightenment*; Victor Nuovo, ed. *John Locke and Christianity: Contemporary Responses to* The Reasonableness of Christianity (Bristol: Thoemmes, 1997).
47. "[W]e have a Sort of People who will acknowledge a God, but he must be such a one as they please to make him; a fine well bred good natur'd Gentleman like Deity, that cannot have the Heart to damn any of his Creatures to an Eternal Punishment, nor could not be so weak as to let the *Jews* crucify his own Son. . . . [T]he Story of our Saviour they look upon as a meer Novel, and the Miracles of the New Testament as a Legend of Priestcraft." *Serious Reflections during the Life and Surprising Adventures of Robinson Crusoe*, 100.
48. The first editions of 1720 and 1723 were printed for private circulation by Dr. Richard Mead; other Latin editions followed in 1726, 1727, 1728, and 1733.
49. *A Treatise concerning the State of the Dead, and of Departed Souls, at the Resurrection. To which is added, An Appendix concerning the future Restoration of the Jews* (London, 1737), I, 376–77, 380. Another, and unattributed, translation.
50. Arguing for God's love as reformative and ultimately restorative were Francis van Helmont, Lady Conway, Henry Hallywell, Archibald Campbell, Thomas Burnet, William Whiston, Almond, *Heaven and Hell*, 153. The *Critical Review* considered the ambiguity of "eternal" relative to Thomas Broughton's "singular" *Prospect of Futurity, in Four Dissertations on the Nature and Circumstances of the Life to Come*, 25 (April 1768): 273.
51. Peter Walmsley, " 'Live to Die, Die to Live': An Introduction," *Eighteenth-Century Fiction* 21:1 (2008): 6; Ralph Houlbrooke, *Death, Religion, and the Family in England, 1480–1750* (Oxford: Clarendon, 1998), 92.
52. Alexander Pope, *Moral Essay IV: Epistle to Burlington*, l. 150; *Moral Essay II: To a Lady*, l. 108, *Poems of Alexander Pope*, ed. John Butt (New Haven, CT: Yale University Press, 1963), 593, 563.

53. Marie Huber, *The World Unmasked*, 1736, in Almond, *Heaven and Hell in Enlightenment England*, 98, 160–61.
54. Catherine Trotter Cockburn, *Philosophical Writings*, ed. Patricia Sheridan (Peterborough, ON: Broadview, 2006), 232.
55. *Adventurer* #107, 13 November 1753, *The Idler and The Adventurer*, ed. W. J. Bate, J. M. Bullitt, L. F. Powell (New Haven, CT: Yale University Press, 1963), 445.
56. Fred Parker, *Scepticism and Literature: An Essay on Pope, Hume, Sterne, and Johnson* (New York: Oxford University Press, 2003), 238–39.
57. *The Dictionary Historical and Critical of Mr. Peter Bayle*, 2nd ed., ed. Mr. [P.] Des Maizeaux, Fellow of the Royal Society, 5 vols. (London, 1734–1738), I, ci.
58. Pierre Cuppé, *Heaven Open to All Men* (London, 1743), xxiv.
59. George Craighead, *The Nature and Place of Hell Discovered: Or, A Fair Conjecture that the SUN is the only Tartarus, or Receptacle of the DAMNED; and that there is both Everlasting Material Fire there to torture the Body, and Inward Sorrow to torment the Soul. In ANSWER to A late, but atheistical Pamphlet, entituled, Heaven open to all Men; or a Treatise solidly proving from Scripture and Reason, that (without unsettling the Practice of Religion) all Men who are, or hereafter will be upon Earth shall be saved, or made finally happy* (Edinburgh, 1748).
60. *Gentleman's Magazine*, 30 (April 1760): 181.
61. David Hartley, *Observations on Man, His Frame, His Duty, and His Expectations*, 2 parts (London, 1749), Preface, I, viii.
62. Alexander Robertson of Struan, *Poems on Various Subjects and Occasions* (Edinburgh, 1752), "Epitaph on John Robertson of Lude, junior," 12; 'A Morning Thought,' 266.
63. Anthony Horneck, *DELIGHT AND JUDGMENT: Or, a Prospect of the Great Day of Judgment, And its Power to damp, and imbitter Sensual Delights, Sports, and Recreations* (London, 1684), 15.
64. Preface to *Sylvae*, 1685, *Works* (Berkeley: University of California Press), III, 11–12.
65. Catherine Trotter Cockburn, *Philosophical Writings*, 203–09; Henry St. John, Viscount Bolingbroke, I, 350; David Hume, "Of a Particular Providence and of a Future State," *Philosophical Essays concerning Human Understanding* (London, 1748), 217.
66. *Theory of Moral Sentiments*, hereafter TMS, III.5.7–9, pp. 166–67.
67. Isabel Rivers, *Reason Grace and Sentiment* II, 260; Smith, TMS, III.5.7, p. 166.
68. "Of a Particular Providence," *Philosophical Essays concerning Human Understanding*, 219.
69. Almond, *Heaven and Hell in Enlightenment England*, 161.
70. *The Adventurer*, #10, ed. John Hawkesworth, 2 vols. (London, 1752–54), I, 59.
71. 19 April 1740, *Contributions to the Champion*, ed. W. B. Coley (Oxford: Clarendon, 2003), 284.
72. In 1783, when hangings were finally concealed, Samuel Johnson complained that the rage of innovation had reached even Tyburn: "The old method was most satisfactory to all parties; the publick was gratified by a procession; the criminal was supported by it. Why is all this to be swept away?" James Boswell, *Life of Samuel Johnson*, ed. David Womersley (New York: Penguin, 2008), 868.
73. Jeremiah Seed, *Discourses on several Important Subjects. To which are added, Eight Sermons Preached at the Lady Moyer's Lecture, in the Cathedral Church of St. Paul,*

London, 2 vols. (London, 1743), Sermon IV. "The Nature and Duration of future Punishments considered; and the Goodness of God fully vindicated; as to that Article against the principal Objections of some late Writers," II, 108, 97. Seed quantifies the argument Robert Sharrock had made about proportion in 1673. For Sharrock, see Almond, *Heaven and Hell in Enlightenment England*, 31.

74. John Leland (1691–1766), *The Advantage and Necessity of the Christian Revelation*, II, 460. Editions also in 1768, 1776, 1818. Priestley used Leland's 1768 edition as one of his authorities in *Disquisitions relating to Matter and Spirit. To which is added, the History of the Philosophical Doctrine concerning the Origin of the Soul, and the Nature of Matter; with its Influence on Christianity, especially with Respect to the Doctrine of the Pre-existence of Christ* (London, 1777).

75. Pierre Cuppé's translator, *Heaven Open to All Men*, xxiv.

76. Bernhard Lang charts Wesley's reading of Swedenborg, who presented him with a copy of *Vera Christiana Religio*. Initially sympathetic, Wesley became profoundly hostile. They never met. *Meeting in Heaven: Modernizing the Christian Afterlife 1600–2000* (New York: Peter Lang, 2011), 133–37.

77. Martin Folkes, president of the Royal Society, had Swedenborg's *De Cultu et Amore Dei*, *A Catalogue of the Entire and Valuable Library of Martin Folkes, Esq. President of the Royal Society and Member of the Royal Academy of Sciences at Paris, Lately Deceased* (London, 1756), 13; the same title appears in Thomas Payne's *Catalogue of A large Collection of the best Books*, 1761. The *Philosophical Transactions, giving some Account of the Present Undertakings, Studies, and Labours of the Ingenious, in many Considerable Parts of the World*, vol. 59, 1769 (London, 1770), reported three books in the "Presents made to the Royal Society in the year 1769, with the names of the donors": Mr. Em. Swedenborg gave *Delitiae Sapientiea; De Unione Mentis & Corporis; Doctrine of the new Church*, xviii. Antoine Grimoald Monnet, *Nouvelle Hydrologie* (Londres, 1772), 210, cites him on Swedish water. James Robson, *A Catalogue of a very Large and Capital Collection of Books* (London, 1772), offering three clerical libraries, included *Doctrine of the New Church*, 1769, 105. *Bibliotheca Westiana: A Catalogue of the Curious and truly Valuable Library of the late James West, President of the Royal Society* (London, 1773), #1598, Swedenborg, *Vera Christiana Religio*, 100; *A Catalogue . . . the late Mr Hall of Magdalen College, Oxford* (London, 1773), *Delitiae sapiente de amore conjugali*, #2237, 64. *A Catalogue . . . Rev Dr William Borlase* (1773) contained *Theosophic Lucubrations on the Nature of Influx*, 1770; Anton Friedrich Bushing, *An Introduction to the Study of Geography* (London, 1778) cites him on mines, p. 69. William Bent's *Catalogue* (1779) had *Heaven and Hell*.

78. *A Treatise Concerning Heaven and Hell Containing A Relation of many Wonderful Things Therein, as heard and seen by the Author, the Honourable Emanuel Swedenborg, Of the Senatorial Order of Nobles in the Kingdom of Sweden*. Now First Translated from the ORIGINAL LATIN (London, Bristol, Exeter, 1778), 198–99.

79. Colleen McDannell and Bernhard Lang, *Heaven: A History* (1988) 2nd. ed. (New Haven, CT: Yale University Press, 2001), 234, 181–227, 269, 282, 302, 323–24. Bernhard Lang, *Meeting in Heaven*, 79–142.

80. Peter Walmsley, "Whigs in Heaven: Elizabeth Rowe's 'Friendship in Death,'" *Eighteenth-Century Studies* 44:3 (2011): 320; Addison, *Spectator #447*, 2 Aug. 1712, *The Spectator*, ed. Donald F. Bond, 5 vols. (Oxford: Clarendon, 1965), IV, 72; Philip Doddridge, *Practical Discourses on Regeneration, in Ten Sermons Preached at Northampton.* "Sermon V. Of the Incapacity of an Unregenerate Person for relishing the Enjoyments of the Heavenly World." Running title: "To endure the Presence of God" (London, 1742), 137–68; Laurence Sterne, "Our Conversation in Heaven," *The Sermons of Laurence Sterne*, ed. Melvyn New (Gainesville, FL: University Press of Florida, 1996), IV, 278–79; V, 315–16.

81. *Fanatical Conversion; Or, Methodism Displayed. A Satire. Illustrated and versified by Notes from J. Wesley's Fanatical Journals . . . unraveling the delusive Craft of that well-invented System of pious Sorcery which turns Lions into Lambs, called, in Derision, METHODISM.* (London 1779); John Clowes, *A Letter of Exhortation and Admonition to all who receive the Testimony of Emanuel Swedenborg* (London, 1783); *Brief Remarks on a late Pamphlet entitled "A Letter of Exhortation and Admonition to all who receive the Testimony of Emanuel Swedenborg"* (Manchester, 1783); A Simple Layman, *A Seasonable Address to those Who receive the Testimony of Emanuel Swedenborg* (London, 1783); Thomas Arnold, M.D., *Observations on the Nature, Kinds, Causes, and Prevention of Insanity, Lunacy, or Madness*, 2 vols. (Leicester, London, 1782), I, 294; Albert M. Lyles, *Methodism Mocked: The Satiric Reaction to Methodism in the Eighteenth Century* (London: Epworth Press, 1960); Misty Anderson, *Imagining Methodism in Eighteenth-Century Britain: Enthusiasm, Belief, and the Borders of the Self* (Baltimore, MD: Johns Hopkins University Press, 2012).

82. John Wesley, *An Extract from the Rev. Mr. John Wesley's Journal, from Jan. 1, 1776 to Aug. 8, 1779* (London 1783), 18, 107.

83. Hannah More, *Works*, 11 vols. (London, 1830), V, 407–08; *An Estimate of the Religion of the Fashionable World. By one of the laity* (London, 1791), 38. As if emerging from one of the sermons Pope describes, she insists, "The locality of Hell, and the existence of an Evil Spirit, are annihilated, or considered as abstract ideas. They are never named without some periphrasis or circumlocution; as if the very names, instead of being awful and terrible, were only vulgar and illiberal," *Estimate*, 34. Bernhard Lang notes that in Stoneham, Massachusetts's, cemetery the traditional tombstone ornament, a winged skull, was replaced between 1760 and 1780, by a winged head, intimating salvation. By 1790 there were no skulls at all. *Meeting in Heaven*, 149–50. When the evangelicals succeeded in restoring hell, the results could be dire. William Cowper's "The Castaway" (1799) finds a believer drowning in gulfs of despair. Satirists claimed that Methodism made its adherents suicidal over failed conversion experiences. The debate over hell continues in Joel Buenting, ed., *The Problem of Hell: A Philosophical Anthology* (Burlington, VT: Ashgate, 2010). James Cain explains "Why I Am Unconvinced by Arguments against the Existence of Hell," 133–44; those around him take its nonexistence as a given.

84. Alexander Pope, "Dying Christian to His Soul," *Poems*, 116–17; John Harvey, *A Collection of Miscellany Poems and Letters, Comical and Serious* (Edinburgh, 1726), "To the Memory of the Illustrious Princess, Anne Dutchess of Hamilton, Who died at her Apartments in

the Palace of Holy-rood-house, August 1724," "To the Memory of the Right Hon William late Earl of Kintore," "To the Memory of the Right Honourable, the late Lady Blantyrea: A Pastoral"; [Elizabeth Thomas], *Poems on Several Occasions. By a Lady* (London, 1726), "To the Pious Memory of Mrs Diana Bridgman, An Ode," "On the Death of the Right Honourable Anne, Lady Dowager de la War"; Peleg Morris, *Leisure Hours well employ'd: Being a Collection of Hymns and Spiritual Poems* (London, 1740), "Hymn XIII: A View of Heaven."

85. Kevin Barry, "Learned Blindness: Irish Counter-Enlightenment," in *The Enlightenment by Night: Essays on After-Dark Culture in the Long Eighteenth Century*, ed. Serge Soupel, Kevin Cope, and Alexander Pettit (New York: AMS Press, 2010), 291–305.
86. "Hymn XI: The Best Choice," Peleg Morris, *Leisure hours well employ'd*, 17–18. Morris's epigraph is from George Herbert, a pleasant reminder that someone still read him, "A verse may find him, that a Sermon flies . . ."
87. Thomas Emlyn, *Funeral Consolations: Or a Plain Discourse from John 14. Ver. 28. Being the First Sermon he Preach'd after the Death of his Wife Mrs. Esther Emlyn: who Died Octob. 13.1701* (Dublin, 1703), 24.
88. D. P. Walker, *The Decline of Hell*, 158–59. William Whiston challenged Burnet's theory with his own. In 1696, he dedicated to Newton his view that after the fall a comet hit the earth and altered paradise by affecting the axis. Identified with Halley's comet, it also caused Noah's flood and is the site for the second death of Revelation. *Astronomical Principles of Religion, Natural and Reveal'd* (London, 1717), 75, 147–48, 152, 155–56.
89. Thomas Burnet, *A Treatise Concerning the State of the Dead, and of Departed Souls, at the Resurrection. To which is added, an Appendix concerning the future Restoration of the Jews* (London, 1737), 352–53, 376–77, 380.
90. Matania Z. Kochani, "One Prophet Interprets Another: Sir Isaac Newton and Daniel," in James E. Force and Richard H. Popkin, eds. *The Books of Nature and Scripture: Recent Essays on Natural Philosophy, Theology, and Biblical Criticism in the Netherlands of Spinoza's Time and the British Isles of Newton's Time* (Dordrecht, The Netherlands: Kluwer, 1994), 105–22.
91. Isaac Watts, *The World to Come: Or, Discourses on the Joys or Sorrows of Departed Souls at Death, and the Glory or Terror of the Resurrection. Whereto is Prefix'd, An Essay toward the Proof of a Separate State of Souls after Death* (London, 1739), 12–13.
92. Kochani, "One Prophet Interprets Another: Sir Isaac Newton and Daniel," 116–19.
93. Robert Hooke, Preface, *Micrographia* (1665) (NY: Dover, 1961), n.p.
94. Jacob Sider Jost, "The Afterlife and *The Spectator*," *SEL* 51:3 (2011): 609–13. See also Jost, *Prose Immortality, 1711–1819* (Charlottesville, VA: University of Virginia Press, 2015).
95. Joseph Addison, *Spectator* #111, July 7, 1711, I, 458–59.
96. Porteus, Bishop of Chester, *Sermons on Several Subjects* (London, 1783), 125–26.
97. *English Review*, 21 (1793): 255.
98. London, 1730. Addison was long dead, but Jacob Tonson the bookseller attached his name and credit to the compilation of *Spectators*.
99. Charles Bonnet (1720–93), *Conjectures concerning the Nature of Future Happiness. Translated from the French of Mons. Bonnet of Geneva* (York, London, 1785), 25.

100. *Spectator* # 635, Dec. 20, 1714, V, 171–72.
101. *Spectator* #635, V, 173.
102. Mary [Lee], Lady Chudleigh, *Essays upon Several Subjects In Prose and Verse* (London, 1710), 44.
103. *Discourses on the Four Last Things, viz. I. Death, II. Judgment, III. Heaven and IV. Hell. And on some Other Subjects Relating thereunto* (Dublin, 1724), 457–59, 472–3, 475.
104. Butler, *The Analogy of Religion, Natural and Revealed, to the Constitution and Course of Nature*, 91.
105. Joseph Priestly, *Letters to a Philosophical Unbeliever. Part. I. Containing An Examination of the principal Objections to the Doctrines of Natural Religion, and especially those contained in the Writings of Mr. Hume*. 2nd. ed. (Birmingham, 1787), 115. Letter VIII "Of the Evidence for the future Existence of Man."
106. Bonnet, *Conjectures*, 11.
107. [William Kenrick], *Epistles Philosophical and Moral* (London, 1759), 334, l.488.
108. *Spectator*, # 111, I, 457.
109. *The Female Spectator*, 4 vols. (London, 1745–46), II, 267–69.
110. *Elements of Criticism*, 3 vols. (Edinburgh, 1762), II, 38.
111. *Gentleman's Magazine* (1800): 1158.
112. *Spectator*, #111, I, 457.
113. Benjamin Martin, *Bibliotheca Technologica: Or, a Philological Library of Literary Arts and Sciences* (London, 1737), 11.
114. David Hartley, *Observations on Man*, II, 385.
115. [Kenrick], *Epistles Philosophical and Moral*, 301–02.
116. Catherine Macaulay Graham, *Letters on Education. With Observations on Religious and Metaphysical Subjects* (Dublin, 1790), 238, 240.
117. *The British Apollo: Containing about Two Thousand Answers to curious Questions in most Arts and Sciences*. 4th. ed. (London, 1740), III, 779–780.
118. *Adventurer*, #120, 2 December 1753, 469–70.
119. Aaron Hill, *Free Thoughts upon Faith: Or the Religion of Nature. A poem, with notes (1746)* ([Liverpool], 1758), 88.
120. [William Kenrick], *Poems Ludicrous, Satirical and Moral* (London, 1768), 151, 161.
121. *Boswell on the Grand Tour—Germany and Switzerland 1764*, 303.
122. [Matthew Turner], *Answer to Dr. Priestley's Letters to a Philosophical Unbeliever. Part I* (London, 1782), 14.
123. Shelley, *Poetical Works*, ed. Thomas Hutchinson (New York: Oxford University Press, 1968), 478–79.
124. *Mr. Asgill's Defence upon his Expulsion*, 46.
125. John Boys, trans. *Aeneid Book VI* (London, 1661), 129, 132. [Sir Robert Howard, attrib.] *History of Religion* (London, 1694), v.
126. Timothy Manlove, d. 1699, *The Immortality of the Soul Asserted, and Practically improved [sic]: Shewing by Scripture, Reason, and the Testimony of the Ancient Philosophers, That the Soul of Man is capable of subsisting and acting in a State of Separation from the Body,*

And how much it concerns us all to prepare for that State (London, 1697), 76; John Leland, *Advantage and Necessity of the Christian Revelation*, I, 452.
127. McDannell and Lang, *Heaven*, 274.
128. W. H. C. Frend, "Edward Gibbon (1737–1794) and Early Christianity," *Journal of Ecclesiastical History* 45 (1994): 662.
129. Tickell, #634, 17 Dec. 1714, *Spectator*, V, 169, modifies #574, 30 July 1714, IV, 565.
130. *Spectator* #166, II, 154.
131. Daniel W. Odell, "Young's *Night Thoughts* as an Answer to Pope's *Essay on Man*," SEL 12:3 (1972): 481–51.
132. Beilby Porteus, Bishop of Chester, *Sermons on Several Subjects*, 134–35.
133. Hugh Blair, *Sermons* (London, 1780), II, 265.
134. *Tatler*, #152, March 10, 1710, II, 356; #156, April 8, 1710, II, 373–78.
135. *Tatler* #15, May 14, 1709, I, 124–32. The child's welcome is contrasted with that of a duelist, a second, entering by the door of the murdered. Socrates draws near him to instruct in the error of his ways. #26, June 9, 1709, I, 203–04.
136. [Richard and Elizabeth Griffith], *A Series of Genuine Letters between Henry and Frances*. 2 vols. (London, 1757), I, 208.
137. William Sherlock, *A Practical Discourse Concerning a Future Judgment*, 10th. ed. (1731), 191.
138. Oct. 27, 1727, Irvin Ehrenpreis, *Swift: The Man, His Works, and the Age* (Cambridge, MA: Harvard University Press, 1983), III, 549.
139. Jonathan Pritchard, "Elizabeth Singer Rowe," *Oxford DNB*; Almond counts fourteen editions between 1733 and 1816, *Heaven and Hell*, 104.
140. Theophilus Rowe, "Life of Mrs. Elizabeth Rowe, *Miscellaneous Works in Prose and Verse of Mrs. Elizabeth Rowe*, xlvi. "See *Bib. Brit.* Tom. Xiii, p. 39."
141. Rowe's devotional writings outstripped Friendship in Death (*FID*) in the early nineteenth century and continued to amass reprints through the 1850s. Paula R. Backscheider, *Elizabeth Singer Rowe and the Development of the English Novel* (Baltimore, MD: Johns Hopkins University Press, 2013), 1–2.
142. Benjamin Boyce, "News from Hell: Satiric Communication with the Nether World in English Writing of the Seventeenth and Eighteenth Centuries," *PMLA* 58:2 (1943): 402–437; Frederick M. Keener, *English Dialogues of the Dead: A Critical History, an Anthology, and a Check List* (New York: Columbia University Press, 1973); Paula R. Backscheider and John J. Richetti, *Popular Fiction by Women 1660–1730: An Anthology* (Oxford: Clarendon, 1996).
143. Peter Walmsley, "Whigs in Heaven," 325.
144. Twain adopts progress-in-knowledge for infants, at a period when mothers assume they will reclaim their infants as infants in heaven. Twain's mother thus incurs a second loss in heaven. He also allows the young to flirt in heaven, like the brother with the lute, but there is no whisper of consummated sexual desire in his American heaven. Twain's missing child is a girl, who excels in knowledge while her mother knows only cranberries. Rowe's child is a boy, a countess's heir, so property feels loss in the eighteenth century, but not the American nineteenth century.

145. "On the Death of my dear Daughter Eliza Maria Chudleigh. A Dialogue between Lucinda and Marissa," *Poems on Several Occasions* (London, 1703), 11, 97.
146. *Poem on the Last Day*, 2nd. ed. (Oxford, 1713), Dedication, n.p. The Rev. J. Mitford observes that the dedication to the queen was cut from Young's subsequent reprinting of the poem. *Poetical Works of Edward Young, with a Memoir* (Boston: Houghton Mifflin, [1854]), "Life of Young," xi, xiii.
147. *Poem on the Last Day*, 2nd. ed. (Oxford, 1713), 56–57.
148. "To a lady on the death of her son," *Gentleman's Magazine*, 6 (1736): 546.
149. "A poem sacred to the memory of a dearly beloved and only daughter, who died in the eleventh year of her age. Written by her mourning father," in *A Collection of Poems on Divine and Moral Subjects, selected from various authors*, ed. William Giles (London, 1775), 82–88, 223.
150. James Boswell, *Boswell in Extremes 1776-1778*, ed. Charles McC. Weis and Frederick A. Pottle (New York: McGraw Hill, 1970), 114.
151. Walmsley, "Whigs in Heaven," 321.
152. Rowe, *FID*, 123–24.
153. *FID*, 117–18.
154. Edward Young, *The Complaint: Or, Night Thoughts on Life, Death, and Immortality*, 8th. ed. (London, 1749), 69.
155. *Diaries, Prayers and Annals*, anno 1752, James Boswell, *Life of Samuel Johnson*, 129–30.
156. Rowe, *Miscellaneous Works*, I, xlviii, xliv.
157. E. Derek Taylor, "Samuel Richardson's *Clarissa* and the Problem of Heaven," in *Theology and Literature in the Age of Johnson*, ed. Melvyn New and Gerard Reedy, S. J. (Newark, DE: University of Delaware Press, 2012), 134–67; Paula R. Backscheider, *Elizabeth Singer Rowe and the Development of the English Novel*, 67.
158. Eliza Haywood, *History of Jemmy and Jenny Jessamy*, ed. John Richetti (Lexington, KY: The University Press of Kentucky, 2005), 156.
159. *Idler* #41, 27 January 1759, *Idler and Adventurer*, ed. W. J. Bate, John M. Bullitt, L. F. Powell (New Haven, CT: Yale University Press, 1963), 130.
160. Samuel Johnson, *Rasselas*, chap. 37.
161. Boswell, *Life of Johnson*, 28 March 1772, 346–47.
162. [Richard and Elizabeth Griffith], *A Series of Genuine Letters between Henry and Frances*, 2 vols. (London, 1757), I, 208, letter cxiii. The quotation reworks Altamont's speech, "[My soul] kindles not with Anger or Revenge;/Love was th'informing, active Fire within,/ Now that is quench'd, the Mass forgets to move,/ And longs to mingle with its kindred Earth." Nicholas Rowe, *The Fair Penitent*, (1703), ed. Malcolm Goldstein (Lincoln: University of Nebraska Press, 1969), 55, Act 4, scene 1, ll.273–76.
163. "Of the Happiness of a Heavenly Conversation," *The Works of the Most Reverend Dr. John Tillotson*, 12 vols. (London, 1743), I, 202; Walmsley, "Whigs in Heaven," 324 and 329n47.
164. William Dodd, ed. *The Visitor*, 2 vols. (London, 1764), Advert, I, A3; II, No. 45, 21–27.
165. Richard Price (1723–91), *Four Dissertations* (London, 1767), editions with additions, 1768, 1772, 1777; William Morgan, *Memoirs of the Life of the Rev. Richard Price* (London 1815), 31.

166. Without actually lying, Johnson was avoiding acknowledging his authorship of Dodd's pleas for his life.
167. William Dodd, *Reflections upon Death*, 105.
168. Dodd, *Mutual Knowledge in a future State; Offered as an Argument of Consolation* (London, 1766), 6–7.
169. David's dying child is the one conceived in adultery with Bathsheba, wife of Uriah the Hittite, whom David ordered murdered. This text indexes the change. Sometime before his death in 1755, Joseph Williams had applied it cautiously to his wife in her death. He says nothing of meeting again, but does cite 2 Samuel, "Lord, hasten the time when *I shall go to her*, since *she shall not return to me!*" Joseph Williams, *Extracts from the Diary, Meditations and Letters of Mr. Joseph Williams of Kidderminster, who died Dec. 21, 1755, aged 63* (Shrewsbury, 1779), 243. By 1782, caution has gone, and confidence reigns: Robert Carter Thelwall closes "all this long disgressive rhapsody on grief with this most consolatory of all reflexions: That though she shall not return to me, I shall go to her." *A Sketch from the Dead; Or, A Monody to the Memory of Mrs. Carter Thelwall* (London, 1782), 24.
170. Dodd, *Mutual Knowledge in a future State*, 4, 6–7, 13–14.
171. Bernhard Lang, "Meeting in Heaven in John Bunyan's *Pilgrim's Progress*," *Tod und Jenseits in der Schriftkultur der Frühen Neuzeit* (Wiesbaden: Harrassowitz in Kommission, 2008), 130. Rptd. *Meeting in Heaven*, 52.
172. Dror Wahrman, *The Making of the Modern Self: Identity and Culture in Eighteenth-Century England* (New Haven, CT: Yale University Press, 2004), 272–78; Philippe Rochat, *Others in Mind: Social Origins of Self-consciousness* (New York: Cambridge University Press), 2009.
173. *TMS*, III.i.3–6, pp. 110–13.
174. *Reflections on the Revolution in France, Writings and Speeches of Edmund Burke, Vol. VIII*, ed. L. G. Mitchell (Oxford: Clarendon, 1989), 61. Price was irate about Burke's accusation. When his sermon was reprinted, he insisted that he had referred not to the October days but to the earlier trip to Paris by the king. "Preface," *Discourse on the Love of Our Country*. He did not consider a possible relationship between the two episodes.
175. *Four Dissertations. III. On the Reasons for expecting that virtuous Men shall meet after Death in a State of Happiness* (London, 1767), 344.
176. Dodd, *Reflections on Death*, 184.
177. *Critical Review*, 23 (March 1767): 238.
178. June 1777, James Boswell, *Life of Johnson*, 602.
179. B. W. Young, "Jortin," *Oxford DNB*.
180. John Jortin, *Sermons on Different Subjects*, 7 vols. (London, 1771), III, 259–64.
181. Jortin, *Sermons*, III, 258.
182. Catherine Talbot, *Essays on various Subjects*, 2nd. ed. (London, 1772), Essay ix, 80–81.
183. William James Mickle (1734–88), *Voltaire in the Shades* (London, 1770), v.
184. Clementina, *Letters Religious and Moral* (London, 1786), 37; G. Wright, ed. *Pleasing Reflections on Life and Manners with Essays, Characters, & Poems, Moral & Entertaining; Principally selected from Fugitive Publications*, 2nd. ed. (London, 1788), 55–56.

185. Hugh Blair, *Sermons*, 3 vols. (London, 1790), "Sermon V: On Death," III, 100–01.
186. Soul reunites with body, not friend with friend, in such works as Thomas Broughton, *A Prospect of Futurity, in Four Dissertations on the Nature and Circumstances of the Life To Come* (London, 1768), viii, 428; Samuel Chandler, *Sermons* (London, 1759–69), 238; Patrick Delany, *Sixteen Discourses upon Doctrines and Duties* (London, 1754), 187; Caleb Fleming, *Of the Search After Soul* (London, 1758), 280; John Dupre, *Sermons on Various Subjects* (London, 1783), 187.

In William Blake's illustrations of 1808 for Robert Blair's *The Grave* (1743), the amorous soul descends into a passionate embrace of its body, as a family meets in heaven. In Blair, the image is horizontal—searching on a level, while Blake swoops on the vertical:

Nor shall the conscious *Soul*
Mistake its Partner; but amidst the Croud
Singling its other Half, into its Arms
Shall rush, with all th'Impatience of a Man
That's new-come Home; who, having long been absent,
With Haste runs over ev'ry different Room,
In Pain to see the whole. Thrice happy Meeting!
Nor *Time*, nor *Death*, shall ever part them more.

(ll. 754–61)

187. James Boswell, *Life of Johnson*, 571, 637.
188. Richard B. Sher, "Hugh Blair," *Oxford Dictionary of National Biography*.
189. Blair, "Sermon XV: On the Sacrament of the Lord's Supper, as a Preparation for Death," III, 322, 324–25.
190. Sher, *Oxford DNB*, quoting T. Somerville, *My Own Llife and Times, 1741–1814*, ed. W. Lee (1861), 167.
191. Polwhele, *Discourses on Different Subjects*, 2 vols. (London, 1791), Discourse X, I, 183–84.
192. In Keener's checklist, most titles mention Styx, Charon, or Shades, except some examples from 1642, 1658, and 1659. Frederick M. Keener, *English Dialogues of the Dead: A Critical History, an Anthology, and a Check List*, 279–92.
193. Regina Janes, "Henry Fielding Reinvents the Afterlife," *Eighteenth-Century Fiction* 23:3 (2011): 495–518.
194. Quevedo, Jr., *A Particular Account of Cardinal Fleury's Journey to the Other World*, quoted in Boyce, "News from Hell," 424.
195. Sterne makes no appearance in McDannell and Lang's *Heaven: A History*.
196. Improbable as this claim seems, ECCO and EEBO searches fail to retrieve the phrase before Sterne. After Sterne, it appears in "On Beneficence: A Poetical Essay" (1764), Edward Burnaby Greene, *Critical Essays* (1770), 294, and Byron's *The Vision of Judgement* (1822), 3.4. Kushner uses the phrase in the first speech in Act III, Scene 7. Sterne's invention is confirmed by the OED, which, after Sterne cites Bellamy's *Family Preacher*, 1776, and observes that Sterne's coinage is later treated as an "actual theological concept."

197. Jane Timbury, *The Story of Le Fevre, from the works of Mr. Sterne* (London, 1787), 23–4: "The accusing spirit, here reluctant soar'd /To Heaven's bright chanc'ry with the offending word:/ But doubting, if to deem the oath a sin,/ Blush'd as he gave the accusation in; / While that angelic being, who's assign'd /T'record the various actions of mankind, /Scarce let the sentence from his pen appear,/ Blotting it out forever with a tear." "On Beneficence: A Poetical Essay" (1764) also retells LeFevre's story.

198. Christians, and Jews, and Turks, and Pagans stand,
    A blended Throng, One Undistinguish'd Band,
    Some who perhaps by mutual Wounds expir'd
    With Zeal for their distinct Persuasions fir'd,
    In mutual Friendship their long Slumber break,
    And Hand in Hand their Saviour's Love partake. (30)

199. *Life of Johnson*, 17 April 1778, 692.
200. As "Edward Search," Abraham Tucker's Lockean afterlife solved such problems as sensory data without organs through special thin vehicles, perhaps referred to by Flann O'Brien in *The Third Policeman*. Pope supplied his epigraph: "The proper study of mankind is man." *The Light of Nature Pursued* (London, 1768), 5 vols.
201. "The Devil and Dr. Hornbook," stanza 2, *The Poems and Songs of Robert Burns*, ed. James Kinsley, 3 vols. (Oxford: Clarendon, 1968), I, 79.
202. "Epitaph on James Grieve, Laird of Boghead, Tarbolton," "Epitaph on my own Friend and my Father's Friend, Wm. Muir in Tarbolton Mill," *Poems and Songs*, I, 39, 47.
203. "Recollections of Ramsay of Ochtertyre," *Poems and Songs*, III, 1540.
204. *TMS* V.2.9, pp. 206–07.
205. *TMS*, I, i. 1. 13, p. 13.
206. Bence Nanay, "Adam Smith's Concept of Sympathy and Its Contemporary Interpretations," *The Philosophy of Adam Smith: Adam Smith Review, volume 5: Essays commemorating the 250th anniversary of The Theory of Moral Sentiments*, ed. Vivienne Brown and Samuel Fleischacker (New York: Routledge, 2010), 101.
207. *TMS* II.ii.3.12n, pp. 91, 91–92n.
208. *TMS*, II.ii.3.12, p. 91.
209. *TMS*, II.ii.3.12n, pp. 91–92n; Appendix II, p. 400.
210. "Small Victories," *The New Yorker*, July 27, 2015, 75.
211. "On Suicide" was also printed and withdrawn. According to Eugene Miller, such hostile critics as William Warburton knew of the essays and alluded to them. They appeared in French translation in 1770, though Hume never knew it. *Essays Moral, Political and Literary*, 577–78n1.
212. "Of the Immortality of the Soul," *EMPL*, 593.
213. The passage first appears in the draft revision of 1759 and in print in editions 2–5, the second edition appearing in 1761. III.2.30–31, p. 128n. Hugh Blair made a similar argument in his sermon, "On our imperfect knowledge of a Future State," *Sermons* (London: 1777), 110–12.

214. *TMS*, VI, iii.3.2., p. 235.
215. *TMS*, III.ii.12, p. 120.
216. Twain's "Extract" elevates an unknown poet superior to Shakespeare and a lame military strategist superior in genius to Napoleon, though he never had an opportunity even to join the army. Both Smith's and Twain's extending Gray's unrealized genius suggests the cultural position long held by Gray's poem. Twain quotes Gray on several occasions and owned Edmund Gosse's biography of Gray. A reader of Hume, he also had some indirect acquaintance with the common sense and sentimental philosophy of the eighteenth century. No evidence uncovered by Americanists suggests he knew Adam Smith, but they may not have looked. Gregg Camfield, *Sentimental Twain: Samuel Clemens in the Maze of Moral Philosophy* (Philadelphia: University of Pennsylvania Press, 1994), 44, 12, 244n16. Alan Gribben, *Mark Twain's Library: A Reconstruction*, 2 vols. (Boston, MA: G. K. Hall, 1980). Smith's "humble hope" nods to Pope.
217. *Palgrave's The Golden Treasury* (New York: Modern Library, 1944), 182–83.
218. *TMS*, III.2.33, p. 132.
219. Ian Simpson Ross, wondering how the atonement endured five editions, does not remark on this passage, although he doubts Smith "put stock in an afterlife" and notes his increasing skepticism as he aged. *The Life of Adam Smith*, 2nd. ed. (New York: Oxford University Press, 2010), 432, 173.
220. "Of the Immortality of the Soul," *EMPL*, 597.
221. *TMS*, III. ii. 34, p. 132.
222. *TMS*, III. ii, 34–35, pp. 132–34.
223. Ian Simpson Ross, *The Life of Adam Smith*, 436.
224. Fania Oz-Salzberger, "Adam Ferguson," *Oxford DNB* (2004, 2009).
225. *Divine Comedy of Dante Alighieri: Inferno*, trans. John Sinclair (New York: Oxford University Press, 1976), 46.
226. *The Poetical Works of Robert Southey*, 10 vols. (Boston: Little Brown, 1873), X, 213, 244–45.
227. Peter Cochran, "One Ton per Square Foot: The Antecedents of *The Vision of Judgement*," *Keats-Shelley Review* 19 (2005): 64.
228. Emrys Jones adds Seneca's *Ludus*, a posthumous attack on the emperor Claudius, and Erasmus's *Junius Exclusus*, perhaps inspired by Seneca, "Byron's Visions of Judgment" *Modern Language Review* 76:1 (1981): 1–19. Erasmus, Jones observes, never acknowledged the authorship of *Julius Exclusus*. John Jortin's edition of 1758–60 made the modern attribution. 9, 11n.
229. William H. Marshall, *Byron, Shelley, Hunt and The Liberal* (Philadelphia: University of Pennsylvania Press, 1960), 126–27; "The King against John Hunt," in *Reports of State Trials: New Series* (London: Eyre and Spottiswoode, 1889), II, 69–104.
230. McDannell and Lang, *Heaven*, 250.

5. WANDÂFURU RAIFU, OR AFTERLIFE INVENTIONS AND VARIATIONS

1. *Tatler*, no. 156, April 1710, II, 378.
2. William Wordsworth, "A Slumber Did My Spirit Seal," *Selected Poems and Prefaces by William Wordsworth*, ed. Jack Stillinger (Boston, MA: Houghton Mifflin, 1965), 113; Percy Bysshe Shelley, "Chorus," from *Hellas, Shelley Poetical Works*, ed. Thomas Hutchinson (New York: Oxford University Press, 1968), 457. The stardust mantra of TED talks and Neil deGrasse Tyson is Carl Sagan's, quoted most recently in *The Smithsonian*, November 2013, 10, "We're made of star-stuff."
3. "Cats Will Kill You First, But Wolves Just Rip You Open," Temple Grandin, interview with Andrew Goldman, *New York Times Magazine*, April 14, 2013, 14.
4. W. H. Auden, "On Reading a Child's Guide to Modern Physics," *Selected Poetry of W. H. Auden*, 2nd. ed. (New York: Vintage, 1971), 214.
5. Dan Cohn-Sherbok and Christopher Lewis, eds., *Beyond Death: Theological and Philosophical Reflections on Life After Death* (New York: St. Martin's Press, 1995), 183–98.
6. Samuel Beckett, *Waiting for Godot* (New York: Grove Press, 1954), 41 [b].
7. Christopher Hitchens, *God Is Not Great: How Religion Poisons Everything* (New York: Twelve Hachette, 2009); Richard Dawkins, *The God Delusion* (Boston, MA: Houghton Mifflin, 2006); George Levine, ed., *Joy of Secularism: Eleven Essays for How We Live Now* (Princeton, NJ: Princeton University Press, 2011); Michael Warner, Jonathan Van Antwerpen, Craig Calhoun, *Varieties of Secularism in a Secular Age* (Cambridge, MA.: Harvard University Press, 2010); Charles Taylor, *A Secular Age* (Cambridge, MA: Harvard University Press, 2007), 362–68, especially 366–68; Craig Calhoun, Mark Juergensmeyer, and Jonathan Van Antwerpen, eds., *Rethinking Secularism* (New York: Oxford University Press, 2011); W. Warren Wagar, ed., *The Secular Mind: Transformations of Faith in Modern Europe* (New York: Holmes and Meier, 1982).
8. Tatyana Tolstaya's *Aetherial Worlds*, trans. Anya Migdal (New York: Alfred A. Knopf, 2018), gliding from disbelief to fictions through desire, would make a distinctive seventh, had it arrived earlier. Her story "Emanuel" is the most interesting account of Swedenborg extant.
9. Etgar Keret, *The Bus Driver Who Wanted to Be God and Other Stories.*, trans. Miriam Shlesinger and others (New York: St Martin's Press, 2001), 181.
10. Christopher Falzon, "On *Being John Malkovich* and Not Being Yourself," in *The Philosophy of Charlie Kaufman*, ed. David LaRocca (Louisville: University of Kentucky Press, 2011), 46–65; Garry L. Hagberg, "The Instructive Impossibility of *Being John Malkovich*," in LaRocca, 169–89; Daniel Shaw, "On Being Philosophical and *Being John Malkovich*," *Journal of Aesthetics and Art Criticism* 64:1 (2006): 111–18; William Young, "Otherwise than *Being John Malkovich*: Incarnating the Name of God," *Literature and Theology* 18:1 (2004): 95–108; Sayantani DasGupta, "Being John Doe Malkovich: Truth, Imagination, and Story in Medicine," *Literature and Medicine* 25:2 (2006): 439–62.
11. Given the magical realist features of *BJM*, the forty-four-year age requirement may have been suggested by the English translation of Gabriel García Márquez's *Cien años de*

soledad. In Spanish, it is said of Melquíades's manuscripts that "no one can read them until they are a hundred years old," that is, the manuscripts must be one hundred years old. In English, a diligent copy-editor corrected a nonexistent error, and Gregory Rabassa's translation was made to read, "no one can read them until he is a hundred years old," that is, the reader must be one hundred years old, as no one ever is in the novel.

12. Three Passovers in the gospel of John, and Luke's statement that Jesus was about thirty when his ministry began, make Jesus thirty plus three at his resurrection.
13. Robert Pogue Harrison, *The Dominion of the Dead* (Chicago: University of Chicago Press, 2003).
14. *Lazar Malkin Enters Heaven* (New York: Penguin, 1986), 39.
15. The west or western wind makes a considerable figure in verse, but Stern probably has in mind the anonymous Tudor poem, in modernized spelling: "Western wind when wilt thou blow, /the small rain down can rain, /Christ if my love were in my arms/ and I in my bed again." Unmodernized: "Westron wynde when wyll thow blow/ the smalle rayne downe can Rayne/ Cryst yf my love were in my Armys/ And I yn my bed Agayne." Charles Frey, "Interpreting 'Western Wind,'" *ELH* 4:3 (1976): 259.
16. Steve Stern, *The Frozen Rabbi* (Chapel Hill, NC: Algonquin Books of Chapel Hill, 2010), 171.
17. For variations on the trope, see Karen Russell, "The Prospectors," *The New Yorker*, June 8 and 15, 2015, 91–101; Margaret Atwood, *Stone Mattress* (New York: Anchor, 2015), 15.
18. The single-appearance trope appears most prominently in Rodgers and Hammerstein's *Carousel* (1945) and its source, Ferenc Molnár's *Liliom: A Legend in Seven Scenes and a Prologue.*
19. George Saunders, *In Persuasion Nation* (New York: Penguin, 2006), 227.
20. J. M. Coetzee, *Elizabeth Costello* (New York: Penguin Books, 2003), 17.
21. Dirk Klopper, " 'We Are Not Made for Revelation': Letters to Francis Bacon in the Postscript to J. M. Coetzee's *Elizabeth Costello*," *English in Africa* 35:2 (2008): 120–21.
22. *Moral Essay I: Epistle to Cobham*, 1734, ll.29–30, 35–40, *The Poems of Alexander Pope*, ed. John Butt (New Haven, CT: Yale University Press, 1963), 551.
23. H. Stefan Schultz, "Hofmannsthal and Bacon: The Sources of the Chandos Letter," *Comparative Literature* 13:1 (1961): 1–15; Reingard Nethersole, "Reading in the In-between: Pre-scripting the 'Postscript' to *Elizabeth Costello*," *Journal of Literary Studies* 21:3–4 (2005): 254–77.
24. Milan Kundera, *Immortality*, trans. Peter Kussi (1990) (New York: HarperCollins, 1992).
25. Not everyone agrees, but surely characters should be more interesting than authors? Does a wife who doesn't want to meet her husband make critics uneasy? François Ricard testifies to her charm in his title, *Agnès's Final Afternoon: An Essay on the Work of Milan Kundera*, trans. Aaron Asher (New York: HarperCollins, 2003). So in *Being John Malkovich,* "John Malkovich" has less character than Cusack-Malkovich or Bean-Malkovich.
26. Ricard, *Agnès's Final Afternoon*, 204–06.
27. Aaron Gerow and Tanaka Junko, "Documentarists of Japan #12: Koreeda Hirokazu," trans. Michael Raine, Yamagata International Documentary Film Festival, web. 14.
28. Aaron Gerow and Tanaka Junko, "Documentarists of Japan #12: Koreeda Hirokazu"; Roger Ebert, "After Life," *Chicago Sun-Times* , Aug. 6, 1999, Rogerebert.com.

29. Taitetsu Unno, *River of Fire, River of Water: An Introduction to the Pure Land Tradition of Shin Buddhism* (New York: Doubleday, 1998), 180; E. A. Burtt, ed. *The Teachings of the Compassionate Buddha*, 188–89.
30. Gabriel M. Paletz and Ayako Saito, "The Halfway House of Memory: An Interview with Hirokazu Kore-eda," *CineAction* (Winter 2003): 58.
31. Timothy Iles, "The Light of Life and Death: The Function of Cinematography and Lighting in Two Films by Kore-eda Hirokazu," *Asian Cinema* 16:1 (2005): 216.
32. David Desser, "*After Life*: History, Memory, Trauma and the Transcendent," *Film Criticism* 35: 2/3 (2011): 52–54. Counting the seconds that elapse in the jump cuts, Desser brilliantly shows how an initially rapid rhythm slows down, breaks up, comes back.
33. A year's seasons pass in the days of one week. Kristi McKim, "Learning to Love What Passes: Sensual Perception, Temporal Transformation, and Epistemic Production in Hirokazu Kore-eda's *After Life*," *Camera Obscura* 68:2 (2008): 79.
34. Desser's figure, "*After Life*: History, Memory, Trauma," 56. The film twice insists on calling the instigation of those riots "false rumors." The allusion, Desser observes, evokes the history of anti-Korean prejudice in Japan, 57.
35. It seems not unreasonable to locate in *WR* a deliberate ideological construction intended to intervene in a current cultural malaise, adapting American happy talk to address a particular social moment in Japan. Tetsuya Ozaki connects a rising Japanese suicide rate in 1998 (from 24,391 to 32,863, remaining above 30,000 ever since) to the Dutch journalist Karel van Wolferen's 1994 *Ningen o kōfuku ni shinai Nihon to iu shisutemu* (Japan: A System That Doesn't Make People Happy) and its concern with contempt for salary men and pornographic manga. David Elliott with Tetsuya Ozaki, *Bye Bye Kitty !!!: Between Heaven and Hell in Contemporary Japanese Art*. New York: Japan Society (New Haven, CT: Yale University Press, 2011), 49, 53, 59. Kore-eda's subsequent films often track recent traumas, carrying into fiction the purposefulness of his earlier documentaries, for example, *Nobody Knows* (2004), *Air Doll* (2009), *I Wish* (2011).
36. Haruo Shirane, ed., *Early Modern Japanese Literature: An Anthology, 1600–1900* (New York: Columbia University Press, 2002), 553.
37. David Desser's otherwise brilliant "*After Life*: History, Memory, Trauma, and the Transcendent," describes Watanabe and Kyoko on the bench as one of the "memory recreations," 49. Lars-Martin Sørensen even says that the memories to be screened are videotaped. "Reality's Poetry: Kore-eda Hirokazu between Fact and Fiction," *Film Criticism* 35:2/3 (2011): 30.
38. Liza Bear, "Hirokazu Koreeda on *Wandafuru raifu (After Life)*," September 7, 1999, www.filmscouts.com.
39. Elaine Sciolino, "Poet's Nightmare in Chinese Prison," *New York Times*, April 10, 2013, C5.
40. Samuel Beckett, "Words and Music," in *The Collected Shorter Plays* (New York: Grove Press, 1984), 131; "Rockaby," 280.
41. Samuel Beckett, *The Collected Shorter Plays*, "Rockaby," 280; "Embers," 91. Beckett's Lethe may be remembering *Tatler* #118, Jan. 10, 1710, II, 201–02. John Partridge reported from the banks of Styx that "Our Time passes away much after the same Manner as it did

when we were among you; Eating, Drinking, and Sleeping, are our chief Diversions. . . . they have several warm Liquors made of the Waters of *Lethe*, with very good Poppy Tea. We that are the sprightly Genius's of the Place, refresh our selves frequently with a Bottle of Mum, and tell Stories till we fall asleep." He wanted a copy of Dodwell against the immortality of the soul in order to rest forever. Dodwell had argued that the soul is not naturally immortal, but immortalized by baptism by a priest in the apostolic succession, thus including Catholics and cutting out dissenters. Henry Dodwell, *An Epistolary Discourse, Proving from the Scriptures and the First Fathers, that the Soul Is A Principle Naturally Mortal: But Immortalized Actually by the Pleasure of God, to Punishment; or, to Reward, by its Union with the Divine Baptismal Spirit. Wherein is Proved, That None have the Power of Giving this Divine Immortalizing Spirit, since the Apostles, but only the Bishops*, (London, 1706).

INDEX

Abhidhamma Pitaka, 153
aborigines, of Australia, 7, 23, 299*n*92
abortion, 10
Abraham, 55
Accusing Spirit which Flew up to Heaven's Chancery with the Oath (Gillray), 241
Acheron, 121
Achilles, 105, 107, 124
action. *See karma*
Acts, Book of, 315
Adam, 314*n*182
Adams, Thomas, 292*n*10
Addison, Joseph, 28, 217–18, 221, 224, 225, 256–57, 341*n*98
Adorno, Theodor, 257–58
adultery, 39, 83, 125, 243, 286, 319*n*252; of David, 345*n*169
Adventurer, The, 212, (Johnson), 208–9, 222
Adventurer, The, 212
Aeneid (Virgil), 45–46, 114–15, 122, 123
Aeschylus, 107
Afghanistan, 22
Afterlife (Frayn), 4
Afterlife (Wandâfuru Raifu) (Kore-eda), xv, xvi, xvii, 258–59, 274, 278–86

"Afterlife" (Gordimer), 2
Afterlife and Other Stories, The (Updike), 2
Agamemnon, 106, 107, 112
Aga of Kish, 55
agent detection, 15, 20
Agni Purana, 146
ahimsa (doing no harm), 150
Ajax, 112
Alexander, Eben, 4, 293*n*7, 318*n*239
Alexander the Great, 35–36, 45, 59
All Is Lost, 260
All Saints Day, 306*n*90
All Souls Day, 306*n*90
Almond, Philip, 212
Amitābha (infinite or immeasurable light), 174–76
Amos, 86–87
Amun, 36, 45
Amenpnufer, 42–43
Analects ("Conversations") (Confucius), 164
Analects of the Warring States, The, 134
Anaximander, 106
ancestor worship, in ancient Israel, 80, in Rome, 113, 122, in China, 162–64
Ancus, 120, 127, 128

angels: heaven for, 9, 214–15; recording, 241
Angels in America (Kushner), 241
angry demons *(ashuras)*, 137, 159, 184
animal cults, of Egypt, 46–47, 304*n*72
animal deaths, in Judea, 82
anima mundi, 126
Anna St. Ives (Holcroft), 334*n*10
Anne (Queen), 228, 253
Annet, Peter, 244–45
annihilation: in Buddhism, 187; in hell, 207; Johnson and, 333*n*6
Antaraya Karma Puja, 149
Anthesteria, 103
Anticleia, 105
Anti-Jacobin Review, 239
Antiochus Epiphanes IV, 90, 92
Apis, 36, 45
apocalypses, 295*n*44
Apollo, 126
Apology (Plato), 109
Apuleius, 45, 46
arhat, 153, 159
Aristophanes, 101, 108
Aristotle, 101, 102, 103, 108–9, 112
Arjuna, 145–46
A'rna, 9
Arsuaga, Juan Luis, 298*n*78
Asclepius, 107
Asgill, John, 202–3, 333*n*92, 334*nn*12–14
Asherah (Queen of Heaven), 77, 80, 312*n*154
ashuras (angry demons), 159
Ashurbanipal, 58–59, 72, 76
Ashurbanipal II, 72
asocial autonomy, 25
Astell, Mary, 226
Athanasian creed, 242, 254
atheism, 7–8, 74, 205–6, 335*n*25
Athenian Oracle, 204
ātman (self), 136–43, 151
Atonement, 248, 348*n*219
Atrahasis, 310*n*136
Atrahasis, 57, 310*n*136
Atwood, Margaret, 206

Auden, W. H., 257
Augustine, 314*n*182
Augustus, 114, 127, 129
austerity, in Hinduism, 141
Austin, R. G., 123
Australia, aborigines of, 7, 23, 299*n*92
Averroes, 126
Avicenna, 126

Baal, 78–79
Babylonia, 20, 48–72; Book of Genesis and, 310*n*135; flood of, 305*n*89; Jewish Bible and, 77–78; Temple and, 77; underworld of, 58
Babyloniaca (Berossus), 59
Babylonian Gilgamesh Epic, The (George), 58, 300*n*1
Bailey, Lee, 4
Bālapandita Sutta (Fools and Wise Men), 156–57
"Bank of Bilgameš," 54–55
Bardo Todrol, 133
Barnes, Julian, 2, 4, 257
Bathsheba, 83, 345*n*169
Bayle, Pierre, 8, 293*n*19
Beckett, Samuel, xv, 287–88, 351*n*41
Beckman, Gary, 310*n*134
Behn, Aphra, 53, 207, 335*n*25
Being Dead (Crace), 257
Being John Malkovich, 258–63, 349*n*11
BEN. See "Bilgameš, Enkidu, and the Netherworld"
Bergson, Henri, 122
Berman, David, 335*n*25
Berossus, 59
Beyond the Pleasure Principle (Freud), 296*n*46
Bhagavad Gita (Song of God), 145–48
bhakti (devotion), 145
Bible: Christian, 75, 183; Hebrew, 76, 77–78, 87, 90. *See also specific books*
Big Questions, Or, Asomatognosia: Whose Hand Is It Anyway (Nilsen), 4
Bilgameš, 50–56, 67, 307*n*104, 307*n*110, 307*n*113, 308*n*123, 308*n*124

"Bilgameš, Enkidu, and the Netherworld" (BEN), 54, 66–69
Blackburne, Francis, 206, 334n19
Blair, Hugh, 225, 238–40
Blair, Robert, 346n186
Blake, William, 213, 255, 346n186
Blessed Isles, 72
Blissful Groves, 125
Blount, Charles, 205, 206–7
bodhisattvas, 153, 160, 175, 185
body mutilation, 22–23
Bold, Frederick, 5
Bolingbroke, Henry St. John, Viscount, 8, 205, 244
Bonnet, Charles, 220
Book of the Great Decrease (Maha Parinibbana Suttanta), 325n94
Books of Going Forth by Day, (Egypt), 32, 35, 38, 40, 47–48
Books of the Dead (Egypt), *see Books of Going Forth by Day*
Book of Rites (Li chi) (Confucius), 165, 167
Book of Songs (Shih Ching), 163
Book of the Dead, of Tibet, 133, 177–80
Book of the Great Decrease (Maha Parinibbana Suttanta), 325n94
Books of Going Forth by Day, 31, 40, 47–48
Books of the Dead, 35, 38
Boswell, James, ix–x, 201, 202, 223, 244
Bowker, John, xvii, 146
Boyer, Pascal, 296n53
Boyers, Peg, 4
Boyse, Joseph, 220, 237
Boy Who Came Back from Heaven, The (Malarkey, K., and Malarkey, A.), 4, 258
Brahmanism, 135, 138–39, 140, 322n41
brahman, 140
Brahmanas, 133, 135
brain, 14, 296n53; consciousness and, 19
brain death, 18
Brandon, S. G. F., 302n22
Bṛhadāraṇyaka Upaniṣad, 138
British Apollo, The, 221–22

Brookner, Anita, 1
Brooks, Albert, 259, 260, 279
Browne, Thomas, 242
Buddha, 152–53, 175–76, 322n37
Buddha field, 175
Buddhism, 6, 7, 18–19, 133–34; annihilation in, 187; in China, 150–77; Christian Bible and, 183; compassion in, 187–88; Daoism and, 173; *dharma* in, 144, 150–51, 184–85; emptiness in, 136, 151, 159–60; enlightenment in, 176, 184–85, 191–92; ghosts in, 137, 158–59; heaven in, 154, 185, 191; hell in, 137, 155–58, 184–85, 191; Hinduism and, 135; Hume and, 324n76; Islam and, 135–36; in Japan, 176, 180–96; *karma* in, 191; Kore-eda and, 258–59, 274, 278–86; middle way of, 194; mindfulness at death in, 175, 186; morality in, 183; reincarnation in, 154–55, 173–74; salvation in, 148, 175; seven treasures in, 156–57; Shinto and, 182; in Tibet, 135. *See also* Pure Land
Bunyan, John, 164, 215, 232, 234
burials, 20–21; in China, 170; in Egypt, 33, 34–35; in Greece, 103; in Judea, 82; in Rome, 7, 113–14; in Sumer, 55
Buried Book, The (Damrosch), 59
Burke, Edmund, 232, 234, 251, 345n174
Burnet, Thomas, 207–8, 216, 341n88
Burns, Robert, 245–47
Burpo, Todd, 4, 293n7
Buson, Yosa, 281
Butler, Joseph, Bishop, 205–6, 220
butterflies, 185, 205–6
Byron, George Gordon, Lord, 252–55

Cabin in the Sky (Minnelli), 259
Cadmus, 107
Caesarion, 114
Cain, James, 340n83
Calvin, John, 100, 204
Camfield, Gregg, 333n3
Canaanites, 80

Canon of Immortality, The (Xian Jing), 169
Capra, Frank, 259
Carnes, Bruce, 7
Carroll, Maureen, 318*n*232
Cassio Dio, 46–47
"Castaway, The" (Cowper), 340*n*83
Cathcart, Thomas, 4, 333*n*92
Catholicism, 19, 244; emancipation of, 254; heaven for, 242; resurrection in, 100; souls in, 203–4
causal agency, 15
CBS/*Vanity Fair* poll, 2
Cerberus, 103, 121
Chāndogya Upanishad, 141, 142
Chapone, Sarah, 230
Charlie Parker's Yardbird, 4
Charvaka school, 142
Chekhov, Antonin, 1
Chief Doorkeeper of the Temple of Amun, 42
Childe, V. Gordon, 22, 33
children's deaths, 55, 226–29, 306*n*90, 314*n*177, 343*n*144
chimpanzees, 16–18, 25–26, 297*nn*63–64
China, 20, 26; ancestor worship in, 162–64; Buddhism in, 133, 150–77; burials in, 170; coffins from, 170; grave goods in, 171; heaven in, 134, 171–72, 242; human sacrifices in, 166, 170; justice in, 172; Shang dynasty in, 162–63; tombs in, 170–72
Chopra, Deepak, 1
Christian Bible, 75, 87, 133, 136, 183, 312*n*152
Christianity, 6, 7, 75–76; on atheism, 335*n*25; in Egypt, 47; Enlightenment and, 9; God of, 133, 136; grave goods and, 301*n*9; hell in, 199–200; in India, 135–36; in Japan, 188–90, 192–93; Lucretius and, 130; parousia of, 131, 334*n*19; Pure Land and, 188; resurrection in, 99–100, 190; reunited in afterlife with friends and family in, 238–40; tombstones in, 23; Virgil and, 115. See also Catholicism; heaven; Jesus
Chronicles of Japan *(Nihongi)*, 180–82
Chrysippus, 113

Chuang Tzu (Zhuangzi), 134, 162, 164, 167–68, 327*n*126
Chubb, Thomas, 205
Chudleigh, Mary (Lee), Lady, 219-20, 228, 335*n*25
Cicero, 46, 101, 113–31
Citragupta, 147
Clarissa (Richardson), 230
Cleanthes, 113
Cleopatra, 114, 305*n*76
Clerk of Destinies, 168
Cockburn, Catherine Trotter, 8
Coetzee, J. M., 243, 258, 269–74, 278, 286, 287, 288
coffins, 170
Coffin Texts, 38, 40, 47
cognitive psychology, 10, 15
Collected Biographies of Immortals (Liexian Zhuan), 167
Collection of Poems on Divine and Moral Subjects, selected from various authors, A (Giles), 229
Collins, Anthony, 205
comfortable doctrine, of Hume, 245–46
compassion: in Buddhism, 174, 187–88; in Christianity, 193; in *Puranas*, 147
Complaint: or, Night Thoughts (Young), 230
Confessions (Rousseau), 237–38
Confucius, 134, 162, 164, 171–72, 192
Congreve, William, 164
consciousness, 19–20; in Hinduism, 143; of plants, 149–50
conservation of matter and energy, 13–14
Consolations in Travel (Davy), 220
"Conversations" *(Analects)* (Confucius), 164
cosmic balance *(maat)*, 40–41
Cowper, William, 201, 340*n*83
Crace, Jim, 257
Creech, Thomas, 115, 335*n*25
cremation, 19, 20, 103, 141
Croesus, 88
cult of the dead, in Judea, 75
Cuppé, Pierre, 209

Curll, Edmund, 207
Cyrus the Persian, 77, 88, 316n194

Daiseishi, 185
Dalley, Stephanie, 309n125
Damrosch, David, 59
Daniel (biblical character), 91–93
Daniel, Book of, 74, 75–76, 216–17
Daniel, Stephen H., 336n32
Dante, xiv, 4, 32, 126, 185, 199, 215, 226, 231, 240, 259, 287; gate of, 253; Lucretius and, 116, 118; Virgil and, 115, 129
dao (way), 165–66
Dao de Jing, 165–66
Daoism, 134, 192; Buddhism and, 173; in China, 169; heaven in, 171–72, 185; hell in, 174; proto-Daoism, 164, 165–68
Darius, 107
David, 74, 83, 345n169
Davies, Philip R., 312n155
Davy, Humphry, 220
Dawes, William, 207
Day of the Dead, 306n90
Death and Heaven (Watts), 232
Death and the Afterlife (Scheffler), 5, 295n44
deathbed, 175, 186, 331n235
death instinct, of Freud, 10
"Death of Bilgameš, The," 67, 71, 308n124
Declaration of Independence, 264
Defending Your Life (Brooks), 259, 260, 279
Defoe, Daniel, 204, 207, 244, 269, 337n47
delayed parousia, 131, 334n19
Democritus, 108–9, 120
Denis the Carthusian, 291n7
Dennett, Daniel, 19, 151
Dennis, John, 207
De rerum natura (On the Nature of Things) (Lucretius), 101, 114
"Descent of Inana, The," 50
Desser, David, 351n37, 351nn32–34
De statu mortuorum et resurgentium tractatus (Burnet), 207–8
Deus Destroyed (Ha Daiusu) (Habian), 189–90

Deuteronomists, 77, 165, 312nn154–55
Deuteronomy, Book of, 81, 85, 89–90, 157
Deuills Banket, The (Adams), 292n10
Devadūta Sutta (The Divine Messengers), 157
De Veritate (Herbert, Edward, of Cherbury, Lord), 204–5
devotion *(bhakti)*, 145
devotion, to Buddha, 175–76
de Waal, Frans, 15, 24
dhamma, 152
Dhānañjāni Sutta, 155–56
Dhaneśhvara, 147
dharma, 133, 144, 148, 150–51, 184–85
Dialogues of the Sea-Gods (Enalioi Dialogoi), 46
"Diamond-Cutter" Perfection of Wisdom Sutra, 133
Dickens, Charles, 229
Dickie, Simon, 9
Dictionary (Johnson), 200–201, 238
Dido, 127
Dionysus, 108
Discourse concerning the Happiness of Good Men, and the Punishment of the Wicked in the Next World, A (Sherlock), 207
Discourses on Different Subjects (Polwhele), 240
"Dispute between a Man and his Ba," 38
Divine Legation of Moses Demonstrated (Warburton), 206
Divine Messengers, The (Devadūta Sutta), 157
Divine Providence (Swedenborg), 218
diviner *(fang shih)*, 171
divining, in Judea, 80–81
Djehuty-hotep, 42
Doctrine of a future STATE's being universally taught, The, 201
Dodd, William, 232–36, 242, 244, 345n166
Doddridge, Philip, 213
Dodwell, Henry, 351n41
doing no harm *(ahimsa)*, 150
doll substitute or slave for the person *(shabtis)*, 41–42
Dominion of the Dead, The (Harrison), 263
Doniger, Wendy, 137, 138–39

"Don Juan in Hell Interlude" (Shaw), 198–99
Dostoyevksy, Fyodor, 7
Douglas, Mary, 57
"Dream of Homer" (Ennius), 123
Dream of Scipio (Cicero), 121–22, 123
Drew, Bernard A., 291*n*5
Dryden, John, 8, 116, 117–18, 121, 205, 206–7, 318*n*239
D'Souza, Dinesh, 1, 11
Duat (Jones, D.), 4
Dumuzi, 78
"Dumuzid's Dream," 51
Dunciad (Pope), 255
Durán, Diego, 306*n*90
Dvigimbara, 149

Eagleman, David, 5
Earbery, Matthias, 207
Earth After Us, The: What Legacy Will Humans Leave in the Rocks? (Zalasiewicz), 295*n*44
Earth Prison, 174
Eastern Zhou, 170–71
Ecclesiastes, Book of, 57, 63, 83–84, 88, 93
Eclogues (Virgil), 122
"Economics in the Afterlife" (Gordon, S.), 5
Eden, 76, 314*n*182
Edict of Horemheb, 303*n*52
Edward, Lord Herbert of Cherbury, 204–5
Egypt: animal cults of, 46–47, 304*n*72; Babylon and, 72; burials in, 33, 34–35; grave goods in, 34–35, 43; Greece and, 35–36, 45–46, 48; Jewish slavery in, 74; justice in, 31–48; legal codes of, 303*n*52; magic spells in, 20, 31; morality in, 26; mummification in, 33, 35, 36, 43–44, 46–47, 48, 301*n*11; pyramids of, 33–34; Rome and, 36, 45; snakes in, 310*n*135; Suez Canal of, 35, 311*n*137; Sumer and Babylon and, 49–51; tombs in, 36–37, 42–43
Eightfold Path, of Buddhism, 152
El, 78
Electra, 107

Electronic Text Corpus of Sumerian Literature (ETCSL), 306*n*96, 306*n*98
Elegy Wrote in a Country Churchyard (Gray), 249–50
elephants, 16
Elijah, 72, 86, 95, 99, 263
Eliot, Charles, 188
Elisha, 83, 99
Elizabeth Costello (Coetzee), 243, 258, 269–74, 278, 287
Eloisa to Abelard (Pope), 227, 263
Elysium, 125–26, 200, 212, 223, 227, 240–41, 251–52
emancipation: in Buddhism, 160–61; of Catholicism, 254
Emlyn, Thomas, 215
Emmaus, 98
empathy, 25
emptiness, in Buddhism, 136, 151, 159–60
Enalioi Dialogoi (Dialogues of the Sea-Gods), 46
end-of-life consultations, 10
Enkidu, 55, 57–68, 71, 75, 137, 307*n*111, 308*n*123
enlightenment: in Buddhism, 152, 153, 176, 184–85, 191–92; happiness and, 197–255; justice and, 210
Enlightenment, Christianity and, 9
Ennius, 123
Enoch, 72
Epic of Gilgamesh (Martinů), 49, 71
Epic of Gilgamesh, The (George), 307*n*113
Epicureans, 112–13
Epicurus, 101, 102, 108–9, 114–30, 287
Er, 110–11, 112, 121–22
Erasing Death: The Science That Is Rewriting the Boundaries between Life and Death (Parnia), 293*n*7
Erasmus, 240, 334*n*18, 348*n*228
Ereshkigal, 50–51, 58, 61, 78, 137
Eriphyle, 105
Essay on Man (Locke), 200
Essay on Sepulchres (Godwin), 203

Essay on the Evidence from Scripture that the Soul, immediately after the Death of the Body, is not in a state of Sleep or Insensibility; but of Happiness or Mercy: and on the Moral Uses of that Doctrine (Polwhele), 240
Essentials of Self-insight (Kanjin ryaku yōshū), 186
Etana, 61
ETCSL. *See* Electronic Text Corpus of Sumerian Literature
Euripides, 107, 108
Eusebius, 334n19
euthanasia, 10
Eve, 85
Everyman, 5
Evidences of the Christian Religion (Addison), 218
evolutionary psychology, 24
Evolution of the Gilgamesh Epic, The (Tigay), 310n134
Exodus, Book of, 81, 85, 316n194
extinction, in Buddhism, 160–61
"Extract from Captain Stormfield's Visit to Heaven" (Twain), 199
Ezekiel, Book of, 76, 88, 314n182

"Fairy-Tale" (Rowe), 226
family, happiness with, 225–40
fang shih (diviner), 171
Fasti (Ovid), 113–14
Female Spectator, The (Haywood), 220–21
Ferguson, Adam, 252
Fielding, Henry, 8, 116, 212, 226, 229, 239, 240, 335n25
Field of Reeds, 38, 41–42, 45
Fields of Mourning, 124
Fiesta de los Muertecitos (Miccailhuitontli), 306n90
Fiesta Grande de los Muertos (Xocotlhuetzi), 306n90
Flynn, C. P., 4
Folkes, Martin, 339n77

food offerings: for ancestor worship, 163; with burials, 21; in Judea, 82
Fools and Wise Men (Bālapandita Sutta), 156–57
ford-makers *(tirthankara),* 148–49
Foucault, Michel, 8
Four Last Things: Death, Judgment, Heaven and Hell (Boyse), 220
Franklin, Benjamin, 202–3, 205, 259, 336n28
Frayn, Michael, 4
Freud, Sigmund, 7, 8, 9, 75, 293n16, 296n46; death instinct of, 10; on religions, 202
friends, happiness with, 225–40
Friendship in Death: Twenty Letters from the Dead to the Living (Rowe), 226–28, 230
Frost, Robert, 276
Frozen Rabbi, The (Stern), 258–59, 264–66
Fudaraku, 175
fundamentalism, 10
"Funeral, The" (Erasmus), 334n18
funeral rituals, 18–22; in Sumer, 54
fusiform gyrus, 14
Future of an Illusion, The (Freud), 8, 9

Gabriel (Hirsch), 13
Gandharvas, 140
Gandhi, Mahatma, 148, 150
Garth, Samuel, 205
Gates Ajar, The (Phelps), 200
Gautama, Siddhartha, 152
Gay, Peter, 200
Genesis, Book of, 57, 59, 80, 287, 312n151, Sumer, Babylonia and 310n135
Gennai, Hiraga, 18–19, 256, 285
Genshin, 174, 184–88, 193, 285
Gentleman's Magazine, 228–29
George, A. R., 58, 63, 67, 69, 300n1, 307n113, 308n124, 310n134
George III (King), 253
Georgics (Virgil), 122–23
ghosts: in Buddhism, 137, 158–59; Confucius and, 165; in Judea, 81, 91
Gibbon, Edward, 130, 244

Giles, William, 229
Gilgamesh, 7, 28–29, 49, 54–71, 300n1; OBV of, 55, 58, 62, 69; *Rig Veda* and, 137; SBV of, 56, 58, 63–64, 309n125
Gillray, James, 241
Glimpses of Heaven (Macdonald), 258
Gobekli Tepe, 21
God, 2, 130–31; of Christianity, Judaism, and Islam, 132, 136; death of, 75; Grove on, 219; Job and, 78; in Judea, 74, 82–83, 85, 87, 98; love of, 226, 337n50; morality and, 8, 308n117; in religions, 201; in Ten Commandments, 86; Wisdom of Solomon and, 101
Godwin, William, 202–3, 244, 259, 334n10
Goethe, Johann Wolfgang von, 237, 274–75, 277
Golden Ass (Apuleius), 46
Golden Splendor Sutra, 182
Goody, Jack, 55
Gordimer, Nadine, 2, 257
Gordon, George, Lord Byron, 252–255
Gordon, Lucie Duff, 36
Gordon, Scott, 5
Gorgias, 111
Gorgon, 103
Gotama, Siddatha, 152
Graham, Catherine Macaulay, 221
Grandin, Temple, 257
Grand One (T'ai i), 171
Grant, Adam, 10
Grave, The (Blair, R.), 346n186
grave goods, 21, 301n9; in China, 171; in Egypt, 34–35, 43; in Greece, 22
Gray, Thomas, 194, 249–50, 348n216
Graziano, Michael, 19
Great Cloud Sutra, 177
Greece, 73, 101–13; burials in, 103; cremation in, 103; Egypt and, 35–36, 45–46, 48; grave goods in, 22; Jews and, 77, 93; justice in, 102, 103–6; severed heads in, 316n209; Wisdom of Solomon and, 94
Greenblatt, Stephen, 116
Greenspoon, Leonard J., 93
Greyson, Bruce, 4

grief, 123, 240; for dead children, 314n177; in primates, 16–18
Griffith, Elizabeth, 231–32
Griffith, Richard, 231–32
Grove, Henry, 218–19, 227, 334n16, 336n35
Guardian, The, 217
Guggenheim, Bill, 260
Guggenheim, Judy, 260
gui, 165
Gulliver's Travels (Swift), 183, 257, 260

Habian, Fukansai, 183, 188–90, 192–93, 206
Ha Daiusu (Deus Destroyed) (Habian), 189–90
Hades, 46, 73, 103, 107, 126
Hadrian, 108
Hallett, Joseph, 336n35
Halley, Edmund, 335n25
Halley's comet, 341n88
Hammurabi's code, 53
Handel, George Frideric, 216, 253
hangings, 212, 338n72
happiness: with family and friends, 225–40; political implications of, 243–45. *See also* enlightenment; heaven
"Happiness of a Future State, The" (Blair, H.), 238
Hardie, Philip, 122
Harrison, Robert Pogue, 263
Hartley, David, 209–10, 221
Hasmoneans, 77
Hawkins, John, 333n6
Haywood, Eliza, 220–21, 231
Heaney, Seamus, 4
heaven: Americans and, 2; for angels, 9, 214–15; in Buddhism, 154, 185, 191; in Catholicism, 203–4; children's deaths and, 343n144; in China, 134, 171–72; Confucius and, 164, 171–72; in Daoism, 171–72, 185; fictionalized, 240–43; Hinduism and, 143–50; Jesus and, 215; knowledge and, 214–25; proto-Daoism and, 166; self-knowledge and, 214–25; Smith, A., on, 245–52; souls and, 214–15; Southey and Byron on, 252–55; Twain on, 199

Heaven: A History (McDannell and Lang), 94
Heaven Can Wait, 259, 260
Heaven Is for Real (Burpo and Vincent), 4, 293*n*7
Hebrew Bible, 75, 76, 77–78, 80, 87, 90, 210, 312*n*152, 315*n*191
Heidegger, Martin, 257–58
Heidegger and a Hippo Walk Through Those Pearly Gates (Cathcart and Klein), 4, 333*n*92
Heidel, Alexander, 49–50
Heike monogatari, 188, 190
Heine, Heinrich, 9
hell, 94, 340*n*83; annihilation in, 207; in Buddhism, 137, 155–58, 184–85, 191; in Catholicism, 203–4; challenges to, 206–7; in Christianity, 199–200; in Daoism, 174; decline of, 214; Hinduism and, 143–50; invention of, 5; Shaw on, 198–99; Wesley on, 212, 213
"Hell, Religion and Cultural Change" (Hull and Bold), 5
Hellas (Shelley), 223
Hello from Heaven! A New Field of Research—After-Death Communication—Confirms That Life and Love Are Eternal (Guggenheim, B., and Guggenheim, J.), 260
Hell Torments Not Eternal. Argumentatively Proved, from the attribute of divine mercy (Curll), 207
Hemingway, Ernest, 274–75
Hena, 77
Herakleitos, 106
Hercules, 72, 102, 103, 105, 106, 108, 124, 312*n*149
Here Comes Mr. Jordan, 259
Hermes, 73
Herodotus, 35, 45, 88, 107–8
Hertz, Robert, 15
Hesiod, 58, 73, 101, 102–4, 125, 312*n*149
Hezekiah, 76, 81
Hilkiah, 312*n*156
Hill, Aaron, 222–23
Hīnayāna, 174

Hīnayānists, 153
Hinduism, 6, 7; Buddhism and, 135; cremation in, 141; heaven and, 143–50; hell and, 143–50; reincarnation in, 136–43; salvation in, 148; *Vedas* of, 133, 135, 139. *See also Puranas*; *Upanishads*
Hirsch, Edward, 13
History of Jemmy and Jenny Jessamy (Haywood), 231
History of the World in 10½ Chapters (Barnes), 2
Hitchens, Christopher, 75, 86, 131
Hobbes, Thomas, 25
Holcroft, Thomas, 334*n*10
Home, Henry, Lord Kames, 221
Homer, 7, 22–23, 58, 59, 101, 102–3, 104–6, 312*n*149; Lucretius and, 116; Plato on, 73, 109–10; Virgil and, 125
Homme Machine, La (Offray de la Mettrie), 206
Hōnen, 184, 187–88
Hōnen's Jōdo-shū (Pure Land School), 183
Hooke, Robert, 215, 217
Horace, 114–15, 122
Horneck, Anthony, 210
Horus, 35
Hosea, 79
Household Assistant, in China, 171
Howard, Robert, 223
Huai-nan tzu, 171
Huber, Marie, 208
Huldah, 76, 88
Hull, Brooks B., 5
Human Relations Area Files, 6–7
human sacrifices, 22, 51, 166, 170
Humbaba, 60
Hume, David, 10, 14, 25, 201–2, 225, 238, 244, 293*n*19, 336*n*35; Buddhism and, 324*n*76; comfortable doctrine of, 245–46; on justice, 211, 248; Lucretius and, 130; Smith, A., and, 247–52; on suicide, 347*n*211
hun (spirit), 165
Hutcheson, Francis, 25
Huwawa, 55, 308*n*123
"Hymn to Demeter," 106

362 INDEX

I Am a Cat (Sōseki), 183, 194–96
I Ching, 170
icons, in Judea, 300n6
Idler (Johnson), 231
Ikram, Salina, 31, 41
Iliad (Homer), 104
Image of the Netherworld in the Sumerian Sources, The (Katz), 307n111
Immortality (Kundera), 258, 274–78
Immortality Defended (Leslie), 11
Inana, 50
incest, 319n252
India, 135–36
individualist selfishness, 25
Indonesia, 19
Inferno (Dante), 116, 118, 126, 240, 253, 259
infinite or immeasurable light (Amitābha), 174–76
In Persuasion Nation (Saunders), 258, 266–69
"Instructions of Ankhsheshonq," 47
Invention of Sacred Tradition, The (Davies), 312n155
Iopas, 123
Ipsos/Reuters poll, 2
Isaiah (biblical character), 81, 94
Isaiah, Book of, 76, 314n182, 316n194
Ishtar, 58, 78
Isis, 45, 49, 305n76
Islam, 6, 7; Buddhism and, 135–36; in Egypt, 47; God of, 133, 136; heaven for, 242; in India, 135–36; sensuality in, 223–24; tombs in, 23
Israel. *See* Judea
Israel, Jonathan, 293n19
Ito, Aiko, 194, 196
It's a Wonderful Life (Capra), 259
Ivvah, 77

Jacob, 80, 88
Jainism, 135, 144, 148–50
Japan: Buddhism in, 176, 180–96; Christianity in, 188–90, 192–93; Kore-eda and, 258–59, 274, 278–86; Pure Land in, 176, 180–96; suicide in, 351n35
Jeremiah, 77, 88, 312n156
Jesus, 75–76; heaven and, 215; ministry beginning of, 350n12; resurrection of, 79, 98–100, 315n191; salvation in, 148
Jewish Bible. *See* Hebrew Bible
Jewish Naturalization Act, 244
Jews, 300n5; Greece and, 77; heaven for, 242; morality of, 90; Rome and, 77; slavery of, in Egypt, 74
Jigoku, 285
jiva (soul), 148, 150
Job (biblical character), 38–39, 78, 82, 88, 131
Job, Book of, 241
Jōdo Shin-shū (True Pure Land School), 183
John, Gospel of, 2, 98–99, 350n12
Johnson, Samuel, 200–201, 208–9, 222, 231, 238, 244; annihilation and, 333n6; Dodd and, 233, 236, 345n166; on hangings, 338n72
Jones, Daniel Alexander, 4
Jones, Emrys, 348n228
Jonze, Spike, 258–59, 260, 286, 287
Jortin, John, 130, 204, 236–37
Joseph, 88
Josiah, 76
Jost, Jacob Sider, 243
Journal of a Voyage to Lisbon, A (Fielding), 116
Journey from This World to the Next (Fielding), 212, 229, 240
Judah, 87, 88
Judaism, 6, 30; in Egypt, 47; God of, 133, 136; in India, 135–36; morality and, 26–27. *See also* Jews
Judea, 73–101; burials in, 82; cult of the dead in, 75; divining in, 80–81; icons in, 300n6; justice in, 87; martyrdom in, 91–101; resurrection in, 91–101; underworld of, 78–79
Julius Caesar, 114, 129
Julius Exclusus (Erasmus), 240

justice, 212; in China, 172; Ecclesiastes and, 83–84; in Egypt, 31–48; enlightenment and, 210; in Greece, 102, 103–6; Hume on, 211, 248; in Judea, 87; Virgil on, 124–25
Juvenal, 46

Kafka, Franz, 259
kalpa, 185
kami (spirits), 182–83
Kanjin ryaku yōshū (Essentials of Self-insight), 186
Kannon, 175
karma (action), 191, 321*n*24; heaven and hell and, 143–50; reincarnation and, 132, 136–43
katabasis, 116
Katha Upanishad, 142–43, 150
Katz, Dina, 58, 307*n*111
Kaufman, Charlie, 260, 286
Kaushītaki Upanishad, 141–42
Keightley, David N., 163
Kenrick, William, 220, 221–22
Keret, Etgar, 260
Kesakambalin, Ajita, 135, 142, 152
Keshin, 150
Khafra, 33
Khufu, 33
Kinkade, Thomas, 259
King, Gregory, 210–11
Klein, Daniel, 4, 333*n*92
"Kneller's Happy Campers" (Keret), 260
knowledge: in Book of Daniel, 216–17; heaven and, 214–25
Knox, Bernard, 122
Kojiki (Record of Ancient Matters), 180–82
Kore-eda, Hirokazu, xv, xvi, xvii, 258–59, 274, 278–86, 287
Kōtatsu, Fujita, 188
Krishna, 145–46
Kundera, Milan, 258, 274–78, 286
Kurzweil, Ray, 334*n*11
Kushner, Tony, 241
Kwannon, 185

KwaZulu-Natal, 21

Lachesis, 112
Lagerwey, John, 173
"Lament for Ur," 50
Land of Darkness, 162
land of the ancestors or gods *(Toko-yo no kuni)*, 181
Land of Ultimate Bliss, 188
Lane, Anthony, 248
Lang, Bernhard, 94, 213, 224, 339*n*76, 340*n*83
Laozi, 134, 162, 327*n*126
Laplanders, 6
Larger Pureland Sutra, 182–83
Larkin, Philip, 4, 256, 287
"Lazar Malkin Enters Heaven" (Stern), 264
Lazarus, 99, 216
Leland, John, 335*n*25, 339*n*74
leopards, 17
Leslie, John, 11
Letters Religious and Moral (Young), 237
Levinas, Emmanuel, 14, 287
Leviticus, Book of, 81, 90
Lex Julia, 319*n*252
Libation Bearers, The (Aeschylus), 107
liberation *(moksha)*, 143–44
Li chi (Book of Rites) (Confucius), 165, 167
Lichtheim, Miriam, 43
Liexian Zhuan (Collected Biographies of Immortals), 167
Life After Death (Segal), 94, 301*n*3
"Life After Death: A Fate Worse than Death" (Wilson, A.), 257
Life After Life (Moody), 4
Life at Death (Ring), 4
Lipit-Ishtar, 52–53
Literary Afterlife (Drew), 291*n*5
Locke, John, 200, 207, 242
Long Discourses, 152–53, 155, 325*n*85
Look of Silence, The (Lane), 248
Lost (TV series), 5
Lost in Translation, 279
Lotus Sutra, 159–61, 175, 184, 188

love, of God, 226, 337n50
Lovely Bones, The, 260
Lucian, 46, 59, 73, 240, 251, 253
Lucius Runnius Pollo, 114
Lucretius, 101, 114–30, 205, 257, 335n25
Ludus (Seneca), 348n228
Luke, Gospel of, 5, 82, 91, 98, 99, 100, 208, 216, 265, 315n91, 350n12
Luther, Martin, 204

maat (cosmic balance), 40–41
Macaulay, Catherine, 239
Maccabees, 91, 94
Macdonald, Gordon, 258
Made in Heaven, 260
magic spells, in Egypt, 20, 31
Mahabharata, 133, 135, 143–44, 147, 323n53
Mahādukkhakkhandha Sutta, 325n99
Mahā Parinibbana Suttanta (Book of the Great Decrease), 325n94
Mahāvastu, 158
Mahavira, 135, 149, 150, 151
Mahāyāna Buddhism, 153–54, 174
Mahīratha, 147
Maimonides, 30, 85
Maitreya, 153
"Makropulos Case, The: Reflections on the Tedium of Immortality" (Williams, B.), 5
Malarkey, Alex, 4, 258
Malarkey, Kevin, 4, 258
Malkovich, John, 261, 263
Man and Superman (Shaw), 198–99
Mandeville, Bernard, 25
Manlove, Timothy, 342n126
Marcellus, 127, 129
Marcus Aurelius, 108, 113
Mark, Gospel of, 91, 94, 96, 98, 99–100, 239
Markandeya Purana, 146, 147
Mark Antony, 114
Marlowe, Christopher, 8
Marsh of Offerings, 38
Martin, Benjamin, 221
Martinů, Bohuslav, 49, 71

martyrdom, in Judea, 91–101
Marx, Karl, 7, 75, 202
Mary Magdalene, 98
Matthew, Book of, 91, 98, 99, 239
McDannell, Colleen, 94, 213, 224
McPherson, Conor, 2
Medusa, 103
Mekhu, 34–35
Mencius, 162, 164
Menelaos, 104
Mesopotamia. *See* Babylonia
Messiah (Handel), 216
metempsychosis, 14, 97, 102, 111, 193, 194, 278, 295n44
Methodism, 202, 212, 213, 243, 340n83
Mexico, Day of the Dead in, 306n90
Miccailhuitontli (Fiesta de los Muertecitos), 306n90
Mickle, William, 237
Micrographia (Hooke), 215, 217
Middle Length Discourses, 152–53, 155, 325–26nn99–100, 325n85
middle way, of Buddhism, 194
Mill, John Stuart, 221
Miller, Eugene, 347n211
Millhauser, Steven, 295n39
Milton, John, 214, 227
Mind Children (Moravec), 11
mindfulness at death, in Buddhism, 175, 186
Minos, 105
Mishnah, 30
moksha (liberation), 143–44
Momus, 46
Monet, Claude, 259
Montesquieu, 223–24
Moody, Raymond, 4
moon, in Hinduism, 141–42
morality, 2, 24–27, 287; atheism and, 74; in Buddhism, 183; God and, 8, 308n117; of Jews, 90; of primates, 24–26; in Sumer, 49, 70–71
moral sense, 25
Moravec, Hans, 11

More, Hannah, 214, 340n83
Morgan, Thomas, 205
"Morning Thought, A" (Robertson), 210
Morris, Peleg, 215
Morrow, Susan Brind, 310n135
Moses, 74, 90
mot, 78–79, 101–2
mourning, 16–18; Confucius on, 167
Mozi, 162
muertecitos, 48, 306n90
mummification: in Egypt, 33, 35, 36, 43–44, 46–47, 48, 301n11; reconstructed faces from, 302n37
Murnane, William J., 302n22
Musicophilia (Sacks), 4
Muslims. *See* Islam
Mutual Knowledge in a future State; Offered as an Argument of Consolation under the Loss of Friends (Dodd), 232–33
Myōshū, 191–93
Myōtei Mondō (Habian), 183
Myth of Er, 110, 121
Myths from Mesopotamia: Creation, The Flood, Gilgamesh, and Others (Dalley), 309n125

Naciketas, 142
Nāgārjuna, 151, 159, 161, 175–76, 187
Nanak, Guru, 136
Nannaya, 71
Natural History (Pliny), 116
Natural History of Religion (Hume), 201–2
Nauri Decree, 303n52
Nawirtum, 71
NDEs. *See* near-death experiences
Neanderthal (Palmer), 298n78
Neanderthals, 20
Near-Death Experience, The (Bailey and Yates), 4
Near-Death Experience, The (Greyson and Flynn), 4
near-death experiences (NDEs), 4
Nebuchadnezzar, 77
necromancers, in Judea, 80

nembutsu (nenbutsu), 185, 186, 192, 193, 285
Ne no kuni (root country), 181
Neuman, Abraham, 91
New Testament, 75, 87; resurrection in, 99
Newton, Isaac, 216–17, 242
Nicheren, 188
Nicole, Pierre, 229–30
Nietzsche, Friedrich, 93
Night Thoughts (Young), 224–25
Nihongi (Chronicles of Japan), 180–83
Nilometers, 32, 301n12
Nilsen, Anders Brekhus, 2
Nilsson, Martin, 89
Nîmes, 45
90 Minutes in Heaven (Piper), 4, 292n6
Ninsun, 68
Nintu, 57
nirvana, 151, 152, 159, 160–61, 191–92
Noah, 206, 310n136, 341n88
Norris, John, 213, 226
Nothing To Be Frightened Of (Barnes), 4, 257
Nouvelle Eloise (Rousseau), 238
Nouvelles de la République des Lettres, 203

Obeyesekere, Gananath, 137
Observations on Man, His Frame, His Duty and His Expectations (Hartley), 209–10
OBV. *See* Old Babylonian Version
Octavian, 47
Odysseus, 59, 62, 104–6, 123, 144
Odyssey (Homer), 59, 104–6
Oedipus at Colonnus (Sophocles), 107
"Of a Particular Providence and a Future State" (Hume), 293n19
Offray de la Mettrie, Julien, 206
"Of National Characters" (Hume), 252
Ōjōyōshū (Genshin), 174, 184, 186–87
Old Babylonian Version (OBV), of *Gilgamesh*, 55, 58, 62, 69, 309n125
"Old Fools, The" (Larkin), 256
Old Testament, 75, 76, 77–78, 80, 84–85, 87, 90, 210, 312n152, 315n191
Olivelle, Patrick, 138

Olshansky, Jay, 7
Omega Point, 11
"On Death" (Blair, H.), 238
100 Schools, 162
O'Neill, Eugene, 264
"On Suicide" (Hume), 347*n*211
"On the Death of a Favorite Cat Drowned in a Bowl of Goldfishes" (Gray), 194
"On the Death of Mr. Thomas Rowe" (Singer Rowe), 227
"On the Immortality of the Soul" (Hume), 249
On the Nature of Things (De rerum natura) (Lucretius), 101, 114
On the reasons for expecting that virtuous Men shall meet after Death in a State of Happiness (Price), 232
Opticks (Newton), 217
Orestes, 106, 107
organ harvesting, 18
Origen, 206, 334*n*19
original sin, 314*n*182
Oroonoko (Behn), 53, 207
Orphic tablets, 85–86
Osiris, 34, 35, 36, 37, 40, 43, 45, 113
Overmyer, Daniel, 173
Ovid, 111, 113–14, 305*n*76
Oxford Dictionary of World Religions, The, 28

Padma Purana, 147
Paine, Tom, 205, 244
Pali canon, 174, 324*n*81, 325*n*87
Palmer, Douglas, 298*n*78
Paradise Lost (Milton), 214
Parés, Josep M., 298*n*78
parinirvana, 152
Parker, Fred, 209
Parliament of the Gods (Thea Ekklesia) (Lucian), 46
Parnia, Samuel, 293*n*7
parousia, 131, 334*n*19
Parsva, 135
Paul (Saint), 46, 75, 79, 100, 314*n*182
Pax Romana, 127

Payne, Thomas, 339*n*77
Penelope, 105
Pepi I, 38, 47
Pepi II, 34
Pérez-González, Alfredo, 298*n*78
Persephone, 103, 106, 126
Persian Letters (Montesquieu), 223–24
Persians (Aeschylus), 107
Persian Wars (Herodotus), 35
2 Peter, Book of, 334*n*19
Peter Bell the Third (Shelley), 245, 255
Phaedo (Plato), 109, 111, 129, 250
Phaedrus (Plato), 109, 111, 122
Phelps, Elizabeth, 200
Philo, 90
Philosophical and Religious Dialogue in the Shades between Mr. Hume and Dr. Dodd, 241
Physics of Immortality, The (Tipler), 11, 295*n*37
Pilgrim's Progress (Bunyan), 232
Pindar, 107
Piper, Don, 4, 292*n*6
plants, in Jainism, 149–50
Platform Sutra, 176
Plato, 72, 101, 102, 109–15, 121, 122, 250; on children's deaths, 55; Cicero and, 114; on Homer, 73, 109–10; morality and, 26; Virgil and, 124–25, 129
Pleasing Reflections on Life and Manners . . . Principally selected from Fugitive Publications (Wright), 237
Pliny, 2, 116
Plutarch, 46
po, 165
Poem on the Last Day (Young), 243, 344*n*146
Political Justice (Godwin), 202–3
Polwhele, Richard, 238, 239–40
Pope, Alexander, 106, 197, 208, 214, 224, 226, 227, 242, 255
Porter, Roy, 201
Porteus, Beilby, 218
Practical Discourse Concerning Death (Walmsley), 207

Prasenajit, 150
"Prayer, in the Prospect of Death, A" (Burns), 246
Price, Richard, 202, 232, 234–35, 244, 345*n*174
Priestley, Joseph, 220, 244, 339*n*74
primates: grief in, 16–18; morality of, 24–26
Principia Mathematica (Newton), 217
pro-lifers, 10
Prometheus, 105
Proof of Heaven (Alexander), 4, 293*n*7
Prophets, second division of Tanakh (Jewish Bible), 76
prophets, in Judea, 80
proto-Daoism, 164, 165–68
Proverbs, Book of, 80
Psalms, Book of, 84–85, 89, 245, 246, 315*n*191
Ptolemies, Egypt and, 36, 43–44, 59
Punic Wars, 122
Puranas, 133, 135, 146–47
Pure Land, 175–77, 285; Christianity and, 188; in Japan, 176, 180–96; *Tenjukoku* and, 330*n*209
Pure Land School (Hōnen's Jōdo-shū), 183
purgatory, 203–4
pyramids, of Egypt, 33–34
Pyramid Texts, 33–34, 37, 38, 40, 48, 302*n*22
Pythagoras, 111

qi (vital energy), 329*n*173
quantum physics, 13–14
Queen of Heaven (Asherah), 77, 80, 312*n*154
Quevedo, Francisco de, 240
Quirke, Stephen, 34, 37
Qur'an, 132

Ra, 34, 49
Rachel, 80
Radical Enlightenment (Israel), 293*n*19
Rama, 147
Ramayana, 133, 143–44
Ramsden, Peter, 19
Rasselas (Johnson), 231
Rawson, Jessica, 170, 171

Reasonableness of Christianity (Locke), 207
rebirth. *See* reincarnation
recording angel, 241
Record of Ancient Matters *(Kojiki)*, 180–82
Redford, Robert, 260
Reed, Joseph, 205, 242–43
"Reflections by a Lady," 198
Reflections on Death (Dodd), 232–33
reincarnation, xiv, 6, 14, 30, 259, 262; in Buddhism, 151–55, 173–74, 285, 324*n*79; in Hinduism, 136–47; in Jainism, 149; in Judaism, 97, 102, 265; *karma* and, 132, 136–45; Plato on, 102, 109, 111; Stoicism, desire for, 113
relics, in Catholicism, 19
Religio Laici (Blount), 205, 206–7
Religio Medici (Browne), 242
religions, 6–7; Freud on, 202; fundamentalism in, 10; God in, 201; Marx on, 202; terminally ill and, 10–11. *See also specific religions*
Republic, The (Plato), 102, 109, 110, 114, 121
"rest in peace," on tombstones, 23
resurrection, 193–94, 300*n*4; of Baal, 79; in Catholicism, 100; in Christianity, 99–100, 190; of Jesus, 79, 98–100, 315*n*191; in Judea, 91–101; reincarnation and, 136–37; of soul, 334*n*19
Revelation, Book of, 87, 129, 341*n*88
Rhadamanthus, 104, 111
Ricard, François, 276
Richardson, Samuel, 230
Rig Veda, 135, 137, 139
Ring, Kenneth, 4
Roach, Mary, 1, 4
Robertson, Alexander, 210
Robin Hood Society, 335*n*25
Robinson Crusoe (Defoe), 204, 207, 269
Rome, 7, 113–31; Egypt and, 36, 45; Jews and, 77; underworld of, 115
root country *(Ne no kuni)*, 181
Rootless Weeds (Gennai), 256, 285
Ross, Ian Simpson, 348*n*219

round of rebirth *(samsara),* 143, 151, 159
Rousseau, Jean-Jacques, 25, 202, 234, 237–38
Rowe, Elizabeth Singer, 218, 226–30, 241, 343*n*141
Ryūnosuke, Akutagawa, 189

Sacks, Oliver, 4
Sacred Eagle Peak, 175
Sacred Theory of the Earth (Burnet), 216
Sadducees, 98
Saigyō, 158
Saint Peter's Lodge: A Serio-Comi-Legendary Tale (Reed), 242–43
Sakadâgâmin, 154
Salmagundi (Gordimer), 257
salvation, 148; in Buddhism, 175
Šamaš (Shamash), 49, 62, 64, 309*n*125, 311*n*142, 313*n*159
Sami, 6, 9
samsara (round of rebirth), 143, 151, 159
Samuel (biblical character), 80, 83
2 Samuel, Book of, 345*n*169
Sandars, N. K., 67
Sappho, 103
Saul, 80–82, 83
Saunders, George, 2, 258, 266–69, 286
SBV. *See* Standard Babylonian Version
Scheffler, Samuel, 5, 7, 286–87, 295*n*44
Scipio Aemilianus Africanus, 122
Scipio Africanus, 120, 122, 127
Scripture of Great Peace (T'ai-p'ing ching), 174
Scythian, 48
Seafarer (McPherson), 2
"Second Olympian Ode" (Pindar), 107
Seed, Jeremiah, 212
Segal, Alan, 94, 301*n*13
self (ātman), 136–43, 151
self (soul), 230
Seneca, 205, 335*n*25, 348*n*228
sensuality, in Islam, 223–24
Sentimental Twain: Samuel Clemens in the Maze of Moral Philosophy (Camfield), 333*n*3

separation, in Buddhism, 160–61
Sepharvaim, 77
Series of Genuine Letters between Henry and Frances, A (Griffith, R., and Griffith, E.), 231–32
Seti I, 303*n*52
seven treasures, in Buddhism, 156–57
severed heads, in Greece, 316*n*209
shabtis (doll substitute or slave for the person), 41–42
Shallum, 312*n*156
Shang dynasty, in China, 162–63
Shaw, George Bernard, 198–99, 257
Shelley, Percy Bysshe, 223, 244, 245, 255
Shema, 89
sheol, 82, 101–2, 103
Sherlock, William, 207, 226
Shermer, Michael, 15–16
Shih Ching (Book of Songs), 163
Shinran, 184, 187–88
Shinto, 6, 135; Buddhism and, 182; Habian and, 192
Shiva, 147, 148
Shuwela, 78
Sider Jost, Jacob, 217
Siduri, 59, 62, 64–65, 67, 71
Sikhism, 136
Singer, Elizabeth. *See* Rowe
Sinuhe, 35
Sisyphus, 105
sitting shivah, 18
skull rings, 20
skulls, on tombstones, 340*n*83
Smith, Adam, 25, 214, 293*n*14; on heaven, 245–52
Smith, Sydney, 198
snakes, in Egypt, 310*n*135
Sobek, 48
Socinians, 244
Socrates, 109, 110, 111, 121, 250
Solomon, 77. *See also* Wisdom of Solomon
Song of God *(Bhagavad Gita),* 145–46, 148
Sophocles, 107

Sorrows of Young Werther (Goethe), 237
Sōseki, Natsume, 183, 194–96
soul, 346*n*186; Calvin on, 204; in Catholicism, 203–4; Confucius and, 165; heaven and, 214–15; immortality of, 342*n*126; Luther on, 204; resurrection of, 334*n*19
soul *(jiva)*, 148, 150
soul (self), 230
Southey, Robert, 252–55
Spectator, The, 217, 218, 238, 341*n*98
spirit *(hun)*, 165
spirits *(kami)*, 182–83
Spook (Roach), 1, 4
"Spuriousness of the Tao, The" (Wang Chong), 168–69
Standard Babylonian Version (SBV), of *Gilgamesh*, 56, 58, 63–64, 309*n*125
"Stanzas on the same Occasion" (Burns), 246
Steele, Richard, 217–18
Stern, Steve, 258–59, 264–66, 286, 287
Sterne, Laurence, 183, 194, 200, 213, 241, 346–47*nn*196–197
St. John, Henry, Viscount Bolingbroke. See Bolingbroke.
Stoics, 101, 112–13; *anima mundi* doctrine of, 126
"Stopping by woods on a snowy evening" (Frost), 276
Styx, 103
Sueños (Quevedo), 240
Suez Canal, 35, 311*n*137
"Sufferer and a Soul, A," 38–40
suffering, in Buddhism, 151–52
suicide, 295*n*39; Hume on, 347*n*211; in Japan, 351*n*35; Methodism and, 340*n*83; Virgil on, 124, 126, 129; to Yellow Springs, 162
Sumer, 20, 26, 48–72, 307*n*104, 307*nn*110–11; Book of Genesis and, 310*n*135; burials in, 55; funeral rituals in, 54; morality in, 49, 70–71; underworld of, 104
Sum: Tales from the Afterlives (Eagleman), 5
Surveiller et punir: Naissance de la prison (Foucault), 8

Swedenborg, Emmanuel, 212–13, 214, 218, 255, 339*n*76, 349*n*8
Swerve, The (Greenblatt), 116
Swift, Jonathan, 18, 183, 226, 257, 260
Synoptic Gospels, 98
Sørensen, Lars-Martin, 351*n*37

Tacitus, 319*n*252
T'ai i (Grand One), 171
Taimouthes, 44
T'ai-p'ing ching (Scripture of Great Peace), 174
T'ai Tsung, 177
Taj Mahal, 23
Talbot, Catherine, 237
Tang Gongfang, 169
Tartarus, 103, 104, 125
Tatler, The, 217, 256
Taylor, E. Derek, 230
Taylor, John, 34, 301*n*11
Ten Canoes, 23, 299*n*92
Ten Commandments, 55, 77, 86, 146
tenjukoku, 180, 330*n*209
Ten Yama Kings, 174
terminally ill, religion and, 10–11
Terror Management Theory, 12–14
Tertullian, 207
Thea Ekklesia (Parliament of the Gods) (Lucian), 46
Thelwall, Robert Carter, 345*n*169
Theogony (Hesiod), 103
theory of mind, 15; consciousness and, 19–20; for primates, 18
Theory of Moral Sentiments (Smith, A.), 25, 214, 247–49, 293*n*14
Theravada Buddhism, 152, 153
Thiel, Peter, 334*n*11
Thomas, Keith, 243
Thoth, 49
Thoughts on Death translated from the Moral Essays of the Messieurs du Port Royal (Nicole), 229–30
Tibet: *Book of the Dead* of, 133, 177–80; Buddhism in, 135

Tickell, Thomas, 218, 224
Tigay, Jeffrey H., 310*n*134
Tillotson, John, 207, 232
Timbury, Jane, 241, 347*n*197
2 Timothy, Book of, 206
Tindal, Matthew, 205
Tipler, Frank J., 11, 295*n*37
tirthankara (ford-makers), 148–49
Titans, 103, 125
Tityos, 105
Tobiason, Isabella, 331*n*235
Tobit, 82
Toko-yo no kuni (land of the ancestors or gods), 181
Toland, John, 205
tombs, 20, 22; in China, 170–72; in Egypt, 36–37, 42–43; in Islam, 23
tombstones, 23, 340*n*83
Tom Jones (Fielding), 226
Tonson, Jacob, 218, 341*n*98
Torah, 74, 76, 77, 88, 90, 312*n*152, 314*n*181
Tories, 244
Tour Magne, 45
tranquility, in Buddhism, 160–61
Tripitaka, 152
Triptolemus, 107
Tristram Shandy (Sterne), 183, 194, 241
Trotter, Catherine, 208
Troy, 127
True Pure Land School (Jōdo Shin-shū), 183
Tucker, Abraham, 245, 347*n*200
Tull, Herman W., 321*n*24
Turkey, 21
Tusculan Disputations (Cicero), 121
Twain, Mark, 199, 242, 249, 257, 333*n*3, 343*n*144; Gray and, 348*n*216
Twelfth Tablet, 54, 57, 59, 63, 66, 67–68
Tylor, Edward B., 296*n*46

underworld: of Babylonia, 58; of Judea, 78–79; of Rome, 115; of Sumer, 104; of Virgil, 123–26, 129
Underworld Assistant, in China, 171

Unis, 37, 38
Unsex'd Females, The (Polwhele), 239
Upanishads, 133, 135, 137, 141–43, 150; Buddha and, 322*n*37; karma in, 321*n*24
Updike, John, 2
"Upon the Death of Her Husband" (Singer), 227
Ur-Namma, 51–52, 53, 62
Ur-shanabi, 65–66
Urukagina's code, 52
Ūta-napišti, 63, 64–65, 71, 309*n*125
utility, 25, 109, 248

Vamana Purana, 146
Van der Toorn, Karel, 312*n*156, 313*n*167
Vedas, 133, 135, 139
Venus, 120
Vermeule, Blakey, 308*n*117
Vinaya-pitaka, 152–53, 158
Vincent, Lynn, 4, 293*n*7
Vipashchit, 147
Virgil, 45–46, 72, 101, 102, 108, 113–31, 250, 305*n*76; on children's deaths, 55; morality and, 26
Vishnu, 147
Vision of Judgment, A (Southey), 252–55
Vision of Judgement, The (Byron), 254–55
Visitor, The (Dodd), 232
vital energy (*qi*), 329*n*173
Voltaire, 205, 223, 251
Voltaire in the Shades (Mickle), 237, 241
Vultures' Peak, 175

Wahrman, Dror, 234
Wakabayashi, Haruko, 330*n*202
wakes, 18
Walmsley, Peter, 207, 227, 229
Walpole, Horace, 194
Wandâfuru Raifu (Afterlife) (Kore-eda), xv, xvi, xvii, 258–59, 274, 278–86
Wang Chong, 162, 165, 168–69, 171–72, 193
Wang Fu, 172–73
Warburton, William, 206, 347*n*211

Washington, George, 253
Watts, Isaac, 204, 232, 237, 244
way *(dao)*, 165–66
"Wayfarer's Night Song II" (Goethe), 275–76
Way of the World (Congreve), 164
Wealth of Nations, The (Smith, A.), 247
Webster, John, 197
Weil, Arlo B., 298*n*78
Wesley, John, 212, 213, 339*n*76
Westerhoff, Jan, 191
Western Zhou, 163
whales, 16
What Dreams May Come, 259, 260, 279
Whigs, 244
Whiston, William, 341*n*88
White, Jeremiah, 206
Why Do We Care about Literary Characters? (Vermeule), 308*n*117
Wilkinson, Toby A.H., 33, 44
Williams, Bernard, 5
Williams, James, 345*n*169
Wilmot, John, Earl of Rochester, 205, 335*n*25
Wilson, A. N., 257
Wilson, Graeme, 194, 196
Winstanley, Gerard, 206
Wisdom of Solomon, 46, 88, 90, 91, 93; Book of Genesis and, 312*n*151; God and, 101; Greece and, 94; Paul and, 100; secret initiations and, 314*n*177
Woolf, Virginia, 277
Wordsworth, William, 246–47
Wright, G., 237

Wristcutters: A Love Story, 259, 260
Wu (Emperor), 171
Wu Hung, 170–71

Xerxes, 120
Xian Jing, 169
Xi Wu, 171
Xocotlhuetzi (Fiesta Grande de los Muertos), 306*n*90

Yama, 144, 147, 157, 177, 330*n*202
Yates, Jenny, 4
Yeats, W. B., 116
Yekutieli, Yuval, 300*n*6
Yellow Emperor, 169
Yellow Springs, 161, 162, 172, 181, 326*n*16
YHWH, 30, 77, 78, 79, 310*n*136
Ying-shih Yü, 168
Young, Edward, 204, 224–25, 230, 237, 243, 253, 344*n*146
Yudhisthira, 144–45, 147
Yūtei, 191, 192

Zalasiewicz, Jan, 295*n*44
Zeller, Anne, 17–18
Zen Buddhism, 174, 188–89
Zeus, 46, 78, 103–4
Zhou, 20
Zhuangzi (Chuang Tzu), 134, 162, 164, 167–68, 327*n*126
Zhu Xi, 164
Ziusudra, 56, 308*n*123, 308–09*n*124
Zoroastrianism, 94, 135–36

GPSR Authorized Representative: Easy Access System Europe, Mustamäe tee
50, 10621 Tallinn, Estonia, gpsr.requests@easproject.com

www.ingramcontent.com/pod-product-compliance
Lightning Source LLC
Chambersburg PA
CBHW021930290426
44108CB00012B/785